The Oxford Starter Spanish Dictionary

Edited by
Ana Cristina Llompart
Jane Horwood
Carol Styles Carvajal

D0669087

Oxford   New York
OXFORD UNIVERSITY PRESS

Oxford University Press, Great Clarendon Street, Oxford OX2 6DP

Oxford New York

Athens Auckland Bangkok Bogota Bombay
Buenos Aires Calcutta Cape Town Dar es Salaam
Delhi Florence Hong Kong Istanbul Karachi
Kuala Lumpur Madras Madrid Melbourne
Mexico City Nairobi Paris Singapore
Taipei Tokyo Toronto Warsaw

and associated companies in
Berlin Ibadan

Oxford is a trade mark of Oxford University Press

© Oxford University Press 1997

First published 1997

British Library Cataloguing in Publication Data
Data available

Library of Congress Cataloging in Publication Data
Data available

ISBN 0-19-860035-6

10   9   8   7   6   5   4   3   2

Typeset by Latimer Trend & Company Ltd
Printed in Great Britain by The Bath Press

Contents

The Oxford Starter Spanish Dictionary

Senior Editors
Ana Cristina Llompart
Jane Horwood
Carol Styles Carvajal

Editors
Haydn Kirnon
Bernadette Mohan

Dictionary know-how
Michael Britton

Introduction

The *Oxford Starter Spanish Dictionary* represents a major departure from traditional dictionaries on several fronts. It looks different; it provides essential information in a totally new way; the two sides of the dictionary have very distinct functions. In all, the *Starter Dictionary* approaches the needs of the English-speaking learner of Spanish from a very different angle, making it a uniquely accessible and user-friendly introduction to the Spanish language.

It looks different

The dictionary page is uncluttered, with a streamlined typeface providing a consistent structure for the information, both in English and Spanish. Subdivisions of text are clearly indicated, using bullet points and Arabic numerals. The move from one language to the other is explicitly indicated with = signs. Points of basic grammar are reinforced using the ! sign, informal Spanish usage is marked with the ✖ symbol, and ✦ indicates words to be used with special care.

It provides information in a new way

Every effort has been made to approach the foreign language from the point of view of the beginner who may be unfamiliar with the conventions of the more traditional bilingual dictionary.

Parts of speech and grammatical terms are given in full, not in abbreviated form, with a glossary providing explanations of all the terms used. Basic grammatical issues and specific points of usage are dealt with in short notes at appropriate points in the text.

Sets of words which behave in a similar way are treated in a consistent manner, and the user is encouraged to cross-refer to different parts of the dictionary, for example to verb tables and usage notes dealing with such concepts as colors, countries, and dates.

The language used in examples and in sense indicators (or signposts to the correct translation) has been carefully screened to ensure maximum clarity. The word list contains all the material a beginner will need, and reflects current American and British English and Latin American and European Spanish in clear, lively examples.

The two sides have distinct functions

Each side of the dictionary is shaped by its specific function. The English–Spanish side is longer, providing the user going into the foreign language with maximum guidance in the form of detailed coverage of essential grammar, clear signposts to the correct translation for a particular context, and a wide selection of example material.

The Spanish–English side is designed to capitalize on what English speakers already know about their language, hence the more streamlined presentation of English-language information. From irregular verb forms to common idiomatic usage such as might be encountered in the media, the *Oxford Starter Spanish Dictionary* provides generous coverage of those aspects of Spanish which are less easy to decode for English speakers. Irregular verbs, adjectives and plurals are all featured in the wordlist, referring the user to the base form where the translations are given.

The Dictionary know-how section in the middle of the dictionary is designed to give help and practice in using the dictionary more effectively.

How to use the dictionary

Every entry in the dictionary tells you whether that particular word is a noun, a verb, an adjective, or another part of speech. If you need help to find out what any part of speech means, look it up in the glossary of grammatical terms on page xi.

If there is more than one part of speech within an entry, numbers are used to separate them. Within each part of speech, different senses are given bullet points (•):

fresco/fresca
1 *adjective*
• (*if it's vegetables*) = fresh
• (*if it's weather, water*) = cool
2 fresco *noun, masculine*
  hace fresco = it's a bit chilly

fish
1 *noun*
• (*an animal*)
  a fish = un pez
• (*as food*)
  fish = pescado (*masculine*)
2 *verb* = pescar

The English–Spanish entries tend to be longer, in order to offer detailed guidance on how to write and speak correctly in Spanish, so it is a good idea to scan the whole entry to find the sense which is closest to the one you need.

Each Spanish verb entry is marked with a number pointing you to the table of Spanish verbs at the back of the dictionary. The number refers to the model verb in the table where you can find the information you need about how to form the tenses:

absorber *verb* [17]
  = to absorb

Cross-references are shown by an arrow ▶. These are especially useful for identifying verb forms which you might not otherwise recognize:

sé ▶ saber

In examples, different words with which a phrase can be used are put in square brackets. This means that it is possible to substitute another word for the alternatives given in the dictionary:

little[1]
1 *adjective* = poco/poca
  little [time | wine | money ...] = poco [tiempo | vino | dinero ...]

Notes giving additional information are designed to help you produce correct Spanish in areas where it is all too easy to forget important points of grammar or usage:

agua *noun, feminine*
  el agua = water

  ! *Note that although* **agua** *is feminine it is preceded by a masculine article in the singular*

her
1 *pronoun*
• (*when used as a direct object*) = la
  I know/don't know her = la conozco/no la conozco

  ! *Note that* **la** *comes before the verb in Spanish*

Boxed usage notes covering certain themes and sets of related words form a very useful feature of this dictionary. Topics covered include dates, the human body, languages, and time of day. In relevant entries, a number refers you to the page with a note on the particular topic:

January *noun* ▶ **p. 192**
  January = enero (*masculine*)

The pronunciation of Spanish

Vowels

a	is between the pronunciation of *a* in English *cat* and *arm*
e	is like *e* in English *bed*
i	is like *ee* in English *see* but a little shorter
o	is like *o* in English *hot* but a little longer
u	is like *oo* in English *too*

Consonants

b	(1) in initial position or after **m** or **n** is like English *b*
	(2) in other positions is between English *b* and English *v*
c	(1) before **e** or **i**: in European Spanish is like *th* in English *thin*; in Latin American Spanish is like *s* in English *stop*
	(2) in other positions is like *c* in English *cat*
ch	is like *ch* in English *chip*
d	(1) in initial position, after **m** or **n**, and after **l** is like English *d*
	(2) in other positions is like *th* in English *this*
f	is like *f* in English *fat*
g	(1) before **e** or **i** is like *ch* in Scottish *loch*
	(2) in initial position is like *g* in English *get*
	(3) in other positions is like (2) but a little softer
h	is silent in Spanish, but see also **ch**
j	is like *ch* in Scottish *loch*
k	is like English *k*
l	is like English *l*, but see also **ll**
ll	is like *lli* in English *million*, except in the River Plate area, where it is like *s* in English *measure*
m	is like English *m*
n	is like English *n*
ñ	is like English *ni* in English *opinion*
p	is like English *p*
q	is like English *k*
r	is rolled; is more strongly rolled when double *r*, or in initial position
s	is like *s* in English *sit*
t	is like English *t*
v	(1) in initial position or after **m** or **n** is like English *b*
	(2) in other positions is between English *b* and English *v*
w	is like *g* in English *get* followed by English *w*
x	is like English *x*
y	is like English *y*
z	in European Spanish is like *th* in English *thin*; in Latin American Spanish is like *s* in English *stop*

Glossary of grammatical terms

Abbreviation A shortened form of a word or phrase

Adjective A word describing a noun: a green shirt = una camisa *verde*

Adverb A word that describes or changes the meaning of a verb, an adjective or another verb: he speaks *quickly* = habla *rápido*

Article The definite article the (= el / la / los / las), and the indefinite article a / an (= un / una), used in front of a noun

Clause A self-contained section of a sentence that contains a subject and a verb

Conditional tense A verb tense that expresses what might happen if something else occurred: he would go = él iría

Conjunction A word used to join clauses together: and = y, because = porque

Consonant A letter representing a sound that can only be used together with a vowel, such as b, c, d; see *Vowel*.

Definite article the (= el / la / los / las)

Direct object The noun or pronoun directly affected by the verb: she bought *the book* = compró *el libro*

Exclamation A sound, word, or remark expressing a strong feeling such as anger, fear, or joy: ouch! = ay!

Feminine One of the two noun genders: la mujer = the woman

Future tense The tense of a verb that refers to something that will happen in the future: I will leave = me iré

Gender One of the two groups of nouns: masculine or feminine

Gerund The part of a verb that in English ends in -*ing* and in Spanish ends in -*iendo* or -*ando*: talking = hablando

Imperative A verb form that is used to express a command: bring your passport with you = traiga el pasaporte

Imperfect tense The tense of a verb that refers to a continuous or habitual action in the past: I was eating / I used to eat = comía

Indefinite article A / an (= un / una)

Indicative A verb form that is used when stating a fact: I can't decide which I prefer no puedo decidir cuál prefiero

Indirect object The noun or pronoun indirectly affected by the verb, at which the direct object is aimed: I gave *him* the book = *le* di el libro

Infinitive The basic part of a verb: cantar = to sing

Masculine One of the two noun genders: el hombre = the man

Noun A word that names a person or thing: chair = silla

Part of speech A grammatical term for the function of a word: noun, verb, adjective, etc are parts of speech

Past participle The part of the verb used to form past tenses: made = hecho

Past simple The tense of a verb that refers to something that happened or was completed in the past: he woke up = se despertó

Plural Of nouns, etc, referring to more than one: the books = los libros

Preposition A word that stands in front of a noun or pronoun, relating it to the rest of the sentence: with = con, for = para

Present tense The tense of a verb referring to something that is happening now: I make = hago

Pronoun A word that stands instead of a noun: he = él, she = ella, mine = mío/mía etc

Reflexive verb A verb whose object is the same as its subject; in Spanish used with a reflexive pronoun, for example bañarse, irse.

Singular Of nouns, etc, referring to just one: the tree = el árbol

Subject The noun or pronoun that causes the action of the verb: *he* wants to do it = *él* lo quiere hacer

Subjunctive A verb form that is used to express a desire, doubt, or unlikelihood: I want you to stay = quiero que te quedes

Tense The form of a verb that tells when the action takes place: present, future, past

Verb A word or phrase which indicates what is being done or what is happening

Vowel A letter representing a sound that can be spoken by itself; a, e, i, o, u

a *preposition*
- (*indicating destination*) = to
  fuimos a la playa = we went to the beach
  se lo di a tu hermano = I gave it to your
  brother
- (*indicating time*) = at
  se fueron a la una = they left at one o'clock
  a la hora de comer = at lunchtime
- (*indicating date*)
  hoy estamos a jueves = today is Thursday
- (*indicating position*)
  está a la derecha = it's on the right
  estábamos sentados a la mesa = we were
  sitting at the table
- (*indicating manner*)
  ir a pie = to go on foot
- (*indicating distance*)
  el pueblo está a 40 km de Leeds = the
  village is 40 km from Leeds
- (*indicating price*)
  las manzanas están a 90 pesos el kilo =
  the apples cost 90 pesos a kilo
- (*used before people or people's names*)
  vi a Juan = I saw Juan
  ¿conoces a su madre? = do you know her
  mother?
- (*after certain verbs*)
  voy a ir = I'm going to go
  empezar a comer = to start eating

abajo *adverb*
- = below
  está en el cajón de abajo = it's in the
  drawer below
  = it's in the bottom drawer
- = downstairs
  viven abajo = they live downstairs
- (*Lat Am*) **abajo de** = under
  abajo de la cama = under the bed

abanico *noun, masculine*
  un abanico = a fan

abarrotería *noun, feminine (Mex)*
  una abarrotería = a grocery store, a grocer's

abarrotero/abarrotera *noun,
masculine/feminine (Mex)*
  un abarrotero/una abarrotera = a
  storekeeper, a grocer

abarrotes *noun, masculine plural (C Am,
Mex)*
  abarrotes = groceries

abecedario *noun, masculine*
  el abecedario = the alphabet

abeja *noun, feminine*
  una abeja = a bee

abierto/abierta *adjective*
- = open
  la puerta estaba abierta = the door was
  open
- (*if it's a faucet*) = running
  dejaste la llave abierta = you left the faucet
  running

abogado/abogada *noun,
masculine/feminine*
  un abogado/una abogada = a lawyer

abordar *verb* 1 (*Mex*)
= to board

abrazar *verb* 4
= to hug

abrazo *noun, masculine*
  un abrazo = a hug
  me dio un abrazo = she gave me a hug
  un abrazo, Juan (*in a letter*) = best wishes,
  Juan

abrebotellas *noun, masculine* (**!** *does
not change in the plural*)
  un abrebotellas = a bottle opener

abrelatas *noun, masculine* (**!** *does not
change in the plural*)
  un abrelatas = a can opener

abreviatura *noun, feminine*
  una abreviatura = an abbreviation

abridor *noun, masculine*
  un abridor = a can opener
  = a bottle opener

abrigo *noun, masculine*
  un abrigo = a coat

abril *noun, masculine*
  abril = April

abrir *verb* 59
- = to open
- = to turn on
  abrir el gas = to turn the gas on

abrocharse *verb* 1
- (*if it's clothes, buttons*) = to do up
  se abrochó la chaqueta = she did up her
  jacket
- (*if it's a seatbelt*) = to fasten

absoluto/absoluta *adjective*
= absolute

absorber verb 17
= to absorb

absurdo/absurda adjective
= absurd

abuelo/abuela noun,
masculine/feminine
un abuelo/una abuela = a
grandfather/grandmother
mis abuelos = my grandparents

aburrido/aburrida adjective
• = bored
• = boring

aburrir verb 41
= to bore
aburrirse
= to get bored

acá adverb
= here
¡ven acá! = come here!

acabar verb 1
• = to finish
acaba a las siete = it finishes at seven
acabé de pintarlo ayer = I finished
painting it yesterday
• = to end
cuando acabó la película = when the film
ended
• acabo de verlo = I've just seen him
acabarse
• = to be over
se acabó el colegio = school is over
• = to run out
• se les acabó el dinero a mis padres = my
parents ran out of money
se nos acabó el pan = we ran out of bread

academia noun, feminine
una academia = a school
una academia de idiomas = a language
school

acampar verb 1
= to camp

acaso adverb
por si acaso = just in case

accidente noun, masculine
un accidente = an accident

aceite noun, masculine
aceite = oil
aceite de oliva = olive oil

aceituna noun, feminine
una aceituna = an olive

acelerador noun, masculine
el acelerador = the accelerator

acento noun, masculine
un acento = an accent

aceptable adjective
= acceptable

aceptar verb 1
= to accept

acera noun, feminine
la acera = the sidewalk, the pavement

acercar verb 2
• = to bring closer/nearer
• = to pass
me acercó un cuchillo = he passed me a
knife
acercarse
• = to get nearer
• = to go/come nearer
acércate un poco = come a bit nearer

acero noun, masculine
acero = steel

ácido/ácida
1 adjective
• = sharp
• = acid
2 ácido noun, masculine
un ácido = an acid

acierta, acierto, etc ▶ acertar

acné noun, masculine
acné = acne

aconsejar verb 1
= to advise
me aconsejó que no fuera = he advised me
not to go

! Note the use of the subjunctive after
aconsejar que

acordarse verb 6
= to remember
acordarse de algo/alguien = to remember
something/someone

acostarse verb 6
= to go to bed
= to lie down

acostumbrado/acostumbrada
adjective
estar acostumbrado/acostumbrada a algo
= to be used to something

acostumbrarse verb 1
acostumbrarse a algo = to get used to
something

actitud noun, feminine
una actitud = an attitude

actividad noun, feminine
una actividad = an activity

activo/activa adjective
= active

acto noun, masculine
  un acto = an act

actor/actriz noun, masculine/feminine
  un actor/una actriz = an actor/actress

actuar verb [11]
  = to act

Acuario noun, masculine
  Acuario = Aquarius

acuario noun, masculine/feminine
  un/una acuario = an Aquarius, an Aquarian

acuerda, acuerdo, etc ▶ acordar

acuerdo noun, masculine
  un acuerdo = an agreement
  llegaron a un acuerdo = they reached an
    agreement
  de acuerdo = all right
  estar de acuerdo = to agree

acuesta, acuesto, etc ▶ acostar

acusar verb [1]
  = to accuse

adaptar verb [1]
  = to adapt
adaptarse
  = to adapt

adecuado/adecuada adjective
  • = suitable
  • = right

adelantar verb [1]
  • (if it's a car) = to overtake
    (if it's an appointment, meeting) = to bring
    forward
  • (if it's a clock) = to put forward

adelante
1 adverb
  • = forward
    se cayó hacia adelante = he fell forward
  • (Lat Am) adelante de = in front of
    adelante de mí = in front of me
2 exclamation
  ¡adelante! = come in!

adelgazar verb [4]
  = to lose weight

además adverb
  • = besides
    no quiero ir, además no tengo dinero = I
      don't want to go; besides, I don't have any
      money
  • = what's more
    llega tarde y, además, no trabaja = he's
      always late, and what's more, he doesn't
      work
  • además de = as well as

adentro adverb
  • = inside
    vamos adentro = let's go inside

  • (Lat Am) adentro de = inside
    adentro de la casa = inside the house

adhesivo/adhesiva adjective
  • = sticky
  • = adhesive

adiós exclamation
  • (on leaving a person or place)
    ¡adiós! = goodbye!
  • (when passing someone in the street)
    ¡adiós! = hello!

adivinar verb [1]
  = to guess

adjetivo noun, masculine
  un adjetivo = an adjective

administración noun, feminine
  la administración = the administration

admiración noun, feminine
  • admiración = admiration
  • un signo de admiración = an exclamation
    point, an exclamation mark

admirar verb [1]
  = to admire

adonde adverb
  = where
  el lugar adonde iban = the place where
    they were going

adónde adverb
  = where
  ¿adónde vas? = where are you going?

adornar verb [1]
  = to decorate

adorno noun, masculine
  un adorno = an ornament
  adornos de Navidad = Christmas
    decorations

adquiera, adquiero, etc ▶ adquirir

adquirir verb [47]
  = to acquire

adrede adverb
  = on purpose

aduana noun, feminine
  la aduana = customs

adulto/adulta
1 adjective
  = adult
2 noun, masculine/feminine
  un adulto/una adulta = an adult

adverbio noun, masculine
  un adverbio = an adverb

aéreo/aérea adjective
  = air
  el tráfico aéreo = air traffic
  el puente aéreo = the shuttle

aeromozo/aeromoza *noun,*
masculine/feminine (*Lat Am*)
  un aeromozo/una aeromoza = a flight
  attendant

aeropuerto *noun, masculine*
  un aeropuerto = an airport

afectar *verb* ⬚1
  = to affect

afeitarse *verb* ⬚1
  = to shave
  = to shave off
  se afeitó la barba = he shaved off his beard

aficionado/aficionada
1 *adjective*
• = keen
  ser aficionado/aficionada a algo = to be
  keen on something
• (*if it's an athlete, a sports player*) = amateur
2 *noun, masculine/feminine*
  un aficionado/una aficionada al fútbol = a
  football fan
  un aficionado/una aficionada a la música
  = a music lover

afortunado/afortunada *adjective*
  = lucky

africano/africana
1 *adjective*
  = African
2 *noun, masculine/feminine*
  un africano/una africana = an African

afuera *adverb*
• = outside
  ¡ven afuera! = come outside!
• (*Lat Am*) **afuera de** = outside
  afuera del edificio = outside the building

afueras *noun, feminine plural*
  las afueras = the outskirts

agarrar *verb* ⬚1
• = to grab
• (*Lat Am*) = to take
• (*Lat Am*) = to catch
  agarrar un resfriado = to catch a cold

agencia *noun, feminine*
  una agencia = an agency

ágil *adjective*
  = agile

agradezca, agradezco, etc
▶ agradecer

agosto *noun, masculine*
  agosto = August

agotado/agotada *adjective*
• (*if it's a person*) = exhausted
• (*if it's a book, record, etc*) = sold out

agotar *verb* ⬚1
  = to use up

agradable *adjective*
  = pleasant

agradecer *verb* ⬚19
  = to thank
  agradecerle algo a alguien = to thank
  someone for something

agradecido/agradecida *adjective*
  = grateful
  le estoy muy agradecida = I am very
  grateful to you

agresivo/agresiva *adjective*
  = aggressive

agrícola *adjective*
  = agricultural

agricultor/agricultora *noun,*
masculine/feminine
  un agricultor/una agricultora = a farmer

agrio/agria *adjective*
  = sour

agua *noun, feminine*
  el agua = water

> ! *Note that although* **agua** *is feminine it is*
> *preceded by a masculine article in the*
> *singular*

  agua mineral con gas/sin gas =
  sparkling/still mineral water

aguacate *noun, masculine*
  un aguacate = an avocado

aguantar *verb* ⬚1
• = to bear
• = to stand
• = to put up with
• = to hold
  aguantar la respiración = to hold one's
  breath

águila *noun, feminine*
  un águila = an eagle

> ! *Note that although* **águila** *is feminine it*
> *is preceded by a masculine article in the*
> *singular*

• **águila o sol** (*Mex*) = heads or tails

aguja *noun, feminine*
• **una aguja** = a needle
• (*of watch, clock*) = a hand

agujero *noun, masculine*
  un agujero = a hole

ahí *adverb*
  = there
  ponlo ahí = put it there

ahogarse *verb* ⬚3
• = to suffocate
• = to drown

A

ahora *adverb*
= now
ahora mismo = right now
por ahora = for the time being

ahorrar *verb* ☐1
= to save

ahorro *noun, masculine*
un ahorro = a saving
mis ahorros = my savings

aire *noun, masculine*
aire = air
aire acondicionado = air-conditioning
al aire libre = outdoors
estar al aire libre = to be outdoors
un concierto al aire libre = an open-air
   concert

ajedrez *noun, masculine*
el ajedrez = chess

ajo *noun, masculine*
ajo = garlic

al

> ! Note that **al** *is a contraction of the*
> *preposition* **a** *and the definite article* **el**

• **ir al cine** = to go to the cinema
   vimos al marido de Elena = we saw Elena's
   husband
• (*used before an infinitive*)
   al verme se puso a llorar = when he saw
   me he started to cry
   tengo que llamarlos al llegar a casa = I
   have to phone them when I get home

ala *noun, feminine*
un ala = a wing

> ! Note that although **ala** *is feminine it is*
> *preceded by a masculine article in the*
> *singular*

alambre *noun, masculine*
alambre = wire

alargar *verb* ☐3
• = to extend
   decidieron alargar las vacaciones = they
   decided to extend their vacation
• = to lengthen
   alargar una falda = to lengthen a skirt
• = to stretch out
   alargó la mano para tomar el libro = she
   stretched out her hand to take the book
alargarse
• = to get longer
   los días se iban alargando = the days were
   getting longer
• = to go on
   la reunión se alargó hasta la noche = the
   meeting went on until night-time

alarma *noun, feminine*
una alarma = an alarm
una alarma contra incendios = a fire alarm

albañil *noun, masculine*
un albañil = a builder
= a bricklayer

albaricoque *noun, masculine* (*Spa*)
un albaricoque = an apricot

alberca *noun, feminine* (*Mex*)
una alberca = a swimming pool

albergue *noun, masculine*
un albergue = a hostel
un albergue juvenil = a youth hostel

albóndiga *noun, feminine*
una albóndiga = a meatball

álbum *noun, masculine*
un álbum = an album

alcachofa *noun, feminine*
una alcachofa = an artichoke

alcalde *noun, masculine*
el alcalde = the mayor

alcaldesa *noun, feminine*
la alcaldesa = the mayoress
= the mayor's wife

alcanzar *verb* ☐4
• = to reach
   no alcanzo al estante de arriba = I can't
   reach the top shelf
• = to catch up with
   corrió para alcanzarlos = she ran to catch
   up with them
• = to pass
   ¿me alcanzas la mantequilla? = can you
   pass me the butter?

alcohol *noun, masculine*
alcohol = alcohol

alcohólico/alcohólica
1 *adjective*
= alcoholic
2 *noun, masculine/feminine*
un alcohólico/una alcohólica = an
   alcoholic

alegrarse *verb* ☐1
= to cheer up
¡alégrate! = cheer up!
• **alegrarse de algo:**
   se alegran de tu éxito = they are happy
   about your success
   me alegro de verte = it's nice to see you
   se alegraron de venir = they were glad they
   had come

alegre *adjective*
• (*if it's a person*) = cheerful
• (*if it's a color*) = bright

alegría *noun, feminine*
alegría = joy
= happiness

alemán/alemana
1 *adjective*
= German
2 *noun, masculine|feminine*
un alemán/una alemana = a German
3 alemán *noun, masculine*
el alemán (*the language*) = German

Alemania *noun, feminine*
Alemania = Germany

alfabeto *noun, masculine*
el alfabeto = the alphabet

alfiler *noun, masculine*
un alfiler = a pin

alfombra *noun, feminine*
• una alfombra = a rug
(*large*) = a carpet
• (*Lat Am: wall to wall*) la alfombra = the
carpet

algo *pronoun*
• = something
quiero preguntarte algo = I want to ask you
something
• = anything
¿vas a comprar algo? = are you going to
buy anything?

algodón *noun, masculine*
algodón = cotton

alguien *pronoun*
• = someone, somebody
alguien me dijo que estaba cerrado =
someone told me that it was shut
• = anyone, anybody
¿llamó alguien? = did anyone phone?

algún *adjective*
▶ alguno/alguna

alguno/alguna

! *Note that* alguno *becomes* algún *before*
masculine singular nouns

1 *adjective*
• (*in affirmative sentences*) = some
algunos alumnos = some pupils
lo haré algún día = I'll do it some day
• (*in questions*) = any
¿quieres ver alguna película en especial?
= do you want to see any movie in
particular?
• alguna cosa = something
= anything
¿trajeron alguna cosa para comer? = did
they bring anything to eat?
• alguna vez = ever
¿has montado alguna vez en globo? =
have you ever been up in a balloon?
• en algún lugar, en algún sitio, en alguna
parte (*in affirmative sentences*) =
somewhere
(*in questions*) =anywhere

2 *pronoun*
siempre hay alguno que falta = there is
always one missing
seguro que a alguno se le olvida = one of
them is bound to forget
¿te queda alguno? = have you any left?
algunos fueron a pie = some went on foot
algunos de ellos = some of them

alimentar *verb* 1
= to feed

alimento *noun, masculine*
alimento = food

allá *adverb*
= there

allí *adverb*
= there

almacén *noun, masculine*
• un almacén = a warehouse
(*a room*) = a storeroom
• (*SC*) un almacén = a grocery store, a
grocer's shop

almendra *noun, feminine*
una almendra = an almond

almíbar *noun, masculine*
el almíbar = syrup

almohada *noun, feminine*
una almohada = a pillow

almorzar *verb* 10
= to have lunch

almuerza, almuerzo, etc ▶ almorzar

almuerzo *noun, masculine*
el almuerzo = lunch

aló *exclamation* (*AmS*)
(*when answering the phone*) = hello?

alojarse *verb* 1
= to stay

alojamiento *noun, masculine*
alojamiento = accommodations,
accommodation

alquilar *verb* 1
• (*from a person or company*)
= to rent
= to hire
• (*to a person or company*)
= to rent out
= to let
= to hire out

alquiler *noun, masculine*
• (*money paid*) = hire charge
= rent
• de alquiler:
un coche de alquiler = a hire car
un apartamento de alquiler = a rented
apartment

C Am Central America   Lat Am Latin America   Mex Mexico

A

alrededor *adverb*
- **a mi alrededor** = around me
  se sentaron alrededor suyo = they sat around her
- **alrededor de** = around
  formaron un círculo alrededor del árbol = they formed a circle around the tree
  llegaron alrededor de las once = they'll arrive at about eleven
- **de alrededor:**
  los pueblos de alrededor son muy bonitos = the surrounding villages are very pretty

alrededores *noun, masculine plural*
los alrededores = the surrounding area
(of a town) = the outskirts
= the surroundings

altavoz *noun, masculine*
un altavoz = a loudspeaker

alternativa *noun, feminine*
una alternativa = an alternative

altitud *noun, feminine*
la altitud = the altitude

alto/alta
1 *adjective*
- *(if it's a person, building)* = tall
- *(if it's a mountain, volume)* = high
- *(if it's the radio)* = loud
2 alto *adverb*
= loud
hablar alto = to speak loudly
3 alto *noun, masculine*
- **el alto** = the height
  tiene 4m de alto = it's 4m high
- **pasarse un alto** *(Méx)* = to go through a red light
  = to go through a stop sign

altura *noun, feminine*
- **la altura** = the height
  tiene 50m de altura = it's 50m high
- **la altura** = the altitude

aluminio *noun, masculine*
aluminio = aluminum, aluminium

alumno/alumna *noun,*
masculine/feminine
- **un alumno/una alumna** = a pupil
- **un alumno/una alumna** = a student

amable *adjective*
= kind

ama de casa *noun, feminine*
un ama de casa = a housewife

> **!** Note that although **ama de casa** is feminine it is preceded by a masculine article in the singular

amanecer 19
1 *verb*
= to get light
estaba amaneciendo = it was getting light

2 *noun, masculine*
el amanecer = dawn, daybreak
al amanecer = at dawn, at daybreak

amanezca ▶ amanecer

amante *noun, masculine/feminine*
un/una amante = a lover

amar *verb*
= to love

amargo/amarga *adjective*
= bitter

amarillo/amarilla
1 *adjective*
= yellow
2 amarillo *noun, masculine*
el amarillo = yellow

ambición *noun, feminine*
la ambición = ambition

ambiente *noun, masculine*
- **el ambiente** = the environment
- *(at work, at a party)*
  el ambiente = the atmosphere

ambiguo/ambigua *adjective*
= ambiguous

ambos/ambas *adjective, pronoun*
= both
ambos libros = both books
me gustan ambas = I like them both

ambulancia *noun, feminine*
una ambulancia = an ambulance

amenaza *noun, feminine*
una amenaza = a threat

amenazar *verb* 4
= to threaten

americano/americana
1 *adjective*
= American
2 *noun, masculine/feminine*
un americano/una americana = an American

amigo/amiga *noun, masculine/feminine*
un amigo/una amiga = a friend

amistad *noun, feminine*
la amistad = friendship

amor *noun, masculine*
el amor = love

amplio/amplia *adjective*
= wide

ancho/ancha
1 *adjective*
- = wide
- *(referring to clothing)*
  siempre lleva jerseys anchos = she always wears baggy sweaters
  esta chaqueta me queda ancha = this jacket is too big for me

2 ancho *noun, masculine*
= width
¿cuánto mide de ancho? = how wide is it?
tiene 30cm de ancho = it is 30cm wide

anciano/anciana
1 *adjective*
= elderly
2 *noun, masculine/feminine*
un anciano/una anciana = an elderly
man/woman
los ancianos = the elderly

ancla *noun, feminine*
un ancla = an anchor

> **!** *Note that although* ancla *is feminine it is preceded by a masculine article in the singular*

andar *verb* 14
• = to walk
tuvimos que ir andando = we had to walk
• = to work
el reloj no anda = the watch doesn't work
• (*Lat Am*) = to ride
andar [**en bicicleta** | **a caballo** | **en moto** ...] = to
ride [a bicycle | a horse | a motorcycle ...]

andén *noun, masculine*
un andén = a platform
(*C Am*) = a sidewalk, a pavement

anduve, anduviste, etc ▶ andar

ángel *noun, masculine*
un ángel = an angel

ángulo *noun, masculine*
un ángulo = an angle

anillo *noun, masculine*
un anillo = a ring

aniversario *noun, masculine*
un aniversario = an anniversary

anoche *adverb*
= last night
antes de anoche = the night before last

anochecer 19
1 *verb*
= to get dark
estaba anocheciendo = it was getting dark
2 *noun, masculine*
el anochecer = dusk
al anochecer = at dusk

anochezca ▶ anochecer

anotar *verb* 1
= to make a note of

antártico/antártica *adjective*
= Antarctic

Antártida *noun, feminine*
la Antártida = Antarctica

ante *preposition*
= before
se puso ante el micrófono = she stood
before the microphone
ante todo = above all

antena *noun, feminine*
una antena (*on a radio, television*) = an
antenna, an aerial
(*of an insect*) = an antenna

antepasado/antepasada *noun,*
masculine/feminine
un antepasado/una antepasada = an
ancestor

anterior *adjective*
= previous
el día anterior = the previous day, the day
before

antes *adverb*
• = before
la noche antes = the night before
antes de Navidad = before Christmas
antes de anoche/ayer = the night/day
before yesterday
• = earlier
ayer llegó antes = yesterday she arrived
earlier
• (*indicating order, priority*)
éste va antes = this one goes first
antes de hacer algo = before doing
something
lo antes posible = as soon as possible

anticonceptivo *noun, masculine*
un anticonceptivo = a contraceptive

anticuado/anticuada *adjective*
= old-fashioned

antiguo/antigua *adjective*
• = old
estos muebles son muy antiguos = this
furniture is very old
• = former
el antiguo campeón = the former
champion
• = ancient
el antiguo Egipto = ancient Egypt

anual *adjective*
= annual

anunciar *verb* 1
• (*if it's a decision, news*) = to announce
• (*if it's a product*) = to advertise

anuncio *noun, masculine*
un anuncio = an advertisement, an ad
(*on TV*) = a commercial
(*on a billboard*) = a poster

año *noun, masculine*
un año = a year
el año que viene = next year
los años 60 = the 60s
un año bisiesto = a leap year
¡Feliz Año Nuevo! = Happy New Year!
¿cuántos años tienes? = how old are you?
tengo trece años = I'm thirteen

A

apagar verb [3]
• (if it's a light, TV) = to turn off
• (if it's a fire, cigarette) = to put out

apagón noun, masculine
un apagón = a power cut, a blackout

aparato noun, masculine
los aparatos eléctricos = electrical
appliances
el dentista y todos sus aparatos = the
dentist and all his equipment

aparcamiento noun, masculine (Spa)
un aparcamiento = a parking lot, a car park

aparcar verb [2] (Spa)
= to park

aparecer verb [19]
= to appear

aparezca, aparezco, etc ▶aparecer

apariencia noun, feminine
apariencia = appearance

apartamento noun, masculine
un apartamento = an apartment, a flat

apartar verb [1]
• = to move away
apartó el coche de la acera = she moved
the car away from the sidewalk
• = to move out of the way
aparté las cajas para poder pasar = I
moved the boxes out of the way so I could
get past
• = to set aside
aparta los que te gusten = set aside the
ones that you like
• apartar los ojos de algo = to take one's eyes
off something
apartarse
• = to move over
¡apártese!, ¡apártate! = move over!
• = to move away
apartarse de la ventana = to move away
from the window

aparte adverb
• = aside, to one side
puso sus libros aparte = he put his books
aside
lo llamó aparte = she called him to one side
• aparte de = apart from

apellido noun, masculine
el apellido = the surname

apenas adverb
• = hardly
apenas podía oírlo = I could hardly hear it
• = hardly ever
apenas viene a vernos = she hardly ever
comes to see us
• = scarcely
hace apenas tres meses que murió = it's
scarcely three months since she died

• apenas el jueves podré ir (Mex) = I won't
be able to go till Thursday
• (meaning shortly afterwards)
apenas había llegado cuando sonó el
teléfono = no sooner had he arrived than
the phone rang

apéndice noun, masculine
el apéndice = the appendix

apetecer verb [19] (Spa)
me apetece ir al cine = I feel like going to
the cinema
haz lo que te apetezca = do whatever you
like

apetezca, apetezco, etc ▶apetecer

apetito noun, masculine
el apetito = appetite

aplastar verb [1]
= to crush, = to squash

aplaudir verb [41]
= to applaud
= to clap

aplauso noun, masculine
un aplauso = a round of applause
aplausos = applause

apodo noun, masculine
un apodo = a nickname

apostar verb [6]
= to bet

apoyar verb [1]
• = to lean
apoya la escalera en la pared = lean the
ladder against the wall
• = to rest
apoyó la cabeza en la almohada = she
rested her head on the pillow
• = to support
todos apoyaron mi decisión = everyone
supported my decision
apoyarse
apoyarse en algo = to lean on something

apoyo noun, masculine
apoyo = support

apreciar verb [1]
• = to be fond of
la aprecio mucho = I am very fond of her
• = to appreciate
aprecio tu interés = I appreciate your
interest

aprender verb [17]
= to learn

apretar verb [7]
• (if it's a lid, bolt) = to tighten
• (if it's a button) = to press

* (*referring to shoes, clothing*)
  estos zapatos me aprietan = these shoes are too tight for me
* = to squeeze
  me apretó la mano = she squeezed my hand
* **apretar el puño** = to clench one's fist
* **apretar el acelerador** = to put one's foot on the accelerator

aprieta, aprieto, etc ▶ apretar

aprobar *verb* 6
* (*if it's an idea, behavior*) = to approve of
* (*if it's a test, subject*) = to pass

apropiado/apropiada *adjective*
= appropiate, suitable

aprovechar *verb* 1
* = to make good use of
  hay que aprovechar bien el tiempo = we have to make good use of our time
* (*other uses*)
  aproveché su visita para devolverle los libros = her visit gave me the chance to return her books to her
  quisiera aprovechar la oportunidad para darle las gracias = I would like to take the opportunity to thank you
  ¡qué aproveche! = enjoy your meal!

aproximado/aproximada *adjective*
= rough
  un cálculo aproximado = a rough estimate

aprueba, apruebo, etc ▶ aprobar

apto/apta *adjective*
= suitable

apuesta, apuesto, etc ▶ apostar

apuntar *verb* 1
* (*if it's a name, address*) = to note down
* (*with your finger etc*) = to point at
  me apuntó con el dedo = she pointed her finger at me
apuntarse
= to put one's name down
  me apunté para ir a la excursión = I put my name down for the trip

aquel/aquella *adjective*
  aquel/aquella = that
  aquellos/aquellas = those
  aquel día = that day
  dame aquellos zapatos = give me those shoes

aquél/aquélla *pronoun*
  aquél/aquélla = that one
  aquéllos/aquéllas = those
  aquélla es la que más me gusta = I like that one the most
  aquéllos son de Juan = those are Juan's

aquello *pronoun*
  ¿qué es aquello de allí? = what's that over there?

aquí *adverb*
  = here
  ven aquí = come here
  lo puse aquí abajo = I put it down here
* **por aquí:**
  por aquí, por favor = this way, please
  creo que está por aquí = I think it's around here
  está por aquí cerca = it's near here

árabe
1 *adjective*
  = Arab
2 *noun, masculine/feminine*
  un/una árabe = an Arab
3 árabe *noun, masculine*
  el árabe (*the language*) = Arabic

araña *noun, feminine*
  una araña = a spider

árbitro/árbitra *noun,*
masculine/feminine
  un árbitro/una árbitra (*in football, boxing*) = a referee
  (*in tennis, baseball*) = an umpire

árbol *noun, masculine*
  un árbol = a tree

arbusto *noun, masculine*
  un arbusto = a bush

archivo *noun, masculine*
  un archivo = an archive
  (*in computing*) = a file

arco *noun, masculine*
* **un arco** = an arch
* (*for shooting arrows, playing the violin*) **un arco** = a bow
* (*Lat Am: in football*) **el arco** = the goal

arder *verb* 17
  = to burn

área *noun, feminine*
  un área = an area

> **!** Note that although **área** *is feminine it is preceded by a masculine article in the singular*

arena *noun, feminine*
  arena = sand

arete *noun, masculine* (*Mex*)
  un arete = an earring

argentino/argentina
1 *adjective*
  = Argentinian
2 *noun, masculine/feminine*
  un argentino/una argentina = an Argentinian

A

argot *noun, masculine*
  argot = slang

Aries *noun, masculine*
  Aries = Aries

aries *noun, masculine|feminine*
  un/una aries = an Aries

aristocracia *noun, feminine*
  la aristocracia = the aristocracy

aritmética *noun, feminine*
  aritmética = arithmetic

arma *noun, feminine*
  un arma = a weapon

> **!** *Note that although* **arma** *is feminine it is preceded by a masculine article in the singular*
> las armas = weapons, arms

armario *noun, masculine*
  un armario = a cupboard
  (*for keeping clothes*) = a closet, a wardrobe

armonía *noun, feminine*
  armonía = harmony

armónica *noun, feminine*
  una armónica = a harmonica

aro *noun, masculine* (*SC*)
  un aro = an earring

aroma *noun, masculine*
  un aroma = an aroma

arpa *noun, feminine*
  un arpa = a harp

> **!** *Note that although* **arpa** *is feminine it is preceded by a masculine article in the singular*

arquitecto/arquitecta *noun, masculine|feminine*
  un arquitecto/una arquitecta = an architect

arquitectura *noun, feminine*
  arquitectura = architecture

arrancar *verb* ②
• = to pull up
  arrancar una planta = to pull up a plant
• = to pull out
  no puedo arrancar este clavo = I can't pull this nail out
• = to tear off
  me arrancó un botón de la chaqueta = he tore a button off my jacket
• = to tear out
  arrancar una hoja de un libro = to tear a page out of a book
• = to start
  arrancó el coche = she started the car
• = to snatch
  me arrancó las llaves de la mano = she snatched the keys from my hand

arrastrar *verb* ①
  = to drag
arrastrarse
  = to crawl

arreglar *verb* ①
• = to mend
• (*if it's a television, washing-machine*) = to repair
• (*if it's a room, the house*) = to straighten (up), to tidy (up)
• = to sort out
  no sé cómo arreglar este asunto = I don't know how to sort this matter out
arreglarse
• = to get ready
  necesito dos minutos para arreglarme = I need two minutes to get ready
• = to get better
  a ver si se arreglan las cosas = let's see if things get better

arriba *adverb*
• = up
  está ahí arriba = it's up there
  ponlo más arriba = put it higher up
• de arriba:
  la parte de arriba = the top part
  el piso de arriba = the apartment above
  = the top apartment
  los vecinos de arriba = the upstairs neighbors
• arriba de (*Lat Am*):
  está arriba del armario = it's on top of the cupboard
  está arriba de mi dormitorio = it's above my bedroom

arriesgarse *verb* ③
• = to take a risk
• = to risk
  se arriesgan a que los despidan = they risk being fired

arrogante *adjective*
  = arrogant

arroz *noun, masculine*
  arroz = rice

arte *noun, masculine*
  el arte = art

> **!** *Note that* **arte** *is generally masculine in the singular and feminine in the plural:*
> las artes = *the arts*

artesanía *noun, feminine*
  artesanía = crafts

artesano/artesana *noun, masculine|feminine*
  un artesano/una artesana = a craftsman/a craftswoman

ártico/ártica *adjective*
  = Arctic

Ártico noun, masculine
  el Ártico = the Arctic
  = the Arctic Ocean

artículo noun, masculine
  el artículo = the article
  el artículo definido = the definite article

artificial adjective
  = artificial

artista noun, masculine/feminine
  un/una artista = artist

asa noun, feminine
  un asa = a handle

> ! Note that although asa is feminine it is
> preceded by a masculine article in the
> singular

asado noun, masculine
  un asado = a roast
  (Lat Am) = a barbecue

asar verb 1
  (if it's meat) = to roast
  (if it's a potato) = to bake

ascensor noun, masculine
  el ascensor = the elevator, the lift

asegurar verb 1
• = to assure
  me aseguró que vendría = she assured me
    that she would come
• = to insure
  aseguraron el cuadro en un millón = they
    insured the painting for a million
asegurarse
  = to make sure
  asegúrate de cerrar la puerta = make sure
    you shut the door

asesino/asesina noun,
masculine/feminine
  un asesino/una asesina = a murderer

asfalto noun, masculine
  el asfalto = asphalt

asfixiar verb
  = to suffocate
• = to smother
asfixiarse
• = to suffocate

así
1 adverb
• = like this
  así es mejor = it's better like this
• = like that
  no te pongas así = don't be like that
2 adjective (! never changes)
  = like that
  él es así = he's like that

asiático/asiática
1 adjective
  = Asian

2 noun, masculine/feminine
  un asiático/una asiática = an Asian

asiento noun, masculine
  un asiento = a seat
  (on a bicycle) = a saddle

asignatura noun, feminine
  una asignatura = a subject

asistir verb 41
  = to attend
  = to go to

asno noun, masculine
  un asno = a donkey

asociación noun, feminine
  una asociación = an association

asociar verb 1
  = to associate
asociarse
  asociarse a algo = to become a member of
    something
  asociarse con alguien = to go into
    partnership with someone

aspecto noun, masculine
• (referring to appearance)
  un niño de aspecto delicado = a delicate-
    looking boy
  tienen un aspecto agradable = they look
    nice
  ¿qué aspecto tienen? = what do they look
    like?
• (referring to health)
  no tienes buen aspecto = you don't look
    well
• un aspecto = an aspect

áspero/áspera adjective
  = rough

aspiradora noun, feminine, **aspirador**
noun, masculine
  una aspiradora, un aspirador = a vacuum
    cleaner, a Hoover®
  pasar la aspiradora, pasar el aspirador =
    to vacuum, to hoover

aspirina noun, feminine
  una aspirina = an aspirin

asterisco noun, masculine
  un asterisco = an asterisk

astrología noun, feminine
  la astrología = astrology

astronauta noun, masculine/feminine
  un/una astronauta = an astronaut

asunto noun, masculine
  un asunto = a matter
  es un asunto personal = it's a personal
    matter
  no es asunto tuyo = it's none of your
    business

---

asustar *verb* 1
= to scare, to frighten
asustarse
= to get scared, to get frightened

atacar *verb*
= to attack

ataque *noun, masculine*
un ataque = an attack
un ataque cardíaco = a heart attack

atar *verb* 1
= to tie
= to tie up
me ataron las manos = they tied my hands up
atarse
= to do up
se ató los zapatos = he did up his shoes

atardecer
1 *verb*
= to get dark
atardecía = it was getting dark
2 *noun, masculine*
el atardecer = dusk
al atardecer = at dusk

atención *noun, feminine*
atención = attention
prestar atención = to pay attention

Atlántico *noun, masculine*
el Atlántico = the Atlantic

atlas *noun, masculine*
un atlas = an atlas

atleta *noun, masculine|feminine*
un/una atleta = an athlete

atlético/atlética *adjective*
= athletic

atletismo *noun, masculine*
el atletismo = athletics

atmósfera *noun, feminine*
la atmósfera = the atmosphere

atómico/atómica *adjective*
= atomic

atracar *verb* 2
• (*if it's a bank*) = to hold up
• (*if it's a person*) = to mug

atraco *noun, masculine*
un atraco (*in a bank*) = a holdup
(*in the street*) = a mugging

atractivo/atractiva *adjective*
= attractive

atrapar *verb* 1
= to catch

atrás *adverb*
• = back
ponlo más atrás = put it further back

• = at the back
con botones atrás = with buttons at the back
quedarse atrás = to be left behind
• (*Lat Am*) **atrás de** = behind
atrás de mí = behind me

atrasado/atrasada *adjective*
• = slow
tengo el reloj atrasado = my watch is slow
• = behind
estamos *or* **vamos atrasados en los preparativos** = we're behind in our preparations

atrasar *verb* 1
• = to postpone
atrasaron el comienzo del curso = they postponed the start of the course
• = to delay
atrasaron la salida del avión = the flight was delayed
• = to put back
atrasar los relojes una hora = to put the clocks back an hour
• = to be slow, to lose time
este reloj atrasa = this clock is slow
atrasarse
• = to be slow, to lose time
este reloj se atrasa = this clock is slow
• = to be late (*Lat Am*)
el vuelo se atrasó = the flight was late

atreverse *verb* 17
= to dare
no me atreví a llamar = I didn't dare call

atrevido/atrevida *adjective*
• = daring
• = sassy, cheeky

atropellar *verb* 1
= to knock down
= to run over

atún *noun, masculine*
el atún = tuna

aula *noun, feminine*
un aula = a classroom
(*in a university*) = a lecture theater

! *Note that although* **aula** *is feminine it is preceded by a masculine article in the singular*

aumentar *verb* 1
= to increase

aumento *noun, masculine*
un aumento = an increase

aun *adverb*
= even
ni aun con una caja más grande = not even with a bigger box
aun así = even so

R Pl River Plate area　　**SC** Southern Cone　　**Spa** Spain

aún *adverb*
* = still
  es aún joven = he is still young
* = yet
  ¿aún no has terminado? = haven't you finished yet?
* = even
  éste es aún más barato = this one is even cheaper

aunque *conjunction*
* = although
* = even though
* = even if
  inténtalo, aunque sólo sea una vez = try it, even if only once

auricular
1 *noun, masculine*
  (of a telephone)
  el auricular = the receiver
2 auriculares *noun, masculine plural*
  los auriculares = the headphones

ausencia *noun, feminine*
  una ausencia = an absence

ausente *adjective*
  = absent

australiano/australiana
1 *adjective*
  = Australian
2 *noun, masculine/feminine*
  un australiano/una australiana = an Australian

austriaco/austriaca,
austríaco/austríaca
1 *adjective*
  = Austrian
2 *noun, masculine/feminine*
  un austriaco/una austriaca = an Austrian

auténtico/auténtica *adjective*
  = genuine, authentic

auto *noun, masculine* (*SC*)
  un auto = a car

autobiografía *noun, feminine*
  una autobiografía = an autobiography

autobús *noun, masculine*
  un autobús = a bus
  (*Lat Am*) = a coach

autocar *noun, masculine* (*Spa*)
  un autocar = a bus, a coach

autógrafo *noun, masculine*
  un autógrafo = an autograph

automático/automática *adjective*
  = automatic

automóvil *noun, masculine*
  un automóvil = a car

autopista *noun, feminine*
  una autopista = an expressway, a motorway

autor/autora *noun, masculine/feminine*
  un autor/una autora = an author

autoridad *noun, feminine*
  autoridad = authority

autoservicio *noun, masculine*
  un autoservicio = a self-service restaurant

autostop *noun, masculine*
  autostop = hitchhiking
  hacer autostop = to hitchhike

avalancha *noun, feminine*
  una avalancha = an avalanche

avanzar *verb* 4
  = to advance

ave *noun, feminine*
  un ave = a bird

> **!** *Note that although* **ave** *is feminine it is preceded by a masculine article in the singular*

avellana *noun, feminine*
  una avellana = a hazelnut

avenida *noun, feminine*
  una avenida = an avenue

aventar *verb* 7 (*Mex*)
  = to throw

aventón *noun, masculine* (*Mex*)
  un aventón = a ride, a lift

aventura *noun, feminine*
  una aventura = an adventure

avería *noun, feminine*
  una avería = a breakdown

aviación *noun, feminine*
  la aviación = aviation

avión *noun, masculine*
  un avión = a plane, an airplane, an aeroplane

avisar *verb* 1
* = to let know
  avísame cuando termines = let me know when you've finished
* = to warn
* (*Mex, Spa*) = to call
  avisar al médico = to call the doctor

aviso *noun, masculine*
* **un aviso** = a notice
* **un aviso** = a warning
  sin previo aviso, sin avisar = without prior warning
* (*Lat Am*) **un aviso** = an advertisement, an advert

avispa *noun, feminine*
  una avispa = a wasp

C Am Central America   **Lat Am** Latin America   **Mex** Mexico

¡ay! *exclamation*
(*expressing pain*) = ouch!, ow!
(*expressing alarm*) = oh dear!

ayer *adverb*
= yesterday
ayer en or (*Spa*) **por** or (*R Pl*) **a la noche** =
last night

ayuda *noun, feminine*
ayuda = help

ayudante *noun, masculine/feminine*
un/una ayudante = an assistant

ayudar *verb* ⓵
= to help

ayuntamiento *noun, masculine*
el ayuntamiento = the town hall

azafata *noun, feminine*
una azafata = a flight attendant, an air
hostess

azúcar *noun, masculine/feminine*
azúcar = sugar

> **!** *Note that* azúcar *is always preceded by
> the masculine article even though it can
> have a feminine adjective:* el azúcar
> morena = *brown sugar*

azucarero *noun, masculine*
un azucarero = a sugar bowl

azul
1 *adjective*
= blue
2 *noun, masculine*
el azul = blue

azulejo *noun, masculine*
un azulejo = a tile

bachillerato *noun, masculine*
el bachillerato = high school education and
diploma

bahía *noun, feminine*
una bahía = a bay

bailar *verb* ⓵
= to dance

bailarín/bailarina *noun,*
masculine/feminine
un bailarín/una bailarina = a dancer

baile *noun, masculine*
• **baile** = dance
un baile nuevo = a new dance

• (*the activity*)
el baile = dancing

bajar *verb* ⓵
• = to go/come down
ya bajo = I'm coming down
el camino baja hasta la playa = the road
goes down to the beach
• = to get down
baja ese libro del estante = get that book
down from the shelf
• = to take down
voy a bajar estas cajas = I'm going to take
down these boxes
• = to bring down
¿me bajas un jersey? = can you bring
down a sweater for me?
• = to lower
bajar la vista/los ojos = to lower one's
eyes
• = to turn down
bajar la televisión = to turn down the
television
• (*if it's temperature, prices*) = to fall
• **bajar la cabeza** = to bow one's head
bajarse
bajarse de un coche = to get out of a car
bajarse del tren = to get off the train

bajo/baja
1 *adjective*
• = short
• (*if it's volume, level, a building*) = low
hablar en voz baja = to speak quietly
2 bajo *preposition*
= under
3 bajo *adverb*
• =low
volar bajo = to fly low
• = quietly, softly
hablar bajo = to speak quietly
4 bajo *noun, masculine*
• **el bajo** = the first floor, the ground floor
• **el bajo** (*of a dress, skirt*) = the hem
(*of trousers*) = the cuff, the turn-up

bala *noun, feminine*
una bala = a bullet

balcón *noun*
un balcón = a balcony

ballena *noun, feminine*
una ballena = a whale

balón *noun, masculine*
un balón = a ball

balonvolea *noun, masculine*
el balonvolea = volleyball

banco *noun, masculine*
• **un banco** = a bank
• **un banco** (*in a park*) = a bench
(*in a church*) = a pew

bandeja *noun, feminine*
una bandeja = a tray

B

bandera noun, feminine
una bandera = a flag

banqueta noun, feminine
• una banqueta = a stool
• (Mex) una banqueta = a sidewalk

bañador noun, masculine (Spa)
un bañador = a swimsuit

bañar verb 1
= to bath
bañarse
= to have a bath

bañera noun, feminine
una bañera = a bath, a bathtub

baño noun, masculine
• un baño = a bath
darse un baño = to have a bath
= to have a swim
• el baño = the bathroom
ir al baño = to go to the bathroom, to go to
the toilet

bar noun, masculine
un bar = a bar

baraja noun, feminine
una baraja = a deck of cards

barata noun, feminine (Mex)
una barata = a sale

barato/barata adjective
= cheap

barba noun, feminine
una barba = a beard
dejarse (la) barba = to grow a beard

barbacoa noun, feminine
una barbacoa = a barbecue
hacer una barbacoa = to have a barbecue

barbilla noun, feminine
la barbilla = the chin

barco noun, masculine
un barco = a boat

barra noun, feminine
• una barra (of chocolate, soap) = a bar
(of deodorant) = a stick
• (for curtains) una barra = a rod
• una barra de pan (Mex, Spa) = a stick, a
French loaf

barrer verb 17
= to sweep

barrera noun, feminine
una barrera = a barrier

barriga noun, feminine
una barriga = a belly, a tummy
echar barriga = to develop a paunch

barrio noun, masculine
un barrio = a neighborhood, a
neighbourhood
el barrio Gótico = the Gothic quarter

barro noun, masculine
barro = mud
(for pottery) = clay

base noun, feminine
• una base = a base
• la base = the basis

bastante
1 adjective
• = enough
¿tenemos bastantes sillas? = do we have
enough chairs?
• = quite a lot of
vino bastante gente = quite a lot of people
came
2 pronoun
= enough
3 adverb
• = enough
no es bastante fuerte = he's not strong
enough
• = quite
es bastante guapa = she's quite pretty
me gusta bastante = I like it quite a lot

bastar verb 1
= to be enough

basura noun, feminine
la basura = the garbage, the rubbish
(container) = the garbage can, the dustbin
tirar algo a la basura = to throw something
away

basurero/basurera
1 noun, masculine/feminine
un basurero/una basurera = garbage
collector, dustman
2 basurero noun masculine
el basurero = the garbage can, the dustbin

batalla noun, feminine
una batalla = a battle

bate noun, masculine
un bate = a bat

batería noun, feminine
• una batería = a battery
• la batería = the drums

batido noun, masculine
un batido = a (milk)shake

batir verb 41
• (if it's eggs) = to beat
• (if it's cream) = to whip
• (if it's a record) = to beat

baúl noun, masculine
un baúl = a trunk
(R Pl: in a car) = a trunk, a boot

bebe/beba noun, masculine/feminine
(R Pl)
un bebe/una beba = a baby

bebé noun, masculine
un bebé = a baby

bebedero noun, masculine (Méx, SC)
    un bebedero = a drinking fountain

beber verb [17]
    = to drink

bebida noun, feminine
    una bebida = a drink

beca noun, feminine
    una beca = a grant
    = a scholarship

béisbol or (Méx) **beisbol** noun,
masculine
    el béisbol, el beisbol = baseball

belga
1 adjective
    = Belgian
2 noun, masculine|feminine
    un|una belga = a Belgian

Bélgica noun, feminine
    Bélgica = Belgium

belleza noun, feminine
    la belleza = beauty

bello|bella adjective
    = beautiful

berenjena noun, feminine
    una berenjena = an eggplant, aubergine

besar verb [1]
    = to kiss

beso noun, masculine
    un beso = a kiss

betabel noun, feminine (Mex)
    una betabel = a beet, a beetroot

Biblia noun, feminine
    la Biblia = the Bible

biblioteca noun, feminine
    una biblioteca = a library

bibliotecario|bibliotecaria noun,
masculine|feminine
    un bibliotecario|una bibliotecaria = a
    librarian

bicho* noun, masculine
• un bicho = a bug
• un bicho = a critter, a creature

bici* noun, feminine
    una bici = a bike

    ! Note that bici is short for bicicleta

bicicleta noun, feminine
    una bicicleta = a bicycle

bien
1 adverb

• = well
    lo has hecho muy bien = you've done it
      very well
    ¿qué tal estás? — muy bien, gracias =
      how are you? — very well, thank you
• = all right, OK
    ¿estás bien? = are you all right?
• = correctly
    contestó bien = he answered correctly
• = good
• = nice
    huele bien = it smells nice
• = properly
    siéntate bien = sit properly
• ¡muy bien! = very good!, well done!
• hablar bien inglés/francés = to speak good
    English/French
• hacer bien:
    hiciste bien llamándome = you did the
      right thing phoning me
• ¡está bien! (agreeing to something) = OK!
2 noun, masculine
• el bien = good
• (Spa: in school) = grade between 6 and 7 on a
    scale of 10

bienvenida noun, feminine
    una bienvenida = a welcome
    darle la bienvenida a alguien = to welcome
      someone

bienvenido|bienvenida adjective
    = welcome

bigote noun, masculine
    un bigote = a mustache, a moustache

bilingüe adjective
    = bilingual

billar noun, masculine
    el billar = billiards

billetera noun, feminine, **billetero** noun,
masculine
    una billetera, un billetero = a wallet, a
      billfold

biografía noun, feminine
    una biografía = a biography

biología noun, feminine
    la biología = biology

biólogo|bióloga noun,
masculine|feminine
    un biólogo|una bióloga = a biologist

biquini noun, masculine
    un biquini = a bikini

birome noun feminine (R Pl)
    una birome = a ballpoint pen

bisabuelo|bisabuela noun,
masculine|feminine
    un bisabuelo|una bisabuela = a great-
      grandfather/a great-grandmother
    mis bisabuelos = my great-grandparents

B

bisnieto/bisnieta *noun,*
masculine/feminine
  un bisnieto/una bisnieta = a great-
    grandson/a great-granddaughter
  mis bisnietos = my great-grandchildren

blanco/blanca
1 *adjective*
  = white
  en blanco y negro = in black and white
2 *noun, masculine/feminine*
  un blanco/una blanca = a white
    man/woman
  los blancos = white people
3 blanco *noun, masculine*
• **el blanco** = the target
  dar en el blanco = to hit the target
• (*the color*) **el blanco** = white

blando/blanda *adjective*
  = soft
  (*if it's meat*) = tender

bloc *noun, masculine*
  un bloc = a writing pad

bloque *noun, masculine*
  un bloque = a block

bloquear *verb* 1
  = to block

blusa *noun, feminine*
  una blusa = a blouse

boca *noun, feminine*
• **la boca** = the mouth
• (*of tunnel*) **la boca** = the entrance
  la boca del metro or (*R Pl*) **subte** = the
    subway entrance, underground entrance
• **boca abajo/arriba** = face up/down
  (*referring to person*) = on one's stomach/on
    one's back

bocadillo *noun, masculine* (*Spa*)
  un bocadillo = a (filled) roll

bocina *noun, feminine*
• **una bocina** = a horn
• (*Lat Am: of a telephone*) **la bocina** = the
  receiver

boda *noun, feminine*
  una boda = a wedding

bodega *noun, feminine*
  una bodega = a wine cellar
  (*selling wine*) = a wine merchant's
  (*C Am*) = a grocery store, a grocer's

bofetada *noun, feminine*
  una bofetada = a slap

boina *noun, feminine*
  una boina = a beret

bola *noun, feminine*
  una bola = a ball
  una bola de nieve = a snowball

boletería *noun, feminine* (*Lat Am*)
  la boletería = the ticket office

boleto *noun, masculine*
  un boleto (*for lottery*) = a ticket
  (*Lat Am: for train, bus, etc*) = a ticket
  (*Mex: for the theater etc*) = a ticket

boli✱ *noun, masculine*
  un boli = a ballpoint pen

  ❗ *Note that boli is short for* **bolígrafo**

bolígrafo *noun, masculine*
  un bolígrafo = a ballpoint pen

bollo *noun, masculine*
  un bollo = a bun

bolsa *noun, feminine*
• una bolsa = a bag
• (*Mex*) una bolsa = a purse, a handbag

bolsillo *noun, masculine*
  un bolsillo = a pocket
  de bolsillo = pocket-size

bolso *noun, masculine*
  (*Spa*) un bolso = a handbag, a purse
  un bolso de viaje = an overnight bag

boludo/boluda✷ *noun,*
masculine/feminine (*R Pl*)
  un boludo/una boluda = an asshole

bomba *noun, feminine*
  una bomba = a bomb

bombero *noun, masculine/feminine,*
bombero/bombera *noun,*
masculine/feminine
  un/una bombero, un bombero/una
    bombera = a firefighter

bombilla *noun, feminine* (*Spa*)
  una bombilla = a light bulb

bombita *noun, feminine* (*R Pl*)
  una bombita = a light bulb

bombón *noun, masculine*
  un bombón = a chocolate
  (*Mex*) = a marshmallow

bonito/bonita *adjective*
  = pretty
  = nice
  = lovely

borde *noun, masculine*
• un borde = an edge
  (*of glass etc*) = a rim
• **al borde de algo**
  = on the brink *or* verge of something

bordo *noun, masculine*
  a bordo = on board

B

borracho/borracha
1 *adjective*
= drunk
2 *noun, masculine/feminine*
un borracho/una borracha = a drunk

borrador *noun, masculine*
• **un borrador** = a (rough) draft
  (*for the blackboard*) = an eraser, a board
    rubber
  (*Mex, Spa: for pencil*) = an eraser, a rubber

borrar *verb* 1
• = to erase, to rub out
• = to white out, to Tipp-Ex® out
• (*if it's the blackboard*) = to clean
• (*from a tape*) = to erase
• (*from a computer*) = to delete

bosque *noun, masculine*
un bosque = a forest
= a wood

bostezar *verb* 4
= to yawn

bota *noun, feminine*
• **una bota** = a boot
• (*for wine*) **una bota** = a small wineskin

botar *verb* 1 (*Lat Am*)
botar algo = to throw something out *or*
  away
botar a alguien✗ (*from a job*) = to fire
  someone
(*from a bar, etc*) = to throw someone out

bote *noun, masculine*
• **un bote** = a boat
• **un bote** (*of marmalade, jelly*) = a jar
  (*of paint*) = a can, a tin
• (*Mex: for garbage*) **un bote** = a trash can, a
  rubbish bin

botella *noun, feminine*
una botella = a bottle

botón *noun, masculine*
un botón = a button
(*of TV, etc*) = a button, a switch
(*Lat Am*) = a badge

boxeador/boxeadora *noun,*
masculine/feminine
un boxeador/una boxeadora = a boxer

boxear *verb* 1
= to box

bragas *noun, feminine plural* (*Spa*)
unas bragas = a pair of panties

bragueta *noun, feminine*
la bragueta (*in trousers*) = fly, flies

brasier *noun, masculine* (*Mex*)
un brasier = a bra

brasileño/brasileña *or* (*Lat Am*)
brasilero/brasilera

1 *adjective*
= Brazilian
2 *noun, masculine/feminine*
un brasileño/una brasileña = a Brazilian

brazo *noun, masculine*
un brazo = an arm

brillante
1 *adjective*
= bright
= shiny
2 *noun, masculine*
un brillante = a diamond

brillar *verb* 1
= to shine
= to sparkle

brisa *noun, feminine*
una brisa = a breeze

británico/británica
1 *adjective*
= British
2 *noun, masculine/feminine*
un británico/una británica = a British
  man/woman

broma *noun, feminine*
una broma = a joke
hacerle *or* **gastarle una broma a alguien** =
  to play a joke on someone

bromear *verb* 1
= to joke

bronce *noun, masculine*
el bronce = bronze

bronceado/bronceada *adjective*
= tanned

bruja *noun, feminine*
una bruja = a witch

brújula *noun, feminine*
una brújula = a compass

buceador/buceadora *noun,*
masculine/feminine
un buceador/una buceadora = a diver

bucear *verb* 1
= to dive

buen *adjective* ▶ bueno/buena

bueno/buena
1 *adjective*

> **!** *Note that* **bueno** *becomes* **buen** *before*
> *masculine singular nouns*

• = good
  son muy buenos conmigo = they are very
    good to me
  ser bueno para [los deportes | los idiomas | la
    física ...] = to be good at [sport | languages |
    physics ...]

- *(in greetings)*
  ¡buenos días! *or (R Pl)* **¡buen día!** = good
  morning
  ¡buen provecho! = enjoy your meal!
- **estar bueno/buena** *(referring to taste)* = to
  be nice
  (referring to condition of food)
  esta leche no está buena = this milk is off
- **¡qué bueno!** *(referring to food)* = it's really
  nice!
- **¡qué bueno!** *(Lat Am)* = great!
2 bueno *adverb*
  = OK, all right
  ¿quieres un café? — bueno = do you want
  a coffee? — OK
- *(other uses)*
  bueno, ya he terminado = well, I have
  finished now
  ¡bueno, basta ya! = right, that's enough!
  ¡bueno! *(Mex: answering the phone)* =
  hello!

buey *noun, masculine*
  un buey = an ox

bufanda *noun, feminine*
  una bufanda = a scarf

búho *noun, masculine*
  un búho = an owl

burbuja *noun, feminine*
  una burbuja = a bubble

burlarse *verb* $\boxed{1}$
  burlarse de algo/alguien = to make fun of
  something/somebody

burro *noun, masculine*
  un burro = a donkey

busca *noun, feminine*
  a *or* **en busca de algo** = in search of
  something

buscar *verb* $\boxed{2}$
- = to look for
- = to look
  buscar en un cajón = to look in a drawer
  (in a book, list) = to look up
- **ir a buscar a alguien** = to go to pick
  someone up

búsqueda *noun, feminine*
  búsqueda = search

buzo *noun, masculine*
  un buzo = a diver

buzón *noun, masculine*
  un buzón = a mailbox, a letterbox

Cc

caballero *noun, masculine*
  un caballero = a gentleman
  caballeros *(in a store)* = menswear
  caballeros *(toilets)* = Gentlemen

caballo *noun, masculine*
  un caballo = a horse
  (in chess) = a knight

cabello *noun, masculine*
  el cabello = the hair

caber *verb* $\boxed{27}$
- = to fit
  la mesa no cabe aquí = the table doesn't fit
  here
  cabe otro más = there's room for one more
- = to hold
  en el estadio caben 100.000 personas =
  the theater holds 100,000 people
- **caber por algo** = to go through something
  no cabe por la puerta = it doesn't go
  through the door

cabeza *noun, feminine*
- **la cabeza** = the head
  se tiró a la piscina de cabeza = he dived
  into the pool
  caí de cabeza = I fell on my head
  lavarse la cabeza = to wash one's hair
- **a la cabeza de**
  = at the top of
  = at the head of
- **cabeza abajo** = upside down
- **una cabeza de ajo(s)** = a head of garlic

cabina *noun, feminine*
  una cabina telefónica *or* **de teléfonos** = a
  telephone box

cabra *noun, feminine*
  una cabra = a goat

cabré, **cabría**, **etc** ▶ caber

cabrón/cabrona⬥
1 *noun, masculine/feminine (Spa)*
  un cabrón/una cabrona = a bastard/a bitch
2 cabrón⬥ *noun, masculine*
  un cabrón = a cuckold

cacahuete, **cacahuate** *noun,*
masculine
  un cacahuete, un cacahuate = a peanut

cacao *noun, masculine*
- **cacao** = cocoa
- *(Spa)* **cacao** = lipsalve

cacerola *noun, feminine*
  una cacerola = a saucepan

---

cada adjective
= each
= every
cada uno = each
cada noche = every night, each night
cada dos días = every two days
cada cierto tiempo = every so often
cada vez más/menos = more and more/less
  and less
cada vez mejor/peor = better and
  better/worse and worse

cadena
1 noun, feminine
• una cadena = a chain
• una cadena (Spa: of radio) = a station
  (Spa: of television) = a channel
• tirar de la cadena = to flush the toilet
• cadena perpetua = life imprisonment
2 cadenas noun, feminine plural
  cadenas = snow chains

cadera noun, feminine
la cadera = the hip

caer verb 28
= to fall
dejar caer algo = to drop something
caerse
= to fall (down)
se me cayó el vaso = I dropped the glass
se le cayó todo el pelo = all his hair has
  fallen out

café noun, masculine
• café = coffee
un café negro or (Spa) solo = a black coffee
un café con leche = a regular coffee, a
  white coffee
un café cortado = a coffee with a dash of
  milk
• un café = a café
• (Mex: the color) el café = brown

cafetera noun, feminine
una cafetera = a coffeepot
una cafetera eléctrica = a coffee maker

caído/caída past participle
= fallen

caiga, caigo, etc ▶ caer

caimán noun, masculine
un caimán = an alligator

caja noun, feminine
• una caja = a box
  (of beer) = a crate
  (of wine) = a case
• una caja (in a shop) = a till
  (in a supermarket) = a checkout
• una caja fuerte = a safe

cajero/cajera noun, masculine/feminine
• un cajero/una cajera = a cashier
  (in a supermarket) = a checkout operator
• un cajero automático = a cash dispenser

cajón noun, masculine
un cajón = a drawer

cajuela noun, feminine (Mex)
la cajuela = the trunk, the boot

calabacín noun masculine or (Mex)
calabacita noun, feminine
una calabacín = a zucchini, a courgette

calamar noun, masculine
un calamar = a squid
calamares a la romana = fried squid in
  batter

calcetín noun, masculine
un calcetín = a sock
unos calcetines = a pair of socks

calculadora noun, feminine
una calculadora = a calculator

caldo noun, masculine
caldo = stock
= broth

calefacción noun, feminine
la calefacción = the heating

calendario noun, masculine
un calendario = a calendar

calentador noun, masculine
un calentador = a heater

calentar verb 7
• = to heat (up)
• (if it's a stove etc) = to give off heat
• (if it's a car) = to warm up
• calentar los músculos = to warm up
calentarse
• = to get hot
• = to get warm

calesita noun, feminine (R Pl)
una calesita = a merry-go-round

calidad noun, feminine
calidad = quality

calienta, caliento, etc ▶ calentar

caliente adjective
• = hot
• = warm

callado/callada adjective
= quiet
quedarse callado = to go quiet
= to keep quiet

callar verb 1
• = to go quiet
• = to be quiet
¡calla! = be quiet!/shut up!
callarse
• = to go quiet
• = to be quiet
¡cállate ya! = be quiet!/shut up!

calle noun, feminine
una calle = a street
calle Lérida n° 9 = 9 Lerida Street

C

calma noun, feminine
  calma = calm
  en calma = calm
  me lo tomé con calma = I took it easy
  ¡tengamos calma! = let's calm down
  = let's keep calm

calor noun, masculine
  el calor = the heat
  tengo mucho calor = I'm very hot
  hace calor = it's hot
  ¡qué calor! = it's so hot

calvo/calva adjective
  = bald

calzoncillos noun, masculine plural
  unos calzoncillos = a pair of underpants

cama noun, feminine
  una cama = a bed
  hacer or (Lat Am) tender la cama = to make
    the bed
  una cama individual or (Lat Am) de una
    plaza = a single bed
  una cama de matrimonio or (Lat Am) de
    dos plazas = a double bed

cámara noun, feminine
  una cámara fotográfica or de fotos = a
    camera
  una cámara de video or (Spa) vídeo = a
    video camera

cambiar verb [1]
• = to change
  cambiar de [coche | canal | trabajo …] = to
    change [cars | channels | jobs …]
  cambiar de idea/opinión = to change one's
    mind
• = to exchange
  quisiera cambiar esta camisa por una
    blusa = I'd like to exchange this shirt for
    a blouse
• te cambio estos sellos por tu póster = I'll
    swap you these stamps for your poster
• cambiar algo de lugar = to move
    something
cambiarse
  = to change
  cambiarse de ropa = to change clothes
  cambiarse de casa = to move house

cambio noun, masculine
• un cambio = a change
  un cambio de horario = a change in the
    timetable
  un cambio para mejor/peor = a change for
    the better/worse
• cambio = change
  me dieron mal el cambio = they gave me
    the wrong change
• el cambio = the exchange rate
  ¿a cuánto está el cambio? = what's the
    exchange rate?
  Cambio (sign in a bank, street) = Bureau de
    Change
• a cambio (de) = in return (for)

caminar verb [1]
  = to walk
  = to go for a walk

camino noun, masculine
• un camino = a road
  = a path, a track
• el camino = the way
  de camino a … = on the way to …
  me queda de camino = it's on my way
  ponerse en camino = to set off

camión noun, masculine
  un camión = a truck, a lorry
  (Mex, C Am) = a bus

camisa noun, feminine
  una camisa = a shirt

camiseta noun, feminine
  una camiseta = an undershirt, a vest
  = a T-shirt

camisón noun, masculine
  un camisón = a nightdress

camote noun masculine (Mex)
  un camote = a sweet potato

campamento noun, masculine
  un campamento = a camp
  irse de campamento = to go camping

campana noun, feminine
  una campana = a bell

campeón/campeona noun,
masculine/feminine
  un campeón/una campeona = a champion

campesino/campesina noun,
masculine/feminine
  un campesino/una campesina = a country
    man/woman
  = a peasant

campo noun, masculine
• el campo = the country
• el campo = the countryside
• el campo = the land
• un campo = a field
  un campo de fútbol = a football field, a
    football pitch
  un campo del golf = a golf course

cana noun, feminine
  una cana = a grey hair

canadiense
1 adjective
  = Canadian
2 noun, masculine/feminine
  un/una canadiense = a Canadian

canal noun, masculine
• un canal = a channel
  = a canal
  el canal de la Mancha = the English
    Channel
• (of television etc) un canal = a channel

C

canario noun, masculine
un canario = a canary

cancelar verb 1
= to cancel

Cáncer noun, masculine
Cáncer = Cancer

cáncer
1 noun, masculine
cáncer = cancer
cáncer de mama = breast cancer
2 noun, masculine|feminine
un/una cáncer = a Cancer, a Cancerian

cancha noun, feminine
una cancha = a court
(Lat Am: for football) = a field, a pitch
(Lat Am: for polo) = a field

canción noun, feminine
una canción = a song
una canción de cuna = a lullaby

cangrejo noun, masculine
un cangrejo = a crab
= a crayfish

canguro
1 noun, masculine
un canguro = a kangaroo
2 noun, masculine|feminine (Spa)
un/una canguro = a babysitter

canica noun, feminine
una canica = a marble

cansado/cansada adjective
• = tired
estoy cansado de pedírtelo = I'm tired of
asking you
• = tiring

cansador adjective (S Am)
= tiring

cansar verb 1
• = to tire (out)
• = to be tiring
• = to bore, to tire
le cansa mucho caminar = he gets very
tired walking
• = to be boring
esta música cansa = this music is boring
cansarse
= to get tired
cansarse de algo/de hacer algo = to get
tired of something/of doing something

cantante noun, masculine|feminine
un/una cantante = a singer

cantar verb 1
= to sing

cantidad noun, feminine
una cantidad = an amount
= a quantity
= a number
¡qué or cuánta cantidad de coches! = what
a lot of cars!
hay cantidad or cantidades de [gente |
peces ...] = there are lots of [people | fish ...]
¿qué or cuánta cantidad de leche pongo?
= how much milk do I add?
¿qué cantidad de niños hay? = how many
children are there?

cantina noun, feminine
• una cantina = a buffet, a cafeteria
• (Lat Am) una cantina = a bar

cañería noun, feminine
una cañería = a pipe

capa noun, feminine
• una capa = a layer
(of paint, varnish) = a coat
• una capa (garment) = a cape

capaz adjective
= capable, able
ser capaz de hacer algo
= to be capable of doing something, to be
able to do something
no fui capaz de terminarlo = I wasn't able to
finish it

capital noun, feminine
una capital = a capital

capitán/capitana
1 noun, masculine|feminine
(in sports)
un capitán/una capitana = a captain
2 capitán noun, masculine|feminine
(in the army)
un/una capitán = a captain

capítulo noun, masculine
un capítulo = a chapter
= an episode

capó noun, masculine
un capó = a hood, a bonnet

Capricornio noun, masculine
Capricornio = Capricorn

capricornio noun, masculine|feminine
un/una capricornio = a Capricorn

cara noun, feminine
la cara = the face
(of record, etc) = the side
tener cara de [enfermo | cansado ...] = to look
[ill | tired ...]
poner cara de [sorpresa | susto | alegría ...] =
to look [surprised | scared | happy ...]
cara o cruz = heads or tails

caracol noun, masculine
un caracol = a snail
(from the sea) = a winkle
(Lat Am) = a conch

carácter *noun, masculine*
  carácter = character
  = nature
  es de carácter bondadoso = he has a kind
    nature
  tener buen/mal carácter = to be good-
    natured/bad-tempered
  tener mucho/poco carácter = to have a lot
    of/not much personality

¡caramba! *exclamation*
• = goodness me!
• = dammit!

caramelo *noun, masculine*
• **un caramelo** = a candy, a sweet
  un caramelo de menta = a mint
• **caramelo** = caramel

caravana *noun, feminine*
• **una caravana** (*of traffic*) = a backup, a
    tailback
• (*Spa*) **una caravana** = a trailer, a caravan

carbón *noun, masculine*
  el carbón = coal

cárcel *noun, feminine*
  la cárcel = jail

cardíaco/cardíaca *adjective* ▶ ataque

carga *noun, feminine*
• **una carga** = a load
    (*of plane, boat*) = a cargo
• (*of pen*) **una carga** = a refill
• (*of weapon*) **una carga** = a charge
• (*responsibility*) **una carga** = a burden

cargado/cargada *adjective*
• = loaded
  el arma estaba cargada = the weapon was
    loaded
  venía cargada de bolsas = she was loaded
    down with bags
• (*if it's coffee*) = strong

cargo *noun, masculine*
• **un cargo** = a post, a position
• **el niño está a mi cargo** = the child is in my
    care
  estoy a cargo de la empresa = I'm in
    charge of the company
• **me da cargo de conciencia** = I feel guilty
    about it
  tener cargo de conciencia = to feel guilty

cariño *noun, masculine*
  cariño = affection
  tenerle cariño a alguien/algo = to be fond
    of someone/something
  tomarle *or* (*Spa*) **cogerle cariño a**
    alguien/algo = to grow fond of
    someone/something
  cariños (*Lat Am*), **con cariño** (*Spa*) (*in*
    letters) = love

cariñoso/cariñosa *adjective*
• = affectionate
• = warm

carnaval *noun, masculine*
  un carnaval = a carnival

carne *noun, feminine*
  carne = flesh
  = meat
  carne molida (*Lat Am*) *or* (*Spa, R Pl*)
    picada = ground beef, mince

carné *noun, masculine*
  un carné = a card
  un carné de identidad = an identity card
  un carné de conducir = a driver's licence, a
    driving licence

carnicería *noun, feminine*
  una carnicería = a butcher's

caro/cara *adjective*
  = expensive
  costar caro = to be expensive
  pagar algo caro (*for a mistake, a misdeed*)
    = to pay dearly for something

carpeta *noun, feminine*
  una carpeta = a folder

carpintero/carpintera *noun,*
masculine/feminine
  un carpintero/una carpintera = a carpenter

carrera *noun, feminine*
• **una carrera** = a race
  echar una carrera = to have a race
  echarle una carrera a alguien = to race
    someone
  las carreras de caballos = the races
  una carrera de relevos = a relay race
• **echar una carrera** = to run
  fui hasta la tienda de una carrera = I ran to
    the shop
• **una carrera** = a degree course
  hace la carrera de derecho = she is
    studying law
• **una carrera** = a career
  su carrera profesional = her professional
    career

carretera *noun, feminine*
  una carretera = a road

carrito *noun, masculine*
  un carrito (*for baggage*) = a trolley
    (*in supermarket*) = a shopping cart, a
    trolley

carro *noun, masculine*
• **un carro** = a cart
• (*Lat Am*) **un carro** = a car
  fui en carro = I went by car
• (*Mex: of a train*) **un carro** = a coach, a
    carriage
  un carro dormitorio = a sleeping
    coach/carriage

carrusel *noun, masculine* (*Lat Am*)
  un carrusel = a merry-go-round

carta *noun, feminine*
- una carta = a letter
  echar una carta (al correo) = to mail a
    letter, to post a letter
  una carta certificada/urgente = a
    registered/express letter
- la carta = the menu
- una carta = a card
  jugar a las cartas = to play cards

cartel *noun, masculine*
  un cartel = a poster
  = a sign

cartelera *noun, feminine*
  la cartelera = the theater/movie listings
  la cartelera de espectáculos = the
    entertainment guide
  la obra sigue en cartelera = the play is still
    on *or* running

cartera *noun, feminine*
  una cartera = a wallet
  (*for documents*) = a briefcase
  (*for school*) = a school bag
  (*S Am*) = a purse, a handbag

cartero/cartera *noun,*
masculine/feminine
  un cartero/una cartera = a mailman/
    mailwoman, a postman/
    postwoman

cartón *noun, masculine*
  cartón = cardboard

casa *noun, feminine*
- una casa = a house
- una casa = an apartment, a flat
- mi casa = my home
  vive en casa de sus padres = he lives at
    his parent's
  están en casa = they are at home

casado/casada *adjective*
  = married
  estar casado con alguien = to be married
    to someone

casarse *verb* 1
  = to get married
  casarse con alguien = to get married to
    someone

cáscara *noun, feminine*
  cáscara = peel
  (*of an egg, a nut*) = shell
  (*of a banana*) = skin

casco
1 *noun, masculine*
- un casco = a helmet
- (*of a horse*) un casco = a hoof
- (*Mex, Spa*) un casco = an empty bottle
2 **cascos** *noun, masculine plural* (*Spa*)
  los cascos = the headphones

caseta *noun, feminine*
- una caseta = a kennel

- (*for guard*) una caseta = a hut
- (*in exhibitions*) una caseta = a stand

casete
1 *noun, masculine/feminine*
  un/una casete = a cassette
2 **casete** *noun, masculine* (*Spa*)
  un casete = a cassette recorder/player

casi *adverb*
- = almost
  casi he terminado = I have almost finished
- = hardly
  no viene casi nunca = she hardly ever
    comes
  casi, casi = almost

caso *noun, masculine*
- un caso = a case
  en todo *or* cualquier caso = in any case
  el caso es que... = the thing is that...
  en caso de = in case of
  yo en tu caso... = if I were you...
- hacer caso de algo = to take notice of
    something
  hacerle caso a alguien = to take notice of
    someone

castaña *noun, feminine*
  una castaña = a chestnut

castaño/castaña *adjective*
  = brown

castañuelas *noun, feminine plural*
  las castañuelas = castanets

castellano/castellana
1 *adjective*
  = Castilian
2 *noun, masculine/feminine*
  un castellano/una castellana = a Castilian
3 **castellano** *noun, masculine*
  el castellano (*the language*) = Castilian
  = Spanish

> ! *Note that Castilian is the official
> language in Spain and the language that,
> with regional variants, is used in Latin
> America. Spanish speakers often use the
> word* castellano *rather than* español *to
> refer to the Spanish language.*

castigar *verb* 3
  = to punish
  castigar a alguien sin salir = to ground
    someone, to keep someone in as a
    punishment

castigo *noun, masculine*
  un castigo = a punishment

castillo *noun, masculine*
  un castillo = a castle
  un castillo de arena = a sandcastle

casualidad *noun, feminine*
  una casualidad = a coincidence
  de *or* **por casualidad** = by chance
  da la casualidad de que... = it so happens
    that...

catalán/catalana
1 *adjective*
  = Catalan
2 *noun, masculine/feminine*
  un catalán/una catalana = a Catalan
3 catalán *noun, masculine*
  el catalán (*the language*) = Catalan

catarata *noun, feminine*
  una catarata = a waterfall

catarro *noun, masculine*
  un catarro = a cold
  agarrarse *or* (*Spa*) **coger un catarro** = to
    catch a cold

catedral *noun, feminine*
  una catedral = a cathedral

categoría *noun, feminine*
  una categoría = a category
  de categoría = first-rate
  de mucha categoría = first-rate
  de poca categoría = second-rate

católico/católica
1 *adjective*
  = Catholic
2 *noun, masculine/feminine*
  un católico/una católica = a Catholic

catorce *number*
• = fourteen
• (*in dates*) = fourteenth
    See **quince** for examples

causa *noun, feminine*
  una causa = a cause
  a causa de algo = due to something

causar *verb* 1
  = to cause

cavar *verb* 1
  = to dig

cayendo ▶ caer

caza *noun, feminine*
  la caza = hunting
  ir de caza = to go hunting

cazadora *noun, feminine* (*Spa*)
  una cazadora = a jacket

cazar *verb* 4
• = to hunt
• = to shoot

cebolla *noun, feminine*
  una cebolla = an onion

ceja *noun, feminine*
  una ceja = an eyebrow

celebración *noun, feminine*
  una celebración = a celebration

celebrar *verb* 1
• = to celebrate
• (*if it's a meeting, an election*) = to hold

celo *noun, masculine* (*Spa*)
  celo = Scotch® tape, Sellotape®

celos *noun, masculine plural*
  celos = jealousy
  sentir *or* **tener celos de alguien** = to be
    jealous of someone
  darle celos a alguien = to make someone
    jealous

celoso/celosa *adjective*
  = jealous

cementerio *noun, masculine*
  un cementerio = a cemetery

cemento *noun, masculine*
  cemento = cement

cena *noun, feminine*
  la cena = dinner, supper
  ¿qué quieres de cena? = what do you
    want for dinner?

cenar *verb* 1
  = to have dinner, to have supper
  les di de cenar = I gave them their dinner
  salir a cenar = to go out for a meal

cenicero *noun, masculine*
  un cenicero = an ashtray

ceniza *noun, feminine*
  la ceniza = ash

centenar *noun, masculine*
  un centenar = a hundred
  centenares de personas = hundreds of
    people

centenario *noun, masculine*
  un centenario = a centenary

centígrado *adjective*
  = centigrade

centímetro *noun, masculine*
  un centímetro = a centimeter, a centimetre

central
1 *adjective*
  = central
2 *noun, feminine*
  la central = (the) head office
  una central nuclear = a nuclear power
    station

centro *noun, masculine*
  el centro = the center, the centre
  un centro comercial = a shopping mall, a
    shopping centre

ceño noun, masculine
  fruncir el ceño = to frown

cepillar verb 1
  = to brush
cepillarse
  = to brush
  se cepilló los dientes = he brushed his
    teeth

cepillo noun, masculine
  un cepillo = a brush
  un cepillo de dientes = a toothbrush
  un cepillo del pelo = a hairbrush

cera noun, feminine
  la cera = wax

cerámica noun, feminine
  cerámica = pottery
  una cerámica = a piece of pottery

cerca adverb
• = nearby
  hay un bar cerca = there is a bar nearby
• = close
  el verano ya está cerca = summer is
    getting close
• cerca de = near
  está cerca del hospital = it's near the
    hospital
  son cerca de las tres = it's almost three
    o'clock

cerdo/cerda
1 noun, masculine/feminine
  un cerdo/una cerda = a pig
2 cerdo noun, masculine
  cerdo = pork

cereal
1 noun, masculine (Lat Am)
  cereal = cereal
2 cereales noun, masculine plural (Spa)
  cereales = cereal

ceremonia noun, feminine
  una ceremonia = a ceremony

cereza noun, feminine
• una cereza = a cherry
• (C Am) una cereza = a coffee bean

cerilla noun, feminine (Spa), **cerillo**
noun, masculine (C Am, Mex)
  una cerilla/un cerillo = a match

cero noun, masculine
  cero = zero, nought
  (in telephone numbers) = zero, oh
  (in football, rugby, etc) = zero, nil
  (in tennis) = love

cerrado/cerrada adjective
• = closed, shut
  cerrado con llave/con cerrojo =
    locked/bolted
• (if it's a faucet) = turned off
• (if it's an envelope) = sealed

• (if it's curtains) = drawn
• (if it's a space) = enclosed
• (if it's an accent) = broad

cerrar verb 7
• = to close, to shut
  cerrar con llave/cerrojo = to lock/to bolt
• (if it's a faucet) = to turn off
• (if it's an envelope) = to seal
cerrarse
  = to close
  se me cerraban los ojos = my eyes were
    closing
  cerrarse de un portazo = to slam shut

certificado/certificada
1 adjective
• = registered
• = certified
2 certificado noun, masculine
  un certificado = a certificate

cerveza noun, feminine
  una cerveza = a beer
  una cerveza de barril = a draught beer
  una cerveza rubia = a lager

césped noun, masculine
  el césped = the grass
  = the lawn

cesta noun, feminine
  una cesta = a basket
  una cesta de Navidad = a Christmas
    hamper

chabacano noun, masculine (Mex)
  un chabacano = an apricot

chaleco noun, masculine
  un chaleco = a vest, a waistcoat
  (knitted) = a sleeveless sweater
  (SC) = a cardigan

champán, noun, masculine, **champaña**
noun, feminine
  el champán, la champaña = champagne

champiñón noun, masculine
  un champiñón = a mushroom

champú noun, masculine
  champú = shampoo

chancho/chancha noun,
masculine/feminine (Lat Am)
  un chancho/una chancha = a pig

chándal noun, masculine (Spa)
  un chándal = a tracksuit

chapa noun, feminine
• una chapa = a metal sheet
• (Spa: of bottle) una chapa = a top
• una chapa = a badge
  (of policeman) = a shield, a badge
• (Lat Am: on door, etc) una chapa = a lock
• (R Pl: of car) una chapa = a license plate, a
    number plate

chaqueta *noun, feminine*
 una chaqueta = a jacket

charco *noun, masculine*
 un charco = a puddle

chavo/chava✶ *noun, masculine/feminine*
(Mex)
 un chavo/una chava = a guy/a girl

checar *verb* 2 *(Mex)*
 = to check

cheque *noun, masculine*
 un cheque = a check, a cheque
 un cheque de viaje = a traveler's check, a
  traveller's cheque
 un cheque sin fondos = a bad check

chequear *verb* 1
• = to check
• *(Lat Am)* = to check in

chequeo *noun, masculine*
 un chequeo = a checkup

chícharo *noun, masculine (Mex)*
 un chícharo = a pea

chicle *noun, masculine*
 un chicle = a piece of chewing gum

chico/chica *noun, masculine/feminine*
 un chico/una chica = a boy/a girl
 = young man/woman
 unos chicos *(boys and girls)* = some
  children/some youngsters

chimenea *noun, feminine*
 una chimenea = a fireplace
 = a chimney

chinche *noun, feminine (C Am, Mex, R Pl)*
 una chinche = a thumbtack, a drawing pin

chincheta *noun, feminine (Spa)*
 una chincheta = a thumbtack, a drawing
  pin

chino/china
1 *adjective*
• = Chinese
• *(Mex)* = curly
2 *noun, masculine/feminine*
• un chino/una china = a Chinese
  man/woman
• *(Mex)* un chino/una china = a curly-haired
  man/woman
3 chino *noun, masculine*
• *(the language)*
 el chino = Chinese
• *(Mex)* chino = curly hair

chispa *noun, feminine*
• una chispa = a spark
• una chispa de [café | agua]✶ = a drop of
  [coffee | water]

chiste
1 *noun, masculine*
 un chiste = a joke
 contar un chiste = to tell a joke
 hacerle un chiste a alguien *(Mex, SC)* = to
  play a joke on someone
2 chistes *noun, masculine plural (R Pl)*
 chistes = comic strips

chocar *verb* 2
 = to crash, to collide
 chocar con *or* contra algo = to run *or* crash
  into something
 chocar contra alguien = to run into
  someone

chocolate *noun, masculine*
 chocolate = chocolate
 chocolate negro = dark chocolate
 chocolate con leche = milk chocolate
 (Lat Am) un chocolate = a chocolate

chocolatina *noun, masculine (Spa)*
 una chocolatina = a chocolate bar

chofer *(Lat Am)*, **chófer** *(Spa)*, *noun,*
masculine
 un chofer, un chófer = a chauffeur
 = a driver

chompipe *noun, masculine (C Am, Mex)*
 un chompipe = a turkey

choque *noun, masculine*
 un choque = a crash, a collision

chuleta *noun, feminine*
 una chuleta = a chop

chupar *verb* 1
• = to suck
• = to absorb
chuparse
 chuparse el dedo = to suck one's thumb

churro *noun, masculine*
 un churro = a strip of fried dough

cicatriz *noun, feminine*
 una cicatriz = a scar

ciclista *noun, masculine/feminine*
 un/una ciclista = a cyclist

ciego/ciega
1 *adjective*
 = blind
 quedarse ciego = to go blind
2 *noun, masculine/feminine*
 un ciego/una ciega = a blind man/woman
 los ciegos = the blind

cielo *noun, masculine*
• el cielo = the sky
• el cielo = heaven

cien *number*
= a/one hundred
cien días = a hundred days
cien por ciento or (*Spa*) **cien** = a hundred
per cent
cien mil = a hundred thousand
ciento uno = one hundred and one

ciencia
1 *noun, feminine*
la ciencia = science
2 ciencias *noun, feminine plural*
ciencias (*subject*) = science

científico/científica
1 *adjective*
= scientific
2 *noun, masculine/feminine*
un científico/una científica = a scientist

ciento *number*
= a/one hundred
ciento veinte = a/one hundred and twenty
cientos de personas = hundreds of people
• **por ciento** = per cent
el tres por ciento = three per cent
See also **tanto**

cierra, cierro, etc ▶ cerrar

cierto/cierta *adjective*
• = true
es cierto = it's true
• = certain
ciertas personas = certain people
en cierta ocasión = once, on one occasion
• **por cierto** = by the way
See also **punto**

cigarrillo *noun, masculine*
un cigarrillo = a cigarette

cima *noun, feminine*
la cima = the top

cinco *number*
• = five
cinco niños = five children
el cinco = (number) five
tengo cinco = I have five (of them)
• (*in dates*) = fifth
hoy es cinco or (*Spa*) **hoy es día cinco** =
today is the fifth
hoy estamos a cinco = today's the fifth
el cinco de mayo = the fifth of May
• (*talking about the time*)
son las cinco = it's five o'clock
las siete y cinco = five after or past seven
cinco para la una or (*R Pl, Spa*) **la una
menos cinco** = five minutes to one
• (*talking about age*)
tengo cinco años = I'm five (years old)
hoy cumplo cinco años = I'm five today
a los cinco años empecé a ir al colegio = I
started school when I was five

cincuenta *number*
• = fifty
cincuenta y uno, cincuenta y dos, *etc*
= fifty-one, fifty-two, etc.
el cincuenta = (number) fifty
hay cincuenta = there are fifty (of them)
• (*talking about age*)
tengo cincuenta años = I'm fifty (years
old)
hoy cumplo cincuenta años = I'm fifty
today
a los cincuenta años dejé de trabajar = I
stopped working when I was fifty

cine *noun, masculine*
• **un cine** = a movie theater, a cinema
ir al cine = to go to the movies, to go to the
cinema
• **el cine** = cinema
el mundo del cine = the world of cinema
• **el cine** = movies, films
el cine mudo = silent movies, silent films
hacer cine = to make movies, to make
films

cinta *noun, feminine*
• **una cinta** = a ribbon
• (*of video, cassette*) **una cinta** = a tape
una cinta virgen = a blank tape
• **una cinta transportadora** = a conveyor belt

cintura *noun, feminine*
la cintura = the waist

cinturón *noun, masculine*
un cinturón = a belt
un cinturón de seguridad = a safety belt

circo *noun, masculine*
un circo = a circus

circunstancia
1 *noun, feminine*
• **una circunstancia** = a reason
por esta circunstancia = for this reason
• **una circunstancia** = a factor
2 circunstancias *noun, feminine plural*
circunstancias = circumstances

ciruela *noun, feminine*
una ciruela = a plum
una ciruela pasa or (*SC*) **seca** = a prune

cirujano/cirujana *noun,
masculine/feminine*
un cirujano/una cirujana = a surgeon

cisne *noun, masculine*
un cisne = a swan

cita *noun, feminine*
• **una cita** = a quotation
• (*with doctor, dentist*) = an appointment
• (*with boyfriend, girlfriend*) = a date
tener una cita con alguien = to have a date
with someone
(*with a friend*) = to have arranged to meet
someone

R Pl River Plate area   SC Southern Cone   Spa Spain

ciudad *noun, feminine*
  una ciudad = a city
  = a town

ciudadano/ciudadana *noun,*
masculine|feminine
  un ciudadano/una ciudadana = a citizen

claro
1 *adjective*
• = clear
  dejar claro algo = to make something clear
• (*if it's a color*) = light
  azul claro = light blue
  ojos claros = green/blue/gray eyes
• (*if it's the sky*) = bright
2 *adverb*
  = clearly
  habla claro = speak clearly
  ¡claro! = of course!
  ¡claro que sí/no! = of course/of course not!
  ¡claro que quieres! = of course you want to!

clase *noun, feminine*
• = kind, sort, type
• = quality
  productos de primera clase = top-quality
    products
• (*in education*) **una clase** = a class, a lesson
  una clase particular = a private lesson
  dar clase de [inglés | latín | música…] (*if it's a*
    a teacher) = to teach [English | Latin |
    music…]
  (*Spa: if it's a pupil*) = to have [English | Latin |
    music…] lessons
• (*room*) **una clase** = a classroom
• (*group of pupils*) **la clase** = the class
• (*social status*) **clase** = class
  clase alta/baja = upper/lower class
• (*when traveling*) **clase** = class
  primera clase = first class
  clase turista/preferente =
    economy/business class

clasificar *verb* 2
  = to classify

clave
1 *noun, feminine*
• **una clave** = a code
  un mensaje en clave = a coded message
• (*in music*) **una clave** = a clef
• **la clave del éxito** = the key to success
2 *adjective* (**!** *never changes*)
  = key

clavo *noun, masculine*
• **un clavo** = a nail
• (*spice*) **un clavo** = a clove

claxon *noun, masculine*
  un claxon = a horn

cliente/clienta *noun,*
masculine|feminine
  un cliente/una clienta = a customer
  (*of company, lawyer, etc*) = a client
  (*at hotel*) = a guest

clima *noun, masculine*
  el clima = the climate

clínica *noun, feminine*
  una clínica = a private hospital

clip *noun, masculine*
• **un clip** = a paperclip
• (*for hair*) **un clip** = a bobby pin, a hairgrip
• **aretes** *or* (*Spa*) **pendientes de clip** = clip-on
  earrings

cobarde
1 *noun, masculine|feminine*
  un/una cobarde = a coward
2 *adjective*
  = cowardly

cobija *noun, feminine* (*Lat Am*)
  una cobija = a blanket

cobrador/cobradora *noun,*
masculine|feminine
  un cobrador/una cobradora (*on bus, train*)
    = a conductor
  (*of debts*) = a collector

cobrar *verb* 1
• = to charge
  me cobraron de más/de menos = they
    overcharged me/undercharged me
  ¿me cobra las cervezas, por favor? = can I
    pay for the beers, please?
• = to earn
  ¿cuánto cobras al mes? = how much do
    you earn a month?
• = to get paid
  mañana cobro = I'm getting paid
    tomorrow
• (*if it's a debt*) = to recover
• (*if it's a check*) = to cash
• (*if it's one's pension, benefits*) = to draw

cobre *noun, masculine*
  el cobre = copper

cocer *verb* 23
  (*if it's vegetables, water*) = to boil
  (*if it's bread*) = to bake
  cocer a fuego lento = to simmer

coche *noun, masculine*
• **un coche** = a car
  fui en coche = I went by car
• (*of train*) **un coche** = a car, a carriage
  un coche cama/restaurante = a
    sleeping/dining car
• **un coche bomberos** = a fire truck, a fire
  engine

cocina *noun, feminine*
• **una cocina** = a stove, a cooker
• (*room*) **una cocina** = a kitchen
• **la cocina española** = Spanish cooking

- **un libro de cocina** = a cookbook, a cookery book

cocinar *verb* 1
= to cook
cocinar a fuego lento = to cook over a low heat

coco *noun, masculine*
un coco = a coconut

cocodrilo *noun, masculine*
un cocodrilo = a crocodile

código *noun, masculine*
un código = a code

codo *noun, masculine*
el codo = the elbow

coger *verb* 20 *(Spa)*

> **!** Note that **coger** is an offensive word in Mexico, River Plate and Venezuela. In those regions the words **agarrar** or **tomar** are used instead

- = to take
me cogió de la mano = he took me by the hand
coger el tren = to take the train
- = to catch
coger una pelota = to catch a ball
coger a un ladrón = to catch a thief
- = to get
coger un resfriado = to catch a cold
coger una entrada = to get a ticket
- = to pick
coger flores = to pick flowers
- **coger algo del suelo** = to pick something up off the floor
- **coger el teléfono** = to answer the phone
cogerse
= to grab hold of
se cogió a la cuerda = she grabbed hold of the rope

cogido/cogida *past participle (Spa)*
= taken
ir cogidos de la mano = to be hand in hand
See also **coger**

coincidencia *noun, feminine*
una coincidencia = a coincidence
se dio la coincidencia de que... = it so happened that...

coincidir *verb* 41
- *(if it's dates, results)* = to coincide
- *(when discussing something)* = to agree

coja, **cojo**, **etc** ▶ **coger**

cojín *noun, masculine*
un cojín = a cushion

cojo/coja
1 *adjective*
= lame
ser cojo = to be lame
estar cojo = to have a limp
ir/andar a la pata coja = to hop

2 *noun, masculine/feminine*
un cojo/una coja = a lame man/woman

col *noun, feminine (Mex, Spa)*
una col = a cabbage
coles de Bruselas = Brussels sprouts

cola *noun, feminine*
- **una cola** = a tail
- *(at bus stop, bank)*
una cola = a line, a queue
hacer cola = to line up, to queue up
ponerse a la cola = to join the line, to join the queue
saltarse la cola *(Mex, Spa)* = to jump the line, to jump the queue
- *(of dress)* **la cola** = the train
- *(for sticking things together)* **cola** = glue

colcha *noun, feminine*
una colcha = a bedspread

colchón *noun, masculine*
un colchón = a mattress

colección *noun, feminine*
una colección = a collection

coleccionar *verb* 1
= to collect

colega *noun, masculine/feminine*
un/una colega = a colleague

colegio *noun, masculine*
un colegio = a school
colegio público = public school *(in USA)*, state school *(in Britain)*

colgado/colgada *past participle*
- *(if it's a lamp etc)* **colgado de algo** = hanging from something
- **el teléfono está mal colgado** = the telephone is off the hook

colgar *verb* 9
- = to hang
(if it's a coat) = to hang up
(if it's a picture) = to put up
- *(when phoning)*
colgar el teléfono = to put the phone down
¡me colgó! = he hung up on me!
no cuelgue, por favor = please hold the line
colgarse
colgarse de algo = to hang from something

coliflor *noun, feminine or (R Pl) noun, masculine*
una coliflor, un coliflor = a cauliflower

colina *noun, feminine*
una colina = a hill

collar *noun, masculine*
un collar = a necklace
(for animal) = a collar

colmo *noun, masculine*
¡esto es el colmo! = this is the limit!
y para colmo = and to make matters worse

colocar *verb* 2
• = to place
colócalo en su lugar = put it in its place
• colocar a alguien = to find/give someone a
  job
colocarse
• = to get a job
• colocarse al lado de la ventana = to
  stand/sit next to the window

colombiano/colombiana
1 *adjective*
= Colombian
2 *noun, masculine/feminine*
un colombiano/una colombiana = a
  Colombian

colonia *noun, feminine*
• una colonia = a colony
• (*Mex*) una colonia = a district
• colonia = (eau de) cologne

coloquial *adjective*
= colloquial

color *noun, masculine*
color = color, colour
¿de qué color es? = what color is it?
de colores = colored, coloured
una televisión en colores *or* (*Spa*) en color
  or (*Mex*) a color = a color television
a todo color = full color, full colour

colorado/colorada *adjective*
= red
ponerse colorado = to turn red

colorear *verb* 1
= to color (in), to colour (in)

columna *noun, feminine*
• una columna = a column
• la columna vertebral = the spine

columpio *noun, masculine*
un columpio = a swing

coma
1 *noun, feminine*
una coma = a comma

> **!** *Note that in Spanish a comma and not a*
> *point is used to mark decimal numbers:*
> *2,7 instead of 2.7* (**dos coma siete** = *two*
> *point seven*)

2 coma *noun, masculine*
coma = coma
en estado de coma = in a coma

comba *noun, feminine* (*Spa*)
una comba = a jump rope, a skipping rope
saltar *or* jugar a la comba = to jump rope,
  to skip

comedia *noun, feminine*
una comedia = a comedy

comedor *noun, masculine*
un comedor = a dining room
(*in school, university*) = a dining hall
(*in factory*) = a canteen

comentario *noun, masculine*
un comentario = a comment

comenzar *verb* 5
= to start, to begin

comer *verb* 17
• = to eat
(*Mex, Spa*) = to have lunch
(*Lat Am*) = to have dinner
¿qué hay de comer? = what's for
  lunch/dinner?
• dar de comer a alguien = to feed someone
• (*in chess, checkers*) = to take

comercio *noun, masculine*
• el comercio = trade
• el comercio = the stores, the shops

cometa *noun, feminine*
una cometa = a kite

cometer *verb* 17
(*if it's a crime*) = to commit
(*if it's a mistake*) = to make

cómic *noun, masculine* (*Spa*)
• un cómic = a comic strip
• un cómic = a comic

cómico/cómica
1 *adjective*
= comic
2 *noun, masculine/feminine*
un cómico/una cómica = a comedy
  actor/actress
un cómico/una cómica = a comedian

comida *noun, feminine*
comida = food
una comida = a meal
(*Mex, Spa*) la comida = lunch
(*Lat Am*) la comida = dinner
hacer la comida (*Mex, Spa*) = to cook
  lunch
(*Lat Am*) = to cook dinner

comienza, comienzo, etc
▶ comenzar

comillas *noun, feminine plural*
comillas = quotation marks, inverted
  commas
entre comillas = in quotation marks, in
  inverted commas

como
1 *adverb*
• = as
duro como una piedra = as hard as rock

* = like
no eres como los demás = you're not like the rest
* = such as, like
países como Grecia, Italia... = countries such as or like Greece, Italy...
* = about
llegaron como a las siete = they arrived about seven
* **como mucho/poco** = at most/least

2 conjunction
* = if
como no estudies no vas a aprobar = if you don't study, you won't pass

> **!** Note the use of the subjunctive after como

* = as, since
como tenía dinero, lo compré = since I had the money, I bought it
* = as
como yo creía = as I thought
* = the way
no me gustó como lo dijo = I didn't like the way he said it

cómo adverb
* = how
¿cómo estás? = how are you
sé cómo lo hizo = I know how he did it
* (in exclamations)
¡cómo has cambiado! = you've really changed!
¡cómo! ¿no lo sabías? = what! you didn't know?
¡cómo no! = of course!
¿cómo? (when you don't understand) = sorry?, pardon?
* **¿cómo es?** = what's he/she/it like?
¿cómo te llamas? = what's your name?

cómodo/cómoda adjective
= comfortable
ponerse cómodo = to make oneself comfortable

compañero/compañera noun, masculine/feminine
un compañero/una compañera = a colleague
un compañero de cuarto = a roommate
un compañero de clase = a schoolmate

compañía noun, feminine
* **compañía** = company
hacerle compañía a alguien = to keep someone company
* **una compañía** = a company, a firm

comparar verb [1]
= to compare

compartir verb [41]
= to share

competencia noun, feminine
* **la competencia** = the competition
* (Lat Am) **una competencia** = a competition

competición noun, feminine (Spa)
una competición = a competition

competir verb [48]
= to compete

compita, compito, etc ▶ competir

completo/completa adjective
= complete
= full
por completo = completely

complicado/complicada adjective
= complicated

comportamiento noun, masculine
comportamiento = behavior, behaviour

comportarse verb [1]
= to behave

compra noun, feminine
una compra = a purchase
las compras or (Spa) **la compra** = the shopping
ir de compras = to go shopping
hacer las compras or (Spa) **la compra** = to do the shopping

comprar verb [1]
= to buy
comprarle algo a alguien = to buy something for someone
= to buy something from someone
le compré un libro para su cumpleaños = I bought him a book for his birthday
le compré su coche viejo = I bought his old car from him

comprender verb [17]
= to understand

computación noun, feminine (Lat Am)
computación = computing

computador noun, masculine,
computadora noun, feminine (Lat Am)
un computador, una computadora = a computer

común adjective
* = common
* **en común:**
hicieron el trabajo en común = they did the work together
tener algo en común = to have something in common

comunicación noun, feminine
* **la comunicación** = communication
* (when phoning)
se cortó la comunicación = I was/we were etc cut off

comunicar verb [2]
* = to communicate
* (Spa: if it's the phone) = to be busy, to be engaged
está comunicando = it's busy

R Pl River Plate area   **SC** Southern Cone   **Spa** Spain

- (*Lat Am: if it's someone phoning*) = to put through
  lo comunico = I'm putting you through

comunidad *noun, feminine*
  una comunidad = a community
  una comunidad de vecinos = a residents' association
  una comunidad autónoma (*in Spa*) = an autonomous region

comunión *noun, feminine*
  la comunión = communion
  hacer la primera comunión = to take one's first communion

con *preposition*
  = with
  córtalo con el cuchillo = cut it with the knife
  pan con mantequilla = bread and butter
  estar casado con alguien = to be married to someone

concha *noun, feminine*
  una concha = a shell

concierto *noun, masculine*
- **un concierto** = a concert
- **un concierto** = a concerto

concurso *noun, masculine*
  un concurso = a competition
  = a contest
  = a quiz

conde/condesa *noun, masculine/feminine*
  un conde/una condesa = a count/a countess

condición *noun, feminine*
  una condición = a condition
  estar en malas condiciones = to be in bad condition
  con la condición de que... = on condition that...

conducir *verb* 43
- = to lead
- = to drive

conductor/conductora *noun, masculine/feminine*
  un conductor/una conductora = a driver

conduje, **condujo** ▶conducir

conduzca, **conduzco**, **etc**
  ▶conducir

conejillo de Indias *noun, masculine*
  un conejillo de Indias = a guinea pig

conejo/coneja *noun, masculine/feminine*
  un conejo/una coneja = a rabbit

conexión *noun, feminine*
  una conexión = a connection

conferencia *noun, feminine*
  una conferencia = a lecture, a talk
- **una conferencia de prensa** = a press conference
- (*Spa*) **una conferencia** = a long-distance call

confianza *noun, feminine*
  confianza = confidence
  de confianza = trustworthy
  tratar a alguien con confianza = to treat someone as a friend
  tener confianza con alguien
  = to trust someone
  = to be friends with someone

confiar *verb* 13
  confiar en alguien/en algo = to trust someone/something
  = to rely on someone/something

confirmar *verb* 1
  = to confirm

confitería *noun, feminine*
- **una confitería** = a cake shop (*also selling candy*)
- (*R Pl*) **una confitería** = a tearoom

confundir *verb* 41
  = to confuse
  confundir algo por algo = to mistake something for something
confundirse
- = to make a mistake/mistakes
  perdona, me he confundido = sorry, I've made a mistake
- = to get confused
  confundirse de [persona | casa | número ...] = to get the wrong [person | house | number ...]

confusión *noun, feminine*
- **una confusión** = a mistake
  = a mix-up
- **confusión** = confusion
  había una gran confusión = there was great confusion

confuso/confusa *adjective*
- = confused
- = confusing

congelador *noun, masculine*
  un congelador = a freezer

congelar *verb* 1
  = to freeze
congelarse
  = to freeze
  = to be freezing
  me estoy congelando = I'm freezing

conjugar *verb* 3
  = to conjugate

conmigo *pronoun*
- = with me
- = to me
  conmigo mismo = with myself
  = to myself

---

conocer verb 19
- = to know
  no las conozco = I don't know them
  conocer a alguien de vista/de oídas = to have seen someone/have heard of someone
  conocer a alguien de nombre = to know someone by name
- = to meet
  ¿dónde se conocieron? = where did you meet?

conocido/conocida
1 adjective
= well-known
2 noun, masculine/feminine
un conocido/una conocida = an acquaintance

conocimiento noun, masculine
- **conocimiento** = knowledge
- **sin conocimiento** = unconscious
  perder/recobrar el conocimiento = to lose/regain consciousness

conozca, conozco, etc ▶ conocer

conseguir verb 57
- = to achieve
- = to get
  conseguí que fuera I got him to go

> ! Note the use of the subjunctive after **conseguir que**

consejo noun, masculine
un consejo = a piece of advice
mis consejos = my advice

conserje noun, masculine/feminine
un/una conserje (in a school) = a custodian, a caretaker
(in a hotel) = a receptionist
(of public building) = a superintendent, a caretaker

considerar verb 1
= to consider

consiga, consigo, consiguiendo, etc ▶ conseguir

consigna noun, feminine
una consigna = a baggage room, a left-luggage office

consigo pronoun
- = with him/her
  Ana no lo llevaba consigo = Ana didn't have it with her
  consigo mismo/misma = with himself/herself
  = to himself/herself
- = with them
  todo lo que tenían consigo = everything they had with them
  consigo mismos = with themselves
  = to themselves

- (referring to you — polite form) = with you
  ¿lleva el pasaporte consigo? = do you have your passport with you?
  consigo mismo/misma = with yourself
  = to yourself

consistir verb 41
consistir en algo = to consist of something

consonante noun, feminine
una consonante = a consonant

constipado/constipada
1 past participle
- **estar constipado** = to have a cold
- (Lat Am) **estar constipado** = to be constipated
2 constipado noun, masculine
un constipado = a cold

construir verb 51
= to build

construya, construyendo, construyo, etc ▶ construir

consultar verb 1
- = to consult
- = to look up

contacto noun, masculine
un contacto = a contact
ponerse en contacto con alguien = to get in touch with someone

contaminación noun feminine
la contaminación = the pollution

contar verb 6
- = to count
  contar hasta diez = to count up to twenty
- = to tell
  cuéntame lo que pasó = tell me what happened
- **contar con alguien/algo** = to count on or rely on someone/something

contenedor noun, masculine
- **un contenedor** = a container
  (for garbage) = a bin
  (for rubble) = a dumpster®, a skip
- **un contenedor de vidrio** = a bottle bank

contenido noun, masculine
el contenido = the contents

contento/contenta adjective
= happy
estamos contentos de verte = we are happy to see you

contestador noun, masculine
un contestador (**automático**) = an answering machine

contestar verb 1
= to answer
= to reply

contigo *pronoun*
* = with you
* = to you
  contigo mismo = with yourself
  = to yourself

continente *noun, masculine*
  un continente = a continent

continuar *verb* [11]
  = to continue, to carry on

contra *preposition*
* = against
  en contra = against
* = into
  chocó contra un árbol = he crashed into a tree
* llevarle la contra a alguien✗ = to contradict someone

contrario/contraria *adjective*
  = opposite
  ser contrario a algo = to be opposed to something
  al contrario = on the contrary
  todo lo contrario = quite the opposite
  llevarle la contraria a alguien✗ = to contradict someone

contrato *noun, masculine*
  un contrato = a contract

control *noun, masculine*
* control = control
* (*in education*) un control = a test

controlar *verb* [1]
  = to control

convencer *verb* [18]
* = to convince
* = to persuade

conveniente *adjective*
* = convenient
* = advisable

convenza, convezco, *etc*
▶ convencer

conversación *noun, feminine*
  una conversación = a conversation

convertir *verb* [46]
  convertir agua en vino = to turn water into wine
  convertir pesos a *or* (*Spa*) en dólares = to convert pesos into dollars
convertirse
  convertirse en un monstro = to become a monster
  (*by magic*) = to turn into a monster
  convertirse al budismo = to convert to Buddhism

convierta, convierto, *etc*
▶ convertir

copa *noun, feminine*
* una copa = a glass (*with a stem*)
* una copa = a drink
  tomar una copa = to have a drink
* (*of tree*) la copa = the top
* (*trophy*) una copa = a cup

copia *noun, feminine*
  una copia = a copy

copiar *verb* [1]
  = to copy
  = to make a copy of
  = to copy down

corazón *noun, masculine*
  el corazón = the heart

corbata *noun, feminine*
  una corbata = a tie

corcho *noun, masculine*
  un corcho = a cork

cordero *noun, masculine*
  un cordero = a lamb

cordón *noun, masculine*
* un cordón = a cord
* un cordón = a (shoe)lace
* (*R Pl*) el cordón de la vereda = the curb, the kerb

coro *noun, masculine*
  un coro = a choir

corona *noun, feminine*
* una corona = a crown
* una corona = a wreath

correcto/correcta *adjective*
  = correct

corredor/corredora *noun, masculine|feminine*
  un corredor/una corredora = a runner
  (*on a bike*) = a cyclist

corregir *verb* [45]
  = to correct
  (*if it's an exam etc*) = to grade, to mark

correo *noun, masculine*
  el correo = the mail, the post
  echar una carta al correo = to mail a letter, to post a letter
  un correo (*Lat Am*) = a post office
  una oficina de correos (*Spa*) = a post office

correr *verb* [17]
  = to run
  subir las escaleras corriendo = to run up the stairs
  salir corriendo de la habitación = to run out of a room
  echar a correr = to start running
  (*in competition*) = to race

✗ in informal situations   C Am Central America   Lat Am Latin America   Mex Mexico

- = to hurry
  ¡corre, vístete! = hurry up, get dressed!
  hacer las cosas corriendo = to do things in a hurry
  me tengo que ir corriendo = I have to rush
- **correr (mucho)** (*if it's a car*) = to go very fast
  (*if it's a driver*) = to drive very fast
- (*if it's curtains*) = to draw
- (*if it's an object*) = to move (along/across *etc*)

corrida *noun, feminine*
  una corrida (de toros) = a bullfight

corriente
1 *adjective*
  = common
  = normal
2 *noun, feminine*
- **la corriente** = the current
- **una corriente (de aire)** = a draft, a draught
  hay *or* (*Spa*) **hace corriente** = there's a draft

corrija, corrijo, etc ▶ corregir
corrompido/corrompida,
corrupto/corrupta *adjective* = corrupt

cortar *verb* [1]
- = to cut
  cortar una rama = to cut off a branch
  cortar un árbol = to chop down a tree
  cortar el césped *or* (*Lat Am*) **el pasto** = to mow the lawn
- (*when on the phone*)
  me cortó = he hung up on me
cortarse
- = to cut oneself
  se cortó el dedo = she cut her finger
  me corté el pelo = I've had my hair cut
  = I cut my hair
- (*when on the phone*)
  se cortó = I was, we were, *etc* cut off

cortaúñas *noun, masculine* (**!** *does not change in the plural*)
  un cortaúñas = a pair of nail clippers

corte *noun, masculine*
- **un corte** = a cut
  un corte de pelo = a haircut
- **un corte de digestión** = a stomach cramp

cortina *noun, feminine*
  una cortina = a curtain

corto/corta *adjective*
  = short

cosa *noun, feminine*
  una cosa = a thing
  ¿cómo van las cosas? = how are things?
  alguna cosa = something
  = anything
  ¿trajeron alguna cosa para comer? = did they bring anything to eat?
  cualquier cosa = anything
  alguna otra cosa = something else
  = anything else
  ¿quiere alguna otra cosa? = would you like anything else?

cosecha *noun, feminine*
  la cosecha = the harvest
  = the crop

coser *verb* [17]
  = to sew

cosquillas *noun, feminine plural*
  tener cosquillas = to be ticklish
  hacerle cosquillas a alguien = to tickle someone

costa *noun, feminine*
  la costa = the coast

costar *verb* [6]
- = to cost
  ¿cuánto cuesta? = how much is it?
  costar mucho *or* **caro** = to be expensive
  costar poco = to be cheap
- = to be hard
  me cuesta entenderlo = I find it hard to understand

costo *or* (*Spa*) **coste** *noun, masculine*
  el costo = the cost

costumbre *noun, feminine*
- **una costumbre** = a habit
  por costumbre = out of habit
  tengo la costumbre de madrugar = I'm in the habit of getting up early
  = I usually get up early
  antes tenía la costumbre de pasear después del trabajo = I used to go for a walk after work
- **una costumbre** = a custom

cotilla✕ (*Spa*)
1 *noun, masculine/feminine*
  un/una cotilla = a gossip
2 *adjective*
  eres muy cotilla = you're such a gossip

cotillear✕ *verb* [1] (*Spa*)
  = to gossip

crear *verb* [1]
  = to create

crecer *verb* [19]
  = to grow
  = to grow up

creer *verb* [26]
  = to believe
  = to think
  ¿tú crees? = do you think so?
  no creo = I don't think so

crema *noun, feminine*
- **una crema** = a cream
- **crema** = *type of custard*
- (*from milk*) **crema** = cream

cremallera *noun, feminine*
  una cremallera = a zipper, a zip
  bajarse la cremallera = to undo one's zipper

creyendo, **creyó**, **etc** ▶ creer

crezca, **crezco**, **etc** ▶ crecer

crimen *noun, masculine*
un crimen = a serious crime
= a murder

cristal *noun, masculine*
el cristal = crystal
(*Spa: material*) **el cristal** = glass
(*Spa: section of window*) **un cristal** = a
window pane

cristiano/cristiana
1 *noun, masculine/feminine*
un cristiano/una cristiana = a Christian
2 *adjective*
= Christian

crítica *noun, feminine*
• **una crítica** = a criticism
• (*of film, play*) **una crítica** = a review
• **la crítica** = the critics

cruce *noun, masculine*
• **un cruce** = a crossing
(*where roads cross*) = a crossroads
• (*between animals, plants*) **un cruce** = a
cross

crucigrama *noun, masculine*
un crucigrama = a crossword

crudo/cruda *adjective*
• = raw
• = underdone

cruel *adjective*
= cruel

cruz *noun, feminine*
una cruz = a cross

cruzar *verb* 4
= to cross
cruzar las piernas = to cross one's legs
cruzarse
cruzarse de brazos = to fold one's arms

cuaderno *noun, masculine*
un cuaderno = a notebook
(*in school*) = an exercise book

cuadra *noun, feminine*
una cuadra = a block

cuadrado/cuadrada
1 *adjective*
= square
2 cuadrado *noun, masculine*
un cuadrado = a square

cuadro *noun, masculine*
• **un cuadro** = a picture
• **una tela a cuadros** = a checked material

cual *pronoun*
el/la cual/los/las cuales = who
= whom
= which
la mayoría de los cuales = most of whom
= most of which
lo cual = which
• **por** *or* **con lo cual** = therefore

cuál
1 *pronoun*
• = which (one)
¿**cuál te llevas?** = which one are you
taking?
• = what
¿**cuál es el problema?** = what's the
problem?
2 *adjective* (*Lat Am*)
= which
= what
¿**en cuál casa vive?** = which house does
she live in?

cualidad *noun, feminine*
una cualidad = a quality

cualquiera
1 *adjective*

> ! *Note that before a noun or noun phrase*
> cualquiera *becomes* cualquier

= any
en cualquier momento = at any moment
un día cualquiera = any day
2 *pronoun*
• = anybody
• = anyone
• (*referring to two people or things*) = either
(*referring to more than two*) = whichever
¿**cual de los dos llevo?** — **cualquiera** =
which one shall I take? — either (of them)
= which one shall I take? — whichever one
you want

cuando *conjunction*
• = when
cuando sea viejo = when I am old

> ! *Note the use of the subjunctive after*
> cuando *to express something that will*
> *happen in the future*

• **cuando quieras, quiera** *etc* = whenever you
want, he/she wants, *etc*
cuando puedas, pueda *etc* = whenever you
can, he/she can *etc*

cuándo *adverb*
= when
¿**desde cuándo vives aquí?** = how long
have you been living here?

cuanto/cuanta
1 *adjective, pronoun*
cuanto/cuanta = as much as
cuantos/cuantas = as many as
unos cuantos [niños | días | casos ...] = a few
[children | days | cases ...]

le di todo cuanto tenía = I gave him everything I had
fueron sólo unos cuantos = only a few went
2 cuanto *adverb*
= as much as
toma cuanto quieras = take as much as you want

> **!** *Note the use of the subjunctive after* cuanto

cuanto antes = as soon as possible
cuanto más/menos = the more/the less
cuanto más tarde mejor = the later the better
en cuanto [llegue | pueda | termine ...] = as soon as [I arrive | I can | I finish ...]

> **!** *Note the use of the subjunctive after* en cuanto

cuánto/cuánta
1 *adjective, pronoun*
cuánto/cuánta = how much
cuántos/cuántas = how many
¿cuánta leche quieres? = how much milk do you want?
¿cuántos libros hay? = how many books are there?
• (*in exclamations*)
¡cuántos niños! = look at all those/these children!
¡cuánto dinero tienes! = you've got so much money!
• (*referring to time*) = how long
¿cuánto (tiempo) tardaste? = how long did you take?
2 cuánto *adverb, pronoun*
• = how much
¿cuánto cuesta? = how much is it?
• (*referring to measurements, size, etc*)
¿cuánto mide de largo? = how long is it?
• (*in exclamations*)
¡cuánto llueve! = it's raining so much!

cuarenta *number*
= forty
See **cincuenta** for examples

cuarto/cuarta *number*
1 = fourth
See **primero** for examples
2 cuarto *noun, masculine*
• **un cuarto** = a room
el cuarto de estar = the living room
el cuarto de baño = the bathroom
• **un cuarto** = a bedroom
el cuarto de los niños = the children's room
• **un cuarto** = a quarter
(*referring to time*) = a quarter
son un cuarto para las dos *or* (*R Pl, Spa*)
son las dos menos cuarto = it's a quarter to two
las tres y cuarto = a quarter after three, a quarter past three

cuatro *number*
• = four

• (*in dates*) = fourth
See **cinco** for more examples

cuatrocientos/cuatrocientas
number
= four hundred
See **quinientos** for examples

cubierto/cubierta
1 *adjective*
= covered
(*it it's the sky*) = overcast
2 cubierto *noun, masculine*
un cubierto = a piece of cutlery
los cubiertos = the cutlery

cubo *noun, masculine*
• **un cubo** = a cube
• (*Spa*) **un cubo** = a bucket
el cubo de la basura (*Spa*) = the garbage can, the dustbin
(*in the kitchen*) = the garbage can, the rubbish bin

cubrir *verb* 59
= to cover

cucaracha *noun, feminine*
una cucaracha = a cockroach

cuchara *noun, feminine*
una cuchara = a spoon
una cuchara de postre = a dessertspoon
una cuchara de servir = a tablespoon

cucharada *noun, feminine*
una cucharada = a spoonful

cucharilla, cucharita *noun, feminine*
una cucharilla de café/té = a coffee spoon/teaspoon

cuchilla *noun, feminine*
una cuchilla = a blade
una cuchilla de afeitar = a razor blade

cuello *noun, masculine*
• **el cuello** = the neck
(*of shirt, dress*) = the collar
• **un cuello alto** = a turtleneck, a polo neck
• **un cuello de pico** = a V neck

cuelga, cuelgo, etc ▶ colgar

cuenta, cuento, etc ▶ contar

cuenta *noun, feminine*
• **una cuenta** = a check, a bill
¿me trae la cuenta, por favor? = could I have the check, please? could I have the bill, please?
• (*at the bank*) **una cuenta** = an account
• **una cuenta** = a sum
hacer cuentas = to do some calculations
• (*in phrases*)
llevar la cuenta de algo = to keep count of something
tener algo en cuenta = to take something into account
más de la cuenta = too much
darse cuenta de algo = to realize something

cuento noun, masculine
* un cuento = a story
* un cuento = a tale
  un cuento de hadas = a fairy tale

cuerda noun, feminine
* una cuerda = a rope
  darle cuerda a un juguete/al reloj = to wind
  a toy/the clock up
* una cuerda = a jump rope, a skipping rope
  saltar a la cuerda = to jump rope, to skip

cuerno noun, masculine
  un cuerno = a horn

cuero noun, masculine
  el cuero = leather

cuerpo noun, masculine
  el cuerpo = the body

cuesta, cueste, etc ▶ costar

cuesta noun, feminine
  una cuesta = a slope
  ir cuesta abajo/cuesta arriba = to go
  uphill/downhill
  llevar algo/a alguien a cuestas = to carry
  something/someone on one's back

cueva noun, feminine
  una cueva = a cave

cueza, cuezo, etc ▶ cocer

cuidado
1 noun, masculine
  hacer algo con cuidado = to do something
  carefully
  tener cuidado con algo/alguien = to be
  careful with something/someone
  ten cuidado de no quemarte = be careful
  you don't burn yourself
  cuidado con el perro = beware of the dog
  cuidado con el escalón = mind the step
2 exclamation
  ¡cuidado! = watch out!/careful!

cuidar verb 1
* = to look after
* = to take care of
  cuidar de algo/alguien = to look after
  something/someone

culo noun, masculine

> **!** Note that **culo** is an offensive word in
> most regions of Latin America

* el culo = the butt, the bum
* (of bottle, glass) el culo = the bottom

culpa noun, feminine
  culpa = fault
  mi, tu, su, etc culpa = my, your, his/her, etc
  fault
  no es culpa tuya = it's not your fault
  echarle la culpa a alguien = to blame
  someone
  tener la culpa de algo = to be to blame for
  something
  por culpa de algo/alguien = because of
  something/someone

culpable
1 adjective
  = guilty
2 noun, masculine|feminine
  el/la culpable = the culprit

cultivar verb 1
  = to cultivate
  = to grow

cultura noun, feminine
  la cultura = culture

cumpleaños noun, masculine
  un cumpleaños = a birthday
  ¡feliz cumpleaños! = Happy Birthday!

cumplir verb 41
* (referring to age, time) = to be
  hoy cumple quince años = she's fifteen
  today
  ¡que cumplas muchos más! = many happy
  returns!
  hoy cumplimos quince años de casados
  (Lat Am) = it's our fifteenth wedding
  anniversary today
* (if it's a jail sentence) = to serve
* (if it's a promise) = to keep
* (if it's an order, a task) = to carry out
* cumplió con su deber = he did his duty

cuna noun, feminine
  una cuna = a crib, a cot

cuñado/cuñada noun,
masculine|feminine
  un cuñado/una cuñada = a brother-/sister-
  in-law

cupe, cupiera, cupo, etc ▶ caber

cura¹ noun, feminine
  una cura = a cure

cura² noun, masculine
  un cura = a priest

curioso/curiosa
1 adjective
  = curious
2 noun, masculine|feminine
  un curioso/una curiosa✱ = a busybody

curita noun, feminine (Lat Am)
  una curita = a Band-Aid®, a sticking plaster

curso noun, masculine
* un curso = a year
* un curso = a course

curva noun, feminine
  una curva = a curve
  (in road) = a bend

cuyo/cuya adjective
  = whose

✱ in informal situations   C Am Central America   Lat Am Latin America   Mex Mexico

Dd

dado *noun, masculine*
un dado = a dice

danés/danesa
1 *adjective*
= Danish
2 *noun, masculine/feminine*
un danés/una danesa = a Dane
3 danés *noun, masculine*
el danés (*the language*) = Danish

daño *noun, masculine*
hacerse daño = to hurt oneself
¿te hiciste daño? = did you hurt yourself?
hacerle daño a alguien = to hurt someone
¿te hace daño el cinturón? = does your belt hurt you?

dar *verb* 15
• = to give
le di mi chaqueta a tu madre = I gave my jacket to your mother
¿me da un paquete de azúcar? = can I have a packet of sugar?
• = to turn on
dar la luz = to turn on the light
• = to say
dar las gracias = to say thank you
• = to give
dales recuerdos de mi parte = give them my regards
darle una noticia a alguien = to break a piece of news to someone
• (*to cause*)
esto da [sed | hambre | calor ...] = this makes you feel [thirsty | hungry | hot ...]
me dio un susto = he gave me a fright
• (*referring to time*)
dieron las cinco = the clock struck five
• dar a:
la ventana da al mar = the window overlooks the sea
la puerta da a la plaza = the door leads to the square
See also **clase** for more examples

darse
darse un baño = to have a bath
darse un golpe = to hit oneself

de *preposition*
• = of
la puerta de la casa = the door of the house
• (*indicating possession, ownership*)
el abrigo de María = María's coat
están en casa de sus padres = they are at their parents'
son de él = they're his
la iglesia del pueblo = the village church
la ciudad de Sevilla = Seville
ciudad de México = Mexico city
• (*indicating origin*) = from
soy de Lima = I'm from Lima
¿cuánto se tarda de aquí a allá? = how long does it take from here to there?
• (*describing people*)
una niña de diez años = a ten-year-old girl
el señor del sombrero = the man with the hat
la chica de la chaqueta verde = the girl in the green jacket
• (*indicating material, content*)
una caja de madera = a wooden box
una botella de vino = a bottle of wine
• (*indicating subject*)
un libro de aventuras = an adventure book
una película de misterio = a thriller
la clase de inglés = the English lesson
• (*indicating authorship*) = by
una canción de los Beatles = a song by the Beatles
• (*with numbers, quantities*)
un billete de cincuenta dólares = a fifty-dollar bill
la mitad de treinta = half of thirty
• (*in comparisons*)
el más grande de todos = the biggest of all
menos de diez = less than ten
• (*in expressions of time*)
viajan de noche = they travel at night
a las siete de la tarde = at seven in the evening

dé ▶ dar

debajo *adverb*
• = underneath
ponte una camiseta debajo = wear a T-shirt underneath
el de debajo = the one underneath
• debajo de = under
debajo de la mesa = under the table
el de debajo de todo = the one at the bottom
por debajo de cero grados = below zero degrees
pasó por debajo de la mesa = he went underneath the table

deber
1 *noun*
un deber = a duty
2 deberes *noun plural*
• (*in school*)
los deberes = homework
3 *verb* 17
= to owe
te debo disculpas = I owe you an apology
• deber hacer algo:
(*when used in the past or conditional*)
debiste or deberías or debías or debieras haber ido = you should have gone
deberías estudiar más = you should study more
(*when used in the present*)

debes portarte bien = you must behave (*when used in the future*)
los estudiantes deberán esforzarse = the students must *or* will have to make an effort

debido/debida *adjective*
debido a algo = due to something

débil *adjective*
= weak

decena *noun, feminine*
una decena = ten
una decena de personas = about ten people

decente *adjective*
= decent

decepcionar *verb* ☐1
= to disappoint
Madrid me decepcionó = I was disappointed with Madrid

decidir *verb* ☐41
= to decide
decidirse
= to make up one's mind

décimo/décima
1 *number*
= tenth
See **primero** *for examples*
2 décimo *noun, masculine*
un décimo = a tenth

decir *verb* ☐53
• = to say
  = to tell
  me lo dijo él = he told me
• (*Spa: when answering the phone*)
  diga *or* (*more polite*) **dígame** = hello?
• (*inviting someone to talk*)
  oye, Ana — dime = hey Ana! — yes?
• **querer decir** = to mean
  ¿qué quiere decir esta palabra? = what does this word mean?

decisión *noun, feminine*
una decisión = a decision

decorar *verb* ☐1
= to decorate

dedo *noun, masculine*
• **un dedo** = a finger
  = a toe
  el dedo pulgar *or* **gordo** (*on the hand*) = the thumb
  (*on the foot*) = the big toe
  el dedo meñique/índice = the small/index finger
• **hacer dedo** = to hitchhike

defecto *noun, masculine*
un defecto = a defect
= a fault
= a flaw
un defecto físico = a physical handicap

defender *verb* ☐21
= to defend
defenderse
= to defend oneself

definición *noun, feminine*
una definición = a definition

dejar *verb* ☐1
• = to leave
  dejé el vaso en la mesa = I left the glass on the table
  dejó el trabajo = he left his job
  ¡déjame en paz! = leave me alone!
• (*to allow*) = to let
  no la dejan ver la tele = they don't let her watch TV
• (*Spa*) = to lend
  ¿me dejas tu coche? = will you lend me your car?, can I borrow your car?
• **dejar de hacer algo**
  = to stop doing something
  = to give up doing something
  ¡deja de preguntar! = stop asking!
  dejar de fumar = to give up smoking
dejarse
• (*Spa*) = to leave
  me dejé las llaves en casa = I left the keys at home
• **dejarse barba** = to grow a beard
  dejarse el pelo largo = to grow one's hair long
• **¡déjate de molestar!** (*Lat Am*) stop being a nuisance

del

> **!** *Note that* **del** *is a contraction of the preposition* **de** *and the article* **el**, *as in la caseta del perro (=* **la caseta de + el perro**). *For usage see* **de**

delantal *noun, feminine*
un delantal = an apron
= a pinafore

delante *adverb*
= in front
estaban delante de mí = they were in front of me
la fila de delante = the front row
• **por delante**:
  se abrocha por delante = it does up at the front
  tienes toda la vida por delante = you have your whole life ahead of you

delegación *noun, feminine*
• **una delegación** = a delegation
• (*Mex*) **una delegación** = a police station

deletrear *verb*
= to spell

delfín *noun, masculine*
un delfín = a dolphin

delgado/delgada *adjective*
= thin

delicado/delicada *adjective*
= delicate

delicioso/deliciosa *adjective*
= delicious

delito *noun, masculine*
un delito = a crime

demás
1 *adjective*
los demás niños = the rest of the children,
(the) other children
2 *pronoun*
¿dónde están los demás? = where are the
others?
ayudar a los demás = to help others
lo demás = the rest

demasiado/demasiada
1 *adjective, pronoun*
demasiado/demasiada = too much
demasiados/demasiadas = too many
hay demasiada luz = there's too much light
había demasiada gente = there were too
many people
demasiadas veces = too often, too many
times
somos demasiados = there are too many
of us
2 demasiado *adverb*
• = too much
comimos demasiado = we ate too much
• = too
es demasiado grande = it's too big
vas demasiado lento = you're going too
slowly

demonio *noun, masculine*
el demonio = the devil

demos, dan, etc ▶ dar

den ▶ dar

dentífrico *noun, masculine*
dentífrico = toothpaste

dentista *noun, masculine/feminine*
un/una dentista = a dentist

dentro *adverb*
• = inside
= indoors
vamos dentro = let's go inside, let's go in
está ahí dentro = it's in there
no se puede fumar dentro = you can't
smoke indoors
de dentro, desde dentro = from the inside
se cierra desde dentro = it locks from the
inside
está pintado por dentro = it's painted on
the inside
• dentro de:

dentro de la caja = in the box, inside the
box
dentro de dos semanas = in two weeks
time
dentro de lo posible = if possible

departamento *noun, masculine*
• (of a company, university) un
departamento = a department
• (Lat Am) un departamento = an apartment,
a flat

depender *verb* 17
= to depend
¿vas a ir? — depende = are you going? — it
depends
depender de algo = to depend on
something

dependiente/dependienta *noun*
masculine/feminine
un dependiente/una dependienta = a sales
clerk , a shop assistant

deporte *noun, masculine*
el deporte = sport
un deporte = a sport
hacer deporte = to play sports

deprisa *adverb*
= fast
escribía muy deprisa = he was writing very
fast
¡deprisa, que llegamos tarde! = quick,
we're late!

derecha *noun, feminine*
• la derecha = the right
fue hacia la derecha = he went right
a la derecha = on the right
manejar or (Spa) conducir por la derecha
= to drive on the right
• la derecha = the right hand
• (in politics) la derecha = the right
ser de derecha or (Spa) de derechas = to
be right-wing

derecho/derecha
1 *adjective*
• = straight
el árbol no crece derecho = the tree isn't
growing straight
siéntate derecho = sit up straight
• = right
la mano derecha = the right hand
2 derecho *adverb*
sigue todo derecho = go straight on
3 derecho *noun, masculine*
• (in law) un derecho = a right
los derechos humanos = human rights
tener derecho a algo/a hacer algo = to
have the right to something/to do
something
¡no hay derecho! = it's not fair!

- *(of a garment, fabric, piece of paper)*
  el derecho = the right side
  póntelo al derecho = put it on right side out

des ▶ dar

desabrochar *verb* 1
- = to undo
  le desabroché el abrigo = I undid his coat
desabrocharse
- = to undo
  se desabrochó la blusa = she undid her blouse
- = to come undone
  se le desabrochó la camisa = his shirt came undone

desagradable *adjective*
= unpleasant

desaparecer *verb* 19
= to disappear

desastre *noun, masculine*
un desastre = disaster

desatornillador *noun, masculine (C Am Mex)*
un desatornillador = a screwdriver

desayunar *verb* 1
= to have breakfast
¿desayunaste ya? = have you already had breakfast?
después de desayunar = after breakfast
normalmente desayuno café = I normally have coffee for breakfast
desayunarse *(Lat Am)*
= to have breakfast
se desayunó con tostadas = she had toast for breakfast

desayuno *noun, masculine*
el desayuno = breakfast

descansar *verb* 1
- = to rest
  necesita descansar = he needs to rest
- *(from work)* = to have a break
  vamos a descansar un rato = let's have a break

descanso *noun, masculine*
un descanso = a rest
necesitas un descanso = you need a rest
- *(from work)* **un descanso** = a break
  hacer un descanso = to take a break
- *(in sport)* **el descanso** = half time
- *(at the theater)* **un descanso** = an interval

desconocido/desconocida
1 *adjective*
- = unknown
- = unrecognizable
  está desconocida *(Spa)* = she's changed so much
2 *noun, masculine/feminine*
un desconocido/una desconocida = a stranger

describir *verb* 60
= to describe

descripción *noun, feminine*
una descripción = a description

descrito ▶ describir

desde *preposition*
- = from
  nos llamó desde Roma = he called us from Rome
  va desde la pared hasta la puerta = it goes from the wall to the window
- = since
  desde las tres en punto = since three o'clock
  desde que llegó aquí = since she arrived here
- = from
  desde tres mil pesos = from three thousand pesos
  desde un principio = right from the start
- **desde luego** = of course

desembarcar *verb* 2
- = to unload
  desembarcaron la carga = they unloaded the cargo
- *(if it's people)* = to disembark
  los pasajeros desembarcaron = the passengers disembarked

desempleado/desempleada
1 *noun, masculine/feminine*
un desempleado/una desempleada = an unemployed person
2 *adjective*
= unemployed

desenchufar *verb* 1
= to unplug

deseo *noun, masculine*
- **un deseo** = a wish
  pide un deseo = make a wish
- **deseo** = desire

desgracia *noun feminine*
una desgracia = a misfortune
tuvo la desgracia de perder la vista = he had the misfortune to lose his sight
por desgracia = unfortunately

desierto/desierta
1 *adjective*
= deserted
2 **desierto** *noun, masculine*
el desierto = the desert

desnudo/desnuda *adjective*
(if it's a person) = naked
(if it's a part of the body) = bare

desobedecer *verb* 19
= to disobey

desobedezca, desobedezco, etc
▶ desobedecer

desobediente
1 *adjective*
= disobedient
2 *noun, masculine/feminine*
eres un/una desobediente = you are very
disobedient

desorden *noun, masculine*
= mess
estaba todo en desorden = everything was
a mess

desorganizado/desorganizada
1 *adjective*
= disorganized
2 *noun, masculine/feminine*
**eres un desorganizado/una
desorganizada** = you are so disorganized

despacho *noun, masculine*
un despacho (*at work*) = an office
(*at home*) = a study

despacio *adverb*
= slowly
¡ve más despacio! = slow down!

despedida *noun, feminine*
una despedida = a goodbye
una fiesta de despedida = a farewell party

despedir *verb* 48
• (*to say goodbye*)
iremos a despedirlos al aeropuerto = we'll
go to see them off at the airport
• (*at work*) = to dismiss, to fire
despedirse
= to say goodbye

despegar *verb* 3
= to take off

despegue *noun, masculine*
= takeoff

despertador *noun, masculine*
un despertador = an alarm clock

despertar *verb* 7
= to wake up
despertarse
= to wake up

despida, despido, etc ▶ despedirse

despierta, despierto, etc
▶ despertar

despierto/despierta *adjective*
= awake

despistado/despistada
1 *adjective*
= absentminded
2 *noun, masculine/feminine*
es una despistada = she's very
absentminded

desplegar *verb* 8
= to unfold

despliega, despliego, etc
▶ desplegar

después *adverb*
= later
= afterwards
quedaron para después = they arranged to
meet later
se lo dijo mucho después = he told her
much later
poco después = shortly afterwards
¿qué dijo después? = what did she say
next?
• **después de** = after
después de la película = after the movie
depués de ir al gimnasio = after going to
the gym
después de todo = after all
después de que hayas hecho los deberes
= when or after you've finished your
homework

! *Note the use of the subjunctive after*
después de que

destino *noun, masculine*
• **el destino** = fate
• (*of a train, plane, traveler*) **destino** =
destination
con destino a = bound for

destornillador *noun, masculine*
un destornillador = a screwdriver

detalle *noun, masculine*
un detalle = a detail

detective *noun, masculine/feminine*
un/una detective = a detective

detergente *noun, masculine*
un detergente = a laundry detergent, a
washing powder
(*SC*) = a dishwashing liquid, a washing-up
liquid

detestar *verb* 1
= to detest

detrás *adverb*
• = behind
vienen detrás = they are coming behind
• **detrás de** = behind
se escondió detrás de un árbol = he hid
behind a tree
• = after
un cigarrillo detrás de otro = one cigarette
after another
• **por detrás:**
se abrocha por detrás = it does up at the
back
nos atacaron por detrás = they attacked us
from behind

deuda noun, feminine
  una deuda = a debt
  tener una deuda = to be in debt

devolver verb 24
• (if it's an object, a book) = to return
• (if it's money) = to refund

devuelto, **devuelvo**, **etc** ▶ devolver

di ▶ dar

día noun, masculine
• **un día** = a day
  ¿qué día es hoy? = what day is it today?
  al or **el día siguiente** = the following day
  el día anterior = the previous day
  el otro día = the other day
  [**una vez** | **dos veces** | **doce horas** …] **al día** =
    [once | twice | twelve hours …] a day
  de día = during the day, in the daytime
  hacerse de día = to get light
  todos los días = every day
  cada día = every day
  un día festivo or (Lat Am) **feriado** = a public
    holiday
  un día libre = a day off
  el día trece de junio = the thirteenth of
    June
  el día de los inocentes = April Fool's day
  el día de los Reyes = the 6th of January
    (when Christmas presents are exchanged in
    Spain)
• (talking about the weather)
  hoy hace un buen día = it is nice today

diablo noun, masculine
  el diablo = the devil

diadema noun, feminine
• **una diadema** = a tiara
• **una diadema** = a hairband

diagrama noun, masculine
  un diagrama = a diagram

diálogo noun, masculine
  un diálogo = a conversation

diamante noun, masculine
  un diamante = a diamond

diario/diaria
1 adjective
• = daily
  clases diarias = daily lessons
• = everyday
  gastos diarios = everyday expenses
• **a diario** = every day
• **de diario** = everyday
  ropa de diario = everyday clothes
2 diario noun, masculine
• **un diario** = a newspaper
• **un diario** = a diary

dibujar verb 1
  = to draw

dibujo noun, masculine
  un dibujo = a drawing
  hizo un dibujo = he drew a picture
  estudiar dibujo = to study drawing
  dibujos animados = cartoons

diccionario noun, masculine
  un diccionario = a dictionary

dice, **dicho**, **etc** ▶ decir

diciembre noun, masculine
  = December

dictado noun, masculine
  un dictado = a dictation

diecinueve number
• = nineteen
• (in dates) = nineteenth
    See **quince** for examples

dieciocho number
• = eighteen
• (in dates) = eighteenth
    See **quince** for examples

dieciséis number
• = sixteen
• (in dates) = sixteenth
    See **quince** for examples

diecisiete number
  = seventeen
• (in dates) = seventeenth
    See **quince** for examples

diente noun, masculine
• **un diente** = a tooth
• **un diente de ajo** = a clove of garlic

diera, **dieras**, **etc** ▶ dar

diez number
• = ten
• (in dates) = tenth
    See **cinco** for examples

diferencia noun, feminine
  una diferencia = a difference
  diferencia de tamaño = difference in size

diferente adjective
  = different

difícil adjective
  = difficult

dificultad noun, feminine
  una dificultad = a difficulty

diga, **digo**, **dije**, **etc** ▶ decir

dimos ▶ dar

Dinamarca noun, feminine
  Dinamarca = Denmark

dinero noun, masculine
  el dinero = money
  dinero suelto (Mex, Spa) = small change
  dinero en efectivo = cash

dinosaurio noun, masculine
  un dinosaurio = a dinosaur

dio ▶ dar

dios noun, masculine
  un dios = a god
  ¡Dios mío! = Good God!
  ¡por Dios! = for God's sake!

dirá, diré, etc ▶ decir

dirección noun, feminine
• = address
  ¿me das tu dirección? = will you give me
    your address?
• = direction
  en dirección contraria = in the opposite
    direction
  van en dirección a Lima = they are heading
    toward Lima

directo/directa adjective
• = direct
• (if it's a train) = through
• en directo = live

director/directora noun,
masculine/feminine
  un director/una directora (of a company) =
    a manager
  (of a school) = a principal, a
    headmaster/headmistress
  (of a play, a film) = a director
  (of a newspaper) = an editor
  (of an orchestra, a choir) = a conductor

disco noun, masculine
  un disco = a record

discoteca noun, feminine
  una discoteca = a disco

disculpa noun, feminine
  una disculpa = an apology
  pedir disculpas = to apologize

disculparse verb [1]
  = to apologize

diseño noun, masculine
  un diseño = a design
  estudiar diseño = to study design

disfraz noun, masculine
• un disfraz = a costume, a fancy dress outfit
• un disfraz = a disguise

disfrutar verb [1]
  = to enjoy

disparo noun, masculine
  un disparo = a shot

distancia noun, feminine
  = distance
  ¿a qué distancia está el pueblo? = how far
    is the village?
  está a poca distancia de la frontera = it's
    near the border

diste ▶ dar

distinto adjective
  = different

distrito noun, masculine
  un distrito = a district
  el Distrito Federal = the Federal District

divertido/divertida adjective
  = funny
  = entertaining

dividir verb [41]
  = to divide
  = to share out

división noun, feminine
  una división = a division

divorciado/divorciada
1 adjective
  = divorced
2 noun, masculine/feminine
  un divorciado/una divorciada = a divorcé, a
    divorcee/a divorcée, a divorcee

doblar verb [1]
• = to fold
• = to bend
• = to double
• (if it's a movie) = to dub
• doblar la esquina = to turn the corner

doble
1 adjective
  = double
• (if it's a whisky, gin, etc) = large
2 noun, masculine
  el doble = twice as many/much
  es el doble de ancho = it's twice as wide

doce number
• = twelve
• (in dates) = twelfth
    See cinco for examples
• (talking about the time)
  son las doce del mediodía = it's twelve
    noon
  son las doce de la noche = it's twelve
    midnight

doceavo/doceava number
  = twelfth
    See primero for examples

docena noun, feminine
  una docena = a dozen
  una docena de huevos = a dozen eggs

doctor/doctora noun,
masculine/feminine
  un doctor/una doctora = a doctor

D

documento *noun, masculine*
un documento = a document

dólar *noun, masculine*
un dólar = a dolar

doler *verb* 22
= to hurt
¿te duele? = does it hurt?
me duele la mano = my hand hurts
me duele la cabeza = I have a headache

dolor *noun, masculine*
un dolor = a pain
un dolor en la espalda = a pain in my back
tengo dolor de muelas/de cabeza = I have
a toothache/a headache

domingo *noun, masculine*
domingo = Sunday
Domingo de Ramos/de Resurrección =
Palm/Easter Sunday
See **miércoles** *for examples*

dominó *noun, masculine*
el dominó = dominoes

don *noun, masculine*
≈ Mr
don Miguel Ferrer ≈ Mr Miguel Ferrer

! *Note that* **don** *can also be used before
first names as a mark of respect*

dona *noun, feminine (Mex)*
• una dona = a donut, a doughnut

donde *adverb*
= where
el lugar donde vivo = the place where I live
el lugar a donde viajaban = the place they
were traveling to
la carretera por donde pasamos = the road
we went along
ponlo donde quieras = put it wherever you
want

! *Note the use of the subjunctive after*
donde

dónde *adverb*
= where
¿dónde vives? = where do you live?
¿dónde queda? = where is it?
¿por dónde se va a la estación? = how do
you get to the station?
no sé por dónde se fueron = I don't know
which way they went

donut *noun, masculine*
un donut = a donut, a doughnut

doña *noun, feminine*
≈ Mrs, Ms
doña Juana Lucas = Mrs Juana Lucas

! *Note that* **doña** *can also be used before
first names as a mark of respect*

dorado/dorada *adjective*
= golden
= gold

dormir *verb* 49
• = to sleep
= to be asleep
• = to get to sleep
no conseguí dormir al niño = I couldn't get
the baby to sleep
dormirse
= to fall asleep
= to get to sleep
= to oversleep
se me ha dormido el brazo = my arm has
gone to sleep

dormitorio *noun, masculine*
un dormitorio *(in a house)* = a bedroom
(in a school, barracks) = a dormitory

dorso *noun, masculine*
el dorso = the back
el dorso [de la mano | del papel | de la carta ...]
= the back [of the hand | paper | letter ...]
nadar de dorso *(Méx)* to swim (the)
backstroke

dos *number*
• = two
• *(in dates)*
= second
See **cinco** *for examples*

doscientos/doscientas *number*
= two hundred
See **quinientos** *for examples*

doy ▶ dar

droga *noun, feminine*
una droga = a drug

drogadicto/drogadicta *noun,
masculine/feminine*
un drogadicto/ una drogadicta = a drug
addict

droguería *noun, feminine (Spa)*
una droguería = *a shop that sells cleaning
materials and products, paint, and other
household items*

ducha *noun, feminine*
una ducha = a shower
darse una ducha = to take a shower

ducharse *verb* 1
= to take a shower

duda *noun, feminine*
• una duda = a doubt
no tengo la menor duda = I have no doubts
whatsoever
tener dudas *or (Spa)* estar en duda sobre
algo = to have doubts about something

* (*in a class, lecture*)
  consultar dudas con el profesor = to sort
    out queries with the teacher
  ¿tiene alguien alguna duda? = does
    anybody have any queries?

dudar *verb* [1]
  = to doubt
  dudo de su honestidad = I doubt his
    honesty
  dudo que venga = I doubt he'll come

  ! *Note the use of the subjunctive after*
  dudar que
  dudaba entre ir o quedarse = he didn't
    know whether to go or to stay

duela, **duelo**, **etc** ▶ doler

dueño/dueña *noun*, *masculine/feminine*
  un dueño/una dueña = an owner

duerma, **duermo**, **etc** ▶ dormir

dulce
1 *adjective*
  = sweet
2 *noun*, *masculine* (*Lat Am*)
  un dulce = a candy, a sweet

duodécimo/duodécima *adjective*
  = twelfth

duque/duquesa *noun*
masculine/feminine
  un duque/una duquesa = a duke/a duchess

durante *preposition*
* = during
  lo leí durante el viaje = I read it during the
    journey
* = for
  trabajaron durante tres semanas = they
    worked for three weeks

durar *verb* [1]
  = to last
  duró mucho = it lasted a long time

duro/dura
1 *adjective*
* = hard
* = harsh
  un castigo duro = a harsh punishment
* = tough
  un régimen duro = a tough regime
* (*referring to food*)
  un huevo duro = a boiled egg
  la carne está dura = the meat is very
    tough
* **ser duro/dura de oído** = to be hard of
    hearing
2 duro *adverb* (*Lat Am*)
  = hard
  estudiar duro = to study hard
3 duro *noun*, *masculine* (*Spa*)
  un duro = a five-peseta coin

Ee

e *conjunction*
  = and

  ! *Note that* e *is used instead of* y *when
  the word that follows starts with* i *or* hi, *as
  in* España e Inglaterra, *and in* padres e
  hijos. *See* y *for uses*

echar *verb* [1]
* = to throw
  échale la pelota = throw him the ball
* = to put in
  echar [gasolina | azúcar | leche …] = to put
    [some gasoline | sugar | milk …] in
* = to give, to serve
  ¿te echo más vino? = can I give you some
    more wine?
* **echar a alguien** (*from a job*) = to fire
    someone
  (*from a bar, theater*) = to throw someone
    out
  (*from school*) = to expel someone
* **echar de menos a alguien** = to miss
    someone

eco *noun*, *masculine*
  un eco = an echo

economía *noun*, *feminine*
  la economía = the economy

económico/económica *adjective*
* = economic
* = economical

ecuador *noun*, *masculine*
  el ecuador = the equator

edad *noun*, *feminine*
  edad = age
  ¿qué edad tiene? = how old is she?
  tengo un hijo de tu edad = I have a boy
    your age

edificio *noun*, *masculine*
  un edificio = a building

edredón *noun*, *masculine*
  un edredón = a quilt
  un edredón nórdico = a continental quilt, a
    duvet

educación *noun*, *feminine*
* = education
  educación física = physical education
* = upbringing
  tuvo una educación muy estricta = he had
    a very strict upbringing
* = manners
  eso es de mala educación = that's bad
    manners

E

educado/educada *adjective*
= polite
una persona bien/mal educada = a
polite/rude person

efectivo/efectiva
1 *adjective*
= effective
2 efectivo *noun, masculine*
efectivo = cash
dinero en efectivo = cash
pagar en efectivo = to pay cash

efecto *noun, masculine*
hacer efecto = to take effect

egoísta
1 *noun, masculine/feminine*
eres un/una egoísta = you are so selfish
2 *adjective*
= selfish

ejemplo *noun, masculine*
un ejemplo = an example
por ejemplo = for example

ejercicio *noun, masculine*
un ejercicio = an exercise
hacer ejercicio = to exercise

ejército *noun, masculine*
un ejército = an army

ejote *noun, masculine* (*Mex*)
un ejote = a green bean

el *masculine article*

> **!** *The plural of* **el** *is* **los**, *and the feminine
> forms are* **la** (*singular*) *and* **las** (*plural*).
> *Note that the masculine article* **el** *is also
> used before feminine nouns which begin
> with an stressed* **a**- *or* **ha**- *sound, such as*
> **el agua**, **el hada**

• = the
prefiero el abrigo rojo = I prefer the red
coat
• **los perros son muy fieles** = dogs are very
loyal
me duele la cabeza = my head hurts
se quitó los zapatos = he took his shoes off
• (*with proper names, titles, and names that
indicate family ties*)
el señor Rodríguez = Mr Rodríguez
el hermano de Julia = Julia's brother
• (*with expressions of time*)
llegan el quince de julio = they arrive on
the fifteenth of July
la semana que viene = next week
voy a visitarla los lunes = I go to visit her
on Mondays
son las siete = it's seven o'clock
• **el/la/los/las de:**
el de Jaime = Jaime's
las del colegio = the ones from the school
la de los ojos verdes = the one with green
eyes
• **el/la /los/las que:**

el que te dije = the one I told you about
los/las que yo llevé = the ones I took
elige el/la que tú quieras = choose
whichever you want
dame el/la que sea = give me any one
invitaré a los/las que yo quiera = I will
invite whoever I want

> **!** *Note the use of the subjunctive after*
> **el/la que**, **los/las que**

él *pronoun*
• = he
• = him
se lo di a él = I gave it to him
él mismo = himself
es de él = it's his

elástico/elástica *adjective*
= elastic

elección *noun, feminine*
• **una elección** = a choice
no tengo elección = I have no choice
• **una elección** = an election
las elecciones municipales = the local
elections

electricidad *noun, feminine*
la electricidad = electricity

electricista *noun, masculine/feminine*
un /una electricista = an electrician

eléctrico/eléctrica *adjective*
= electric
= electrical

electrónico/electrónica *adjective*
= electronic

elefante *noun, masculine*
un elefante = an elephant

elegir *verb* 45
= to choose

elepé *noun, masculine*
un elepé = an LP

elija, **elijo**, **elijiendo**, **etc ▶** elegir

ella *pronoun*
• = she
• = her
se lo di a ella = I gave it to her
ella misma = herself
es de ella = it's hers

ellas *pronoun*
• = they
• = them
See **ellos** *for examples*

ello *pronoun*
= it
ocúpate de ello = take care of it

ellos/ellas *pronoun*
- = they
- = them
  se lo dí a ellos/ellas = I gave it to them
  ellos mismos/ellas mismas = themselves
  es de ellos/ellas = it's theirs

elote *noun, masculine (C Am, Mex)*
un elote = a corncob, an ear of corn

embarazada
1 *adjective*
= pregnant
quedar *or (Spa)* quedarse embarazada = to get pregnant
está embarazada de seis meses = she's six months pregnant
2 *noun, feminine*
una embarazada = a pregnant woman

embarcar *verb* 2
(onto a plane) = to board
(onto a boat) = to embark

embotellamiento *noun, masculine*
un embotellamiento = a traffic jam

emergencia *noun, feminine*
una emergencia = an emergency

empanada *noun, feminine*
una empanada *(Lat Am)* = a pastry
(Spa) = a pie

empate *noun, masculine*
un empate *(in sports)* = a tie, a draw
(in an election) = a tie

empecé ▶ empezar

empeorar *verb* 1
- = to get worse
- = to make worse

empezar *verb* 5
= to begin, to start

empiece, **empieza**, **empiezo**, **etc**
▶ empezar

empleado/empleada *noun*
masculine/feminine
un empleado/una empleada = an employee
(in an office) = an office worker, a clerk
(in a shop) = a clerk, a shop assistant

empleo *noun, masculine*
un empleo = a job
estar sin empleo = to be unemployed

empujar *verb* 1
= to push

en *preposition*
- = in
  = into
  en primavera = in spring
  meterse en la cama = to get into bed
- = on
  en la mesa = on the table

- = at
  viven en el número quince = they live at number fifteen
  ahora está en casa = she's at home now
  en la noche *(Lat Am)* = at night
- = by
  en [coche | barco | avión …] = by [car | boat | plane …]
  iba en bicicleta = she was riding a bike

encendedor *noun, masculine*
un encendedor = a lighter

encender *verb* 21
- = to switch on
  = to turn on
  encender [la televisión | la calefacción | la luz …] = to turn on [the television | the heating | the light …]
- = to light
  encender [el fuego | una vela | una cigarrillo …] = to light [the fire | a candle | a cigarette …]

encendido/encendida *adjective*
- *(if it's a television, radio)* = on
- *(if it's a fire, match, etc.)* = lit, lighted

enchufar *verb* 1
- = to plug in
  enchufar la plancha = to plug the iron in
- = to switch on
  = to turn on

enchufe *noun, masculine*
un enchufe = a plug

enciclopedia *noun, feminine*
una enciclopedia = an encyclopedia

encienda, **enciendo**, **etc** ▶ encender

encima *adverb*
- = on
  le puse una piedra encima = I put a stone on it
  lo dejé ahí encima = I left it up there
- encima de:
  encima de la mesa = on the table
  está encima del refrigerador = it's on top of the fridge
  su sala está encima de mi cuarto = her living-room is over my bedroom
- el de encima = the top one
- por encima de:
  = above
  = over
  por encima de las rodillas = above the knees
  por encima de la valla = over the fence
  temperaturas por encima de veinte grados = temperatures over twenty degrees

encontrar verb [6]
= to find
no lo encuentro = I can't find it
encontrarse
• = to find
me encontré una cartera = I found a wallet
• = to meet
se encontraron en la calle = they met on the beach

encuentra, **encuentro**, **etc**
▶ encontrar

enemigo/enemiga noun, masculine/feminine
un enemigo/una enemiga = an enemy

energía noun, feminine
energía = energy
la energía eléctrica = electricity

enero noun, masculine
= January

enfadado/enfadada adjective (Spa)
= angry
= annoyed

enfadar verb [1] (Spa)
= to make angry
= to annoy
me hizo enfadar = he made me angry
enfadarse
= to get angry
= to get annoyed

enfermarse verb [1] (Lat Am)
= to fall ill

enfermedad noun, feminine
una enfermedad = an illness
= a disease

enfermero/enfermera noun, masculine/feminine
un enfermero/una enfermera = a nurse

enfermo/enferma
1 adjective
= ill
= sick
caer enfermo/enferma = to fall ill
2 noun, masculine/feminine
un enfermo/una enferma = a sick person

enfrente adverb
= opposite
está enfrente del cine = it's opposite the movie house

engordar verb [1]
• = to put on weight
he engordado mucho = I have put on a lot of weight
• = to be fattening

enhorabuena noun, feminine
¡enhorabuena! = congratulations!
darle la enhorabuena a alguien = to congratulate someone

enojado/enojada adjective (Lat Am)
= angry
= annoyed

enojar verb [1] (Lat Am)
= to make angry
= to annoy
me hizo enojar = he made me angry
enojarse
= to get angry
= to get annoyed

enorme adjective
= enormous

ensalada noun, feminine
una ensalada = a salad

ensaladera noun, feminine
una ensaladera = a salad bowl

ensayo noun, masculine
un ensayo = a test
(for a play) = a rehearsal
(a short piece of writing) = an essay

enseguida adverb
= at once, straight away

enseñanza noun, feminine
= teaching
= education

enseñar verb [1]
• = to teach
• = to show
¿me enseñas las fotos? = will you show me the photographs?

ensuciar verb [1]
= to get dirty
ensuciarse
te has ensuciado la cara = you've got your face dirty
me ensucié la camisa de café = I got coffee on my shirt

entender verb [21]
= to understand
te entendí mal = I misunderstood you
dar a entender = to imply
entiende mucho de [fotografía | motos | jardinería ...] = he knows a lot about [photography | bikes | gardening ...]

entero/entera adjective
• = whole
la semana entera = the whole week
• (not broken) = intact
• (if it's milk) = full-cream

entienda, **entiendo**, **etc** ▶ entender

entonces adverb
= then

entrada noun, feminine
• = entry
'prohibida la entrada' = 'no entry'

- = entrance
  sólo hay una entrada = there's only one entrance
- = ticket
  = admission
  'entrada libre' = 'free admission', 'open to the public'
- (*Spa: when buying a house, a car*)
  una entrada = a deposit

entrar *verb* 1
  = to come in
  = to go in
  déjame entrar = let me in
- **entrar en:**
  = to go into
  entramos en *or* (*Lat Am*) **a la cocina** = we went into the kitchen
  = to fit into
  no entra en el cajón = it doesn't fit in the drawer
  = to join
  entrar en *or* **a una organización** = to join an organization
- = to start
  entro a trabajar a las nueve = I start work at nine

entre *preposition*
- = between
  se puso entre ellos dos = he stood between them
- = among
  entre amigos = among friends
  entre otras cosas = among other things
- = in
  entre paréntesis = in parentheses *or* brackets
- = by
  dividir veinte entre cinco = to divide twenty by five

entregar *verb* 3
- = to give
  = to hand over
- **entregar un paquete** = to deliver a parcel
- **entregarle un premio a alguien** = to present someone with a prize
entregarse
  = to surrender

entrenador/entrenadora *noun*,
masculine/feminine
  un entrenador/una entrenadora = a coach

entrenar *verb* 1
  = to train

entrevista *noun, feminine*
  una entrevista = an interview

enviar *verb* 13
  = to send

envolver *verb* 24
  = to wrap

envuelto ▶ envolver

episodio *noun, masculine*
  un episodio = an episode

época *noun, feminine*
  época = time
  = times
  = age

equilibrio *noun, masculine*
  equilibrio = balance
  mantener/perder el equilibrio = to keep/lose one's balance

equipaje *noun, masculine*
  equipaje = baggage, luggage
  equipaje de mano = hand baggage, hand luggage

equipo *noun, masculine*
  un equipo = a team

equivocado/equivocada *adjective*
  = wrong

equivocarse *verb* 2
  = to make a mistake
  = to be wrong
  me equivoqué = I made a mistake
  me equivoqué de casa/teléfono = I got the wrong house/number
  en eso se equivoca = he's wrong about that

era, erais, eras, eres, etc ▶ ser

error *noun, masculine*
  un error = a mistake

eructar *verb* 1
  = to burp

eructo *noun, masculine*
  un eructo = a burp

es ▶ ser

esa *adjective*
  = that

ésa *pronoun*
  = that one

esas *adjective*
  = those

ésas *pronoun*
  = those ones

escala *noun, feminine*
- (*when traveling*) **una escala** = a stopover
  hacer escala en Roma = to stop over in Rome
- (*in music*) **una escala** = a scale

escalera *noun, feminine*
- **una escalera** = a staircase
  una escalera de incendios = a fire escape
  una escalera mecánica = an escalator
- **una escalera (de mano)** = a ladder

E

escalón *noun, masculine*
un escalón = a step

escalofrío *noun, masculine*
un escalofrío = a shiver
tener escalofríos = to shiver

escándalo *noun, masculine*
* un escándalo = a scandal
* un escándalo = a racket
armar un escándalo = to make a racket

escaparate *noun, masculine (Spa)*
un escaparate = a shop window

escaparse *verb* 1
= to escape

escarabajo *noun, masculine*
un escarabajo = a beetle

escena *noun, feminine*
una escena = a scene

escenario *noun, masculine*
un escenario = a stage

esclavo/esclava *noun,*
masculine/feminine
un esclavo/una esclava = a slave

escoba *noun, feminine*
una escoba = a broom

escocés/escocesa
1 *adjective*
= Scottish
* (*if it's whisky*) = Scotch
* (*if it's a pattern*) = tartan
2 *noun, masculine/feminine*
un escocés/una escocesa = a Scot

Escocia *noun, feminine*
= Scotland

escoger *verb* 20
= to choose

escoja, **escojo**, etc ▶ escoger

escolar
1 *adjective*
= school
las vacaciones escolares = the school
    vacation *or* holidays
2 *noun masculine/feminine*
un/una escolar = a schoolboy/-girl

esconder *verb* 17
= to hide
esconderse
= to hide

escondido/escondida *adjective*
= hidden

Escorpión, **Escorpio** *noun, masculine*
Escorpion = Scorpio

escorpión, **escorpio** *noun,*
masculine/feminine
un/una escorpión, un/una escorpio
= a Scorpio

escribir *verb* 60
* = to write
* = to spell

escrito ▶ escribir

escritor/escritora *noun,*
masculine/feminine
un escritor/una escritora = a writer

escuchar *verb* 1
= to listen
= to listen to

escuela *noun, feminine*
una escuela = a school

escupir *verb* 41
= to spit
me escupió = he spat at me

ese/esa *adjective*
= that

ése/ésa *pronoun*
= that one

esfuerzo *noun, masculine*
un esfuerzo = an effort
hacer un esfuerzo = to make an effort

eso *pronoun*
= that
por eso = that's why
¡eso es! = that's it!

esos/esas *adjective*
= those

ésos/ésas *pronoun*
= those (ones)

espacio *noun, masculine*
= space
= room

espaguetis *noun, masculine plural*
los espaguetis = spaghetti

espalda *noun, feminine*
le espalda = the back
de espaldas:
estaba de espaldas a la ventana = she had
    her back to the window
me puse de espaldas a la clase = I stood
    with my back to the class
nadar de espaldas = to swim (the)
    backstroke

espantapájaros *noun, masculine*
un espantapájaros = a scarecrow

España *noun, feminine*
España = Spain

español/española
1 *adjective*
= Spanish
2 *noun, masculine/feminine*
un español/una española = a Spaniard

---

3 español noun, masculine
el español (the language) = Spanish

espárrago noun, masculine
espárrago = asparagus

especia noun, feminine
una especia = a spice

especial adjective
= special
en especial = especially
= in particular

espectáculo noun, masculine
• un espectáculo (on television, at a theater etc) = a show
• un espectáculo = a sight

espejo noun, masculine
un espejo = a mirror
el espejo retrovisor = the rear-view mirror

espera noun, feminine
una espera = a wait
una lista de espera = a waiting list
una sala de espera = a waiting room

esperar verb [1]
• = to wait
= to wait for
la estuve esperando tres horas = I was waiting for her for three hours
• = to expect
los espero a eso de las diez = I'm expecting them at around ten o'clock
• = to hope
eso espero, espero que sí = I hope so
espero que te guste = I hope you like it

! Note the use of the subjunctive after esperar que

espeso/espesa adjective
= thick

espinaca noun, feminine
las espinacas = spinach

esponja noun, feminine
una esponja = a sponge

esposo/esposa noun, masculine/feminine
un esposo/una esposa = a husband/a wife

espuma noun, feminine
espuma = foam
(of beer) = froth
(of soap) = lather
(for styling hair) = mousse

esqueleto noun, masculine
un esqueleto = a skeleton

esquí noun, masculine
• un esquí = a ski
• (sport) el esquí = skiing
hacer esquí = to ski
esquí acuático = water-skiing

esquiar verb [13]
= to ski

esquimal
1 adjective
= Eskimo
2 noun, masculine/feminine
un/una esquimal = an Eskimo

esquina noun, feminine
una esquina = a corner

esta adjective
= this

ésta pronoun
= this (one)

está ▶ estar

estación noun, feminine
• una estación = a station
una estación de buses/de tren = a bus/train station
una estación de servicio = a gas station, a petrol station
• una estación de esquí = a ski resort
• una estación = a season

estacionar verb [1] (Lat Am)
= to park

estadio noun, masculine
un estadio = a stadium

estado noun, masculine
• un estado = a state
• estado = condition
el cuadro está en buen estado = the picture is in good condition
en mal estado (if it's food) = to be off
(if it's a house, road) = to be in a bad state
• estado civil = marital status

Estados Unidos noun, masculine plural
(los) Estados Unidos (de América) = the United States (of America)

estáis ▶ estar

estanco noun, masculine
un estanco = a tobacconist's

estanque noun, masculine
un estanque = a pond

estante noun, masculine
un estante = a shelf

estar verb [16]
• = to be
últimamente está muy amable = he's being very nice lately
¿cómo estás? = how are you?
estoy [alegre | enfermo | cansado ...] = I'm [happy | ill | tired ...]
está de viaje = he's away on a trip
están sin trabajo = they're unemployed
¿dónde está Juan? = where is Juan?
estaré allí tres días = I'll be there for three days
estar [casado | soltero | divorciado ...] (Spa) = to be [married | single | divorced ...]

E

está casada con un inglés = she's married to an Englishman

hoy estamos a tres de enero = it's the third of January today

¿a cuánto están los tomates? = how much are the tomates

• (*Spa: referring to how clothes suit or fit you*) = to be

me está largo = it's too long for me

no te está bien = it doesn't fit you

• (*as auxiliary verb*) = to be

está mintiendo = he's lying

estába dormido = he was sleeping

está roto = it's broken

estarse

• = to keep

¡estáte quieto! = keep still!

• se está bien al sol = it's nice in the sun

estatua *noun, feminine*
una estatua = a statue

este *noun, masculine*
• el este = the east
al este de Quito = to the east of Quito
• = easterly
vientos del este = easterly winds

este/esta *adjective*
= this

éste/ésta *pronoun*
= this (one)

esté, estén ▶ estar

estéreo *noun, masculine*
un estéreo = a stereo

estés ▶ estar

estilo *noun, masculine*
un estilo = a style
o algo por el estilo = or something like that
eran todos por el estilo = they were all similar

estirar *verb* 1
= to stretch

esto *pronoun*
= this
¿de quién es esto? = whose is this?

estómago *noun*
el estómago = the stomach

estornudar *verb* 1
= to sneeze

estoy ▶ estar

estrecho/estrecha *adjective*
= narrow
= tight
un pasillo estrecho = a narrow corridor
estos pantalones me quedan estrechos = these trousers are too tight for me

estrella *noun, feminine*
una estrella = a star

estrellarse *verb* 1
= to crash

estricto/estricta *adjective*
= strict

estropear *verb* 1
• (*if it's a plan, holiday*) = to spoil
• (*if it's a television, car, toy*) = to break
• (*if it's a dress, carpet*) = to ruin

estructura *noun feminine*
una estructura = a structure

estudiante *noun, masculine/feminine*
un/una estudiante = a student

estudiar *verb* 1
= to study
= to learn
estudiar inglés = to study English
estudiar la lección = to learn the lesson

estudio
1 *noun, masculine*
• un estudio = a study
el estudio de la naturaleza = the study of nature
estudios de derecho = law studies
• estudio de mercado = market research
• un estudio = a studio apartment
un estudio (*for artist, photographer, etc; room in a house*) = a study
2 estudios *noun, masculine plural*
= education

estufa *noun, feminine*
• una estufa = a heater
una estufa eléctrica/de gas = an electric heater/a gas heater
• (*Mex*) una estufa = a stove, a cooker

estúpido/estúpida
1 *adjective*
= stupid
2 *noun, masculine/feminine*
es un estúpido/una estúpida = he's/she's really stupid

estuve, estuvo, etc ▶ estar

etapa *noun, feminine*
una etapa = a stage
por *or* en etapas = in stages

etcétera *noun, masculine*
= etcetera, and so on

etiqueta *noun, masculine*
una etiqueta = a label
= a price tag

Europa *noun, feminine*
Europa = Europe

europeo/europea
1 *adjective*
= European

2 *noun, masculine or feminine*
un europeo/una europea = a European

evitar *verb* ☐1
= to avoid
= to prevent
no se puede evitar = it can't be avoided
si puedo/puede evitarlo = if I can help it/if
you, he, she can help it

exacto/exacta *adjective*
* = exact
= accurate
son 1.000 pesos exactos = that's 1,000
pesos exactly

exagerar *verb* ☐1
= to exaggerate

examen *noun, masculine*
un examen = an exam, a test
hacer un examen = to take an exam
aprobar *or* pasar un examen = to pass an
exam
un examen de recuperación (*Spa*) = a
retake exam, a resit
un examen tipo test = a multiple-choice
test
los exámenes finales = the finals

excelente *adjective*
= excellent

excepto *preposition*
= except

excusa *noun, feminine*
una excusa = an excuse

existir *verb* ☐41
= to exist
no existen pruebas = there's no evidence

éxito *noun, masculine*
un éxito = a success
(*song*) = a hit
tener éxito = to succeed
(*if it's a song*) = to be a hit

experiencia *noun, feminine*
una experiencia = an experience
tengo mucha experiencia = I have a lot of
experience

experto/experta *noun,*
masculine/feminine
un experto/una experta = an expert

explicar *verb* ☐2
= to explain

explotar *verb* ☐1
= to explode

exportar *verb* ☐1
= to export

exposición *noun, feminine*
una exposición = an exhibition
(*of a subject*) = a presentation

expresión *noun, feminine*
una expresión = an expresion

exterior
1 *adjective*
* = outer
la capa exterior = the outer layer
la parte exterior del objeto = the outside of
the object
* = foreign
la política exterior = foreign policy
2 *noun, masculine*
el exterior = the outside, the exterior

externo/externa *adjective*
= external

extinguidor *noun, masculine* (*Lat Am*)
un extinguidor = a fire extinguisher

extintor *noun, masculine* (*Spa*)
un extintor = a fire extinguisher

extranjero/extranjera
1 *adjective*
= foreign
2 *noun, masculine/feminine*
un extranjero/una extranjera = a foreigner
3 extranjero *noun, masculine*
estar en el extranjero = to be abroad

extrañar *verb* ☐1
* me extraña que no te lo haya dicho = I'm
suprised that *or* I find it surprising that
he hasn't told you

> ! *Note the use of the subjunctive after*
> extrañar que

* (*Lat Am*) = to miss
extrañar a un amigo = to miss a friend

extraño/extraña
1 *adjective*
= strange
2 *noun, masculine/feminine*
un extraño/una extraña = a stranger

extremo/extrema
1 *adjective*
= extreme
2 extremo *noun, masculine*
* un extremo = an extreme
* (*of rope, corridor, etc*) un extremo = an end

E

Ff

fábrica noun, feminine
una fábrica = a factory

fácil adjective
= easy

factura noun, feminine
una factura = a bill

facultad noun, feminine
• una facultad = a faculty
la Facultad de Medicina = the Faculty of
Medicine
• la facultad = university
ir a la facultad = to go to university

falda noun, feminine
una falda = a skirt

falla noun, feminine
una falla = a flaw
(Lat Am: of a machine etc) = a fault

fallar verb [1]
• = to miss
me falló la puntería, fallé el tiro = I missed
• = to fail
fallaron los frenos = the brakes failed
• = to go wrong
el plan falló = the plan went wrong
• fallarle a alguien = to let someone down

fallo noun, masculine (Spa) ▶ falla

falso/falsa adjective
= false
= fake

falta noun, feminine
• una falta de ortografía = a spelling mistake
• (in school) una falta = an absence
ponerle falta a alguien = to mark someone
as absent
• (in football) una falta = a foul
• falta de algo = lack of something
falta de [cariño | dinero | tiempo ...] = lack of
[love | money | time ...]
falta de educación = lack of manners
eso es una falta de educación = that's bad
manners
• hacer falta:
hace falta revisarlo = it needs to be
revised
no hace falta que te quedes = you don't
need to stay

! Note the use of the subjunctive after
hacer falta que

nos hace falta más dinero = we need more
money
ya no me hace falta = I don't need it any
more
le hace mucha falta = he really needs it

faltar verb [1]
• = to be missing
faltan dos niños = there are two children
missing
• (talking about time)
faltan dos horas para llegar = it's another
two hours before we arrive
¿les falta mucho para terminar? = do you
have long to go before you finish?
aún falta mucho tiempo para las
vacaciones = the vacation is still a long
way away
• les falta [disciplina | dinero | apoyo ...] = they
lack [discipline | money | support ...]
me falta cuerda = I need more rope

fama noun, feminine
la fama = fame
fama = reputation
tener fama de [gracioso | despistado | cruel ...]
= to have a reputation for being [funny |
absent-minded | cruel ...]
tener buena/mala fama = to have a
good/bad reputation

familia noun, feminine
la familia = the family

familiar
1 adjective
• = familiar
• = family
2 noun, masculine/feminine
un/una familiar = a relative

famoso/famosa adjective
= famous, well-known

fantasía noun, feminine
fantasía = fantasy
= imagination

fantasma noun, masculine
un fantasma = a ghost

fantástico/fantástica adjective
= fantastic

farmacia noun, feminine
• una farmacia = a pharmacy, a chemist's
• (as a subject) farmacia = pharmacy
estudiar farmacia = to study pharmacy

farola noun, feminine
una farola = a street light

favor noun, masculine
un favor = a favor, a favour
estar a favor de algo = to be in favor of
something

favorito/favorita adjective
= favorite, favourite

febrero noun, masculine
febrero = February

---

fecha *noun, feminine*
  una fecha = a date
  **¿qué fecha es hoy?, ¿a qué fecha
    estamos?** = what's the date today?
  el año pasado por estas fechas = this time
    last year
  fecha de caducidad *(for medicines)* =
    expiration date, expiry date
  (for food) = use-by date

feliz *adjective*
  = happy

femenino/femenina
1 *adjective*
  = feminine
  = women's
  = female
2 femenino *noun, masculine*
  el femenino = the feminine

feo/fea *adjective*
  = ugly

feria *noun, feminine*
• **una feria** = a fair
• *(Mex)* **feria** = small change

feriado/feriada *adjective (Lat Am)* ▶ día

ferretería *noun, feminine*
  una ferretería = a hardware store, an
    ironmonger's

ferrocarril *noun, masculine*
  un ferrocarril = a railroad, a railway

festivo/festiva *adjective* ▶ día

fiarse *verb* 13
  = to trust
  = to believe
  fiarse de alguien = to trust someone
  no te fíes de lo que dice = don't believe
    what he says

fideo
1 *noun, masculine*
  un fideo = a noodle
2 fideos *noun, masculine plural (R Pl)*
  fideos = pasta

fiebre *noun, feminine*
• **fiebre** = temperature
  tener fiebre = to have a fever, to have a
    temperature
• *(an illness)* **una fiebre** = a fever

fiesta *noun, feminine*
• **una fiesta** = a party
• **una fiesta** = a holiday
  hoy es fiesta = today's a holiday

figura *noun, feminine*
  una figura = a figure

fijo/fija *adjective*
• = fixed
• *(if it's a job, an employee)* = permanent

fila *noun, feminine*
  una fila = a row
  = a line

fin *noun, masculine*
  el fin = the end
  un fin de semana = a weekend
  a fin de mes/año = at the end of the
    month/year
  a fines de abril/siglo = at the end of
    April/the century
  al fin, por fin = at last
  en fin, ya veremos = well, we'll see

final
1 *adjective*
  = final
2 *noun, masculine*
• **el final** = the end
  (of a movie) = the ending
• **al final**
  = at the end
  = in the end
  a finales de [mes | año | semana ...] = at the
    end of [the month | year | week ...]
2 *noun, feminine*
  una final = a final

finlandés/finlandesa
1 *adjective*
  = Finnish
2 *noun, masculine/feminine*
  un finlandés/una finlandesa = a Finn
3 finlandés *noun, masculine*
  el finlandés *(the language)* = Finnish

firmar *verb* 1
  = to sign

física *noun, feminine*
  la física = physics

flama *noun, feminine (Mex)*
  una flama = a flame

flan *noun, masculine*
  un flan = a crème caramel

flauta *noun, feminine*
  una flauta = a flute
  una flauta dulce = a recorder

flecha *noun, feminine*
  una flecha = an arrow

fleco *noun, masculine (Mex)* ▶ flequillo

flequillo *noun, masculine*
  un flequillo = bangs, a fringe

flojo/floja
1 *adjective*
• = loose, slack
• *(if it's coffee, tea)* = weak
• *(if it's wind)* = light
• *(Lat Am: if it's a person)* **flojo/floja ✱** = lazy

F

- **estar flojo en** [inglés | química | matemáticas …] = to be weak at [English | chemistry | maths …]
2 *noun, masculine/feminine (Lat Am)*
  un flojo/una floja✖ = a lazybones

flor *noun, feminine*
  una flor = a flower

florero *noun, masculine*
  un florero = a vase

floristería *noun, feminine*
  una floristería = a flower shop

flotar *verb* 1
  = to float

foco *noun, masculine*
  un foco = a spotlight
  (*Mex*) = a light bulb

folleto *noun, masculine*
  un folleto = a leaflet, a flier
  = a brochure
  = a booklet

fondo *noun, masculine*
- **el fondo** = the bottom
  un pozo sin fondo = a bottomless well
- (*of a corridor, road*) **el fondo** = the end
  al fondo del pasillo = at the end of the corridor
- (*of a room*) **el fondo** = the back
- **a fondo** = in depth
  = thoroughly
- **en el fondo** = deep down

fontanero/fontanera *noun, masculine/feminine (Spa)*
  un fontanero/una fontanera = a plumber

forma *noun, feminine*
- **una forma** = a shape
  tiene forma redonda = it's round
- **forma** = way
  esa no es forma de contestar = that's no way to answer
  es mi forma de ser = that's the way I am
- (*Mex: a paper*) **una forma** = a form
- **estar/ponerse en forma** = to be/get fit

formal *adjective*
- = formal
- = reliable
- = well-behaved

formar *verb* 1
- = to form
- = to make up

fortuna *noun, feminine*
- **una fortuna** = a fortune
- **por fortuna** = fortunately

fósforo *noun, masculine*
  un fósforo = a match

foto *noun, feminine*
  una foto = a photo
  sacar *or* **tomar** *or* (*Spa*) **hacer una foto** = to take a photo

fotocopia *noun, feminine*
  una fotocopia = a photocopy

fotografía *noun, feminine*
- **una fotografía** = photograph
- (*the art*) **la fotografía** = photography

fotógrafo/fotógrafa *noun, masculine/feminine*
  un fotógrafo/una fotógrafa = a photographer

fracasar *verb* 1
  = to fail

fracaso *noun, masculine*
  un fracaso = a failure

frágil *adjective*
  = fragile

frambuesa *noun, feminine*
  una frambuesa = a raspberry

francés/francesa
1 *adjective*
  = French
2 *noun, masculine/feminine*
  un francés/una francesa = a Frenchman/Frenchwoman
3 francés *noun, masculine*
  el francés (*the language*) = French

Francia *noun, feminine*
  France = France

frase *noun, feminine*
  una frase = a sentence
  = a phrase

frazada *noun, feminine (Lat Am)*
  una frazada = a blanket

frecuente *adjective*
  = frequent
  = common
  no es muy frecuente = it doesn't happen very often

fregadero *noun, masculine*
  un fregadero = a sink

fregar *verb* 8
  = to wash

fregona *noun, feminine (Spa)*
  una fregona = a mop

freír *verb* 61
  = to fry

freno *noun, masculine*
  un freno = a brake
  el freno de mano = the handbrake
  poner/quitar el freno = to put on/release the brake

✖ in informal situations　　　　**C Am** Central America　**Lat Am** Latin America　**Mex** Mexico

frente
1 *noun, feminine*
  la frente = the forehead
2 *noun, masculine*
  el frente = the front
  al frente:
  dar un paso al frente = to move one step
    forward
  pasar al frente (*Lat Am*) = to go/come up to
    the front
  al frente de la empresa = in charge of the
    company

fresa *noun, feminine*
  una fresa = a strawberry

fresco/fresca
1 *adjective*
• (*if it's vegetables*) = fresh
• (*if it's weather, water*) = cool
2 **fresco** *noun, masculine*
  hace fresco = it's a bit chilly

fría, frío, etc ▶ freír

friega, friego, friegue, etc ▶ fregar

frigorífico *noun, masculine* (*Spa*)
  un frigorífico = a fridge

frío/fría
1 *adjective*
  = cold
2 **frío** *noun, masculine*
  hace frío = it's cold
  tener frío, pasar frío = to be cold
  ¡tengo tanto frío! = I'm so cold!
  tomar *or* (*Spa*) coger frío = to catch cold

frito/frita *adjective*
  = fried

frontera *noun, feminine*
  la frontera = the border

fruta *noun, feminine*
  fruta = fruit

frutero *noun, masculine*
  un frutero = a fruit bowl

frutilla *noun, feminine* (*SC*)
  una frutilla = a strawberry

fruto *noun, masculine*
  un fruto = a fruit
  frutos secos = nuts and dried fruits

fue ▶ ser, ir

fuego *noun, masculine*
• fuego = fire
  hacer fuego = to light a fire
  prenderle fuego a algo = to set fire to
    something
• fuego = a light
  ¿me da fuego? = could you give me a
    light?
  fuegos artificiales = fireworks
    See also cocer, cocinar

fuente *noun, feminine*
  una fuente = a spring
  = a fountain

fuera, fuéramos, etc ▶ ser, ir

fuera *adverb*
• = out
  = outside
  por fuera:
  es verde por fuera = it's green on the
    outside
  pintamos la casa por fuera = we painted
    the outside of the house
  fuera de la casa = outside the house
  fuimos a comer fuera = we went out for a
    meal
  fuera de juego = offside
• = away
  = abroad

fueron ▶ ser, ir

fuerte
1 *adjective*
• = strong
• (*if it's rain, a meal*) = heavy
• (*if it's an increase*) = big
• (*if it's a pain, cold*) = bad
• (*if it's a noise*) = loud
2 *adverb*
• = hard
• = tight, tightly
  apretar una tuerca = to screw a bolt in
    tightly
• = loud, loudly
  poner la música fuerte = to turn the music
    up loud

fuerza *noun, feminine*
  fuerza = force
  = strength
  tengo mucha fuerza = I'm very strong
  a la fuerza = by force

fui, fuimos, fuiste, etc ▶ ser, ir

fumador/fumadora *noun,*
masculine/feminine
  un fumador/una fumadora = a smoker

fumar *verb* ①
• = to smoke

función *noun, feminine*
• una función = a function
• (*at a theater*) una función = a performance

funcionar *verb* ①
  = to work

furgoneta *noun, feminine*
  una furgoneta = a van

furioso/furiosa *adjective*
  = furious

fusil *noun, masculine*
  un fusil = a rifle

futbito *noun, masculine* (*Spa*)
  futbito = five-a-side football

F

fútbol or (C Am, Mex) **futbol** noun, masculine
  fútbol = soccer, football

futbolín
1 noun, masculine
  futbolín = table football
2 futbolines noun, masculine plural (Spa)
  los futbolines = the local amusement arcade

futbolista noun, masculine|feminine
  un/una futbolista = a footballer

futuro noun, masculine
  el futuro = the future

Gg

gafas noun, feminine plural
  gafas = glasses
  llevar or usar gafas = to wear glasses

galería noun, feminine
  una galería = a gallery

Gales noun, masculine
  Gales, el país de Gales = Wales

galés/galesa
1 adjective
  = Welsh
2 noun, masculine|feminine
  un galés/una galesa = a Welshman/a Welshwoman
3 galés noun, masculine
  el galés (the language) = Welsh

gallego/gallega
1 adjective
  = Galician
2 noun, masculine|feminine
  un gallego/una gallega = a Galician
3 gallego noun, masculine
  el gallego (the language) = Galician

galleta noun, feminine
  una galleta = a cookie, a biscuit
  = a cracker

gallina noun, feminine
  una gallina = a hen

gallo noun, masculine
  un gallo = a cock

gamba noun, feminine (Spa)
  una gamba = a shrimp, a prawn

gana noun, feminine
  no me da la gana = I don't want to
  haz lo que te dé la gana = do as you please
  hacer algo de buena/mala gana = to do something willingly/unwillingly
  hacer algo sin ganas = to do something half-heartedly
  tener ganas de hacer algo
  = to feel like doing something
  = to look forward to doing something

ganador/ganadora
1 adjective
  = winning
2 noun, masculine|feminine
  un ganador/una ganadora = a winner

ganar verb 1
• = to earn
• = to win

gancho noun, masculine
  un gancho = a hook

ganso/gansa noun, masculine|feminine
  un ganso/una gansa = a goose

garage (Lat Am), **garaje** (Spa) noun, masculine
  un garage = a garage

garantía noun, feminine
  una garantía = a guarantee

garbanzo noun, masculine
  un garbanzo = a chickpea

garganta noun, feminine
  la garganta = the throat
  me duele la garganta = I have a sore throat

gas noun, masculine
  gas = gas

gaseosa noun, feminine
  una gaseosa = a soda, a lemonade

gasolina noun, feminine
  gasolina = gas, petrol

gasolinera noun, feminine
  una gasolinera = a gas station, a petrol station

gastar verb 1
• = to spend
• = to use
  gastaron toda el agua = they used (up) all the water

gasto noun, masculine
  un gasto = an expense

gato/gata noun, masculine|feminine
  un gato/una gata = a cat

---

gemelo/gemela
1 *adjective*
= twin
hermanos gemelos = twin brothers
2 *noun, masculine/feminine*
un gemelo/una gemela = a twin
3 **gemelos** *noun, masculine plural*
unos gemelos = a pair of binoculars
4 **gemelo** *noun, masculine*
un gemelo = a cuff link

Géminis *noun, masculine*
Géminis = Gemini

géminis *noun, masculine/feminine*
un/una géminis = a Gemini, a Geminian

generación *noun, feminine*
una generación = a generation

general
1 *adjective*
= general
en general = in general, on the whole
por lo general = generally, usually
2 *noun, masculine/feminine*
un/una general = a general

generoso/generosa *adjective*
= generous

genio *noun, masculine*
• genio = temper
tener mal genio = to be bad-tempered
estar de mal genio = to be in a bad mood
• un genio = a genius

gente *noun, feminine*
gente = people
había mucha gente = there were a lot of
people

geografía *noun, feminine*
la geografía = geography

gerente *noun, masculine/feminine*
un/una gerente = a manager

gesto *noun, masculine*
un gesto = a gesture

gigante/giganta *noun,*
masculine/feminine
un gigante/una giganta = a giant

gilipollas *noun, masculine/feminine*
(Spa) (**!** *does not change in the plural*)
un/una gilipollas = a jerk

gimnasia *noun, feminine*
la gimnasia = gymnastics
hice dos horas de gimnasia = I worked out
for two hours

gimnasio *noun, masculine*
un gimnasio = gymnasium, gym

girar *verb* 1
= to turn

gitano/gitana *noun, masculine/feminine*
un gitano/una gitana = a gypsy

globo *noun, masculine*
• un globo = a balloon
• un globo terráqueo = a globe

gobierno *noun, masculine*
un gobierno = a government

gol *noun, masculine*
un gol = a goal

golfo *noun, masculine*
un golfo = a gulf
el Golfo de México = the Gulf of Mexico

golpe *noun, masculine*
• un golpe = a blow
me di un golpe en la cabeza = I banged my
head
le dio un golpe en la espalda = she hit him
on the back
• un golpe = a knock
• la ventana se cerró de un golpe = the
window slammed shut

golpear *verb* 1
= to bang
= to beat
= to hit

goma *noun, feminine*
• goma = rubber
• una goma (**elástica**) = a rubber band, an
elastic band
• una goma (**de borrar**) = an eraser, a
rubber
• goma de pegar = glue

gorra *noun, feminine*
una gorra = a cap

gorro *noun, masculine*
un gorro = a cap

gota *noun, feminine*
una gota = a drop

gozar *verb* 4
= to enjoy
gozar de algo/haciendo algo = to enjoy
something/doing something

grabadora *noun, feminine*
una grabadora = a tape recorder

grabar *verb*
= to tape

gracia *noun, feminine*
una gracia = a joke
tener gracia = to be funny
hacerle gracia a alguien = to make
someone laugh
= to amuse someone
no me hace gracia = I don't find it
funny

G

* **¡muchas gracias!** = thank you very much!
  darle las gracias a alguien = to thank
    somebody
  gracias a alguien/algo = thanks to
    somebody/something

grado *noun, masculine*
  un grado = a degree
  tres grados bajo cero = three degrees
   below zero

gramática *noun, feminine*
  la gramática = grammar

gramo *noun, masculine*
  un gramo = a gram

gran ▶ grande

Gran Bretaña *noun, feminine*
  Gran Bretaña = Great Britain

grande *adjective*

> **!** *Note that* **grande** *becomes* **gran** *before
> singular nouns*

* = big, large
  una gran cantidad = a large quantity
* = great
  es un gran escritor = he's a great writer
* (*referring to age*)
  cuando sea grande = when I grow up
  mi hijo ya es grande = my son is grown up
  See also **parte**

granizado *noun, masculine*
  un granizado = *a drink served on crushed ice*
  un granizado de limón = *an iced lemon
   drink*

granja *noun, feminine*
  una granja = a farm

grapa *noun, feminine*
  una grapa = a staple

grapadora *noun, feminine*
  una grapadora = a stapler

grapar *verb* 1
  = to staple

grasa *noun, feminine*
  grasa = grease
  = fat

grasiento/grasienta *adjective*
  = greasy

gratis *adjective, adverb*
  = free

grave *adjective*
  = serious
  está grave = he's seriously ill

Grecia *noun, feminine*
  Grecia = Greece

griego/griega
1 *adjective*
  = Greek

2 *noun, masculine/feminine*
  un griego/una griega = a Greek
3 griego *noun, masculine*
  el griego (*the language*) = Greek

grifo *noun, masculine* (*Spa*)
  un grifo = a faucet, a tap

gripe *or* (*Mex*) **gripa** *noun, feminine*
  gripe = flu
  tener gripe = to have the flu

gris
1 *adjective*
  = gray, grey
2 *noun, masculine*
  el gris = gray, grey

gritar *verb* 1
  = to shout

grito *noun, masculine*
  un grito = a shout
  = a cry

grueso/gruesa *adjective*
  = thick

grupo *noun, masculine*
  un grupo = a group

guante *noun, masculine*
  un guante = a glove

guapo/guapa *adjective*
  = good-looking

guardabarros *noun, masculine* (**!** *does
not change in the plural*)
  un guardabarros (*on a car*) = a fender, a
   mudguard
  (*on a bicycle*) = a mudguard

guardar *verb* 1
* = to keep
* = to put away

guardia *noun, masculine/feminine*
  un/una guardia = a police officer, a
   policeman/a policewoman

guarro/guarra✗ *adjective* (*Spa*)
  = filthy

guau *exclamation*
  ¡guau! = woof!, bow-wow!

güero/güera✗ *adjective* (*Mex*)
  = blond, blonde

guerra *noun, feminine*
  una guerra = a war
  la Primera/Segunda Guerra Mundial = the
   First/Second World War

guía
1 *noun, feminine*
  una guía = a guide, a guidebook
  una guía turística = a tourist guide
  una guía telefónica = a telephone
   directory

2 *noun, masculine|feminine*
un/una **guía** = a guide

guiar *verb* [13]
= to guide

guiñar *verb* [1]
= to wink

guiño *noun, masculine*
un **guiño** = a wink

guisante *noun, masculine (Spa)*
un **guisante** = a pea

guitarra *noun, feminine*
una **guitarra** = a guitar

gusano *noun, masculine*
un **gusano** = a worm

gustar *verb* [1]
me **gusta** nadar = I like swimming
la película no me **gustó** = I didn't like the movie
le **gustan** los perros = he/she likes dogs

gusto *noun, masculine*
• **gusto** = taste
 tiene buen **gusto** = he has good taste
• = pleasure
 mucho *or* tanto **gusto** = pleased to meet you

ha ▶ haber

haba *noun, feminine*
un **haba** = a broad bean

 ! *Note that although* haba *is feminine it is preceded by a masculine article in the singular*

habéis ▶ haber

haber *verb* [29]
• (*used to form past tenses*) = to have
 han **terminado** = they have finished
 no lo había **visto** = I hadn't seen it
• **hay** = there is
 = there are
 no hay **suficiente** = there isn't enough
 hay tres **entradas** = there are three entries
• hay que:
 hay que **revisarlo** = it needs revising
 hay que **comprar** pan = we have to buy bread
 hay que **hacerlo** = it must be done
• gracias — no hay de qué = thank you — don't mention it

habitación *noun, feminine*
una **habitación** = a bedroom
(*in a hotel*) = a room
una **habitación** individual = a single room

habitante *noun, masculine|feminine*
un/una **habitante** = an inhabitant

hablar *verb*
• = to speak
 hablar italiano = to speak Italian
• = to talk
 hablar de algo/alguien = to talk about something/someone

habrán, **habré**, **etc** ▶ haber

hacer *verb* [30]
• = to make
 hacer [la cama | la cena | un vestido …] = to make [the bed | dinner | a dress …]
 hacer un esfuerzo = to make an effort
• = to do
 ¿qué **haces** aquí? = what are you doing here?
 hacer los deberes = to do one's homework
• (*when talking about the weather*)
 hace [frío | calor | sol …] = it's [cold | hot | sunny …]
 hizo mal tiempo *or* (*Spa*) **hizo** malo = the weather was bad
• (*when talking about time*)
 hace dos años que no nos vemos = we haven't seen each other for two years
 me jubilé **hace** cinco años = I retired two years ago
 ¿**hace** mucho que esperas? = have you been waiting long?
 desde **hace**/desde **hacía** = for
 no la había visto desde **hacía** dos años = I hadn't seen her for two years

hacerse
• = to make
 se **hace** ella misma la ropa = she makes her own clothes
 se va a **hacer** un traje para la boda = he is going to have a suit made for the wedding
• = to become
 = to get
 se **hizo** famosa = she became famous
 hacerse viejo = to get old
• **hacerse** daño = to hurt oneself

hacia *preposition*
• = toward(s)
 íbamos **hacia** la playa = we were going toward(s) the beach
• = at about
 llegará **hacia** las dos = he'll arrive at about 2 o'clock

haga, **hago**, **etc** ▶ hacer

hamaca noun, feminine
• una **hamaca** = a hammock
• (R Pl) una **hamaca** = a swing
 = a rocking chair

hambre noun, feminine
 el **hambre** = hunger

> ! Note that although **hambre** is feminine it
> is preceded by a masculine article in the
> singular

 tener **hambre** = to be hungry
 tengo **hambre** = I'm hungry

hamburguesa noun, feminine
 una **hamburguesa** = a hamburger

han ▶ haber

harán, **haré**, **etc** ▶ hacer

harina noun, feminine
 la **harina** = flour

harto/harta
1 adjective
 = fed up
 estar **harto** de algo = to be fed up with
 something
2 harto adverb (Lat Am)
• = very
 es **harto** difícil = it's very difficult
• = a lot
 comimos **harto** = we ate a lot

has ▶ haber

hasta
1 preposition
• = until, till
 esperé **hasta** las tres = I waited until three
 no será or (Mex) será publicado **hasta**
 mayo = it won't be published till May
• = as far as
 nadaron **hasta** la roca = they swam as far
 as the rock
• = up to
 el ascensor sólo sube **hasta** el tercer piso
 = the elevator only goes up to the third
 floor
• = down to
 el pelo le llega **hasta** la cintura = her hair
 goes down to her waist
• **hasta** [mañana | luego | esta tarde ...] = see you
 [tomorrow | later | this afternoon ...]
2 adverb
 = even
 hasta yo lo sé hacer = even I can do it

hay ▶ haber

haz ▶ hacer

he ▶ haber

hebilla noun, feminine
 una **hebilla** = a buckle

hecho/hecha
1 past participle of hacer
• = made
 está **hecho** de madera = it's made of wood
 hecho a mano = handmade
• = done
 la cena aún no está **hecha** = dinner is not
 ready yet
2 adjective
 un filete de carne bien **hecho**/poco **hecho**
 (Spa) = a well-done/rare steak
3 hecho noun, masculine
 un **hecho** = a fact

helado/helada
1 adjective
• = frozen
 el lago está **helado** = the lake is frozen
• = freezing
 estoy **helada** = I'm freezing
2 helado noun, masculine
 un **helado** = an ice cream

helicóptero noun, masculine
 un **helicóptero** = a helicopter

hemos ▶ haber

herida noun, feminine
 una **herida** = an injury
 = a wound

herido/herida adjective
 = injured
 = wounded

hermanastro/hermanastra noun,
masculine/feminine
 un **hermanastro** = a stepbrother
 = a half brother
 una **hermanastra** = a stepsister
 = a half sister

hermano/hermana noun,
masculine/feminine
 un **hermano**/una **hermana** = a brother/a
 sister
 ¿tienes **hermanos**? = do you have any
 brothers or sisters?

hermoso/hermosa adjective
 = beautiful

héroe noun, masculine
 un **héroe** = a hero

heroína noun, feminine
 una **heroína** = a heroine

herramienta noun, feminine
 una **herramienta** = a tool

hervir verb **46**
 = to boil

hice ▶ hacer

hielo noun, masculine
 hielo = ice
 un cubito de **hielo** = an ice cube

hierba noun, feminine
* la hierba = the grass
* una hierba = a herb

hierro noun, masculine
hierro = iron

hierve, hiervo, etc ▶ hervir

hígado noun, masculine
el hígado = the liver

hijo/hija noun, masculine/feminine
un hijo/una hija = a son/a daughter
¿tienes hijos? = do you have any children?

hilo noun, masculine
hilo = thread

himno noun, masculine
un himno = a hymn
el himno nacional = the national anthem

hipo noun, masculine
hipo = hiccups
tener hipo = to have hiccups

hipopótamo noun, masculine
un hipopótamo = a hippopotamus

hispanohablante
1 adjective
= Spanish-speaking
2 noun, masculine/feminine
un/una hispanohablante = a Spanish
speaker

historia noun, feminine
* la historia = history
* una historia = a story

histórico/histórica adjective
* = historical
* = historic

hizo ▶ hacer

hoja noun, feminine
* una hoja = a leaf
* (of paper) una hoja = a sheet

hola exclamation
¡hola! = hello!

holá exclamation (R Pl)
(when answering the phone) hello?

Holanda noun, feminine
Holanda = Holland

holandés/holandesa
1 adjective
= Dutch
2 noun, masculine/feminine
un holandés/una holandesa = a
Dutchman/a Dutchwoman
3 holandés noun, masculine
el holandés (the language) = Dutch

hombre noun, masculine
un hombre = a man

hombro noun, masculine
el hombro = the shoulder

honesto/honesta adjective
= honest

honor noun, masculine
honor = honor, honour

hora noun, feminine
* una hora = an hour
horas de consulta/visita (at the doctor's or
dentist's) = surgery/visiting hours
* la hora = the time
siempre empieza a la misma hora = it
always begins at the same time
¿tiene hora, por favor? = have you got the
time, please?
¿me da la hora? = can you tell me the
time?
¿qué hora es? = what time is it?
* pedir hora con el médico = to make an
appointment at the doctor's

horario noun, masculine
un horario (for trains, airplanes) = a
schedule, a timetable
(at school) = a timetable
horario de atención al público (in a shop or
bank) = opening hours

horizonte noun, masculine
el horizonte = the horizon

hormiga noun, feminine
una hormiga = an ant

hormigón noun, masculine
hormigón = concrete

horno noun, masculine
un horno = an oven
un horno microondas = a microwave oven

horóscopo noun, masculine
el horóscopo = the horoscope

horrible adjective
= horrible, awful

hospital noun, masculine
un hospital = a hospital

hostal noun, masculine
un hostal = a cheap hotel

hotel noun, masculine
un hotel = a hotel

hoy adverb
= today
hoy en día = nowadays, these days
el diario de hoy = today's newspaper
los jóvenes de hoy = the youth of today

hube, hubo, etc ▶ haber

hueco/hueca
1 adjective
= hollow

H

2 hueco noun, masculine
un hueco = a space
= a hollow

huela, **huelo**, **etc** ▶ oler

huelga noun, feminine
una huelga = a strike
estar en huelga or (Spa) de huelga = to be
on strike
ir a la huelga or hacer huelga or (Spa)
ponerse en huelga = to go on strike

hueso noun, masculine
un hueso = a bone

huésped noun, masculine/feminine
un/una huésped = a guest

huevo noun, masculine
un huevo = an egg
un huevo duro/frito = a hard-boiled/fried
egg
huevos revueltos = scrambled eggs

huir verb 51
= to flee, to escape

hule noun, masculine (Mex)
hule = rubber

humano/humana
1 adjective
= human
un ser humano = a human being
2 noun, masculine/feminine
los humanos = human beings, humans

húmedo/húmeda adjective
= damp
= wet
= moist

humo noun, masculine
= smoke
= fumes

humor noun, masculine
• = mood
estar de buen/mal humor = to be in a
good/bad mood
• = humor, humour

hundir verb 41
= to sink
hundirse
= to sink

huracán noun, masculine
un huracán = a hurricane

hurra exclamation
¡hurra! = hurrah!, hooray!

huyas, **huyo**, **etc** ▶ huir

I i

iba, iban, etc ▶ ir

ida noun, feminine
la ida = the outward journey
a la ida = on the way there
un boleto (Lat Am) or (Spa) billete de ida y
vuelta = a round trip ticket, a return
ticket

idea noun, feminine
una idea = an idea

idéntico/idéntica adjective
= identical

identidad noun, feminine
identidad = identity
un documento de identidad = an identity
card

idioma noun, masculine
un idioma = a language

idiota
1 adjective
= stupid
2 noun, masculine/feminine
un/una idiota = an idiot

ido/ida ▶ ir

iglesia noun, feminine
una iglesia = a church

igual
1 adjective
son los dos iguales = they are both the
same
es igual al mío = it's the same as mine
mi abrigo es igual a or que éste = my coat
is the same as this one
2 adverb
• = equally
cantan igual de bien = they both sing
equally well
• = the same
se escriben igual = they are written the
same
• = maybe
igual se ha perdido = maybe he's got lost
• es igual de alto/inteligente/gordo que yo
= he's as tall/intelligent/fat as I am
• igual que = just like, the same as
se llama Juan, igual que yo = his name is
Juan, just like mine

ilegal adjective
= illegal

ilusión noun, masculine
• una ilusión = an illusion

* **mi mayor ilusión es volar en globo** = my greatest dream is to fly in a balloon
  hacerse ilusiones = to build up one's hopes
* **me hace mucha ilusión ir** (*Spa*) = I am looking forward to going
  ¡qué ilusión! (*Spa*) = how wonderful!

ilustración *noun, feminine*
  una ilustración = an illustration

imagen *noun, feminine*
  una imagen = an image

imaginación *noun, feminine*
  la imaginación = the imagination

imbécil
1 *adjective*
  = stupid
2 *noun, masculine|feminine*
  un/una imbécil = an idiot

impaciente *adjective*
  = impatient

impermeable *noun, masculine*
  un impermeable = a raincoat

impersonal *adjective*
  = impersonal

importación *noun, feminine*
  importación = importation
  artículos de importación = imported goods
  las importaciones = imports

importancia *noun, feminine*
  importancia = importance
  sin importancia = unimportant
  no tiene importancia = it doesn't matter

importante *adjective*
  = important

importar *verb* 1
* = to matter
  no importa = it doesn't matter
  no me importa ir sola = I don't mind going on my own
  no me importa lo que ellos digan = I don't care what they say
* = to import

imposible *adjective*
  = impossible

incluido/incluida *adjective*
  somos diez, los niños incluidos = there are ten of us including the children
  todo incluido = all in, all inclusive

incluir *verb* 51
  = to include

incluso *adverb*
  = even

incluya, incluyo, etc ▶ incluir

incómodo/incómoda *adjective*
  = uncomfortable

inconveniente *noun, masculine*
  un inconveniente = a problem
  = a drawback

incorrecto/incorrecta *adjective*
  = incorrect

increíble *adjective*
  = incredible

independencia *noun, feminine*
  independencia = independence

independiente *adjective*
  = independent

indicar *verb* 2
  = to show
  = to indicate
  = to point out

índice *noun, masculine*
* **un índice** = an index
* **el índice** = the index finger, the forefinger

indio/india
1 *adjective*
  = Indian
2 *noun*
  un indio/una india = an Indian

individual *adjective*
* = individual
* (*if it's a bed, a room*) = single

individuo/individua *noun, masculine|feminine*
  un individuo/una individua = an individual
  = a person

industria *noun, feminine*
  una industria = an industry

infarto *noun, masculine*
  un infarto = a heart attack

inferior *adjective*
* = lower
* = inferior

infierno *noun, masculine*
  el infierno = hell

influencia *noun, feminine*
  influencia = influence

informal *adjective*
* = informal, casual
* = unreliable

informar *verb* 1
  = to inform

informática *noun, feminine*
  la informática = computing

ingeniero/ingeniera *noun, masculine|feminine*
  un ingeniero/una ingeniera = an engineer

Inglaterra *noun, feminine*
  Inglaterra = England

I

R Pl River Plate area   SC Southern Cone   Spa Spain

inglés/inglesa
1 *adjective*
= English
2 *noun, masculine/feminine*
un inglés/una inglesa = an Englishman/Englishwoman
3 inglés *noun, masculine*
el inglés (*the language*) = English

ingrediente *noun, masculine*
un ingrediente = an ingredient

inicial *adjective*
= initial

injusto/injusta *adjective*
= unfair

inmigración *noun, masculine*
inmigración = immigration

inmigrante *noun, masculine/feminine*
un/una inmigrante = an immigrant

inocente *adjective*
• = innocent
• = naive

inolvidable *adjective*
= unforgettable

insecto *noun, masculine*
un insecto = an insect

insistir *verb* 41
= to insist

inspector/inspectora *noun,*
masculine/feminine
un inspector/una inspectora = an inspector

instalar *verb* 1
= to install
= to put in
= to put up
= to put

instante *noun, masculine*
un instante = a moment

instituto *noun, masculine*
• **un instituto** = an institute
• (*Spa*) **un instituto** = a high school, a secondary school

instrucción
1 *noun, feminine*
una instrucción = an instruction
2 instrucciones *noun, feminine plural*
instruciones = directions

instructor/instructora *noun,*
masculine/feminine
un instructor/una instructora = an instructor

instrumento *noun, masculine*
un instrumento = an instrument

insuficiente
1 *adjective*

• = insufficient
• = inadequate
• = poor
2 *noun, masculine* (*Spa*)
un insuficiente = a fail

insulto *noun, masculine*
un insulto = an insult

inteligencia *noun, feminine*
la inteligencia = intelligence

inteligente *adjective*
= intelligent

intención *noun, feminine*
una intención = an intention
no fue mi intención = I didn't mean to
tener buenas intenciones = to mean well

intentar *verb* 1
= to try

intercambio *noun, masculine*
un intercambio = an exchange

interés *noun, masculine*
interés = interest
tener interés en algo = to be interested in something

interesante *adjective*
= interesting

interesar *verb* 1
no me interesa la política = I am not interested in politics
le interesa oír tu opinión = he's interested in hearing your opinion
interesarse
= to show an interest

interior
1 *adjective*
• = inner
= inside
• = domestic
2 *noun, masculine*
el interior = the inside
= the interior

intermedio
1 *adjective*
• = intermediate
• = medium
2 *noun, masculine*
un intermedio = a break
= an interval

internacional *adjective*
= international

internado *noun, masculine*
un internado = a boarding school

---

interno/interna
1 *adjective*
• = internal
= inner
• = domestic
2 *noun, masculine/feminine*
un interno/una interna = a boarder

intérprete *noun, masculine/feminine*
un/una intérprete = an interpreter

interrumpir *verb* 41
= to interrupt

interruptor *noun, masculine*
un interruptor = a switch

íntimo/íntima *adjective*
= intimate
= private
un amigo íntimo = a close friend

inundación *noun, feminine*
una inundación = a flood

inútil
1 *adjective*
= useless
2 *noun, masculine*
un/una inútil = a good-for-nothing

invasión *noun, feminine*
una invasión = an invasion

inventar *verb* 1
= to invent
inventarse
= to make up

invento *noun, masculine*
un invento = an invention

invernadero *noun, masculine*
un invernadero = a greenhouse
el efecto invernadero = the greenhouse
effect

investigación *noun, feminine*
una investigación = an investigation
(*scientific*) = a piece of research

invierno *noun, masculine*
el invierno = winter

invisible *adjective*
= invisible

invitación *noun, feminine*
una invitación = an invitation

invitado/invitada *noun,*
masculine/feminine
un invitado/una invitada = a guest

invitar *verb* 1
= to invite
te invito a una copa = I'll buy you a drink
me invitó a comer a un restaurante = he
took me out for a meal
esta vez te invito yo = this time it's is on
me, this time it's my treat

ir *verb* 54
• = to go
fuimos a México = we went to Mexico
vamos a casa = let's go home
ir [a pie | en coche | en tren ...] = to go [on foot |
by car | by train ...]
fui a ayudarla = I went to help her
¿qué tal van las cosas? = how are things
going?
• = to come
¡ya voy! = I'm coming!
• = to be
iba con su novio = she was with her
boyfriend
• = to have
iba con un peinado muy raro = she had a
really strange hairstyle
• ir a hacer algo:
voy a estudiar medicina = I'm going to
study medicine
vete a comprar pan = go and buy some
bread
• ir haciendo algo:
voy acostumbrándome = I'm getting used
to it
vete vistiéndote = start getting dressed
• ¡vamos! = come on!
• ¡vaya!:
¡vaya, si es Fernando! = what a surprise,
it's Fernando!
¡vaya, se rompió! = oh, dear! it has broken
irse
• = to leave
nos fuimos a las siete = we left at seven
irse de casa = to leave home
• = to go
me voy al trabajo = I'm going to work

Irlanda *noun, feminine*
Irlanda = Ireland

irlandés/irlandesa
1 *adjective*
= Irish
2 *noun, masculine/feminine*
un irlandés/una irlandesa = an
Irishman/Irishwoman

irregular *adjective*
= irregular

isla *noun, feminine*
una isla = an island

italiano/italiana
1 *adjective*
= Italian
2 *noun, masculine/feminine*
un italiano/una italiana = an Italian
3 italiano *noun, masculine*
el italiano (*the language*) = Italian

izquierda *noun, feminine*
* **la izquierda** = the left
  ir hacia la izquierda = to go left
  a la izquierda = on the left
  manejar or (*Spa*) **conducir por la izquierda**
    = to drive on the left
* **la izquierda** = the left hand
* (*in politics*) **la izquierda** = the left
  ser de izquierda or (*Spa*) **izquierdas** = to be
    left-wing

izquierdo/izquierda *adjective*
  = left

Jj

jabón *noun, masculine*
  el jabón = the soap

jabonera *noun, feminine*
  una jabonera = a soapdish

jaguar *noun, masculine*
  un jaguar = a jaguar

jalar *verb* [1]
* (*Lat Am*) = to pull
* (*Mex*) = to take

jamás *adverb*
  = never
  nunca jamás = never ever
  = never again

jamón *noun, masculine*
  el jamón = ham
  jamón cocido, jamón (de) York = cooked
    ham
  jamón serrano = *type of cured ham similar to
    Parma ham*

Japón *noun, masculine*
  (**el**) **Japón** = Japan

jardín *noun, masculine*
* **un jardín** = a garden
* **un jardín de niños** or (*Spa*) **de infancia** = a
    nursery school

jardinero/jardinera *noun,
  masculine/feminine*
  un jardinero/una jardinera = a gardener

jarra *noun, feminine*
  una jarra = a pitcher, a jug

jarro *noun, masculine*
  un jarro = a pitcher, a jug

jaula *noun, feminine*
  una jaula = a cage

jefe/jefa *noun, masculine/feminine*
  un jefe/una jefa = a boss
  (*of a department*) = a head
  (*of a group*) = a leader
  jefe de estado/gobierno = head of
    state/government

jerez *noun, masculine*
  el jerez = sherry

jersey *noun, masculine*
  un jersey = a sweater, a jumper

Jesucristo *noun, masculine*
  Jesucristo = Jesus Christ

jícama *noun, feminine* (*Mex*)
  una jícama = a yam bean

jirafa *noun, feminine*
  una jirafa = a giraffe

jitomate *noun, masculine* (*Mex*)
  un jitomate = a tomato

joven
1 *adjective*
  = young
2 *noun, masculine/feminine*
  un/una joven = a young man/young
    woman
  los jóvenes de hoy = the young people of
    today

joya *noun, feminine*
  una joya = a piece of jewelry, a piece of
    jewellery
  mis joyas = my jewelry

joyería *noun, feminine*
  una joyería = a jeweler's, a jeweller's

jubilado/jubilada
1 *adjective*
  = retired
2 *noun, masculine/feminine*
  un jubilado/una jubilada = a pensioner

judía *noun, feminine* (*Spa*)
  una judía = a bean
  una judía verde = a green bean

judío/judía
1 *adjective*
  = Jewish
2 *noun, masculine/feminine*
  un judío/una judía = a Jew

juega, juego, etc ▶ jugar

juego *noun, masculine*
* **un juego** = a game
* **hacer juego con algo** = to match
    something
* (*of knives, plates*) **un juego** = a set

juegue ▶ jugar

jueves *noun, masculine* (**!** *does not
  change in the plural*)
  el jueves = Thursday
  See **miércoles** *for more examples.*

juez noun, masculine|feminine
un/una juez = a judge

jugador/jugadora noun,
masculine|feminine
un jugador/una jugadora = a player

jugar verb 12
= to play
jugar tenis or (R Pl, Spa) al tenis = to play
tennis
jugar a las cartas = to play cards

jugo noun, masculine
jugo = juice
jugo de naranja = orange juice

juguete noun, masculine
un juguete = a toy

juguetería noun, feminine
una juguetería = a toy store, a toyshop

julio noun, masculine
julio = July

jungla noun, feminine
la jungla = the jungle

junio noun, masculine
junio = June

juntar verb 1
• = to put together
juntaron todos los pupitres = they put all
the desks together
• = to join
hay que juntar los dos extremos = you
have to join the two ends
• (Lat Am) = to collect
juntar sellos = to collect stamps
juntarse
• = to move closer together
• = to get together

junto/junta adjective, adverb
• = together
ponlos juntos = put them together
lo queremos hacer juntos = we want to do
it together
viven juntas = they live together
• junto a = by, next to
• junto con = with

justicia noun, feminine
la justicia = justice

justo/justa
1 adjective
• = fair
• = tight
me queda un poco justo = it's a bit tight for
me
• = right
la cantidad justa = the right amount
• = just enough
tengo el dinero justo = I have just enough
money

2 justo adverb
= just
justo donde yo pensaba = just where I
thought
llegó justo a las 8 = he arrived at 8 o'clock
exactly

juventud noun, feminine
la juventud = young people
(period) = youth

juzgar verb 3
= to judge

kilo noun, masculine
un kilo = a kilo

kilogramo noun, masculine
un kilogramo = a kilogram

kilómetro noun, masculine
un kilómetro = a kilometer, a kilometre

kiosco noun, masculine
un kiosco = a newsstand
(selling sweets, cigarettes) = a kiosk

la
1 feminine article
= the
la niña = the girl
See **el** for more examples
2 pronoun
• = her
la vi ayer = I saw her yesterday
• = it
la vas a romper = you're going to break it

labio noun, masculine
un labio = a lip

lado noun, masculine
un lado = a side
en el lado derecho = on the right-hand side
de un lado a otro = from one place to
another
la casa de al lado = the house next door
al lado de = next to
a mi lado = next to me
de lado = sideways
duerme de lado = he sleeps on his side
en otro lado = somewhere else

en todos lados = everywhere
en algún lado = somewhere
en cualquier lado = anywhere
en ningún lado = nowhere
= anywhere
por un lado..., pero por otro (lado)... = on
the one hand..., but on the other hand...

ladrar verb 1
= to bark

ladrillo noun, masculine
un ladrillo = a brick

ladrón/ladrona noun,
masculine/feminine
un ladrón/una ladrona = a thief
= a burglar
= a bank robber

lagarto noun, masculine
un lagarto = a lizard

lago noun, masculine
un lago = a lake

lágrima noun, feminine
una lágrima = a tear

lamer verb 17
= to lick

lámpara noun, feminine
una lámpara = a lamp

lana noun, feminine
la lana = wool

langosta noun, feminine
una langosta = a lobster

lanzar verb 4
• = to throw
• = to launch

lapicera noun, feminine (SC)
una lapicera = a pen

lápiz noun, masculine
un lápiz = a pencil
a lápiz = in pencil
lápices de colores = crayons
un lápiz de ojos = an eyeliner
un lápiz de labios = a lipstick

largo/larga
1 adjective
= long
2 **largo** noun, masculine
el largo = the length
¿cuánto mide de largo? = how long is it?
a lo largo de = along
(referring to time) = throughout

las plural feminine article, pronoun
See **los/las** for examples

lástima noun, feminine
una lástima = a pity, a shame
¡qué lástima! = what a shame!

lata noun, feminine
• una lata = a can, a tin
• una lata✱ = a pain
¡qué lata! = what a pain!

látigo noun, masculine
un látigo = a whip

latín noun, masculine
el latín = Latin

latino/latina adjective
= Latin

lavabo noun, masculine
un lavabo = a washbowl, a washbasin

lavadora noun, feminine
una lavadora = a washing machine

lavandería noun, feminine
una lavandería = a Laundromat ®, a
launderette

lavaplatos noun, masculine (! does not
change in the plural)
un lavaplatos = a dishwasher

lavar verb 1
= to wash
lavarse
= to wash (oneself), to have a wash
lavarse el pelo = to wash one's hair

lavatorio noun, masculine (SC)
un lavatorio = a washbowl, a washbasin

lavavajillas noun, masculine (! does not
change in the plural)
un lavavajillas (detergent) = a dish liquid,
a washing-up liquid
(machine) = a dishwasher

lazo noun, masculine
• un lazo = a bow
• un lazo = a ribbon

le pronoun
• = him/her
= to him/her
• (referring to you — polite form) = you
= to you
• = it
hay que ponerle más fertilizante = you
have to give it more fertilizer

> ! Note that sometimes the only thing that
> will indicate whether **le** is translated by
> him, her, you or it is the context

tengo que decirle algo = I have to tell
him/her/you something

> ! Note that **le** becomes **se** when it's
> followed by another pronoun: **se lo dije**
> and not **le lo dije**

lección noun, feminine
una lección = a lesson

leche noun, feminine
la leche = milk
leche descremada or (Spa) desnatada =
  skim milk, skimmed milk

lechuga noun, feminine
una lechuga = a lettuce

lectura noun, feminine
la lectura = reading

leer verb 26
= to read

lejos adverb
= far
lejos de = far from
de or desde lejos = from a distance

lengua noun, feminine
• la lengua = the tongue
• lengua = language

lenguaje noun, masculine
un lenguaje = a language

lente
1 noun, masculine or feminine
un/una lente = a lens
lentes de contacto = contact lenses
2 lentes noun, masculine plural (Lat Am)
lentes = glasses
llevar or usar lentes = to wear glasses

lenteja noun, feminine
una lenteja = a lentil

lentilla noun, feminine (Spa)
una lentilla = a contact lens

lento/lenta adjective
= slow

Leo noun, masculine
Leo = Leo

leo noun, masculine|feminine
un/una leo = a Leo

león/leona noun, masculine|feminine
un león/una leona = a lion/a lioness

leopardo noun, masculine
un leopardo = a leopard

les pronoun
• = them
  = to them
• = you
  = to you

> **!** Note that sometimes the only thing that
> will indicate whether **les** is translated by
> them or you is the context

tengo que pedirles un favor = I have to ask
  them a favor
(referring to you) = I have to ask you a
  favour

> **!** Note that **les** becomes **se** when it's
> followed by another pronoun: se lo dije
> and not les lo dije

letra noun, feminine
• una letra = a letter
• letra = handwriting
  tener buena letra = to have good
    handwriting
• (of a song) la letra = the words

letrero noun, masculine
un letrero = a sign, a notice

levantar verb 1
= to lift
= to raise
= to pick up
levantarse
= to stand up
= to get up

ley noun, feminine
una ley = a law

leyó ▶ leer

liberar verb 1
= to free
= to liberate

libertad noun, feminine
la libertad = freedom

Libra noun, masculine
Libra = Libra

libra
1 noun, feminine
una libra = a pound
2 noun, masculine|feminine
un/una libra = a Libra, a Libran

libre adjective
= free

librería noun, feminine
• una librería = a bookstore, a bookshop
• (Spa) una librería = a bookcase

libro noun, masculine
un libro = a book

líder noun, masculine|feminine, or (Mex)
líder, lideresa noun, masculine|feminine
un/una líder = a leader

ligero/ligera adjective
• = light
• = slight

límite noun, masculine
un límite = a limit

limpiaparabrisas noun, masculine
(**!** does not change in the plural)
el limpiaparabrisas = the windshield
  wipers, the windscreen wipers

limpiar verb 1
= to clean

limpieza noun, feminine
limpieza = cleanliness
= cleaning
hacer la limpieza = to do the cleaning
limpieza en seco = drycleaning

L

limpio/limpia *adjective*
= clean

lindo/linda *adjective*
* = cute
* = lovely
* (*Lat Am*) = nice

línea *noun, feminine*
una línea = a line

linterna *noun, feminine*
una linterna = a flashlight, a torch

líquido *noun, masculine*
un líquido = a liquid

liso/lisa *adjective*
* = flat
* = smooth
* (*if it's hair*) = straight

lista *noun, feminine*
* una lista = a list
  una lista de espera = a waiting list
* (*at school*) **la lista** = the roll call, the register
  pasar lista = to take the roll call , to take the register

listo/lista *adjective*
* = clever
* **estar listo/lista** = to be ready

literatura *noun, feminine*
la literatura = literature

litro *noun, masculine*
un litro = a liter, a litre

llama *noun, feminine*
* una llama = a flame
* (*animal*) **una llama** = a llama

llamada *noun, feminine*
una llamada = a call
una llamada a cobro revertido *or* (*Mex*) **por cobrar** = a collect call, a reverse-charge call

llamar *verb* ⬜1
* = to call
* = to phone, to call, to ring
  llamar a alguien por teléfono = to phone someone
llamarse
= to be called
¿cómo te llamas? = what's your name?

llano/llana *adjective*
= flat

llanta *noun, feminine* (*Lat Am*)
una llanta = a tire, a tyre

llave *noun, feminine*
* una llave = a key
* (*a tool*) **una llave** = a wrench, a spanner
* (*Lat Am*) **una llave** = a faucet, a tap
* **la llave del gas** = the gas jet, the gas tap
* (*in music*) **una llave** = a clef

llavero *noun, masculine*
un llavero = a key ring

llegada *noun, feminine*
la llegada = the arrival

llegar *verb* ⬜3
* = to arrive
  llegaron a Francia = they arrived in France
  llegar a casa = to get home
  llegar tarde/temprano = to be late/early
  llegar a tiempo = to be on time
  no me llegó la carta = I didn't get the letter
  ¿**falta mucho para llegar?** = is there much further to go?
* = to reach
  ¿**llegas a la estantería de arriba?** = can you reach the top shelves?
* **llegar hasta** = to come up/down to
  = to go up/down to
  el agua llegó hasta la ventana = the water came up to the window
  el camino llega hasta el pueblo = the road goes up to the village
* **llegar a ser** = to become

llenar *verb* ⬜1
* = to fill
  = to fill up
  llena la botella de agua = fill the bottle with water
  llenó el suelo de basura = he covered the floor with garbage
* = to fill out, to fill in

lleno/llena *adjective*
= full
lleno de = full of
= covered with

llevar *verb* ⬜1
* = to take
* = to carry
* = to wear
  llevaré un vestido rojo = I'll wear a red dress
* **no llevo dinero** = I don't have any money on me
* = to lead
  el camino que lleva a la playa = the road that leads to the village
* (*referring to time*)
  llevo una semana estudiando = I've been studying for a week
  ¿**cuánto tiempo llevas en Inglaterra?** = how long have you been in England?
  me llevó mucho (tiempo) = it took me a long time
* (*referring to age*)
  le llevo cuatro años a mi marido = I'm four years older than my husband
llevarse
* = to take
  se llevó mis llaves = he took my keys
* **llevarse bien/mal con alguien** = to get on/not to get on with someone

llorar *verb* 1
= to cry

llover *verb* 22
= to rain

llueva, **llueve** ▶ llover

lluvia *noun, feminine*
la lluvia = the rain

lo
1 *article*
lo interesante es... = the interesting thing
is...
prefiero lo dulce = I prefer sweet things
• lo de:
lo de Ana me preocupa = I'm worried
about Ana
lo de su hijo fue terrible = what happened
to his son was terrible
todo esto es lo de Juan = all this is Juan's
iremos a lo de María *(R Pl)* = we'll go to
María's
• lo mío, lo tuyo, *etc*:
todo esto es lo mío = all this is mine
• lo que = what
eso no es lo que yo dije = that's not what I
said
lo que sea = whatever
2 *pronoun*
• = him
lo vi ayer = I saw him yesterday
• = it
lo vas a romper = you are going to break it
ya lo sé = I know

lobo *noun, masculine*
un lobo = a wolf

local *noun, masculine*
el local = the premises

loco/loca
1 *adjective*
= crazy, mad
2 *noun, masculine|feminine*
un loco/una loca = a madman/madwoman

lograr *verb* 1
• = to achieve
• = to manage
lograr que alguien haga algo = to get
someone to do something

! *Note the use of the subjunctive after*
lograr que

lomo *noun, masculine*
• el lomo = the back
• *(of a book)* el lomo = the spine
• *(of meat)* lomo = loin of pork
(of beef) = sirloin steak

loncha *noun, feminine*
una loncha = a slice

loro/lora *noun, masculine|feminine*
un loro/una lora = a parrot

los/las
1 *article*
= the
See **el** *for examples*
2 *pronoun*
= them

lotería *noun, feminine*
la lotería = the lottery
jugar a la lotería = to play the lottery

lucha *noun, feminine*
una lucha = a fight
= a struggle
lucha libre = wrestling

luchar *verb* 1
• = to fight
• = to struggle
• = to wrestle

luego *adverb*
• = later
• = then, afterwards
• *(Mex)* = soon
= quickly

lugar *noun, masculine*
• un lugar = a place
en algún lugar = somewhere
en cualquier lugar = anywhere
en ningún lugar = nowhere
= anywhere
en otro lugar = somewhere else
• lugar = position
en primer/último lugar *(in a race etc)* = in
first/last position
(when listing reasons etc) = first/last of all
• en lugar de = instead of
• yo en tu lugar = if I were you

lujo *noun, masculine*
un lujo = a luxury
de lujo = luxury

luna *noun, feminine*
la luna = the moon

lunes *noun, masculine* (! *does not change
in the plural*)
el lunes = monday
See **miércoles** *for more examples*

luz *noun, feminine*
• la luz = the light
las luces = the lights
• la luz = electricity

L

Mm

macarrones *noun, masculine plural*
macarrones = macarroni

macedonia *noun, feminine*
una macedonia (**de frutas**) = a fruit salad

maceta *noun, feminine*
una maceta = a flowerpot

machista
1 *adjective*
= sexist
2 *noun, masculine*
un machista = a sexist

madera *noun, feminine*
madera = wood
= lumber, timber
una madera = a piece of wood
una mesa de madera = a wooden table

madre *noun, feminine*
una madre = a mother

madrina *noun, feminine*
una madrina (*of a baby*) = a godmother
(*at a wedding*) = woman who accompanies the
  groom, usually his mother

madrugada *noun, feminine*
la madrugada = dawn, daybreak
a las tres de la madrugada = at three
  o'clock in the morning

madrugar *verb* ③
= to get up early

maduro/madura *adjective*
• (*if it's a fruit*) = ripe
• (*if it's a person*) = mature

maestro/maestra *noun,*
masculine/feminine
un maestro/una maestra = a teacher
(*of a discipline, an art*) = a master

magdalena *noun, feminine* (*Spa*)
una magdalena = a cup cake, a fairy cake

magia *noun, feminine*
la magia = magic

mágico/mágica *adjective*
= magic

magnético/magnética *adjective*
= magnetic

magnetofón, **magnetófono** *noun,*
masculine
un magnetofón = a tape recorder

magnífico/magnífica *adjective*
= wonderful

mago/maga *noun, masculine/feminine*
un mago/una maga = a magician

Majestad *noun, feminine*
Su Majestad = His/Her Majesty

mal
1 *adjective* (**!** *never changes*)

> **!** *Note that* mal *is the shortened form of*
> malo, *used before a masculine noun*

• = bad
  un mal día = a bad day
• = ill
• = wrong
2 *adverb*
• = badly
• = wrongly
  entender mal = to misunderstand
  el café me hace mal (*Lat Am*) = coffee
    doesn't agree with me
• te oigo muy mal = I can hardly hear you
• el pescado huele/sabe mal = the fish
    smells/tastes bad
  olía muy mal allí dentro = there was a
    horrible smell in there
• portarse mal = to misbehave
• ¡menos mal! = thank goodness!
3 *noun, masculine*
  el mal = evil

maleducado/maleducada
1 *adjective*
= rude
2 *noun, masculine/feminine*
ser un maleducado/una maleducada = to
  be rude

maleta *noun, feminine*
una maleta = a suitcase
hacer la(s) maleta(s) = to pack

maletero *noun, masculine*
el maletero = the trunk, the boot

maletín *noun, masculine*
un maletín = a briefcase
(*of a doctor*) = a bag

malla *noun, feminine*
• una malla = a leotard
• (*R Pl*) una malla (**de baño**) = a swimsuit

malo/mala
1 *adjective*
• = bad
• = poor
  mala calidad = poor quality
  ser malo para los deportes/los idiomas =
    to be bad at sports/languages
• = naughty
  eres muy malo = you are very naughty
• el guiso esta malo (*referring to condition of
    food*) = the stew has gone bad *or* is off
    (*referring to taste*) = the stew doesn't taste
    nice
• estar malo (*Mex, Spa*) = to be sick, ill

---

mamáˣ *noun, feminine*
  mamá = mom, mommy; mum, mummy

mancha *noun, feminine*
  una mancha = a stain

manchar *verb* [1]
  = to mark, to stain
mancharse
  = to get dirty
  me manché los pantalones = I got my
    trousers dirty

mandar *verb* [1]
• = to send
  mandar una postal = to send a postcard
• le gusta mandar = he likes telling people
    what to do
• (*Lat Am*) mandé a arreglar el coche = I'm
    having my car fixed
  me mandaron venir = they sent for me
• ¿mande? (*Mex*) = sorry?, pardon?

mandarina *noun, feminine*
  una mandarina = a mandarin, a tangerine

mandíbula *noun, feminine*
  la mandíbula = the jaw

manejar *verb* [1]
• (*if it's a machine, a tool*) = to handle
• (*Lat Am*) = to drive

manera *noun, feminine*
  manera = way
  a mi manera, a tu manera, *etc* = my way,
    your way, *etc*
  de ninguna manera = no way
  de todas maneras = anyway
  de cualquier manera = anyway
  = any which way, any old how
  es su manera de ser = that's the way he is
  no hay manera de [abrirlo | entenderlo |
    saberlo …] = it is impossible to [open |
    understand | know …]

manga *noun, feminine*
  una manga = a sleeve

mango *noun, masculine*
• (*of a knife etc*) un mango = a handle
• (*fruit*) un mango = a mango

manguera *noun, feminine*
  una manguera = a hose

manillar *noun, masculine* (*Spa*)
  el manillar = the handlebars

mano *noun, feminine*
• una mano = a hand
  decir adiós con la mano = to wave goodbye
  dame la mano = give me your hand

(*when congratulating someone*) = shake
    my hand
  ir de la mano = to be hand in hand
  tener algo a mano = to have something at
    hand
  está a mano derecha/izquierda = it's on the
    right-/left-hand side
  hacer algo a mano = to do something by
    hand
  echarle una mano a alguien = to give
    someone a hand
  de segunda mano = second hand
• (*of paint*) una mano = a coat

manta *noun, feminine*
  una manta = a blanket

manteca *noun, feminine*
• = fat
• = lard
• (*R Pl*) = butter

mantel *noun, masculine*
  un mantel = a tablecloth

mantendrá, **mantendría**, **etc**
▶ mantener

mantener *verb* [37]
  = to keep

mantengo, **mantenga**, **etc**
▶ mantener

mantequilla *noun, feminine*
  mantequilla = butter

mantuve, **mantuvo**, **etc** ▶ mantener

manzana *noun, feminine*
  una manzana = an apple

mañana
1 *noun, feminine*
  la mañana = the morning
  en la *or* (*Spa*) por la *or* (*R Pl*) a la mañana =
    in the morning
  a la mañana siguiente = the following
    morning
  a las ocho de la mañana = at eight o'clock
    in the morning
2 *adverb*
  = tomorrow
  pasado mañana = the day after tomorrow
  mañana por la mañana = tomorrow
    morning

mapa *noun, masculine*
  un mapa = a map

maquillaje *noun, masculine*
  maquillaje = makeup

maquillarse *verb* [1]
  = to put one's makeup on

máquina *noun, feminine*
  una máquina = a machine
  una máquina fotográfica *or* de fotos = a
    camera
  una máquina de escribir = a typewriter
  escribir algo a máquina = to type
    something

M

maquinilla noun, feminine (Spa)
una maquinilla (**de afeitar**) = an electric
razor

mar noun, masculine
el mar = the sea
por mar = by sea

maratón noun, masculine|feminine
un/una maratón = a marathon

maravilla noun, feminine
una maravilla = a wonder
es una maravilla = it's wonderful

maravilloso/maravillosa adjective
= wonderful
= marvelous, marvellous

marca noun, feminine
una marca = a mark
(for products) = a brand, a make
(in sports) = a record
un producto de marca = a brand-name
product
ropa de marca = designer clothes

marcar verb ⟨2⟩
• = to mark
• (when phoning) = to dial
• (in sports) = to score
• = to say
el reloj marcaba las seis = the clock said
six o'clock

marco noun, masculine
• (currency) un marco = a mark
• (for pictures) un marco = a frame

marea noun, feminine
la marea = the tide

mareado/mareada adjective
• = sick, queasy
• = dizzy, giddy

marear verb ⟨1⟩
• = to make ... feel sick or queasy
• = to make ... feel dizzy or giddy
• (with questions, explanations) = to confuse
marearse
= to feel sick
= to get dizzy

margarina noun, feminine
margarina = margarine

margarita noun, feminine
una margarita = a daisy

margen noun, masculine
el margen = the margin

marido noun, masculine
un marido = a husband

marina noun, feminine
la marina = the navy

marinero noun, masculine
un marinero = a sailor

mariposa noun, feminine
una mariposa = a butterfly

marisco noun, masculine
los mariscos or (Spa) el marisco = seafood

mármol noun, masculine
el mármol = marble

marrón
1 adjective
= brown
2 noun, masculine
el marrón = brown

martes noun, masculine (! does not
change in the plural)
el martes = Tuesday
See **miércoles** for more examples

martillo noun, masculine
un martillo = a hammer

marzo noun, masculine
marzo = March

más
1 adjective|adverb
• = more
necesito más tiempo = I need more time
es más valiente/organizado que yo = he's
braver/more organized than me
más de tres días = more than three days
no me lo digas más = don't tell me any
more
más alto que yo = taller than me
más negro que el carbón = as black as coal
no voy a esperar más = I am not going to
wait any longer
• el jugador de más altura/habilidad = the
tallest/most skillful player
el que más me gusta = the one I like the
best
• nadie más que tú = only you
no tiene más que veinte mil pesetas = he
only has twenty thousand pesetas
• = else
¿algo más? = anything else?
nada más = nothing else
¿qué más quieres? = what else do you
want?
• (in exclamations) = so
¡este camino es más largo! = this road is so
long!
¡qué agua más limpia! = this water is so
clean!
• de más:
hay cinco copias de más = there are five
copies too many
¿alguien tiene una entrada de más? = does
anyone have a spare ticket?
• más o menos = more or less
2 preposition
más = plus
dos más cuatro son seis = two plus four is
six

masculino
1 *adjective*
  = male
  = men's
  = masculine
2 *noun, masculine*
  el **masculino** = the masculine

matar *verb* 1
  = to kill
matarse
• = to kill oneself
• = to get killed

matemáticas *noun, feminine*
  las **matemáticas** = mathematics, math,
  maths

material
1 *adjective*
  = material
2 *noun, masculine*
  material = material
  = equipment

matrícula *noun, feminine*
• (*for a course*) la **matrícula** = registration
• (*for a car*) una **matrícula** = a license
  number, a registration number
  = a license plate, a number plate

matrimonio *noun, masculine*
• el **matrimonio** = marriage
• un **matrimonio** = a married couple

mayo *noun, masculine*
  mayo = May

máximo/máxima *adjective*
  = maximum

mayonesa *noun, feminine*
  la **mayonesa** = mayonnaise

mayor
1 *adjective*
• = greater/greatest
  mi **mayor deseo** = my greatest wish
  la **mayor parte del tiempo** = most of the
  time
• (*Spa*) = bigger/biggest
  un **tamaño mayor** = a bigger size
• = older/oldest
  es el **hermano mayor** = he's the oldest
  brother
  ella es bastante mayor que yo = she's quite
  a bit older than me
• = grown-up
  cuando los niños sean mayores = when
  the children are grown-up
  las **personas mayores** = grown-ups
  hacerse mayor = to grow up
  ser mayor de edad = to be of age
• (*Spa*) = higher
  una **mayor temperatura** = a higher
  temperature
• **al por mayor** = wholesale

2 *noun, masculine/feminine*
  el **mayor**/la **mayor** = the oldest
3 **mayores** *noun, masculine plural*
  los **mayores** (*adults*) = the grown-ups
  (*old*) = the elderly

mayoría *noun, feminine*
  la **mayoría** = the majority
  la **mayoría de** = most (of)

mayúscula *noun, feminine*
  una **mayúscula** = a capital letter
  con *or* **en mayúsculas** = in capital letters

me *pronoun*
• = me
  = to me
  me lo dijo = she told me
  me lo dio = she gave it to me
  me lavé la cara = I washed my face
  me puse el abrigo = I put my coat on
• (*when someone else does the action*)
  me tengo que cortar el pelo = I have to
  have my hair cut
• = myself
  tengo que cuidarme = I have to look after
  myself
  no me he movido de aquí = I haven't
  moved from here

mecánica *noun, feminine*
  mecánica = mechanics

mecánico/mecánica
1 *adjective*
  = mechanical
2 *noun, masculine/feminine*
  un **mecánico**/una **mecánica** = a mechanic

mecedora *noun, feminine*
  una **mecedora** = a rocking chair

mechero *noun, masculine* (*Spa*)
  un **mechero** = a lighter

medalla *noun, feminine*
  una **medalla** = a medal

media
1 *noun, feminine*
• la **media** = the average
• (*garment*) una **media** = a stocking
  (*Lat Am*) = a sock
2 **medias** *noun, feminine plural*
• **medias** = pantyhose, tights
• **a medias**:
  hicimos el trabajo a medias = we did the
  work between the two of us
  pagamos a medias = we paid half each
  See also **medio**

mediados *noun, masculine plural*
  a mediados de = in the middle of

medianoche *noun, feminine*
  la **medianoche** = midnight
  a medianoche = at midnight

M

medicamento noun, masculine
un medicamento = a medicine

medicina noun, feminine
medicina = medicine

médico/médica noun,
masculine|feminine
un/una médico, un médico/una médica = a doctor

medida noun, feminine
una medida = a measure
(size) = a measurement

medio/media
1 adjective
• = half
• medio paquete = half a packet
media pensión = half board
a medio camino = halfway
• = average
la temperatura media = the average temperature
• (referring to time)
las cinco y media = half past five
media hora = half an hour
tres días y medios = three and a half days
2 adverb
= half
estaba medio dormido = he was half asleep
3 medio noun, masculine
• un medio = a way
ése es el medio de ganar = that's the way to win
por cualquier medio = by any means
por todos los medios = by all possible means
por medio de = through
• el medio = the middle
me gusta el del medio = I like the one in the middle
ponerse en medio = to get in the way
quitarse de en medio or del medio = to get out of the way
• los medios de comunicación = the media
• medios (económicos) = means, resources

medio ambiente noun, masculine
el medio ambiente = the environment

mediodía noun, masculine
mediodía = midday, noon, lunchtime
a mediodía = at midday, at lunchtime

medir verb [48]
• = to measure
• (referring to height) ¿cuánto mides? = how tall are you?
mido 1,80 m = I'm 1.80 m

Mediterráneo noun, masculine
el Mediterráneo = the Mediterranean

mejicano/mejicana
▶ mexicano/mexicana

mejilla noun, feminine
la mejilla = the cheek

mejillón noun, masculine
un mejillón = a mussel

mejor
1 adjective
= better/best
cuanto más grande mejor = the bigger the better
es mejor que no vengan = it's better if they don't come
mi mejor amiga = my best friend
2 adverb
• = better/best
ahora canta mejor = he sings better now
el que mejor trabaja = the best worker
el que mejor funciona = the one that works the best
lo mejor que puedo = as best as I can
• (when giving suggestions)
mejor no vamos = it's better if we don't go
mejor siéntate ahí = you'd be better sitting over there
• a lo mejor = maybe
a lo mejor se han perdido = maybe they have got lost
3 noun, masculine|feminine
el/la mejor = the best (one)

mejorar verb [1]
= to improve

mellizo/melliza
1 adjective
= twin
2 noun, masculine|feminine
un mellizo/una melliza = a twin, a twin brother/sister

melocotón noun, masculine (Spa)
un melocotón = a peach

melón noun, masculine
un melón = a melon

membrillo noun, masculine
un membrillo = a quince

memoria noun, feminine
la memoria = memory
aprenderse algo de memoria = to learn something by heart

mencionar verb [1]
= to mention

mendigo/mendiga noun,
masculine|feminine
un mendigo/una mendiga = a beggar

menor
1 adjective
• = less
de menor importancia = of less importance
• = smaller/smallest
el menor detalle = the smallest detail

• = younger/youngest
mi hermano menor = my younger brother
soy la menor del grupo = I'm the youngest of the group
es bastante menor que yo = he's quite a bit younger than me
el menor [esfuerzo | ruido | gasto …] posible = as little [effort | noise | expense…] as possible
2 *noun, masculine/feminine*
el/la menor = the younger/youngest
un/una menor = a minor

menos
1 *adjective/adverb*
= less
= fewer
gastar menos dinero = to spend less money
tengo menos que tú = I have less than you
cada vez menos = less and less
el menos dañado de todos = the least damaged of all
el que menos se queja = the one who complains the least
tiene menos errores = it has fewer mistakes
el que tiene menos empleados = the one with the fewest employees
menos de tres dólares = less than three dollars
hay cinco copias de menos = we're five copies short
al menos = at least
por lo menos = at least
a menos que = unless
¡menos mal! = thank goodness!
2 *preposition*
• = except
todos menos éste = all of them except this one
• (*R Pl Spa: when telling the time*)
las doce menos cinco = five of *or* to twelve
• (*in temperatures, math*) = minus
tres grados bajo cero = minus three degrees
trece menos cinco son ocho = thirteen minus five is eight

mensaje *noun, masculine*
un mensaje = a message

menta *noun, feminine*
menta = mint
un caramelo de menta = a mint

mente *noun, feminine*
la mente = the mind

mentir *verb* 46
= to lie

mentira *noun, feminine*
una mentira = a lie

mentiroso/mentirosa *noun, masculine/feminine*
un mentiroso/una mentirosa = a liar

menú *noun, masculine*
un menú = a menu
el menú del día = the set menu

menudo/menuda *adjective*
• = small
• (*Spa: in exclamations*)
¡menudo coche! = what a fantastic car!
• **a menudo** = often

mercado *noun, masculine*
un mercado = a market

merecer *verb* 19
= to deserve
merecerse
= to deserve

merendar *verb* 7
= to have a snack in the afternoon
merendamos leche con galletas = we had milk and biscuits in the afternoon

merezca, merezco, etc ▶ merecer

merienda, meriendo, etc
▶ merendar

mermelada *noun, feminine*
mermelada = jam
= marmalade
mermelada de naranja = marmalade

M

mero/mera✗
1 *adjective* (*C Am, Mex*)
uno mero = just one
en la mera esquina = right on the corner
el mero día de su cumpleaños = the very day of his birthday
2 mero *adverb* (*Mex*)
= nearly, almost
ya mero llegamos = we are almost there

mes *noun, masculine*
un mes = a month
el mes pasado/que viene = last/next month
dos veces al *or* **por mes** = twice a month

mesa *noun, feminine*
una mesa = a table
sentarse a la mesa = to sit at the table
poner/quitar la mesa = to lay/clear the table

mestizo/mestiza
1 *adjective*
= (of) mixed race
2 *noun, masculine/feminine*
un mestizo/una mestiza = a man/woman of mixed race

metal *noun, masculine*
el metal = metal

metálico/metálica *adjective*
• = metal, metallic
• **en metálico** = in cash

---

meter *verb* 17
* = to put
  mete estos papeles en el cajón = put these papers in the drawer
* = to fit
  podemos meter dos más en el coche = we can fit two more in the car
* **meter un gol** = to score a goal
meterse
* = to get in/into
  se metió en el coche = she got into the car
  se me metió jabón en los ojos = I got soap in my eyes
* = to get involved
  no te metas en lo que no te importa = mind your own business

método *noun, masculine*
  un método = a method

métrico *adjective*
  = metric

metro *noun, masculine*
* **un metro** = a meter, a metre
* **el metro** = the subway, the underground

mexicano/mexicana
1 *adjective*
  = Mexican
2 *noun, masculine/feminine*
  un mexicano/una mexicana = a Mexican

mezcla *noun, feminine*
  una mezcla = a mixture, a mix
  (of coffee, tea) = a blend

mezclar *verb* 1
* = to mix
* = to get mixed up
mezclarse
  mezclarse con alguien = to mix with someone
  mezclarse en algo = to get mixed up in something

mi *adjective*
  = my

mí *pronoun*
  = me
  es mejor para mí = it's better for me
  me lo dijo a mí = he told me
* **mí mismo/mí misma** = myself
  sólo pensaba en mí mismo = I was only thinking of myself

micrófono *noun, masculine*
  un micrófono = a microphone

microondas *noun, masculine* (**!** *does not change in the plural*)
  un microondas = a microwave

microscopio *noun, masculine*
  un microscopio = a microscope

mida, **midiendo midió**, **mido**, **etc**
▶ medir

miedo *noun, masculine*
  miedo = fear
  tener miedo = to be scared, to be afraid
  tener miedo de hacer algo = to be afraid of doing something
  me da miedo la oscuridad = I'm afraid of the dark
  le da miedo volar = he's afraid of flying
  no me da miedo = I'm not afraid

miel *noun, feminine*
  la miel = honey

miembro
1 *noun, masculine*
  un miembro = a limb
2 *noun, masculine/feminine*
  un/una miembro = a member

mienta, **miento, etc** ▶ mentir

mientras
1 *adverb*
* = in the meantime
  mientras tanto = in the meantime
* **mientras más tiene, más quiere** (*Lat Am*) = the more he has, the more he wants
2 *conjunction*
* = while
  disfrútalo mientras dure = enjoy it while it lasts
* = as long as
  mientras no se oponga = as long as he/she doesn't object

  ! *Note the use of the subjunctive after the conjunction* mientras

miércoles *noun, masculine* (**!** *does not change in the plural*)
  miércoles = Wednesday
  llegaron el miércoles = they arrived on Wednesday
  el miércoles pasado = last Wednesday
  el miércoles próximo *or* **que viene** = next Wednesday
  todos los miércoles = every Wednesday
  un miércoles sí y otro no = every other Wednesday
  Miércoles de Ceniza = Ash Wednesday

miga *noun, feminine*
  una miga = a crumb
  migas de pan = breadcrumbs

mil *number*
  = a/one thousand
  veinte mil dólares = twenty thousand dollars
  miles de personas = thousands of people
  mil cincuenta = one thousand and fifty

milagro *noun, masculine*
  un milagro = a miracle

mili✻ *noun, feminine* (*Spa*)
  la mili = military service

✻ in informal situations   **C Am** Central America   **Lat Am** Latin America   **Mex** Mexico

milímetro *noun, masculine*
  un milímetro = a millimeter, a millimetre

militar
1 *adjective*
  = military
2 *noun, masculine|feminine*
  un/una militar = a soldier

milla *noun, feminine*
  una milla = a mile

millón *number*
  un millón = a million

millonario/millonaria *noun,*
masculine|feminine
  un millonario/una millonaria = a
    millionaire

minoría *noun, feminine*
  una minoría = a minority

mintamos, **mintió**, **etc** ▶ mentir

minúscula *noun, feminine*
  una minúscula = a small *or* lower-case
    letter
  con *or* en minúsculas = in small letters

minúsculo/minúscula *adjective*
  • = minute, tiny
  • letra minúscula = small *or* lower-case letter

minusválido/minusválida
1 *adjective*
  = disabled
2 *noun, masculine|feminine*
  un minusválido/una minusválida = a
    disabled man/woman

minuto *noun, masculine*
  un minuto = a minute

mío/mía
1 *adjective*
  = mine
  mío/mía/míos/mías = mine
2 *pronoun*
  el mío/la mía/los míos/las mías = mine
    See **tuyo** for more examples

mirada *noun, feminine*
  una mirada = a look
  = a glance
  echarle una mirada a algo = to look at
    something
  = to glance at something
  bajar la mirada = to look down

mirar *verb* [1]
  • = to look
  miré abajo = I looked down
  mirar por la ventana = to look through the
    window
  ¡mira qué cuadro! = look at that picture!
  • = to watch
  mirar una película = to watch a movie
  • mirar fijamente = to stare

mirarse
  mirarse en el espejo = to look at oneself in
    the mirror

mismo/misma
1 *adjective*
  • = same
  en el mismo lugar = in the same place
  lo mismo = the same (thing)
  yo mismo/tú mismo, *etc* = myself/yourself,
    etc
  • very
  en este mismo momento = at this very
    moment
2 *pronoun*
  el mismo/la misma = the same one
  los mismos/las mismas = the same ones
  da lo mismo = it doesn't matter
  me da lo mismo uno que otro = I don't
    mind *or* care which one
3 mismo *adverb*
  = just
  = right
  ahí mismo = just there
  ahora mismo = right now
  enfrente mismo del cine = right opposite
    the movie house
  ayer mismo lo vi = I saw him just yesterday
  lo haré hoy mismo = I'll do it today

misterio *noun, masculine*
  un misterio = a mystery

misterioso/misteriosa *adjective*
  = mysterious

mitad *noun, feminine*
  una mitad = a half
  la mitad del dinero = half (of) the money
  partir algo por la mitad = to split
    something in half
  llénalo hasta la mitad = fill it halfway
  a mitad de precio = half-price
  a mitad de camino = halfway
  en la mitad de la película = halfway
    through the movie
  a *or* en la mitad de la reunión = in the
    middle of the meeting

mito *noun, masculine*
  un mito = a myth

mochila *noun, feminine*
  una mochila = a backpack

mocos *noun, masculine plural*
  tener mocos = to have a runny nose
  límpiate los mocos = wipe your nose

moda *noun, feminine*
  la moda = fashion
  ir a la moda = to be trendy
  estar de moda = to be in fashion
  pasarse de moda = to go out of fashion

modales *noun, masculine plural*
  modales = manners

M

modelo
1 *noun, masculine*
un modelo = a model
2 *noun, masculine/feminine*
un/una modelo = a model

moderno/moderna *adjective*
= modern

modesto/modesta *adjective*
= modest

modo *noun, masculine*
modo = way
no hay otro modo = there's no other way
a mi modo, a tu modo, *etc* = my way, your
way, *etc*
de todos modos = anyway
'modo de empleo' = 'instructions for use'
ni modo✖ (*Lat Am*) = no way

mojar *verb* [1]
• = to get...wet
• = to dip
mojarse
• = to get wet
• = to wet
mojarse el pelo = to wet one's hair

molestar *verb* [1]
• = to bother
deja de molestar a tu hermano = stop
bothering your brother
me molesta que no me ayuden = it annoys
me that they don't help me

> ! Note use of the subjunctive after
> molestar que

• = to disturb
'no molestar' = 'do not disturb'
• (*when asking permission*)
¿te molesta si abro la ventana? = do you
mind if I open the window?
molestarse
• = to get upset
• molestarse en hacer algo = to bother to do
something

molestia *noun, feminine*
• una molestia = a feeling of discomfort
• ¿podría apartarse un poco si no es
molestia? = would you mind moving
away a little?
• no es ninguna molestia = it's no trouble at
all
tomarse la molestia de hacer algo = to
take the trouble to do something

molesto/molesta *adjective*
• = annoying
= unpleasant
• estar molesto/molesta con alguien = to be
upset with someone

molino *noun, masculine*
un molino = a mill
un molino de agua/viento = a
watermill/windmill

momento *noun, masculine*
un momento = a moment
= a minute
a partir de ese momento = from that
moment on
cuando llegue el momento = when the
time comes
de momento = at the moment
de un momento a otro = any minute now
en cualquier momento = at any time
en este momento = right now
por el momento = for the time being

moneda *noun, feminine*
• una moneda = a coin
• la moneda mexicana = the Mexican
currency

monedero *noun, masculine*
un monedero = a change purse, a purse

monja *noun, feminine*
una monja = a nun

monje *noun, masculine*
un monje = a monk

mono/mona
1 *adjective*
= pretty
= lovely
= cute
2 *noun, masculine/feminine*
un mono/una mona = a monkey

monopatín *noun, masculine*
un monopatín = a skateboard
= a scooter

monstruo *noun, masculine*
un monstruo = a monster

montaña *noun, feminine*
• una montaña = a mountain
• una montaña rusa = a roller coaster

montar *verb* [1]
• = to ride
montar a caballo = to ride a horse
montar en bicicleta = to ride a bicycle
• = to get on/in
montar en un coche = to get in a car
• = to assemble
• montar un negocio = to set up a business
• montar una tienda = to put up a tent
montarse
= to get on/in
montarse en el coche/en el tren = to get in
the car/on the train

montón *noun, masculine*
• un montón = a pile
un montón de hojas = a pile of leaves
• un montón de✖ = loads of
un montón de llamadas = loads of calls

monumento *noun, masculine*
un monumento = a monument

---

morder verb 22
= to bite

mordisco noun, masculine
un mordisco = a bite
dar un mordisco = to bite

moreno/morena adjective
= brown
= dark
piel morena = brown/dark skin
ser moreno/morena (referring to skin) = to
be dark
(referring to hair) = to be dark-haired
estar moreno/morena = to be brown, to be
tanned

morir verb 62
= to die
morirse
= to die
me muero de frío = I'm freezing
se murió de frío = he died of cold

mora noun, feminine
una mora = a blackberry

moro/mora
1 adjective
= Moorish
2 noun, masculine/feminine
un moro/una mora = a Moor
(Spa) = a North African

mosca noun, feminine
una mosca = a fly

mostaza noun, feminine
mostaza = mustard

mostrador noun, masculine
un mostrador (in a shop) = a counter
(in a pub) = a bar
(at the airport) = a check-in desk

mostrar verb 6
= to show

motivo noun, masculine
un motivo = a reason
= a cause

moto✗ noun, feminine
una moto = a bike

! Note that moto is short for motocicleta

motocicleta noun, feminine
una motocicleta = a motorcycle

motor noun, masculine
un motor = an engine

mover verb 22
= to move
moverse
= to move

movimiento noun, masculine
un movimiento = a movement
estar en movimiento = to be in motion

muchacho/muchacha noun,
masculine/feminine
un muchacho/una muchacha = a boy/a girl

muchedumbre noun, feminine
una muchedumbre = a crowd

mucho/mucha
1 adjective
• mucho/mucha = much, a lot of
muchos/muchas = many, a lot of
• tengo [mucha sed | mucho sueño | mucho
frío …] = I'm very [thirsty | tired | cold …]
hace mucho calor = it's very hot
• (referring to time)
hace mucho tiempo = a long time ago
por mucho tiempo = for a long time
2 pronoun
• mucho/mucha = much, a lot
muchos/muchas = many, a lot
muchos de ellos se quejaron = many or a
lot of them complained
• mucho (referring to time)
hace mucho que se fueron = it's a long
time since they went away
aún falta mucho para las vacaciones = the
vacation is still a long way off
queda mucho para llegar = it's still a long
way/time before we get there
no se quedó mucho = he didn't stay long
3 mucho adverb
= much, a lot
hemos gastado mucho = we've spent a lot
eso es mucho para nosotros = that's too
much for us
no me gusta mucho = I don't like it much
mucho antes/después = long before/after
como mucho = at most
ni mucho menos = far from it
trabajan mucho = they work very hard
lo siento mucho = I'm very sorry

mudanza noun, feminine
una mudanza = a move, a removal
estar de mudanza = to be in the process of
moving

mudarse verb 1
= to move

mudo/muda
1 adjective
= dumb
2 noun, masculine/feminine
un mudo/una muda = a mute

mueble noun, masculine
un mueble = a piece of furniture
los muebles = the furniture

muela noun, feminine
una muela = a (back) tooth

muera, muero, etc ▶ morir

muerda, muerdo, etc ▶ morder

muerte noun, feminine
la muerte = death

M

muerto/muerta
1 *adjective*
= dead
muerto/muerta de✶:
muerto/muerta de cansancio/de sueño =
dead tired
muerto/muerta de frío = freezing cold
muerto/muerta de hambre = starving
muerto/muerta de sed = dying of thirst
2 *noun, masculine|feminine*
un muerto/una muerta = a dead
man/woman
hubo tres muertos en el incendio = three
people died in the fire

muestra, muestro, etc ▶ mostrar

mueva, muevo, etc ▶ mover

mujer *noun, feminine*
• **una mujer** = a woman
• **mi mujer** = my wife

muleta *noun, feminine*
una muleta = a crutch
andar con muletas = to be on crutches

multa *noun, feminine*
una multa = a fine
ponerle una multa a alguien = to fine
someone

multiplicar *verb* 2
= to multiply

mundial
1 *adjective*
= world
de fama mundial = world-famous
2 *noun, masculine*
el mundial = the world championship

mundo *noun, masculine*
el mundo = the world
todo el mundo = the whole world
= everybody

municipal *adjective*
• = municipal
• = local

muñeca *noun, feminine*
• **una muñeca** = a doll
• **la muñeca** = the wrist

muñeco *noun, masculine*
• **un muñeco** = a doll
= a toy animal
• **un muñeco de nieve** = a snowman

muralla *noun, feminine*
una muralla = a wall

murciélago *noun, masculine*
un murciélago = a bat

muriendo, murió ▶ morir

murmullo *noun, masculine*
un murmullo = a murmur

murmurar *verb* 1
• = to mutter
• = to whisper
• = to gossip

muro *noun, masculine*
un muro = a wall

músculo *noun, masculine*
un músculo = a muscle

museo *noun, masculine*
un museo = a museum

música *noun, feminine*
la música = music

musical *adjective*
= musical

músico/música *noun,*
masculine|feminine
un músico/una música = a musician

muslo *noun, masculine*
un muslo = a thigh
(*of chicken*) = a leg

musulmán/musulmana
1 *adjective*
= Muslim
2 *noun, masculine|feminine*
un musulmán/una musulmana = a Muslim

muy *adverb*
• = very
es muy tarde = it's very late
son muy trabajadores = they work very
hard
muy bien = very well
Muy Sr mío, Muy Sra mía (*in formal letters*)
= Dear Sir/Madam
• = too
es muy grande para mí = it's too big for me

Nn

nacer *verb* 19
= to be born

nacimiento *noun, masculine*
un nacimiento = a birth
es sordo de nacimiento = he was born deaf

nación *noun, feminine*
una nación = a nation

nacional *adjective*
• = national
• = domestic

nacionalidad *noun, feminine*
nacionalidad = nationality

---

nada
1 *pronoun*
• **nada** = nothing
  = anything
  no pasó nada = nothing happened
  no necesito nada = I don't need
    anything
  ¿no quieres nada de París? = don't you
    want anything from Paris?
• (*Spa: in tennis*) **nada** = love
  quince nada = fifteen love
• **de nada** (*to someone who has said 'thank
    you'*) = you're welcome
• **nada más** = just
  uno nada más = just one
• **nada más** = nothing else
  = anything else
  no compramos nada más = we didn't buy
    anything else
  nada más gracias = that's all, thank you
2 *adverb*
  = at all
  no estudia nada = he doesn't study at all

nadar *verb* 1
  = to swim
    See **espalda, dorso, pecho**

nadie *pronoun*
  = nobody
  = anybody
  nadie vino *or* **no vino nadie** = nobody came
  no vi a nadie = I didn't see anybody

nafta *noun, feminine* (*R Pl*)
  nafta = gas, petrol

naipe *noun, masculine*
  un naipe = a card

naranja
1 *noun, feminine*
  una naranja = an orange
2 *adjective* (**!** *never changes*)
  = orange
3 *noun, masculine*
  el naranja (*the color*) = orange

nariz *noun, feminine*
  la nariz = the nose

nata *noun, feminine* (*Spa*)
  nata = cream

natación *noun, feminine*
  la natación = swimming

naturaleza *noun, feminine*
  la naturaleza = nature

navaja *noun, feminine*
• **una navaja** = a penknife
  = a knife
• (*for shaving*) **una navaja** = a razor

navegar *verb* 3
  = to sail

Navidad *noun, feminine*
  la Navidad = Christmas
  feliz Navidad = Merry Christmas, Happy
    Christmas

nazca, nazco, etc ▶ **nacer**

necesario/necesaria *adjective*
  = necessary
  no es necesario que preguntemos = we
    don't need to ask

  ! *Note the use of the subjunctive after* **ser
  necesario que**

necesidad *noun, feminine*
• **una necesidad** = a need
  no hay necesidad = there's no need
• **la necesidad** = necessity

necesitar *verb* 1
  = to need

negativo/negativa *adjective*
  = negative

negocio *noun, masculine*
• **un negocio** = a business
  un viaje de negocios = a business trip
• (*SC*) **un negocio** = a store, a shop

negro/negra
1 *adjective*
  = black
2 *noun, masculine/feminine*
  un negro/una negra = a black man/woman
3 **negro** *noun, masculine*
  el negro = black

nervioso/nerviosa *adjective*
• = nervous
  poner nervioso/nerviosa a alguien = to
    make somebody nervous
  (*to irritate*) = to get on someone's nerves
• = worked up
  ponerse nervioso/nerviosa = to get worked
    up

neumático *noun, masculine*
  un neumático = a tire, a tyre

nevar *verb* 7
  = to snow

nevera *noun, feminine*
  una nevera = a fridge

ni *conjunction*
  no me escribió ni me telefoneó = he didn't
    ring me nor did he phone me
  allí no está ni aquí tampoco = it's not there
    and not here either
  ni yo mismo lo sé = not even I know
  ni ... ni ... = neither ... nor ...
  ni siquiera la conozco = I don't even know
    her

nido *noun, masculine*
  un nido = a nest

niebla noun, feminine
la niebla = fog
hay niebla = it's foggy

nieto/nieta noun, masculine|feminine
un nieto/una nieta = a grandson/granddaughter
mis nietos = my grandchildren

nieva, **nieve**, **etc** ▶ nevar

nieve noun, feminine
la nieve = the snow

ningún adjective
▶ ninguno/ninguna

ninguno/ninguna
1 adjective

> **!** Note that ninguno becomes ningún before masculine singular nouns

no veo ningún animal = I don't see any animals
no hay ninguna razón = there is no reason
2 pronoun
• = neither
ninguno de los dos vino = neither of them came
• = none
¿cuál quieres? — ninguno = which one do you want? — none of them

niño/niña noun, masculine|feminine
un niño/una niña = a boy/girl

nivel noun, masculine
un nivel = a level

no adverb
= no
= not
no te muevas = don't move
tu eres Pedro ¿no? = you're Pedro, aren't you?
no me gusta nada = I don't like it at all
no salen nunca = they never go out
no gastaron nada = they didn't spend anything

noche noun, feminine
la noche = the night
= the evening
esta noche = tonight
= this evening
a las nueve de la noche = at nine o'clock in the evening
en la or (Spa) por la or (RPl) a la noche = in the evening/at night
el martes en la noche = Tuesday evening/night
[trabajar | conducir | estudiar ...] de noche = [to drive | work | study ...] at night
hacerse de noche = to get dark
¡buenas noches! (as a greeting) = good evening!
(when leaving, going to bed) = good night!

Nochebuena noun, feminine
la Nochebuena = Christmas Eve

Nochevieja noun, feminine
la Nochevieja = New Year's Eve

nocturno/nocturna adjective
• = night
• = evening

nomás✱ adverb (Lat Am)
así nomás = just like that
es aquí nomás = it's just here
pase nomás = come on in

nombre noun, masculine
• un nombre = a name
• (printed on a form) nombre = first name
• (in grammar) un nombre = a noun

nordeste, noreste noun, masculine
el nordeste = the north-east

norma noun, feminine
una norma = a rule

normal adjective
• = normal
• = ordinary

noroeste noun, masculine
el noroeste = the north-west

norte noun, masculine
el norte = the north
See **este** for more examples

noruego/noruega
1 adjective
= Norwegian
2 noun, masculine|feminine
un noruego/una noruega = a Norwegian
3 noruego noun, masculine
el noruego (the language) = Norwegian

nos pronoun
• = us
= to us
nos lo dijo = he told us
nos lo dio = he gave it to us
vamos a lavarnos las manos = let's wash our hands
nos pusimos los abrigos = we put our coats on
• (when someone else does the action)
nos tenemos que hacer ropa = we have to have some clothes made
• = ourselves
nos tenemos que cuidar más = we have to look after ourselves more
nos divertimos mucho = we had a good time
• = each other
nos queremos = we love each other

nosotros/nosotras pronoun
• = we

- = us
  nos lo dijo a nosotras = he told us
  nosotros mismos = ourselves

nota *noun, feminine*
- **una nota** = a note
- (*in school*) **una nota** = a grade, a mark
  sacar buenas notas = to get good
    grades/marks
  tomar nota de algo = to write something
    down

notar *verb* ⊡
  = to notice
  se nota que ... = you can tell that ...

noticia *noun, feminine*
  una noticia = a piece of news
  tengo una noticia = I have some news
  escuchar las noticias = to listen to the
    news
  tener noticias de alguien = to hear from
    someone

novecientos/novecientas *number*
  = nine hundred
    See **quinientos** for examples

novela *noun, feminine*
  una novela = a novel

noveno/novena *number*
  = ninth
    See **primero** for examples

noventa *number*
  = ninety
    See **cincuenta** for examples

noviembre *noun, masculine*
  noviembre = November

novio/novia *noun, masculine/feminine*
- **un novio/una novia** = a boyfriend/
    girlfriend
- **un novio/una novia** = a fiancé/a fiancée
- **el novio/la novia** = the groom/bride
  los novios = the bride and groom

nube *noun, feminine*
  una nube = a cloud

nublado/nublada *adjective*
  = cloudy
  está nublado = it's cloudy

nuca *noun, feminine*
  la nuca = the back of the neck

nudillo *noun, masculine*
  un nudillo = a knuckle

nudo *noun, masculine*
  un nudo = a knot
  hacer un nudo = to tie a knot

nuera *noun, feminine*
  una nuera = a daughter-in-law

nuestro/nuestra
1 *adjective*
  nuestro/nuestra/nuestros/nuestras = our
2 *pronoun*
  **el nuestro/la nuestra/los nuestros/las
    nuestras** = ours
    See **tuyo** for more examples

nueve *number*
- = nine
- (*in dates*) = ninth
    See **cinco** for examples

nuevo *adjective*
  = new

nuez *noun, feminine*
- **una nuez** = a walnut
- **la nuez** = the Adam's apple

número *noun, masculine*
  un número = a number
  (*of shoes*) = a size

nunca *adverb*
  = never
  = ever
  casi nunca = hardly ever
  nunca más = never again
  nunca jamás = never ever
  = never again

ñapa *noun, feminine (Lat Am)*
  = *small amount of extra goods given free*

ñoño /ñona *adjective*
  = drippy, wet

o *conjunction*
  = or
  diez o doce = ten or twelve

obedecer *verb* ⊡⊙
- = to obey
- = to do as one is told

obedezca, obedezco, etc
▶ obedecer

obediente *adjective*
= obedient

objeto *noun, masculine*
un objeto = an object

obligar *verb* ③
obligar a alguien a hacer algo = to make
someone do something, to force someone
to do something

obra *noun, feminine*
• una obra = a deed
• (*in a theater*) una obra = a play
(*literary, artistic*) = a work
• una obra = a building site
estamos de obras = we are having some
building work done
la calle está en obras = there are
roadworks in the street

obrero/obrera *noun, masculine|feminine*
un obrero/una obrera = a worker

observación *noun, feminine*
una observación = an observation

obstáculo *noun, masculine*
un obstáculo = an obstacle

obstante: no obstante *conjunction*
= nevertheless

obtendré, obtendría, etc ▶ obtener

obtener *verb* ③⑦
= to obtain
= to get

obtenga, obtengo, obtuve, etc
▶ obtener

obvio/obvia *adjective*
= obvious

ocasión *noun, feminine*
una ocasión = an occasion
= an opportunity

océano *noun, masculine*
un océano = an ocean

ochenta *number*
= eighty
See cincuenta *for examples*

ocho *number*
• = eight
• (*in dates*) = eighth
See cinco *for examples*

ochocientos/ochocientas *number*
= eight hundred
See quinientos *for examples*

octavo/octava *number*
= eighth
See primero *for examples*

ocupado/ocupada *adjective*
• (*if it's a person*) = busy

• (*if it's a telephone*) = busy, engaged
• (*if it's a seat*) = taken

ocurrir *verb* ④①
= to happen
¿qué les ha ocurrido? = what's happened
to them?
ocurrirse
se me ha ocurrido que... = it's just occurred
to me that...
si se te ocurre algo... = if you think of
anything...

odiar *verb* ①
= to hate

oeste *noun, masculine*
el oeste = the west
See este *for more examples*

ofender *verb* ⑰
= to offend
ofenderse
= to take offense

oferta *noun, feminine*
una oferta = an offer
estar de oferta = to be on offer

oficial *adjective*
= official

oficina *noun, feminine*
una oficina = an office
la oficina de información y turismo = the
tourist information office

ofrecer *verb* ⑲
= to offer

ofrezca, ofrezco, etc ▶ ofrecer

oído *noun, masculine*
• el oído = the ear
se lo dije al oído = I whispered it in her ear
• el oído = hearing

oiga, oigo, etc ▶ oír

oír *verb* ⑤⑤
• = to hear
• = to listen to
me gusta oír música = I like to listen to
music

ojalá *exclamation*
¡ojalá vengan! = I hope they come!
¡ojalá fuera mía! = I wish it was mine!

! *Note the use of the subjunctive after*
ojalá

ojo
1 *noun, masculine*
• un ojo = an eye
• el ojo de la cerradura = the keyhole
2 *exclamation*
¡ojo! = careful!

ola *noun, feminine*
una ola = a wave

oler *verb* 25
= to smell
oler a algo = to smell of something

olimpiada, **olimpíada** *noun, feminine*
la olimpiada, las olimpiadas = the Olympics

olla *noun, feminine*
una olla = a pot
una olla a presión = a pressure cooker

olor *noun, masculine*
un olor = a smell

olvidar *verb* 1
= to forget
olvidarse
olvidarse de algo/de hacer algo = to forget something/to do something

ombligo *noun, masculine*
el ombligo = the navel, the belly button

omitir *verb* 41
= to omit, to leave out

once *number*
• = eleven
• (*in dates*) = eleventh
See **cinco** for examples

onceavo/onceava *number*
= eleventh

operación *noun, feminine*
una operación = an operation

operar *verb* 1
= to operate (on)
operarse
= to have an operation
se operó del corazón = he had a heart operation

opinar *verb* 1
• = to think
• = to express an opinion

opinión *noun, feminine*
una opinión = an opinion

oportunidad *noun, feminine*
• **una oportunidad** = an opportunity
• (*Lat Am*) **una oportunidad** = an occasion

oposición *noun, feminine*
• **oposición** = opposition
• (*Spa*) **una oposición** = a public competitive exam

optimista
1 *adjective*
= optimistic
2 *noun, masculine/feminine*
un/una optimista = an optimist

orden
1 *noun, masculine*
orden = order
por orden alfabético = in alphabetical order

2 *noun, feminine*
una orden = an order

ordenador *noun, masculine* (*Spa*)
un ordenador = a computer

ordenar *verb* 1
• = to put in order
• = to straighten up, to tidy up
• (*Lat Am*) = to order

oreja *noun, feminine*
una oreja = an ear

organización *noun, feminine*
una organización = an organization

organizar *verb* 4
= to organize

orgullo *noun, masculine*
orgullo = pride

orgulloso/orgullosa *adjective*
= proud

oriente *noun, masculine*
el oriente = the east

oro *noun, masculine*
el oro = gold

orquesta *noun, feminine*
una orquesta = an orchestra
= a band

ortografía *noun, feminine*
ortografía = spelling

os *pronoun* (*Spa*)
• = you
= to you
os lo dijo = he told you
os lo di = I gave it to you
lavaos las manos = wash your hands
¿os habéis puesto los abrigos? = have you put your coats on?
• (*when someone else does the action*)
os tenéis que cortar el pelo = you have to have your hair cut
• = yourselves
os tenéis que cuidar más = you have to look after yourselves more
¿os lo pasasteis bien? = did you have a good time?
• = each other
¿os veis mucho? = do you see each other often?

oscuro *adjective*
= dark

oso *noun, masculine*
un oso = a bear

otoño *noun, masculine*
el otoño = the fall, the autumn

O

---

otro/otra
1 *adjective*
  otro/otra = another
  = other
  otros/otras = other
  = another
  el otro día = the other day
  dame otro vaso = give me another glass
  me trajeron otros libros/otros dos libros =
    they brought me some other/another two
    books
  otra cosa = something else
  (*in the negative*) = nothing else
  = anything else
  otra vez = again
2 *pronoun*
  otro/otra = another (one)
  otros/otras = others
  el otro, la otra = the other (one)

oveja *noun, feminine*
  una oveja = a sheep

oxidado/oxidada *adjective*
  = rusty

oxígeno *noun, masculine*
  el oxígeno = oxygen

oyendo, oyó ▶ oír

ozono *noun, masculine*
  el ozono = ozone

Pp

paciencia *noun, feminine*
  paciencia = patience

paciente
1 *adjective*
  = patient
2 *noun, masculine/feminine*
  un/una paciente = a patient

padre *noun, masculine*
  un padre = a father
  mis padres = my parents

padrino *noun, masculine*
  el padrino (*of a baby*) = the godfather
  (*at a wedding*) = man who gives away and
    accompanies the bride, usually her father

pagar *verb* 3
  • = to pay
  • = to pay for

página *noun, feminine*
  una página = a page

pago *noun, masculine*
  un pago = a payment

país *noun, masculine*
  un país = a country

Países Bajos *noun, masculine plural*
  los Países Bajos = the Netherlands

paisaje *noun, masculine*
  el paisaje = the landscape, the scenery

paisano/paisana *noun,*
masculine/feminine
  un paisano/una paisana = a fellow
    countryman/countrywoman

paja *noun, feminine*
  • **paja** = straw
  • (*for drinking through*) **una paja** = a straw

pájaro *noun, masculine*
  un pájaro = a bird

pala *noun, feminine*
  una pala = a shovel
  = a spade

palabra *noun, feminine*
  una palabra = a word

palacio *noun, masculine*
  un palacio = a palace

paleta *noun feminine*
  • **una paleta** = a paletta
  • (*Lat Am*) **paleta** = beach tennis
  • (*Mex*) **una paleta** (**helada**) = a Popsicle®, an
    ice lolly

pálido/pálida *adjective*
  = pale
  ponerse pálido = to go pale

palito helado *noun, masculine* (*R Pl*)
  un palito helado = a Popsicle®, an ice lolly

palmera *noun, feminine*
  una palmera = a palm tree

palo *noun, masculine*
  • **un palo** = a stick
  • (*in golf*) **un palo** = a club

paloma *noun, feminine*
  una paloma = a dove
  = a pigeon

palomitas de maíz *noun, feminine*
plural
  palomitas de maíz = popcorn

pan *noun, masculine*
  el pan = bread
  pan integral = wholemeal bread
  un pan = a loaf of bread
  un pan de molde = a tin loaf

panadería *noun, feminine*
  una panadería = a bakery

---

pánico *noun, masculine*
pánico = panic

panorama *noun, masculine*
un panorama = a view

pantaletas *noun, feminine plural (C Am, Mex)*
unas pantaletas = a pair of panties, a pair of knickers

pantalla *noun, feminine*
• una pantalla (*in a cinema, of a computer*) = a screen
• (*of a lamp*) una pantalla = a lampshade

pantalón *noun, masculine,* **pantalones** *noun, masculine plural*
un pantalón, unos pantalones = a pair of pants, a pair of trousers

pañal *noun, masculine*
un pañal = a diaper, a nappy

pañuelo *noun, masculine*
• un pañuelo = a handkerchief
• un pañuelo = a scarf

papa *noun, feminine (Lat Am)*
una papa = a potato
papas fritas = French fries, chips
= potato chips, potato crisps

papá* *noun, masculine*
papá = dad, daddy
mis papás = my mom and dad, my mum and dad

papel *noun, masculine*
• papel = paper
un papel = a piece of paper
papel de aluminio = tinfoil
papel de envolver *or* de regalo = wrapping paper
papel higiénico = toilet paper
• (*in a movie, a play*) un papel = a role

papelera *noun, feminine or (SC)*
papelero *noun, masculine*
una papelera, un papelero = a waste-paper basket
= a litter basket, a litter bin

papelería *noun, feminine*
una papelería = a stationery store, a stationer's

paquete *noun, masculine*
un paquete = a parcel, a packet

par
1 *adjective*
= even
2 *noun, masculine*
un par = a pair
un par de preguntas = a couple of questions

para *preposition*
• = for
¿para qué es? = what's it for?
• = by
debe estar listo para mañana = it must be ready by tomorrow
• = to
es muy grande para llevarlo = it's too big to carry
• (*indicating direction*)
van para [casa | el aeropuerto | Sevilla ...] = they are going [home | to the airport | to Seville ...]
• (*Lat Am: when telling the time*)
son cinco para las siete = it is five to seven
• para que = so that

parabrisas *noun, masculine (**!** does not change in the plural)*
un parabrisas = a windshield, a windscreen

paracaídas *noun, masculine (**!** does not change in the plural)*
un paracaídas = a parachute

parachoques *noun, masculine (**!** does not change in the plural)*
un parachoques = a bumper, a fender

parado/parada
1 *adjective*
• (*Spa*) = unemployed
• estar parado/parada (*Lat Am*) = to be standing
2 *noun, masculine/feminine (Spa)*
un parado/una parada = an unemployed person
3 parada *noun, feminine*
una parada = a stop
una parada de autobús = a bus stop
una parada de taxis = a taxi stand, a taxi rank

paradero *noun, masculine (Lat Am)*
un paradero = a bus stop

paraguas *noun, masculine (**!** does not change in the plural)*
un paraguas = an umbrella

paraíso *noun, masculine*
el paraíso = paradise

parar *verb* 1
• = to stop
parar de hacer algo = to stop doing something
• (*in sports*) = to save
• (*Lat Am*) = to stand (up)
• (*Lat Am*) = to go on strike
pararse
• = to stop
• (*Lat Am*) = to stand up

parchís *noun, masculine (Spa)*
parchís = ludo

P

parecer verb 19
• = to seem
= to look
parece de metal = it looks like metal
al parecer, según parece = apparently
parece ser que = it seems that
parece que va a llover = it looks like it's going to rain
parece mentira = it is difficult to believe
• me parece mal = I don't think it's right
nos parece necesario = we think it's necessary
¿qué te parece el plan? = what do you think of the plan?

parecerse
parecerse a algo = to be like something
parecerse a alguien = to look like someone
= to be like someone

parecido/parecida adjective
• = similar
• = alike
ser parecido/parecida a alguien = to look like someone
= to be like someone

pared noun, feminine
una pared = a wall

pareja noun, feminine
• una pareja = a pair
= a couple
• mi pareja = my partner

parezca, parezco, etc▶ parecer

pariente noun, masculine/feminine
un/una pariente = a relative

parlamento noun, masculine
el parlamento = parliament

paro noun, masculine
• (at work) un paro = a strike
estar de or en paro = to be on strike
• (Spa) el paro = unemployment
estar en paro = to be unemployed

párpado noun, masculine
un párpado = an eyelid

parque noun, masculine
un parque = a park
un parque de atracciones or (R Pl) de diversiones = an amusement park

párrafo noun, masculine
un párrafo = a paragraph

parrilla noun, feminine
una parrilla = a grill
a la parrilla = grilled

parte noun, feminine
• parte = part
esta parte del país = this part of the country
la gran or mayor parte del tiempo = most of the time
en alguna parte = somewhere, anywhere
en cualquier parte = anywhere
en otra parte = somewhere else
en todas partes = everywhere

• una parte = a share
mi parte del premio = my share of the prize
• ¿de parte de quién? = who's calling? (on the phone)
dale recuerdos de mi parte = give him my regards

participar verb 1
= to participate, to take part

partida noun, feminine
una partida = a game

partido noun, masculine
• un partido = a match
• un partido = a party
• (Lat Am) un partido de ajedrez = a game of chess

pasa noun, feminine
una pasa = a raisin

pasado/pasada
1 adjective
• = last
el sábado pasado = last Saturday
pasados dos meses = after two months
• (when telling the time)
son las tres pasadas = it's past three o'clock
2 pasado noun, masculine
el pasado = the past

pasajero/pasajera noun, masculine/feminine
un pasajero/una pasajera = a passenger

pasaporte noun, masculine
un pasaporte = a passport

pasar verb 1
• = to go/come past
pasaron tres autobuses seguidos = three buses went past one after the other
pasar por un lugar = to go past a place
pasaré por su oficina mañana = I'll stop by at her office tomorrow
dejar pasar a alguien = to let someone through
pasar por la aduana = to go through customs
• = to come/go in
¡pase! = come in!
• = to cross
pasar la frontera = to cross the border
• (when talking about time) = to pass
pasaron tres días = three days passed
ha pasado mucho tiempo = it's been a long time
• = to spend
¿dónde vas a pasar las Navidades? = where are you going to spend Christmas?
pasarlo bien/mal = to have a good/bad time
• = to happen
¿qué pasó? = what happened?
¿qué pasa? = what's the matter?
les ha debido pasar algo = something must have happened to them

---

C Am Central America   Lat Am Latin America   Mex Mexico

• = pass
¿me pasas la sal? = can you pass me the salt?
pasarse
• = to go too far
pasarse de estación/de casa = to go past the station/house
• (*if it's fruit*) = to go bad
(*if it's milk, fish*) = to go off

pasatiempo *noun, masculine*
un pasatiempo = a hobby

Pascua *noun, feminine*
la Pascua = Easter

pasear *verb* $\boxed{1}$
= to walk
= to go for a walk
llevar al perro a pasear = to take the dog for a walk
pasear en bicicleta = to go for a ride
pasear en coche = to go for a drive

paseo *noun, masculine*
un paseo = a walk
= a ride
= a drive
ir a dar un paseo = to go for a walk
ir a dar un paseo en bicicleta = to go for a ride
ir a dar un paseo en coche = to go for a drive

pasillo *noun, masculine*
un pasillo = a corridor

paso *noun, masculine*
• **un paso** = a step
dar un paso = to take a step
paso a paso = step by step
oí pasos = I heard footsteps
• **de paso** = on the way
= in passing
me pilla de paso = it's on my way
mencionar algo de paso = to mention something in passing
• 'ceda el paso' = 'yield', 'give way'
'prohibido el paso' = 'no entry'
• **un paso de cebra** = a zebra crossing
un paso de peatones = a crosswalk, a pedestrian crossing
un paso subterráneo = an underpass

pasta *noun, feminine*
• **una pasta** = a paste
• (*food*) **la pasta** = pasta
• (*Spa*) **una pasta** = a cookie, a biscuit

pastel *noun, masculine*
un pastel = a cake

pastelería *noun, feminine*
una pastelería = a cake shop

pastilla *noun, feminine*
• **una pastilla** = a tablet, a pill
• (*of soap*) **una pastilla** = a bar

pata *noun, feminine*
una pata = a leg
(*of a cat, dog*) = a paw

patada *noun, feminine*
una patada = a kick

patata *noun, feminine* (*Spa*)
una patata = a potato
See **papa** for examples

patín *noun, masculine*
un patín = a roller skate
= an ice skate

patinar *verb* $\boxed{1}$
• = to skate
• = to ice-skate
• = to skid
• = to slip

patio *noun, masculine*
un patio = a courtyard
= a playground

pato/pata *noun, masculine/feminine*
una pato/una pata = a duck

pausa *noun, feminine*
una pausa = a pause, a break
hacer una pausa = to have a break

pavo/pava *noun, masculine/feminine*
un pavo/una pava = a turkey
un pavo real = a peacock

payaso/payasa *noun, masculine/feminine*
un payaso/una payasa = a clown

paz *noun, feminine*
la paz = peace
dejar a alguien en paz = to leave someone alone
hacer las paces = to make (it) up

peatón *noun, masculine*
un peatón = a pedestrian

peca *noun, feminine*
una peca = a freckle

pecado *noun, masculine*
un pecado = a sin

pecho *noun, masculine*
el pecho = the chest
= the breast
nadar de pecho = to do (the) breaststroke

pechuga *noun, feminine*
la pechuga = the breast

pedal *noun, masculine*
un pedal = a pedal

pedazo *noun, masculine*
un pedazo = a piece, a bit
hacerse pedazos = to smash to pieces

P

pedir verb 48
* = to ask
  me pidió información = she asked me for
    information
  les pedí que me ayudasen = I asked them
    to help me
* (in a restaurant) = to order

pegamento noun, masculine
  pegamento = glue

pegar verb 3
* = to hit
  pegarle a alguien = to hit someone
* (if it's a stamp) = to stick
* (if it's a broken object) = to glue (together)
pegarse
  = to stick
  no se pega = it doesn't stick

pegatina noun, feminine (Spa)
  una pegatina = a sticker

peinado noun, masculine
  un peinado = a hairstyle

peinar verb 1
  = to comb
  = to brush
peinarse
  = to comb one's hair
  = to brush one's hair

peine noun, masculine
  un peine = a comb

pelar verb 1
  = to peel
  = to shell

peldaño noun, masculine
  un peldaño = a step

pelea noun, feminine
* una pelea = a fight
* una pelea = an argument

pelear verb 1
* = to fight
* = to quarrel
pelearse
* = to fight
* = to quarrel

película noun, feminine
  una película = a movie, a film
  una película cómica or de risa = a comedy
  una película de terror = a horror movie
  una película de suspense (Spa) or (Lat
    Am) de suspenso = a thriller

peligro noun, masculine
  un peligro = a danger
  estar en peligro/fuera de peligro = to be in
    danger/out of danger

peligroso/peligrosa adjective
  = dangerous

pelirrojo/pelirroja adjective
  = red-haired, ginger

pellizcar verb
  = to pinch

pelo noun, masculine
* el pelo = hair
  tiene el pelo rubio = he has blond hair
* (of an animal) = fur

pelota noun, feminine
  una pelota = a ball

peluca noun, feminine
  una peluca = a wig

peluquería noun, feminine
  una peluquería = a hairdresser's

peluquero/peluquera noun,
masculine/feminine
  un peluquero/una peluquera = a
    hairdresser

pena noun, feminine
* = sadness
* = pity, shame
  sentir or tener pena = to feel sad
  me da pena que no estén aquí = I'm sad
    that they are not here
  ¡qué pena que se haya roto! = what a
    shame it has broken!

  ! Note the use of the subjunctive after
  pena que

* (Lat Am)
  ¡qué pena! = how embarrassing!
  le da pena pedírselo = he is embarrassed to
    ask her
* merecer or valer la pena = to be worth it
* la pena de muerte = the death penalty

pendejo/pendeja✶ noun,
masculine/feminine (Lat Am)
  un pendejo/una pendeja = a nerd

penique noun, masculine
  un penique = a penny

pensamiento noun, masculine
  un pensamiento = a thought

pensar verb 7
  = to think
  pensar en algo = to think about something

pensión noun, feminine
* una pensión = a pension
* una pensión = a guesthouse
  pensión completa = full board

peor
1 adjective
  = worse/worst
2 adverb
  = worse
3 noun, masculine/feminine
  el/la peor = the worst (one)

pepino noun, masculine
un pepino = a cucumber

pequeño/pequeña
1 adjective
• = small, little
un paquete pequeño = a small parcel
un niño pequeño = a little boy
• = young
es muy pequeño para ir solo = he's too
young to go on his own
mi hermano pequeño = my younger
brother
2 noun, masculine/feminine
un pequeño/una pequeña = a small
boy/girl
el pequeño/la pequeña = the younger
= the youngest

pera noun, feminine
una pera = a pear

perder verb 21
• = to lose
• = to miss
perder [un tren | una oportunidad | un vuelo …]
= to miss [a train | an opportunity | a flight …]
• perder (el) tiempo = to waste time
perderse
= to get lost

pérdida noun, feminine
una pérdida = a loss
una pérdida de tiempo = a waste of time

perdón
1 noun, masculine
perdón = forgiveness
pedirle perdón a alguien = to apologize to
someone
2 ¡perdón! exclamation
= sorry!
= excuse me!

perdonar verb 1
= to forgive
perdonarle algo a alguien = to forgive
someone for something
perdona or (more polite) perdone = sorry
= excuse me

perejil noun, masculine
el perejil = parsley

perezoso/perezosa adjective
= lazy

perfeccionar verb 1
• = to improve
• = to perfect

perfecto/perfecta adjective
= perfect

perfume noun, masculine
un perfume = a perfume

periódico noun, masculine
un periódico = a newspaper

periodista noun, masculine/feminine
un periodista/una periodista = a journalist

periodo, **período** noun, masculine
un periodo = a period

perla noun, feminine
una perla = a pearl

permanecer verb 19
= to remain

permanente
1 adjective
= permanent
2 noun, feminine or (Mex) noun, masculine
una/un permanente = a perm

permanezca, **permanezco**, etc
▶ permanecer

permiso noun, masculine
• permiso = permission
• un permiso = a permit
• un permiso = a leave
estar de permiso = to be on leave
• con permiso (when entering) = may I come
in?
(when wishing to get past) = excuse me

permitir verb 41
= to allow, to let
¿me permite? = may I?

pero conjunction
= but

perro/perra noun, masculine/feminine
• un perro/una perra = a dog
• un perro caliente = a hot dog

persiana noun, feminine
una persiana = a blind

persona noun, feminine
una persona = a person
muchas personas = a lot of people

personaje noun, masculine
un personaje = a character

persuadir verb 41
= to persuade

pertenecer verb 19
= to belong

pertenezca, **pertenezco**, etc
▶ pertenecer

pesa noun, feminine
una pesa = a weight
hacer pesas = to do weightlifting

pesadilla noun, feminine
una pesadilla = a nightmare

P

pesado/pesada
1 *adjective*
- = heavy
- **un libro muy pesado** = a very tedious book
  Juan es muy pesado✗ = Juan is a pain in
  the neck *or* such a bore
2 *noun, masculine|feminine*
  ser un pesado/una pesada✗ = to be a pain
  in the neck *or* a bore

pesar *verb* 1
- = to weigh
- = to be heavy
  ¿te pesa mucho? = is it too heavy for you?

pesca *noun, feminine*
  la pesca = fishing
  ir de pesca = to go fishing

pescadería *noun, feminine*
  una pescadería = a fish shop, a
  fishmonger's

pescado *noun, masculine*
- **el pescado** = fish
- **un pescado** = a fish

pescador/pescadora *noun,*
masculine|feminine
  un pescador/una pescadora = a
  fisherman/fisherwoman

pescar *verb* 2
- = to fish
  ir a pescar = to go fishing
- = to catch
  pescar un salmón = to catch a salmon

pesero *noun, masculine (Mex)*
  un pesero = a minibus

peseta *noun, feminine*
  una peseta (*Spanish currency*) = a peseta

pesimista
1 *adjective*
  = pessimistic
2 *noun, masculine|feminine*
  un/una pesimista = a pessimist

peso *noun, masculine*
- **un peso** = a weight
- **un peso** = a (pair of) scales
- (*currency in many Latin American
  countries*) **un peso** = a peso

pestaña *noun, feminine*
  una pestaña = an eyelash

petaca *noun, feminine (Mex)*
  una petaca = a suitcase

pétalo *noun, masculine*
  un pétalo = a petal

petróleo *noun, masculine*
  el petróleo = oil

pez *noun, masculine*
  un pez = a fish
  un pez de colores = a goldfish

piano *noun, masculine*
  un piano = a piano

picadura *noun, feminine*
  una picadura = a bite
  = a sting

picante *adjective*
  = hot, spicy

picar *verb* 2
- = to bite
- = to sting
- (*if it's carrots, onions etc*) = to chop
- (*R Pl, Spa*) = to grind, to mince

pico *noun, masculine*
- (*of a bird*) **un pico** = a beak
- (*of a mountain*) **un pico** = a peak
- **y pico** = and a bit
  dos años y pico = two years and a bit

pida, pido, pidió, etc ▶ pedir

pie *noun, masculine*
  un pie = a foot
  ir a pie = to go on foot
  estar de pie = to be standing
  ponerse de pie = to stand up

piedra *noun, feminine*
  una piedra = a stone

piel *noun, feminine*
  piel (*of a person, fruit*) =skin
  (*of a potato, lemon*) = peel
  (*of a fox, rabbit*) = fur

piensa, pienso etc ▶ pensar

pierna *noun, feminine*
  una pierna = a leg

pieza *noun, feminine*
- **una pieza** = a piece
  (*of an engine*) = a part
- (*Lat Am*) **una pieza** = a bedroom
  (*in a hotel*) = a room

pijama *noun, masculine*
  un pijama = a pair of pajamas, a pair of
  pyjamas

pila *noun, feminine*
- (*for a torch, radio, etc*) **una pila** = a battery
- (*in the kitchen*) **una pila** = a sink

píldora *noun, feminine*
  una píldora = a pill

pileta *noun, feminine (R Pl)*
- **una pileta** = a sink
  = a washbowl, a washbasin
- **una pileta** = a swimming pool

piloto *noun, masculine|feminine*
  un/una piloto = a pilot

pimentón *noun, masculine*
  el pimentón = paprika

---

pimienta noun, feminine
la pimienta = pepper

pimiento noun, masculine
un pimiento = a pepper

pimpón noun, masculine
el pimpón = ping-pong

pinchar verb 1
* = to prick
= to be prickly
* = to burst
= to puncture
= to get a puncture

pinchazo noun, masculine
un pinchazo = a puncture

pino noun, masculine
un pino = a pine tree

pinta noun, feminine
* una pinta = a pint
* ¡qué pinta más buena!✱ = it looks really delicious!
tiene pinta de estudiante✱ = he looks like a student

pintar verb 1
= to paint

pintor/pintora noun, masculine/feminine
un pintor/una pintora = a painter

pintura
1 noun, feminine
pintura = painting
= paint
2 **pinturas** noun, feminine plural (Mex, Spa)
pinturas = color crayons

pinza
1 noun, feminine
* (of a crab) una pinza = a pincer
* (for hair) una pinza = a bobby pin, a hairgrip
* (for laundry) una pinza = a clothespin, a clothes peg
2 **pinzas** noun, feminine plural
unas pinzas = a pair of tweezers

piña noun, feminine
* una piña = a pineapple
* un piña = a pine cone

pipa noun, feminine
una pipa = a pipe

pirámide noun, feminine
una pirámide = a pyramid

pisar verb 1
pisar a alguien = to step on someone's foot
pisar algo = to step on/in something

piscina noun, feminine
una piscina = a swimming pool

Piscis noun, masculine
Piscis = Pisces

piscis noun, masculine/feminine
un/una piscis = a Pisces

piso noun, masculine
* piso = floor
el primer piso = the second floor (US English), the first floor (British English)
un edificio de cinco pisos = a five-story building
* (Spa) un piso = an apartment, a flat

pista noun, feminine
* (in a mystery, riddle) una pista = a clue
* (for racing) una pista = a track
* (for dancing) = a dance floor
* una pista de esquí = a ski slope
una pista de hielo = an ice rink
una pista de tenis (Spa) = a tennis court

pistola noun, feminine
una pistola = a gun

pitar or (Lat Am) **pitear** verb 1
* = to whistle
* (in a car) = to hoot

pito noun, masculine
un pito = a whistle

piyama noun, masculine/feminine (Lat Am)
un/una pyjama = a pair of pajamas, a pair of pyjamas

pizarra noun, feminine
una pizarra = a blackboard

placer noun, masculine
placer = pleasure

plan noun, masculine
un plan = a plan

plancha noun, feminine
* una plancha = an iron
* a la plancha = grilled

planchar verb 1
= to iron
= to do the ironing

planear verb 1
= to plan

planeta noun, masculine
un planeta = a planet

plano
1 adjective
= flat
2 noun, masculine
un plano = a map, a plan

planta noun, feminine
* una planta = a plant
* (of a building) una planta = a floor
* la planta del pie = the sole of the foot

plantar verb 1
= to plant

P

plasticina® (SC) ▶ plastilina

plástico noun, masculine
el plástico = plastic

plastilina® noun, feminine
la plastilina = Plasticine®

plata noun, feminine
• la plata = silver
• (S Am) plata = money
tener mucha plata = to have a lot of money

plataforma noun, feminine
una plataforma = a platform

plátano noun, masculine
• un plátano = a banana
• un plátano = a plantain

platicar verb [2]
• (C Am, Mex) = to talk
• (Mex) = to tell

plato noun, masculine
un plato = a plate
(for a cup) = a saucer
(for food) = a dish
el primer/segundo plato = the first/second course

playa noun, feminine
la playa = the beach
= the seaside

playera noun, feminine
• (Spa) una playera = a canvas shoe
• (Mex) una playera = a T-shirt

plaza noun, feminine
• (in a town) una plaza = a square
• (Spa) una plaza = a market
• (on a bus, plane) una plaza = a seat
• (on a course) una plaza = a place
• (at work) una plaza = a position
una plaza de toros = a bullring

plegar verb [8]
= to fold

pleno/plena adjective
en pleno centro = right in the middle
= right in the center
en pleno invierno = in the middle of winter
a plena luz del día = in broad daylight

pliega, **pliego**, **pliegue**, **etc** ▶ plegar

plomo noun, masculine
el plomo = lead

pluma noun, feminine
• una pluma = a feather
• una pluma = a pen
una pluma atómica (Mex) = a ballpoint pen

plural
1 noun, masculine
el plural = the plural
2 adjective
= plural

población noun, feminine
• la población = the population
• una población = a city
= a town
= a village

pobre
1 adjective
= poor
2 noun, masculine/feminine
un/una pobre = a poor man/woman

pobreza noun, feminine
la pobreza = poverty

poco/poca
1 adjective
poco/poca = little, not much
pocos/pocas = few, not many
con poco entusiasmo = with little enthusiasm
unos pocos días = a few days
2 pronoun
• poco/poca = little, not much
pocos/pocas = a few/not many
he comprado poco = I haven't bought much
pocos lo saben = only a few know about it
un poco = a little (bit)
poco a poco = little by little, gradually
• por poco = nearly
por poco se cae = he nearly fell
• hace poco que vive aquí = she hasn't lived here for very long
ya falta poco = it won't be long now
se quedó poco = he didn't stay long
3 poco adverb
me gusta poco = I don't like it much
son muy poco responsables = they're very irresponsible
es poco interesante = it is not very interesting

poder
1 noun
el poder = power
2 verb [31]
• = to be able to
no puedo levantarlo = I can't lift it
¿puedo entrar? = may I come in?, can I come in?
• podrías haberte hecho daño = you could have hurt yourself
puede que no lo sepa = he might not know
¿cómo has podido hacerme esto? = how could you do this to me?
podríamos ir al cine = we could go to the movies
• puede ser = it might be
puede que vengan... = maybe they'll come...

! Note the use of the subjunctive after puede que

podrá, **podré**, **podría**, **etc** ▶ poder

podrido/podrida *adjective*
= rotten

poema *noun*, *masculine*
un poema = a poem

poesía *noun*, *feminine*
• la poesía = poetry
• una poesía = a poem

poeta, **poeta/poetisa** *noun*,
masculine/feminine
un poeta/una poeta, un poeta/una poetisa
= a poet

polaco/polaca
1 *adjective*
= Polish
2 *noun*, *masculine/feminine*
un polaco/una polaca = a Pole
3 **polaco** *noun*, *masculine*
el polaco (*the language*) = Polish

policía
1 *noun*, *masculine/feminine*
un/una policía = a policeman/policewoman
2 *noun*, *feminine*
la policía = the police

política *noun*, *feminine*
• la política = politics
• una política = a policy

político/política
1 *noun*, *masculine/feminine*
un político/una política = a politician
2 *adjective*
• = political
• mi familia política = my in-laws

pollito *noun*, *masculine*
un pollito = a chick

polo *noun*, *masculine*
• el polo norte/sur = the North/South Pole
• (*sport*) el polo = polo
• (*Spa*) un polo = a Popsicle®, an ice lolly

Polonia *noun*, *feminine*
Polonia = Poland

polución *noun*, *feminine*
la polución = pollution

polvo
1 *noun*, *masculine*
• = dust
• = powder
2 **polvos** *noun*, *masculine plural*
polvos = face powder

pomelo *noun*, *masculine*
un pomelo = a grapefruit

ponchar *verb* 1 (*Mex*)
se nos ponchó una llanta = we had a
puncture

pondría, **pondrías**, **etc** ▶ poner

poner *verb* 32
• = to put
ponlo en el cajón = put it in the drawer
• = to put on
ponle el abrigo al niño = put the baby's coat
on
• = to give
¿te pongo un poco más? = shall I give you
a bit more?
• poner la tele = to put the TV on
• = to set
pon el despertador a las siete = set the
alarm for seven
• poner una tienda = to open a shop
• poner una película (*Spa*) = to show a movie
• poner a alguien [nervioso | contento | triste ...]
= to make someone [nervous | happy | sad ...]
ponerse
• = to become
ponerse enfermo = to get sick, to fall ill
ponerse contento = to cheer up
• = to put on
se puso los zapatos = he put his shoes on
• ponerse de pie = to stand up
• ponerse a hacer algo = to start doing
something
se puso a cantar = he started singing
• ponerse al teléfono (*Spa*) = to come to the
phone

ponga, **pongo**, **etc** ▶ poner

poni *noun*, *masculine*
un poni = a pony

popular *adjective*
= popular

por *preposition*
• = by
por avión = by plane
uno por uno = one by one
• = for
lo hice por ti = I did it for you
• = because of
no salimos por la lluvia = we didn't go out
because of the rain
• (*indicating position*)
por la derecha = on the right
viajar por el mundo = to travel around the
world
pasamos por el museo = we went past the
museum
pasar por la puerta = to go through the
door
• por la mañana = in the morning
por la noche = at night
vino por el día = he came for the day
• por teléfono = on the telephone
lo dijeron por el radio = it was on the radio
• = per
cinco libras por hora = five pounds per
hour *or* an hour

P

- **por qué** = why
  ¿por qué no lo dijiste? = why didn't you say
  so before?
- **por eso** = that's why
  por eso no vino = that's why he didn't come
- **por supuesto** = of course
- **por si (acaso)** = (just) in case

porcentaje noun, masculine
  un porcentaje = a percentage

poro noun, masculine (Mex)
  un poro = a leek

porque conjunction
  = because

portero/portera noun,
masculine|feminine
  un portero/una portera = a porter
  = a superintendent, a caretaker

portugués/portuguesa
1 adjective
  = Portuguese
2 noun, masculine|feminine
  un portugués/una portuguesa = a
  Portuguese
3 portugués noun, masculine
  el portugués (the language) = Portuguese

posibilidad noun, feminine
  una posibilidad = a possibility
  tener muchas posibilidades de hacer algo
  = to have a good chance of doing
  something

posible
1 adjective
  = possible
  hacer todo lo posible = to do one's best
2 adverb
  lo antes posible = as soon as possible
  lo hice lo mejor posible = I did my best

posición noun, feminine
  una posición = a position

positivo/positiva adjective
  = positive

posterior adjective
- = rear, back
  la parte posterior = the back, the rear
- = later

postizo/postiza adjective
  = false

postre noun, masculine
  un postre = a dessert

pozo noun, masculine
  un pozo = a well

practicar verb ②
  = to practice, to practise

precio noun, masculine
  un precio = a price

precioso/preciosa adjective
- = beautiful
- = precious

preciso/precisa adjective
- = precise
  el lugar preciso = the precise spot
  en el momento preciso = at the right
  moment
- **es preciso que vayas** = you must go, you
  have to go
  no es preciso que lo cambies = there's no
  need for you to change it

  ! Note the use of the subjunctive after **ser**
  preciso que

  si es preciso = if necessary

preferir verb ㊻
  = to prefer
  preferiría no verla = I would rather not see
  her

prefiera, prefiero, etc▶ preferir

pregunta noun, feminine
  una pregunta = a question
  hacer una pregunta = to ask a question

preguntar verb ①
  = to ask
  el jefe ha estado preguntado por ti = the
  boss has been asking for you
  le pregunté por su madre = I asked after
  his mother
preguntarse
  = to wonder

premio noun, masculine
  un premio = a prize

prender verb ⑰
- = to light
  prender un cigarrillo = to light a cigarette
  prenderle fuego a algo = to set fire to
  something
- (Lat Am) = to switch on, to turn on

prensa noun, feminine
  la prensa = the press, the newspapers

preocupar verb ①
  = to worry
preocuparse
  = to worry, to get worried

preparación noun, feminine
- **preparación** = preparation
- (for a job)
  ¿que preparación tiene? = what
  experience does he have?
  = what has he studied?
- (in sports) **preparación** = training

preparar verb ①
  = to prepare
prepararse
  = to get ready

---

preposición *noun, feminine*
una preposición = a preposition

presencia *noun, feminine*
presencia = presence

presentar *verb* 1
• = to introduce
les presentó a su mujer = he introduced
them to his wife
• = to present
presentar un programa = to present a
program
presentarse
• = to introduce oneself
• = to take
presentarse a un examen = to take an
exam
• presentarse a un concurso = to enter a
competition

presente *noun, masculine*
el presente = the present

presidencia *noun, feminine*
la presidencia = the presidency
= the chairmanship

presidente/presidenta *noun,*
masculine/feminine
un presidente/una presidenta = a president
= a chairman/chairwoman

preso/presa
1 *adjective*
estar preso/presa = to be in prison
2 *noun, masculine/feminine*
un preso/una presa = a prisoner

préstamo *noun, masculine*
un préstamo = a loan

prestar *verb* 1
= to lend
prestarle algo a alguien = to lend
something to someone
¿me prestas tu coche? = can I borrow your
car?

presumido/presumida
1 *adjective*
= conceited
= arrogant
= vain
2 *noun, masculine/feminine*
ser un presumido/una presumida = to be
vain

presumir *verb* 41
= to show off

primavera *noun, feminine*
la primavera = spring

primer *adjective* ▶ primero/primera

primero/primera *number*

> **!** *Note that* primero *becomes* primer
> *before masculine singular nouns*

= first
el primero/la primera = the first
de primera calidad = top quality
• (*in dates*) = first

primo/prima *noun, masculine/feminine*
un primo/una prima = a cousin

princesa *noun, feminine*
una princesa = a princess

principal *adjective*
= main
lo principal = the main thing

príncipe *noun, masculine*
un príncipe = a prince
los príncipes = the prince and princess

principiante/principianta *noun,*
masculine/feminine
un principiante/una principianta = a
beginner

principio *noun, masculine*
el principio = the beginning
al principio = at the beginning

prisa *noun, feminine*
prisa = hurry, rush
tener prisa = to be in a hurry
darse prisa = to hurry
meter prisa a alguien = to rush someone
de prisa ▶ deprisa

prisión *noun, feminine*
una prisión = a prison

prisionero/prisionera *noun,*
masculine/feminine
un prisionero/una prisionera = a prisoner

privado/privada *adjective*
= private

privilegio *noun, masculine*
un privilegio = a privilege

probable *adjective*
= probable, likely
poco probable = unlikely

probar *verb* 6
• = to try
nunca he probado el vodka = I have never
tried vodka
• = to taste
¿has probado la salsa? = have you tasted
the sauce?
• = to test
probar una máquina = to test a machine
• = to prove
probó su inocencia = he proved his
innocence
probarse
= to try on

P

problema noun, masculine
un problema = a problem

proceso noun, masculine
un proceso = a process

producir verb 43
= produce

producto noun, masculine
un producto = a product

produje, **produzca**, **etc** ▶ producir

profesión noun, feminine
una profesión = a profession

profesional adjective
= professional

profesor/**profesora** noun,
masculine/feminine
un profesor/una profesora = a teacher
(at a university) = a professor, a lecturer
un profesor/una profesora particular = a
private tutor

profundo/**profunda** adjective
= deep

programa noun, masculine
un programa = a program, a programme
(in school, college etc) = a syllabus, a
curriculum

progresar verb 1
= to progress

progreso noun, masculine
el progreso = progress

prohibido/**prohibida** adjective
= forbidden
'prohibido pisar el césped' = 'keep off the
grass'
'prohibido el paso', 'prohibida la entrada'
= 'no entry'
'prohibido fumar' = 'no smoking'

prohibir verb 52
• = to forbid
= to ban
te lo prohíbo = I forbid you
'se prohíbe fumar' = 'no smoking'

promesa noun, feminine
una promesa = a promise

prometer verb 17
= to promise

pronombre noun, masculine
un pronombre = a pronoun

pronto adverb
• = soon
= quickly
lo más pronto posible = as soon as possible
termínalo pronto = finish it quickly
de pronto = suddenly

• (Spa) = early
se levantan pronto = they get up early

pronunciar verb 1
= to pronounce

propina noun, feminine
una propina = a tip

propio/**propia** adjective
• = own
mi propio hijo = my own son
• = himself/herself
la propia dueña los atendió = the owner
herself served them

propósito noun, masculine
un propósito = an intention, a purpose
a propósito = on purpose
= by the way

protección noun, feminine
protección = protection

proteger verb 20
= to protect

protestante
1 adjective
= Protestant
2 noun, masculine/feminine
un/una protestante = a Protestant

provecho noun, masculine
provecho = benefit
sacar provecho de algo = to benefit from
something
¡buen provecho! = enjoy your meal!

proverbio noun, masculine
un proverbio = a proverb

próximo/**próxima** adjective
= next

proyecto noun, masculine
un proyecto = a plan
= a project

proyector noun, masculine
un proyector = a projector

prueba noun, feminine
• una prueba = a proof
• una prueba = a test

prueba, **pruebo**, **etc** ▶ probar

psicólogo/**psicóloga** noun,
masculine/feminine
un psicólogo/una psicóloga = a
psychologist

psiquiatra noun, masculine/feminine
un/una psiquiatra = a psychiatrist

pub noun, masculine
un pub = a bar that is open till late at night and
has music

publicar verb 2
= to publish

publicidad *noun, feminine*
• la publicidad = publicity
• la publicidad = the advertisements
  = advertising
  después de la publicidad = after the break
  = after this message

público/pública
1 *adjective*
  = public
2 **público** *noun, masculine*
  el público = the public
  = the audience

pude, pudo, etc ▶ poder

pudrirse *verb* 63
  = to rot

pueblo *noun, masculine*
• un pueblo = a village
• el pueblo = the people

pueda, puedo, etc ▶ poder

puente *noun, masculine*
  un puente = a bridge

puerco/puerca
1 *adjective*
  puerco/puerco✱ = dirty
2 *noun, masculine/feminine*
  un puerco/una puerca = a pig
3 **puerco** *noun, masculine (Mex)*
  puerco = pork

puerta *noun, feminine*
• una puerta = a door
• una puerta = a gate
  la puerta de embarque *(at an airport)* = the
  gate

puerto *noun, masculine*
  un puerto = a port, a harbor, a harbour

pues *conjunction*
  pues, no sabía = oh, I didn't know
  pues mira, se hace así = you see, it's done
  like this
  pues no = well, no
  pues si no te gusta, no lo compres = if you
  don't like it, don't buy it
  ¡pues claro que iré! = of course I'll go!

puesto¹ *noun, masculine*
• un puesto = a position, a place
  en primer puesto = in first position
• *(at work)* un puesto = a job
• un puesto de periódicos = a newspaper
  stand

puesto²**/puesta** *adjective*
• *(if it's the table)* = laid
• llevaba el sombrero puesto = he had his
  hat on
  no lo envuelva, me lo llevo puesto = don't
  wrap it, I'll wear it now

pulgada *noun, feminine*
  una pulgada = an inch

pulgar *noun, masculine*
• el pulgar = the thumb
• el pulgar = the big toe

pulir *verb* 41
  = to polish

pulmón *noun, masculine*
  el pulmón = the lung

pulpo *noun, masculine*
  un pulpo = an octopus

pulsera *noun, feminine*
  una pulsera = a bracelet

pulso *noun, masculine*
• pulso = pulse
  tomarle el pulso a alguien = to take
  someone's pulse
• tener buen pulso = to have a steady hand
  me tiembla el pulso = my hand is shaking

punta *noun, feminine*
  una punta = a point
  = a tip
  = an end
  sacar punta a un lápiz = to sharpen a
  pencil

puntada *noun, feminine*
  una puntada = a stitch

puntilla *noun, feminine*
  de *or (Lat Am)* en puntillas = on tiptoe

punto *noun, masculine*
• un punto = a point
  hasta cierto punto = up to a point
  un punto de vista = a point of view
• un punto = a dot
  un punto (**final**) = a period, a full stop
  un punto y coma = a semicolon
  dos puntos = a colon
  puntos suspensivos = suspension points,
  dot, dot, dot
• un punto = a stitch
• estar a punto de hacer algo
  = to be about to do something
  = to be on the verge of doing something
• *(Spa)* hacer punto = to knit
  de punto *(Spa)* = knitted
• llegar en punto = to arrive on the dot

puntuación *noun, feminine*
• puntuación = punctuation
• *(in exams)* puntuación = grades, marks

puntual *adjective*
  = punctual
  llegar puntual = to arrive on time

puñetazo *noun, masculine*
  un puñetazo = a punch

puño *noun, masculine*
• un puño = a fist
• *(of a shirt)* un puño = a cuff
• *(of an umbrella)* un puño = a handle

P

pupitre noun, masculine
un pupitre = a desk

puré noun, masculine
puré = purée
= mash

puro[1] noun, masculine
un puro = a cigar

puro[2]/**pura** adjective
= pure

puse, **puso**, etc ▶ poner

puta• noun, feminine
una puta = a whore

puzzle noun, masculine
un puzzle = a jigsaw (puzzle)

Qq

que
1 pronoun
• = who, that
la chica que trabaja conmigo = the girl
who works with me
• = which, that
la casa que compraron = the house they
bought
See **el** for translations of **el que**/**la que**/**los
que**/**las que**
2 conjunction
• = that
dijo que no vendría = he said (that) he
wouldn't come
• = than
es más alto que yo = he's taller than me
• (when expressing a wish)
¡que te diviertas! = have a good time!
¡que no llame! = I hope she doesn't phone!

! Note the use of the subjunctive after
que

qué
1 pronoun
= what
¿qué es esto? = what's this?
no sé qué decir = I don't know what to say
¿qué tal van las cosas?, ¿qué tal? = how
are things?
¡qué de libros! = what a lot of books!
¡qué va! = no way!
2 adjective
• = what
¿qué hora es? = what time is it?
• (in exclamations) = what a
¡qué playa más limpia! = what a clean
beach!

3 adverb
= how
¡qué bonito! = how beautiful!
¡qué bien! = great!

quebrar verb [7]
= to break
quebrarse
= to break
se quebró un brazo (Lat Am) = he broke his
arm

quedar verb [1]
• = to be left
no queda pan = there is no bread left
me quedan treinta libras = I have thirty
pounds left
quedan tres minutos para el final = there
are three minutes left to the end
aún queda mucho tiempo = there's still
plenty of time
nos quedan tres kilómetros = we still have
three kilometers to go
te queda media hora = you have half an
hour left
• (when talking about clothes, color, etc)
me queda grande = it's too big for me
te queda muy bien = it suits you
• (Spa)
quedamos en el bar = we arranged to meet
at the bar
¿quedamos esta tarde? = shall we meet
this afternoon?
quedarse
• = to stay
• quedarse con algo = to keep something
• quedarse + adjective:
quedarse ciego = to go blind
quedarse callado/quieto = to keep
still/quiet
quedarse sentado = to remain or stay
seated
quedarse dormido = to fall asleep
quedarse solo = to be left alone
• me quedé mirando = I sat/stood there
watching

queja noun, feminine
una queja = a complaint

quejarse verb [1]
= to complain
quejarse de algo = to complain about
something

quemadura noun, feminine
una quemadura = a burn

quemar verb [1]
• = to burn
• = to scald
• = to burn down
• = to be hot
quemarse
• = to burn oneself

me quemé la lengua = I burnt my tongue
- = to scald oneself
- = to get (sun)burnt
- = to burn
- = to burn down

querer *verb* 34
- = to love
  te quiero = I love you
- = to want
  ¿quieres verlos? = do you want to see them?
  quiere que la ayudemos = she wants us to help her

> **!** *Note the use of the subjunctive after* querer que

- **quiero** *or* **quisiera una habitación doble** = I would like a double room
  quisiera preguntarle... = I would like to ask you...
- **querer decir** = to mean
- **lo hice sin querer** = I didn't mean to do it
  hacer algo queriendo = to do something on purpose
quererse
  = to love each other

querido/querida *adjective*
  = dear

querrá, querré, querría, etc
▶ querer

quesadilla *noun, feminine (Mex)*
  una quesadilla = *a tortilla filled with a savory mixture and topped with melted cheese*

queso *noun, masculine*
  queso = cheese

quien *pronoun*
  = who
  = whom
  = that
  fue ella quien me lo pidió = she's the one who asked me
  la persona con quien hablé = the person I spoke to

quién *pronoun*
- = who
- = which
  ¿quién de ellos es el dueño? = which of them is the owner?
  ¿de quién es este libro? = whose book is this?

quiera, quiere, etc ▶ querer

quieto/quieta *adjective*
  = still

química *noun, feminine*
  la química = chemistry

quince *number*
- = fifteen
  quince niños = fifteen children
  el quince = (number) fifteen
  tengo quince = I have fifteen (of them)
- (*in dates*) = fifteenth
  hoy es quince *or* (*Spa*) **hoy es día quince** = today is the fifteenth
  hoy estamos a quince = today's the fifteenth
  el quince de mayo = the fifteenth of May
- (*talking about age*) =fifteen
  tengo quince años = I'm fifteen (years old)
  hoy cumplo quince años = I'm fifteen today
  a los quince años cambié de colegio I changed schools at fifteen

quinceañero/quinceañera *noun, masculine/feminine*
  un quinceañero/una quinceañera = a teenager

quincena *noun, feminine*
  una quincena = two weeks, a fortnight

quiniela
1 *noun, feminine (Spa)*
  una quiniela = a sports lottery ticket (*in USA*), a pools coupon (*in Britain*)
2 quinielas *noun, feminine (Spa)*
  las quinielas = the sports lottery (*in USA*), the pools (*in Britain*)

quinientos/quinientas *number*
  = five hundred
  quinientos uno, quinientos dos, etc = five hundred and one, five hundred and two, *etc*

quinto/quinta
1 *adjective*
  = fifth
    See **primero** *for examples*
2 quinto *noun, masculine*
  un quinto = a fifth

quiosco *noun, masculine*
  un quiosco = a newsstand
  = an ice-cream stand
  = a drinks stand
  = a kiosk

quise, quiso, etc ▶ querer

quitar *verb* 1
  = to take off
  = to remove
  = to take away
  quitarle algo a alguien = to take something from someone
quitarse
- = to take off
  quitarse los zapatos = to take one's shoes off
- (*if it's a pain*) = to go away

quizá, quizás *adverb*
  = perhaps

Q

Rr

rábano noun, masculine
un rábano = a radish

rabia noun, feminine
• rabia = anger
me pegó con rabia = he hit me in anger
me da rabia su actitud = his attitude drives
me mad, his attitude really annoys me
le da rabia no haberte visto = he's really
upset not to have seen you
me da rabia tener que irme ahora = what a
shame I have to go now
¡qué rabia! = how annoying!
(expressing disappointment) = what a
shame!
• (disease) la rabia = rabies

rabo noun, masculine
un rabo (of animal) = a tail
(of fruit, leaf) = a stalk

racimo noun, masculine
un racimo = a bunch

ración noun, feminine
una ración = a portion

radiador noun, masculine
un radiador = a radiator

radio noun, masculine (Lat Am) or (Spa,
SC) noun, feminine
un/una radio = radio
escuchar el/la radio = to listen to the radio

raíz noun, feminine
una raíz = a root
echar raíces = to take root

rallar verb [1]
= to grate

rama noun, feminine
una rama = a branch

rana noun, feminine
una rana = a frog

rápido/rápida adjective
= quick, swift

raqueta noun, feminine
una raqueta = a racket

raro/rara adjective
• = strange, odd
• = rare

rasguño noun, masculine
un rasguño = a scratch

rata noun, feminine
una rata = a rat

rato noun, masculine
un rato = a while
hace (un) rato que te llamó = he rang you a
while ago
hace (un) rato que está ahí = she's been
there for a while
al rato = after a while
al poco rato = soon afterwards
a ratos = on and off
en mis ratos libres = in my spare time
pasar un buen/mal rato = to have a
great/bad time

ratón noun, masculine
un ratón = a mouse

raya noun, feminine
• una raya = a line
• (in designs) una raya = a stripe
una camiseta a rayas = a striped T-shirt
• (in hair) la raya = the part, the parting
llevar la raya a un lado or (Lat Am) a un
costado = to have a side part or parting

rayar verb [1]
= to scratch

rayo noun, masculine
un rayo (of sun, light) = a ray
(in storms) = a bolt/flash of lightning
un rayo láser = a laser beam
rayos X = X-rays

raza noun, feminine
una raza = a race
un perro de raza = a pedigree dog

razón noun, feminine
una razón = a reason
tener razón = to be right
no tener razón = to be wrong

reacción noun, feminine
una reacción = a reaction

real adjective
• = real
• = true
• = royal

realidad noun, feminine
la realidad = reality
hacerse realidad = to become true
en realidad = actually

rebaja
1 noun, feminine
una rebaja = a reduction
2 **rebajas** noun, feminine plural
las rebajas = the sales
estar de rebajas = to have a sale on

rebajar verb [1]
• = to reduce
se lo rebajo a cincuenta dólares = I'll
reduce it to fifty dollars for you
me rebajó dos mil pesetas = he gave me a
two thousand pesetas discount
• = to bring down
rebajar el precio = to bring down the price

rebanada noun, feminine
  una rebanada = a slice

rebelde
1 adjective
• = rebel
• = rebellious
2 noun, masculine|feminine
  un/una rebelde = a rebel

rebobinar verb
  = to rewind

rebotar verb 1
  (if it's a ball) = to bounce
  (if it's a bullet) = to ricochet
  rebotó en la pared = it bounced/ricocheted
    off the wall

recado noun, masculine
  un recado = a message

recámara noun, feminine (Mex)
  una recámara = a bedroom

recepción noun, feminine
  la recepción = reception

recepcionista noun,
masculine|feminine
  un/una recepcionista = a receptionist

receta noun, feminine
• (for cooking) **una receta** = a recipe
• (from the doctor) **una receta** = a
    prescription

recibir verb 41
• = to receive
  recibir ayuda = to receive help
• = to meet
  fuimos a recibirlos a la estación = we went
    to meet them at the station
• = to welcome
  me recibieron con los brazos abiertos =
    they welcomed me with open arms

recibo noun, masculine
  un recibo = a receipt

recién adverb
• **el recién nacido/la recién nacida** = the
    newborn baby
  los recién llegados = the newcomers
  los recién casados = the newlyweds
  'recién pintado' = 'wet paint'
• (Lat Am) = just
  recién llego = I've just arrived

reciente adjective
  = recent

recoger verb 20
• (if it's fruit, information) = to collect
• (from the floor) = to pick up
• (if it's a person, a parcel) = to pick up, to
    fetch
• (if it's garbage) = to take away
• (if it's a room, a house) = to straighten (up),
    to tidy (up)

• (if it's the table) = to clear
recogerse
  recogerse el pelo = to tie one's hair back

recomendar verb 7
  = to recommend

recompensa noun
  una recompensa = a reward

reconocer verb 19
• (if it's a person, place) = to recognize
• (if it's a mistake) = to admit

reconozca etc ▶ reconocer

récord noun, masculine
  un récord = a record
  batir un récord = to break a record

recordar verb 6
• = to remember
• **recordarle algo a alguien**
  = to remind someone about something
  = to remind someone of something
  me recuerda a su madre = she reminds me
    of her mother
  recuérdame que la llame mañana =
    remind me to phone her tomorrow

  ! Note the use of the subjunctive after
  recordar que

recreo noun, masculine
  el recreo = the recess, the break

rectángulo noun, masculine
  un rectángulo = a rectangle

recto/recta
1 adjective
  = straight
2 recto adverb
  siga todo recto = carry straight on

recuerda, recuerdo, etc ▶ recordar

recuerdo
1 noun, masculine
• **un recuerdo** = a memory
• **un recuerdo** = a souvenir
2 recuerdos noun, masculine plural
  recuerdos = regards
  dale recuerdos de mi parte = give him my
    regards

redacción noun, feminine
  una redacción = an essay

redondo/redonda adjective
• = round
• (Mex: if it's a ticket) = round-trip, return

reducir verb 43
  = to reduce

reduje, reduzca, reduzco, etc
▶ reducir

R

reemplazar verb 4
= to replace

referirse verb 46
= to refer

refiera, refiero, refiramos, refirió, etc ▶ referirse

reflejo
1 adjective
= reflex
2 noun, masculine
• un **reflejo** = a reflex
tener **reflejos rápidos** = to have fast reflexes
• (in the mirror) un **reflejo** = a reflection
3 **reflejos** noun, masculine plural
reflejos = highlights

refrán noun, masculine
un **refrán** = a saying

refresco noun, masculine
un **refresco** = a soft drink

regadera noun, feminine
• una **regadera** = a watering can
• (Mex) una **regadera** = a shower
= a shower head

regalar verb 1
• = to give (as a gift)
• = to give away

regalo noun, masculine
un **regalo** = a gift, a present

regañar verb 1
= to tell off, to scold

regar verb 8
= to water

régimen noun, masculine
un **régimen** = a diet
ponerse a **régimen** = to go on a diet

región noun, feminine
una **región** = a region

registro noun, masculine
• (book) un **registro** = register
• (office) un **registro** = a registry
un **registro civil** = a registry, a registry office
• (by the police) un **registro** = a search

regla noun, feminine
• una **regla** = a rule
• (for measuring) una **regla** = a rule, a ruler
• (in a woman) la **regla** = the period
tener la **regla**, estar con la **regla** = to have one's period
• en **regla** = in order

regresar verb 1
• = to return, to come/go back
• (Lat Am) = to return, to give back
= to send back

regreso noun, masculine
regreso = return

regular
1 adjective
• = regular
• = poor
2 adverb
¿qué tal va el trabajo? — **regular** = how's work going? — so-so
lee **regular** = her reading is not very good

reina noun, feminine
la **reina** = the queen

reino noun, masculine
un **reino** = a kingdom
el **Reino Unido** = the United Kingdom

reír verb 50
= to laugh
echarse a **reír** = to burst out laughing
reírse
= to laugh
reírse de algo/alguien = to laugh at something/someone
reírse a carcajadas = to roar with laughter

reja noun, feminine
una **reja** = a grille
= a railing

relación noun, feminine
una **relación** (between facts, events) = a connection
(between people) = a relationship
relaciones **diplomáticas/comerciales** = diplomatic/trade relations
relaciones **públicas** = public relations

relacionar verb 1
= to relate
relacionarse
relacionarse con alguien = to mix with someone

relajar verb 1
= to relax
relajarse
= to relax

relámpago noun, masculine
un **relámpago** = a flash of lightning
un viaje/una visita **relámpago** = a lightning trip/visit

religión noun, feminine
la **religión** = religion

religioso/religiosa adjective
= religious

relleno/rellena
1 adjective
(if it's a cake) = filled
(if it's a chicken, pepper, etc) = stuffed
2 **relleno** noun, masculine
relleno (for cakes) = filling
(for chicken, peppers, etc) = stuffing

reloj noun, masculine
un **reloj** = a clock
= a watch
un **reloj de sol** = a sundial
un **reloj despertador** = an alarm clock
un **reloj de pulsera** = a wristwatch

relojería noun, feminine
una **relojería** = a watchmaker's

remedio noun, masculine
• un **remedio** = a remedy
(for a problem) = a solution
si no hay más **remedio** = if there's no other
option
no tener más **remedio que** ... = to have no
other option but ...
• (Lat Am) un **remedio** = a medicine

remitente
1 noun, masculine|feminine
el/la **remitente** = the sender
2 noun, masculine
el **remitente** = the return address

remolacha noun, feminine
una **remolacha** = a beet, a beetroot

remover verb 22
• (if it's soil) = to turn over
• (Spa: if it's a salad) = to toss
• (Spa: if it's a liquid) = to stir

remueva, remuevo, etc ▶ remover

renglón noun, masculine
un **renglón** = a line

rentar verb 1 (Mex)
= to rent

reparar verb 1
• = to repair
• = to mend

repartir verb 41
• (if it's post, goods) = to deliver
• (if it's money) = to share out
• (if it's leaflets) = to hand out
• (in card games) = to deal

repasar verb 1
• = to check
• (for an exam) = to review, to revise

repaso noun, masculine
un **repaso** = a review, a revision
darle un **repaso a los apuntes** = to review
one's notes, to revise one's notes

repente: de repente adverb
= suddenly, all of a sudden

repentino/repentina adjective
= sudden

repetir verb 48
• = to repeat
• = to do/say again
• (when eating) = to have a second helping
• (in school) = to repeat a year

repita, repitió, repito, etc ▶ repetir

repollo noun, masculine
un **repollo** = a cabbage

reportaje noun, masculine
un **reportaje** (in the newspaper) = an article
(on television) = a report
(Lat Am) = an interview

reportero/reportera noun,
masculine|feminine
un **reportero**/una **reportera** = a reporter

representante noun,
masculine|feminine
un/una **representante** = a representative
(of actor, actress) = an agent

representar verb 1
• = to represent
• (if it's a play) = to perform
• (if it's a role) = to play

república noun, feminine
una **república** = a republic

resbalar verb 1
• = to slip
• (if it's the floor) = to be slippery
resbalarse
= to slip
resbalarse con algo = to slip on something

reserva noun, feminine
una **reserva** = a reservation

reservar verb 1
= to reserve, to book

resfriado noun, masculine
un **resfriado** = a cold
agarrar or (Spa) **coger un resfriado** = to
catch a cold

residencia noun, feminine
• **residencia** = residence
• (for students) una **residencia** = a
dormitory, a hall of residence
una **residencia de ancianos** = an old
people's home

respaldo noun, masculine
el **respaldo** = the back

respecto noun, masculine
respecto a, con respecto a = with regard
to, regarding

respetable adjective
= respectable

respetar verb 1
= to respect

respeto noun, masculine
respeto = respect

respirar verb 1
= to breath
respirar hondo = to take a deep breath

R

responder verb 17
* = to answer, to reply
* = to respond

responsabilidad noun, feminine
responsabilidad = responsibility

responsable
1 adjective
= responsible
2 noun, masculine|feminine
el/la responsable (in a shop, office) = the person in charge
(of a mistake, crime) = the person responsible

respuesta noun, feminine
una respuesta = an answer, a reply

restar verb 1
= to subtract, to take away

restaurante noun, masculine
un restaurante = a restaurant

resto
1 noun, masculine
el resto = the rest
2 restos noun, masculine plural
los restos = the remains
(of food) = the leftovers

resultado noun, masculine
el resultado = the result
dar resultado = to work

resultar verb 1
* (if it's a plan, idea) = to work
* resultar [fácil | aburrido | caro ...] = to be [easy | boring | expensive ...]

resumen noun, masculine
un resumen = a summary

retraso noun, masculine
un retraso = a delay
el vuelo de Caracas lleva retraso = the flight from Caracas is delayed
llegaron con veinte minutos de retraso = they arrived twenty minutes late

retrato noun, masculine
un retrato = a portrait

reunión noun, feminine
una reunión = a meeting
(of friends) = a gathering

reunirse verb 64
= to meet

revancha noun, feminine
* la revancha = revenge
tomarse la revancha = to take (one's) revenge
* (when playing games) la revancha = the return game

revelar verb 1
* (if it's a secret) = to reveal
* (if it's a photograph) = to develop

reverso noun, masculine
el reverso (of paper, cloth) = the back
(of coin, medal) = the reverse

revés noun, masculine
* el revés (of paper, material) = the back
(of garment) = the inside
* al revés = upside down
= inside out
= back to front
= the other way around
= the wrong way around
* del revés = inside out

revisar verb 1
* (if it's a machine, document) = to check
* (Lat Am) = to search, to go through

revisión noun, feminine
una revisión = a check
(of an installation) = an inspection
(medical) = a checkup
(Spa: for a car) = a service

revisor/revisora noun, masculine|feminine (Spa)
un revisor/una revisora = a ticket inspector

revista noun, feminine
una revista = a magazine

revolución noun, feminine
una revolución = a revolution

revolver verb 24
= to stir

rey noun, masculine
un rey = a king
los reyes (the couple) = the King and Queen
los Reyes Magos = the Three Wise Men

rezar verb 4
= to pray
rezar una oración = to say a prayer

ría, **rían**, **etc ▶** reír

rico/rica
1 adjective
= rich
* (if it's food) = nice
* (if it's a baby, a puppy) = sweet, cute
2 noun, masculine|feminine
los ricos = the rich

ridículo noun, masculine
hacer el ridículo = to make a fool of oneself
dejar or poner a alguien en ridículo = to make someone look stupid

ridículo/ridícula adjective
= ridiculous

ríe, **ríen**, **etc ▶** reír

riega, **riego**, **riegue**, **etc ▶** regar

riesgo noun, masculine
un riesgo = a risk
correr un riesgo = to run a risk, to take a risk

---

rifa noun, feminine
  una rifa = a raffle

rincón noun, masculine
  un rincón = a corner
  un bonito rincón de España = a beautiful
    spot in or corner of Spain
  estará en cualquier rincón = it could be
    anywhere
  mirar por todos los rincones = to look in
    every nook and cranny

riña noun, feminine
• una riña = a quarrel, a row
• una riña = a fight

riñón
1 noun, masculine
  un riñón = a kidney
2 riñones noun, masculine plural
  los riñones = the lower part of the back
  me duelen los riñones = my back hurts

río noun, masculine
  un río = a river

rió ▶ reír

riqueza noun, feminine
  la riqueza = wealth

risa
1 noun, feminine
  la risa = laughter
  ¡qué risa! = what a laugh!
  darle risa a alguien = to make someone
    laugh
  me da risa pensarlo = thinking about it
    makes me laugh
  me dio la risa = I started laughing
  morirse de la risa = to die laughing
    See also película
2 risas noun, feminine plural
  risas = laughter

ritmo noun, masculine
• el ritmo = the rhythm
  llevar el ritmo = to keep time
• el ritmo = the pace, the speed
  a este ritmo = at this pace

rizo noun, masculine
  un rizo = a curl

robar verb [1]
  = to steal
  = to rob
  = to break into
  = to rip off

robo noun, masculine
  un robo = a robbery
  = a theft
  = a burglary
  = a break-in
  = a rip-off

roca noun, feminine
  una roca = a rock

rodaja noun, feminine
  una rodaja = a slice
  en rodajas = sliced

rodear verb [1]
  = to surround

rodilla noun, feminine
  una rodilla = a knee
  ponerse de rodillas = to kneel down

rojo/roja
1 adjective
  = red
  ponerse rojo = to blush
  al rojo vivo = red hot
2 rojo noun, masculine
  el rojo = red

rollo noun, masculine
• un rollo = a roll
• (Spa) un rollo✹ = a bore, a pain
  sus padres son un rollo = his parents are a
    bore or a real pain
  un rollo de libro = a really boring book

romántico/romántica adjective
  = romantic

rompecabezas noun, masculine (**!** does
not change in the plural)
  un rompecabezas = a jigsaw (puzzle)
  = a puzzle, a riddle

romper verb [40]
• = to break
• (if it's paper, material) = to tear
• (if it's shoes) = to wear out
• romper con alguien = to split up with
    someone
romperse
  = to break
  se rompió un brazo = he broke his arm

ron noun, masculine
  el ron = rum

roncar verb [2]
  = to snore

ronronear verb [1]
  = to purr

ropa noun, feminine
  la ropa = clothes
  ropa interior = underwear

ropero noun, masculine
  un ropero = a wardrobe

rosa
1 noun, feminine
  una rosa = a rose
2 adjective (**!** never changes)
  = pink
3 noun, masculine
  el rosa (the colour) = pink

R

rosado/rosado
1 *adjective*
= pink
2 rosado *noun, masculine*
• (*wine*) un rosado = a rosé
• (*the colour*) el rosado = pink

rosario *noun, masculine*
un rosario = a rosary

roto/rota *adjective*
= broken
(*if it's paper, material*) = torn
(*if it's shoes*) = worn-out

rotulador *noun, masculine* (*Spa*)
un rotulador = a felt-tip pen

rubio/rubia *adjective*
= blond

rueda *noun, feminine*
una rueda = a wheel
= a tire, a tyre
se me pinchó una rueda = I got a puncture

ruedo *noun, masculine*
el ruedo = the bullring

rugir *verb* 44
= to roar

ruido *noun, masculine*
un ruido = a noise

ruidoso/ruidosa *adjective*
= noisy

ruina *noun, feminine*
ruina = ruin
estar en la ruina = to be ruined
en ruinas = in ruins

rulo *noun, masculine*
un rulo = a curler, a roller
(*SC*) = a curl

rumbo *noun, masculine*
rumbo = direction
(*of boat, plane*) = course
poner rumbo a = to set course for
un avión con rumbo a Santiago = a plane
bound for Santiago

rumor *noun, masculine*
un rumor = a rumor, a rumour
corre el rumor de que se va = there's a
rumor going around that he's leaving

ruso/rusa
1 *adjective*
= Russian
2 *noun, masculine/feminine*
un ruso/una rusa = a Russian
3 ruso *noun, masculine*
el ruso (*the language*) = Russian

ruta *noun, feminine*
una ruta = a route

rutina *noun, feminine*
la rutina = the routine
las preguntas de rutina = the routine
questions

Ss

sábado *noun, masculine*
el sábado = Saturday
See **miércoles** *for more examples*

sábana *noun, feminine*
una sábana = a sheet

saber *verb* 35
• = to know
no se sabe = nobody knows
¡y yo qué sé!, ¡qué sé yo! = how should I
know?
• = to find out
¿cómo lo supo? = how did she find out?
• saber hacer algo = to know how to do
something
no sé nadar = I can't swim
• saber de alguien = to hear from someone
¿qué sabes de Ana? = have you heard
from Ana?
• saber a algo = to taste of something
sabe bien/dulce = it tastes nice/sweet
saber mal = to have a nasty taste
sabe a limón = it tastes of lemon
saberse
saberse algo de memoria = to know
something by heart

sabor *noun, masculine*
un sabor = a taste, a flavor, a flavour

sabrá, sabré, sabría, etc ▶ saber

sabroso/sabrosa *adjective*
• (*if it's food*) = delicious
• (*Lat Am*) sabroso/sabrosa✘ = nice

sacacorchos *noun, masculine* (**!** *does
not change in the plural*)
un sacacorchos = a corkscrew

sacapuntas *noun, masculine* (**!** *does not
change in the plural*)
un sacapuntas = a pencil sharpener

sacar *verb* 2
• = to take (out), to get (out)
sacar al perro a pasear = to take the dog
out for a walk
• = to put out
sacó la cabeza por la ventana = he put his
head out of the window

✘ *in informal situations*   **C Am** Central America   **Lat Am** Latin America   **Mex** Mexico

* = to take off
  no puedo sacar la tapa = I can't take the lid
  off
* (*if it's a ticket, passport*) = to get
* (*if it's a book, record*) = to bring out
* (*if it's a conclusion*) = to draw
* (*if it's a photograph*) = to take
* (*if it's a stain*) = to remove
sacarse
* = to take out
  sacarse las manos de los bolsillos = to
  take one's hands out of one's pockets
  se sacó una muela = he had his tooth out
* = to get
  se sacó el carnet de identidad = he's got
  his identity card
  me saqué una buena nota en el examen
  (*Lat Am*) = I got a good grade *or* mark in
  the exam
* = to take off
  se sacó los zapatos = he took his shoes off

sacerdote *noun, masculine*
  un sacerdote = a priest

saco *noun, masculine*
* **un saco** = a sack
  un saco de dormir = a sleeping bag
* (*Lat Am*) **un saco** = a jacket

sacudir *verb* 41
* = to shake
* = to shake off
* (*Mex, SC*) = to dust
sacudirse
  = to brush
  = to brush off

Sagitario *noun, masculine*
  Sagitario = Sagittarius

sagitario *noun, masculine|feminine*
  un/una sagitario = a Sagittarius

sagrado/sagrada *adjective*
  = holy
  = sacred

sal *noun, feminine*
  la sal = salt

sala *noun, feminine*
  una sala = a room
  (*in a hospital*) = a ward
  una sala de estar = a living room
  una sala de espera = a waiting room
  una sala de exposiciones = a gallery

salado/salada *adjective*
  = salty

salario *noun, masculine*
  un salario = a salary

salchicha *noun feminine*
  una salchicha = a sausage

**saldrá, saldré, saldría, salga,
salgo, etc ▶ salir**

salida *noun, feminine*
* **la salida** = the exit
* (*of plane, train*) **la salida** = the departure
* **a la salida** = on the way out

salir *verb* 56
* = to go out
  salen todas las noches = they go out every
  night
* = to come out
  sal de ahí = come out of there
* = to leave
  salen mañana = they're leaving tomorrow
* = to turn out
  todo salió bien = everything turned out OK
* = to work out
  sale a 3.000 pesos cada uno = it works out
  at 3.000 pesos each
* (*referring to the way one does something*)
  no me sale = I can't do it
  le sale muy bien la paella = he makes a
  really good paella
* **me salió un grano** = I have a spot
  te está saliendo sangre = you're bleeding
salirse
* = to come off
  se salió el asa = the handle came off
* = to leave
  salirse del colegio = to leave school
* = to leak
  se sale el gas = the gas is leaking
* = to overflow
  el agua se salió de la bañera = the bathtub
  overflowed

salmón
1 *noun, masculine*
* **un salmón** = a salmon
* **el salmón** (*the color*) = salmon pink
2 *adjective* (**!** *never changes*)
  = salmon pink

salón *noun, masculine*
* (*in a hotel*) **un salón** = a reception room
* (*Spa*) **un salón** = a living room
* (*Mex*) **un salón** = a classroom
* **un salón de belleza** = a beauty salon

salpicadera *noun, feminine* (*Mex*)
  ▶ guardabarros

salpicar *verb* 2
  = to splash

salsa *noun, feminine*
* **una salsa** = a sauce
* **salsa** = gravy

saltamontes *noun, masculine* (**!** *does
not change in the plural*)
  un saltamontes = a grasshopper

saltar *verb* 1
* = to jump
  saltó al suelo = he jumped onto the floor
saltarse

S

- (*if it's a line, page, etc*) = to skip, to miss
  saltarse un stop/un semáforo = to go
  through a stop sign/a red light

salto *noun, masculine*
  un salto = a jump, a leap
  (*of a bird, a kangaroo, etc*) = a hop
  (*from a diving board*) = a dive
  dar saltos = to jump, to leap
  (*if it's a bird, kangaroo, etc*) = to hop
  dar saltos de alegría = to jump for joy
  se levantó de un salto de la silla/la cama =
  he jumped up from his chair/out of bed

salud *noun, feminine*
  la salud = health
  estar bien de salud = to be in good health
  ¡salud! (*when drinking*) = cheers!
  (*Lat Am: when someone sneezes*) = bless
  you!

saludar *verb* [1]
  = to greet
  = to say hello to
  lo/la saluda atentamente (*in letters*) = yours
  faithfully

saludo
1 *noun, masculine*
  un saludo = a greeting
2 **saludos** *noun, masculine plural*
  saludos = regards

salvaje *adjective*
  = wild

salvar *verb* [1]
  = to save
salvarse
  = to survive

salvavidas *noun, masculine* (**!** *does not
change in the plural*)
  un salvavidas = a life jacket

salvo: a salvo *adverb*
  estar a salvo = to be safe

San *adjective*
  = Saint

sandalia *noun, feminine*
  una sandalia = a sandal

sandía *noun, feminine*
  una sandía = a watermelon

sangrar *verb* [1]
  = to bleed

sangre *noun, feminine*
  la sangre = blood
  me salió *or* (*Spa*) **me hice sangre** = I bled

sano/sana *adjective*
  = healthy
  sano y salvo = safe and sound

santo/santa
1 *adjective*
  = holy
  Santo Tomás = Saint Thomas
2 *noun, masculine/feminine*
  un santo/una santa = a saint
3 **santo** *noun, masculine*
  mi santo = my saint's day

sapo *noun, masculine*
  un sapo = a toad

sarampión *noun, masculine*
  el sarampión = measles

sardina *noun, feminine*
  una sardina = a sardine

sargento *noun, masculine/feminine*
  un/una sargento = a sergeant

sartén *noun, feminine or* (*Lat Am*) *noun,
masculine/feminine*
  una/un sartén = a frying pan

sastre *noun, masculine/feminine*
  un/una sastre = a tailor

satisfacción *noun, feminine*
  satisfacción = satisfaction

satisfecho/satisfecha *adjective*
- = satisfied
- = pleased

saxofón *noun, masculine*
  un saxofón = a saxophone

se *pronoun*
- = himself/herself/itself
  se quemó = he burnt himself
  se lavó la cara = he/she washed his/her
  face
- = themselves
  se quemaron = they burnt themselves
  se vistieron = they got dressed
- (*referring to you — polite form*)
  = yourself/yourselves
  no se culpe = don't blame yourself
  ¿se hicieron daño? = have you hurt
  yourselves?
- (*when someone else does the action*)
  se cortaron el pelo = they had their hair
  cut
  se va a operar = he's/she's going to have an
  operation
- = each other
  se ayudan mucho = they help each other a
  lot
- (*impersonal use*)
  se ve bien desde aquí = you can see well
  from here
  se está bien allí = it's nice there
- (*passive use*)
  se dice que... = it is said that...
  se vendió rápidamente = it was sold very
  quickly

C Am Central America   **Lat Am** Latin America   **Mex** Mexico

• (*in instructions*)
  se calienta la leche = heat the milk

> ! Note that **se** *is used also in many pronominal verbs, such as* **irse, caerse, subirse, volverse,** *etc. Many of these verbs are reflexive in Spanish but not in English:* **se cayó** = he fell down. *See these verbs for meaning and use.*

• = him/her
  = to him/her
  se lo dije = I told her
• = them
  = to them
  se lo di a los dos = I gave it to both of them
  See **le, les** *for more information*

sé ▸ saber

secador *noun, masculine*
  un secador (de pelo) = a hairdryer

secadora *noun, feminine*
• **una secadora** = a tumble dryer
• (*Mex*) **una secadora** = a hairdryer

secar *verb* 2
  = to dry
secarse
• = to dry up
• = to dry
  se secó las lágrimas = he dried his tears

sección *noun, feminine*
• **una sección** = a section
• (*in a shop, company*) **una sección** = a department

seco/seca *adjective*
  = dry
  = dried

secretario/secretaria *noun, masculine/feminine*
• **un secretario/una secretaria** = a secretary
• (*Mex*) **un secretario/una secretaria** = a secretary of state, a minister

secreto *noun, masculine*
  un secreto = a secret

secuestrar *verb* 1
• = to kidnap
• = to hijack

sed *noun, feminine*
  sed = thirst
  tener sed = to be thirsty

seda *noun, feminine*
  seda = silk

seguida: en seguida *adverb*
• = at once, straightaway

seguir *verb* 57
• = to follow
  seguir a alguien = to follow someone

• = to carry on, to continue
  seguir adelante = to carry on
  sigue trabajando en un colegio = he is still working at a school

según
1 *preposition*
• = according to
• = depending on
  según cómo me sienta = depending on how I feel

> ! Note the use of the subjunctive after **según como**

2 *adverb*
  = it depends
  ¿vas a ir? — según = will you go? — it depends
3 *conjunction*
  = as
  según vayan terminando = as they finish

> ! Note the use of the subjunctive after **según**

segundo/segunda
1 *number*
  = second
  See **primero** *for examples*
2 segundo *noun, masculine*
• **un segundo** = a second
• **el segundo** = the main course

seguridad *noun, feminine*
• = safety
• = security
• = certainty
  no lo sé con seguridad = I don't know for certain
• **seguridad en uno mismo** = self-confidence

seguro/segura
1 *adjective*
• = safe
• = secure
• = sure
  ¿es seguro que vienen? = are they coming for sure?
2 seguro *adverb*
  las tiene él seguro = he's definitely got them
3 seguro *noun, masculine*
  un seguro = an insurance

seis *number*
• = six
• (*in dates*) = sixth
  See **cinco** *for examples*

seiscientos/seiscientas *number*
  = six hundred
  See **quinientos** *for examples*

selección *noun, feminine*
  una selección = a selection
  la selección (nacional) = the national team

sello *noun, masculine*
  un sello = a stamp

S

selva noun, feminine
la selva = the jungle

semáforo noun, masculine
un semáforo = a set of traffic lights
pasarse or (Spa) saltarse un semáforo en
rojo = to go through a red light

semana noun, feminine
una semana = a week
la semana pasada/que viene = last/next
week
entre semana = during the week
la Semana Santa = Easter

semanal adjective
= weekly

sembrar verb 7
• = to sow
• = to plant

semilla noun, feminine
una semilla = a seed

sencillo/sencilla
1 adjective
= simple
= straightforward
2 sencillo noun, masculine
• (Mex) sencillo = change
• (Mex, Spa) un sencillo = a one-way ticket, a
single (ticket)
• (a record) un sencillo = a single

sensación noun, feminine
una sensación = a feeling

sensato/sensata adjective
= sensible

sensible adjective
= sensitive

sentado/sentada adjective
= seated
= sitting

sentar verb 7
• = to sit
• = to suit
la chaqueta te sienta bien = the jacket
suits you
• el café me sienta mal = coffee doesn't agree
with me
sentarse
= to sit (down)

sentido noun, masculine
• un sentido = a sense
(of a word) = a meaning
• (of a road, someone moving) un sentido = a
direction
una calle de sentido único = a one-way
street
• estar sin sentido = to be unconscious
quedarse sin sentido = to lose
consciousness

sentimiento noun, masculine
un sentimiento = a feeling

sentir verb 46
• = to feel
sentir frío = to feel cold
siento alegría = I feel happy
• = to hear
sentí un ruido = I heard a noise
• siento lo que ha pasado = I am sorry about
what has happened
lo siento mucho = I'm very sorry
sentirse
= to feel

seña
1 noun, feminine
una seña = a sign
les hice señas para que se callaran = I
gestured to them to be quiet
2 señas noun, feminine plural
unas señas = an address

señal noun, feminine
una señal = a sign
= a mark
= a signal

señor/señora
1 noun, masculine/feminine
un señor/una señora = a gentleman/a lady
el Señor García = Mr García
la Señora de García = Mrs García
¡oiga, señora! = excuse me, (madam)!
2 señora noun, feminine
mi señora = my wife

señorita noun, feminine
una señorita = a young lady
la Señorita García = Miss or Ms García

sepa, sepan, etc ▶ saber

separado/separada adjective
• = separate
• = separated

separar verb 1
• = to separate
• = to move away
separa la silla de la pared = move the chair
away from the wall
separarse
= to get separated

septiembre noun, masculine
= September

séptimo/séptima number
= seventh
See **primero** for examples

sequía noun, feminine
una sequía = a drought

ser verb 36
- = to be
  es [flaco | muy amable | soltero …] = he's [thin | very kind | single …]
  ¿cómo son? = what are they like?
  = what do they look like?
  soy ingeniero = I'm an engineer
  era verano = it was summer
  ¿cuánto es? = how is that (altogether)?
  es de madera = it's wooden
  eso es = that's right
- (passive use)
  fue despedido = he was fired
- a no ser que = unless
- como/donde/cuando sea = however/wherever/whenever
  lo que sea = whatever
- o sea = so
  = that is
  o sea que no fuiste = so you didn't go
  toda mi familia, o sea, mis padres mi hermana y yo = all my family, that is my parents, my sister, and I

será, **seré**, **sería**, **etc** ▶ ser

serie noun, feminine
  una serie = a series

serio/seria adjective
  = serious
  en serio = seriously
  lo digo en serio = I'm serious, I mean it

serpiente noun, feminine
  una serpiente = a snake
  una serpiente (de) cascabel = a rattlesnake

servicio noun, masculine
- un servicio = a service
- los servicios = the restroom, the toilet(s)
- el servicio militar = military service

servilleta noun, feminine
  una servilleta = a napkin

servir verb 48
- = to serve
  servir la comida = to serve the food
- = to be used for
  sirve para sujetar los libros = it can be used to hold the books
  ¿para qué sirve? = what's it for?
  esto no sirve = this is no good
  no sirves para nada = you're useless
servirse
  (if it's food) = to help oneself (to)

sesenta number
  = sixty
  See **cincuenta** for examples

sesión noun, feminine
  una sesión = a session
  (of a movie) = a showing
  (of a play) = a performance

setecientos/setecientas number
  = seven hundred
  See **quinientos** for examples

setenta number
  = seventy
  See **cincuenta** for examples

sexo noun, masculine
  el sexo = the sex

sexto/sexta
1 number
  = sixth
  See **primero** for examples
2 **sexto** noun, masculine
  un sexto = a sixth

si conjunction
- = if
  si tu quieres = if you want
  si lo hubiese sabido… = if only I had known…

  ! Note the use of the subjunctive after si

- = whether
  no sé si comprarlo o no = I don't know whether to buy it or not

sí[1] adverb
  = yes
  ¿lo conoces? — sí = do you know him? — yes, I do
  él no ha estado pero yo sí = he's never been there but I have

sí[2] personal pronoun
- = himself/herself/itself
  sí (mismo)/sí (misma) = himself/herself
  sólo piensa en sí (mismo) = he only thinks of himself
- (referring to you — polite form)
  = yourself/yourselves
  léalo para sí/léanlo para sí = read it to youself/read it to yourselves
- entre sí = between themselves
  = among themselves

sida, **SIDA** noun, masculine
  el sida = AIDS

sidra noun, feminine
  la sidra = cider

siempre adverb
  = always
  como siempre = as usual
  lo de siempre = the usual thing
  desde siempre = always
  siempre que… = whenever…

sienta, **siento**, **etc** ▶ sentarse, sentir

sierra noun, feminine
- una sierra = a saw
- la sierra = the (range of) mountains
  la sierra de Guadarrama = the Guadarrama mountain range

S

siesta *noun, feminine*
  una siesta = a siesta, a nap
  echarse✶ *or* **dormir la siesta** = to have a
  nap

siete *number*
• = seven
• (*in dates*) = seventh
   See **cinco** *for examples*

siga, sigan, etc ▶ seguir

siglo *noun, masculine*
  un siglo = a century

significado *noun, masculine*
  el significado = the meaning

significar *verb* ②
  = to mean

signo *noun, masculine*
  un signo = a sign
  un signo de admiración = an exclamation
  point, an exclamation mark
  un signo de interrogación = a question
  mark

sigo, sigue ▶ seguir

siguiente
1 *adjective*
  = following
  = next
2 *noun, masculine/feminine*
  el/la siguiente = the next one

siguió ▶ seguir

silbar *verb* ①
• = to whistle
• = to boo

silbato *noun, masculine*
  un silbato = a whistle

silbido *noun, masculine*
  un silbido = a whistle

silencio *noun, masculine*
  el silencio = the silence
  ¡silencio! = quiet!

silla *noun, feminine*
  una silla = a chair
  una silla de ruedas = a wheelchair
  una silla de montar = a saddle

sillón *noun, masculine*
  un sillón = an armchair

símbolo *noun, masculine*
  un símbolo = a symbol

simpático/simpática *adjective*
• = nice
• = friendly

simple *adjective*
  = simple

sin *preposition*
  = without
  aún está sin terminar = it's not finished yet

sincero/sincera *adjective*
  = sincere

singular *noun, masculine*
  el singular = the singular

sino *conjunction*
  = but

sinónimo
1 *adjective*
  = synonymous
2 *noun, masculine*
  un sinónimo = a synonym

sintieron, sintió ▶ sentir

sinvergüenza *noun, masculine/feminine*
  un/una sinvergüenza = a scoundrel

sirena *noun, feminine*
• una sirena = a siren
• (*in children's stories*) una sirena = a
   mermaid

sistema *noun, masculine*
  un sistema = a system

sitio *noun, masculine*
• un sitio = a place
   en algún sitio = somewhere
   en ningún sitio = nowhere
   en cualquier sitio = anywhere
   en otro sitio = somewhere else
• (*to sit*) un sitio = a seat
• (*space*) sitio = room
   no hay sitio = there's no room
   hacer sitio = to make room
• (*Mex*) un sitio = a taxi stand, a taxi rank

situación *noun, feminine*
  una situación = a situation
  = a position

situado/situada *adjective*
  = situated

sobra
1 de sobra *adjective/adverb*
• = plenty of
   con dinero de sobra = with plenty of
   money
• = spare
   tengo una entrada de sobra = I have a
   spare ticket
• = very well
   lo sabes de sobra = you know very well
• **estar de sobra:**
   aquí estamos de sobra = we are not
   wanted/needed here
2 sobras *noun, feminine plural*
  sobras = leftovers

sobrar *verb* 1
- = to be left over
  sobró vino de la fiesta = there was wine left over from the party
  me sobran cinco mil pesetas de ayer = I have five thousand pesetas left from yesterday
- = to be too much/too many
  sobra dinero = there's too much money
  sobran dos entradas = there are two tickets too many
  me sobran dos cartas = I have two cards too many
  nos sobra tiempo = we have plenty of time
- **tú aquí sobras** = you're not wanted/needed here
- **y aún nos sobran diez dólares** = and we still have ten dollars to spare

sobre
1 *noun, masculine*
- **un sobre** = an envelope
- **un sobre de sopa** = a packet of soup
2 *preposition*
- = on
  está sobre la mesa = it's on the table
- = over
  el avión pasó sobre la ciudad = the plane flew over the city
- = about
  un libro sobre la guerra = a book about the war
- = above
  sobre el nivel del mar = above sea level
  sobre todo = above all

sobresaliente *noun, masculine* (*Spa*)
  un sobresaliente = *an 8.5/a 9 out of 10*

sobrevivir *verb* 41
  = to survive

sociedad *noun, feminine*
  la sociedad = society
  una sociedad anónima = a limited company

socio/socia *noun, masculine/feminine*
  un socio/una socia = a member
  (*in a company*) = a partner

socorro *noun, masculine*
  socorro = help

sofá *noun, masculine*
  un sofá = a sofa

sois ▶ ser

sol *noun, masculine*
- **el sol** = the sun
  al salir/al ponerse el sol = at dawn/sunset
  hace sol = it's sunny
  tomar el sol = to sunbathe
- (*Peruvian currency*) **un sol** = a sol

solamente ▶ sólo

soldado *noun, masculine/feminine*
  un/una soldado = a soldier

soleado/soleada *adjective*
  = sunny

soler *verb* 22
- (*in the present*)
  suele llover = it usually rains
  suelen venir los lunes = they usually come on Mondays
- (*in the past*)
  solían salir juntos = they used to go out together

sólido/sólida *adjective*
- = solid
- = sound

solo/sola *adjective*
- = alone
  quedarse solo = to be left alone
  estar a solas = to be alone
- = lonely
- = by oneself
  lo hice sola = I did it by myself

sólo *adverb*
  = only

soltar *verb* 6
- = to let go
  me soltó la mano = she let go of my hand
- = to let out
  suelta un poco de cuerda = let out a bit of rope
  soltó un grito = he let out a cry
- **soltar a un prisionero** = to release a prisoner
- **soltar una carcajada** = to burst out laughing
soltarse
- = to let go
  no te sueltes de la mano = don't let go of my hand
- (*if it's a dog*) = to get loose
- (*if it's a knot*) = to come undone
- **soltarse el pelo** = to let one's hair down

soltero/soltera
1 *adjective*
  = single
2 *noun, masculine/feminine*
  un soltero/una soltera = a single man/woman

solución *noun, feminine*
  una solución = a solution

solucionar *verb* 1
  = to solve

sombra *noun, feminine*
- **una sombra** = a shadow
- **la sombra** = the shade
- **sombra de ojos** = eyeshadow

S

sombrero noun, masculine
un **sombrero** = a hat
un **sombrero** de copa = a top hat

sombrilla noun, feminine
una **sombrilla** = a parasol
= a sunshade

somos, **son** ▶ ser

sonar verb [6]
* = to sound
suena bonito = it sounds nice
¿qué suena? = what's that noise
me suena ese nombre = that name sounds
    familiar to me
* (if it's an alarm) = to go off
(if it's a telephone, bell) = to ring
sonarse
sonarse la nariz = to blow one's nose

sonido noun, masculine
un **sonido** = a sound

sonreír verb [50]
= to smile

sonría, **sonríe**, **sonrió**, **etc** ▶ sonreír

sonrisa noun, feminine
una **sonrisa** = a smile

sopa noun, feminine
una **sopa** = a soup

soplar verb [1]
* = to blow
* = to blow out

sorbo noun, masculine
un **sorbo** = a sip

sordo/sorda
1 adjective
= deaf
2 noun, masculine/feminine
un **sordo**/una **sorda** = a deaf man/woman

sordomudo/sordomuda
1 adjective
= deaf and dumb
2 noun, masculine/feminine
un **sordomudo**/una **sordomuda** = a deaf-
mute

sorprender verb [17]
* = to surprise
la sorprendí robando el dinero = I caught
    her stealing the money
* = to catch (unawares)
sorprenderse
= to be surprised

sorprendido/sorprendida adjective
= surprised

sorpresa noun, feminine
una **sorpresa** = a surprise

sospecha noun, feminine
una **sospecha** = a suspicion

sospechar verb [1]
= to suspect

sospechoso/sospechosa adjective
= suspicious

sostén noun, masculine
un **sostén** = a bra

sostener verb [37]
= to hold

soy ▶ ser

su adjective
* = his/her/its
* = their
* (referring to you — polite form)
= your

> ! Note that sometimes the only thing that
> will indicate whether **su** is translated by
> his, her, its, their or your is the context:
> ¿es éste su coche? = is this his/her car?
> = is this their car?
> = is this your car?

* (impersonal use)
cada uno tiene que traer su (propia) tienda
    = everyone has to bring their own tent

suave adjective
* = soft
* = smooth
* = gentle

subida noun, feminine
una **subida** = a rise

subir verb [41]
* = to go/come up
subir las escaleras = to go up the stairs
subir a un coche = to get into a car
* = to put up
el gobierno subió los precios = the
    government put up prices
* = to take/bring up
subí las cajas al piso de arriba = I took the
    boxes upstairs
sube el cuadro un poco más = put the
    picture a bit higher
* (if it's the volume) = to turn up
sube el radio = turn up the radio
* (if it's a curtain, blind) = to raise
* (if it's the temperature) = to rise
* (if it's the tide) = to come in
subirse
* = to climb
subirse a un árbol = to climb (up) a tree
* subirse a un avión = to get on a plane

subjuntivo noun, masculine
el **subjuntivo** = the subjunctive

submarino noun, masculine
un **submarino** = a submarine

subrayar verb [1]
= to underline

subte✕ *noun, masculine (R Pl)*
  el subte = the subway, the underground

  ❗ *Note that* **subte** *is short for* **subterráneo**

subterráneo/subterránea
1 *adjective*
  = underground
2 subterráneo *noun, masculine (R Pl)*
  el subterráneo = the subway, the
    underground

suburbio *noun, masculine*
  • **un suburbio** = a suburb
  • (*poor area*) = a slum

suceder *verb* 17
  • (*if it's an event*) = to happen
  • (*to the throne*) = to succeed

suceso *noun, masculine*
  un suceso = an event
  = an incident

suciedad *noun, feminine*
  la suciedad = dirt

sucio/sucia *adjective*
  = dirty

sucursal *noun, feminine*
  una sucursal (*of a bank*) = a branch
  (*of a company*) = an office

sudadera *noun, feminine*
  una sudadera = a sweatshirt

sudar *verb* 1
  = to sweat

sudeste *noun, masculine*
  el sudeste = the south-east

sudoeste *noun, masculine*
  el sudoeste = the south-west

sudor *noun, masculine*
  sudor = sweat, perspiration

Suecia *noun, feminine*
  Suecia = Sweden

sueco/sueca
1 *adjective*
  = Swedish
2 *noun, masculine|feminine*
  un sueco/una sueca = a Swede
3 sueco *noun, masculine*
  el sueco (*the language*) = Swedish

suegro/suegra *noun,*
masculine|feminine
  un suegro/una suegra = a father-in-law/
    a mother-in-law
  mis suegros = my parents-in-law

suela, suelas, etc ▶ soler

sueldo *noun, masculine*
  un sueldo = a salary

suelo *noun, masculine*
  el suelo = the floor

suelo ▶ soler

suelta, suelte, suelto, etc ▶ soltar

suelto/suelta
1 *adjective*
  = loose
2 suelto *noun, masculine (Mex, Spa)*
  suelto = small change

suena, suene, sueno, etc ▶ sonar

sueña, sueñe, sueño, etc ▶ soñar

sueño *noun, masculine*
  un sueño = a dream
  tener sueño = to be sleepy
  darle sueño a alguien = to make someone
    feel sleepy

suerte *noun, feminine*
  = luck
  dar buena/mala suerte = to bring good/bad
    luck
  una número de (la) suerte = a lucky
    number
  por suerte = fortunately
  echar algo a suertes (*Spa*) = to toss for
    something

suéter *noun, masculine*
  un suéter = a sweater

suficiente
1 *adjective*
  = enough
2 *noun, masculine (Spa)*
  un suficiente = a pass

sufrir *verb* 41
  • = to suffer
  • **sufrir un accidente** = to have an accident
  • **sufrir un cambio** = to undergo a change

sugerencia *noun, feminine*
  una sugerencia = a suggestion

sugerir *verb* 46
  = to suggest

sugiera, sugiero, sugirieron, etc
▶ sugerir

suicidarse *verb* 1
  = to commit suicide

suicidio *noun, masculine*
  un suicidio = a suicide

Suiza *noun, feminine*
  Suiza = Switzerland

suizo/suiza
1 *adjective*
  = Swiss
2 *noun, masculine|feminine*
  un suizo/una suiza = a Swiss

S

sujeto/sujeta *adjective*
= secured
= fastened
tener sujeto a alguien = to have hold of someone

suma *noun, feminine*
una suma = a sum

sumar *verb* 1
= to add (up)

supe, **supiste**, **etc** ▶ saber

superar *verb* 1
• to exceed
• (*if it's a difficulty*) = to overcome
(*if it's a trauma*) = to get over
• (*if it's a record*) = to beat

superior *adjective*
• = superior
• = top
• = upper

supermercado *noun, masculine*
un supermercado = a supermarket

superstición *noun, feminine*
una superstición = a superstition

supersticioso/supersticiosa
adjective
= superstitious

supervisar *verb* 1
= supervise

superviviente *noun, masculine/feminine*
un/una superviviente = a survivor

supondrá, **supondré**, **supondría**,
etc ▶ suponer

suponer *verb* 32
= to suppose
supongamos que... = let's suppose that...

suponga, **supongo**, **etc** ▶ suponer

suprimir *verb* 41
• = to supress
• = to delete

supuesto: por supuesto
= of course

supuse, **supuso** ▶ suponer

sur *noun, masculine*
el sur = the south
See **este** *for more examples*

sureste *noun, masculine*
▶ sudeste

suroeste *noun, masculine*
▶ sudoeste

suspender *verb* 17
• = to suspend
• (*Spa*) = to fail

suspense *noun, masculine* (*Spa*)
suspense = suspense
See also **película**

suspenso *noun, masculine*
• (*Lat Am*) **suspenso** = suspense
See also **película**
• (*Spa*) **un suspenso** = a fail

suspirar *verb* 1
= to sigh

suspiro *noun, masculine*
un suspiro = a sigh

sustancia *noun, feminine*
una sustancia = a substance

sustantivo *noun, masculine*
un sustantivo = a noun

sustituir *verb* 51
• = to replace
• = to stand in for
• = to substitute

sustituto/sustituta *noun,
masculine/feminine*
un sustituto/una sustituta = a replacement
(*temporary*) = a substitute
(*for a doctor*) = a covering doctor, a locum

susto *noun, masculine*
un susto = a fright

susurrar *verb* 1
= to whisper

sutil *adjective*
= subtle

suyo/suya *adjective, pronoun*
• suyo/suya/suyos/suyas = his/hers/its
el coche no es suyo = the car isn't his/hers
• suyo/suya/suyos/suyas = theirs
fueron con un amigo suyo = they went
with a friend of theirs
• (*referring to you — polite form*)
suyo/suya/suyos/suyas = yours
perdone, ¿es esto suyo? = excuse me, is
this yours?

> **!** *Note that sometimes the only thing that
> will indicate whether* suyo/suya/suyos/
> suyas *is translated by* his, hers, its, theirs
> *or* yours *is the context:*
> **usé las suyas** = I used his/hers
> = I used theirs
> = I used yours

tabaco *noun, masculine*
tabaco = tobacco
(*Spa*) = cigarettes

tacaño/tacaña
1 *adjective*
= mean
2 *noun, masculine/feminine*
un tacaño/una tacaña = a skinflint

tachar *verb* 1
= to cross out

taco *noun, masculine*
• un taco = a taco
• (*SC*) un taco = a heel
• (*Spa*) un taco✖ = a swearword

tacón *noun, masculine*
un tacón = a heel
= a high heel
zapatos de tacón = high-heeled shoes

tal
1 *adjective*
• = such (a)
nunca dije tal cosa = I never said such a
thing
en tales circunstancias = in such
circumstances
• en tal caso = in that case
• un tal García = someone called García
2 *adverb*
• ¿qué tal estás✖? = how are you?
¿que tal es la película✖? = what's the movie
like?
• tal vez = maybe
• tales como... = such as...

talento *noun, masculine*
talento = talent

talla *noun, feminine*
una talla = a size

taller *noun, masculine*
un taller = a workshop
(*for cars*) = a garage, a repair shop

talón *noun, masculine*
el talón = the heel

tamaño *noun, masculine*
tamaño = size

también *adverb*
= also, too, as well

tambor *noun, masculine*
un tambor = a drum

tampoco *adverb*
él tampoco lo sabe = he doesn't know it
either
él no va ni yo tampoco = he isn't going and
neither am I

tan *adverb*
• = so
es tan inteligente = he's so clever
• = such
era un trabajo tan difícil = it was such a
difficult job
¡qué paisaje tan bonito! = what a lovely
landscape!
• ¿qué tan ricos son? (*Lat Am*) = how rich
are they?
• tan [alto | rico | listo ...] como... = as [tall | rich |
clever ...] as...

tanque *noun, masculine*
un tanque = a tank

tanto/tanta
1 *adjective*
tanto/tanta = so much
tantos/tantas = so many
tanto vino = so much wine
tantos coches = so many cars
tanta cantidad = so much
tanto tiempo = so long
no hace tanto tiempo = it hasn't been so
long
tanto/tanta...como... = as much... as...
tantos/tantas...como... = as many... as...
tanto/tanta... que... = so much... that...
tantos/tantas... que... = so many... that...
2 *pronoun*
• tanto/tanta = so much
tantos/tantas = so many
no necesitamos tanto/tantos = we don't
need so much/so many
• tanto = so long
hace tanto que no los veo = I haven't seen
them for so long
• por lo tanto = therefore
• entre tanto, mientras tanto = in the
meantime
3 tanto *adverb*
• = so
me alegro tanto = I'm so glad
• = so much
tanto como = as much as
• = so long
siempre tardas tanto = you always take so
long
• = so often
no salen tanto = they don't go out so often
• ¿qué tanto te gusta? (*Lat Am*) = how much
do you like it?
4 **tanto** *noun masculine*
• un tanto (*in sports*) = a point
(*in football*) = a goal
• un tanto por ciento = a percentage

T

R Pl River Plate area   SC Southern Cone   Spa Spain

tapa
1 *noun, feminine*
 una tapa (*of a jar, box*) = a lid
  (*of a book*) = a cover
2 tapas *noun, feminine plural* (*Spa*)
 tapas (*food*) = tapas

tapar *verb* ⟨1⟩
• = to cover
• = to put the lid/top on
• = to fill
 tapar un agujero = to fill a hole
• = to block
 estás tapando la luz = you are blocking the
  light
 quítate, me estás tapando = move, you are
  in my way

tapete *noun, masculine* (*Mex*)
 un tapete = a carpet

tapón *noun, masculine*
 un tapón (*of a bottle*) = a cork
  (*for the sink, bath, etc*) = a plug
  (*Spa: of bottle*) = a top

taquilla *noun, feminine*
 la taquilla = the ticket office
  = the box office

tardar *verb* ⟨1⟩
• = to take
 se tarda tres horas en llegar = it takes
  three hours to get there
 ¡cuánto tardan! = they are taking so long!
 tardaron mucho tiempo = they took a long
  time
• = to be long
 no tardo nada = I won't be long

tarde
1 *noun, feminine*
 = afternoon
 = evening
 en la *or* (*Spa*) **por la** *or* (*RPl*) **a la tarde** = in
  the afternoon
 = in the evening
 ¡buenas tardes! = good afternoon/evening!
2 *adverb*
 = late
 llegar tarde = to be late
 hacerse tarde = to get late
 se me hace tarde, mejor me voy = it's
  getting late, I'd better go
 tarde o temprano = sooner or later

tarea *noun, feminine*
• **una tarea** = a task
 las tareas de la casa = the housework
• (*in school*) **la tarea** *or* (*Lat Am*) **las tareas** =
  homework

tarjeta *noun, feminine*
 una tarjeta = a card

tarta *noun, feminine* (*Spa*)
 una tarta = a cake

Tauro *noun, masculine*
 Tauro = Taurus

tauro *noun, masculine/feminine*
 un/una tauro = a Taurus, a Taurean

taxista *noun, masculine/feminine*
 un/una taxista = a taxi driver

taza *noun, feminine*
 una taza = a cup

te *pronoun*
• = you
 = to you
 te lo dije = I told you
 te lo di ayer = I gave it to you yesterday
 ¿te lavaste la cara? = did you wash your
  face?
 ponte el abrigo = put your coat on
• (*when someone else does the action*)
 tienes que cortarte el pelo = you have to
  have your hair cut
• = yourself
 cuídate = look after yourself
 muévete = move

té *noun, masculine*
 té = tea

teatro *noun, masculine*
 el teatro = the theater, the theatre

tebeo *noun, masculine* (*Spa*)
 un tebeo = a comic

techo *noun, masculine*
 el techo = the ceiling
  (*Lat Am: of a house*) = the roof

tecla *noun, feminine*
 una tecla = a key

técnico/técnica
1 *adjective*
 = technical
2 *noun, masculine/feminine*
 un técnico/una técnica = a technician

tecnología *noun, feminine*
 la tecnología = technology

tejado *noun, masculine*
 el tejado = the roof

tejer *verb* ⟨17⟩
• = to weave
• = to knit

tela *noun, feminine*
 tela = material, fabric, cloth
 una tela = a piece of material

telaraña *noun, feminine*
 una telaraña = a spider's web
  = a cobweb

tele✸ *noun, feminine*
 la tele = the TV, the telly

 ! *Note that* **tele** *is short for* **televisión**
 See **televisión** *for more examples*

telediario noun, masculine (Spa)
  el telediario = the news

telefonear verb 1
  = to phone, to telephone, to call

teléfono noun, masculine
• un teléfono = a telephone
• un teléfono = a phone number

telegrama noun, masculine
  un telegrama = a telegram

telenovela noun, feminine
  una telenovela = a soap opera

telescopio noun, masculine
  un telescopio = a telescope

televisión noun, feminine
• la televisión = the television
  ver (la) televisión = to watch television
• una televisión = a television (set)

televisor noun, masculine
  un televisor = a television (set)

tema noun, masculine
  un tema = a subject, a topic
  (in music) = a theme

temblar verb 7
• = to tremble
• = to shake
• (with cold) = to shiver
• (if it's the ground, a building) = to shake
• ¡está temblando! (Lat Am) = it's an
   earthquake!

temer verb 17
• = to fear
• = to be afraid of
  no temas = don't be afraid
temerse
  = to be afraid
  me temo que no es posible = I'm afraid
   that's not possible

temperatura noun, feminine
  la temperatura = the temperature

temprano adverb
  = early

tender verb 21
• = to hang out
  tender la ropa = to hang the washing out
• tender la cama (Lat Am) = to make the bed
• tiende a enojarse = he tends to get
   annoyed
tenderse
  = to lie down

tenedor noun, masculine
  un tenedor = a fork

tendrá, **tendré**, **tendría**, **etc** ▶ tener

tener verb 37
• = to have
  tuvimos una pelea = we had a fight
  tengo la gripe = I have the flu
  tiene el pelo corto = she has long hair

• = to be
  tengo cuarenta años = I'm forty years old
  tiene dos metros de alto = it is two meters
   tall
  tener paciencia/cuidado = to be
   patient/careful
  tener [frío | hambre | calor ...] = to be [cold |
   hungry | hot ...]
  tener celos de alguien = to be jealous of
   someone
• = to feel
  tener sueño = to feel sleepy
• tener que hacer algo = to have to do
   something
  tienes que estudiar más = you must study
   more
  tendría que preguntárselo a mi madre = I
   would have to ask my mother
• tener + past participle:
  lo tengo terminado = I've already finished
   it
  nos tiene preocupados = we are worried
   about him

tenga, **tengo**, **etc** ▶ tener

tenis noun, masculine
  el tenis = tennis
  tenis de mesa = table tennis

tenista noun, masculine/feminine
  un/una tenista = a tennis player

tensión noun, feminine
• tensión = tension
• tensión = voltage
• (Spa) la tensión = blood pressure

teñir verb 65
  = to dye
teñirse
  = to dye one's hair

tercer adjective
▶ tercero/tercera

tercero/tercera number

> ! Note that tercero becomes tercer
> before masculine singular nouns
> = third
>   See primero for examples

terminar verb 1
• = to finish
  terminar de hacer algo = to finish doing
   something
• = to end up
  vas a terminar en la cárcel = you're going
   to end up in jail
  terminó aceptándolo = he accepted it in
   the end
  terminó disculpándose = he ended up
   apologizing
• termina en punta = it is pointed

T

terminarse
- = to be over
  se nos terminó el pan = we ran out of
  bread

termómetro noun, masculine
un termómetro = a thermometer
ponerle el termómetro a alguien = to take
someone's temperature

ternero/ternera
1 noun, masculine/feminine
un ternero/una ternera = a calf
2 ternera noun, feminine
ternera = veal

terraza noun, feminine
- una terraza = a balcony
- una terraza = a roof terrace
- una terraza = an area with tables outside a bar
  or café where people can sit

terremoto noun, masculine
un terremoto = an earthquake

terrible adjective
= terrible

terreno noun, masculine
terreno = land
un terreno = a piece of land

territorio noun, masculine
territorio = territory

terror noun, masculine
terror = terror

terrorismo noun, masculine
el terrorismo = terrorism

tesoro noun, masculine
un tesoro = a treasure

tetera noun, feminine
una tetera = a teapot
(Lat Am) = a kettle

texto noun, masculine
un texto = a text

ti personal pronoun
- = you
  es para ti = it's for you
  no me apetece, ¿y a ti? = I don't feel like it,
  do you?
- ti (mismo)/ti (misma) = yourself
  sólo piensas en ti (mismo) = you only
  think of yourself

tiburón noun, masculine
un tiburón = a shark

tiembla, **tiemblo**, **etc▶** temblar

tiempo
1 noun, masculine
- tiempo = time

¡cuánto tiempo sin verte! = I haven't seen
  you for ages!
a tiempo = on time
al mismo tiempo = at the same time
al poco tiempo = shortly afterwards
por un tiempo = for a while
hace mucho tiempo que no los veo = I
  haven't seen them for a long time
¿cuánto tiempo hace que lo conoces? =
  how long have you known him for?
- (in grammar) el tiempo = the tense
- tiempo = weather
  hace buen tiempo = the weather is nice
- el primer tiempo (in sports) = the first half
2 tiempos noun, masculine plural
en mis tiempos = in my time
en aquellos tiempos = in those days

tienda, **tiendo**, **etc▶** tender

tienda noun, feminine
- una tienda = a store, a shop
- una tienda de campaña = a tent

tierra noun, feminine
tierra = land
= earth, soil
= ground
tomar tierra = to land
la Tierra = the Earth

tigre/tigresa noun, masculine/feminine
un tigre/una tigresa = a tiger/a tigress

tijera noun, feminine
una(s) tijera(s) = a pair of scissors
dame las tijeras = pass me the scissors

timbre noun, masculine
- un timbre = a bell
- (Mex) un timbre = a stamp

tímido/tímida adjective
= shy

tinta noun, feminine
tinta = ink

tinto
1 adjective
= red
2 noun, masculine
el tinto = red wine

tintorería noun, feminine
una tintorería = a dry cleaner's

tiña, **tiñeron**, **tiño**, **tiñó**, **etc▶** teñir

tío/tía noun, masculine/feminine
un tío/una tía = an uncle/an aunt
mis tíos = my aunt and uncle

tiovivo noun, masculine (Spa)
un tiovivo = a merry-go-round

típico/típica adjective
- = typical
- = traditional

---

tipo noun, masculine
- **tipo** = kind, sort
  = type
- **el tipo** = the body, the figure

tirar verb 1
- = to throw
- = to throw away
- = to knock over
  tirar una puerta abajo = to knock a door down
- **tirar de la cuerda** = to pull the rope
- **verde tirando a azul** = bluish green

tirarse
  = to throw oneself
  tirarse al agua = to jump into the water
  tirarse de cabeza = to dive in head first

tirita noun, feminine (Spa)
  una tirita = a Band-Aid®, a sticking plaster

tiro noun, masculine
  un tiro = a shot
  le dispararon or **le pegaron un tiro** = they shot him

títere
1 noun, masculine
  un títere = a puppet
2 títeres noun, masculine plural
  unos títeres = a puppet show

título noun, masculine
- **un título** = a title
- (of chapter) **un título** = a heading
- (in education) **un título** = a degree

tiza noun, feminine
  tiza = chalk
  una tiza = a (piece of) chalk

tlapalería noun, feminine (Mex)
  una tlapalería = a hardware store

toalla noun, feminine
  una toalla = a towel

tobillo noun, masculine
  un tobillo = an ankle

tobogán noun, masculine
  un tobogán = a slide

tocadiscos noun, masculine
  un tocadiscos = a record player

tocar verb 2
- = to touch
  me tocó la mano = he touched my hand
- (at the door) = to knock
- **tocar un disco/un instrumento** = to play a record/an instrument
- **tocar el timbre** = to ring the bell
- = to blow
  tocar una bocina = to blow a horn
- **les tocó la lotería** = they won the lottery
- **te toca fregar los platos/jugar** = it's your turn to do the dishes/to play

tocarse
  = to touch
  tocarse la nariz = to touch one's nose

tocino noun, masculine
- **tocino** = pork fat
- (Lat Am) **tocino** = bacon

todavía adverb
- = yet
- = still
- = even
  todavía mejor = even better

todo/toda
1 adjective
- = all
  todo mi dinero = all my money
- = whole
  toda la semana = the whole week
2 pronoun
- = everything
  yo pago por todo = I'll pay for everything
- = all
  ¿han llegado ya todos? = are they all there?
- **ante todo** = above all
- **un poco de todo** = a bit of everything
- **sobre todo** = especially
  = above all
- **todo lo que quieras** = as much as you like
  = for as long as you like
3 todo adverb
  = all
  = completely

tomar verb 1
- = to take
  me tomó del brazo = she took me by the arm
  tomar el tren = to take the train
- (when handing something to someone)
  toma, tus llaves = here are your keys
- (Spa) = to have
  ¿qué quieres tomar? = what are you going to have?
- (Lat Am) = to drink

tomarse
- = to take
  tomarse unas vacaciones = to take a vacation
- **tomarse una foto** (Lat Am) = to have one's picture taken

tomate noun, masculine
  un tomate = a tomato

tonelada noun, feminine
  una tonelada = a ton

tono noun, masculine
- **tono** = tone
- **un tono** = a shade

tontería noun, feminine
  eso es una tontería = that's silly

T

tonto/tonta
1 *adjective*
= silly
2 *noun, masculine|feminine*
un tonto/una tonta = a fool
hacer el tonto (*Spa*) = to play the fool

torcer *verb* 23
• = to twist
me torció el brazo = he twisted my arm
• = to turn
tuerce a la derecha = turn to the right
torcerse
= to twist
= to sprain

torcido/torcida *adjective*
• = crooked
• = twisted
• = bent
• = sprained
tengo el tobillo torcido = I've twisted my ankle

torero/torera *noun, masculine|feminine*
un torero/una torera = a bullfighter

tormenta *noun, feminine*
una tormenta = a storm

tornillo *noun, masculine*
un tornillo = a screw

toro
1 *noun, masculine*
un toro = a bull
2 toros *noun, masculine plural*
los toros = bullfighting

toronja *noun, feminine* (*Lat Am*)
una toronja = a grapefruit

torpe *adjective*
= clumsy

torre *noun, feminine*
• **una torre** = a tower
= an apartment block, a tower block
• (*in chess*) **una torre** = a rook, a castle

torta *noun, feminine*
• **una torta** (*Lat Am*) = a pie
(*Mex*) = a sandwich
(*SC*) = a cake

tortilla *noun, feminine*
una tortilla = a tortilla
= an omelet, an omelette
una tortilla de papas (*Lat Am*) or (*Spa*) **de patatas** = a Spanish omelet, a Spanish omelette

tortuga *noun, feminine*
una tortuga = a tortoise
= a turtle

torturar *verb* 1
= to torture

tos *noun, feminine*
tos = cough
me dio (la) tos = I started coughing

toser *verb* 17
= to cough

tostada *noun, feminine*
• **una tostada** = a piece of toast
tostadas = toast
• (*Mex*) **una tostada** = a fried corn tortilla

tostador *noun, masculine,* **tostadora** *noun, feminine*
un tostador, una tostadora = a toaster

tostar *verb* 6
• = to toast
• = to roast

total
1 *adjective*
= total
2 *noun, masculine*
el total = the total
en total = altogether

trabajador/trabajadora
1 *adjective*
= hard-working
2 *noun, masculine|feminine*
un trabajador/una trabajadora = a worker

trabajar *verb* 1
= to work

trabajo *noun, masculine*
• **el trabajo** = work
estar sin trabajo = to be out of work
el trabajo de la casa = the housework
• **un trabajo** = a job
• (*in school*) **un trabajo** = a project
= an essay

tractor *noun, masculine*
un tractor = a tractor

tradición *noun, feminine*
la tradición = tradition

tradicional *adjective*
= traditional

traducción *noun, feminine*
una traducción = a translation

traducir *verb* 43
= to translate

traductor/traductora *noun, masculine|feminine*
un traductor/una traductora = a translator

traduje, traduzca, traduzco, etc
▶ traducir

traer *verb* 33
= to bring
me trajo a casa = he brought me home

tráfico noun, masculine
el tráfico = the traffic

tragar verb ③
= to swallow
tragarse
= to swallow

tragedia noun, feminine
una tragedia = a tragedy

trágico/trágica adjective
= tragic

traiga, traigo, traje, etc ▶ traer

traje noun, masculine
un traje = a suit
(in the theater) = a costume
un traje de baño = a pair of swimming
   trunks
= a swimsuit

trampa noun, feminine
una trampa = a trap
hacer trampa(s) = to cheat

trampolín noun, masculine
un trampolín = a springboard
= a diving board

tranquilo/tranquila adjective
= quiet
= calm

transformar verb ①
= to transform
transformarse
= to be transformed

transparente adjective
= transparent

transporte noun, masculine
el transporte = transportation, transport

tranvía noun, masculine
un tranvía = a streetcar, a tram

trapo noun, masculine
un trapo = a cloth
un trapo del polvo = a dust cloth, a duster

tras preposition
• = after
• = behind

trasero/trasera adjective
= back
= rear

trasnochar verb ①
= to stay up late
= to stay up all night

tratar verb ①
• = to treat
   tratar algo con cuidado = to be careful
      with something
• to try
   tratar de hacer algo = to try to do
      something

tratarse
tratarse de algo = to be about something

través: a través de preposition
• = through
• = across

travieso/traviesa adjective
= naughty

trece number
• = thirteen
• (in dates) = thirteenth
   See **quince** for examples

treinta number
• = thirty
• (in dates) = thirtieth
   See **cinco** and **cincuenta** for examples

tren noun, masculine
un tren = a train

trenza noun, feminine
una trenza = a braid, a plait

trepar verb ①
= to climb (up)

tres number
• = three
• (in dates)
   = third
   See **cinco** for examples

trescientos/trescientas number
= three hundred
   See **quinientos** for examples

triángulo noun, masculine
un triángulo = a triangle

trigo noun, masculine
el trigo = wheat

trillizos/trillizas noun,
masculine/feminine plural
trillizos/trillizas = triplets

trimestre noun, masculine
un trimestre = a quarter
(in education) = a term

triple
1 adjective
= triple
2 noun, masculine
es el triple de caro = it's three times more
   expensive

tripulación noun, feminine
la tripulación = the crew

triste adjective
= sad
= gloomy

tristeza noun, feminine
tristeza = sadness

T

triunfo noun, masculine
un triunfo = a triumph

trofeo noun, masculine
un trofeo = a trophy

trombón noun, masculine
un trombón = a trombone

trompeta noun, feminine
una trompeta = a trumpet

tronco noun, masculine
un tronco = a trunk
= a log

trono noun, masculine
el trono = the throne

tropezar verb [5]
= to trip
tropezar con algo = to trip over something
tropezarse
= to trip
tropezarse con algo = to trip over
something

trópico noun, masculine
el trópico = the tropics

tropiece, tropiezo, etc ▶ tropezar

trozo noun, masculine
un trozo = a piece

trucha noun, feminine
una trucha = a trout

truco noun, masculine
un truco = a trick

trueno noun, masculine
un trueno = a clap of thunder
truenos = thunder

tu adjective
= your

tú pronoun
= you
tú (mismo)/tú (misma) = yourself

tubo noun, masculine
un tubo = a tube

tuerza, tuerzo ▶ torcer

tuesta, tueste, tuesto, etc ▶ tostar

tumba noun, feminine
una tumba = a grave
= a tomb

tumbar verb [1]
= to knock down
tumbarse
= to lie down

turismo noun, masculine
el turismo = tourism
hacer turismo = to travel
= to go sightseeing
= to tour

turista noun, masculine|feminine
un/una turista = a tourist

turno noun, masculine
un turno = a turn
(at work) = a shift

turrón noun, masculine
turrón = type of nougat eaten at Christmas

tutear verb [1]
= to address someone using the familiar **tú** form
tutearse
= to address each other using the familiar **tú**
form

tutor/tutora noun, masculine|feminine
un tutor/una tutora = a course tutor, a class
teacher
(at university) = a tutor

tuvo, tuvieron, tuviste, etc ▶ tener

tuyo/tuya
1 adjective
tuyo/tuya/tuyos/tuyas = yours
eso es un problema tuyo = that's your
problem
un amigo tuyo = a friend of yours
2 pronoun
el tuyo/la tuya/los tuyos/las tuyas = yours

Uu

u conjunction

> **!** Note that **u** is used instead of **o** before
> **o-** or **ho-**

= or
diez u once = ten or eleven

último/última
1 adjective
• = last
• = latest
• (in a pile) = top
2 noun, masculine|feminine
el último/la última = the last one
(in a pile) = the top one
3 último adverb (SC)
= last

últimamente adverb
= recently, lately

un/una article
• un/una = a, an
unos/unas = some, a few
una mesa = a table
compró unos vasos = he bought some
glasses
unos días = a few days

- **unos/unas** (*to express approximate number*) = about
  unas tres horas = about three hours
  See also **uno/una**

único/única
1 *adjective*
- = only
  es hijo único = he's an only child
- = unique
2 *noun, masculine|feminine*
  el único/la única = the only one

unidad *noun, feminine*
  una unidad = a unit

unido/unida *adjective*
- = close
- = united

uniforme
1 *adjective*
  = uniform
2 *noun, masculine*
  un uniforme = a uniform

Unión Europea *noun, feminine*
  la Unión Europea = the European Union

unir *verb* 41
  = to join
unirse
  = to join together

universidad *noun, feminine*
  una universidad = a university

uno/una
1 *adjective, pronoun*

> **!** *Note that* **uno** *becomes* **un** *before masculine singular nouns*

- = one
  tienen un solo hijo = they only have one son
  uno en uno = one by one
- **unos/unas**
  = some
  unos lo sabían y otros no = some knew and some didn't
  = about
  unos dos kilos = about two kilos
2 uno *number*
- **el uno** = (number) one
- (*Spa: in dates*) = first
  See **cinco** *for more examples*

uña *noun, feminine*
  una uña = a nail

urgencia
1 *noun, feminine*
  una urgencia = an emergency
2 urgencias *noun, feminine plural*
  urgencias = accident and emergency

urgente *adjective*
  = urgent

usado/usada *adjective*
- = worn
- = secondhand

usar *verb* 1
- = to use
- = to wear

uso *noun, masculine*
  uso = use

usted *pronoun*

> **!** *Note that this is the polite singular form of address, but in Colombia and Chile it is also used instead of the familiar form of address* **tú**

  = you
  usted (mismo)/usted (misma) = yourself

ustedes *plural pronoun*

> **!** *Note that this is both the polite and the familiar plural form of address, except in Spain where the familiar form of address is* **vosotros**

  = you
  ustedes (mismos)/ustedes (mismas) = yourselves

utensilio *noun, masculine*
  un utensilio = a utensil
  = a tool

útil *adjective*
  = useful

uva *noun, feminine*
  una uva = a grape

vaca *noun, feminine*
  una vaca = a cow

vacaciones *noun, feminine plural*
  unas vacaciones = a vacation, a holiday
  las vacaciones de verano = the summer vacation, the summer holidays

vacío/vacía *adjective*
  = empty

vagón *noun, masculine*
  un vagón = a coach, a car, a carriage

vainilla *noun, feminine*
  vainilla = vanilla

valdrá, valdré, valdría, etc ▶ valer

valer *verb* 38
- = to be worth
- = to cost

valga, valgo, etc ▶ valer

válido/válida *adjective*
= valid

valiente *adjective*
= brave

valle *noun, masculine*
un valle = a valley

valor *noun, masculine*
* valor = courage
* valor = value

vanidoso/vanidosa *adjective*
= vain

vano/vana *adjective*
= vain
en vano = in vain

vapor *noun, masculine*
vapor = steam

vaquero
1 *noun, masculine*
un vaquero = a cowboy
2 vaqueros *noun, masculine plural*
unos vaqueros = a pair of jeans

variedad *noun, feminine*
variedad = variety

varón
1 *noun, masculine*
un varón = a man, a male
tuvieron un varón = they had a boy
2 *adjective*
= male

vasco/vasca
1 *adjective*
= Basque
2 *noun, masculine|feminine*
un vasco/una vasca = a Basque
3 vasco *noun, masculine*
el vasco (*the language*) = Basque

vaso *noun, masculine*
un vaso = a glass

vecino/vecina
1 *adjective*
= neighboring, neighbouring
2 *noun, masculine|feminine*
un vecino/una vecina = a neighbor, a
neighbour

vegetariano/vegetariana
1 *adjective*
= vegetarian
2 *noun, masculine|feminine*
un vegetariano/una vegetariana = a
vegetarian

vehículo *noun, masculine*
un vehículo = a vehicle

veía, veían, etc ▶ ver

veinte *number*
* = twenty

* (*in dates*) = the twentieth
See **cinco** *and* **cincuenta** *for examples*

vela *noun, feminine*
* una vela = a candle
* (*on a ship*) una vela = a sail

velocidad *noun, feminine*
velocidad = speed

vena *noun, feminine*
una vena = a vein

vencer *verb* 18
* = to beat
* = to overcome

venda *noun, feminine*
una venda = a bandage

vendedor/vendedora *noun, feminine*
un vendedor/una vendedora = a
stallholder
= a salesclerk, a shop assistant
= a salesman/saleswoman

vender *verb* 17
= to sell
'se vende' = 'for sale'

vendrá, vendré, vendría, etc
▶ venir

veneno *noun, masculine*
un veneno = a poison

venenoso/venenosa *adjective*
= poisonous

venga, vengo, etc ▶ venir

venir *verb* 58
* = to come
venir por *or* (*Spa*) a por alguien = to come
to pick someone up
venir por *or* (*Spa*) a por algo = to come to
pick up something
* = to come back
no vengas tarde = don't come back late
* [la semana | el mes | el año …] que viene =
next [week | month | year …]

venta *noun, feminine*
una venta = a sale
estar en venta = to be for sale

ventaja *noun, feminine*
una ventaja = an advantage

ventana *noun, feminine*
una ventana = a window

ventanilla *noun, feminine*
* (*of a vehicle*) una ventanilla = a window
* (*at a theater, cinema, etc*) la ventanilla =
the box office

ventilador *noun, masculine*
un ventilador = a fan

ver *verb* 39
- = to see
  no lo veo = I can't see it
- = to watch
  ver (la) televisión = to watch television
- **a ver**:
  a ver, ¿cuál es el problema? = okay, what's the problem?
  ¿a ver? = let's see

verse
= to meet (up)
= to see each other

verano *noun, masculine*
el verano = the summer

verbo *noun, masculine*
un verbo = a verb

verdad *noun, feminine*
- **la verdad** = the truth
  ser verdad = to be true
- **éste es mejor ¿verdad?** = this one is better, isn't it?
  tú lo sabes ¿verdad? = you know it, don't you?
- **de verdad** = really
  = real
  ¿de verdad que la viste? = did you really see her?
  de verdad que lo siento = I am really sorry
  una pistola de verdad = a real gun

verdura *noun, feminine*
una verdura = a vegetable

verde
1 *adjective*
= green
2 *noun, masculine*
el verde = green

vereda *noun, feminine* (SC)
la vereda = the sidewalk, the pavement

vergüenza *noun, feminine*
- **vergüenza** = embarrassment
  me da vergüenza pedírselo = I'm embarrassed to ask her
- **vergüenza** = shame
  no tienes vergüenza = you have no shame

verso *noun, masculine*
un verso = a verse

vestíbulo *noun, masculine*
un vestíbulo = a hall
= a lobby
= a foyer

vestido/vestida
1 *adjective*
= dressed
siempre va bien vestido = he is always well dressed
iba vestida de verde = she was wearing green
2 vestido *noun, masculine*
un vestido = a dress

vestir *verb* 48
= to dress

vestirse
= to dress, to get dressed

veterinario/veterinaria *noun, masculine/feminine*
un veterinario/una veterinaria = a veterinarian, a veterinary surgeon

vez *noun, feminine*
una vez más = one more time
dos veces = twice
tres veces al mes = three times a month
lo vi una vez = I saw it once
a la vez = at the same time
a veces = sometimes
de vez en cuando = from time to time, now and again
érase una vez = once upon a time

vía *noun, feminine*
la vía = the track
la vía férrea = the railroad track, the railway track

viaje *noun, masculine*
un viaje = a journey, a trip
están de viaje = they are away

viajero/viajera *noun, masculine/feminine*
un viajero/una viajera = a traveler, a traveller
= a passenger

víctima *noun, feminine*
una víctima = a victim

victoria *noun, feminine*
una victoria = a victory
(*in sports*) = a win

vida *noun, feminine*
la vida = life

video *or* (*Spa*) **vídeo**, *noun, masculine*
un video, un vídeo = a video
= a video cassette recorder
= a videotape, a videocassette

videocámara *noun, feminine*
una videocámara = a video camera

videoclub *noun, masculine*
un videoclub = a video library

videojuego *noun, masculine*
un videojuego = a video game

vidrio *noun, masculine*
- **vidrio** = glass
- (*Lat Am*) **un vidrio** = a window pane
  limpiar los vidrios = to clean the windows

viejo/vieja
1 *adjective*
= old
2 *noun, masculine/feminine*
un viejo/una vieja = an old man/an old woman

viento noun, masculine
  el viento = the wind

viernes noun, masculine (**!** does not
change in the plural)
  el viernes = Friday
  Viernes Santo = Good Friday
    See **miércoles** for more examples

villancico noun, masculine
  un villancico = a carol

vinagre noun, masculine
  el vinagre = vinegar

vine, viniste, vino, etc ► venir

vino noun, masculine
  el vino = wine

violencia noun, feminine
  la violencia = violence

violento/violenta adjective
  = violent

violín noun, masculine
  un violín = a violin

Virgo noun, masculine
  Virgo = Virgo

virgo noun, masculine/feminine
  un/una virgo = a Virgo, a Virgoan

visa noun, feminine or (Spa) **visado** noun,
masculine
  una visa, un visado = a visa

visita noun, feminine
  una visita = a visit
    = a visitor

visitar verb [1]
  = to visit

víspera noun, feminine
  la víspera = the day before
  la víspera del accidente = the day before
    the accident

vista noun, feminine
• la vista = sight, eyesight
  ¡hasta la vista! = see you!
• una vista = a view

vistieron, vistió, etc ► vestir

visto past participle ► ver

vitamina noun, feminine
  una vitamina = a vitamin

viudo/viuda noun, masculine/feminine
  un viudo/una viuda = a widower/a widow

vivir verb [41]
• = to live
• = to be alive

vivo/viva adjective
• = alive
• un concierto en vivo = a live concert

vocabulario noun, masculine
  el vocabulario = the vocabulary

volante noun, masculine
  un volante = a steering wheel

volar verb [6]
  = to fly

volcán noun, masculine
  un volcán = a volcano

vóleibol, voleibol noun, masculine
  el vóleibol = volleyball

voltear verb [1] (Lat Am)
• = to turn over
• = to turn inside out
voltearse
  = to turn around

voltereta noun, feminine
  una voltereta = a somersault

volumen noun, masculine
  el volumen = the volume

voluntad noun, feminine
  la voluntad = the will
  fuerza de voluntad = willpower

voluntario/voluntaria
1 adjective
  = voluntary
2 noun, masculine/feminine
  un voluntario/una voluntaria = a volunteer

volver verb [24]
• = to go/come back
  volví a mi país = I went back to my country
• = to be back
  volveré a las cinco = I'll be back at five
• volver a hacer algo = to do something
    again
volverse
• = to turn around
• = to become
  se ha vuelto muy presumido = he's become
    very vain

vosotros/vosotras personal pronoun
(Spa)
  = you
  vosotros mismos/vosotras mismas =
    yourselves

votar verb [1]
  = to vote

voto noun, masculine
  un voto = a vote

voz noun, feminine
  una voz = a voice
  en voz alta/baja = in a loud/quiet voice

vuelo noun, masculine
  un vuelo = a flight

vuelta noun, feminine
• una vuelta = a turn
  dale otra vuelta = give it another turn
• dar una vuelta = to go for a walk/drive
• la vuelta = the return
  a la vuelta = on the way back

- **dar (la) vuelta a algo:**
  dar (la) vuelta a la esquina = to turn the corner
  dar (la) vuelta a la página = to turn the page
  dar (la) vuelta al colchón = to turn the mattress over
  dar (la) vuelta a un vaso = to turn a glass upside down/the right way up
  dar vuelta a la llave = to turn the key
- **dar vueltas alrededor de algo** = to go around something
  dar la vuelta al mundo = to go around the world

vuelva, vuelvo, etc ▶ volver

vuestro/**vuestra** (Spa)
1 adjective
vuestro/vuestra/vuestros/vuestras = your
2 pronoun
el vuestro/la vuestra/los vuestros/las vuestras = yours
See **tuyo** *for more examples*

wáter noun, masculine
el wáter = the toilet

xilófono noun, masculine
un xilófono = a xylophone

y conjunction
= and
Pepe y Laura = Pepe and Laura
son las seis y veinte = it's twenty after six, it's twenty past six

a las diez y media = at ten thirty
cincuenta y cinco = fifty-five

ya
1 adverb
- = already
  ya lo he hecho = I've done it already
- = now
  ha estado enfermo pero ya está mejor = he's been ill but he's better now
- **¡ya voy!** = I'm coming!
  ¡ya casi está! = it's almost ready
- (referring to the future)
  ya veremos = we'll see
  ya lo terminarás = you'll get it finished
- (in negative sentences)
  = any more, any longer
  ya no está enfadada = she's not angry any more
- (in interrogative sentences) = yet
  ¿ya se decidió? = has he decided yet?
- (to emphasize)
  ¡ya lo sé! = I know!
  ¡ya lo creo! = you bet!
- (to show that you understand)
  esto va aquí — ya = this goes here — right or I see
- **ya que** = since
2 exclamation
  ¡ya! (ironic) = of course

yate noun, masculine
un yate = a yacht

yema noun, feminine
- **una yema** = a yolk
- **una yema** = a fingertip

yerno noun, masculine
un yerno = a son-in-law

yo pronoun
- = I
  yo que tú = if I were you
- = me
  soy yo = it's me
  yo (mismo)/yo (misma) = myself

yogur noun, masculine
un yogur = a yogurt, yoghurt

yudo noun, masculine
yudo = judo

zanahoria noun, feminine
una zanahoria = a carrot

zapallo noun, masculine (SC)
un zapallo = a pumpkin

W
X
Y
Z

zapatería noun, feminine
  una **zapatería** = a shoe store, a shoe
  shop

zapatero/zapatera noun,
masculine/feminine
  un **zapatero**/una **zapatera** = a shoe-
  maker

zapatilla noun, feminine
  una **zapatilla** = a slipper
  (for sports) = a sneaker, a trainer
  (Mex) = a woman's shoe

zapato noun, masculine
  un **zapato** = a shoe

zíper noun, masculine (C Am, Mex)
  un **zíper** = a zipper, a zip

zodíaco, **zodiaco** noun, masculine
  el **zodíaco** = the Zodiac

zona noun, feminine
  una **zona** = an area
  = a zone

zoológico noun, masculine
  un **zoológico** = a zoo

zorro/zorra noun, masculine/feminine
  un **zorro**/una **zorra** = a fox/a vixen

zumbido noun, masculine
  un **zumbido** = buzzing

zumo noun, masculine (Spa)
  zumo = juice
  zumo de naranja = orange juice

zurdo/zurda
1 adjective
  = left-handed
  = left-footed
2 noun, masculine/feminine
  un **zurdo**/una **zurda** = a left-hander
  = a left-footed person

Dictionary know-how

This section contains a number of short exercises which will help you to use your
dictionary more effectively. You will find answers to all of the exercises at the end of
the section.

1 Noun or adjective?

Here is an extract from a Spanish advertisement for swimming pool installation.
See if you can find thirteen different nouns and underline them, and nine different
adjectives and circle them (or make two lists). If you are not sure of some words,
look them up in the Spanish/English half of the dictionary and see if the term
'noun' or 'adjective' is used to describe them.

> ### ¿TE GUSTA NADAR? ¿TE GUSTA LA SENSACIÓN DE TIRARTE AL AGUA PURA, AZUL, LIMPIA Y PROFUNDA?
>
> *ask*   *own*   *enjoy*
>
> Ya puedes. En tu propia casa. Más de tres millones de españoles ya gozan
> de este lujo con nuestras modernas piscinas de diseño original y precio
> económico. Tenemos veinte años de experiencia en instalar piscinas
> cubiertas y por lo tanto ahora somos expertos en este campo.
>
> Venga, permítete el lujo. Lánzate.
>
> *luxury*

2 Which gender?

Here are some English nouns which appear in the English–Spanish half of the
dictionary. Find out what their Spanish equivalents are and make two separate lists,
masculine nouns and feminine nouns.

bag	hat	shop	door
pencil	animal	tiger	island
train	library	magic	nickname
milk	mussel	pear	rain
belt	saucer	thunderstorm	parents
waitress	worm		

3 **Spot the pronoun**

Each of the following phrases appears in the Spanish–English half of this dictionary in entries where a pronoun is the headword. In each one, underline the pronoun(s) and give the English equivalent(s).

¿de quién es esto?

lo vi ayer

la vas a romper

me lo dio

¿te lavaste la cara?

tengo que pedirles un favor

ocúpato de ello

es para ti

4 **Where's the verb?**

Rearrange the following to form correct sentences and underline the verb in each case. Some variations in the word order may be possible.

te para despacio entienda que habla

de cinco tren minutos el dentro llegará

el tienda recuerda la Roberto no de nombre

una lado del siempre verano mar alquilamos al en casa

su en columpio primo jardín mi tiene un rojo

5 **Spot the adverb**

Here is a list of seventeen Spanish words. Eleven of them are adverbs and six are not. Underline the ones which are not, or make a list, and say what they are. If you are not sure of some of them, look them up in the Spanish–English half of the dictionary.

abajo	caso	entrevista	mente
abeja	delante	fuera	mientras
acaso	deprisa	incluso	prisa
además	enseguida	limpiaparabrisas	recién
afuera			

6 **Subject or object?**

We have left out the subjects and objects from this account in Spanish. Choose suitable words from the list below in order to complete it. When you have finished, list the subjects and objects separately. Remember, word order is much more flexible in Spanish than in English.

> .... del pueblo salieron varias veces a cazar .... pero siempre logró escaparse. Todas las noches arrancaba .... que se cultivaban en los campos. Al final .... atraparon .... cerca del pueblo y .... metieron en una jaula. Sin embargo esa noche, mientras .... celebraba ...., un nino travieso soltó al pobre animal. .... del pueblo estaban tan preocupadas que no dejaron salir a .... , de manera que .... del niño travieso se vio obligado a ofrecer .... de 2.000 rupias a quien le trajera la cola del animal.

la gente	las plantas
sus niños	el padre
el elefante peligroso	lo
los habitantes	una recompensa
las madres	unos jóvenes
lo	una fiesta

7 **Word search**

Here is a grid in which are hidden the following twelve Spanish words: agarrar, amor, ancho, diente, eso, gusano, hija, morder, nieve, silla, sucio, vaso. They may appear horizontally, vertically or diagonally, and in either direction. When you have found them, ring them, then list them in their correct categories (masculine nouns, feminine nouns, etc)

H	E	T	N	E	I	D	A	J	U
R	A	P	R	E	D	R	O	M	A
E	A	W	I	G	H	O	S	I	L
I	V	R	E	U	E	S	O	M	L
P	O	E	R	S	N	H	A	B	I
S	H	N	I	A	Y	I	Z	O	S
G	C	O	R	N	G	J	E	U	T
E	N	U	T	O	P	A	C	H	U
V	A	S	O	X	L	I	F	A	N
S	I	L	N	A	O	J	R	D	E

8 **Accents are important**

Here is part of a letter typed by somebody who does not know how to find the accents on a word processor. Use your dictionary to help you put them in:

Querida Teresa:

Muchas gracias por las flores que recibi ayer. Son preciosas.

Esta manana me encontre con Carmen en la calle Mayor ¿sabes que? hace poco conocio a un pintor ingles y esta a punto de irse con el a Londres. Ademas termino la carrera y se consiguio una beca para seguir estudiando alli. Es increible, ¿no? Claro que es una persona simpatica, pero es muy timida y encima bastante fea, la pobrecita. Bueno, pues ¿tu como estas? ¿Que piensas hacer en el verano? ¿Por que no vienes con nosotros a la playa?, siempre lo pasamos muy bien alli . . . .

9 **Find the ending**

Use your knowledge of Spanish and the dictionary, in particular the verb tables on pages 339–52, to give the correct form of the verb in parentheses.

¿Cuánto (**ganar**) ud.?
How much do you earn?

Normalmente (**almorzar**) a las doce
I usually have lunch at twelve o'clock

(**Pedir**) la cuenta
He asked for the bill

Tú lo (**ver**) más tarde
You'll see him later

(**Jugar**) con los niños en el jardín
She used to play with the children in the garden

(**Llegar**) el domingo
I arrived on Sunday

(**Pertenecer**) a ese club
I belong to that club

10 **Find the preposition**

Use your dictionary to find the English for the following Spanish sentences and underline the English and Spanish prepositions.

Dejé de fumar hace seis meses

El mantel estaba cubierto de manchas

Los obligó a abrir la caja fuerte

Es muy mala para la química

Iba acompañada de su madre

11 **Find the verb**

Some words in English can be both nouns and verbs e.g. race. In this exercise you have to find the following English words in the English–Spanish half of the dictionary and then give the Spanish for the verb only.

answer	**insult**	**finish**
block	**joke**	**rest**
camp	**kiss**	**sentence**
dance	**laugh**	**trick**
envy	**market**	**video**
fish	**notice**	**water**
glue	**paint**	**yell**

12 **Choosing the right word**

Very often you cannot use a word exactly as it is given in the dictionary. In the case of adjectives, you have to make sure that you select the form which is appropriate to the noun you are using. Use your dictionary and your own knowledge to find the correct form of the adjective to match the nouns in the following sentences.

Mi padre es .... pero mi madre es .... (*Irish*) (*German*)

Tienen una casa .... con unas habitaciones .... (*beautiful*) (*huge*)

Carmen es muy .... pero sus hermanos son .... (*tall*) (*short*)

Raquel y su madre están muy .... allí (*happy*)

Es muy .... idea (*good*)

Las inmigrantes .... llevaban pañuelos ....
(*Russian*) (*old*) (*white*)

La rabia es una de las enfermedades más .... de controlar (*difficult*)

13 **Translating phrasal verbs**

Use your dictionary to find the correct translation for the following English sentences containing phrasal verbs.

a button came off my jacket

to take down a poster

to give up smoking

I took off my shoes

to get worked up

14 **Form the subjunctive**

It's important not to be afraid of the subjunctive, because it is so common in Spanish. Using the English–Spanish side of the dictionary and the verb tables on page 339–52, translate these sentences into Spanish.

stay here until I call you [referring to one person]

I'll walk unless it rains

you needn't send the letter today

put this helmet on so that you don't hurt yourself

it's likely that they'll lose

it's no wonder he hasn't got a girlfriend

15 **Falsos amigos**

Some Spanish words look the same as, or very similar to English words, but in fact have a different meaning. These are known as 'falsos amigos' or false friends. Use your dictionary to find the meanings of the following Spanish words:

asistir	**librería**
avisar	**quieto**
embarazada	**remover**
éxito	**sensible**
fábrica	**suceso**
largo	**wáter**

16 **False friends**

Now use your dictionary to find a Spanish meaning for each of these English 'lookalikes'.

to advise	library
assistance	quiet
embarrassed	remove
exit	sensible
fabric	success
large	water

17 **Male or female?**

Many Spanish nouns also have a feminine form. This is particularly true of words denoting an occupation—un abogado, una abogada. Some simply change from -o to -a for the feminine form, but not all do. Use your dictionary to find the feminine form of the following nouns:

un soldado	un policía
un director	un presidente
un actor	un bailarín
un poeta	un astronauta

18 **Find the sentence**

Use your dictionary to find the Spanish equivalents of the following English sentences

(a) I'd like to change jobs
(b) we arrived at the right time
(c) before the train leaves
(d) he's not up yet
(e) her work means a lot to her

(f) what's happening?
(g) how long is the movie?
(h) the meal came to 25 dollars
(i) stamps sold here
(j) painting is great fun

19 **Which meaning?**

Some words have more than one meaning and it's important to check that you have chosen the right one. In this dictionary the different meanings of a word are marked by a bullet point •

We have given you one meaning of the Spanish words below. Use your dictionary to find another one.

un departamento	• a department	**una llama**	• a flame
una escala	• a stopover	**manejar**	• to handle
formal	• formal	**raro**	• strange
importar	• to matter	**repasar**	• to check
justo	• fair	**sentar**	• to sit
una lata	• a can	**la tensión**	• voltage

20 **Crossword**

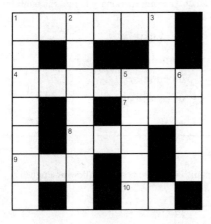

Across

1 to avoid
4 we go out, leave
  we went out, left
7 bear
8 without
9 celery with the end cut off
10 yes

Down

1 to teach
2 church
3 rivers
5 monkeys
6 alone

Answers

1

Nouns: sensación, agua, casa, millones, españoles, lujo, piscinas, diseño, precio, años, experiencia, expertos, campo

Adjectives: pura, azul, limpia, profunda, propia, modernas, original, económico, cubiertas

2

Masculine nouns: sombrero, tigre, animal, apodo, platillo, mejillón, cinturón, padres, gusano, tren, làpiz

Feminine nouns: bolsa, tienda, puerta, isla, leche, biblioteca, magia, pera, lluvia, tormenta eléctrica, camarera, (mesera, moza)

3

¿de quien es **esto**?
whose is this?

lo vi ayer
I saw him yesterday

la vas a romper
you're going to break it

me lo dio
she gave it to me

¿**te** lavaste la cara?
did you wash your face?

tengo que pedir**les** un favor
I have to ask them a favor

ocúpate de **ello**
take care of it

es para **ti**
it's for you

4

habla despacio para que te **entienda**

el tren **llegará** dentro de cinco minutos

Roberto no **recuerda** el nombre de la tienda

en verano siempre **alquilamos** una casa al lado del mar

mi primo **tiene** un columpio rojo en su jardín

5

abeja, entrevista, mente, prisa are feminine nouns

caso, limpiaparabrisas are masculine nouns

6

Los habitantes del pueblo salieron varias veces a cazar el elefante peligroso pero siempre logró escaparse. Todas las noches arrancaba las plantas que se cultivaban en los campos. Al final lo atraparon unos jóvenes cerca del pueblo y lo metieron en una jaula. Sin embargo, esa noche, mientras la gente celebraba una fiesta, un niño travieso soltó al pobre animal. Las madres del pueblo estaban tan preocupadas que no dejaron salir a sus niños, de manera que el padre del niño travieso se vio obligado a ofrecer una recompensa de 2.000 rupias a quien le trajera la cola del animal.

Subjects: los habitantes, unos jóvenes, la gente, las madres, el padre

Objects: el elefante peligroso, las plantas, lo, lo, una fiesta, sus niños

7

amor, diente, gusano, vaso are masculine nouns

hija, nieve, silla are feminine nouns

ancho, sucio are adjectives

agarrar, morder are verbs

eso is a pronoun

8

Querida Teresa:

Muchas gracias por las flores que recibí ayer. Son preciosas. Esta mañana me encontré con Carmen en la calle Mayor ¿sabes que? Hace poco conoció a un pintor inglés y está a punto de irse con él a Londres. Además terminó la carrera y se consiguió una beca para seguir estudiando allí. Es increíble,¿no? Claro que es una persona simpática, pero es muy tímida y encima bastante fea, la pobrecita. Bueno, pues ¿tú cómo estás? ¿Qué piensas hacer en el verano? ¿Por qué no vienes con nosotros a la playa? siempre lo pasamos muy bien allí ...

9

gana

almuerzo

pidió

verás

jugaba

llegué

pertenezco

10

Dejé **de** fumar hace seis meses
I gave up smoking six months ago

El mantel estaba cubierto **de** manchas
The tablecloth was covered in stains

Los obligó **a** abrir la caja fuerte
He forced them to open the safe

Es muy mala **para** la química
She is very bad at chemistry

Iba acompañada **de** su madre
She was accompanied by her mother

11

contestar insultar terminar acabar
bloquear bromear descansar
acampar besar sentenciar
bailar reírse engañar
envidiar comercializar grabar
pescar notar regar
pegar pintar gritar

12

irlandés alemana
preciosa enormes
alta bajos
contentas
buena
rusas viejas blancos
difíciles

13

se le cayó un botón a la chaqueta
quitar un cartel
dejar de fumar
me quité los zapatos
exaltarse

14

quédate aquí hasta que te llame
quédese aquí hasta que lo/la llame [polite form]

iré a pie a no ser que llueva

no hace falta que mandes la carta hoy

pónte este casco para que no te hagas daño
póngase este casco para que no se haga daño
[polite form]

es probable que pierdan

no es de extrañar que no tenga novia

15

asistir = *to attend*
avisar = *to let know*
embarazada = *pregnant*
éxito = *success*
fábrica = *factory*
largo = *long*
librería = *bookstore, bookshop*
quieto = *still*
remover = *to stir, to turn over, to toss*
sensible = *sensitive*
suceso = *event, incident*
wáter = *toilet*

16

assistance = ayuda
embarrassed = avergonzado
exit = salida
fabric = tela, tejido
large = grande
library = biblioteca
quiet = silencioso, tranquilo
remove = quitar
sensible = sensato, prudente, cómodo y
práctico
success = éxito
water = agua

17

una soldado
una directora
una actriz
una poetisa, una poeta
una policía
una presidenta
una bailarína
una astronauta

18

(a) quisiera cambiar de trabajo

(b) llegamos en un buen momento

(c) antes de que salga el tren

(d) no se ha levantado todavía

(e) su trabajo es muy importante para ella

(f) ¿qué pasa?

(g) ¿cuánto dura la película?

(h) la comida costó 25 dolares

(i) los sellos se venden aquí

(j) la pintura es una gran diversión

19

un departamento	a department an apartment
una escala	a stopover a scale
formal	formal reliable well-behaved
importar	to matter to import
justo	fair tight right just enough
una lata	a can a pain (nuisance)
una llama	a flame a llama
manejar	to handle to drive
raro	strange rare
repasar	to check to review, revise
sentar	to sit to suit
la tensión	voltage tension blood pressure

20

a, an *indefinite article*
a = un/una
he's a dentist = es dentista
what a good idea! = ¡qué buena idea!

> **!** a *is not translated before a person's*
> *profession, or in the phrase* **what a**

ability *noun*
ability = capacidad (*feminine*)
he doesn't have the ability to do it = no
tiene capacidad para hacerlo

able *adjective*
• (*having the ability*)
to be able to [stand up | travel | work ...] =
poder [levantarse | viajar | trabajar ...]
• (*capable*) = capaz
an able pupil = un alumno capaz

aboard
1 *preposition* = a bordo de
2 *adverb*
to go aboard = subir a bordo

about

> **!** About *is often used in combinations*
> *with verbs, for example,* **mess about, run**
> **about.** *To find the correct translations for*
> *this type of verb, look up the separate*
> *dictionary entries at* **mess, run** *etc*

1 *preposition*
• (*on the subject of*) = sobre
it's a book about the First World War = es
un libro sobre la Primera Guerra Mundial
he wants to see you about something =
quiere verte acerca de algo
I know nothing about this matter = no sé
nada (con) respecto a este asunto
2 *adverb*
• (*approximately*) = como
I have about 5 dollars left = me quedan
como 5 dólares
we left at about seven o'clock = nos
fuimos como a las siete
• (*on the point of*)
to be about to = estar a punto de
to be about to go = estar a punto de ir

above
1 *preposition* = encima de
his room is above the kitchen = su cuarto
está encima de la cocina
above all = sobre todo
2 *adverb*
I have the room above = ocupo el cuarto de
arriba
children aged twelve and above = niños a
partir de 12 años

abroad *adverb*
to travel abroad = viajar al extranjero
to live abroad = vivir en el extranjero

absent *adjective*
= ausente
to be absent from school = faltar al colegio

accent *noun*
an accent = un acento
with a Mexican accent = con acento
mexicano

accept *verb*
= aceptar

accident
1 *noun*
an accident = un accidente
by accident (*by chance*) = por casualidad
(*unintentionally*) = sin querer

accommodation,
accommodations (*US English*) *noun*
accommodation = alojamiento (*masculine*)
hotel accommodation = alojamiento en
hotel

accompany *verb*
= acompañar

account *noun*
• (*in a bank*)
an account = una cuenta
• **to take something into account** = tomar
algo en cuenta

accountant *noun*
an accountant = un contador/una
contadora (*Lat Am*), un/una contable
(*Spa*)

accurate *adjective*
an accurate watch = un reloj preciso
are these measurements accurate? =
¿estas medidas son exactas?
an accurate description = una descripción
exacta

accuse *verb*
= acusar
to accuse someone of lying = acusar a
alguien de mentir

across *preposition*

> **!** *The combination of a verb of movement*
> + **across** *is translated by the verb* **cruzar**

to go across the street = cruzar la calle
to run across the street = cruzar la calle
corriendo

- (*through*)
  a journey across the desert = un viaje a través del desierto
- (*on the other side of*)
  she lives across the street = vive al otro lado de la calle

act *verb*
- (*to take action*) = actuar
- (*to perform as an actor*) = actuar

activity *noun*
  an activity = una actividad

actor *noun*
  an actor = un actor

actress *noun*
  an actress = una actriz

actually *adverb*
- (*in fact*)
  I haven't actually read the book yet = la verdad es que no he leído el libro todavía
- (*really*) = de verdad
  did he actually say that? = ¿de verdad dijo eso?
- (*exactly*) = exactamente
  what actually happened? = ¿qué pasó exactamente?

adapt *verb*
- (*if it's a play, an engine etc*) = adaptar
- (*to get used to*) = adaptarse
  she quickly adapted to the new school = pronto se adaptó al nuevo colegio

add *verb*
- = añadir
  you have to add lemon juice = hay que añadir jugo de limón
- (*in arithmetic*) = sumar

address *noun*
  an address = una dirección
  (*on a form*) = un domicilio

adhesive *noun*
  an adhesive = un adhesivo

adjust *verb*
- (*if it's an instrument*) = ajustar
- (*to get used to*) = adaptarse
  it takes time to adjust to a new job = se necesita tiempo para adaptarse a un trabajo nuevo

administration *noun*
  administration = administración (*feminine*)

admire *verb*
  = admirar

admission *noun*
  (*price of entry*)
  admission = entrada (*feminine*)

admit *verb*
- (*to recognize, to confess*) = admitir, reconocer

- **to be admitted to hospital** = ingresar en el hospital

adolescent *noun*
  an adolescent = un/una adolescente

adopt *verb*
  = adoptar

adore *verb*
  = adorar
  she adores her grandparents = adora a sus abuelos
  they adore traveling abroad = les encanta viajar al extranjero

adult *noun*
  an adult = un adulto/una adulta

advance *noun*
  in advance = con antelación
  to pay in advance = pagar por adelantado

advantage *verb*
- (*a positive point*)
  an advantage = una ventaja
  to have an advantage over someone = tener ventaja sobre alguien
- **to take advantage of an opportunity** = aprovechar una oportunidad
  they are taking advantage of you = se están aprovechando de ti

adventure *noun*
  an adventure = una aventura

advert, advertisement *noun*
  an advert, an advertisement = un anuncio, un aviso (*Lat Am*)

advertising *noun*
  advertising = publicidad (*feminine*)

advice *noun*
  advice = consejos (*masculine plural*)
  a piece of advice = un consejo

advise *verb*
  = aconsejar
  to advise someone to stay = aconsejarle a alguien que se quede

  ! *Note the use of the subjunctive after* aconsejarle a alguien que

aerial *noun* (*British English*)
  an aerial = una antena

aeroplane *noun* (*British English*)
  an aeroplane = un avión

affect *verb*
  (*to have an effect*) = afectar a
  this doesn't affect me = esto no me afecta

afford *verb*
  I'd like to go, but I can't afford it = me gustaría ir, pero no puedo permitirme el lujo
  he can't afford a car = no le alcanza el dinero para comprar un coche

---

afraid *adjective*
* (*scared*)
  to be afraid = tener miedo
  I'm afraid of mice = les tengo miedo a los ratones
* (*expressing a regret*)
  I'm afraid I can't go with you = me temo que no te puedo acompañar

Africa *noun* ▶ **p. 187**
  Africa = África (*feminine*)

African ▶ **p. 187**
1 *noun*
  an African = un africano/una africana
2 *adjective* = africano/africana

after ▶ **p. 319**
1 *preposition*
* = después de
  they left after breakfast = se fueron después del desayuno
  the day after tomorrow = pasado mañana
  after all = después de todo
* (*US English—when talking about time*)
  it's twenty after four = son las cuatro y veinte
2 *adverb* = después
  soon after = poco después
3 *conjunction*
  after we finished, we went to bed = después de que terminamos, nos acostamos
  after seeing the movie, I went home = después de ver la película, me fui a casa

afternoon *noun* ▶ **p. 319**
  an afternoon = una tarde
  Friday afternoon = el viernes en la tarde, el viernes por la tarde (*Spa*)
  in the afternoon = en la tarde, por la tarde (*Spa*)
  at six o'clock in the afternoon = a las seis de la tarde
  good afternoon = buenas tardes

aftershave *noun*
  an aftershave = una loción para después de afeitarse, un aftershave

afterward (*US English*), **afterwards** (*British English*) *adverb*
  = después
  they left not long afterwards = se fueron poco después

again *adverb*
  = otra vez, de nuevo
  are you going to do it again? = ¿lo vas a hacer otra vez?, ¿lo vas a hacer de nuevo?

  ! *Very often there will be a specific Spanish verb to translate the idea of doing something 'again'—e.g.* **start again** *= recomenzar, to do the work again = rehacer el trabajo etc*

  she read the letter again = releyó la carta
  to begin again = volver a empezar

against *preposition*
* (*close to*) = contra
  she left her bike against the wall = dejó la bicicleta contra la pared
* (*not in favor of*) = en contra de
  to be against hunting = estar en contra de la caza

age *noun* ▶ **p. 154**
  age = edad (*feminine*)

agree *verb*
* (*to have the same opinion*) = estar de acuerdo
  I don't agree with you = no estoy de acuerdo contigo
* (*to give one's consent*)
  we agreed to meet next week = quedamos en encontrarnos la semana que viene
* (*to reach a decision*)
  to agree on a price = ponerse de acuerdo en un precio

ago *adverb*
  a month/two years ago = hace un mes/dos años

agreement *noun*
  an agreement = un acuerdo

agriculture *noun*
  agriculture = agricultura (*feminine*)

ahead *adverb*
* (*in advance*)
  they went on ahead = se adelantaron
* (*in front*)
  he was ahead of us = estaba delante de nosotros
  to be ahead of the other pupils = estar más avanzado/avanzada que los demás alumnos

AIDS *noun*
  AIDS = el sida, el SIDA

aim
1 *noun*
* (*a purpose*)
  an aim = un objetivo
* (*when using a weapon*)
  to take aim at someone = apuntarle a alguien
2 *verb*
* **to aim to win** (*to try*) = intentar ganar
  (*to intend*) = tener la intención de ganar
* **to aim a gun at someone** = apuntarle a alguien con una pistola

air
1 *noun*
  air = aire (*masculine*)
2 *verb*
  (*if it's clothes, linen*) = airear, orear
  to air a room = ventilar una habitación

air-conditioning *noun*
  the air-conditioning = el aire acondicionado

Age

Where English says **to be X years old**, Spanish says **tener X años** (*to have X years*).

How old?

how old are you?	= ¿cuántos años tienes?
what age is she?	= ¿qué edad tiene?
he is twenty years old	= tiene veinte años
he is twenty	
he is twenty years of age	

Aged

he was aged twenty	= tenía veinte años
a baby aged eleven months	= un bebé de once meses

Younger/older/the same age

he is younger than you	= es más joven que tú
she is older than John	= es mayor que John
he's two years older than me	= es dos años mayor que yo
she's the same age as me	= tiene la misma edad que yo

X-year-old

a fifty-year-old	= una persona de cincuenta años
a five-year-old	= un niño/una niña de cinco años

Approximate ages

he is about thirty	= tiene alrededor de treinta años, tiene unos treinta años
she's in her forties	= tiene cuarenta y tantos
she's in her early forties	= tiene poco más de cuarenta años
she's in her late forties	= tiene cerca de cincuenta años

---

aircraft *noun*
  an aircraft = un avión

air force *noun*
  the air force = la fuerza aérea

air hostess *noun*
  an air hostess = una azafata, una aeromoza (*Lat Am*)

airline *noun*
  an airline = una línea aérea

airmail *noun*
  airmail = correo aéreo (*masculine*)
  by airmail = por vía aérea

airplane *noun* (*US English*)
  an airplane = un avión

airport *noun*
  an airport = un aeropuerto

alarm *noun*
  an alarm = una alarma

alarm clock *noun*
  an alarm clock = un despertador

album *noun*
  an album = un álbum

alcohol *noun*
  alcohol = alcohol (*masculine*)

alike *adjective*
  = parecido/parecida

alive *adjective*
  = vivo/viva

all
1 *adjective*
  = todo/toda (+ *singular*), todos/todas (+ *plural*)
  all the boys/girls = todos los chicos/todas las chicas
2 *pronoun*
  = todo
  that's all = eso es todo
3 *adverb*
  to be all alone = estar completamente solo/sola

---

allergic *adjective*
  to be allergic to something = ser
    alérgico/alérgica a algo

allergy *noun*
  an allergy = una alergia

allow *verb*
  = permitir
  'smoking is not allowed' = 'no se permite
    fumar'

allowance *noun*
  (*from parents*) **a monthly allowance** = una
    mensualidad, una mesada (*Lat Am*)

all right *adjective*
  • (*when giving an opinion*)
  the play was all right = la obra no estaba
    mal
  • (*when talking about health*) = bien
  are you all right? = ¿estás bien?
  • (*when asking for an opinion*)
  is it all right if I go? = ¿está bien si me voy?
  • (*when agreeing*) = de acuerdo

almond *noun*
  an almond = una almendra

almost *adverb*
  = casi
  I've almost finished = casi he terminado
  they almost missed the plane = por poco
    pierden el avión, casi pierden el avión

alone
  1 *adjective* = solo/sola
  2 *adverb*
  to live alone = vivir solo/sola

along *preposition*
  = por
  she walked along the sidewalk = caminó
    por la acera
  there are benches along the street = hay
    bancos a lo largo de la calle

aloud *adverb*
  = en voz alta

already *adverb*
  = ya
  it's already eight o'clock = ya son las ocho

also *adverb*
  = también

alternative *noun*
  an alternative = una alternativa

although *conjunction*
  = aunque

altogether *adverb*
  (*in total*) = en total

always *adverb*
  = siempre

amateur *noun*
  an amateur = un/una amateur

amazed *adjective*
  = asombrado/asombrada

amazing *adjective*
  = increíble

ambassador *noun*
  an ambassador = un embajador/una
    embajadora

ambition *noun*
  ambition = ambición (*feminine*)

ambitious *adjective*
  = ambicioso/ambiciosa

ambulance *noun*
  an ambulance = una ambulancia

America *noun* ▶ **p. 187**
  • (*the USA*)
  America = Estados Unidos (*masculine
    plural*), Norteamérica (*feminine*)
  • (*the continent*)
  America = América (*feminine*)

American ▶ **p. 187**
  1 *noun*
  an American = un/una estadounidense, un
    norteamericano/una norteamericana
  2 *adjective*
  an American city = una ciudad
    norteamericana
  the American embassy = la embajada de
    los Estados Unidos

among, amongst *preposition*
  • (*in the midst of*) = entre
  I found it among the newspapers = lo
    encontré entre los periódicos
  • (*one of*)
  **Japan is among the richest countries in
    the world** = el Japón es uno de los países
    más ricos del mundo

amount *noun*
  an amount = una cantidad

amusement park *noun*
  an amusement park = un parque de
    diversiones, un parque de atracciones
    (*Spa*)

amusing *adjective*
  = divertido/divertida

an *indefinite article* ▶ **a**

ancestor *noun*
  an ancestor = un antepasado/una
    antepasada

anchor *noun*
  an anchor = un ancla (*feminine*)

and *conjunction*

    ! *Note that the usual translation* y
    becomes e *when it precedes a word
    beginning with* i- *or* hi-

  • = y

she visited France and Spain = visitó Francia y España
Pedro and Isabel = Pedro e Isabel
bread and butter = pan con mantequilla
I'll go and see = iré a ver
• (*in numbers*)
  a hundred and ten = ciento diez
  nine hundred and seventy-two = novecientos setenta y dos

angel *noun*
  an angel = un ángel

anger *noun*
  anger = ira (*feminine*), enojo (*masculine*), enfado (*masculine*) (*Spa*)

angry *adjective*
  = enojado/enojada, enfadado/enfadada (*Spa*)
  to be angry with someone = estar enojado con alguien, estar enfadado con alguien (*Spa*)
  to get angry = enojarse, enfadarse (*Spa*)

animal *noun*
  an animal = un animal

ankle *noun* ▶ p. 235
  the ankle = el tobillo

anniversary *noun*
  an anniversary = un aniversario
  a wedding anniversary = un aniversaria de boda de casados

announcement *noun*
  an announcement = un anuncio

annoy *verb*
  = molestar

annoyed *adjective*
  = enojado/enojada, enfadado/enfadada (*Spa*)
  are you annoyed with me? = ¿estás enojado conmigo?, ¿estás enfadado conmigo? (*Spa*)

annoying *adjective*
• (*if it's a person*) = pesado/pesada
• (*if it's a noise*) = molesto/molesta

annual
1 *noun*
  (*a book*)
  an annual = un anuario
2 *adjective* = **anual**

anonymous *adjective*
  = anónimo/anónima

another
1 *adjective* = otro/otra
  another 25 copies = otras 25 copias
  I'll come back another day = vuelvo otro día
2 *pronoun* = otro/otra

answer
1 *noun*

• (*a reply*)
  an answer = una respuesta
  there's no answer (*at the door, on the phone*) = no contestan
• (*a solution*)
  an answer = una solución
2 *verb* = contestar
  to answer a question = contestar una pregunta
  she answered the phone = contestó el teléfono
  would you answer the door? = ¿puedes abrir la puerta?

answer back
  = contestar

answering machine *noun*
  an answering machine = un contestador automático

ant *noun*
  an ant = una hormiga

antenna *noun*
  (*of a television or radio*)
  an antenna = una antena

antique *noun*
  an antique = una antigüedad

anxious *adjective*
• (*worried*) = preocupado/preocupada
  he is anxious about the exam results = está preocupado por los resultados de los exámenes
• (*keen*)
  to be anxious to do something = estar deseoso/desosa de hacer algo

any
1 *adjective*
• (*in questions*)
  is there any sugar? = ¿hay azúcar?
  do you have any money? = ¿tienes dinero?
• (*with a negative*)
  we don't have any beer = no tenemos cerveza
  she doesn't have any brothers = no tiene hermanos
• (*whatever*) = cualquier
  come any day you want = ven cualquier día que quieras
2 *pronoun*
  I need some ink—do you have any? = necesito tinta–¿tienes?
  I don't have any = no tengo

anybody, anyone *pronoun*
• (*in questions*)
  is there anybody at home? = ¿hay alguien en casa?
• (*with the negative*) = nadie
  there isn't anybody there = no hay nadie allí
  they don't want anybody to know = no quieren que nadie lo sepa

---

C Am Central America   Lat Am Latin America   Mex Mexico

- (*everybody*)
  anybody can come = puede venir
  cualquiera

anything *pronoun*
- (*in questions*) = algo
  do you have anything to eat? = tienes algo
  para comer?
- (*with the negative*) = nada
  he doesn't want to do anything = no quiere
  hacer nada
- (*everything*)
  he would do anything for her = haría
  cualquier cosa por ella

anyway *adverb*
= de todos modos

anywhere *adverb*
- (*in questions*)
  have you seen my shoes anywhere? = has
  visto mis zapatos por algún lado?
  are you going anywhere tonight? = ¿vas a
  algún lado esta noche?
- (*with the negative*)
  I can't find them anywhere = no los
  encuentro por ningún lado
  you're not going anywhere = no vas a ir a
  ningún lado
- (*any place*)
  we can go anywhere = podemos ir a
  cualquier lado

apart *adjective*
  they don't like to be apart = no les gusta
  estar separados
  apart from = aparte de

apartment *noun*
  an apartment = un apartamento, un
  departamento (*Lat Am*), un piso (*Spa*)

apartment building, **apartment house** (*US English*) *noun*
  an apartment building = un edificio de
  apartamentos, un edificio de
  departamentos (*Lat Am*), una casa de
  pisos (*Spa*)

ape *noun*
  an ape = un simio

apologize *verb*
= pedir perdón
  we apologize for the delay = rogamos
  disculpen el retraso

apology *noun*
  an apology = una disculpa

appear *verb*
- (*to seem*) = parecer
  she appears to be happy = parece estar
  contenta
- (*to come into view*) = aparecer

appendix *noun*
  the appendix = el apéndice

appetite *noun*
  appetite = apetito (*masculine*)

applaud *verb*
= aplaudir

applause *noun*
  applause = aplausos (*masculine plural*)
  a round of applause = un aplauso

apple *noun*
  an apple = una manzana

appliance *noun*
  an appliance = un aparato
  electrical appliances = electrodomésticos
  (*masculine plural*)

application *noun*
  (*for a job*)
  an application = una solicitud

application form *noun*
  an application form = una solicitud

apply *verb*
  (*to send a job application*)
  to apply for a job = solicitar un trabajo

appointment *noun*
  an appointment (*arrangement to meet*) =
  una cita
  (*with doctor, hairdresser*) = una hora, una
  cita (*Lat Am*)
  to make an appointment = concertar una
  cita
  **I have an appointment at the doctor's at
  one o'clock** = tengo hora con el médico a
  la una, tengo cita con el médico a la una

appreciate *verb*
- (*to be grateful for*) = agradecer
  I appreciate your concern = agradezco tu
  interés
- (*if it's good food or wine*) = apreciar

approach *verb*
= acercarse
  to approach someone/something =
  acercarse a alguien/algo

approve *verb*
  my mother doesn't approve of him = a mi
  madre no le gusta
  they approved of the idea = la idea les
  parecía muy buena

approximately *adverb*
  it is approximately 10 kilometers from here
  = está a unos diez kilómetros de aquí
  at approximately 5 o'clock = a eso de las
  cinco

apricot *noun*
  an apricot = un chabacano (*Mex*), un
  damasco (*SC*), un albaricoque (*Spa*)

April *noun* ▶ **p. 192**
  April = abril (*masculine*)

---

apron *noun*
an apron = un delantal

aquarium *noun*
an aquarium = un acuario

Aquarius *noun*
• (*the sign*)
Aquarius = Acuario
I'm Aquarius = soy Acuario, soy de Acuario
• (*a person*)
an Aquarius = un/una acuario

arch *noun*
an arch = un arco

architect *noun*
an architect = un arquitecto/una arquitecta

architecture *noun*
architecture = arquitectura (*feminine*)

area *noun*
an area (*of country*) = una zona
(*of city*) = un barrio

argue *verb*
= discutir
to argue about money = discutir por el dinero
to argue about politics = discutir de política

argument *noun*
• (*a quarrel*)
an argument = una discusión
to have an argument with someone = discutir con alguien
• (*reasons for or against*)
an argument = un argumento

Aries *noun*
• (*the sign*)
Aries = Aries
I'm Aries = soy Aries, soy de Aries
• (*a person*)
an Aries = un/una aries

arithmetic *noun*
arithmetic = aritmética (*feminine*)

arm *noun* ▶ p. 235
the arm = el brazo

armchair *noun*
an armchair = un sillón

arms *noun*
arms = armas (*feminine plural*)

army *noun*
the army = el ejército
to be in the army = ser militar

around
1 *preposition* = alrededor de
they were sitting around the table = estaban sentados alrededor de la mesa
to go around the world = dar la vuelta alrededor del mundo

2 *adverb*

> ! Around *often occurs in combinations with verbs, eg* run around, turn around *etc. To find the correct translations for this type of verb, look up the separate dictionary entries at* run, turn *etc*

• (*approximately*) = como
I have around 5 dollars left = me quedan unos 5 dólares
I'll be there at around four o'clock = estaré allí como a las cuatro
• (*available, nearby*)
will you be around tomorrow? = vas a estar aquí mañana?
they live around here = viven por aquí

arrange *verb*
to arrange a vacation in Italy = organizar unas vacaciones en Italia
to arrange an appointment = concertar una cita
they arranged to meet later = quedaron en encontrarse más tarde

arrangement *noun*
to make an arrangement *or* arrangements to leave early = quedar en irse temprano

arrest *verb*
= detener

arrival *noun*
the arrival = la llegada

arrive *verb*
= llegar

arrow *noun*
an arrow = una flecha

art *noun*
art = arte (*masculine*)
(*as school subject*) = expresion artística (*feminine*)

art gallery *noun*
an art gallery = un museo de Bellas Artes

artificial *adjective*
= artificial

artist *noun*
an artist = un artista/una artista

artistic *adjective*
= artístico

arts *noun*
the arts = las artes

as
1 *conjunction*
• (*like*) = como
she arrived late as usual = llegó tarde como siempre
let's leave the room as it is = dejemos el cuarto así como está
• (*because, since*) = como
as you were out, I left a message = como habías salido, dejé un mensaje

---

C Am Central America   Lat Am Latin America   Mex Mexico

A

* (*while*) = mientras
  I watched him as he counted the money =
    lo vigilé mientras contaba el dinero
  I used to live there as a child = vivía allí
    cuando era niño/niña
* (*when used with the same*)
  my coat is the same as yours = mi abrigo
    es igual que el tuyo
  they have the same car as us = tienen el
    mismo coche que nosotros
2 *preposition*
  she works as a receptionist = trabaja de
    recepcionista
  he was dressed as a pirate = estaba
    vestido de pirata
3 *adverb*
  I'm as tired as you = estoy tan cansada
    como tú
  I ran as fast as possible = corrí lo más
    rápido que pude
  as for = en cuanto a
  as for us = en cuanto a nosotros
  as from tomorrow = a partir de mañana

ash *noun*
  ash = ceniza (*feminine*)

ashamed *adjective*
  to be ashamed = estar
    avergonzado/avergonzada
  he is ashamed of what he has done = está
    avergonzado de lo que ha hecho

ashtray *noun*
  an ashtray = un cenicero

Asia *noun* ▶ p. 187
  Asia = Asia (*feminine*)

Asian ▶ p. 187
1 *noun*
  an Asian = un asiático/una asiática
2 *adjective* = asiático/asiática

ask *verb*
  to ask = preguntar
  he asked me my name = me preguntó mi
    nombre
  to ask permission to go outside = pedir
    permiso para salir
  to ask someone to call = pedirle a alguien
    que llame

  ! *Note the use of the subjunctive after*
  pedirle a alguien que

  to ask a question = hacer una pregunta
* (*to invite*)
  to ask a friend to dinner = invitar a un
    amigo a cenar
* (*to inquire*)
  did you ask about the plane tickets? =
    ¿preguntaste por los boletos de avión?
ask for
  to ask for money = pedir dinero
  to ask for someone (*on the phone*) =
    preguntar por alguien

asleep *adjective*
  to be asleep = estar dormido/dormida
  to fall asleep = dormirse

aspirin *noun*
  an aspirin = una aspirina

assassinate *verb*
  = asesinar

assemble *verb*
* (*gather*) = reunirse
* (*construct*) = armar

assignment *noun*
  (*for school*)
  an assignment = un trabajo

assistance *noun*
  assistance = ayuda (*feminine*)

assistant *noun*
* (*a helper*)
  an assistant = un ayudante/una ayudante
* (*British English—in a shop*) ▶ shop
    assistant

association *noun*
  an association = una asociación

assume *verb*
  = suponer

assure *verb*
  = asegurar

astronaut *noun*
  an astronaut = un astronauta/una
    astronauta

at *preposition*
* (*when talking about position or place*) = en
  at home = en casa

  ! *You will find translations for phrases
  like* at the top, at the front of, at the
  back of *etc in the entries for* top, front,
  back *etc*

* (*at the house, shop, practice of*)
  we'll be at Laura's = estaremos en casa de
    Laura, estaremos donde Laura (*Lat Am*)
  I have an appointment at the dentist's =
    tengo cita con el dentista
* (*when talking about time*) = a
  it starts at 7 o'clock = empieza a las siete
* (*when talking about age*) = a
  at four years of age = a los cuatro años

  ! *There are many verbs which involve the
  use of* at, *such as* look at, laugh at *etc.
  For translations look up the separate
  dictionary entries for* look, laugh *etc*

athlete *noun*
  an athlete = un atleta/una atleta

athletics *noun*
  athletics (*in the US*) = los deportes
  (*in Britain*) = el atletismo

Atlantic *noun*
  the Atlantic = el Atlántico

atlas *noun*
  an atlas = un atlas

atmosphere noun
(air)
the atmosphere = la atmósfera

attach verb
to be attached to the wall = estar
sujeto/sujeta a la pared
to attach a letter to an application =
adjuntar una carta a una solicitud

attack
1 verb = atacar
2 noun
an attack = un ataque

attempt
1 verb = intentar
to attempt to break the world record =
intentar batir el récord mundial
2 noun
an attempt = un intento
to make an attempt to escape = intentar
escapar

attend verb
to attend a wedding = asistir a una boda
to attend the village school = ir a la escuela
del pueblo

attention noun
attention = atención (feminine)
to get someone's attention = atraer la
atención de alguien
to pay attention to someone/something =
prestar atención a alguien/algo

attic noun
an attic (used for storage) = un desván, un
altillo
(used as accommodation) = un ático

attitude noun
an attitude = una actitud

attract verb
= atraer
to attract someone's attention = atraer la
atención de alguien

attractive adjective
= atractivo/atractiva

audience noun
• (at a cinema, theater, or concert)
the audience = el público
• (for a radio or TV program)
the audience = la audiencia

August noun ▶ p. 192
August = agosto (masculine)

aunt noun
an aunt = una tía

au pair noun
an au pair = una au pair

Australia noun ▶ p. 187
Australia = Australia (feminine)

Australian ▶ p. 187
1 noun
an Australian = un australiano/una
australiana
2 adjective = australiano/australiana

Austria noun ▶ p. 187
Austria = Austria (feminine)

Austrian ▶ p. 187
1 noun
an Austrian = un austríaco/una austríaca,
un austriaco/una austriaca
2 adjective = austríaco/austríaca,
austriaco/austriaca

author noun
an author (of an article) = un autor/una
autora
(of a book) = un escritor/una escritora

authority noun
• (power)
authority = autoridad (feminine)
• the authorities = las autoridades

autograph noun
an autograph = un autógrafo

automatic adjective
= automático/automática

autumn noun
autumn = otoño (masculine)
in autumn = en el otoño

available adjective
(on sale)
there are places available on the 6
o'clock flight = hay asientos disponibles
en el vuelo de las seis
tickets for the concert are still available =
todavía quedan entradas para el
concierto

average
1 noun
an average = un promedio, una media
2 adjective = medio/media

avoid verb
• (to prevent) = evitar
to avoid making noise = evitar hacer
ruido
• (to keep away from)
to avoid someone = evitar a alguien

awake adjective
= despierto/despierta
I'm wide awake now = estoy totalmente
despierta ahora
they kept me awake all night = no me
dejaron dormir en toda la noche

award
1 noun
(a prize)
an award = un premio

2 *verb*
he was awarded first prize = le otorgaron el primer premio

aware *adjective*
* (*conscious*)
  to be aware of a problem = ser consciente de un problema, estar consciente de un problema (*Mex*)
* (*up to date*)
  to be aware of what's happening = estar al tanto de lo que está pasando

away *adverb*
* (*absent*)
  John is away today = John no está hoy
* (*when talking about distances*)
  to be far away = estar muy lejos
  Boston is 80 km away = Boston está a 80 km de aquí

> **!** Away *is often used in combinations with verbs, for example,* go away, run away. *To find the correct translations for this type of verb, look up the separate dictionary entries at* go, run *etc*

awful *adjective*
* the movie was awful = la película fue terrible
  the weather was awful = hacía muy mal tiempo
* (*unwell*)
  I feel awful = me siento muy mal, me siento fatal

awkward *adjective*
it's a very awkward situation = es una situación muy incómoda
I felt very awkward = me sentí muy incómodo

ax (*US English*), **axe** (*British English*) *noun*
an axe = un hacha (*feminine*)

Bb

baby *noun*
a baby = un bebé, un niño/una niña, un bebe/una beba (*R Pl*)

baby buggy, **baby carriage** *noun* (*US English*)
a baby buggy = un cochecito

babysitter *noun*
a babysitter = un/una babysitter, un/una canguro (*Spa*)

back
1 *noun*

* (*a part of the body*) ▶ **p. 235**
  the back = la espalda
* (*the rear of something*)
  at the back of the shop = en el fondo de la tienda
  the back of a chair = el respaldo de una silla
  the back of a car = la parte trasera de un coche
* (*the reverse side of something*)
  write your name on the back of the check = escriba su nombre al dorso del cheque
2 *adverb*

> **!** Back *is often used in combinations with verbs, for example,* come back, get back, give back *etc. To find the correct translations for this type of verb, look up the separate dictionary entries at* come, get, give *etc*

to be back = estar de vuelta
I'll be back in five minutes = vuelvo dentro de cinco minutos
* (*before in time*)
  back in February = en febrero
  back in 1972 = (ya) en 1972
3 *verb*
(*support*)
= respaldar, apoyar
back down = volverse atrás

back door *noun*
the back door = la puerta trasera

background *noun*
* (*of a picture or photograph*)
  the background = el fondo
* (*of a person*)
  she is from a poor background = su familia es pobre

back seat *noun*
the back seat = el asiento trasero

back to front *adverb*
your sweater is on back to front = te has puesto el suéter al revés

backward (*US English*), **backwards** (*British English*) *adverb* = hacia atrás

bacon *noun*
bacon = tocino (*masculine*), bacon (*masculine*) (*Spa*), panceta (*feminine*) (*R Pl*)

bad *adjective*
* (*not good*)
  = malo/mala

> **!** Note that malo *becomes* mal *when it appears before a masculine singular noun*

a bad movie = una película mala
that's not a bad idea = no es mala idea
how was the play?—not bad = ¿qué tal la obra?—no estaba mal

* (*serious*) = grave
  a bad accident = un accidente grave
* (*wicked*) = malo/mala

badge *noun*
* **a badge** = una chapa, un botón (*Lat Am*)
  (*worn by a policeman*) = una placa de policía

badly *adverb*
* (*not well*) = mal
  he did badly in his exams = le fue mal en los exámenes
* (*seriously*)
  he was badly injured = resultó gravemente herido

badminton *noun* ▶ **p. 306**
  badminton = bádminton (*masculine*)

bad-tempered *adjective*
  to be bad-tempered = tener mal genio

bag *noun*
* **a bag** = una bolsa
* (*baggage*)
  she packed her bags = hizo las maletas

baggage *noun*
  baggage = equipaje (*masculine*)

bake *verb*
* **to bake bread** = hacer pan
  to bake a dish in the oven = hacer una comida al horno
* (*to make cakes or bread*)
  he likes baking (*making cakes*) = le gusta hacer pasteles
  (*making bread*) = le gusta hacer pan

baker *noun*
  a baker = un panadero/una panadera

bakery *noun*
  a bakery = una panadería

balance
1 *noun*
* (*physical*)
  balance = equilibrio (*masculine*)
* (*in a bank account*)
  a balance = un saldo
2 *verb*
* (*to place*) = mantener en equilibrio
* (*remain steady*) = mantener el equilibrio

balcony *noun*
  a balcony = un balcón

bald *adjective*
  = calvo, pelón (*Mex*), pelado (*SC*)
  to go bald = quedarse calvo (*or* pelón *etc*)

ball *noun*
* (*for playing football, rugby, tennis, cricket or basketball*)
  a ball = una pelota, un balón
* (*for playing baseball or golf*)
  a ball = una pelota, una bola

* (*a dance*)
  a ball = un baile

ballet *noun*
  ballet = ballet (*masculine*)

balloon *noun*
  a balloon = un globo

ballpoint pen *noun*
  a ballpoint pen = un bolígrafo, una pluma atómica (*Mex*), una birome (*R Pl*)

ban *verb*
  = prohibir

banana *noun*
  a banana = un plátano, una banana (*R Pl*), un banano (*C Am*)

band *noun*
  (*a musical group*)
  a band = un grupo

bandage
1 *noun*
  a bandage = un vendaje
2 *verb* = vendar

Band-Aid® *noun* (*US English*)
  a Band-Aid = una curita®, una tirita® (*Spa*)

bang
1 *noun*
* (*a loud noise*)
  a bang = un estrépito
* (*an explosion*)
  a bang = una explosión
2 *verb*
* (*to hit*)
  he banged his head on the ceiling = se dio un golpe en la cabeza con el techo
  he banged his fist on the table = golpeó la mesa con el puño
* (*to shut loudly*)
  she banged the door = dio un portazo

bangs *noun* (*US English*)
  bangs = flequillo (*masculine*), cerquillo (*masculine*) (*Lat Am*), fleco (*masculine*) (*Mex*)

bank *noun*
* (*a financial institution*)
  a bank = un banco
* (*of a river or lake*)
  the bank = la orilla

bank account *noun*
  a bank account = una cuenta bancaria

bank holiday *noun* (*British English*)
  a bank holiday = un día festivo, un día feriado (*Lat Am*)

bank note *noun*
  (*British English*)
  a bank note = un billete de banco

bankrupt *adjective*
= en bancarrota
to go bankrupt = quebrar

bank statement *noun*
a bank statement = un estado de cuenta

baptize *verb*
= bautizar

bar *noun*
• (*a place*)
  a bar = un bar
• (*a counter*)
  a bar = una barra
• (*on a cage or window*)
  a bar = un barrote
• **a bar of soap** = una pastilla de jabón, una barra de jabón (*R Pl*)
  a bar of chocolate = una barra de chocolate

barbecue *noun*
• (*a cooking utensil*)
  a barbecue = una barbacoa, un asador (*Lat Am*)
• (*a social occasion*)
  a barbecue = una barbacoa, un asado (*Lat Am*)

barbed wire, barbwire (*US English*) *noun*
  barbed wire = alambre de púas (*masculine*), alambre de espino (*masculine*) (*Spa*)

bare *adjective*
• (*uncovered*)
  to have bare feet = estar descalzo/decalza
  the walls were bare = las paredes estaban desnudas
• (*empty*) = vacío/vacía

barely *adverb*
= apenas

bargain
1 *noun*
• (*a cheap thing*)
  a bargain = una ganga
• (*a business agreement*)
  a bargain = un trato
2 *verb*
• (*to haggle*) = regatear
• (*to negotiate*) = negociar

bark
1 *noun*
• (*of a dog*)
  a bark = un ladrido
• (*of a tree*)
  the bark = la corteza
2 *verb* = ladrar

barmaid *noun*
  a barmaid = una mesera, una camarera (*Spa*)

barman *noun* (*British English*)
  a barman = un barman, un camarero (*Spa*)

barn *noun*
  a barn = un granero

barrel *noun*
  a barrel = un barril

barricade *noun*
  a barricade = una barricada

barrier *noun*
  a barrier = una barrera

barrister *noun*
  a barrister = un abogado/una abogada

bartender *noun* (*US English*)
  a bartender = un barman, un camarero (*Spa*)

base
1 *noun*
• (*the bottom part of something*)
  the base of a wall = la base de una pared
  the base of a tree/a lamp = el pie de un árbol/una lámpara
• (*a place*)
  a base = una base
2 *verb*
  she is based in London = tiene su base en Londres
  the film is based on a true story = la película está basada en una historia real

baseball *noun* ▶ p. 306
  baseball = béisbol (*masculine*)

basement *noun*
  a basement = un sótano

basic *adjective*
= básico/básica

basically *adverb*
= básicamente

basin *noun*
• (*for washing up*)
  a basin = una palangana
• (*a washbasin*)
  a basin = un lavabo

basis *noun*
  (*for action or negotiation*)
  basis = base (*feminine*)

basket *noun*
  a basket = una canasta, una cesta

basketball *noun* ▶ p. 306
  basketball = baloncesto (*masculine*), básquetbol (*masculine*) (*Lat Am*)

bat *noun*
• (*animal*)
  a bat = un murciélago
• (*for playing baseball or cricket*)
  a bat = un bate

bath *noun*
• (*a wash*)
  to have a bath, to take a bath (*US English*)
  = bañarse

- (*a tub*)
  a bath = una bañera, una tina (*Lat Am*)
  he's in the bath = se está bañando

bathroom *noun*
  a bathroom = un cuarto de baño

battery *noun*
  a battery (*for a radio, a clock or a torch*) = una pila
  (*for a car*) = una batería

battle *noun*
  a battle = una batalla

bay *noun*
  a bay = una bahía

be *verb*
- (*describing permanent qualities*) = ser
  she is [young | tall | rich …] = es [joven | alta | rica …]
  it is Monday = es lunes
  it is late = es tarde
- (*describing transitional state or mood*) = estar
  I'm [worried | sad | okay …] = estoy [preocupado | triste | bien …]
  the water was hot = el agua estaba caliente
  the car is broken = el coche está estropeado

  ! *Note that* ser *and* estar *can imply fine differences in meaning:* es delgado = *he is thin, implying that he has always been thin;* está delgado = *he is thin, implying that he has lost weight recently;* las manzanas son buenas = *apples are good, talking about apples in general;* las manzanas están buenas = *the apples are good, referring to the particular apples that the speaker has*

- (*exist*)
  there is/are = hay
  there is a tree/there are three trees in the garden = hay un árbol/tres árboles en el jardín
- (*describing a job*) = ser
  I am a journalist = soy periodista
- (*talking about health*) = estar
  how are you = ¿cómo estás?
  I'm very well = estoy muy bien
- (*talking about cost*)
  how much is it? = ¿cuánto cuesta?, ¿cuánto es?
- (*to be situated*) = estar
  where is the library? = ¿dónde está la biblioteca?
- (*talking about going to a place or traveling*)
  I've never been to Greece = nunca he estado en Grecia
- (*in the following expressions* to be *is translated by* tener)
  I'm hot/cold = tengo calor/frío
  to be hungry/thirsty = tener hambre/sed
  to be afraid = tener miedo
  how old are you? = ¿cuántos años tienes?
  I'm 30 = tengo 30 años

- (*talking about the weather*)
  the weather is fine = hace buen tiempo
  it's hot/cold today = hace calor/frío hoy
- (*in continuous sentences*)
  he is reading = está leyendo
  it was snowing = nevaba, estaba nevando
  we are going to Paris tomorrow = mañana vamos a París
- (*in passive sentences*)
  it was built in 1903 = fue construido en 1903, se construyó en 1903, lo construyeron en 1903
  the house has been sold = la casa se ha vendido
  it is known that … = se sabe que …

  ! *The passive is less common in Spanish than it is in English; passive sentences in English are more usually translated using the pronoun* se, *or the third person plural, as shown in the examples above*

- (*in questions at the end of sentences*)
  it's a lovely house, isn't it? = es una casa muy linda, ¿verdad?

  ! *See* estar *and* ser *for a fuller treatment of the uses of these verbs*

beach *noun*
  a beach = una playa

bead *noun*
  a bead = una cuenta

beak *noun*
  a beak = un pico

beam *noun*
- (*made of wood*)
  a beam = una viga
- (*of light*)
  a beam = un rayo

bean *noun*
  a bean = un frijol, un poroto (*SC*), una alubia (*Spa*)

bear
1 *noun*
  a bear = un oso
2 *verb*
- (*to tolerate a person*) = aguantar
- (*to tolerate a sight, a noise, a taste or a smell*) = soportar
- (*to carry*) = llevar

beard *noun*
  a beard = una barba

bearded *adjective*
  = barbudo/barbuda

beat *verb*
- (*to hit*) = pegar
- (*to be victorious over*) = ganarle a
  she beat me at tennis = me ganó al tenis
beat up = pegarle a
  to beat someone up = pegarle a alguien

beautiful adjective
• (if it's scenery) = precioso/preciosa, hermoso/hermosa
• (if it's a woman or child) = precioso/preciosa

beauty noun
beauty = belleza (feminine)

because
1 conjunction = porque
2 **because of** = debido a

become verb
to become President = asumir la presidencia
to become rich = hacerse rico
they became friends = se hicieron amigos

bed noun
a bed = una cama
to go to bed = acostarse

bedroom noun
a bedroom = un dormitorio, un cuarto, una pieza (Lat Am), una recámara (Mex)

bee noun
a bee = una abeja

beef noun
beef = carne de vaca (feminine), carne de res (feminine) (Mex), ternera (feminine) (Spa)

beer noun
• (the product)
beer = cerveza (feminine)
• (a glass of beer)
a beer = una cerveza

beet (US English), **beetroot** (British English) noun
a beet = una remolacha, un betabel (Mex)

before
1 preposition
• (in time) = antes de
before Christmas = antes de Navidad
the day before yesterday = anteayer
• (in front of)
= ante
the match took place before a crowd of five thousand spectators = el partido se desarrolló ante cinco mil espectadores
2 adverb
= antes
two weeks before = dos semanas antes
3 conjunction
I would like to see him before I go = quisiera verlo antes de irme
before the train leaves = antes de que salga el tren

❗ Note the use of the subjunctive after antes de que

beg verb
• (to beg for food or money) = mendigar

• (to ask) = pedir
I beg your pardon = le pido perdón

beggar noun
a beggar = un mendigo/una mendiga

begin verb
= empezar, comenzar
to begin work, to begin working = empezar a trabajar, comenzar a trabajar
to begin with (at first) = al principio
(first of all) = para empezar

beginner noun
a beginner = un/una principiante

beginning noun
the beginning = el comienzo, el principio
in the beginning = al principio
at the beginning of May = al principio de Mayo

behalf noun
in behalf of (US English), on behalf of (British English)
I am phoning in behalf of my sister = llamo de parte de mi hermana
he was acting in her behalf = actuaba en representación de ella

behave verb
= comportarse
to behave oneself = comportarse bien

behavior (US English), **behaviour** (British English) noun
behavior = comportamiento (masculine)

behind
1 preposition = detrás de, atrás de (Lat Am)
2 adverb
• to stay behind = quedarse
he looked behind = miró hacia atrás
• (late)
he is behind with his work = está atrasado con el trabajo

beige adjective ▶ p. 183
= beige (❗ never changes), beis (❗ never changes) (Spa)

Belgian ▶ p. 187
1 noun
a Belgian = un/una belga
2 adjective = belga

Belgium noun ▶ p. 187
Belgium = Bélgica (feminine)

belief noun
a belief = una creencia

believe verb
= creer
to believe in God = creer en Dios

bell noun
• (in a church)
a bell = una campana

• (*on a door or bicycle*)
   a bell = un timbre

belong *verb*
• (*to be the property of*)
   to belong to = pertenecer a
• (*to be a member of*)
   to belong to a club = ser socio de un club
   to belong to a union = estar afiliado/afiliada a un sindicato
• (*to be kept or stored*) = ir
   those plates belong in the kitchen = esos platos van en la cocina

belongings *noun*
   belongings = pertenencias (*feminine plural*)

below
1 *preposition* = debajo de, abajo de (*Lat Am*)
2 *adverb*
   the room below = el cuarto de abajo

belt *noun*
   a belt = un cinturón

bench *noun*
   a bench = un banco

bend
1 *noun*
   (*turning in a road*)
   a bend = una curva
2 *verb*
• (*to bow*)
   to bend one's leg = doblar la pierna
• (*to make something crooked*)
   to bend = torcer
• (*to lean forward or stoop*)
   to bend = inclinarse
   she bent forward = se inclinó hacia adelante
bend down = agacharse

beneath
1 *preposition* = bajo
2 *adverb*
   the room beneath = el cuarto de abajo

benefit
1 *noun*
   (*advantage*)
   a benefit = una ventaja
2 *verb*
   to benefit someone = beneficiar a alguien

bent *adjective*
   = torcido/torcida

berry *noun*
   a berry = una baya

beside *preposition*
   = al lado de, junto a
   he is sitting beside me = está sentado a mi lado, está sentado junto a mí
   I live beside the sea = vivo a la orilla del mar

best
1 *noun*
   the best = el mejor/la mejor
   she did her best to convince me = hizo todo lo que pudo para convencerme
2 *adjective* = mejor
   the best restaurant in town = el mejor restaurante de la ciudad
3 *adverb*
   blue suits you best = el azul es el color que mejor te queda
   I did it as best I could = lo hice lo mejor que pude

bet
1 *noun*
   a bet = una apuesta
2 *verb* = apostar
   to bet on a horse = apostar a un caballo

betray *verb*
   = traicionar

better
1 *adjective* = mejor
   her new film is better than the rest = su nueva película es mejor que las demás
   to get better = mejorar
2 *adverb* = mejor
   he speaks French better than I do = habla francés mejor que yo

between
1 *preposition* = entre
   between now and next year = de aquí al año que viene
2 *adverb*
   in between = en medio

beware *verb*
   beware! = ¡atención!
   beware of the dog! = ¡cuidado con el perro!

beyond *preposition*
   = más allá de

bicycle *noun*
   a bicycle = una bicicleta

big *adjective*
• (*large*) = grande

   ! Note that **grande** *becomes* **gran** *when it is used before a singular noun*

   a big garden = un jardín grande, un gran jardín
• (*important or considerable*)
   a big mistake = un gran error
• (*older*) = mayor

bike *noun*
   a bike = una bici✖

bikini *noun*
   a bikini = un bikini

bilingual *adjective*
   = bilingüe

✖ in informal situations   C Am Central America   Lat Am Latin America   Mex Mexico

bill *noun*
* (*in a restaurant*)
  a bill = una cuenta, una adición (*R Pl*)
* (*for gas, electricity, telephone, repairs*)
  a bill = una factura
* (*in a hotel or guesthouse*)
  a bill = una cuenta
* (*US English—paper money*)
  a bill = un billete

billion *noun*
* (*US English—a thousand million*)
  a billion = mil millones (*masculine plural*)
* (*British English—a million million*)
  a billion = un billón

bin *noun*
  a bin (*in a kitchen*) = un cubo de basura, un
  tacho de basura (*SC*), un bote de basura
  (*Mex*)
  (*for wastepaper*) = una papelera

binoculars *noun*
  binoculars = gemelos (*masculine plural*)

biology *noun*
  biology = biología (*feminine*)

bird *noun*
  a bird (*small*) = un pájaro, (*large*) = un ave
  (*feminine*)

birth *noun*
  a birth = un nacimiento
  she gave birth to a boy = dio a luz a un
  niño

birthday *noun*
  a birthday = un cumpleaños
  happy birthday! = ¡feliz cumpleaños!

biscuit *noun* (*British English*)
  a biscuit = una galleta, una galletita (*R Pl*)

bishop *noun*
  a bishop = un obispo

bit *noun*
* (*a piece*)
  a bit = un pedazo, un trozo
* (*a little*)
  a bit = un poco
  a bit expensive = un poco caro

bite
1 *noun*
* (*from a dog or snake*)
  a bite = una mordedura
* (*from an insect*)
  a bite = una picadura
2 *verb*
* (*of a person or dog*) = morder
  she bites her nails = se come las uñas
* (*of an insect*) = picar

bitter *adjective*
  = amargo/amarga

black *adjective* ▶ p. 183
  = negro/negra

blackberry *noun*
  a blackberry = una mora

blackboard *noun*
  a blackboard = una pizarra

blackcurrant *noun*
  a blackcurrant = una grosella negra

blackmail
1 *noun*
  blackmail = chantaje (*masculine*)
2 *verb* = chantajear

bladder *noun*
  the bladder = la vejiga

blade *noun*
  (*of a knife or sword*)
  a blade = una hoja
  a blade of grass = una brizna de hierba

blame
1 *noun*
  to put the blame on someone = echarle la
  culpa a alguien
2 *verb*
  to blame someone for something = echarle
  a alguien la culpa de algo

blank *adjective*
  a blank sheet of paper = una hoja de papel
  en blanco
  a blank cassette = una cinta virgen

blanket *noun*
  a blanket = una manta, una cobija (*Lat
  Am*), una frazada (*Lat Am*)

blast *noun*
  a blast = una explosión

blaze
1 *noun*
  (*in a building or street*)
  a blaze = un incendio
2 *verb* = arder

bleach *noun*
  bleach = lejía (*feminine*), cloro (*masculine*)
  (*Lat Am*), blanqueador (*masculine*) (*Mex*)

bleed *verb*
  = sangrar
  his nose is bleeding = le sangra la nariz

bless *verb*
  = bendecir

blind
1 *adjective* = ciego/ciega
  to go blind = quedarse ciego/ciega
2 *verb*
* (*to make someone lose their sight*) = dejar
  ciego/ciega
* (*to dazzle*) = deslumbrar
3 *noun*
  (*on a window*)
  a blind = una persiana

blink *verb*
= parpadear

blister *noun*
a blister = una ampolla

blizzard *noun*
a blizzard = una ventisca

block
1 *noun*
• (*a large piece*)
a block = un bloque
• (*a building*)
a block of flats (*British English*) = un edificio de apartamentos, un edificio de departamentos (*Lat Am*), una casa de pisos (*Spa*)
an office block = un edificio de oficinas
2 *verb*
(*to obstruct*) = bloquear
block out
to block out the light = tapar la luz
block up
to block up a hole = tapar un agujero

blond, blonde
1 *noun*
a blond = un rubio/una rubia, un güero✱/una güera✱ (*Mex*)
2 *adjective* = rubio/rubia, güero✱/güera✱ (*Mex*)

blood *noun*
blood = sangre (*feminine*)

bloom *verb*
= florecer

blouse *noun*
a blouse = una blusa

blow
1 *verb* = soplar
the wind was blowing = soplaba el viento
the referee blew his whistle = el árbitro hizo sonar el silbato
2 *noun*
a blow = un golpe
his death was a terrible blow for her = su muerte fue un golpe terrible para ella
blow out
to blow out a candle = apagar una vela
blow up
• (*in an explosion*)
they blew up the building = hicieron saltar el edificio por los aires
• (*to inflate*)
to blow up a balloon = inflar un globo, hinchar un globo (*Spa*)

blue *adjective* ▶ p. 183
= azul

blunt *adjective*
(*not sharp*)
= desafilado/desafilada

blush *verb*
= sonrojarse

board
1 *noun*
• (*a piece of wood*)
a board = una tabla
• (*a committee*)
a board = una junta
• (*for chess or checkers*)
a board = un tablero
• (*a blackboard*)
a board = una pizarra
• (*accommodation*)
board and lodging = comida y alojamiento
• on board = a bordo
2 *verb*
to board a [plane | ship | train ...] = embarcarse

boarding card, boarding pass *noun*
a boarding card = una tarjeta de embarque, un pase de abordar (*Mex*)

boarding school *noun*
a boarding school = un internado

boast *verb*
= alardear

boat *noun*
a boat = un barco

body *noun* ▶ p. 235
the body = el cuerpo
a dead body = un cadáver

boil *verb*
• to boil water = hervir agua
to boil an egg = cocer un huevo
• (*to come to the boil*) = hervir

boiled egg *noun*
a boiled egg (*soft*) = un huevo pasado por agua, un huevo tibio (*Mex*), (*hard*) un huevo duro

boiler *noun*
a boiler = una caldera

boiling *adjective*
boiling water = agua hirviendo

bolt
1 *noun*
• (*a lock*)
a bolt = un pestillo
• (*a screw*)
a bolt = un perno
2 *verb*
to bolt a door = cerrar una puerta con pestillo

bomb
1 *noun*
a bomb = una bomba
2 *verb* = bombardear

bond *noun*
a bond = un lazo

bone *noun*
• a bone = un hueso
• (*of a fish*)
  a bone = una espina

bonnet *noun*
• (*a baby's hat*)
  a bonnet = un gorrito
• (*a lady's hat*)
  a bonnet = un sombrero (de ala pequeña)
• (*British English—of a car*)
  the bonnet = el capó, el capote (*Mex*)

bonus *noun*
• (*a payment*)
  a bonus = una bonificación
• (*an advantage*)
  a bonus = una ventaja

book
1 *noun*
  a book = un libro
2 *verb*
  to book [a room | a seat | a table ...] = reservar
  [un cuarto | un asiento | una mesa ...]
  the flight is fully booked = el vuelo está
  completo

bookcase *noun*
  a bookcase = una biblioteca, una librería
  (*Spa*), un librero (*Mex*)

booking *noun*
  a booking = una reserva, una reservación
  (*Lat Am*)
  to make a booking = hacer una reserva,
  hacer una reservación

bookshop, **bookstore** (*US English*)
noun
  a bookshop = una librería

boom *noun*
  (*in the economy*)
  a boom = un boom

boot *noun*
• (*footwear*)
  a boot = una bota
• (*British English—of a car*)
  the boot = el maletero, la cajuela (*Mex*), el
  baúl (*R Pl*)

border
1 *noun*
• (*a frontier*)
  a border = una frontera
• (*an edge*)
  a border = un borde
2 *verb*
  (*if it's a country*) = limitar con
  Chile borders Argentina = Chile limita con
  Argentina

bore *verb*
  = aburrir

bored *adjective*
  = aburrido/aburrida
  to be bored = estar aburrido/aburrida
  to get bored = aburrirse

boredom *noun*
  boredom = aburrimiento (*masculine*)

boring *adjective*
  = aburrido/aburrida
  to be boring = ser aburrido/aburrida

born *adjective*
  to be born = nacer

borrow *verb*
  I borrowed some money from him = le pedí
  prestado dinero
  can I borrow your keys? = ¿me prestas las
  llaves?, ¿me dejas las llaves? (*Spa*)

boss *noun*
  the boss = el jefe/la jefa

bossy *adjective*
  = mandón/mandona

both
1 *adjective*
  both books are red = ambos libros son
  rojos, los dos libros son rojos
  both my sons = mis dos hijos
2 *pronoun* = ambos/ambas, los dos/las dos
3 *conjunction*
  both Anne and Brian came = tanto Anne
  como Brian vinieron
  both in Europe and America = tanto en
  Europa como en los Estados Unidos

bother *verb*
• (*to worry*) = preocupar
• (*to inconvenience*) = molestar
  I'm sorry to bother you = siento molestarla
• (*to take the trouble*)
  you needn't bother to wait = no hace falta
  que esperes
  please don't bother = no te molestes

bottle *noun*
  a bottle = una botella

bottle opener *noun*
  a bottle opener = un abrebotellas, un
  destapador (*Lat Am*)

bottom
1 *noun*
• (*the lowest part*)
  the bottom of the hill/stairs = el pie de la
  colina/las escaleras
  at the bottom of the page = al final de la
  página
  at the bottom of the garden = al fondo del
  jardín
• (*the underside*)
  the bottom (*of a box*) = la parte de abajo
  (*of a bottle*) = el fondo
• to be bottom of the class = ser el último/la
  última de la clase

R Pl River Plate area   SC Southern Cone   Spa Spain

- (*part of the body*)
  the bottom = el trasero
2 *adjective*
  the bottom shelf = el estante de abajo

bounce *verb*
  (*of a ball*) = rebotar, picar (*Lat Am*), botar
  (*Mex, Spa*)

bound *adjective*
- **it was bound to happen** = tenía que
  suceder
  it's bound to create problems = seguro que
  va a crear problemas
- (*heading in the direction of*)
  a train bound for London = un tren con
  rumbo a Londres

boundary *noun*
  a boundary = un límite

bow[1] *noun*
- (*a knot*)
  a bow = un lazo, un moño (*Lat Am*)
- (*a weapon*)
  a bow = un arco

bow[2]
1 *noun*
  a bow = una reverencia, una venia (*SC*)
2 *verb*
  (*as a mark of respect*) = hacer una
  reverencia, hacer una venia (*SC*)

bowl
1 *noun*
- (*for food*)
  a bowl = un cuenco
  a fruit bowl = un frutero, una frutera (*SC*)
  a salad bowl = una ensaladera
- (*for washing*)
  a bowl = una palangana
2 *verb*
  (*in sports*) = lanzar

bowling *noun*
  bowling = bolos (*masculine plural*),
  bowling (*masculine*)

box *noun*
  a box = una caja

boxer *noun*
  a boxer = un boxeador

boxing *noun*
  boxing = boxeo (*masculine*)

boy *noun*
  a boy = un chico, un niño

boyfriend *noun*
  a boyfriend = un novio

bra *noun*
  a bra = un sostén, un brasier (*Mex*), un
  sujetador (*Spa*)

bracelet *noun*
  a bracelet = una pulsera

bracket *noun*
  a bracket = un paréntesis

braid *noun*
  (*US English—in hair*)
  a braid = una trenza

brain *noun*
  the brain = el cerebro

brake
1 *noun*
  a brake = un freno
  (*in a car*) = un freno de mano
2 *verb* = frenar

branch *noun*
- (*of a tree*)
  a branch = una rama
- (*of a shop or business*)
  a branch = una sucursal

brand *noun*
  (*a make*)
  a brand = una marca

brand-new *adjective*
  = flamante

brandy *noun*
  brandy = coñac (*masculine*)

brass *noun*
  brass = latón (*masculine*)

brave *adjective*
  = valiente

Brazil *noun* ▶ **p. 187**
  Brazil = (el) Brasil

bread *noun*
  bread = pan (*masculine*)

break
1 *noun*
- (*a pause*)
  a break = un descanso
  to take a break = tomarse un descanso
- (*a holiday*)
  the summer break = las vacaciones de
  verano
2 *verb*
- (*to crack, smash or damage*) = romper
- (*to become damaged*) = romperse
- (*to injure*)
  he broke his arm = se rompió el brazo, se
  quebró el brazo (*Lat Am*)
- (*not to keep*)
  to break a promise = no cumplir una
  promesa
  to break the rules = infringir las reglas
- (*to tell*)
  I had to break the news to her = me tocó a
  mí darle la noticia
break down
  (*to stop working*) = estropearse,
  descomponerse (*Lat Am*)

break in
  the thieves broke in through a window =
    los ladrones se metieron por una ventana
break into
  to break into a car = entrar en un coche
    (para robar)
  our house was broken into = nos entraron
    a robar
break out
• (to start suddenly)
  the fire broke out in the basement = el
    incendio se declaró en el sótano
• (to escape) = escaparse
break up
• (to disperse)
  the crowd broke up = la muchedumbre se
    dispersó
• (if it's a couple) = romper

breakfast noun
  breakfast = desayuno (masculine)
  to have breakfast = desayunar

breast noun
  a breast = un pecho

breath noun
  breath = aliento (masculine)
  to be out of breath = estar sin aliento
  to hold one's breath = aguantar la
    respiración
  to have bad breath = tener mal aliento

breathe verb
  = respirar

breed
1 noun
  a breed = una raza
2 verb
  (to rear) = criar

breeze noun
  a breeze = una brisa

brew verb
• (if it's beer) = fabricar
• (if it's tea) = preparar

bribe verb
  to bribe someone = sobornar a alguien

brick noun
  a brick = un ladrillo
  a brick wall = una pared de ladrillo

bride noun
  a bride = una novia

bridge noun
  a bridge = un puente

brief adjective
  = breve

bright adjective
  bright blue = azul vivo (! never changes)
  the light was too bright = la luz estaba
    demasiada fuerte
  this room is not very bright = no hay
    mucha luz en este cuarto

brilliant adjective
  (very clever) = brillante

bring verb
• (take along) = traer
  he brought me flowers = me trajo flores
• (to transport)
  to bring someone home = traer a alguien a
    casa
• (to lead) = llevar
  the path brings you to the village = el
    camino lleva al pueblo
bring back
• (to return) = devolver
• (to take home) = traer
bring down
  to bring down prices = bajar los precios
bring up
  (to raise and educate) = criar

Britain noun ▶ p. 187
  (Great) Britain = Gran Bretaña (feminine)

British ▶ p. 187
1 plural noun
  the British = los británicos
2 adjective = británico/británica

broad adjective
• (wide) = ancho/ancha
• (wide-ranging)
  a broad range of programs = una amplia
    gama de programas
• in broad daylight = a plena luz del día

broadcast
1 noun
  a broadcast = una transmisión, un
    programa
2 verb = transmitir

brochure noun
  a brochure = un folleto

broil verb (US English)
  = asar a la parrilla, asar al grill

broiler noun (US English)
  a broiler = una parrilla, un grill

broke adjective
  to be broke = estar pelado✗/pelada✗

broken adjective
  = roto/rota
• (if it's a bone) roto/rota, quebrado/quebrada
    (Lat Am)

bronze
1 noun
  bronze = bronce (masculine)
2 adjective = de bronce

brooch noun
  a brooch = un prendedor

broom noun
  a broom = una escoba

brother noun
a brother = un hermano

brother-in-law noun
a brother-in-law = un cuñado

brown adjective ▶ p. 183
- (if it's eyes, clothes, shoes) = marrón (**!** never changes), café (**!** never changes) (Mex)
- (it it's someone's hair) = castaño/castaña
- (if it's natural skin color) = moreno/morena
- (tanned) = bronceado/bronceada
- brown rice/bread = arroz/pan integral
  brown sugar = azúcar morena

bruise
1 noun
a bruise = un moretón
2 verb
I bruised my knee = me magullé la rodilla

brush
1 noun
- (for hair, teeth, clothes, shoes)
  a brush = un cepillo
- (a broom)
  a brush = una escoba
- (for painting)
  a (**paint**)brush (small) = un pincel, (large) = una brocha
2 verb = cepillar
  she brushed her hair = se cepilló el pelo
  I brushed my teeth = me cepillé los dientes

bubble noun
- (of air or gas)
  a bubble = una burbuja
- (of soap)
  a bubble = una pompa
  to blow bubbles = hacer pompas

bucket noun
a bucket = un balde, un cubo (Spa), una cubeta (Mex)

build verb
= construir

builder noun
a builder (a contractor) = un/una contratista
(a laborer) = un/una albañil

building noun
a building = un edificio

built-in adjective
= empotrado/empotrada

built-up adjective
= urbanizado/urbanizada

bulb noun
- (a light bulb)
  a bulb = una bombilla, una bombita (R Pl), una bujía (C Am), un foco (Mex)
- (of a plant)
  a bulb = un bulbo

Bulgaria noun ▶ p. 187
Bulgaria = Bulgaria (feminine)

bull noun
a bull = un toro

bullet noun
a bullet = una bala

bulletin noun
a bulletin = un boletín

bully
1 noun
a bully = un matón/una matona
2 verb
to bully someone = intimidar a alguien

bump
1 noun
- (on a part of the body or on a surface)
  a bump = un golpe
- (a jolt)
  a bump = una sacudida
2 verb
  he bumped his head = se dio un golpe en la cabeza
  he bumped into the door = se dio contra la puerta

bumpy adjective
a bumpy road = una calle llena de baches

bun noun
- (sweet)
  a bun = un bollo
- (bread roll)
  a bun = un panecillo, un bolillo (Mex)

bunch noun
a bunch of flowers = un ramo de flores
a bunch of grapes = un racimo de uvas
a bunch of keys = un manojo de llaves

bundle noun
a bundle of clothes (tied up) = un lío de ropa, (loose) = una pila de ropa
a bundle of letters = un paquete de cartas

bunk noun
a bunk = una litera

burden noun
a burden = una carga

bureaucrat noun
a bureaucrat = un/una burócrata

burger noun
a burger = una hamburguesa

burglar noun
a burglar = un ladrón/una ladrona

burglar alarm noun
a burglar alarm = una alarma antirrobo

burglary noun
a burglary = un robo

C Am Central America   Lat Am Latin America   Mex Mexico

burn
1 *noun*
  a burn = una quemadura
2 *verb*
  • **to burn** = quemar
  to burn garbage = quemar basura
  to burn one's fingers = quemarse los dedos
  • (*when cooking*)
  I've burnt the toast = se me quemaron las
  tostadas
  • **a burning building** = un edificio en llamas
burn down = incendiar
  the house burned down = la casa se
  incendió

burst *verb*
  = reventar
  to burst a balloon = reventar un globo
  the pipe burst = la cañería se reventó
  • **to burst into tears** = echarse a llorar
  • **to burst into a room** = irrumpir en un
  cuarto
burst out
  to burst out laughing = echarse a reír

bury *verb*
  = enterrar

bus *noun*
  a bus = un autobús, un bus, un camión
  (*C Am, Mex*)

bush *noun*
  a bush = un arbusto

business *noun*
  • (*commercial activities*)
  business = negocios (*masculine*)
  she has gone to London on business = fue
  a Londres por negocios
  • (*a company*)
  a business = un negocio
  • (*a trade or profession*)
  the insurance business = el negocio de los
  seguros
  the hotel business = la industria hotelera
  • (*matters that concern a person*)
  that's my business = eso es asunto mío
  it's none of your business = no te metas en
  lo que no te importa

businessman *noun*
  a businessman = un hombre de negocios

businesswoman *noun*
  a businesswoman = una mujer de
  negocios

bus stop *noun*
  a bus stop = una parada, un paradero (*Lat
  Am*)

busy *adjective*
  • (*occupied*) = ocupado/ocupada
  • (*full of activity*)
  he leads a very busy life = tiene una vida
  muy ajetreada
  • (*full of people or traffic*)
  the town is very busy on Saturdays = los
  sábados hay mucho movimiento en la
  ciudad
  a busy market = un mercado muy
  concurrido
  • (*if it's a phone*) (*US English*)
  to be busy = estar ocupado, estar
  comunicando (*Spa*)

but
1 *conjunction* = pero
  not one but two = no uno sino dos
2 *preposition*
  we have nothing to drink but water = no
  tenemos nada que beber salvo agua
  they invited everyone but Tom = invitaron
  a todos menos a Tom

butcher *noun*
  a butcher = un carnicero/una carnicera

butter *noun*
  butter = mantequilla (*feminine*), manteca
  (*feminine*) (*R Pl*)

butterfly *noun*
  a butterfly = una mariposa

button *noun*
  a button = un botón

buy *verb*
  = comprar
  he bought me a book = me compró un
  libro

buzz *verb*
  (*if it's a bee, fly etc*) = zumbar

by *preposition*
  • **we entered by the back door** = entramos
  por la puerta trasera
  he was bitten by a dog = lo mordió un
  perro
  to pay by check = pagar con cheque
  • **by oneself** = solo/sola
  she did it by herself = lo hizo sola
  • (*by means of*)
  to travel by bus = viajar en autobús
  we went there by bicycle = fuimos allí en
  bicicleta
  • (*beside*)
  it's by the door = está al lado de la puerta
  by the sea = junto al mar
  • (*used to indicate the painter or author*) = de
  a book by Charles Dickens = un libro de
  Charles Dickens.
  • (*when talking about time*)
  will it be ready by five o'clock? = ¿estará
  listo para las cinco?
  he should be here by now = ya debería
  estar aquí

- (*indicating an amount, a rate*)
  to increase by 20% = subir en un veinte
    por ciento
  to pay by the hour = pagar por hora
- (*in measurements*) = por
  20 meters by 20 meters = 20 metros por 20
    metros

cab *noun*
  a cab = un taxi

cabbage *noun*
  a cabbage = un repollo, una col (*Mex, Spa*)

cabin *noun*
- (*in a boat*)
  a cabin = un camarote
- (*in a plane*)
  a cabin = una cabina
- (*a house made of wood*)
  a cabin = una cabaña

cable *noun*
  a cable = un cable

cable TV *noun*
  cable TV = televisión por cable (*feminine*),
    cablevisión (*feminine*) (*Lat Am*)

café *noun*
  a café = un café

cage *noun*
  a cage = una jaula

cake *noun*
  a cake = un pastel, una tarta (*Spa*), una
    torta (*SC*)

calculator *noun*
  a calculator = una calculadora

calendar *noun*
  a calendar = un calendario

calf *noun*
- (*a young cow*)
  a calf = un ternero/una ternera
- (*part of the leg*)
  the calf = la pantorrilla

call
1 *verb*
- (*to name*) = llamar
  he's called Philip = se llama Philip
- (*to describe as*)
  he called me a liar = me llamó mentiroso
- (*to call out to*) = llamar
- (*to telephone*)
  to call someone = llamar a alguien

- (*to summon*) = llamar
  to call a taxi = llamar un taxi
- (*to arrange*)
  to call a meeting = convocar una reunión
- (*to pay a visit*) = pasar
- (*to stop en route*)
  the train calls at Reading = el tren para en
    Reading
2 *noun*
  a call = una llamada
  to give someone a call = llamar a alguien
call back
- (*to return*) = volver a pasar
- (*to phone back*) = volver a llamar
call off = suspender
call on
  (*to visit*)
  to call on someone = pasar a visitar a
    alguien
call up = llamar (por teléfono)

call box *noun* (*British English*)
  a call box = una cabina telefónica

calm
1 *adjective*
  she's a very calm person = es una persona
    muy tranquila
  keep calm! = ¡calma!
2 *noun*
  calm = calma (*feminine*)
3 *verb*
- **to calm someone** = calmar a alguien
- (*to become less violent*) = calmarse
  calm down = calmarse

camel *noun*
  a camel = un camello

camera *noun*
- (*for taking photographs*)
  a camera = una cámara, una máquina
    fotográfica
- (*in TV studio*)
  a (television) camera = una cámara

camp
1 *noun*
- (*group of tents, huts*)
  a camp = un campamento
  a holiday camp = una colonia de
    vacaciones
2 *verb* = acampar
  to go camping = ir de camping

campsite *noun*
  a campsite = un camping

can[1] *verb*
- (*to have the ability*) = poder
  can you come? = ¿puedes venir?
- (*with verbs of perception*)
  I can hear you better now = ahora te oigo
    mejor
  can they see us? = ¿nos ven?

! *When talking about seeing, hearing, and understanding, you do not translate* can
- (*to be allowed*) = poder
  can I smoke? = ¿puedo fumar?
- (*to know how to*) = saber
  she can swim = sabe nadar
  can you speak German? = ¿sabes (hablar) alemán?
- (*when asking, offering or suggesting*) = poder
  can I help you? = ¿te puedo ayudar?

can² *noun*
  a can = una lata, un bote (*Spa*)

Canada *noun* ▶ **p. 187**
  Canada = (el) Canadá

Canadian ▶ **p. 187**
1 *noun*
  a Canadian = un/una canadiense
2 *adjective* = canadiense

canal *noun*
  a canal = un canal

cancel *verb*
  = cancelar

cancer *noun*
- (*the disease*)
  cancer = cáncer (*masculine*)
- (*the sign*)
  Cancer = Cáncer
  I'm Cancer = soy Cáncer, soy de Cáncer
- (*a person*)
  a Cancer = un/una cáncer

candle *noun*
- (*in a room, restaurant, on a cake*)
  a candle = una vela
- (*in a church*)
  a candle = un cirio, una veladera (*Mex*)

candy *noun* (*US English*)
- (*confectionery*)
  candy = golosinas (*feminine plural*)
- (*a sweet*)
  a candy = un caramelo, un dulce (*Mex*)

canoe *noun*
  a canoe = una canoa

can opener *noun*
  a can opener = un abrelatas

cap *noun*
- (*with a peak*)
  a cap = una gorra
- (*for a pen, marker, bottle*)
  a cap = una tapa

capable *adjective*
  = capaz
  to be capable of = ser capaz de
  to be capable of doing something = ser capaz de hacer algo

capital
1 *noun*
- (*money, wealth*)
  capital = capital (*masculine*)
- (*a city*)
  the capital = la capital
- (*a letter*)
  a capital = una mayúscula
2 *adjective*
  a capital letter = una letra mayúscula

Capricorn *noun*
- (*the sign*)
  Capricorn = Capricornio
  I'm Capricorn = soy Capricornio, soy de Capricornio
- (*a person*)
  a Capricorn = un/una capricornio

capsize *verb*
  = volcarse

captain *noun*
- (*of a ship, sports team*)
  the captain = el capitán/la capitana
- (*of an airplane*)
  the captain = el/la comandante

capture *verb*
  = capturar

car *noun*
- **a car** = un coche, un carro (*Lat Am*), un auto (*SC*)
- (*American English—of a train*)
  a car = un vagón

caravan *noun* (*British English*)
  a caravan = una caravana, un rulot (*Spa*), una casa rodante (*SC*)

card *noun*
- (*for greetings, correspondence*)
  a card = una tarjeta
- (*for playing games*)
  a card = una carta

care
1 *noun*
  care = cuidado (*masculine*)
  to take care crossing the street = tener cuidado al cruzar la calle
  to take care of the children = cuidar a los niños
2 *verb*
  I don't care = me da igual
  to care about someone/something = preocuparse por alguien/algo

career *noun*
  a career = una carrera

careful *adjective*
  (*cautious*) = cuidadoso/cuidadosa, prudente
  to be careful = tener cuidado

careless *adjective*
  to be careless = ser descuidado/descuidada

C

carousel *noun*
* (*a merry-go-round*)
  a carousel = unos caballitos, un carrusel
  (*Lat Am*), una calesita (*R Pl*), un tiovivo
  (*Spa*)
* (*for baggage*)
  a carousel = una cinta transportadora, un
  carrusel (*Spa*)

car park *noun* (*British English*)
  a car park = un aparcamiento, un
  estacionamiento (*Spa*)

carpenter *noun*
  a carpenter = un carpintero/una carpintera

carpet *noun*
* (*covering the entire floor*)
  a carpet = una alfombra (de pared a pared),
  una moqueta (*Spa*), una moquette (*R Pl*)
* (*a mat*)
  a carpet = una alfombra, un tapete (*Mex*)

carriage *noun*
* (*horse-drawn*)
  a carriage = un carruaje, un coche
* (*British English—of a train*)
  a carriage = un vagón

carrot *noun*
  a carrot = una zanahoria

carry *verb*
* (*to hold*) = llevar
* (*to move*)
  to carry the baggage upstairs = subir el
  equipaje
  to carry the boxes downstairs = bajar las
  cajas

carry on
* (*to continue*) = seguir
  carry on working, carry on with your work
  = sigue trabajando

cartoon *noun*
  (*a movie*)
  a cartoon = unos dibujos animados

case¹ *noun*
  it's raining? in that case I'm taking a taxi =
  ¿llueve? en ese caso voy a tomar un taxi
  in case = por si
  keep the rest in case you need it later =
  guarda el resto por si la necesitas más
  tarde

case² *noun*
* (*a suitcase*)
  a case = una maleta, una petaca (*Mex*),
  una valija (*R P*)
* (*for glasses*)
  a case = un estuche
* (*a crate*)
  a case = una caja

cash
1 *noun*
  cash = dinero en efectivo (*masculine*)
2 *verb* = cobrar

cash desk *noun* (*British English*)
  a cash desk = una caja

cassette *noun*
  a cassette = una cinta, un/una cassette

cassette player *noun*
  a cassette player = un pasacintas, un
  cassette (*Spa*)

castle *noun*
  a castle = un castillo

cat *noun*
  a cat = un gato/una gata

catch *verb*
* (*to capture*)
  to catch a fish = pescar un pez
  to catch a rabbit = atrapar un conejo
  to catch a thief = pillar a un ladrón, agarrar
  a un ladrón, coger a un ladrón (*Spa*)
* (*to take hold of*) = agarrar, coger (*Spa*)
  to catch the ball = agarrar la pelota, coger
  la pelota (*spa*)
* (*to trap, snag*)
  he caught his finger in the door = se pilló
  el dedo en la puerta, se agarró el dedo en
  la puerta (*Lat Am*)
* (*to get or take*)
  to catch the plane to Madrid = tomar *or*
  (*Spa*) coger el avión a Madrid
* (*to take by surprise*)
  to catch someone stealing = pillar a
  alguien robando, coger a alguien
  robando (*Spa*)
* (*to hear*) = oír
* to catch flu = contagiarse de gripe
  to catch a cold = resfriarse

catch up
  you'll have to work very hard to catch up =
  tendrás que trabajar mucho para ponerte
  al día
  to catch up with someone = alcanzar a
  alguien

caterpillar *noun*
  a caterpillar = una oruga, un azotador
  (*Mex*)

cathedral *noun*
  a cathedral = una catedral

cattle *noun*
  cattle = ganado (*masculine*)

cauliflower *noun*
  a cauliflower = una coliflor

cause
1 *noun*
  (*of an accident, a death*)
  the cause = la causa
2 *verb*
  = causar

cautious *adjective*
  = cauteloso/cautelosa

cave *noun*
a cave = una cueva

CD *noun*
a CD = un disco compacto, un compact-disc

CD player *noun*
a CD player = un (reproductor de) compact-disc

ceiling *noun*
a ceiling = un techo

celebrate *verb*
= celebrar, festejar

celery *noun*
celery = apio (*masculine*)

cell *noun*
(*in a prison*)
a cell = una celda

cellar *noun*
a cellar = un sótano

cement *noun*
cement = cemento (*masculine*)

cemetery *noun*
a cemetery = un cementerio

center (*US English*), **centre** (*British English*) *noun*
• (*a place for meetings, activities*)
a center = un centro
• (*the middle*)
the center = el centro

centimeter (*American English*), **centimetre** (*British English*) *noun*
a centimeter = un centímetro

central heating *noun*
central heating = calefacción central (*feminine*)

centre *noun* (*British English*) ▶ center

century *noun* ▶ p. 192
a century = un siglo

certain *adjective*
• (*sure*) = seguro/segura
no-one knows for certain = nadie lo sabe con seguridad
• (*particular*) = cierto/cierta
they only open on certain days = sólo abren ciertos días

certainly *adverb*
will you be able to help us?—certainly = ¿podrás ayudarnos?—desde luego

certificate *noun*
a certificate = un certificado

chain *noun*
• a chain = una cadena

• (*a series of shops*)
a chain = una cadena

chair *noun*
a chair = una silla

chalk *noun*
chalk = tiza (*feminine*)

champagne *noun*
champagne = champán (*masculine*), champaña (*feminine*)

champion *noun*
a champion = un campeón/una campeona

championship *noun*
a championship = un campeonato

chance *noun*
• (*likelihood*)
a chance = una posibilidad
there is a chance that she'll agree = es posible que acepte

! *Note the use of the subjunctive after* es posible que

• (*an opportunity*)
a chance = una oportunidad
to have the chance to travel abroad = tener la oportunidad de viajar al extranjero
• by chance = por casualidad

change
1 *noun*
a change = un cambio
• (*a different experience*)
let's go to the cinema for a change = vamos al cine para variar
• (*cash*)
change = cambio (*masculine*), sencillo (*masculine*) (*Lat Am*), feria (*feminine*) (*Mex*)
2 *verb*
• (*to become different, make different*) = cambiar
to change color = cambiar de color
• (*to replace*) = cambiar
to change a tire = cambiar un neumático
• (*to exchange in a shop*) = cambiar
• (*to switch*) = cambiar de
I'd like to change jobs = quisiera cambiar de trabajo
• (*when talking about one's clothes*) = cambiarse
to get changed = cambiarse
• (*when using transport*) = cambiar
• (*when dealing with foreign currency*) = cambiar

changing room *noun* (*British English*)
• (*in a swimming pool, sports center*)
a changing room = un vestuario, un vestidor (*Mex*)
• (*in a store*)
a changing room = un probador

channel *noun*
(*a TV station*)
a channel = un canal

Channel *noun*
the (English) Channel = el Canal de la
Mancha

Channel Tunnel *noun*
the Channel Tunnel = el Eurotúnel

chapter *noun*
a chapter = un capítulo

character *noun*
(*in a book, play or film*)
a character = un personaje

charge
1 *verb*
• (*to ask a price or payment*)
to charge someone for delivery = cobrarle
a alguien por la entrega
they'll charge you for the gasoline = te
cobrarán la gasolina
• (*to run*)
the bull charged at us = el toro arremetió
contra nosotros
2 *noun*
• (*a price or fee*)
a charge = un cobro
• in charge
who is the person in charge? = ¿quién es
el/la responsable?
she's in charge of the organization = está a
cargo de la organización

charming *adjective*
= encantador/encantadora

charter flight *noun*
a charter flight = un vuelo chárter

chase *verb*
= perseguir

chat
1 *verb* = charlar, conversar (*Lat Am*), platicar
(*Mex*)
2 *noun*
a chat = una charla, una conversación (*Lat
Am*), una plática (*Mex*)

cheap *adjective*
= barato/barata

cheat
1 *verb* = hacer trampa(s)
2 *noun*
a cheat = un tramposo/una tramposa

check
1 *verb*
• (*to verify*) = comprobar
• (*to inspect*) = revisar
2 *noun*
• (*an inspection for quality, security*)
a check = una revisión

• (*US English—a bill*)
the check = la cuenta, la adición (*R Pl*)
• (*US English—in banking*)
a check = un cheque
check in
• (*at the airport*) = facturar el equipaje,
chequear el equipaje (*Lat Am*)
• (*at a hotel*) = registrarse
check out
to check out of the hotel = irse del hotel

checkbook *noun* (*US English*)
a checkbook = una chequera, un talonario
(de cheques) (*Spa*)

checkers *noun* (*US English*) ▶ **p. 306**
checkers = damas (*feminine plural*)

checkout *noun*
a checkout = una caja

checkup *noun*
a checkup = un chequeo
to have a checkup = hacerse un chequeo

cheek *noun* ▶ **p. 235**
(*part of the body*)
the cheek = la mejilla

cheeky *adjective*
= descarado/descarada

cheerful *adjective*
= alegre

cheese *noun*
cheese = queso (*masculine*)

chef *noun*
a chef = un jefe/una jefa de cocina

chemist *noun*
(*British English—in a shop*)
a chemist = un farmacéutico/una
farmacéutica
a chemist's = una farmacia

chemistry *noun*
chemistry = química (*feminine*)

cheque *noun* (*British English*)
a cheque = un cheque

chequebook *noun* (*British English*)
a chequebook = una chequera, un
talonario (de cheques) (*Spa*)

cherry *noun*
a cherry = una cereza

chess *noun* ▶ **p. 306**
chess = ajedrez (*masculine*)

chest *noun* ▶ **p. 235**
(*part of the body*)
the chest = el pecho

chestnut
1 *noun*
a chestnut = una castaña

2 adjective ▶ **p. 183**
= castaño/castaña

chest of drawers noun
a chest of drawers = una cómoda

chew verb
to chew food = masticar la comida
to chew gum = mascar chicle

chewing gum noun
chewing gum = chicle (masculine)

chicken noun
• (the bird)
a chicken = un pollo
• (the meat)
chicken = pollo (masculine)

child noun
• a child = un niño/una niña
a group of children = un grupo de niños
• (a son or daughter)
a child = un hijo/una hija
have you any children? = ¿tiene hijos?

chilly adjective
= frío/fría

chimney noun
a chimney = una chimenea

chin noun ▶ **p. 235**
the chin = la barbilla

china noun
china = loza (feminine)
(fine china) = porcelana (feminine)

China noun ▶ **p. 187**
China = (la) China

Chinese ▶ **p. 187, p. 245**
1 adjective = chino/china
a Chinese (man/woman) = un chino/una
china
2 noun
• (the language)
Chinese = chino (masculine)
• (the people)
the Chinese = los chinos

chips noun
• (US English—in packet)
chips = papas fritas (feminine plural) (Lat
Am), patatas fritas (feminine plural) (Spa)
• (British English—French fries)
chips = papas fritas (feminine plural) (Lat
Am), patatas fritas (feminine plural) (Spa)

chocolate noun
chocolate = chocolate (masculine)
a chocolate = un bombón, un chocolate
(Lat Am)

choice noun
• (an option)
a choice = una elección
we had no choice = no tuvimos más
remedio

• (a selection)
a choice = un surtido, una selección

choir noun
a choir = un coro

choke
1 verb
to choke = asfixiarse
to choke someone = estrangular a alguien
2 noun
(of a car)
the choke = el choke, el estárter, el
ahogador (Mex), el cebador (R Pl)

choose verb
= elegir, escoger

chore noun
a chore = una tarea

christen verb
= bautizar

Christian name noun
a Christian name = un nombre de pila

Christmas noun
Christmas = Navidad (feminine)
Christmas (Day) = el día de Navidad
Merry Christmas! = ¡Feliz Navidad!

Christmas carol noun
a Christmas carol = un villancico

Christmas Eve noun
Christmas Eve = Nochebuena (feminine)

church noun
a church = una iglesia

cigarette noun
a cigarette = un cigarrillo

cigarette lighter noun
a cigarette lighter = un encendedor, un
mechero (Spa)

cinema noun
a cinema = un cine

circle noun
a circle = un círculo

circumstances noun
circumstances = circunstancias (feminine
plural)
under the circumstances = dadas las
circunstancias

circus noun
a circus = un circo

citizen noun
• (of a country)
a citizen = un ciudadano/una ciudadana
• (of a city or town)
a citizen = un/una habitante

city noun
a city = una ciudad

civilized *adjective*
= civilizado/civilizada

civil servant *noun*
a civil servant = un empleado público/una
empleada pública, un funcionario/una
funcionaria (del Estado)

clap
1 *verb* = aplaudir
2 *noun*
• (*applause*)
to give someone a clap = aplaudir a
alguien
• a clap of thunder = un trueno

clarinet *noun*
a clarinet = un clarinete

class *noun*
• (*a group of students*)
a class = una clase
• (*a lesson*)
a class = una clase
• (*a group of people in society*)
a social class = una clase social

classical *adjective*
= clásico/clásica

classroom *noun*
a classroom = un aula (*feminine*), una
clase

claw *noun*
a claw (*of a cat, tiger*) = una garra
(*of a crab, lobster*) = una pinza

clay *noun*
clay = arcilla (*feminine*)

clean
1 *adjective* = limpio/limpia
2 *verb* = limpiar
to have a jacket cleaned = hacer limpiar
una chaqueta
clean up = limpiar
to clean up after someone = limpiar lo que
ensucia alguien

clear
1 *adjective*
• (*easy to understand, making sense*)
= claro/clara
• (*obvious*)
it is clear that no one is happy = está claro
que nadie está contento
• (*easy to see or hear*)
the photo is not very clear = la foto no está
muy nítida
she has a clear voice = tiene una voz clara
• (*transparent*) = transparente
• (*with no rain or cloud*) =
despejado/despejada
• (*free, not blocked—if it's a road or space*)
= despejado/despejada

• (*free from spots*)
she has very clear skin = tiene muy buen
cutis
2 *verb*
• (*to remove obstacles, to empty*)
to clear the table = levantar la mesa, quitar
la mesa (*Spa*)
to clear the building = desalojar el edificio
to clear the snow off the road = quitar la
nieve del camino
can you clear your books out of the way?
= ¿puedes quitar los libros de en medio?
to clear one's throat = carraspear
clear away
to clear away the books and toys = recoger
los libros y los juguetes
clear up
• if the weather clears up, we'll go out = si
despeja, saldremos
• to clear up the kitchen = arreglar la cocina

clever *adjective*
• (*intelligent*) = inteligente
to be clever at mathematics = ser
bueno/buena para las matemáticas
• (*smart*) = ingenioso/ingeniosa
a clever idea = una idea ingeniosa
• (*skillful*) = hábil

client *noun*
a client = un/una cliente

climate *noun*
a climate = un clima

climb *verb*
to climb (up) a tree = trepar a un árbol
we climbed to the top = subimos hasta la
parte de arriba
to climb a mountain = escalar una montaña
to climb over a wall = pasar por encima de
una pared

clinic *noun*
• (*in state hospital*)
a clinic = un consultorio
• (*private hospital*)
a clinic = una clínica

cloakroom *noun*
(*for coats*)
a cloakroom = un guardarropa

clock *noun*
a clock = un reloj

close¹
1 *adjective*
• (*near*) = próximo/próxima, cercano/cercana
• (*as a friend or relation*)
a close relation = un pariente cercano
he's a close friend = es un amigo íntimo
• it's very close today = está muy pesado hoy
2 *adverb*
the station is very close = la estación está
muy cerca
to live close (by) = vivir muy cerca
come closer, I can't see you = acércate,
que no te veo

• **close to** (*when talking about location*) = cerca de
• **close to** (*when talking about a situation*)
  to be close to tears = estar a punto de llorar

**close² ** *verb*
= cerrar
close down = cerrar

closed *adjective*
= cerrado/cerrada

closet *noun* (*US English*)
  (*a cupboard*)
  a closet = un armario, un placard (*R Pl*)
  (*for clothes*)
  a closet = un armario, un closet (*Lat Am*), un placard (*R Pl*)

cloth *noun*
• (*material*)
  cloth = tela (*feminine*)
• (*for household use*)
  a cloth = un trapo

clothes *noun*
  clothes = ropa (*feminine*)

cloud *noun*
  a cloud = una nube

cloudy *adjective*
= nublado

clown *noun*
  a clown = un payaso/una payasa

club *noun*
• (*an association*)
  a club = un club
• (*a nightclub*)
  a club = un club nocturno
• (*for playing golf*)
  a club = un palo de golf

clue *noun*
• (*in an investigation*)
  a clue = una pista
• (*in a crossword*)
  a clue = una clave

clumsy *adjective*
= torpe

coach
1 *noun*
• (*British English—a bus*)
  a coach = un autobús, un autocar (*Spa*), un ómnibus (*R Pl*)
• (*a person in charge of training*)
  a coach = un entrenador/una entrenadora
• (*British English—of a train*)
  a coach = un vagón
2 *verb* = entrenar

coal *noun*
  coal = carbón (*masculine*)

coat *noun*
• (*a garment*)
  a coat (*for men*) = un abrigo, un sobretodo (*R Pl*), (*for women*) = un abrigo, un tapado (*R Pl*)
• (*of an animal*)
  the coat = el pelaje
• **a coat of paint/dust** = una capa de pintura/polvo

coat hanger *noun*
  a coat hanger = una percha

cobweb *noun*
  a cobweb = una telaraña

cocktail *noun*
  a cocktail = un cóctel

cocoa *noun*
  (*the drink*)
  cocoa = chocolate (*masculine*), cocoa (*feminine*) (*Lat Am*)

coconut *noun*
  a coconut = un coco

coffee *noun*
• (*the product*)
  coffee = café (*masculine*)
• (*a cup of coffee*)
  a coffee = un café

coffin *noun*
  a coffin = un ataúd, un cajón (*Lat Am*)

coin *noun*
  a coin = una moneda

coincidence *noun*
  a coincidence = una casualidad, una coincidencia

Coke® *noun*
• (*the product*)
  Coke® = Coca-Cola® (*feminine*)
• (*a glass or can of Coke®*)
  a coke = una Coca-Cola®

cold
1 *adjective* = frío/fría
  to be cold, to feel cold = tener frío
  I am very cold = tengo mucho frío
  it's cold in the classroom = hace frío en el aula
  you'll get cold if you don't come in = te vas a enfriar si no entras
2 *noun*
• (*lack of heat*)
  the cold = el frío
• (*illness*)
  a cold = un resfriado, un constipado (*Spa*), un resfrío (*SC*)
  to have a cold = estar resfriado

collapse *verb*
= derrumbarse
  the building collapsed = el edificio de derrumbó
  she collapsed onto the floor = cayó desplomada al suelo

R Pl River Plate area   **SC** Southern Cone   **Spa** Spain

collar *noun*
* (*on a shirt or jacket*)
  a collar = un cuello
* (*for a pet*)
  a collar = un collar

colleague *noun*
  a colleague = un/una colega

collect *verb*
* (*to gather*)
  to collect information = reunir información
* (*to make a collection of*) = coleccionar,
  juntar (*Lat Am*)
  he collects stamps = colecciona
  estampillas, junta estampillas
* (*to pick up*) = recoger
  will you come and collect us? = ¿vendrás a
  recogernos?
* (*to take away*) = recoger
  they collect the mail at midday = recogen el
  correo al mediodía

collection *noun*
* (*a set of collected objects*)
  a collection = una colección
* (*money collected for charity, in church*)
  a collection = una colecta

college *noun*
* (*university*)
  a college = una universidad
* (*for vocational training*)
  a college = una escuela, un instituto

collide *verb*
  to collide (**with someone/something**) =
  chocar (con alguien/algo)

collision *noun*
  a collision = un choque

color (*US English*), **colour** (*British
English*)
1 *noun* ▶ **p. 183**
  a color = un color
  what color is the car? = ¿de qué color es el
  coche?
2 *verb* = colorear

color film (*US English*), **colour film**
(*British English*) *noun*
  a color film = una película de color

colorful (*US English*), **colourful** (*British
English*) *adjective*
  = de colores muy vivos

color television (*US English*), **colour
television** (*British English*) *noun*
  a color television = una televisión en
  colores, una televisión en color (*Spa*)

comb
1 *noun*
  a comb = un peine

2 *verb*
  to comb one's hair = peinarse

come *verb*
* to come = venir
  I'm coming! = ¡ya voy!
  be careful when you come down the stairs
  = ten cuidado al bajar la escalera
  he won't come into the house = no entrará
  en la casa, no entrará a la casa (*Lat Am*)
  he's coming for me at 10 o'clock = me
  viene a buscar a las 10
* (*to reach*)
  turn left when you come to the traffic lights
  = doble a la izquierda cuando llegue al
  semáforo
* (*to attend*)
  will you be able to come to the meeting? =
  ¿podrá venir a la reunión?
* (*to be a native or product of*)
  she comes from Italy = es italiana
  the strawberries all come from Spain =
  todas las fresas vienen de España
* (*referring to a position in a contest*)
  to come first = llegar el primero/la primera
come around
  (*to visit*) = venir
  they're coming around for dinner this
  evening = vienen a cenar esta tarde
come back = volver, regresar
come down
* (*descend*) = bajar
* (*to be reduced*) = bajar
come in
* (*to enter*) = entrar
* (*to arrive*) = llegar
  the train comes in at 5 o'clock = el tren
  llega a las 5
come off
  a button came off my jacket = se le cayó un
  botón a la chaqueta
come on
* (*to start to work*) = encenderse
* (*when encouraging someone*)
  come on, hurry up! = ¡vamos, date prisa!
come out
* (*to go out*) = salir
* (*to become available*) = salir
  the magazine comes out every month = la
  revista sale todos los meses
* (*to fall out*)
  one of my contact lenses came out = se
  me cayó uno de los lentes de contacto
* (*to wash out*) = salir
* (*be revealed*) = revelarse, salir a la luz
come round (*British English*) ▶ **come
around**
come to
  (*to amount to*)
  the meal came to 25 dollars = la comida
  costó 25 dólares
come up
* (*ascend*) = subir
  to come up to someone = acercársele a
  alguien

>te all

Colors

Adjectives

There are no significant differences between Spanish and English as regards the uses of adjectives of color.

what color is it/are they? ¿de qué color es/son?
it's blue es azul
it's a blue dress es un vestido azul

Nouns

In Spanish the names of colors are all masculine. They always preceded by the definite article:

I prefer blue prefiero **el** azul
blue doesn't go with brown **el** azul no combina con **el** marrón

When it follows a preposition:

do you have it in blue? ¿lo tienen **en** azul?
she was dressed in blue estaba vestida **de** azul
the man in blue el hombre **de** azul

When talking about shades of color:

deep/dark blue azul intenso/oscuro
a light blue hat un sombrero azul claro

• (*to occur*)
something came up and I couldn't go = surgió algo y no pude ir

comfortable *adjective*
= cómodo/cómoda

comforter *noun* (*American English*)
a comforter = un edredón

commercial
1 *adjective* = comercial
2 *noun*
a commercial = un anuncio, una aviso (*Lat Am*)

commit *verb*
• (*to carry out*)
to commit a crime = cometer un delito
to commit suicide = suicidarse
• **to commit oneself** = comprometerse

common
1 *adjective*
• (*widespread*) = común
it's a common problem = es un problema común
2 *noun*
in common = en común
we have nothing in common = no tenemos nada en común

communicate *verb*
= comunicarse

community *noun*
a community = una comunidad

company *noun*
• (*a business*)
a company = una compañía, una empresa
• (*the presence of other people*)
company = compañía (*feminine*)

compare *verb*
= comparar
to compare Spain with Italy = comparar España con Italia
compared with, compared to = comparado/comparada con, en comparación con

compartment *noun*
a compartment = un compartimento

compass *noun*
a compass = una brújula

competition *noun*
• (*rivalry*)
competition = competencia (*feminine*)
• (*rival people or products*)
the competition = la competencia
• (*a contest*)
a competition (*sporting*) = una competencia, una competición (*Spa*), (*non-sporting*) = un concurso

complain *verb*
= quejarse
to complain about the noise = quejarse por el ruido

complete
1 *adjective*
(*total*)

it was a complete disaster = fue un desastre total
this is a complete waste of time = esto es una absoluta pérdida de tiempo
2 *verb*
• (*to finish*) = terminar, acabar
• (*to fill in*) = llenar
to complete a form = llenar un formulario

completely *adverb*
= completamente

complicate *verb*
= complicar

complicated *adjective*
= complicado/complicada

compliment
1 *noun*
a compliment = un cumplido
2 *verb*
to compliment someone = felicitar a alguien

comprehensive (**school**) *noun*
(*British English*)
a comprehensive (**school**) = un instituto de enseñanza secundaria

compulsory *adjective*
= obligatorio/obligatoria

computer *noun*
a computer = una computadora (*Lat Am*), un computador (*Lat Am*), un ordenador (*Spa*)

computing *noun*
computing = informática (*feminine*), computación (*feminine*)

concentrate *verb*
(*to pay attention*) = concentrarse

concerned *adjective*
• (*anxious*) = preocupado/preocupada
to be concerned about someone = estar preocupado/preocupada por alguien
• (*involved*)
to be concerned with something = ocuparse de algo

concert *noun*
a concert = un concierto

concrete *noun*
concrete = hormigón (*masculine*), concreto (*masculine*) (*Lat Am*)

condemn *verb*
• (*to sentence*)
to condemn someone to death = condenar a alguien a muerte
• (*to censure*)
= condenar

condition *noun*
• (*physical state*)
condition = estado (*masculine*), condiciones (*feminine plural*)
the car is in good condition = el coche está en buen estado, el coche está en buenas condiciones
• **on condition that** = con la condición de que
you can go on condition that her parents bring you home = pudes ir con la condición de que sus padres te traigan a casa

> **!** *Note the use of the subjunctive after* con la condición de que

conductor *noun*
• (*of an orchestra*)
a conductor = un director/una directora de orquesta
• (*a bus conductor*)
a conductor = un cobrador/una cobradora

cone *noun*
• (*the shape*)
a cone = un cono
• (*for ice-cream*)
a cone = un cucurucho, un barquillo (*Mex*)

confectionery *noun*
confectionery = productos de confitería (*masculine*)

conference *noun*
• (*for business, for academics*)
a conference = una conferencia
• (*of a political party*)
a conference = un congreso

confidence *noun*
• (*trust*)
confidence = confianza (*feminine*)
to have confidence in someone = tener confianza en alguien
• (*self-confidence*)
confidence = confianza en sí mismo/misma (*feminine*)

confident *adjective*
(*self-confident*) = seguro/segura de sí mismo/misma

confidential *adjective*
= confidencial

conflict *noun*
a conflict = un conflicto

confused *adjective*
to get confused = confundirse
I'm confused = estoy confundido/confundida

confusing *adjective*
= confuso/confusa

congratulate *verb*
= felicitar

congratulations *noun*
  congratulations! = ¡enhorabuena!,
  ¡felicitaciones! (*Lat Am*)

connection *noun*
* (*a link between events, statements*)
  a connection = una conexión
* (*in travel*)
  I missed my connection = perdí la
  conexión, perdí la combinación

conquer *verb*
  = conquistar

conscious *adjective*
* (*awake*) = consciente
* (*aware*) = consciente

consequence *noun*
  a consequence = una consecuencia

considerate *adjective*
  = atento/atenta

consideration *noun*
  to take something into consideration =
  tomar algo en cuenta

construct *verb*
  = construir

consult *verb*
  = consultar

contact
1 *noun*
  contact = contacto (*masculine*)
  to be in contact with someone = estar en
  contacto con alguien
2 *verb* = ponerse en contacto con

contact lens *noun*
  a contact lens = un lente de contacto (*Lat
  Am*), una lentilla (*Spa*)

contain *verb*
  = contener

container *noun*
  a container = un recipiente

content *adjective*
  to be content with something =
  contentarse con algo

contents *noun*
* (*of a bag, box, jar*)
  the contents = el contenido
* (*of a book*)
  the contents = el índice de materias

contest *noun*
  a contest (*sporting*) = una competencia,
  una competición (*Spa*), (*non-sporting*) =
  un concurso

continent *noun*
  (*large mass of land*)
  a continent = un continente

continental quilt *noun* (*British English*)
  a continental quilt = un edredón

continue *verb*
  = continuar, seguir
  to continue to talk, to continue talking =
  continuar hablando, seguir hablando

continuous *adjective*
  = continuo/continua

contraceptive *noun*
  a contraceptive = un anticonceptivo

contract
1 *noun*
  a contract = un contrato
2 *verb* = contraerse

contradict *verb*
  = contradecir

contradiction *noun*
  a contradiction = una contradicción

contrast *noun*
  a contrast = un contraste

contribute *verb*
* (*to give money*) = contribuir
* (*to participate*)
  to contribute to a discussion = participar
  en una discusión

control
1 *noun*
  to be in control of an organization = dirigir
  una organización
  to lose control of a car = perder el control
  de un coche
  she lost control and started shouting =
  perdió el control y empezó a gritar
2 *verb*
  (*to be in charge of*)
  to control a region = controlar una región
  to control traffic = dirigir el tráfico

convenient *adjective*
* (*useful, practical*) = práctico/práctica
  it's more convenient to take the bus = es
  más práctico tomar el autobús
* (*suitable*) = conveniente
  it's a convenient place to meet = es un
  lugar conveniente para encontrarse

conversation *noun*
  a conversation = una conversación

convince *verb*
  = convencer

cook
1 *verb*
* (*to prepare food*)
  I like to cook = me gusta cocinar
  to cook a meal = preparar una comida
  to cook the vegetables = preparar las
  verduras
* (*to be cooked in the oven*) = hacerse
2 *noun*
  a cook = un cocinero/una cocinera

C

cookbook *noun*
a cookbook = un libro de cocina

cooker *noun* (*British English*)
a cooker = una cocina, una estufa (*Mex*)

cookery book *noun* (*British English*)
a cookery book = un libro de cocina

cookie *noun* (*US English*)
a cookie = una galleta, una galletita (*R Pl*)

cooking *noun*
cooking = cocina (*feminine*)
to do the cooking = cocinar

cool
1 *adjective*
• (*fresh, not hot*) = fresco/fresca
it's much cooler today = hace mucho más
fresco hoy, está mucho más fresco hoy
a cool drink = una bebida fresca
• (*calm*) = tranquilo/tranquila
stay cool! = ¡tranquilo!
2 *verb*
leave the soup to cool = dejar enfriar la
sopa
cool down
• (*to get colder*) = enfriarse
• (*to calm down*) = calmarse

cooperate *verb*
= cooperar

cope *verb*
how do you cope without a washing
machine? = ¿cómo te las arreglas sin
lavadora?
I can't cope = no puedo más

copper *noun*
(*the metal*)
copper = cobre (*masculine*)

copy
1 *noun*
• (*an imitation*)
a copy = una copia
• (*a book, newspaper*)
a copy = un ejemplar
2 *verb* = copiar
copy down, copy out = copiar

cork *noun*
• (*in a bottle*)
a cork = un corcho
• (*the material*)
cork = corcho (*masculine*)

corkscrew *noun*
a corkscrew = un sacacorchos

corn *noun*
• (*US English—maize*)
corn = maíz (*masculine*)
• (*British English—wheat*)
corn = trigo (*masculine*)
• (*on the toe or foot*)
a corn = un callo

corner *noun*
• (*of a room, a cupboard*)
a corner = un rincón
• (*of a street, a page, a table*)
a corner = una esquina
• (*in football, hockey*)
a corner = un córner

corpse *noun*
a corpse = un cadáver

correct
1 *adjective* = correcto/correcta
the correct answer/pronunciation = la
respuesta/la pronunciación correcta
2 *verb* = corregir

corridor *noun*
a corridor = un pasillo

cost *verb*
= costar
how much does it cost? = ¿cuánto cuesta?

costume *noun*
• (*a style of dress*)
a costume = un traje
• (*for party, disguise*)
a costume = un disfraz

cosy *adjective* (*British English*)
= acogedor/acogedora

cot *noun* (*British English*)
a cot = una cuna

cottage *noun*
a cottage = una casita

cottage cheese *noun*
cottage cheese = requesón (*masculine*)

cotton *noun*
• (*the material*)
cotton = algodón (*masculine*)
• (*the thread*)
cotton = hilo (*masculine*)
• (*US English—absorbent cotton*)
cotton = algodón (*masculine*)

cotton wool *noun* (*British English*)
cotton wool = algodón (*masculine*)

cough
1 *verb* = toser
2 *noun*
a cough = una tos
to have a cough = tener tos

could *verb*
• (*had the ability*)
I couldn't move = no me podía mover
• (*knew how to*)
she could read at the age of 3 = sabía leer a
los 3 años
I couldn't speak German = no sabía hablar
alemán

Countries, cities, and nationalities

In Spanish, countries ending in an unstressed **-a** are feminine (*España, Gran Bretaña, Francia* etc).
All other countries are masculine (*Egipto, Chile, Canadá*).

While the use of the definite article before the name of a country is not generally necessary,
there are some countries which are always preceded by the definite article:

La India	= India
El Reino Unido	= the United Kingdom
El Salvador	= El Salvador

Cities which end in an unstressed **-a** are feminine (*Mérida, Lima, Valencia* etc), and the rest are
masculine (*Londres, París, Madrid*)

The continents are all feminine: *África, Asia, Europa, América*.

Nationalities

Note the different use of capital letters in English and Spanish; adjectives and nouns never have
capital letters in Spanish:

a Spanish student	= un estudiante español
a Spaniard	= un español

English sometimes has a special word for a person of a specific nationality; in Spanish the same
word is almost always both an adjective and a noun:

Danish	= danés
a Dane	= un danés
the Danes	= los daneses

---

* (*with verbs of perception*)
  I couldn't see a thing = no veía nada
  he could hear them = los oía
  they couldn't understand me = no me
    entendían

  ! *When talking about seeing, hearing,
  and understanding, you do not translate*
  could

* (*when implying that something might have
  happened*)
  you could have died! = ¡podrías haberte
    matado!
* (*when indicating a possibility*)
  they could be wrong = puede que estén
    equivocados

  ! *Note the use of the subjunctive after*
  puede que

  a bike could be useful = una bicicleta
    podría ser útil
* (*when asking, offering, or suggesting*)

  ! *The conditional is often used in Spanish
  to make polite requests, suggestions etc*
  could I speak to Annie? = ¿podría hablar
    con Annie?
  we could ask Gary = podríamos
    preguntarle a Gary

count *verb*
  = contar
  **there will be five of us counting the
    children** = seremos cinco, los niños
    incluidos

count on
  to count on someone = contar con alguien

counter *noun*
* (*where customers are served*)
  a counter (*in a shop*) = un mostrador
    (*in a bank, post office*) = una ventanilla
    (*in a bar*) = una barra
* (*for a board game*)
  a counter = una ficha

country *noun*
* (*a state*)
  a country = un país
* (*the countryside*)
  the country = el campo

countryside *noun*
  the countryside = el campo

couple *noun*
* (*when counting*)
  a couple = un par
  a couple of days = un par de días
* (*two people*)
  a couple = una pareja
  (*if married*) = un matrimonio

courage *noun*
  courage = valor (*masculine*)

course *noun*
* (*a series of lessons or lectures*)
  a course = un curso

* (*part of a meal*)
  a course = un plato
  the main course = el plato fuerte, el plato principal
* **of course** = claro, por supuesto
  of course not = claro que no, por supuesto que no

court *noun*
* (*a lawcourt*)
  a court = un tribunal, (*the building*) = un juzgado
* (*for playing sports*)
  a court = una cancha (*Lat Am*), una pista (*Spa*)
  a tennis court = una cancha de tenis, una pista de tenis

courtyard *noun*
  a courtyard = un patio

cousin *noun*
  a cousin = un primo/una prima

cover
1 *verb*
* (*to protect*) = cubrir
* (*to coat*) = cubrir
  to be covered in spots = estar cubierto/cubierta de manchas
* (*to insure*) = asegurar
  to be covered against theft = estar asegurado/asegurada contra el robo
2 *noun*
* (*a lid*)
  a cover = una tapa, una cubierta
* (*for a cushion, comforter*)
  a cover = una funda
* (*a blanket*)
  a cover = una manta, una cobija (*Lat Am*), una frazada (*Lat Am*)
* (*on a book, an exercise book*)
  a cover = una tapa, una cubierta
* (*of a magazine*)
  a cover = una portada

cow *noun*
  a cow = una vaca

coward *noun*
  a coward = un/una cobarde

cowboy *noun*
  a cowboy = un vaquero

cozy *adjective* (*US English*)
  = acogedor/acogedora

crab *noun*
  a crab = un cangrejo, una jaiba (*Lat Am*)

crack
1 *verb*
* (*to damage*) = rajar
* (*to get damaged*) = rajarse
  the mirror cracked during the move = el espejo se rajó durante la mudanza

* (*to get broken*) = cascarse
  one of the eggs cracked = uno de los huevos se cascó
2 *noun*
  a crack = una rendija
  (*in a wall, a pavement*) = una grieta
  (*in a cup, a mirror*) = una rajadura

cradle *noun*
  a cradle = una cuna

crafty *adjective*
  = astuto/astuta

cramp *noun*
  a cramp = un calambre, una rampa (*Spa*)
  I've got (a) cramp in my leg = me ha dado un calambre en la pierna

crane *noun*
  (*machine*)
  a crane = una grúa

crash
1 *noun*
* (*an accident*)
  a crash = un accidente, un choque
  to have a car crash = tener un accidente de automóvil
* (*a loud noise*)
  a crash = un estrépito
2 *verb*
  to crash into a tree = estrellarse contra un árbol
  the plane crashed = el avión se estrelló

crate *noun*
  a crate = un cajón (de embalaje), una jaula

crawl *verb*
  (*to move on one's hands and feet*) = arrastrarse
  (*of a baby*) = gatear

crayon *noun*
  (*a pencil*)
  a crayon = un lápiz de color
  (*made of wax*)
  a crayon = una crayola®, un crayón (*Mex, R Pl*)

crazy *adjective*
  = loco/loca
  to go crazy = volverse loco/loca
  to be crazy about someone = estar loco/loca por alguien

cream
1 *noun*
* (*to eat*)
  cream = crema (de leche) (*feminine*), nata (*feminine*) (*Spa*)
* (*lotion*)
  cream = crema (*feminine*)
2 *adjective* ▶ **p. 183**
  = color crema (**!** *never changes*)

create *verb*
= crear
to create a good impression = causar una
buena impresión

creative *adjective*
= creativo/creativa

crèche *noun* (*British English*)
a crèche = una guardería

credit
1 *noun*
(*in business, banking*)
credit = crédito (*masculine*)
2 *verb*
to credit money to an account = depositar
dinero en una cuenta, ingresar dinero en
una cuenta (*Spa*)

credit card *noun*
a credit card = una tarjeta de crédito

crib *noun* (*American English*)
a crib = una cuna

crime *noun*
• (*a criminal act*)
a crime (*a wrongful act*) = un delito
(*a murder*) = un crimen
• (*in society in general*)
crime = delincuencia (*feminine*)

criminal *noun*
a criminal = un/una delincuente, (*serious*)
= un/una criminal

crisis *noun*
a crisis = una crisis

crisps *noun* (*British English*)
crisps = papas fritas (*feminine plural*) (*Lat
Am*), patatas fritas (*feminine plural*) (*Spa*)

criticize *verb*
= criticar

crooked *adjective*
a crooked line = una línea torcida, una
línea chueca (*Lat Am*)
the picture is crooked = el cuadro está
torcido, el cuadro está chueco (*Lat Am*)

cross
1 *verb*
• (*to go across*) = cruzar
to cross the road = cruzar la calle
• (*other uses*)
to cross one's legs = cruzar las piernas
our letters crossed = nuestras cartas se
cruzaron
2 *noun*
a cross = una cruz
3 *adjective* (*British English*)
= enojado/enojada (*Lat Am*),
enfadado/enfadada (*Spa*)
to get cross = enojarse (*Lat Am*), enfadarse
(*Spa*)

cross off = tachar
cross out = tachar

crossroads *noun*
a crossroads = un cruce

crosswalk *noun* (*US English*)
a crosswalk = un paso de peatones

crossword *noun*
a crossword = un crucigrama, unas
palabras cruzadas (*SC*)

crow *noun*
a crow = un cuervo

crowd
1 *noun*
• (*a large number of people*)
a crowd = una muchedumbre, un gentío
• (*the people watching a game or play*)
the crowd = el público
2 *verb*
they crowded into the hall = entraron en
tropel a la sala

crowded *adjective*
a crowded train = un tren abarrotado de
gente, un tren lleno de gente
the beach was too crowded = había
demasiada gente en la playa

crown *noun*
a crown = una corona

cruel *adjective*
= cruel

cruelty *noun*
cruelty = crueldad (*feminine*)

cruise *noun*
a cruise = un crucero
to go on a cruise = hacer un crucero

crush *verb*
= aplastar

crust *noun*
the crust = la corteza, la costra
a crust of bread = un mendrugo

crutch *noun*
a crutch = una muleta
to be on crutches = andar con muletas

cry
1 *verb* = llorar
2 *noun*
a cry = un grito
cry out = gritar

cub *noun*
a cub = un cachorro

cucumber *noun*
a cucumber = un pepino

cuddle *noun*
a cuddle = un abrazo

cuff *noun*
  a cuff = un puño

cul-de-sac *noun*
  a cul-de-sac = una calle sin salida, una calle cortada (*R Pl*)

culprit *noun*
  the culprit = el/la culpable

culture *noun*
* culture = cultura (*feminine*)
* (*a civilization or society*)
  a culture = una cultura

cunning *adjective*
  = astuto/astuta

cup *noun*
* a cup = una taza
* (*a trophy*)
  a cup = una copa

cupboard *noun*
  a cupboard = un armario

curb *noun*
  (*on a sidewalk*)
  the curb = el bordillo (de la acera), el borde de la banqueta (*Mex*), el cordón de la vereda (*R Pl*)

cure
1 *verb* = curar
2 *noun*
  (*for an illness*)
  a cure = una cura

curious *adjective*
  = curioso/curiosa

curl *noun*
  a curl = un rizo, un rulo (*SC*), un chino (*Mex*)

curly *adjective*
  = rizado/rizada, crespo/crespa (*SC*), chino/china (*Mex*)

currency *noun*
  a currency = una moneda

current *noun*
  (*flow of electricity, water*)
  the current = la corriente

curry *noun*
* (*a dish*)
  a curry = un curry
* (*the powder*)
  curry = curry (*masculine*)

curtain *noun*
  a curtain = una cortina

cushion *noun*
  a cushion = un cojín, un almohadón

custard *noun* (*British English*)
  custard = natillas (*feminine plural*)

custom *noun*
  a custom = una costumbre

customer *noun*
  a customer = un/una cliente

customs *noun*
  customs = aduana (*feminine*)
  to go through customs = pasar por la aduana

cut
1 *verb* = cortar
  cut the bread into small pieces = corta el pan en trocitos
  to cut one's finger = cortarse el dedo
  to have one's hair cut = cortarse el pelo
2 *noun*
* (*a wound*)
  a cut = un tajo, un corte
* (*a reduction*)
  a cut = un recorte
cut down
  to cut down a tree = cortar un árbol, talar un árbol
cut out
  to cut a photo out of a magazine = recortar una foto de una revista
cut up = cortar en pedazos

cute *adjective*
* (*sweet*) = mono/mona, cuco/cuca, rico/rica (*SC*)
* (*US English—attractive*) = guapo/guapa
* (*US English—cunning*) = listo/lista, vivo/viva (*Lat Am*)

cutlery *noun*
  cutlery = cubiertos (*masculine plural*)

CV *noun* (*British English*)
  a CV = un currículum, un historial personal

cycle *verb*
  to cycle to school = ir a la escuela en bicicleta
  to go cycling = salir en bicicleta

cycling *noun*
  cycling = ciclismo (*masculine*)

cyclist *noun*
  a cyclist = un/una ciclista

cynical *adjective*
  = cínico/cínica

Czech Republic *noun* ▶ p. 187
  the Czech Republic = la República Checa

C Am Central America Lat Am Latin America Mex Mexico

Dd

dad, Dad *noun*
  Dad = papá (*masculine*)

daddy *noun*
  my daddy = mi papi

daffodil *noun*
  a daffodil = un narciso

daisy *noun*
  a daisy = una margarita

damage
1 *noun*
  damage = daño (*masculine*)
  the storm did a lot of damage = la
    tormenta causó grandes daños
2 *verb*
  to damage a building = dañar un edificio
  smoking seriously damages your health =
    fumar perjudica seriamente la salud

damp
1 *noun*
  damp = humedad (*feminine*)
2 *adjective* = húmedo/húmeda

dance
1 *noun*
  a dance = un baile
2 *verb* = bailar

dancer *noun*
  a dancer = un bailarín/una bailarina

dancing *noun*
  dancing = baile (*masculine*)

Dane *noun* ▶ p. 187
  a Dane = un danés/una danesa

danger *noun*
  danger = peligro (*masculine*)
  to be in danger = estar en peligro

dangerous *adjective*
  = peligroso/peligrosa

Danish ▶ p. 187, p. 245
1 *noun*
  (*the language*)
  Danish = el danés
2 *adjective* = danés/danesa

dark
1 *noun*
  the dark = la oscuridad
2 *adjective*
• (*lacking in light*) = oscuro/oscura
  it's getting dark = está oscureciendo, se está
    haciendo de noche
• (*if it's a color or piece of clothing*) =
    oscuro/oscura
  a dark blue dress = un vestido azul oscuro

• (*if it's a person's hair*) = oscuro/oscura
• (*if it's a person's coloring*) = moreno/morena

darkness *noun*
  darkness = oscuridad (*feminine*)

darling *noun*
  my darling = mi amor

dart *noun* ▶ p. 306
  a dart = un dardo
  to play darts = jugar a los dardos

date
1 *noun* ▶ p. 192
  a date = una fecha
2 *verb* = fechar
  the letter is dated February 1 = la carta está
    fechada el 1 de febrero

daughter *noun*
  a daughter = una hija

daughter-in-law *noun*
  a daughter-in-law = una nuera

dawn *noun*
  dawn = el amanecer

day *noun* ▶ p. 192
  a day = un día

day care center *noun* (*US English*)
  a day care center = una guardería

daylight *noun*
  in broad daylight = a plena luz del día

dazzle *verb*
  = deslumbrar

dead
1 *adjective* = muerto/muerta
  the dead man/woman = el muerto/la
    muerta
2 *noun*
  the dead = los muertos

deaf *adjective*
  = sordo/sorda

deal
1 *noun*
• (*a business agreement*)
  a deal = un acuerdo
• (*when talking about an amount or quantity*)
  a great deal of = muchísimo/muchísima
2 *verb*
  to deal the cards = dar las cartas, repartir
    las cartas
deal with
  to deal with a problem = ocuparse de un
    problema

dear
1 *adjective*
• (*expensive*) = caro/cara

Dates

The days of the week

The names of the days of the week begin with a lower case letter in Spanish:

Monday	= lunes	*Thursday*	= jueves	*Sunday*	= domingo
Tuesday	= martes	*Friday*	= viernes		
Wednesday	= miércoles	*Saturday*	= sábado		

They are preceded by an article in spoken Spanish. Note that **on** is not translated.

the course starts on Tuesday = el curso empieza el martes
we don't work on Saturdays = no trabajamos los sábados

The months of the year

The names of the months of the year begin with a lower case letter in Spanish:

January	= enero	*May*	= mayo	*September*	= septiembre *or* setiembre
February	= febrero	*June*	= junio	*October*	= octubre
March	= marzo	*July*	= julio	*November*	= noviembre
April	= abril	*August*	= agosto	*December*	= diciembre

The names of the months can be preceded by **el mes de**:

I spent May in Vienna = pasé el mes de mayo en Viena

Years and decades

The years after 1000 are referred to in thousands rather than hundreds:

1936 = mil novecientos treinta y seis   *1492* = mil cuatrocientos noventa y dos

When referring to decades, the plural article is used:

the sixties = los sesenta
the nineties = los noventa

Centuries

Ordinal numbers are used for the first to the ninth centuries:

the 4th century = el siglo cuarto   *the 8th century* = el siglo octavo

For the tenth century both the cardinal and the ordinal numbers are acceptable:

the 10th century = el siglo décimo, el siglo diez

From the 11th century onward, cardinal numbers are used.

the 12th century = el siglo doce   *the 20th century* = el siglo veinte

Dates

Unlike English, Spanish uses cardinal numbers for the date:

today is the 6th = hoy es seis

In most other contexts, the article **el** is required:

my birthday is on May 6 = mi cumpleaños es el 6 de mayo
she died on February 10th = murió el diez de febrero

Note that the ordinal number is preferred for the first day of the month in Latin America, whereas the use of the cardinal number is more common in Spain.

February 1st = el primero de febrero (*Lat Am*)   = el uno de febrero (*Spa*)

Asking the date

what's the date?	= ¿a cuánto estamos?
it's the 6th	= estamos a seis
what's the date today?	= ¿qué fecha es hoy?
today is November 20th	= hoy es 20 de noviembre
what day is it today?	= ¿qué día es hoy?
today is Monday	= hoy es lunes *or* estamos a lunes

- (*in letter writing*) = querido/querida
  Dear Anne = Querida Anne
  Dear Sir/Madam = Estimado
  Señor/Estimada Señora, Muy señor
  mío/señora mía
- (*loved*) = querido/querida
  Paul is a very dear friend = Paul es un
  amigo muy querido
  2 *exclamation*
  oh dear! = ¡ay por Dios!

death *noun*
  death = muerte (*feminine*)

debit *verb*
  = debitar

debt *noun*
  a debt = una deuda
  to be in debt = tener deudas

decade *noun* ▶ p. 192
  a decade = una década

December *noun* ▶ p. 192
  December = diciembre (*masculine*)

decide *verb*
  = decidir

decision *noun*
  a decision = una decisión

deck *noun*
- (*of a ship*)
  the deck = la cubierta
- a deck of cards (*US English*) = una baraja,
  un mazo de cartas (*SC*)

declare *verb*
  = declarar

decorate *verb*
- (*with ornaments*) = adornar, decorar (*Lat
  Am*)
- to decorate a house (*with paint*) = pintar
  una casa, (*with wallpaper*) = empapelar
  una casa

decoration *noun*
- (*the act*)
  decoration = decoración (*feminine*)
- (*an ornament*)
  a decoration = un adorno

dedicated *adjective*
  to be dedicated to something = estar
  dedicado/dedicada a algo

deep *adjective*
  = profundo/profunda
  how deep is the lake? = ¿qué profundidad
  tiene el lago?
  the lake is 20 meters deep = el lago tiene
  20 metros de profundidad

deer *noun*
  a deer = un ciervo

defeat
  1 *noun*
  a defeat = una derrota
  2 *verb*
  to defeat the enemy = derrotar al enemigo,
  vencer al enemigo
  the team was defeated = el equipo sufrió
  una derrota

defense (*US English*), **defence** (*British
English*) *noun*
  a defense = una defensa

defend *verb*
  = defender

definite *adjective*
- (*precise*) = definitivo/definitiva
  a definite answer = una respuesta
  definitiva
- (*obvious*)
  a definite improvement = una clara mejora
- (*certain*) = seguro/segura

definitely *adverb*
  it's definitely true = es indudablemente
  cierto
  she definitely said she would come =
  seguro que dijo que vendría

definition *noun*
  a definition = una definición

defy *verb*
  = desafiar

degree *noun*
- (*from university*)
  a degree = un título
- (*in measurements*)
  a degree = un grado

deliberate *adjective*
  = deliberado/deliberada

deliberately *adverb*
  = adrede, a propósito

delicatessen *noun*
  a delicatessen = una charcutería, una
  fiambrería (*SC*), una salchichonería
  (*Mex*)

delicious *adjective*
  = delicioso/deliciosa

delighted *adjective*
  = encantado/encantada

deliver *verb*
  to deliver goods = entregar mercancías
  to deliver the mail = repartir el correo

demand
  1 *noun*
- (*a request*)
  a demand = una petición, un pedido (*Lat
  Am*)

• (*a claim*)
a demand = una exigencia
2 *verb* = exigir

demolish *verb*
= demoler, derribar

demonstration *noun*
• (*by protesters*)
a demonstration = una manifestación
• (*of a new machine or model etc*)
a demonstration = una demostración

Denmark *noun* ▶ p. 187
Denmark = Dinamarca (*feminine*)

dentist *noun*
a dentist = un dentista/una dentista

deny *verb*
= negar

department *noun*
• (*a part of a firm or institution*)
a department = un departamento
• (*a division of government*)
a department = un ministerio, una
secretaría (*Mex*)
• (*in a large store*)
a department = una sección
• (*in a university*)
a department = un departamento, una
facultad
• (*in a school*)
a department = un departamento

department store *noun*
a department store = unos grandes
almacenes, una tienda de departamentos
(*Mex*)

departure *noun*
departure = salida (*feminine*)

depend *verb*
to depend on someone/something =
depender de alguien/algo

deposit
1 *noun*
• (*an initial payment on a purchase*)
a deposit = una entrega inicial, una
entrada (*Spa*)
• (*paid when renting a house or apartment*)
a deposit = un depósito
• (*in a bank account*)
a deposit = un depósito, un ingreso (*Spa*)
2 *verb* = depositar

depressed *adjective*
= deprimido/deprimida

depression *noun*
depression = depresión (*feminine*)

deprive *verb*
to deprive someone of something = privar
a alguien de algo

depth *noun*
depth = profundidad (*feminine*)
to examine something in depth = estudiar
algo a fondo

deputy
1 *noun*
a deputy (*second-in-command*) = un
segundo/una segunda
(*substitute*) = un/una suplente
2 *adjective*
the deputy director = el subdirector/la
subdirectora

describe *verb*
= describir

description *noun*
a description = una descripción

desert
1 *noun*
a desert = un desierto
2 *verb*
• (*to abandon*) = abandonar
• (*if it's a soldier*) = desertar

deserve *verb*
= merecer

design
1 *noun*
a design = un diseño
the design of a machine/room = el diseño
de una máquina/un cuarto
2 *verb*
= diseñar
the house was designed for a hot climate
= la casa fue diseñada para un clima
cálido
to design clothes = diseñar ropa

designer *noun*
a designer = un diseñador/una diseñadora
a fashion designer = un diseñador/una
diseñadora de modas

desire
1 *noun*
desire = deseo (*masculine*)
2 *verb* = desear

desk *noun*
• (*piece of furniture*)
a desk = un escritorio
• (*of a pupil in a classroom*)
a desk = un pupitre
• (*in a hotel*)
the desk = la recepción

despair *noun*
despair = desesperación (*feminine*)
in despair = en la desesperación

desperate *adjective*
= desesperado/desesperada

dessert *noun*
a dessert = un postre

destroy *verb*
= destruir

destruction *noun*
destruction = destrucción (*feminine*)

detached *adjective*
a detached house (*British English*) = una casa no adosada

detail *noun*
a detail = un detalle
to go into details = entrar en detalles

detailed *adjective*
= detallado/detallada

detective *noun*
• a (police) detective = un/una agente oficial
• a private detective = un/una detective

determined *adjective*
= decidido/decidida
he was determined to go ahead = estaba decidido a seguir adelante

develop *verb*
• (*to elaborate*) = desarrollar
• (*to grow*) = desarrollarse

development *noun*
• (*the act of developing*)
development = desarrollo (*masculine*)
• (*a change*)
there has been a development in the situation = ha cambiado la situación

devil *noun*
the devil = el diablo, el demonio

dew *noun*
dew = rocío (*masculine*)

dial
1 *noun*
• (*of a clock or watch*)
a dial = una esfera
• (*of a telephone*)
a dial = un disco
2 *verb* = marcar, discar (*Lat Am*)

diamond *noun*
a diamond = un diamante

diaper *noun* (*US English*)
a diaper = un pañal

diary *noun*
• (*for writing personal thoughts*)
a diary = un diario
• (*for appointments*)
a diary = una agenda

dice *noun*
a dice = un dado

dictionary *noun*
a dictionary = un diccionario

die *verb*
= morir

diet *noun*
a diet = un régimen, una dieta
to be/go on a diet = estar/ponerse a régimen, estar/ponerse a dieta

difference *noun*
a difference = una diferencia

different *adjective*
= diferente, distinto/distinta

difficult *adjective*
= difícil

difficulty *noun*
a difficulty = una dificultad

dig *verb*
= cavar
dig up
to dig up a garden = levantar un jardín

dilute *verb*
= diluir

dining room *noun*
a dining room = un comedor

dinner *noun*
a dinner = una cena, una comida (*Lat Am*)
to have dinner = cenar, comer (*Lat Am*)

direct
1 *adjective* = directo/directa
2 *adverb* = directamente
3 *verb*
• (*when giving directions*)
could you direct me to the post office? = ¿me podría indicar el camino a la oficina de correos?
• (*if it's a movie or a play*) = dirigir

direction *noun*
• (*the way*)
direction = dirección (*feminine*)
• (*to show someone how to get somewhere*)
directions = indicaciones (*feminine plural*)

director *noun*
• (*of a movie or play*)
a director = un director/una directora
• (*of a company*)
a director = un directivo/una directiva

dirt *noun*
dirt = suciedad (*feminine*), mugre (*feminine*)

dirty *adjective*
= sucio/sucia
to get dirty = ensuciarse

disadvantage *noun*
a disadvantage = un inconveniente, una desventaja

disagree *verb*
= no estar de acuerdo
I disagree with you = no estoy de acuerdo contigo

disappear verb
= desaparecer

disappoint verb
= decepcionar

disappointing adjective
= decepcionante

disappointment noun
disappointment = decepción (feminine)

disapprove verb
to disapprove of an idea = desaprobar una idea
she disapproves of his friends = no tiene buen concepto de sus amigos

disaster noun
a disaster = un desastre

discipline noun
discipline = disciplina (feminine)

disco noun
a disco = una discoteca

discover verb
= descubrir

discovery noun
a discovery = un descubrimiento

discuss verb
to discuss politics = hablar de política

disease noun
a disease = una enfermedad

disguise
1 noun
a disguise = un disfraz
2 verb = disfrazar
she disguised herself as a witch = se disfrazó de bruja

disgust
1 noun
disgust = asco (masculine)
2 verb = darle asco a

disgusting adjective
= asqueroso/asquerosa

dish noun
a dish = un plato
to wash the dishes = fregar los platos, lavar los trastes (C Am, Mex)

dishonest adjective
= deshonesto/deshonesta

dishwasher noun
a dishwasher = un lavaplatos, un lavavajillas

disk noun
(in computing)
a disk = un disco

dislike verb
I dislike him = no me gusta
they disliked the idea = no les gusta la idea

dismiss verb
• (from a job) = despedir
• (to reject)
to dismiss an idea = descartar una idea

disobey verb
= desobedecer

display
1 noun
(of objects for sale)
a book display = una exposición de libros
2 verb
(put on show) = exponer

dispute noun
• (a controversy, clash)
a dispute = una polémica, una controversia
• (a quarrel)
a dispute = una disputa

disrupt verb
to disrupt someone's routine = desbaratar la rutina de alguien
to disrupt the traffic = afectar al tráfico

distance noun
distance = distancia (feminine)

distant adjective
= distante, lejano/lejana

distinguish verb
= distinguir

distract verb
= distraer

distressed adjective
= afligido/afligida

distribute verb
= repartir, distribuir

disturb verb
don't disturb him, he's busy = no lo molestes , que está ocupado
that noise is disturbing me = ese ruido me molesta

disturbing adjective
• (worrying, upsetting) = inquietante
• (alarming) = alarmante

dive
1 noun
(from a diving board)
a dive = un salto, un clavado (Lat Am)
2 verb
• (from a height) = tirarse, echarse un clavado (Lat Am)
he dived into the water = se tiró al agua
• (under surface) = sumergirse
to go diving = ir a hacer submarinismo

divide verb
= dividir
six divided by two is three ($6 \div 2 = 3$) = seis dividido entre dos es igual a tres, seis dividido por dos es igual a tres ($6 \div 2 = 3$)

diving board *noun*
a diving board = un trampolín

division *noun*
division = división (*feminine*)

divorce
1 *noun*
a divorce = un divorcio
2 *verb*
to divorce someone = divorciarse de alguien
to get divorced = divorciarse

DIY *noun* (*British English*)
DIY = bricolaje (*masculine*)

dizzy *adjective*
to feel dizzy = estar mareado/mareada

do *verb*
• to do = hacer
what has he done with the newspaper? = ¿qué hizo con el periódico?
to do the cooking = preparar la comida
• (*when used as an auxiliary verb*)
do you speak English? = ¿hablas inglés?
I don't like cats = no me gustan los gatos
do you eat fish?—yes, I do = ¿comes pescado?—sí
I didn't do anything = no hice nada
don't shut the door! = ¡no cierres la puerta!
I love chocolate—so do I = me encanta el chocolate—a mí también
who wrote it?—I did = ¿quién lo escribió?—yo
he lives in London, doesn't he? = vive en Londres, ¿verdad?
• (*to be enough*)
ten pounds will do = con diez libras está bien
that box will do = esa caja está bien
• (*to perform*)
he did well/badly = le fue bien/mal
do up
• (*fasten*) = abrochar
• to do up a house = arreglar una casa
do with
it's got something to do with computers = tiene algo que ver con las computadoras
it has nothing to do with you = no tiene nada que ver contigo
do without
I can do without the television = puedo prescindir de la televisión

dock *noun*
a dock = una dársena

doctor *noun*
a doctor = un médico/una médica, un doctor/una doctora

document *noun*
a document = un documento

dog *noun*
a dog = un perro/una perra

doll *noun*
a doll = una muñeca

dollar *noun*
a dollar = un dólar

dolphin *noun*
a dolphin = un delfín

dominate *verb*
= dominar

donation *noun*
a donation = un donativo, una donación

donkey *noun*
a donkey = un burro, un asno

door *noun*
a door = una puerta

doorbell *noun*
a doorbell = un timbre

dormitory *noun*
a dormitory = un dormitorio

dose *noun*
a dose = una dosis

double
1 *adjective*
• (*if it's an amount or helping*) = doble
• (*when spelling or giving a number*)
Anne is spelt with a double 'n' = Anne se escribe con dos enes
three double five (*British English*) = tres cinco cinco
2 *adverb*
= el doble
he is double my age = tiene el doble de mi edad
3 *noun*
(*in tennis*)
doubles = dobles (*masculine plural*)
4 *verb*
= doblar

double bed *noun*
a double bed = una cama de matrimonio, una cama de dos plazas (*Lat Am*)

double-decker *noun*
a double-decker = un autobús de dos pisos

double room *noun*
a double room = una habitación doble

doubt
1 *noun*
doubt = duda (*feminine*)
there is no doubt that he is innocent = no cabe duda de que es inocente
2 *verb* = dudar
I doubt that he will come = dudo que venga

! Note the use of the subjunctive after dudar que

dough *noun*
dough = masa (*feminine*)

D

doughnut, **donut** (US English) noun
a doughnut = un dónut, una dona (Mex)

down

> ! Down is often used in combinations with verbs, for example, cool down, fall down, sit down. To find the correct translations for this type of verb, look up the separate dictionary entries at cool, fall, sit etc.

1 adverb
down in Brixton = en Brixton
to go down = bajar
they've gone down to the country = se fueron al campo
I'm down here! = ¡estoy aquí abajo!
where is he?—down there = ¿dónde está?—está allí abajo
2 preposition
to go down a street = bajar por una calle
he ran down the slope = corrió cuesta abajo
the library is just down the street = la biblioteca está un poco más allá

downstairs adverb
= abajo
he's downstairs = está abajo
to go downstairs = bajar las escaleras

dozen noun
a dozen = una docena
a dozen eggs = una docena de huevos

draft noun (US English)
(cold air)
a draft = una corriente de aire

drag verb
= arrastrar

drain
1 noun
• (a pipe)
a drain = un sumidero, un resumidero (Lat Am)
• (a plughole)
a drain = un desagüe
2 verb
to drain the vegetables = escurrir las verduras

drama noun
• (theater)
drama = teatro (masculine)
• (a play)
a drama = un drama

dramatic adjective
= dramático/dramática

drapes noun (US English)
drapes = cortinas (feminine plural)

draught (British English) noun ▶ draft

draughts noun (British English) ▶ p. 306
draughts = damas (feminine plural)

draw
1 verb
• (with a pen or pencil)
to draw = dibujar
to draw a picture = hacer un dibujo
to draw a line = trazar una línea
she drew his portrait = le hizo un retrato
• (to pull)
to draw the curtains = correr las cortinas
• (to remove) = sacar
he drew a knife from his pocket = sacó una navaja del bolsillo
• (to attract) = atraer
• (in a football match or game of tennis) = empatar
• (if it's a date or event)
to draw near = acercarse
2 noun
• (in sport)
a draw = un empate
• (in a lottery)
a draw = un sorteo

draw up
to draw up a contract = redactar un contrato

drawer noun
a drawer = un cajón, una gaveta (Mex)

drawing noun
a drawing = un dibujo

dream
1 noun
a dream = un sueño
2 verb = soñar

dress
1 noun
a dress = un vestido
2 verb
• (to put one's clothes on) = vestirse
• (to put clothes on someone) = vestir

dress up
• (to put on smart clothes) = ponerse elegante
• (to put on a costume) = disfrazarse

dressing gown noun
a dressing gown = una bata

dried adjective
dried fruits/flowers = frutas/flores secas
dried milk = leche en polvo

drill
1 noun
a drill = un taladro
(of a dentist) = un torno
2 verb
to drill a hole in the wall = hacer un agujero con un taladro en la pared

drink
1 verb = beber, tomar (Lat Am)
2 noun
• a drink = una bebida
to have a drink of milk = tomar un poco de leche

C Am Central America   Lat Am Latin America   Mex Mexico

• (*alcohol*)
  drink = bebida (*feminine*)
  to have a drink = tomar una copa

drive
1 *noun*
• (*in a car*)
  to go for a drive = ir a dar un paseo en
    coche
• (*a path*)
  a drive = un camino
2 *verb*
  (*in a vehicle*) = manejar, conducir (*Spa*)
  to drive a car = manejar un coche
  he drives to work = va a trabajar en coche
  she drove me home = me llevó a casa en
    coche

driver *noun*
  a driver = un/una chofer (*Lat Am*), un/una
    chófer (*Spa*)

driver's license (*US English*), driving
licence (*British English*) *noun*
  a driver's license, a driving licence = una
    licencia de conducción, un permiso de
    conducir (*Spa*), una licencia (de
    manejar) (*C Am, Mex*)

drop
1 *noun*
• (*of liquid*)
  a drop = una gota
• (*a decrease*)
  a drop in temperature = un descenso de la
    temperatura
2 *verb*
• (*to fall*) = caerse
• (*to let fall*)
  she dropped her bag (*accidentally*) = se le
    cayó la bolsa, (*intentionally*) = dejó caer la
    bolsa
• **the temperature has dropped** = la
    temperatura ha bajado
drop in = pasar
  he dropped in to see me = pasó a verme
drop out
  to drop out of school = abandonar los
    estudios
  he dropped out of the race = abandonó la
    carrera

drought *noun*
  a drought = una sequía

drown *verb*
• (*to die*) = ahogarse, morir ahogado
• (*to kill*) = ahogar

drug
1 *noun*
• (*an addictive substance*)
  a drug = una droga
  to be on drugs = drogarse
• (*a medicine*)
  a drug = un medicamento

2 *verb*
  to drug someone = drogar a alguien

drug addict *noun*
  a drug addict = un drogadicto/una
    drogadicta

druggist *noun* (*American English*)
  a drugggist = un farmacéutico/una
    farmacéutica

drugstore *noun* (*US English*)
  a drugstore = *un establecimiento que vende
    medicamentos, cosméticos, periódicos y una
    gran variedad de artículos*

drum *noun*
  a drum = un tambor
  she plays the drums = toca la batería

drunk *adjective*
  to be drunk = estar borracho/borracha

dry
1 *adjective* = seco/seca
2 *verb*
  to dry wet clothes = secar la ropa mojada
  the clothes took a long time to dry = la
    ropa tardó en secarse
  to dry oneself = secarse
  he dried his hands = se secó las manos
  to dry the dishes = secar los platos

dryer *noun*
• (*for clothes*)
  a dryer = una secadora
• (*for hair*)
  a hair = un secador, una secadora (*Mex*)

duchess *noun*
  a duchess = una duquesa

duck
1 *noun*
• (*the bird*)
  a duck = un pato/una pata
• (*the meat*)
  duck = pato (*masculine*)
2 *verb*
  (*to lower one's head*)
  to duck = agachar la cabeza

due *adjective*
• (*owing or owed*)
  the balance due = el saldo pendiente
• (*expected*)
  the train is due at 2 o'clock = el tren tiene
    prevista su llegada a las dos

duke *noun*
  a duke = un duque

dull *adjective*
• (*if it's a color*) = apagado/apagada
• (*if it's a person or book*) =
    aburrido/aburrida
• (*if it's the weather*) = gris

dumb *adjective*
(*unable to speak*) = mudo/muda

dump *verb*
= tirar, botar (*Lat Am except R Pl*)

during *preposition*
= durante

dusk *noun*
dusk = anochecer (*masculine*)

dust
1 *noun*
dust = polvo (*masculine*)
2 *verb*
to dust the furniture = quitarles el polvo a
los muebles, sacudir los muebles (*Mex,
SC*)

dustbin *noun* (*British English*)
a dustbin = un cubo de la basura, un tacho
de la basura (*SC*), un bote de la basura
(*Mex*)

dustman *noun* (*British English*)
a dustman = un basurero

dustpan *noun*
a dustpan = una pala, un recogedor

Dutch ▶ **p. 187, p. 245**
1 *noun*
• (*the language*)
Dutch = holandés (*masculine*)
• (*the people*)
the Dutch = los holandeses
2 *adjective* = holandés/holandesa

duty *noun*
• (*moral obligation*)
duty = deber (*masculine*), obligación
(*feminine*)
• (*a task*)
to take up one's duties = asumir las
funciones
• to be on duty (*if it's a policeman, fireman*) =
estar de servicio, (*if it's a nurse, doctor*) =
estar de turno, estar de guardia
• (*a tax*)
a duty = un impuesto

duvet *noun* (*British English*)
a duvet = un edredón

dye
1 *noun*
dye = tintura (*feminine*)
2 *verb* = teñir
she dyed the dress red = tiñó el vestido de
rojo
to dye one's hair = teñirse el pelo

Ee

each
1 *adjective* = cada (**!** *never changes*)
each time I see him = cada vez que lo veo
2 *pronoun* = cada uno/cada una
they are ten dollars each = cuestan diez
dólares cada uno

each other *pronoun*
to love each other = quererse el uno al otro
to help each other = ayudarse el uno al
otro

eager *adjective*
I am eager to meet him = tengo muchas
ganas de conocerlo

eagle *noun*
an eagle = un águila (*feminine*)

ear *noun* ▶ **p. 235**
an ear = una oreja

early
1 *adverb* = temprano
to get up early = levantarse temprano
earlier in the year = más temprano en el
año
I'm a bit early = llegué un poco temprano
2 *adjective*
to have an early lunch = almorzar
temprano
to take the early train = tomar el primer
tren

earn *verb*
= ganar

earring *noun*
an earring = un pendiente, un arete (*Lat
Am*), un aro (*SC*)

earth *noun*
earth = tierra (*feminine*)
the earth = la tierra

earthquake *noun*
an earthquake = un terremoto

easily *adverb*
= fácilmente

east
1 *noun*
east = este (*masculine*)
the East (*of a country*) = el Este
(*the Orient*) = el Oriente
2 *adjective* = este (**!** *never changes*)
the east coast = la costa este
an east wind = un viento del este
3 *adverb*
it is east of Dallas = está al este de Dallas
we went east = fuimos hacia el este

Easter *noun*
  Easter = Pascua (*feminine*)
  at Easter = en Semana Santa

Easter egg *noun*
  an Easter egg = un huevo de Pascua

easy *adjective*
  = fácil

eat *verb*
  = comer

echo *noun*
  an echo = un eco

economic *adjective*
  = económico/económica

economy *noun*
  the economy = la economía

economy class *noun*
  economy class = clase turista (*feminine*)

edge *noun*
- (*of a road, table, object*)
  the edge = el borde
- (*of a lake, a river*)
  the edge = la orilla
- (*of a blade or knife*)
  the edge = el filo

educate *verb*
  = educar

education *noun*
  education = educación (*feminine*)

effect *noun*
  an effect = un efecto

effective *adjective*
  = eficaz

effort *noun*
  an effort = un esfuerzo
  to make an effort = hacer un esfuerzo,
  esforzarse

egg *noun*
  an egg = un huevo

eggcup *noun*
  an eggcup = una huevera

Egypt *noun* ▶ p. 187
  Egypt = Egipto (*masculine*)

eight *number* ▶ p. 154, p. 319
  eight = ocho (*masculine*) (**!** *never changes*)
  see also five

eighteen *number* ▶ p. 154, p. 319
  eighteen = dieciocho (*masculine*) (**!** *never
  changes*) *see also* five

eighth
1 *adjective* = octavo/octava
2 *noun* ▶ p. 192
  (*a part*)
  an eighth = una octava parte

eighty *number* ▶ p. 154
  eighty = ochenta (*masculine*) (**!** *never
  changes*) *see also* five

either
1 *pronoun*
  take either (of them) = toma cualquiera de
  los dos
  which one do you want?—I don't want
  either of them = ¿cuál quieres?—no quiero
  ninguna de las dos
2 *adjective*
  take either road = toma cualquiera de las
  dos rutas
  I can't see either child = no veo a ninguno
  de los niños
3 *adverb* = tampoco
  I can't do it either = yo tampoco puedo
  hacerlo
4 *conjunction*
  they are coming on either Tuesday or
  Wednesday = vienen el martes o el
  viernes

elastic band *noun* (*British English*)
  an elastic band = una goma (elástica), una
  liga (*Mex*), una gomita (*R Pl*)

elbow *noun* ▶ p. 235
  the elbow = el codo

elder *adjective*
  = mayor

elderly *adjective*
  = anciano/anciana
  an elderly man/woman = un anciano/una
  anciana

eldest *adjective*
  = mayor
  the eldest son/daughter = el hijo/la hija
  mayor
  I'm the eldest = soy el/la mayor

elect *verb*
  = elegir

election *noun*
  an election = unas elecciones

electric *adjective*
  = eléctrico/eléctrica

electrician *noun*
  an electrician = un/una electricista

electricity *noun*
  electricity = electricidad (*feminine*)

elegant *adjective*
  = elegante

element *noun*
  (*a part or a unit*)
  an element = un elemento

elephant *noun*
  an elephant = un elefante

E

elevator noun (US English)
an elevator = un ascensor

eleven number ▶ p. 154, p. 319
eleven = once (masculine) (**!** never changes) see also five

else adverb
someone else = otro/otra, otra persona
something else = otra cosa
nothing else = nada más
everyone else = todos los demás/todas las demás
everything else = todo lo demás
what else did he say? = ¿qué más dijo?
was anybody else at the meeting? = ¿había alguien más en la reunión?
take your umbrella or else you'll get wet = lleva el paraguas o si no te vas a mojar

elsewhere adverb
to go/search elsewhere = ir a/buscar en otro lugar
elsewhere in Britain = en otras partes de Gran Bretaña

embark verb
(when sailing) = embarcar(se)

embarrass verb
= avergonzar
to feel embarrassed = sentirse avergonzado/avergonzada

embarrassment noun
embarrassment = vergüenza (feminine)

embassy noun
an embassy = una embajada

emerge verb
• (if it's a person or animal) = salir
he emerged from the building = salió del edificio
• (to become apparent) = surgir
a new problem has emerged = ha surgido un problema nuevo

emergency noun
• an emergency = una emergencia
in an emergency = en caso de emergencia
it's an emergency! = ¡es una situación de emergencia!
• (medical)
an emergency = una urgencia

emergency exit noun
an emergency exit = una salida de emergencia

emigrate verb
= emigrar

emotion noun
emotion = emoción (feminine)

emotional adjective
• (if it's a person) = emotivo/emotiva
• (if it's a scene or moment) = conmovedor/conmovedora

emperor noun
an emperor = un emperador

emphasize verb
= enfatizar

employ verb
= emplear

employee noun
an employee = un empleado/una empleada

employer noun
an employer = un empleador/una empleadora

employment noun
employment = empleo (masculine)

empty
1 adjective = vacío/vacía
2 verb = vaciar

encourage verb
= animar
she/it ∼d me to carry on = me animó a seguir adelante

encyclop(a)edia noun
an encyclop(a)edia = una enciclopedia

end
1 noun
• (the final part)
the end = el fin
at the end of the year = a fin de año
at the end of May = a fines de mayo
in the end I telephoned him = al final lo llamé por teléfono
• (the furthest part)
the end of a stick/rope = el extremo de un palo/una cuerda, la punta de un palo/una cuerda
at the end of the street = al final de la calle
at the end of the garden = al fondo del jardín
2 verb
• (to finish) = terminar, acabar
to end a novel = terminar una novela
• (to come to an end) = terminar, acabar

endure verb
• (to survive) = soportar
• (to last) = perdurar

enemy noun
an enemy = un enemigo/una enemiga

energetic adjective
• (full of energy) = lleno/llena de energía
• (requiring energy) = enérgico/enérgica

energy noun
energy = energía (feminine)

engaged adjective
• (if it's a couple)
to get engaged = prometerse, comprometerse (Lat Am)
they are engaged = están prometidos, están comprometidos

- (*if it's a phone*) (*British English*)
  to be engaged = estar ocupado, estar comunicando (*Spa*)

engagement *noun*
- **an engagement** (*a pledge to marry*) = un compromiso
  (*period as fiancés*) = un noviazgo
- (*an appointment*)
  an engagement = un compromiso

engine *noun*
- (*of a car or airplane*)
  an engine = un motor
- (*of a train*)
  an engine = una locomotora

engineer *noun*
  an engineer = un ingeniero/una ingeniera

England *noun* ▶ p. 187
  England = Inglaterra (*feminine*)

English ▶ p. 187, p. 245
1 *noun*
- (*the people*)
  the English = los ingleses
- (*the language*)
  English = inglés (*masculine*)
2 *adjective* = inglés/inglesa

Englishman *noun* ▶ p. 187
  an Englishman = un inglés

Englishwoman *noun* ▶ p. 187
  an Englishwoman = una inglesa

enjoy *verb*
  = disfrutar de
  he enjoys life = disfruta de la vida
  to enjoy oneself = divertirse
  he enjoys traveling = le gusta viajar

enjoyable *adjective*
  = agradable

enormous *adjective*
  = enorme

enough
1 *pronoun*
  we have had enough to eat = hemos comido bastante
  that's enough = basta
  I've had enough = estoy harto/harta
2 *adverb*
  is it big enough? = ¿es lo suficientemente grande?
  you don't go out enough = no sales lo suficiente
3 *adjective* (*singular*) = bastante, suficiente
  (*plural*) = bastantes, suficientes
  have you enough money? = ¿tienes bastante dinero?
  there aren't enough chairs = no hay suficientes sillas

ensure *verb*
  = asegurar

enter *verb*
- (*to go into*) = entrar en, entrar a (*Lat Am*)
  he entered the room = entró en el cuarto, entró al cuarto (*Lat Am*)
- (*to come in*) = entrar
  they were unable to enter = no pudieron entrar
- (*to participate in*)
  to enter a competition = presentarse a un concurso
  to enter a race = inscribirse en una carrera

entertain *verb*
- (*of a book, film, show*) = entretener
- (*of a host*)
  to entertain guests = recibir a los invitados

enthusiasm *noun*
  enthusiasm = entusiasmo (*masculine*)

enthusiastic *adjective*
  = entusiasta
  to be enthusiastic about something = estar entusiasmado/entusiasmada con algo

entrance *noun*
  an entrance = una entrada

entry *noun*
  entry = entrada (*feminine*)

envelope *noun*
  an envelope = un sobre

environment *noun*
  the environment = el medio ambiente

envy
1 *noun*
  envy = envidia (*feminine*)
2 *verb* = envidiar

episode *noun*
  (*of a story, TV series*)
  an episode = un capítulo, un episodio

equal
1 *adjective* = igual
2 *verb* = ser igual a
  six and four equals 10 = 6 más 4 es igual a 10

equality *noun*
  equality = igualdad (*feminine*)

equator *noun*
  the equator = el ecuador

equipment *noun*
  equipment = equipo (*masculine*)
  sports equipment = artículos de deportes (*masculine plural*)

eraser *noun*
  an eraser = una goma (de borrar)

error *noun*
  an error = un error

escalator *noun*
  an escalator = una escalera mecánica

E

escape
1 *noun*
- (*from prison*)
  an escape = una fuga
- (*of gas, air*)
  an escape = un escape
2 *verb*
  (*from a place*) = escaparse

especially *adverb*
= especialmente

essay *noun*
(*written by a pupil or student*)
an essay = una redacción

essential *adjective*
= esencial

establish *verb*
= establecer

estimate
1 *noun*
- (*rough calculation*)
  an estimate = un cálculo estimado
- (*a quote for a client*)
  an estimate = un presupuesto
2 *verb* = calcular
  the estimated time of arrival = la hora
  prevista de llegada

eternal *adjective*
= eterno/eterna

eurocheque *noun*
a eurocheque = un eurocheque

Europe *noun* ▶ **p. 187**
Europe = Europa (*feminine*)

European ▶ **p. 187**
1 *noun*
a European = un europeo/una europea
2 *adjective* = europeo/europea

European Union *noun*
the European Union = la Unión Europea

even¹ *adverb*
- **he didn't even try** = ni siquiera lo intentó
  she even works when she's on vacation =
  trabaja incluso cuando está de vacaciones
- (*used to emphasize a comparison*)
  it's even colder today = hoy hace más frío
  todavía
  he's even richer than her = es todavía más
  rica que ella

even² *adjective*
- (*flat or smooth*) = plano/plana
  an even surface = una superficie plana
- (*when talking about numbers*) = par
  an even number = un número par

evening *noun* ▶ **p. 319**
the evening (*before dark*) = la tarde, (*after
  dark*) = la noche
Friday evening = el viernes en la
  tarde/noche, el viernes por la tarde/noche
  (*Spa*)
in the evening = en la tarde/la noche, por la
  tarde/la noche (*Spa*)
at 6 o'clock in the evening = a las seis de la
  tarde
good evening = buenas tardes/buenas
  noches

event *noun*
an event = un acontecimiento

eventually *adverb*
= finalmente, al final

ever *adverb*
- (*at any time*)
  nothing ever happens here = nunca pasa
  nada aquí
  nobody will ever know = nadie lo sabrá
  nunca
  have you ever been to Greece? = ¿has
  estado alguna vez en Grecia?
  I hardly ever go there = casi nunca voy allí
- (*always*)
  as ever = como siempre

every *adjective*
every time I meet her = cada vez que la
  encuentro
every day = cada día
every second day, every other day = un
  día sí y otro no, un día por medio (*SC*)

everybody *pronoun*
everybody = todos, todo el mundo

everyday *adjective*
= de todos los días

everyone *pronoun* ▶ everybody

everything *pronoun*
everything = todo

everywhere *adverb*
we looked for it everywhere = lo buscamos
  por todos lados
they go everywhere by car = van a todos
  lados en coche

evidence *noun*
- (*proof*)
  evidence = pruebas (*feminine plural*)
- **to give evidence** = prestar declaración

evil
1 *noun*
evil = mal (*masculine*)
2 *adjective* = malvado/malvada

exact *adjective*
= exacto/exacta

exactly *adverb*
= exactamente

exaggerate *verb*
= exagerar

exaggeration *noun*
exaggeration = exageración (*feminine*)

exam *noun*
an exam = un examen

examination *noun*
(*at school*)
an examination = un examen

examine *verb*
= examinar

example *noun*
an example = un ejemplo
for example = por ejemplo

excellent *adjective*
= excelente

except *preposition*
= menos

exception *noun*
an exception = una excepción

exchange
1 *noun*
(*of information, students*)
an exchange = un intercambio
2 *verb*
to exchange something for something =
cambiar algo por algo

excite *verb*
= excitar

excited *adjective*
= entusiasmado/entusiasmada
to get excited = entusiasmarse

exciting *adjective*
= emocionante

exclude *verb*
= excluir

excuse
1 *noun*
• (*to justify something*)
an excuse = una excusa
to make excuses = poner excusas
• (*a pretext*)
an excuse = una excusa, un pretexto
2 *verb*
• (*to forgive*) = disculpar, perdonar
excuse me! = ¡discúlpame!, ¡perdóname!
• (*to justify*) = excusar, justificar

execute *verb*
= ejecutar

exercise
1 *noun*
• (*a piece of work*)
an exercise = un ejercicio
• (*to keep fit*)
exercises = ejercicios (*masculine plural*)

2 *verb*
(*to keep fit*) = hacer ejercicio

exercise book *noun*
an exercise book = un cuaderno

exhaust *noun*
(*of a car*)
the exhaust = el tubo de escape, el caño de
escape (*R Pl*), el mofle (*C Am*)

exhausted *adjective*
= agotado/agotada

exhibition *noun*
an exhibition = una exposición

existence *noun*
existence = existencia (*feminine*)

exit *noun*
an exit = una salida

exotic *adjective*
= exótico/exótica

expect *verb*
= esperar

expense *noun*
expense = gasto (*masculine*)
they had a good laugh at my expense = se
partieron de risa a costa mía

expenses *noun*
expenses = gastos (*masculine plural*)

expensive *adjective*
= caro/cara

experience
1 *noun*
an experience = una experiencia
2 *verb*
to experience happiness/pain =
experimentar alegría/dolor

expert *noun*
an expert = un experto/una experta

explain *verb*
= explicar

explanation *noun*
an explanation = una explicación

explode *verb*
• (*to go off*) = explotar, estallar
• (*to set off*) = explosionar

exploit *verb*
= explotar

explore *verb*
= explorar

explosion *noun*
an explosion = una explosión

export
1 *noun*
an export = un artículo de exportación
2 *verb* = exportar

expose verb
• (to reveal) = poner al descubierto
• (to uncover or display) = exponer

express
1 adjective
  an express train = un tren expreso, un tren rápido
2 verb = expresar
  to express oneself = expresarse

expression noun
  an expression = una expresión

extent noun
• (of knowledge, wealth)
  extent = amplitud (feminine)
• (of damage)
  extent = alcance (masculine)
• (degree)
  to a certain extent = hasta cierto punto
  to a large extent = en gran parte

external adjective
  = externo/externa

extinct adjective
• (if it's an animal or species) = extinto/extinta
  to become extinct = extinguirse

extra
1 noun
• (an additional thing)
  an extra = un extra
• (an actor in a film) = un/una extra
2 adjective
  I need an extra bed = necesito una cama más
  I brought an extra pair = traje un par de más
3 adverb
  to pay extra = pagar más

extraordinary adjective
  = extraordinario/extraordinaria

extravagant adjective
• (if it's a person) = derrochador/derrochadora

extreme
1 noun
  an extreme = un extremo
2 adjective = extremo/extrema

extremely adverb
  = extremadamente

eye noun ▶ p. 235
  an eye = un ojo

eyebrow noun
  an eyebrow = una ceja

eyelash noun
  an eyelash = una pestaña

eyelid noun
  an eyelid = un párpado

eye shadow noun
  eye shadow = sombra de ojos (feminine)

eyesight noun
  eyesight = vista (feminine)

Ff

fabric noun
  a fabric = una tela, un tejido

face
1 noun
• (of a person) ▶ p. 235
  the face = la cara
  to make a face = hacer una mueca
• (of a clock or watch)
  the face = la esfera, la carátula (Méx)
2 verb
• (to be opposite)
  the house facing ours = la casa que está frente a la nuestra
• (to look toward)
  my room faces the sea = mi cuarto da al mar
• (if it's a building)
  to face north = estar orientado al norte
• (to confront)
  to be faced with a problem = enfrentarse a un problema
  face up to = hacer frente a

fact noun
  a fact = un hecho
  in fact = de hecho

factory noun
  a factory = una fábrica

fade verb
• (if it's a fabric) = perder color, desteñirse
• (if it's a color) = apagarse
• (if it's an image or sound) = fundirse

fail verb
• (not to succeed)
  he tried to prevent the accident but he failed = intentó evitar el accidente pero falló
• (in an exam) = ser reprobado/reprobada (Lat Am), suspender (Spa)
  he failed the exam = fue reprobado en el examen, suspendió el examen
• (not to allow to pass)
  to fail a candidate = reprobar a un candidato (Lat Am), suspender a un candidato (Spa)
• (not to work)
  the brakes failed = fallaron los frenos

failure *noun*
- (*an unsuccessful person*)
  a failure = un fracaso
- (*a breakdown*)
  engine failure = falla mecánica (*feminine*),
    fallo mecánico (*masculine*) (*Spa*)
  a power failure = un apagón

faint
1 *verb*
= desmayarse
2 *adjective*
- (*if it's a light or sound*) = débil
- (*if it's a hope*) = ligero/ligera

fair
1 *noun*
  a fair = una feria
2 *adjective*
- (*if it's hair*) = rubio/rubia, güero✖/güera✖
    (*Mex*)
- (*if it's skin*) = blanco/blanca
- (*just or reasonable*) = justo/justa
- tomorrow the weather will be fair =
    mañana hará buen tiempo

fair-haired *adjective*
= rubio/rubia, güero✖/güera✖ (*Mex*)

fairly *adverb*
(*rather*) = bastante

fairy *noun*
  a fairy = un hada (*feminine*)

fairy story, fairy tale *noun*
  a fairy story = un cuento de hadas

faith *noun*
- (*religious belief*)
  faith = fe (*feminine*)
- (*confidence*)
  faith = confianza (*feminine*)
  to have faith in someone = tener fe en
    alguien

faithful *adjective*
= fiel

fall
1 *noun*
- (*of a person or object*)
  a fall = una caída
- (*a decrease*)
  a fall in prices = una bajada de precios
  a fall in temperatures = un descenso de las
    temperaturas
- the fall of the government = la caída del
    gobierno
- (*US English—autumn*)
  the fall = el otoño
  in the fall = en el otoño
2 *verb*
- (*physically*) = caerse
  to fall down the stairs = caerse por las
    escaleras
- (*to decrease*) = bajar

- (*become*)
  to fall asleep = dormirse
  to fall in love with someone = enamorarse
    de alguien
fall down
- (*of a person*) = caerse
- (*of a building*) = venirse abajo
fall off = caerse
fall out = caerse
  his hair is falling out = se le cae el pelo
fall over = caerse

false *adjective*
- (*not true*) = falso/falsa
- (*fake*) = postizo/postiza
  false teeth = dentadura postiza (*feminine*)

familiar *adjective*
= familiar
  that name sounds familiar to me = ese
    nombre me suena

family *noun*
  a family = una familia

famous *adjective*
= famoso/famosa

fan *noun*
- (*hand-held*)
  a fan = un abanico
- (*mechanical*)
  a fan = un ventilador
- (*an enthusiast*)
  a jazz fan = un aficionado/una aficionada
    al jazz
  an Oasis fan = un/una fan de Oasis
  a rugby fan = un/una hincha de rugby

fancy *adjective*
  a fancy hotel = un hotel de lujo
  fancy clothes = la ropa fina

fancy dress *noun* (*British English*)
  fancy dress = disfraz (*masculine*)

fantastic *adjective*
  (*wonderful*) = fantástico/fantástica

fantasy *noun*
- (*a dream*)
  a fantasy = un sueño
- (*unreality*)
  a fantasy = una fantasía

far
1 *adverb*
- (*in distance*) = lejos
  it's very far = está muy lejos
  how far is Leicester from London? = ¿a
    qué distancia está Leicester de Londres?,
    ¿qué tan lejos está Leicester de Londres?
    (*Lat Am*)
- (*in time*)
  I can't remember that far back = no
    recuerdo cosas tan lejanas
  Christmas isn't far away = falta poco para
    Navidad

R Pl River Plate area   SC Southern Cone   Spa Spain

- (*very much*)
  far better = muchísimo mejor
  far more = muchísimo más
- **by far**
  he's by far the tallest = es con mucho el
  más alto, es (de) lejos el más alto (*Lat Am*)
- **so far** = hasta ahora
2 *adjective*
- (*extreme*) = extremo/extrema
  the far north/south = el extremo norte/sur
- (*other*)
  at the far end of the room = al otro extremo
  de la habitación

fare *noun*
- (*on a bus or on the subway*)
  the fare = el precio del boleto (*Lat Am*), el
  precio del billete (*Spa*)
- (*on a train or plane*)
  the fare = el precio del pasaje, el precio del
  billete (*Spa*)

farm *noun*
  a farm (*small*) = una granja, (*large*) = una
  hacienda

farmer *noun*
  a farmer = un agricultor/una agricultora

farther
1 *adverb*
  it was farther than I thought = estaba más
  lejos de lo que pensaba
  the train drew farther and farther away = el
  tren alejaba cada vez más
2 *adjective*
  at the farther end of the street = al otro
  extremo de la calle

fascinate *verb*
  = fascinar

fascinating *adjective*
  = fascinante

fashion *noun*
  fashion = moda (*feminine*)
  to be in/go out of fashion = estar/pasar de
  moda

fashionable *adjective*
- (*if it's clothes or designs*) = a la moda
- (*if it's places, people, or ideas*) = de moda

fast
1 *adjective*
- (*not slow*)
  = rápido/rápida
- (*if it's a clock or watch*)
  my watch is five minutes fast = mi reloj
  (se) adelanta cinco minutos
2 *adverb* = rápido, rápidamente
3 *verb* = ayunar

fasten *verb*
  to fasten a coat = abrochar un abrigo
  to fasten one's shoelaces = atarse los
  cordones, amarrarse los cordones (*Lat
  Am*), amarrarse las agujetas (*Mex*)
  fasten your seatbelts = abróchense los
  cinturones

fat
1 *adjective* = gordo/gorda
  to get fat = engordar
2 *noun*
  fat = grasa (*feminine*)

fatal *adjective*
  a fatal accident = un accidente fatal
  a fatal mistake = un error de consecuencias
  fatales

father *noun*
  a father = un padre

Father Christmas *noun*
  Father Christmas = Papá Noel (*masculine*)

father-in-law *noun*
  a father-in-law = un suegro

fattening *adjective*
  to be fattening = engordar

faucet *noun* (*US English*)
  a faucet = una llave, una canilla (*R Pl*), un
  grifo (*Spa*)

fault *noun*
- (*responsibility*)
  fault = culpa (*feminine*)
  it's my fault = yo tengo la culpa
- (*a defect*)
  a fault (*in goods*) = una falla
  (*in a machine*) = una falla, un fallo (*Spa*)
  (*in a person*) = un defecto

favor (*US English*), **favour** (*British
English*)
1 *noun*
- (*a kind act*)
  a favor = un favor
  he did me a favor = me hizo un favor
- (*advantage*)
  the circumstances are in his favor = las
  circunstancias están a su favor
- **in favor of**
  to be in favor of = estar a favor de
2 *verb*
- (*to benefit*) = favorecer
- (*to prefer*) = estar a favor de
- (*to treat specially*)
  to favor someone = favorecer a alguien

favorite (*US English*), **favourite** (*British
English*)
1 *adjective* = preferido/preferida
2 *noun*
- (*in a race or contest*)
  the favorite = el favorito/la favorita

- (*a person*)
  a favorite = un preferido/una preferida

fax
1 *noun*
  a fax = un fax
2 *verb* = faxear

fear
1 *noun*
  fear = miedo (*masculine*)
2 *verb* = temer

feast *noun*
  a feast = un banquete

feather *noun*
  a feather = una pluma

February *noun* ▶ p. 192
  February = febrero (*masculine*)

fed up *adjective*
  = harto/harta
  I'm fed up with this situation = estoy harta
  de esta situación

fee *noun*
  an admission fee = una entrada
  a membership fee = una cuota (de socio)
  school fees = cuota del colegio (*feminine*),
  colegiatura (*feminine*) (*Mex*)
  a doctor's fees = los honorarios de un
  médico

feeble *adjective*
  = débil

feed *verb*
- (*to give food to*) = dar de comer a
- (*to eat*) = comer

feel *verb*
- (*emotionally, physically*)
  to feel sad = sentirse triste
  to feel hot/cold = tener calor/frío
  I don't feel very well = no me siento muy
  bien
  I didn't feel any pain = no sentí ningún
  dolor
- (*to touch*) = tocar
- (*to want*)
  I feel like a glass of water = tengo ganas de
  tomar un vaso de agua, me apetece un
  vaso de agua (*Spa*)
  I don't feel like it = no tengo ganas, no me
  apetece (*Spa*)

feeling *noun*
- (*emotional*)
  a feeling of sadness = una sensación de
  tristeza
  I have a feeling he's right = tengo la
  sensación de que tiene razón
- (*physical*)
  a feeling = una sensación

female
1 *adjective*

- (*when talking about animals*) = hembra
- (*when talking about humans*) =
  femenino/femenina
2 *noun*
- (*a woman*)
  a female = una mujer
- (*an animal*)
  a female = una hembra

feminine
1 *noun*
  (*in grammar*)
  the feminine = el femenino
2 *adjective* = femenino/femenina

feminist
1 *noun*
  a feminist = una feminista/un feminista
2 *adjective* = feminista

fence *noun*
  (*around a garden, field etc*)
  a fence = una cerca, un cerco (*Lat Am*)

ferry *noun*
  a ferry = un transbordador

fertile *adjective*
  = fértil

festival *noun*
- (*a holiday or feast*)
  a festival = una fiesta
- (*an artistic or theatrical event*)
  a festival = un festival

fetch *verb*
  (*to go and get*) = ir a buscar

fever *noun*
  fever = fiebre (*feminine*)

few
1 *adjective*
- (*not many*) = pocos/pocas
  the few people who came = las pocas
  personas que vinieron, los pocos que
  vinieron
- (*several*)
  over the next few days = durante los
  próximos días
  fewer people = menos gente
2 *pronoun* = pocos/pocas
  there are so few of them = son tan pocos
  fewer than ten people = menos de diez
  personas
3 a few
  a few houses = algunas casas
  a few of them = algunos de ellos
  I would like a few more = quisiera unos
  cuantos más

fiber (*US English*), fibre (*British English*)
- (*a material*)
  a fiber = una fibra
- (*in diet*)
  fiber = fibra (*feminine*)

fiction *noun*
fiction = ficción (*feminine*)

fiddle *verb*
to fiddle with something = juguetear con
algo

field *noun*
a field = un campo

fierce *adjective*
= feroz

fifteen *number* ▶ p. 154, p. 319
fifteen = quince (*masculine*) (**!** *never
changes*) *see also* five

fifth
1 *adjective* = quinto/quinta
2 *noun* ▶ p. 192
(*a part*)
a fifth = una quinta parte

fifty *number* ▶ p. 154, p. 319
fifty = cincuenta (*masculine*) (**!** *never
changes*) *see also* five

fight
1 *noun*
• (*physical*)
a fight = una pelea
• (*a quarrel*)
a fight = una pelea
• (*a struggle*)
a fight = una lucha
2 *verb*
• (*physically*) = pelear
• (*to quarrel*) = pelear
• (*to struggle*) = luchar
• (*to combat*)
to fight poverty = luchar contra la pobreza
• (*to engage in*)
to fight a war = librar una guerra

fighting *noun*
• (*between armies*)
fighting = enfrentamientos (*masculine
plural*)
• (*brawling*)
fighting = peleas (*feminine plural*)

figure *noun*
• (*a number*)
a figure = una cifra
• (*a person*)
a figure = una figura
• (*referring to a person's body*)
to have a good figure = tener buena
figura, tener buen tipo

file
1 *noun*
• (*for papers or documents*)
a file = una carpeta
• (*in computing*)
a file = un archivo

• (*for nails*)
a (**nail**) **file** = una lima (de uñas)
• **in single file** = en fila india
2 *verb*
• **to file a document** = archivar un
documento
• **to file one's nails** = limarse las uñas

filing cabinet *noun*
a filing cabinet = un archivero, un
archivador (*Mex*)

fill *verb*
• (*to make full*) = llenar
• (*to become full*) = llenarse
fill in = rellenar

film
1 *noun*
• (*in cinema or television*)
a film = una película
• (*for a camera*)
a film = una película (fotográfica)
2 *verb* = filmar

filthy *adjective*
= mugriento/mugrienta

final
1 *adjective*
• (*last*) = último/última
• (*definitive*)
the final result = el resultado final
2 *noun*
(*in sport*)
a final = una final

finally *adverb*
= finalmente

finance
1 *noun*
• (*funds*)
finance = financión (*feminine*),
financiamiento (*masculine*) (*Lat Am*)
2 *verb* = financiar

financial *adjective*
(*referring to a system*) =
financiero/financiera
financial difficulties = dificultades
económicas

find *verb*
= encontrar
I found it hard to concentrate = me
resultaba difícil concentrarme
find out
to find out the truth = descubrir la verdad
if he ever finds out = si algún día se llega a
enterar

fine
1 *adjective*
• (*very good, excellent*)
a fine novel = una novela excelente
the weather is fine = hace buen tiempo
a fine day = un día estupendo

- (*in good health or spirits*)
  I feel fine = estoy muy bien
2 *adverb* = muy bien
3 *noun*
  a fine = una multa
4 *verb*
  to fine someone = multar a alguien

finger *noun* ▶ **p. 235**
  a finger = un dedo

fingernail *noun*
  a fingernail = una uña

fingerprint *noun*
  a fingerprint = una huella digital

finish
1 *verb*
- (*to end*) = terminar, acabar
  I've finished writing my book = terminé de escribir mi libro
- (*to come to an end*) = terminar, acabar
2 *noun*
- (*the end*)
  the finish = el fin, el final
- (*in a race*)
  the finish = la llegada

Finland *proper noun* ▶ **p. 187**
  Finland = Finlandia (*feminine*)

fire
1 *noun*
  fire = fuego (*masculine*)
  to set fire to a house = prenderle fuego a una casa
  to be on fire = estar en llamas
  to catch fire = prender fuego
- (*an accident*)
  a fire = un incendio
2 *verb*
- (*to shoot*)
  to fire at someone = dispararle a alguien
  to fire a gun = disparar una pistola
- (*to dismiss*) = despedir

fire department (*US English*), **fire brigade** (*British English*) *noun*
  the fire department = el cuerpo de bomberos

fire engine *noun* (*British English*) ▶ **fire truck**

fire extinguisher *noun*
  a fire extinguisher = un extinguidor (*Lat Am*), un extintor (*Spa*)

firefighter *noun*
  a firefighter = un/una bombero

fireman *noun*
  a fireman = un bombero

fireplace *noun*
  a fireplace = una chimenea

fire truck *noun* (*US English*)
  a fire truck = un coche de bomberos, un carro de bomberos (*Mex*), un autobomba (*R Pl*)

fireworks *noun*
  fireworks = fuegos artificiales (*masculine plural*)

firm
1 *noun*
  a firm = una empresa, una firma, una compañía
2 *adjective* = firme

first
1 *noun* ▶ **p. 192**
- (*in a sequence or group*)
  the first = el primero/la primera
- (*the beginning*)
  at first = al principio
2 *adjective* = primero/primera

> ! *Note that* primero *becomes* primer *when it appears before a masculine singular noun*

  the first day = el primer día
  at first sight = a primera vista
3 *adverb*
- (*before others*)
  to arrive first = llegar primero
  he came first in the exam = sacó la mejor nota en el examen
- (*to begin with*) = primero, en primer lugar
  first of all = primero, en primer lugar
- (*for the first time*) = por primera vez

first aid *noun*
  first aid = primeros auxilios (*masculine plural*)

first class *adverb*
  to travel first class = viajar en primera clase

first-class *adjective*
  a first-class hotel = un hotel de primera clase
  a first-class stamp (*British English*) = una estampilla urgente (*Lat Am*), un timbre urgente (*Mex*), un sello urgente (*Spa*)

first floor *noun*
  the first floor (*US English*) = la planta baja (*British English*) = el primer piso

first name *noun*
  a first name = un nombre de pila

fish
1 *noun*
- (*an animal*)
  a fish = un pez
- (*as food*)
  fish = pescado (*masculine*)
2 *verb* = pescar

fisherman *noun*
a fisherman = un pescador

fishing *noun*
fishing = pesca (*feminine*)
to go fishing = ir a pescar

fist *noun*
a fist = un puño

fit
1 *adjective*
* (*suitable, appropriate*)
he's not fit to be king = no es digno de ser
rey
the water is not fit to drink = el agua no es
potable
2 *noun*
a fit = un ataque
he had a fit = le dio un ataque
a fit of coughing = un acceso de tos
3 *verb*
* (*to be the right size*)
it fits me perfectly = me queda perfecto
these shoes don't fit = estos zapatos no me
quedan bien
* (*to match*)
it fits your description = cuadra con tu
descripción
fit in
* (*into a room, car etc*)
will you all fit in? = ¿van a caber todos?

fitness *noun*
(**physical**) fitness = estado físico
(*masculine*)

five *number* ▶ **p. 154, p. 319**
five = cinco (*masculine*) (**!** *never changes*)
five apples = cinco manzanas
I have five of them = tengo cinco
two fives are ten (2 × 5 = 10) = dos
(multiplicado) por cinco (son) diez (2 ×
5 = 10)

fix *verb*
* (*to repair*) = arreglar
* (*to establish*) = fijar
to fix [a date | price | limit ...] = fijar [una fecha |
un precio | un límite ...]

fizzy *adjective*
= gaseoso/gaseosa

flag *noun*
a flag = una bandera

flame *noun*
a flame = una llama

flash
1 *noun*
* (*from a light*)
a flash = un destello
* (*in photography*)
a flash = un flash
2 *verb*
* (*to shine*) = destellar

* to flash one's headlights = hacer una señal
con los faros

flashlight *noun* (*US English*)
a flashlight = una linterna

flask *noun*
(*for tea or coffee*)
a flask = un termo

flat
1 *adjective*
* (*if it's a surface*) = plano/plana
* to have a flat tire = tener una rueda
desinflada
2 *noun* (*British English*)
a flat = un apartamento, un departamento
(*Lat Am*), un piso (*Spa*)

flatter *verb*
* (*to please*) = halagar
* (*to praise excessively*) = adular

flavor (*US English*), **flavour** (*British
English*)
1 *noun*
a flavor = un sabor
2 *verb* = sazonar

flaw *noun*
a flaw = un defecto

flea *noun*
a flea = una pulga

flee *verb*
= huir
they fled the country = huyeron del país

flesh *noun*
flesh = carne (*feminine*)

flexible *adjective*
= flexible

flicker *verb*
(*if it's a flame, light, or image*) = parpadear

flight *noun*
* (*in a plane*)
a flight = un vuelo
* (*of a bird*)
flight = vuelo (*masculine*)

flight attendant *noun*
a flight attendant = un/una sobrecargo, un
aeromozo/una aeromoza (*Lat Am*)

float *verb*
* (*in water*) = flotar
* (*in the air*) = flotar en el aire

flock *noun*
* (*of sheep, goats, geese*)
a flock = un rebaño
* (*of birds*)
a flock = una bandada

flood
1 *noun*
(*of a river*)
a flood = una inundación
2 *verb*
- (*to overflow*) = desbordarse
- (*to fill with water*) = inundar

floor *noun*
- (*of a room, a vehicle*)
the floor = el suelo
- (*a story*)
a floor = un piso

florist *noun*
a florist = un/una florista

flour *noun*
flour = harina (*feminine*)

flow
1 *verb*
blood flowed from the wound = sangre le salía de la herida
the river flows into the sea = el río desemboca en el mar
2 *noun*
the flow of traffic = la circulación

flower
1 *noun*
a flower = una flor
2 *verb* = florecer, florear (*Mex*)

flu *noun*
flu = gripe (*feminine*), gripa (*feminine*) (*Mex*)

fluent *adjective*
he speaks fluent Spanish = habla español con fluidez

fluff *noun*
fluff = pelusa (*feminine*)

fluid *noun*
- (*in biology, chemistry*)
a fluid = un fluido
- (*liquid nourishment*)
a fluid = un líquido

flush *verb*
to flush the toilet = tirar de la cadena, jalarle a la cadena (*Lat Am except SC*)

flute *noun*
a flute = una flauta

fly
1 *verb*
- (*if it's a bird, insect, airplane, kite etc*) = volar
- (*if it's an air passenger*) = ir en avión
- (*if it's a pilot*)
to fly a plane = pilotar un avión, pilotear un avión (*Lat Am*)
- **the ship was flying the British flag** = el barco llevaba la bandera británica

2 *noun*
a fly = una mosca
fly away = irse volando

foam *noun*
foam = espuma (*feminine*)

focus
1 *noun*
- (*in photography*)
the picture is not in focus = la foto está desenfocada
- (*the center*)
he was the focus of attention = fue el centro de atención
2 *verb*
- **to focus a camera** = enfocar una cámara
- (*to concentrate*)
to focus on employment = concentrarse en la cuestión del paro

fog *noun*
fog = niebla (*feminine*)

foggy *adjective*
it was foggy = había niebla

fold
1 *verb* = plegar, doblar
he folded his arms = cruzó los brazos
2 *noun*
(*in fabric, paper, skin*)
a fold = un pliegue

follow *verb*
= seguir
she followed him into the room = entró en el cuarto tras él
the winners were as follows . . . = los ganadores fueron los siguientes . . .

following
1 *adjective* = siguiente
2 *preposition*
following the accident = tras el accidente

fond *adjective*
to be fond of someone = tenerle cariño a alguien

food *noun*
food = comida (*feminine*)

fool
1 *noun*
a fool = un/una idiota
2 *verb*
to fool someone = engañar a alguien

foolish *adjective*
= tonto/tonta

foot *noun*
- (*of a person*) ▶ **p. 235**
the foot = un pie
on foot = a pie, andando
- (*of an animal*)
the foot = la pata

F

- (*in measurements*)
  a foot = un pie (= *30.48 cm*)

football *noun* ▶ p. 306
- (*soccer*) = fútbol (*masculine*), futbol (*masculine*) (*Mex*)
- (*American football*) = fútbol americano (*masculine*), futbol americano (*masculine*) (*Mex*)

footprint *noun*
  a footprint = una huella

footstep *noun*
  a footstep = un paso

for *preposition*
- = para
  the letter is for me = la carta es para mí
  to work for a company = trabajar para una compañía
  we went for a swim = fuimos a nadar
  he was criticized for his behavior = fue criticado por su comportamiento
  it's impossible for me to stay = me es imposible quedarme
- (*when talking about time*)
  I haven't seen him for three years = hace tres años que no lo veo
  he will be in Chicago for a year = va a estar en Chicago por un año
  she read for two hours = leyó durante dos horas
  I've been waiting for three hours = hace tres horas que estoy esperando
- (*indicating distance*)
  we drove for 80 kilometers = hicimos 80 kilómetros
- (*indicating the cost or amount of something*)
  he bought it for 50 pounds = lo compró por 50 libras
- (*representing*)
  what is the Spanish for 'badger' = ¿cómo se dice 'badger' en español?

forbid *verb*
  = prohibir
  he forbade the children to go out = a los niños les prohibió salir

force
1 *noun*
  force = fuerza (*feminine*)
  by force = a la fuerza
- (*in the police or military*)
  the police force = la policía
  the (armed) forces = las fuerzas armadas
2 *verb*
  he forced them to accept = los obligó a aceptar
force open
  = forzar

forecast
1 *noun*
  forecast = previsión (*feminine*)
  the weather forecast = el pronóstico del tiempo
2 *verb*
- (*if it's a result*) = prever
- (*if it's the weather*) = pronosticar

forehead *noun*
  the forehead = la frente

foreign *adjective*
  = extranjero/extranjera

foreigner *noun*
  a foreigner = un extranjero/una extranjera

forest *noun*
  a forest = un bosque

forever *adverb*
- (*for all time*) = para siempre
- (*always*) = siempre
  he is forever complaining = siempre se está quejando

forge *verb*
  = falsificar

forgery *noun*
  a forgery = una falsificación

forget *verb*
  = olvidar, olvidarse de

forgive *verb*
  = perdonar
  she forgave him for what he had done = le perdonó por lo que había hecho

fork *noun*
  a fork = un tenedor

form
1 *noun*
- (*a type or kind*)
  form = forma (*feminine*)
- (*a document*)
  a form = un formulario
- (*a shape*)
  a form = una forma
- (*referring to mood or fitness*)
  form = forma (*feminine*)
  to be in good form = estar en buena forma
- (*British English—a class in a school*)
  a form = un año
2 *verb*
- (*to create*) = formar
- (*to become created*) = formarse

formal *adjective*
- (*official*) = formal
- (*not casual*)
  formal dress = traje de etiqueta (*masculine*)
- (*if it's language*) = formal

former *adjective*
• (*previous*) = antiguo/antigua

> ! *antiguo/antigua come before the noun*
the former Prime Minister = la antigua
   primera ministra
his former wife = su ex-esposa

formula *noun*
  a formula = una fórmula

fortnight *noun* (*British English*)
  a fortnight = quince días (*masculine plural*)

fortunate *adjective*
  = afortunado/afortunada

fortunately *adverb*
  = afortunadamente

fortune
• (*wealth*)
  a fortune = una fortuna
• (*luck*)
  fortune = suerte (*feminine*)
  to tell someone's fortune = decirle la
   buenaventura a alguien

forty *number* ▶ p. 154, p. 319
  forty = cuarenta (*masculine*) (! *never
   changes*) *see also* five

forward
1 *adjective*
• (*at the front*) = hacia adelante
• (*cheeky*) = descarado/descarada
2 *adverb* (*US English*)
  = hacia adelante
3 *verb*
  to forward a letter = enviar una carta

forwards *adverb* (*British English*)
  = hacia adelante

fossil *noun*
  a fossil = un fósil

found *verb*
  = fundar

foundation *noun*
• (*a basis*)
  a foundation = una base
• (*in building*)
  foundations = cimientos (*masculine plural*)
• (*a cosmetic*)
  foundation = base (*feminine*)

founder *noun*
  the founder = el fundador/la fundadora

fountain *noun*
  a fountain = una fuente

four *number* ▶ p. 154, p. 319
  four = cuatro (*masculine*) (! *never
   changes*) *see also* five

fourteen *number* ▶ p. 154, p. 319
  fourteen = catorce (*masculine*) (! *never
   changes*) *see also* five

fourth
1 *adjective* = cuarto/cuarta
2 *noun* ▶ p. 192
  (*a part*)
  a fourth = una cuarta parte

fox *noun*
  a fox = un zorro

fraction *noun*
  a fraction = una fracción

fracture
1 *noun*
  a fracture = una fractura
2 *verb*
  he fractured his leg = se fracturó la pierna

fragile *adjective*
  = frágil

fragment *noun*
  a fragment = un fragmento

frame
1 *noun*
• (*of a picture, door, window*)
  a frame = un marco
• (*of a tennis racket*)
  a frame = la montura
• (*for glasses*)
  frames = el/la armazón
2 *verb* = enmarcar

France *noun* ▶ p. 187
  France = Francia (*feminine*)

frank *adjective*
  = franco/franca

fraud *noun*
  fraud = fraude (*masculine*)

freckle *noun*
  a freckle = una peca

free
1 *adjective*
• (*in liberty*) = libre
  to set someone free = dejar a alguien en
   libertad, poner a alguien en libertad
• (*not costing anything*) = gratis
• (*not occupied, available*) = libre
  is this seat free? = ¿está libre este asiento?
2 *adverb*
  (*without payment*) = gratis
3 *verb*
• (*if it's an animal*) = soltar
• (*if it's a person*) = dejar en libertad, poner
  en libertad

freedom *noun*
  freedom = libertad (*feminine*)

freeze *verb*
• (*in cold weather*) = helarse, congelarse
• (*when preserving food*) = congelar

F

- (*to feel cold*)
  I'm freezing = estoy helado/helada, estoy congelado/congelada
  to freeze to death = morir congelado/congelada
- (*to fix at a certain level*)
  to freeze prices = congelar los precios

freezer *noun*
  a freezer = un congelador

French ▶ p. 187, p. 245
1 *noun*
- (*the people*)
  the French = los franceses (*masculine plural*)
- (*the language*)
  French = francés (*masculine*)
2 *adjective* = francés/francesa

French fries *noun*
  French fries = papas fritas (*feminine plural*) (*Lat Am*), patatas fritas (*feminine plural*) (*Spa*)

Frenchman *noun* ▶ p. 187
  a Frenchman = un francés

Frenchwoman *noun* ▶ p. 187
  a Frenchwoman = una francesa

frequent *adjective*
  = frecuente

frequently *adverb*
  = con frecuencia

fresh *adjective*
  = fresco/fresca

freshen up *verb*
  = arreglarse

Friday *noun* ▶ p. 192
  Friday = viernes (*masculine*)

fridge *noun*
  a fridge = un refrigerador (*Lat Am*), un frigorífico (*Spa*), una heladera (*R Pl*)

fried *adjective*
  = frito/frita

friend *noun*
  a friend = un amigo/una amiga
  to make friends = hacer amigos

friendly *adjective*
- (*if it's a person*) = simpático/simpática
- (*if it's a smile, gesture, letter etc*) = amable

friendship *noun*
  friendship = amistad (*feminine*)

fright *noun*
  to give someone a fright = darle un susto a alguien

frighten *verb*
  = asustar

frightened *adjective*
  = asustado/asustada
  to be frightened = tener miedo
  she is frightened of dogs = les tiene miedo a los perros

frightening *adjective*
  = espantoso/espantosa

fringe *noun* (*British English*)
  a fringe = un flequillo, un cerquillo (*Lat Am*), un fleco (*Mex*)

frog *noun*
  a frog = una rana

from *preposition*
- (*referring to a point of origin*) = de
  he is from London = es de Londres
  the journey from Manchester to Birmingham = el viaje de Manchester a Birmingham
  we live ten minutes from the city center = vivimos a diez minutos de la ciudad
- (*referring to a point in time*)
  the shop is open from 8am to 6pm = la tienda está abierta desde las 8 de la mañana hasta las 6 de la tarde
  from June to August = desde junio hasta agosto
  from then on = a partir de ahí
  50 years from now = dentro de cincuenta años
- (*because of*)
  from experience I would say that . . . = según mi experiencia diría que . . .
  I know him from work = lo conozco del trabajo

front
1 *noun*
- the front of a building = la fachada de un edificio, el frente de un edificio
- (*of a garment*)
  the front = la delantera
- (*the forward section*)
  the front = el frente, la parte delantera
  sit in front = siéntate delante
- in front of = delante de
2 *adjective*
  = delantero/delantera
  the front seat = el asiento delantero
  the front wheel = la rueda delantera

front door *noun*
  the front door = la puerta de la calle

frontier *noun*
  a frontier = una frontera

front page *noun*
  the front page = la primera plana

front seat *noun*
  the front seat = el asiento delantero

frost *noun*
- (*sub-zero temperature*)
  frost = helada (*feminine*)

- (*frozen dew*)
frost = escarcha (*feminine*)
frost over = helarse, cubrirse de escarcha

frosty *adjective*
= helado/helada

frown *verb*
= fruncir el ceño

frozen *adjective*
= congelado/congelada

fruit *noun*
fruit = fruta (*feminine*)
a piece of fruit = una fruta

frustrate *verb*
= frustrar

frustrating *adjective*
= frustrante

fry *verb*
= freír

frying pan *noun*
a frying pan = una sartén, un sartén (*Lat Am*)

fuel *noun*
fuel = combustible (*masculine*)

fulfill (*US English*), **fulfil** (*British English*)
verb
to fulfill a duty = cumplir con un deber
to fulfill an ambition = hacer realidad una ambición

full *adjective*
- = lleno/llena
the streets were full of people = las calles estaban llenas de gente
- (*completely booked*) = lleno/llena
the train was full = el tren estaba lleno
- (*complete*)
you don't know the full story = no conoces toda la historia
to pay the full price = pagar el precio íntegro
his full name = su nombre completo
- (*maximum*)
at full speed = a toda velocidad

full moon *noun*
a full moon = una luna llena

full stop *noun* (*British English*)
a full stop = un punto

full-time *adverb*
= a tiempo parcial

fumes *noun*
fumes = gases (*masculine plural*)

fun *noun*
fun = diversión (*feminine*)
to have fun = divertirse
painting is great fun = la pintura es una gran diversión

function
1 *noun*
- (*a purpose or role*)
a function = una función
- (*a reception*)
a function = una recepción
2 *verb* = funcionar

fund
1 *noun*
- (*a reserve of money*)
a fund = un fondo
- (*cash reserves*)
funds = fondos (*masculine plural*)
2 *verb* = financiar

funeral *noun*
a funeral = un entierro

funny *adjective*
- (*amusing*) = divertido/divertida
- (*bizarre*) = raro/rara
it's funny that he hasn't phoned = es raro que no haya llamado

> ! Note the use of the subjunctive after es raro que

fur
1 *noun*
- (*on an animal*)
fur = pelaje (*masculine*)
- (*on a coat or jacket*)
fur = piel (*feminine*)
2 *adjective* = de piel, de pieles (*Spa*)

furious *adjective*
= furioso/furiosa

furnish *verb*
= amueblar, amoblar (*Lat Am*)

furniture *noun*
furniture = muebles (*masculine plural*)
a piece of furniture = un mueble

further
1 *adverb*
it was further than I thought = estaba más lejos de lo que pensaba
how much further is it? = ¿cuánto más allá queda?
- (*to a greater extent*)
prices fell even further = los precios bajaron aún más
2 *adjective*
(*additional*)
without further delay = sin perder más tiempo

fuss
1 *noun*
a fuss = un escándalo
to make a fuss = hacer un escándalo
2 *verb* = preocuparse

future

1 *noun*
   the future = el futuro
   in future = de ahora en adelante
2 *adjective* = futuro/futura

Gg

gale *noun*
   (*a wind*)
   a gale = un vendaval

gallery *noun*
* (*a museum*)
   a gallery = un museo
* (*a commercial showcase*)
   a gallery = una galería (de arte)

game *noun*
   a game = un juego
   a game of football/tennis = un partido de fútbol/tenis
   a game of chess = una partida de ajedrez, un partido de ajedrez (*Lat Am*)

games *noun* ▶ p. 306
   (*British English—in school*)
   games = deportes (*masculine plural*)

game show *noun*
   a game show = un programa concurso

gang *noun*
* (*a group of friends, young people*)
   a gang = una pandilla
* (*a group of criminals*)
   a gang = una banda, una pandilla

gap *noun*
* a gap (*in a fence or hedge*) = un hueco
   (*between buildings, cars*) = un espacio
* (*a period of time*)
   a gap = un intervalo, una interrupción

garage *noun*
* (*for parking*)
   a garage = un garaje, un garage (*Lat Am*), una cochera (*Mex*)
* (*for repairing cars, selling point*)
   a garage = un taller, un garage (*Lat Am*)
* (*British English—for fuel*)
   a garage = una gasolinera, una estación de nafta (*R Pl*)

garbage *noun* (*US English*)
   garbage = basura (*feminine*)

garbage can *noun* (*US English*)
   a garbage can = un cubo de la basura, un tacho de la basura (*SC*), un bote de la basura (*Mex*)

garbage collector, **garbage man**
noun (*US English*)
   a garbage collector = un basurero

garden *noun*
   a garden = un jardín

gardener *noun*
   a gardener = un jardinero/una jardinera

gardening *noun*
   gardening = jardinería (*feminine*)

garlic *noun*
   garlic = ajo (*masculine*)

garment *noun*
   a garment = una prenda (de ropa)

gas *noun*
* gas = gas (*masculine*)
* (*US English—petrol*)
   gas = gasolina (*feminine*), nafta (*feminine*) (*R Pl*)

gasoline *noun* (*US English*)
   gasoline = gasolina (*feminine*), nafta (*feminine*) (*R Pl*)

gas station *noun* (*US English*)
   a gas station = una gasolinera, una estación de nafta (*R Pl*)

gate *noun*
* (*an entrance*)
   a gate (*to a garden*) = una verja, una cancela (*Spa*), un portón (*SC*)
   (*to a town, a prison*) = una puerta
   (*to a field*) = un portón, una tranquera (*Lat Am*)
* (*in an airport*)
   a gate = una puerta de embarque

gather
* (*to come together*) = reunirse
* (*to collect*) = juntar, recoger

gay *adjective*
   = homosexual, gay (**!** *never changes*)

gear *noun*
* (*in a vehicle, on a bike*)
   a gear = una marcha, un cambio
   to be in first gear = estar en primera
* (*equipment*)
   gear = equipo (*masculine*)
* (*clothing*)
   my football gear = mi ropa de fútbol

Gemini *noun*
* (*the sign*)
   Gemini = Géminis
   I'm Gemini = soy Géminis, soy de Géminis
* (*a person*)
   a Gemini = un/una géminis

general
1 *noun*
* a general = un/una general
* in general = en general
2 *adjective* = general

general knowledge *noun*
general knowledge = cultura general
  (*feminine*)

generation *noun*
a generation = una generación

generous *adjective*
= generoso/generosa

genius *noun*
a genius = un genio

gentle *adjective*
• (*if it's a heat, a breeze, a murmur*) = suave
• (*if it's a person*) = dulce

gentleman *noun*
• (*a man*) = un señor
• (*a polite man*) = un caballero

genuine *adjective*
(*real*) = auténtico/auténtica

geography *noun*
geography = geografía (*feminine*)

germ *noun*
a germ = un microbio, un germen

German ▶ p. 187, p. 245
1 *adjective* = alemán/alemana
2 *noun*
• (*a person*)
a German = un alemán/una alemana
• (*the language*)
German = alemán (*masculine*)

Germany *noun* ▶ p. 187
Germany = Alemania (*feminine*)

get *verb*

> ! *The word* **get** *is extremely common in English and does not have a multi-purpose Spanish equivalent. This entry covers the most frequent uses of* **get** *but to find translations for other expressions using* **get**—*to get angry, to get better, to get wet etc, look up the entries at* **angry, better, wet** *etc*

• (*to become*)
to get old = envejecer
to get worried = preocuparse
to get jealous = ponerse celoso/celosa
the situation is getting complicated = la
  situación se complica

> ! *Note that there is very often a single verb translation for the English* | **get** + **adjective**

• (*to ask or persuade*)
I'll get him to lend me the money = le
  pediré que me preste el dinero
get her to call me = dile que me llame
• (*to cause to be done or happen*)
to get the car cleaned = hacer limpiar el
  coche
you got your hair cut = te cortaste el pelo

• (*to arrive*) = llegar
I called when we got there = llamé cuando
  llegamos allí
• (*to be*)
you'll get killed = te vas a matar
a few chairs got broken = se rompieron
  unas cuantas sillas
• (*to obtain*)
I got a job in publishing = conseguí un
  trabajo en el campo editorial
to get a present for someone, to get
  someone a present = comprarle un
  regalo a alguien
I'll get something to eat at the station =
  comeré algo en la estación
get some rest = descansa un poco
• (*to receive*) = recibir
I got a letter from Mark = recibí una carta
  de Mark
to get good marks = sacar buenas notas
• (*to fetch*) = buscar
he's gone to get help = fue a buscar ayuda
• (*to prepare*)
to get breakfast = preparar el desayuno
• (*to experience*)
to get a shock = llevarse un shock
• (*to have the opportunity*)
I hope I get to use the computer = espero
  poder usar la computadora
• (*to catch or fall ill with*) = agarrar, coger
  (*Spa*)
she got a cold = se resfrió
• (*to use for transport*)
we can get the train = podemos tomar el
  tren, podemos coger el tren (*Spa*)
• (*to make progress*)
to be getting somewhere = avanzar

> ! *For the translation of* **to have got** (*meaning to have*), *see the entries* **have** *and* **got**. *For a translation of* **I've got to** [go | work | eat *etc* …] *see the entry* **got**

get about ▶ **get around**
get across
(*to cross*) = cruzar
get along
• (*to cope*) = arreglárselas
• (*to have a good relationship*) = llevarse bien
I get along well with her = me llevo bien
  con ella
get around
I need a car to get around = necesito un
  coche para desplazarme
get away
(*to escape*) = escaparse
get back
• (*to return*) = volver, regresar
• (*to regain*)
did you get your money back? = ¿te
  devolvieron el dinero?
get in
(*to enter*) = entrar
get off
• (*to leave a bus or train*) = bajarse
he fell as he was getting off the train = se
  cayó al bajar del tren
• (*to remove*) = quitar

G

get on
- (*to climb aboard a bus or train*) = subirse
  to get on the train = subirse al tren
- (*to have a good relationship*) = llevarse bien
  I get on well with her = me llevo bien con
  ella

get out
- (*to leave*) = salir
- (*to bring out*) = sacar
  to get the furniture out of the house = sacar
  los muebles de la casa

get over
  (*to recover from*)
  to get over a shock = reponerse de un
  shock

get through
  (*to contact by phone*)
  to get through to someone = comunicarse
  con alguien

get together = reunirse
get up = levantarse

ghost *noun*
  a ghost = un fantasma

giant *noun*
  a giant = un gigante/una giganta

gift *noun*
- (*a present*)
  a gift = un regalo
- (*a talent*)
  a gift = un don
  he has a gift for languages = tiene talento
  para los idiomas

ginger
1 *noun*
  ginger = jengibre (*masculine*)
2 *adjective* ▶ p. 183
  she has ginger hair = es pelirroja
  a ginger cat = un gato rojizo

girl *noun*
- (*a baby or child*)
  a girl = una niña
- (*a young woman*)
  a girl = una chica, una muchacha

girlfriend *noun*
- (*in a couple*)
  a girlfriend = una novia
- (*a female friend*)
  a girlfriend = una amiga

give *verb*
  to give = dar
  I gave him the photos = le di las fotos
  I gave them to him = se los/las di
  give me the newspapers = dame los
  periódicos
  give them to me = dámelos/dámelas
- (*to pass on*)
  to give someone a message = darle un
  mensaje a alguien
- (*to allow*) = dar
  I was given two weeks to do the work = me
  dieron dos semanas para hacer el trabajo

give away
- (*to give*) = regalar
- (*to reveal*) = revelar
give back = devolver, regresar (*Lat Am*)
give in = ceder
give out = repartir
give up
- to give up smoking = dejar de fumar
  to give up a job = renunciar a un empleo
- (*to surrender*)
  to give oneself up to the police =
  entregarse a la policía
give way
- (*to collapse*) = ceder, romperse
- (*British English—when driving*) = ceder el
  paso

glad *adjective*
  I am very glad to see you = me alegro
  mucho de verte
  I'm glad that you're coming = me alegro de
  que vengas

  ! *Note the use of the subjunctive after*
  alegrarse de que

glass *noun*
- (*the material*)
  glass = vidrio (*masculine*), cristal
  (*masculine*) (*Spa*)
- (*for drinking*)
  a glass = un vaso

glasses *noun*
  glasses = gafas (*feminine plural*), lentes
  (*masculine plural*) (*Lat Am*), anteojos
  (*masculine plural*) (*Lat Am*)

glitter *verb*
  = relumbrar

globe *noun*
- (*the earth*)
  the globe = el globo
- (*a model of the earth*)
  a globe = un globo terráqueo

gloomy *adjective*
- (*dark*) = sombrío/sombría
- (*sad*) = lúgubre

glove *noun*
  a glove = un guante

glow
1 *noun*
  a glow = un brillo
2 *verb*
  (*to give off light*) = brillar
  the lamp glowed = la lámpara brillaba, la
  lámpara resplandecía

glue
1 *noun*
  glue = goma de pegar (*feminine*),
  pegamento (*masculine*)
2 *verb*
  (*to stick*) = pegar

go
1 *verb*

> ! Generally, **to go** *is translated by* ir(se). *There are a great many verbs such as* go away, go back, go round *etc., which are listed at the end of this entry. For translations of expressions like* I'm going to [leave | go to London | learn to drive …] *see the entry* going

- (*to get from one place to another*) = ir
  where are you going? = ¿dónde vas?, ¿adónde vas?
  we went to the cinema = fuimos al cine
  to go shopping = ir de compras
  let's go and see them, let's go see them = vamos a verlos
  to go into a room = entrar en un cuarto, entrar a un cuarto (*Lat Am*)
- (*to leave*)
  he's going at the end of the month = se va a fin de mes
  the train goes at 6 o'clock = el tren sale a las seis
- (*when talking about time*)
  the time goes quickly = el tiempo pasa volando
  there are only three days to go before Christmas = faltan sólo tres días para Navidad
- (*to disappear*)
  the money's gone (*spent*) = el dinero se acabó
  I left my bike here and now it's gone = dejé mi bici aquí y ahora ha desaparecido
- (*to become*)
  to go red = enrojecerse
  to go pale = palidecer
  to go blind = quedarse ciego/ciega
  to go mad, to go crazy = volverse loco/loca
- (*in polite enquiries*)
  how's it going? = ¿qué tal?
  everything's going very well = todo va muy bien
  how did the exam go? = ¿qué tal el examen?
- (*match*)
  the skirt and blouse go well together = la falda y la blusa combinan bien
  the dress doesn't really go with your jacket = en realidad el vestido no queda bien con tu chaqueta
- **two burgers to go** = (*US English*) = dos hamburguesas para llevar

2 *noun*
- (*a turn*)
  a go = un turno
  it's your go = te toca a ti
- (*a try*)
  to have a go at doing something = intentar hacer algo
  have another go = inténtalo de nuevo
go across = cruzar
go after = perseguir
go ahead = seguir adelante
go along = ir

go around
- **to go around a corner** = doblar una esquina
- (*to walk around, to visit*)
  to go around the museums = visitar los museos
- (*to become known*)
  there's a rumor going around that you're leaving = corre el rumor de que te vas
- (*to be enough*)
  is there enough bread to go around? = ¿hay suficiente pan para todo el mundo?
go away = irse
go back = volver, regresar
  to go back to sleep = volverse a dormir
go by = pasar
go down = bajar
go for
- (*to attack*) = atacar
go in
- (*to enter*) = entrar
- (*to return inside*) entrar de nuevo
go off
- (*to explode*) = estallar
- (*to ring*) = sonar
  my alarm clock didn't go off = no sonó el despertador
- (*to leave*) = irse
- (*to go bad, sour*) = echarse a perder
- (*to be switched off*) = apagarse
go on
- (*to continue*) = seguir
  to go on talking = seguir hablando
- (*to happen*) = pasar
  what's going on? = ¿qué pasa?
- (*to be switched on*) = encenderse, prenderse (*Lat Am*)
go out
- (*to leave the house*) = salir
  to go out for a walk = salir a dar un paseo
- (*as a boyfriend, girlfriend*)
  to go out with someone = salir con alguien
- (*to be switched off, to stop burning*) = apagarse
go over
- (*to check*) = revisar
- (*to revise*) = repasar
go round (*British English*) ▶ **go around**
go through
- (*to experience*)
  to go through a difficult time = pasar por un período difícil
- (*to search*) = registrar, revisar (*Lat Am*)
go up
- (*by stairs, elevator*) = subir
  he went up to bed = subió a dormir
- (*to rise*) = subir, aumentar
go without = pasar sin

goal *noun*
- (*the structure*)
  the goal = la portería, el arco (*Lat Am*)

G

- (*a point*)
  a goal = un gol
- (*an objective*)
  a goal = una meta

goalkeeper *noun*
  a goalkeeper = un portero/una portera, un arquero/una arquera (*Lat Am*)

goat *noun*
  a goat = una cabra

god *noun*
  a god = un dios
  God = Dios

goddaughter *noun*
  a goddaughter = una ahijada

goddess *noun*
  a goddess = una diosa

godfather *noun*
  a godfather = un padrino

godmother *noun*
  a godmother = una madrina

godson *noun*
  a godson = un ahijado

going
  (*expressing the near future*)
  to be going to = ir a
  I'm going to leave = voy a irme
  this peace is not going to last = esta paz no va a durar
  we were going to phone you = te íbamos a llamar

gold
1 *noun*
  (*the metal*)
  gold = oro (*masculine*)
2 *adjective* = de oro

goldfish *noun*
  a goldfish = un pez de colores

golf *noun* ▶ p. 306
  golf = golf (*masculine*)

golf course *noun*
  a golf course = un campo de golf, una cancha de golf (*Lat Am*)

good
1 *adjective*
  good = bueno/buena

  ! Note that **bueno** becomes **buen** when it appears before a masculine singular noun

  a good book = un buen libro
  we've got some good news = tenemos buenas noticias
  he's good at chemistry = es bueno para la química
  to have good eyesight = tener buena vista
  spinach is good for you = las espinacas son buenas para la salud
  I don't feel too good = no me siento muy bien

if the weather's good, we'll go out = si hace buen tiempo saldremos
- (*talking about food*)
  the coffee is very good = el café está muy bueno, el café está buenísimo
  that tastes good = eso tiene buen sabor
  the cake looks good = el pastel tiene buena pinta
- (*well-behaved*)
  the dog's very good = el perro es muy bueno
  be good! = ¡pórtate bien!
2 *noun*
- (*use*)
  it's no good complaining = no sacarás nada con quejarte
  the change will do you good = el cambio te hará bien
- **for good** = para siempre
3 *exclamation*
- (*when pleased, satisfied*)
  good! = ¡qué bueno!
- (*when praising, encouraging*)
  good! = ¡muy bien!

goodbye *noun, exclamation*
  goodbye = adiós

good-looking *adjective*
  = guapo/guapa, buen mozo/buena moza (*Lat Am*)

goodnight *exclamation*
  goodnight = buenas noches

goods *noun*
  (*items for sale*)
  goods = artículos (*masculine plural*), mercancías (*feminine plural*)

goose *noun*
  a goose = un ganso

gooseberry *noun*
  a gooseberry = una grosella espinosa

gorilla *noun*
  a gorilla = un gorila

gossip
1 *noun*
- (*harmful talk*)
  gossip = chismes (*masculine plural*), cotilleo✖ (*masculine*) (*Spa*)
  to have a gossip = chismorrear✖, cotillear✖ (*Spa*)
- (*a person*)
  a gossip = un chismoso/una chismosa
2 *verb* = chismorrear✖, cotillear✖ (*Spa*)

got: to have got *verb* (*British English*)
- (*to have*) = tener
  I've got a lot of work to do = tengo mucho trabajo que hacer
  have you got a cold? = ¿estás resfriada?
- (*to be obliged*)
  to have got to = tener que
  I have got to work = tengo que trabajar

government *noun*
a government = un gobierno

GP *noun*
a GP = un médico/una médica de medicina general

grab *verb*
to grab someone by the arm = agarrar a alguien del brazo
he tried to grab my purse = intentó arrebatarme el monedero

graceful *adjective*
= lleno/llena de gracia

grade *noun*
• (*quality of an object, a material*)
the grade = la calidad
• (*a mark*)
a grade = una nota
• (*US English—a class*)
a grade = un año, un curso

grade school *noun* (*US English*)
grade school = escuela primaria (*feminine*)

gradually *adverb*
= poco a poco, de a poco (*Lat Am*)

gram, gramme *noun*
a gram = un gramo

grammar *noun*
grammar = gramática (*feminine*)

grandchild *noun*
a grandchild = un nieto/una nieta
the grandchildren = los nietos

granddaughter *noun*
a granddaughter = una nieta

grandfather *noun*
a grandfather = un abuelo

grandmother *noun*
a grandmother = una abuela

grandparents *noun*
grandparents = abuelos (*masculine plural*)

grandson *noun*
a grandson = un nieto

grape *noun*
a grape = una uva

grapefruit *noun*
a grapefruit = una toronja (*Lat Am*), un pomelo (*SC, Spa*)

grass *noun*
• grass = hierba (*feminine*)
• (*the lawn*)
the grass = el césped, la hierba, el pasto (*Lat Am*), la grama (*C Am*)

grasshopper *noun*
a grasshopper = un saltamontes

grateful *adjective*
= agradecido/agradecida

grave *noun*
a grave = una tumba, una sepultura

graveyard *noun*
a graveyard = un cementerio, un panteón (*Mex*)

gray (*US English*) *adjective* ▶ p. 183
• = gris
• (*used of hair*)
to have gray hair = ser canoso/canosa, tener el pelo canoso
she is going gray = le están saliendo canas

grease *noun*
grease = grasa (*feminine*)

greasy *adjective*
your hands are greasy = tienes las manos grasientas
a greasy overall = un overol cubierto de grasa
to have greasy hair = tener el pelo graso, tener el pelo grasoso (*Lat Am*)

great *adjective*
• (*when stressing size, amount, importance*)
= grande
the great cities of Europe = las grandes ciudades de Europa
a great improvement = una gran mejora

> ! Note that grande *becomes* gran *before a singular noun*

• (*when showing enthusiasm*)
it's a great idea = es una idea estupenda
(that's) great! = ¡qué bien!, ¡fenomenal!

Great Britain *noun* ▶ p. 187
Great Britain = Gran Bretaña (*feminine*)

great-grandfather *noun*
a great-grandfather = un bisabuelo

great-grandmother *noun*
a great-grandmother = una bisabuela

Greece *noun* ▶ p. 187
Greece = Grecia (*feminine*)

greedy *adjective*
= glotón/glotona

Greek ▶ p. 187, p. 245
1 *adjective* = griego/griega
2 *noun*
• (*a person*)
a Greek = un griego/una griega
• (*the language*)
Greek = griego (*masculine*)

green *adjective* ▶ p. 183
= verde

greenhouse *noun*
a greenhouse = un invernadero

grey *adjective* (*British English*) ▶ gray

greyhound *noun*
a greyhound = un galgo

grief *noun*
grief = dolor (*masculine*)

grill
1 *noun*
- (*British English—on a stove*)
a grill = un grill, un gratinador
- (*on a barbecue*)
a grill = una parrilla
2 *verb*
- (*British English—to cook on a stove*) =
hacer al grill
- (*to cook over charcoal*) = hacer a la parrilla

grin
1 *noun*
a grin = una sonrisa
2 *verb* = sonreír

grind *verb*
(*if it's coffee or wheat*) = moler
(*US English—if it's meat*) = moler, picar
(*R Pl, Spa*)

groan *verb*
to groan (*in pain*) = gemir
(*when annoyed*) = gruñir

grocer *noun*
a grocer = un tendero/una tendera, un
abarrotero/una abarrotera (*Mex*), un
almacenero/una almacenera (*SC*)
a grocer's shop (*British English*) = una
tienda de comestibles, una tienda de
abarrotes (*C Am, Mex*), un almacén (*SC*)

grocery *noun*
a grocery = una tienda de comestibles, una
tienda de abarrotes (*C Am, Mex*), un
almacén (*SC*)

ground *noun*
- the ground = el suelo
to get up off the ground = levantarse
- (*a piece of land*)
a piece of ground = un terreno

ground beef *noun* (*US English*)
ground beef = carne molida (*feminine*),
carne picada (*feminine*) (*R Pl, Spa*)

ground floor *noun* (*British English*)
the ground floor = la planta baja

grounds *noun*
- (*part of a property*)
grounds = parque (*masculine*), jardines
(*masculine plural*)
- (*reasons*)
to have grounds for complaint = tener
motivo de queja

group *noun*
- (*a number of people*)
a group = un grupo

- (*a musical band*)
a group = un grupo, un conjunto

grow *verb*
- (*to get big, strong*) = crecer
- (*to cultivate*) = cultivar
- (*to get long*) = crecer
my nails are growing = mis uñas están
creciendo
- (*to let grow*)
to grow a beard = dejarse la barba
- (*to become*) = volverse
to grow old = envejecerse
- (*to increase in size, importance*)
the population will grow = la población va a
aumentar

grow up = hacerse mayor

grumble *verb*
= refunfuñar
to grumble about the weather = quejarse
del tiempo

guarantee
1 *verb* = garantizar
2 *noun*
a guarantee = una garantía

guard
1 *verb*
to guard the president = proteger al
presidente
to guard the palace = vigilar el palacio
2 *noun*
- (*in a prison*)
a guard = un carcelero/una carcelera
- (*at a bank*)
a guard = un/una guarda de seguridad
- (*in the army*)
a guard = una guardia
to be on guard = estar de guardia

guard dog *noun*
a guard dog = un perro guardián

guess *verb*
= adivinar
guess who's here? = ¿adivina a quién está
aquí?
to guess right = acertar, atinar(le) (*Mex*)

guest *noun*
- (*a person invited to stay*)
a guest = un invitado/una invitada
- (*a client at a hotel*)
a guest = un/una huésped

guesthouse *noun* (*British English*)
a guesthouse = una pensión

guide
1 *noun*
- (*a book*)
a guide = una guía

- (*a person*)
  a guide = un/una guía
  a tour guide = un/una guía de turismo,
    un/una guía de turistas (*Mex*)
  2 *verb* = guiar

guidebook *noun*
  a guidebook = una guía

guided tour *noun*
  a guided tour = una visita guiada

guilty *adjective*
  = culpable

guitar *noun*
  a guitar = una guitarra

gum *noun*
- (*part of the body*) ▶ **p. 235**
  the gum = la encía
- (*chewing gum*)
  gum = chicle (*masculine*)
  a piece of gum = un chicle
- (*British English — glue*)
  gum = goma de pegar (*feminine*)

gun *noun*
- (*a pistol*)
  a gun = una pistola
- (*a rifle*)
  a gun = un fusil, una escopeta

gym *noun*
  (*a gymnasium*)
  a gym = un gimnasio

gymnasium *noun*
  a gymnasium = un gimnasio

gymnastics *noun*
  gymnastics = gimnasia (*feminine*)

gypsy *noun*
  a gypsy = un gitano/una gitana

habit *noun*
  a habit = una costumbre

hail
  1 *noun*
  hail = granizo (*masculine*)
  2 *verb* = granizar

hair *noun*
- (*on head*) ▶ **p. 235**
  hair = pelo (*masculine*)
  to have black hair = tener el pelo negro
- (*a single strand*)
  a hair = un pelo

- (*on the body*)
  hair = vello (*masculine*)
- (*on an animal*)
  the hair = el pelo

hairbrush *noun*
  a hairbrush = un cepillo

haircut *noun*
  a haircut = un corte de pelo
  to have a haircut = cortarse el pelo

hairdresser *noun*
  a hairdresser = un peluquero/una
    peluquera
  a hairdresser's (*shop*) = una peluquería

hairdrier *noun*
  a hairdrier = un secador, una secadora
    (*Mex*)

hairstyle *noun*
  a hairstyle = un peinado

half
  1 *noun*
- **half** = mitad (*feminine*)
  to cut something in half = cortar algo por la
    mitad
- (*in fractions*)
  a half = un medio
- (*a period in a game*)
  a half = un tiempo
  2 *adjective*
- (*when talking about quantities*)
  half a liter of milk = medio litro de leche
  two and a half cups of flour = dos tazas y
    media de harina
  3 *pronoun*
- (*when talking about quantities, numbers*)
  he has already spent half of his salary = ya
    gastó la mitad de su sueldo
  half the pupils walk to school = la mitad de
    los alumnos van al colegio a pie
- (*when talking about time, age*) ▶ **p. 319**
  an hour and a half = una hora y media
  it's half (past) three = son las tres y media
  he's three and a half = tiene tres años y
    medio
  4 *adverb*
  the bottle is half empty = la botella está
    medio vacía
  the door was half closed = la puerta estaba
    entreabierta

half an hour *noun*
  half an hour = media hora (*feminine*)

half hour *noun*
  a half hour = media hora (*feminine*)

half term *noun* (*British English*)
  half term = vacaciones de mitad de
    trimestre (*feminine plural*)

hall *noun*
- (*in a house, an apartment*)
  a hall = un vestíbulo, una entrada
- (*for public events*)
  a hall = una sala, un salón

H

ham noun
ham = jamón (masculine)

hamburger noun
- (a burger)
  a hamburger = una hamburguesa
- (US English—ground beef)
  hamburger = carne molida (feminine),
  carne picada (feminine) (R Pl, Spa)

hammer
1 noun
a hammer = un martillo
2 verb = martillear

hand
1 noun
- (part of the body) ▶ p. 235
  the hand = la mano
  they were holding hands = iban de la
  mano, iban tomados de la mano, iban
  cogidos de la mano (Spa)
- (help)
  to lend a hand = echar una mano
- (on a clock or watch)
  a hand = una manecilla
- on the one hand . . ., on the other . . . = por
  un lado . . ., por otro lado . . .
2 verb
to hand a book to someone, to hand
someone a book = pasarle un libro a
alguien
hand around
to hand around the biscuits = pasar las
galletas
hand in = entregar
hand out = repartir, distribuir
hand over = entregar
hand round (British English) ▶ hand
around

handbag noun
a handbag = una cartera, un bolso (Spa),
una bolsa (Mex)

handbrake noun
- (US English—on a bicycle)
  a handbrake = un freno (de pastilla)
- (British English—in a car)
  a handbrake = un freno de mano

handicapped adjective
= minusválido/minusválida
mentally handicapped = minusválido
psíquico/minusválida psíquica

handkerchief noun
a handkerchief = un pañuelo

handle
1 noun
a handle (on a door) = un picaporte
(on a drawer) = un tirador
(on a bag) = un asa (feminine)
(on a cup, a saucepan) = un asa (feminine)
(on a spade, a knife) = un mango
2 verb

- (to deal with, cope with)
  to handle a situation = manejar una
  situación
- (to control, manage)
  to handle a car = manejar un coche
  to know how to handle children = saber
  tratar a los niños

handlebars noun
the handlebars = el manillar, el manubrio
(Lat Am)

handsome adjective
= guapo/guapa, buen mozo/buena moza
(Lat Am)

handwriting noun
handwriting = letra (feminine)

handy adjective
the guidebook was very handy = la guía
resultó ser muy útil
to come in handy = venir muy bien

hang verb
- (to attach to a hook, coat hanger, line)
  to hang a picture on the wall = colgar un
  cuadro en la pared
  to hang clothes in a wardrobe = colgar la
  ropa en un ropero
- (to be attached)
  there was a lightbulb hanging from the
  ceiling = la bombilla colgaba del techo
- (to kill) = ahorcar
  he was hanged = lo ahorcaron
hang on
(to wait) = esperar
hang on to
she was hanging on to the rope = se
aferraba a la cuerda
hang out
your shirt is hanging out = tienes la camisa
afuera
to hang out the washing = tender la ropa
hang up
- (to attach to a hook, coat hanger) = colgar
- (to put the phone down) = colgar, cortar
  (SC)

happen verb
= pasar, suceder, ocurrir
what's happening? = ¿qué pasa?
what happened to you? = ¿qué te pasó?

happy adjective
to make someone happy = hacer feliz a
alguien
to be happy (with something) = estar
contento/contenta (con algo)

harbor (US English), **harbour** (British
English) noun
a harbor = un puerto

hard
1 adjective

C Am Central America   Lat Am Latin America   Mex Mexico

- (*firm, stiff*) = duro/dura
  to go hard = endurecerse
- (*difficult*) = difícil
  it's hard to understand = es difícil de
    entender
- (*harsh, tough*)
  a hard winter = un invierno crudo, un
    invierno severo
  hard luck! = ¡mala suerte!
  she's a hard woman = es una mujer muy
    dura
2 *adverb*
  to work hard = trabajar duro
  they hit him hard = le pegaron muy fuerte

hard-boiled *adjective*
  a hard-boiled egg = un huevo duro

hardly *adverb*
  (*barely*) = apenas

hardware *noun*
- (*for computers*)
  hardware = hardware (*masculine*)
- (*for use in the home, garden*)
  hardware = ferretería (*feminine*)

hardware store (*US English*),
hardware shop (*British English*) *noun*
  a hardware store = una ferretería, una
    tlapalería (*Mex*)

hardworking *adjective*
  = trabajador/trabajadora

hare *noun*
  a hare = una liebre

harm
1 *verb*
  to harm someone = hacerle daño a alguien
  to harm the environment = dañar el medio
    ambiente
2 *noun*
  to do harm to someone = hacerle daño a
    alguien
  there's no harm in trying = nada se pierde
    con intentar

harmful *adjective*
  a harmful gas = un gas nocivo
  the harmful effects of alcohol = el efecto
    perjudicial del alcohol

harmless *adjective*
  = inofensivo/inofensiva

harp *noun*
  a harp = un arpa (*feminine*)

harsh *adjective*
  a harsh climate = un clima riguroso
  to live in harsh conditions = vivir en
    condiciones duras
  a harsh light = una luz fuerte

harvest *noun*
  the harvest (*of wheat, fruit*) = la cosecha
  (*of grapes*) = la vendimia

hat *noun*
  a hat = un sombrero

hatch *verb*
  (*if it's a chick*) = salir del cascarón

hate *verb*
  = odiar

hatred *noun*
  hatred = odio (*masculine*)

haunted *adjective*
  = embrujado/embrujada

have
1 *verb*
- **to have, to have got** (*British English*) =
    tener
  she has a dog = tiene un perro
- (*to eat, drink, smoke*)
  to have a sandwich = comer un sándwich
  to have a glass of wine = tomar una copa
    de vino
  to have a cigarette = fumar un cigarrillo
  to have dinner = cenar, comer (*Lat Am*)
- (*to get*)
  I had a letter from Bob yesterday = recibí
    una carta de Bob ayer
  we have had no news from her = no hemos
    tenido noticias suyas
- (*to hold or organize*)
  to have a party = hacer una fiesta
  to have a meeting = hacer una reunión
- (*to spend*)
  I'll have a good time in Paris = lo voy a
    pasar bien en París
- (*to suffer*)
  to have flu = tener gripe
  to have a headache = tener dolor de
    cabeza
- (*to get something done*)
  to have the house painted = hacer pintar
    la casa
  she had her hair cut = se cortó el pelo
- (*to give birth to*) = tener
2 *auxiliary verb*
- (*when used to form a past tense*)
  I've lost my bag = he perdido la bolsa,
    perdí la bolsa (*Lat Am*)
  have you seen Tom? = ¿has visto a Tom?,
    ¿viste a Tom? (*Lat Am*)
  I had seen her = la había visto
  they have arrived = han llegado, llegaron
    (*Lat Am*)
- (*in questions and short answers*)
  you've met her, haven't you? = ya la
    conoces ¿no?
  you haven't lost the key, have you? = ¡no
    habrás perdido la llave
3 **to have to** = tener que
  I have to study = tengo que estudiar
have on
  to have a coat on = tener puesto un abrigo

H

hay *noun*
  hay = heno (*masculine*)

hazelnut *noun*
  a hazelnut = una avellana

he *pronoun*
  he = él
  he went to the theater = fue al teatro
  he did it = él lo hizo
  I work in London but he doesn't = yo
    trabajo en Londres pero él no

> **!** *Although* **él** *is given as the translation of*
> he, *it is in practice used only for*
> *emphasis, or to avoid ambiguity*

head
1 *noun*
- (*part of the body*) ▶ **p. 235**
  the head = la cabeza
- (*the front or the top*)
  at the head of the list = a la cabeza de la
    lista, encabezando la lista
- (*the top part of an object, tool*)
  the head of a nail = la cabeza de un clavo
  the head of a hammer = la cabeza de un
    martillo
- (*British English—a principal*)
  a head = un director/una directora
- (*a person in charge*)
  the head (*of an organization*) = el
    director/la directora
  (*of a family, government*) = el jefe/la jefa
2 *verb*
- (*to be in charge of*)
  to head a team = capitanear un equipo
- (*to be bound for*)
  I was heading home = me dirigía a casa
  where are you heading?, where are you
    headed? = ¿para dónde vas?
- (*in football*)
  to head the ball = cabecear el balón
head for
  I headed for the exit = me dirigí hacia la
    salida

headache *noun*
  a headache = un dolor de cabeza

headlamp, headlight *noun*
  a headlamp = un faro, un foco (*Lat Am*)

headline *noun*
- (*in a newspaper*)
  a headline = un titular
- (*on TV, radio*)
  the news headlines = el resumen
    informativo

headphones *noun*
  a pair of headphones = unos auriculares,
    unos cascos (*Spa*)

headquarters *noun*
  the headquarters (*of a company*) = la
    oficina central

(*of an army*) = el cuartel

headteacher *noun* (*British English*)
  a headteacher = un director/una directora

heal *verb*
  to heal someone = curar a alguien
  the wound has healed = la herida ha
    cicatrizado

health *noun*
  health = salud (*feminine*)
  to be in good health = estar bien de salud

healthy *adjective*
- (*in good health*) = sano/sana
- (*good for the health*) = sano/sana, saludable

heap *noun*
  a heap = un montón, una pila

hear *verb*
- to hear = oír
- (*to learn, discover*)
  to hear the news = enterarse de lo que ha
    pasado
  did you hear who won? = ¿sabes quién
    ganó?
- (*to listen to*) = escuchar
- (*to have news from*)
  we haven't heard from her = no sabemos
    nada de ella
hear of
  I've never heard of the place = nunca he
    oído hablar del lugar

heart *noun*
- (*part of the body*) ▶ **p. 235**
  the heart = el corazón
- (*the center*)
  the office is right in the heart of London =
    la oficina se encuentra en el corazón de
    Londres
- (*when talking about knowledge*)
  by heart = de memoria

heart attack *noun*
  a heart attack = un ataque al corazón, un
    infarto

heat
1 *verb*
  to heat some water = calentar agua
  to heat a house = calefaccionar una casa
2 *noun*
- (*warmth*)
  the heat = el calor
- (*on a cooker*)
  to cook at a low heat = cocinar a fuego
    lento
- (*a round in a sporting contest*)
  a heat = una (prueba) eliminatoria
heat up
  to heat up some soup = calentar un poco
    de sopa

heater *noun*
  a heater = un calentador, un calefactor, una
    estufa

C Am Central America   **Lat Am** Latin America   **Mex** Mexico

heating *noun*
heating = calefacción (*feminine*)

heatwave *noun*
a heatwave = una ola de calor

heaven *noun*
heaven = cielo (*masculine*)

heavy *adjective*
• (*in weight*)
  to be heavy = pesar mucho, ser
    pesado/pesada
  how heavy is it? = ¿cuánto pesa?
• (*in quantity, intensity*)
  the traffic is very heavy = la circulación
    está muy densa
  to be a heavy smoker = fumar mucho
• (*with rich ingredients*) = pesado/pesada
  a heavy meal = una comida pesada

hedge *noun*
a hedge = un seto

hedgehog *noun*
a hedgehog = un erizo

heel *noun*
• (*part of the foot*) ▶ **p. 235**
  the heel = el talón
• (*part of a shoe*)
  a heel = un tacón, un taco (*SC*)

height *noun*
• (*of a person*)
  height = estatura (*feminine*)
• (*of a building or tree*)
  height = altura (*feminine*)

helicopter *noun*
a helicopter = un helicóptero

hell *noun*
hell = infierno (*masculine*)

hello *exclamation*
hello (*when greeting someone*) = hola
(*on the phone*) = sí, aló (*S Am*), diga (*Spa*),
  bueno (*Mex*), holá (*R Pl*)
Catherine says hello = Catherine te manda
  saludos

helmet *noun*
a helmet = un casco

help
1 *verb*
• (*to be of assistance*) = ayudar
  to help someone to escape = ayudar a
    alguien a escapar
  can I help you? (*in a shop*) = ¿qué desea?
• (*to serve*)
  to help oneself = servirse
• (*to avoid*)
  she couldn't help laughing = no pudo
    contener la risa
  I just can't help it = no lo puedo remediar
2 *exclamation*
help! = ¡socorro!

3 *noun*
help = ayuda (*feminine*)
the map wasn't much help = el mapa no
  sirvió mucho

help out
I helped him out = le di una mano

helpful *adjective*
• (*willing to help*) = amable, servicial
• (*useful*) = útil

helpless *adjective*
• (*defenseless*) = indefenso/indefensa
• (*having no power*)
  to be helpless to do something = ser
    incapaz de hacer algo
• (*through disability*)
  the accident left her helpless = el
    accidente la dejó incapacitada

hem *noun*
a hem = un dobladillo

hen *noun*
(*chicken*)
a hen = una gallina

her
1 *pronoun*
• (*when used as a direct object*) = la
  I know/don't know her = la conozco/no la
    conozco

  ! Note that la *comes before the verb in*
  Spanish

• (*when used as an indirect object*) = le
  I never talk to her = nunca le hablo
  I wrote her a letter = le escribí una carta

  ! Note that le *comes before the verb in*
  Spanish

• (*when used as an indirect object pronoun*
  together with a direct object pronoun) =
  se
  I gave it to her = se lo di
  he's not going to say it to her = no se lo va
    a decir

  ! Note that se *comes before the direct*
  object pronoun

• (*when telling someone to do something*)
  catch her! = ¡atrápenla!
  give the money to her = dale el dinero (a
    ella)
  give them to her = dáselos

  ! Note that la, le, *and* se *come after the*
  verb in Spanish

• (*when telling someone not to do*
  something)
  don't look at her! = ¡no la mires!
  don't give her my phone number! = ¡no le
    des mi número de teléfono!
  don't show them to her! = ¡no se los
    muestres!

! Note that **la**, **le** and **se** come before the verb in Spanish

- (when used after prepositions and with to be) = ella
 we did it for her = lo hicimos por ella
 I have nothing against her = no tengo nada en contra de ella, no tengo nada en contra suya
 she had her dog with her = tenía el perro consigo
 it's her = es ella
2 adjective
 = su (+ singular), sus (+ plural)

! For **her** used with parts of the body, ▶ **p. 235**

herb noun
 a herb = una hierba, un yuyo (R Pl)

herd noun
 a herd (of cattle) = una manada, una tropa (R Pl)
 (of goats) = un rebaño
 (of pigs) = una manada

here adverb
- (at a point close to the person speaking) = aquí, acá
 I'm up here = estoy aquí arriba
- (when drawing attention to something)
 here's the bus stop = aquí está la parada de autobuses
 here they are = aquí están
 here comes the train = aquí viene el tren
- (when giving something)
 here, take my pencil = toma, te doy mi lápiz
 here's my telephone number = aquí tienes mi número de teléfono
- (present)
 she's not here at the moment = no está en este momento

hers pronoun
 hers (singular) = suyo/suya, de ella
 (plural) = suyos/suyas, de ella
 they're hers = son suyos/suyas, son de ella
 hers is blue = el suyo/la suya es azul, el/la de ella es azul
 a friend of hers = un amigo suyo, un amigo de ella

herself pronoun
- (translated by a reflexive verb in Spanish)
 she didn't hurt herself = no se hizo daño, no se lastimó (Lat Am)
 she bought herself a hat = se compró un sombrero
- (used for emphasis)
 she said it herself = lo dijo ella misma
 she did it by herself = lo hizo sola

hesitate verb
 = dudar
 don't hesitate to tell her = no dude en decírselo

hi exclamation
 hi! = ¡hola!

hiccup, **hiccough** noun
 to have hiccups = tener hipo

hide verb
- (to conceal)
 = esconder
 to hide (oneself) = esconderse
- (to keep secret) = ocultar
 she couldn't hide her joy = no pudo ocultar su alegría

hide and seek noun
 to play hide and seek = jugar al escondite, jugar a las escondidas (Lat Am)

hideous adjective
 = espantoso/espantosa

hiding place noun
 a hiding place = un escondite, un escondrijo

hi-fi noun
 a hi-fi = un equipo de alta fidelidad, un hi-fi

high
1 adjective
- (having great height) = alto/alta
 the mountains are high = las montañas son altas
 how high is the tower? = ¿qué altura tiene la torre?
 it's 200 meters high = tiene 200 metros de altura, tiene 200 metros de alto
- (in number, intensity, speed)
 prices are high = los precios son altos
 the train travels at a high speed = el tren viaja a alta velocidad
- (in quality)
 the standard is very high = el nivel es muy alto
- (shrill)
 to have a high voice = tener una voz aguda
 a high note = una nota alta
2 adverb
 (when talking about a place)
 don't go any higher or you'll fall = no subas más o te vas a caer

high heels noun
 high heels = zapatos de tacón alto (masculine plural), zapatos de taco alto (masculine plural) (SC)

Highlands noun
 the Highlands = las Highlands, las tierras altas

highlights noun
- (on TV, radio)
 the match highlights = las jugadas más importantes del partido

- (*in hair*)
  highlights = reflejos (*masculine plural*),
  luces (*feminine plural*) (*Mex*), claritos
  (*masculine plural*) (*R Pl*)

high school *noun* (*US English*)
  a high school = un colegio secundario
  mixto, un liceo (*SC*), un instituto (*Spa*)

highway *noun*
  a highway (*US English*) = una carretera
  (*British English*) = una vía pública

hijack *verb*
  = secuestrar

hike
1 *noun*
  a hike = una caminata, una excursión
2 *verb*
  to go hiking = ir de caminata, ir de
  excursión

hill *noun*
  a hill (*low*) = una colina, un cerro
  (*high*) = una montaña
- (*a slope*)
  a hill = una cuesta

him *pronoun*
- (*when used as a direct object*) = lo
  I know/don't know him = lo conozco/no lo
  conozco

  ! *Note that* lo *comes before the verb in
  Spanish*

- (*when used as an indirect object*) = le
  she never talks to him = no le habla nunca
  I wrote him a letter = le escribí una carta

  ! *Note that* le *comes before the verb in
  Spanish*

- (*when used as an indirect object pronoun
  together with a direct object pronoun*) =
  se
  I have to give them to him = tengo que
  dárselos
  he's not going to say it to him = no se lo va
  a decir

  ! *Note that* se *comes before the direct
  object pronoun*

- (*when telling someone to do something*)
  catch him! = ¡atrápenlo!
  give the money to him = dale el dinero
  give it to him = dáselo

  ! *Note that* lo, le, *and* se *come after the
  verb in Spanish*

- (*when telling someone not to do
  something*)
  don't look at him! = ¡no lo mires!
  don't give him my phone number! = ¡no le
  des mi número de teléfono!
  don't show them to him! = ¡no se los
  muestres!

  ! *Note that* lo, le, *and* se *come before the
  verb in Spanish*

- (*when used after prepositions and with* to
  be) = él
  we did it for him = lo hicimos por él
  I've got nothing against him = no tengo
  nada en contra de él, no tengo nada en
  contra suya
  he had his dog with him = tenía el perro
  consigo
  it's him = es él

himself *pronoun*
- (*translated by a reflexive verb in Spanish*)
  he wants to enjoy himself = quiere
  divertirse
  he bought himself a hat = se compró un
  sombrero
- (*used for emphasis*)
  he said it himself = lo dijo él mismo
  he did it by himself = lo hizo solo

hip *noun* ▶ **p. 235**
  the hip = la cadera

hire
1 *verb*
- (*to rent*) = alquilar
- (*to lend for payment*) = alquilar
- (*to employ*) = contratar
2 *noun*
  car hire (*British English*) = alquiler de
  coches (*masculine*)
  boats for hire = se alquilan barcos
hire out (*British English*)
  = alquilar

his
1 *adjective*
  = su (+ *singular*), sus (+ *plural*)

  ! *For* his *used with parts of the body,*
  ▶ **p. 235**

2 *pronoun* (*singular*) = suyo/suya, de él
  (*plural*) = suyos/suyas, de él
  they're his = son suyos/suyas, son de él
  his is blue = el suyo/la suya es azul, el/la de
  él es azul
  a friend of his = un amigo suyo, un amigo
  de él

history *noun*
  history = historia (*feminine*)

hit
1 *verb*
- (*to strike*)
  to hit a tennis ball = darle a una pelota de
  tenis
  to hit someone on the head = pegarle a
  alguien en la cabeza
  don't hit me! = ¡no me pegues!
  to hit one's head on the door = pegarse en
  la cabeza con la puerta
- (*to have a collision with, to knock down*)
  I hit the tree = choqué con el árbol
  he was hit by a truck = lo atropelló un
  camión

H

R Pl **River Plate area**   SC **Southern Cone**   Spa **Spain**

- (*strike*)
  to hit a target = dar en un objetivo
  the port was hit = bombardearon el puerto
  2 *noun*
  a hit = un éxito
  to be a big hit = tener mucho éxito

hitchhike *verb*
  = hacer autostop, hacer dedo, ir de aventón
  (*Mex*)

hitchhiker *noun*
  a hitchhiker = un/una autoestopista

hoarse *adjective*
  = ronco/ronca

hobby *noun*
  a hobby = un pasatiempo, un hobby

hold
1 *verb*
  to hold someone's hand = tomar a alguien
    de la mano, agarrar a alguien de la mano,
    coger a alguien de la mano (*Spa*)
  they were holding hands = iban de la
    mano
  he was holding some coins in his hand =
    tenía unas monedas en la mano
- (*to arrange*)
  to hold a meeting = celebrar una reunión
  the party will be held in the school = la
    fiesta tendrá lugar en la escuela
- (*to have*)
  to hold the world record = tener el récord
    mundial
  to hold a Spanish passport = tener
    pasaporte español
- (*other uses*)
  to hold someone responsible = hacer
    responsable a alguien de algo
  hold the line please = no cuelgue, por
    favor, no corte, por favor (*SC*)
2 *noun*
  to get hold of the ball = agarrar la pelota,
    coger el balón (*Spa*)
  to get hold of someone = localizar a
    alguien, ubicar a alguien (*Lat Am*)
hold back
  to hold back the tears = contener las
    lágrimas
hold on
- (*to wait*) = esperar
  hold on please (*on phone*) = no cuelgue,
    por favor, no corte, por favor (*SC*)
- (*so as not to fall*)
  hold on tight! = ¡agárrate fuerte!
hold on to
  to hold on to someone/something =
    agarrarse a alguien/algo
hold up
- (*to raise*) = levantar
- (*to delay*)
  to hold someone up = retrasar a alguien
- (*to rob*) = atracar, asaltar

hole *noun*
- (*in clothes, material*)
  a hole = un agujero
- (*in the ground*)
  a hole = un hoyo
- (*in a wall*)
  a hole = un boquete
- **a rabbit hole** = una madriguera
  a mouse hole = una ratonera

holiday *noun*
- (*British English—a vacation*)
  a holiday = unas vacaciones
  to go on holiday = ir de vacaciones
  the school holidays = las vacaciones
    (escolares)
- (*a national or religious festival*)
  a (public) holiday = un día festivo, un
    feriado (*Lat Am*)

Holland *noun* ▶ p. 187
  Holland = Holanda (*feminine*)

home
1 *noun*
  a home (*a house, a place to live*) = una casa
    (*a family environment*) = un hogar
  to leave home = irse de casa
- (*native country*)
  home = patria (*feminine*)
- (*for elderly people*)
  a retirement home = una residencia de
    ancianos
- **at home** (*in one's house*) = en casa
- **at home** (*comfortable*)
  to feel at home = sentirse a gusto
  make yourselves at home = pónganse
    cómodos, están en su casa
2 *adverb*
  to go home (*to one's house*) = volver a casa
    (*to one's home country*) = volver a su país
  I met her on my way home = me encontré
    con ella cuando volvía a casa
  to be home = estar en casa

homeless *adjective*
  to be homeless = estar sin hogar, estar sin
    techo

home-made *adjective*
  = hecho/hecha en casa

homesick *adjective*
  he is homesick (*for his family*) = echa de
    menos a su familia, extraña a su familia
    (*Lat Am*)
  (*for his country*) = echa de menos a su país,
    extraña a su país (*Lat Am*)

homework *noun*
  homework = deberes (*masculine plural*),
    tareas (*feminine plural*)

homosexual *noun*
  a homosexual = un homosexual/una
    homosexual

---

honest *adjective*
* (*trustworthy*)
  honest = honesto/honesta,
  honrado/honrada
* (*frank, sincere*) = sincero/sincera
  to be honest, I'd rather stay here = para
  serte sincero, prefiero quedarme aquí

honestly *adverb*
  to answer a question honestly = contestar
  sinceramente a una pregunta
  I honestly don't know = de verdad que no
  lo sé

honey *noun*
  honey = miel (*feminine*)

honeymoon *noun*
  a honeymoon = una luna de miel
  to go to Greece on honeymoon = irse a
  Grecia de luna de miel

honor (*US English*), **honour** (*British
English*)
1 *noun*
  honor = honor (*masculine*)
  it's a great honor for us to meet them =
  conocerlos es un gran honor para
  nosotros
2 *verb*
* (*to show respect for*)
  **I would be honored to represent my
  country** = representar a mi país sería un
  honor para mí
* **to honor a promise** = cumplir con una
  promesa

hood *noun*
* (*to cover the head*)
  a hood = una capucha
* (*US English—of a car*)
  the hood = el capó, el capoté (*Mex*)

hoof *noun*
  a hoof (*of a horse*) = un casco, una pezuña
  (*Mex*), un vaso (*R Pl*)
  (*of a cow*) = una pezuña

hook *noun*
* (*for hanging clothes*)
  a hook = una percha, un gancho
* (*for hanging pictures*)
  a hook = un gancho
* (*for fastening a garment*)
  a hook = un ganchito
* (*on the telephone*)
  to leave the phone off the hook = dejar el
  teléfono descolgado

Hoover®, **hoover** (*British English*)
1 *noun*
  a Hoover = una aspiradora, un aspirador
2 *verb* = pasar la aspiradora, aspirar (*Lat Am*)
  to hoover the house = pasar la aspiradora
  por la casa, aspirar la casa

hop *verb*
* (*to jump on one leg*) = saltar a la pata coja,
  saltar con un solo pie
* (*to move lightly*)
  the bird hopped up to me = el pájaro se me
  acercó dando saltitos

hope
1 *verb* = esperar
  I hope it's true = espero que sea verdad

  > ! *Note that* **esperar que** *is followed by the
  > subjunctive*

  to hope to travel abroad = esperar viajar al
  extranjero
  I hope so/not = espero que sí/no
2 *noun*
* (*the belief that things will work out*)
  hope = esperanza (*feminine*)
* (*a chance*)
  a hope = una esperanza

hopeless *adjective*
  (*without hope of success*)
  a hopeless attempt = un intento
  desesperado
  it's hopeless! = ¡es inútil!

horizon *noun*
  the horizon = el horizonte

horn *noun*
* (*on a car, bus*)
  a horn = un claxon, una bocina
  to blow the horn = tocar el claxon, tocar la
  bocina
* (*of an animal*)
  a horn = un cuerno, un asta (*feminine*), un
  cacho (*S Am*)
* (*musical instrument*)
  a horn = un cuerno

horoscope *noun*
  a horoscope = un horóscopo

horrible *adjective*
  = horrible

horror *noun*
  horror = horror (*masculine*)

horse *noun*
  a horse = un caballo

hose *noun*
  a hose (*for watering the garden*) = una
  manguera
  (*for putting out fires*) = una manguera
  contra incendios

hospital *noun*
  a hospital = un hospital
  to be in hospital = estar en el hospital, estar
  hospitalizado/hospitalizada, estar
  internado/internada (*SC*)

hospitality *noun*
  hospitality = hospitalidad (*feminine*)

H

host noun
* (to guests, visitors)
  a host = un anfitrión/una anfitriona
* (on a radio or TV program)
  a host = un presentador/una presentadora

hostage noun
  a hostage = un/una rehén
  to take someone hostage = tomar a
  alguien como rehén

hostel noun
* (for refugees, workers, young people)
  a hostel = un hogar
* (a youth hostel)
  a hostel = un albergue juvenil

hostess noun
* (to guests, visitors)
  a hostess = una anfitriona
* (an air hostess)
  a hostess = una azafata, una aeromoza
  (Lat Am)
* (on a radio or TV program)
  a hostess = una presentadora

hostile adjective
  = hostil

hot adjective
* (very warm)
  to be hot, to feel hot = tener calor
  it's too hot in the office = hace demasiado
  calor en la oficina
  it gets very hot in the summer = hace
  mucho calor en el verano
  a hot climate = un clima cálido
  a hot meal = una comida caliente
* (strong, with a lot of spice) = picante

hot dog noun
_ a hot dog = un perro caliente, un pancho
  (R Pl)

hotel noun
  a hotel = un hotel

hour noun ▶ p. 319
  an hour = una hora
  I earn £2 an hour = gano 2 libras por hora

house noun
  a house = una casa
  the bike is at my house = la bicicleta está
  en mi casa

housewife noun
  a housewife = un ama de casa (feminine)

housework noun
  housework = tareas domésticas (feminine
  plural)

housing development (US English),
housing estate (British English) noun
  a housing development, a housing estate
  = un conjunto residencial, una
  urbanización (Spa)

hovercraft noun
  a hovercraft = un aerodeslizador

how
1 adverb
* (in what way) = cómo
  how do you spell your name? = ¿cómo se
  escribe su nombre?
  I know how [to swim | to ride a horse | to
  skate ...] = yo sé [nadar | cabalgar | patinar ...]
  she showed me how to send a fax = me
  enseñó cómo mandar un fax
* (in polite questions)
  how are you? = ¿cómo estás?
  how's the job going? = ¿cómo marcha el
  trabajo?
  how was your holiday? = ¿qué tal las
  vacaciones?
  how do you do? = ¡mucho gusto!
* (in questions requiring specific information)
  how tall are you? = ¿cuánto mides?
  how old is he? = ¿cuántos años tiene?,
  ¿qué edad tiene?
* (in exclamations) = qué
  how strange = ¡qué raro!
* how about Friday? = ¿qué te parece el
  viernes?
  I'd love to go, how about you? = me
  encantaría ir ¿y a ti?
2 conjunction
  I still don't know how she did it = todavía
  no sé cómo lo hizo

however adverb
  (nevertheless) = sin embargo, no obstante

hug verb
  = abrazar

huge adjective
  = enorme

human adjective
  = humano/humana

human being noun
  a human being = un ser humano

humid adjective
  = húmedo

humor (US English), **humour** (British
English) noun
  humor = humor (masculine)
  a good sense of humor = un buen sentido
  del humor

humorous adjective
  a humorous book = un libro humorístico
  a humorous remark = un comentario
  gracioso

hundred number ▶ p. 154
  one hundred, a hundred = cien (masculine)
  (! never changes)
  one hundred people = cien personas
  one hundred and ninety-eight = ciento
  noventa y ocho

The human body

When it is clear who owns the part of the body being mentioned, Spanish tends to use the definite article, where English uses a possessive adjective:

*he closed **his** eyes*	= cerró **los** ojos
*she raised **her** arm*	= levantó **el** brazo

For expressions such as *he hurt his ankle* or *she brushed her teeth*, where the action involves more than the simple movement of a body part, use a reflexive verb in Spanish:

*she **has broken her** leg*	= **se ha roto** la pierna
*he **was washing his** hair*	= **se lavaba** el pelo

Note also the following:

*she touched **my** arm*	= me tocó **el** brazo
	(*literally* she touched to me the arm)

Describing people

When describing people, Spanish mainly uses the verb **tener**:

his hair is long	= tiene el pelo largo
he has long hair	= tiene el pelo largo
the boy with long hair	= el niño de pelo largo
her eyes are green	= tiene (los) ojos verdes
she has green eyes	= tiene (los) ojos verdes
his nose is red	= tiene la nariz roja
he has a red nose	= tiene la nariz roja

Illnesses, aches and pains

where does it hurt?	= ¿dónde te duele?
his leg hurts	= le duele la pierna
I have a bad back	= me duele la espalda
I have a sore throat	= tengo dolor de garganta
he had a heart attack	= le dio un ataque al corazón

! Ciento *is used to translate* one hundred *in numbers between 101 and 199*

two hundred = doscientos/doscientas
two hundred and fifty = doscientos cincuenta (**!** *never changes*)
three hundred = trescientos/trescientas
four hundred = cuatrocientos/cuatrocientas
five hundred = quinientos/quinientas
six hundred = seiscientos/seiscientas
seven hundred = setecientos/setecientas
eight hundred = ochocientos/ochocientas
nine hundred = novecientos/novecientas

Hungary *noun* ▶ **p. 187**
  Hungary = Hungría (*feminine*)

hungry *adjective*
  to be hungry = tener hambre

hunter *noun*
  a hunter = un cazador/una cazadora

hunting *noun*
  hunting = caza (*feminine*)
  to go hunting = ir de caza

hurrah, **hurray** *exclamation*
  hurrah! = ¡hurra!

hurry
1 *verb*
  to hurry = darse prisa, apurarse (*Lat Am*)
  to hurry someone = meter prisa a alguien, apurar a alguien (*Lat Am*)
2 *noun*
  to be in a hurry = tener prisa, estar apurado/apurada (*Lat Am*)
  she was in a hurry to leave = tenía prisa por irse, estaba apurada por irse (*Lat Am*)
  I did my homework in a hurry = hice los deberes deprisa, hice las tareas apurado (*Lat Am*)

hurt
1 *verb*
• (*to injure*)
  to hurt oneself = hacerse daño, lastimarse (*Lat Am*)
  to hurt one's leg = hacerse daño en la pierna, lastimarse la pierna (*Lat Am*)
  many people were hurt = hubo muchos heridos
• (*to be painful*)
  my throat hurts = me duele la garganta

• (*to cause emotional pain*)
to hurt someone's feelings = ofender a
alguien
2 *adjective*
she was badly hurt = estaba gravemente
herida
to feel hurt = sentirse dolido/dolida

husband *noun*
a husband = un marido, un esposo

hut *noun*
• (*a shed*)
a hut = una cabaña
• (*for living in*)
a hut = una choza

hygienic *adjective*
= higiénico/higiénica

hypnotize *verb*
= hipnotizar

hysterical *adjective*
= histérico/histérica

I i

I *pronoun*
I = yo
I went to the theater = fui al teatro
I did it = yo lo hice
I was singing, he was playing the piano =
yo cantaba y él tocaba el piano

! *Although* yo *is given as the translation
of* I, *it is in practice used only for
emphasis or to avoid ambiguity*

ice
1 *noun* = hielo (*masculine*)
2 *verb*
to ice a cake = glasear un pastel

ice cream *noun*
• (*the product*)
ice cream = helado (*masculine*)
• (*on a stick or cone*)
an ice cream = un helado

ice rink *noun*
an ice rink = una pista de hielo

ice skating *noun*
ice skating = patinaje sobre hielo
(*masculine*)

icing *noun*
icing = glaseado (*masculine*)

idea *noun*
an idea = una idea
I haven't the slightest idea! = ¡no tengo ni
la menor idea!

identical *adjective*
= idéntico/idéntica

identity card *noun*
an identity card = un carné de identidad

idiot *noun*
an idiot = un idiota/una idiota

if *conjunction*
= si
if you like = si quieres
if you see him don't speak to him = si lo
ves no le hables
if I were rich, I would travel = si fuera rica,
me iría de viaje
I wonder if they will come = me pregunto si
vendrán
if I were you, I wouldn't go = yo que tú, no
me iría

ignore *verb*
to ignore a person = ignorar a alguien
to ignore a problem = no hacer caso de un
problema
to ignore the rules = hacer caso omiso de
las reglas

ill *adjective*
= enfermo/enferma
to be ill = estar enfermo/enferma
to fall ill = caer enfermo/enferma,
enfermarse (*Lat Am*)

illegal *adjective*
= ilegal

illness *noun*
an illness = una enfermedad

illustration *noun*
an illustration = una ilustración

imagination *noun*
imagination = imaginación (*feminine*)

imagine *verb*
= imaginar(se)

imitate *verb*
= imitar

immediately *adverb*
= inmediatamente

immigrant
1 *noun*
an immigrant = un/una inmigrante
2 *adjective*
an immigrant worker = un obrero
inmigrante
an immigrant community = una
comunidad de inmigrantes

C Am Central America   Lat Am Latin America   Mex Mexico

impatient *adjective*
= impaciente
to get impatient = impacientarse

import
1 *verb* = importar
2 *noun*
an import = un artículo de importación

important *adjective*
= importante

impossible *adjective*
= imposible

impress *verb*
to impress someone = causarle una buena
impresión a alguien
we were impressed by your work = tu
trabajo nos causó muy buena impresión

impression *noun*
an impression = una impresión

improve *verb*
• (*to make better*) = mejorar
she wants to improve her Spanish = quiere
mejorar su español
• (*to get better*) = mejorar
the situation has improved = la situación
ha mejorado

improvement *noun*
an improvement = una mejora

in
1 *preposition*
• (*in a place or position*) = en
in the house = en la casa
he went in the shop = entró en la tienda,
entró a la tienda (*Lat Am*)
I read it in the newspaper = lo leí en el
periódico
the woman in the photograph = la mujer
de la foto
there's a letter in it = tiene una carta
adentro
in Ireland = en Irlanda
in Rome = en Roma
• (*dressed in*)
the woman in the red skirt = la mujer de la
falda roja
she was dressed in black = estaba vestida
de negro
• (*showing the way in which something is
done*) = en
written in Spanish = escrito en castellano
in a low voice = en voz baja
• (*during*)
in October = en octubre
in the night = durante la noche
at two o'clock in the morning/afternoon = a
las dos de la mañana/de la tarde
• (*within*) = dentro de
I'll be ready in ten minutes = estaré listo
dentro de diez minutos

• (*with superlatives*)
the biggest city in the world = la ciudad
más grande del mundo
• (*other uses*)
in the rain = bajo la lluvia
one in ten = uno de cada diez
to cut something in two = cortar algo en
dos
2 *adverb*
• (*indoors*)
to come in = entrar
• (*at home*)
tell him I'm not in = dile que no estoy

inch *noun*
an inch = una pulgada (*2,54 cm*)

incident *noun*
an incident = un incidente, un episodio

include *verb*
= incluir

including *preposition*
they all liked it, including Paul = a todos les
gustó, incluso a Paul

income *noun*
income = ingresos (*masculine plural*)

income tax *noun*
income tax = impuesto sobre la renta
(*masculine*)

incompetent *adjective*
= incompetente

inconsiderate *adjective*
= desconsiderado/desconsiderada

inconvenient *adjective*
= inconveniente

incorrect *adjective*
an incorrect answer = una respuesta
incorrecta
that is incorrect = eso es incierto

increase
1 *verb* = aumentar
to increase someone's salary =
aumentarle el sueldo a alguien
to increase in value = aumentar de valor
2 *noun*
an increase = un aumento
a price increase = un aumento de precio

incredible *adjective*
= increíble

independent *adjective*
= independiente

India *noun* ▶ p. 187
India = la India

Indian ▶ p. 187
1 *noun*
• (*a person from India*)
an Indian = un indio/una india

- (*a Native American*)
  an **Indian** = un/una indígena, un indio/una india
2 *adjective*
- (*of India*) = indio/india
- (*of America*) = indígena, indio/india

indicate *verb*
  = indicar

indigestion *noun*
  to have **indigestion** = tener indigestión

individual
1 *noun*
  an **individual** = un individuo
2 *adjective* = individual

indoor *adjective*
  (*if it's a pool or court*) = cubierto/cubierta, techado/techada

indoors *adverb*
  = dentro, adentro (*Lat Am*)

industrial *adjective*
  = industrial

industry *noun*
  an **industry** = una industria

inevitable *adjective*
  = inevitable

infant *noun*
- (*a baby*)
  an **infant** = un bebé, un niño/una niña
- (*British English—a young child*)
  an **infant** = un niño/una niña

infection *noun*
  an **infection** = una infección

influence
1 *noun*
  an **influence** = una influencia
2 *verb*
  to **influence a person** = influir a una persona
  to **influence someone's decision** = influir en la decisión de alguien

inform *verb*
- (*to tell, to give information to*) = informar
- (*to denounce*)
  to **inform on someone** = delatar a alguien

informal *verb*
- (*if it's a person or a person's manner*) = informal
- (*if it's a discussion or interview*) = informal
- (*if it's language*) = coloquial, familiar

information *noun*
  information = información (*feminine*)
  a piece of **information** = un dato

information desk *noun*
  the **information desk** = el mostrador de información

ingredient *noun*
  an **ingredient** = un ingrediente

inhabitant *noun*
  an **inhabitant** = un/una habitante

injection *noun*
  an **injection** = una inyección

injured *adjective*
  = herido/herida

injury *noun*
  an **injury** = una herida

ink *noun*
  ink = tinta (*feminine*)

inn *noun*
- (*a hotel*)
  an **inn** = una hostería
- (*a tavern*)
  an **inn** = una taberna

innocent *adjective*
  = inocente

inquiry *noun*
- (*a question*)
  to **make inquiries about prices** = pedir información sobre precios
- (*an investigation*)
  an **inquiry** = una investigación

insect *noun*
  an **insect** = un insecto

inside
1 *noun*
- the **inside** = el interior
- to put a shirt on **inside out** = ponerse una camisa al revés
2 *preposition* = dentro de
  inside the house = dentro de la casa
3 *adverb* = dentro, adentro (*Lat Am*)
4 *adjective* = interior

inspect *verb*
  to **inspect a school/a factory** = inspeccionar una escuela/una fábrica
  to **inspect the evidence** = inspeccionar las pruebas

inspector *noun*
- (*of a school*)
  an **inspector** = un inspector/una inspectora
- (*in the police*)
  a police **inspector** = un inspector/una inspectora (de policía)
- (*British English—of passengers' tickets*)
  an **inspector** = un inspector/una inspectora, un revisor/una revisora (*Spa*)

instead *adverb*
- we didn't drive there: we walked **instead** = en vez de ir allí en coche fuimos a pie
- **instead of** = en vez de, en lugar de

instruction *noun*
an instruction = una instrucción
'instructions for use' = 'instrucciones',
'modo de empleo'

instrument *noun*
an instrument = un instrumento

insult
1 *noun*
an insult = un insulto
2 *verb* = insultar

insurance *noun*
insurance = seguro (*masculine*)

insure *verb*
= asegurar
to insure something against theft =
asegurar algo contra robo

intelligent *adjective*
= inteligente

intend *verb*
to intend to do something = pensar hacer
algo

interest
1 *noun*
• (*felt by a person*)
interest = interés (*masculine*)
• (*financial*)
interest = interés (*masculine*)
2 *verb* = interesar

interested *adjective*
= interesado/interesada
they are very interested = están muy
interesados
I am interested in politics = me interesa la
política

interesting *adjective*
= interesante

interfere *verb*
to interfere in someone's affairs =
entrometerse en los asuntos de alguien
she's always interfering = ella siempre se
entromete
he doesn't want these problems to
interfere with his work = no quiere que
estos problemas afecten a su trabajo

intermission *noun*
(*during a performance*)
the intermission = el intermedio

internal *adjective*
= interno/interna

international *adjective*
= internacional

interpreter *noun*
an interpreter = un/una intérprete

interrupt *verb*
= interrumpir

interval *noun*
• (*in time or space*)
an interval = un intervalo
at regular intervals = a intervalos regulares
• (*British English—during a performance*)
the interval = el intermedio
(*in a play*) = el entreacto

interview
1 *noun*
an interview = una entrevista
2 *verb*
to interview someone = entrevistar a
alguien

into *preposition*
• (*when referring to a place or location*)
to go into the house = entrar en la casa,
entrar a la casa (*Lat Am*)
to get into a car = subir a un coche
to get into bed = subir a la cama
• (*indicating change or alteration*)
to translate a letter into Spanish = traducir
una carta al castellano
• (*in division*)
five into twenty goes five times = veinte
dividido por cinco es cinco, veinte
dividido entre cinco es cinco

introduce *verb*
• (*when people meet*) = presentar
he introduced me to Peter = me presentó a
Peter
• (*on radio or television*)
to introduce a program = presentar un
programa
• to introduce [a law | change | reform ...] =
introducir [una ley | un cambio | una
reforma ...]

introduction *noun*
• (*to a book*)
an introduction = una introducción
• (*to a speech*)
an introduction = una presentación
• the introduction of a law = la introducción
de una ley

invade *verb*
= invadir

invent *verb*
= inventar

invention *noun*
an invention = un invento

investigate *verb*
= investigar

investigation *noun*
an investigation = una investigación

invisible *adjective*
= invisible

invitation *noun*
an invitation = una invitación

I

invite *verb*
= invitar

involved *adjective*
he was involved in an accident = se vio
envuelto en un accidente
to be involved in a project = participar en
un proyecto

Ireland *noun* ▶ p. 187
Ireland = Irlanda (*feminine*)

Irish ▶ p. 187, p. 245
1 *noun*
• (*the people*)
the Irish = los irlandeses
• (*the language*)
Irish = irlandés (*masculine*)
2 *adjective* = irlandés/irlandesa

iron
1 *noun*
• (*the metal*)
iron = hierro (*masculine*), fierro
(*masculine*) (*Lat Am*)
• (*for clothes*)
an iron = una plancha
2 *verb* = planchar

irritating *adjective*
= irritante

island *noun*
an island = una isla

it *pronoun*
• (*when used as a subject*)
where is the newspaper?—it's on the table
= ¿dónde está el periódico?—está en la
mesa
where is it? (*of an object*) = ¿dónde está?
(*of a place*) = ¿dónde queda?
• (*when used as a direct object*) = lo/la
that's my book/pen and I need it = ése/ésa
es mi libro/pluma y lo/la necesito

! Note that lo and la come before the
verb in Spanish

• (*when telling someone to do something*)
that's my book/pen—give it to me = ése/ésa
es mi libro/pluma–dámelo/la

! Note that lo and la come after the verb
in Spanish

• (*when telling someone not to do
something*)
that's my book/pen—don't give it to him! =
ése/ésa es mi libro/pluma–¡no se lo/la des!

! Note that lo and la come after the verb
in Spanish

• (*in impersonal constructions*)
who is it? = ¿quién es?
it's me = soy yo
it's a nice house = es una casa linda
it's [difficult | easy | complicated ...] = es [difícil |
fácil | complicado ...]
it's cold/warm = hace frío/calor

• (*where it is used after a preposition*)
I've heard about it = he oído hablar de ello

Italian ▶ p. 187, p. 245
1 *noun*
• (*a person*)
an Italian = un italiano/una italiana
• (*the language*)
Italian = italiano (*masculine*)
2 *adjective* = italiano/italiana

Italy *noun* ▶ p. 187
Italy = Italia (*feminine*)

itchy *adjective*
my leg is itchy = me pica la pierna

its *adjective*
= su (+ *singular*), sus (+ *plural*)
its nose = su nariz

itself *pronoun*
• (*translated by a reflexive verb in Spanish*) =
se
the cat washed itself = el gato se lavaba
• (*used for emphasis*)
the house itself is quite large = la casa en sí
(misma) es bastante grande
by itself = solo

Jj

jacket *noun*
a jacket (*formal*) = una chaqueta
(*casual*) = una americana, un saco (*Lat
Am*)

jail
1 *noun*
a jail = una cárcel, una prisión
2 *verb*
to jail someone = encarcelar a alguien

jam *noun*
jam = mermelada (*feminine*), dulce
(*masculine*) (*R Pl*)

January *noun* ▶ p. 192
January = enero (*masculine*)

Japan *noun* ▶ p. 187
Japan = (el) Japón

Japanese ▶ p. 187, p. 245
1 *noun*
• (*the people*)
the Japanese = los japoneses
• (*the language*)
Japanese = japonés (*masculine*)
2 *adjective* = japonés/japonesa

jar *noun*
  a jar = un tarro, un bote

jaw *noun* ▶ p. 235
  the jaw = la mandíbula

jazz *noun*
  jazz = jazz (*masculine*)

jealous *adjective*
  = celoso/celosa
  he is jealous of her = le tiene celos

jeans *noun*
  (a pair of) jeans = unos vaqueros, unos
  jeans, unos tejanos (*Spa*), unos
  pantalones de mezclilla (*Mex*)

Jesus *noun*
  Jesus = Jesús

jet *noun*
  (*a plane*)
  a jet = un avión

jewelry (*US English*), **jewellery** (*British
English*) *noun*
  jewelry = alhajas (*feminine plural*), joyas
  (*feminine plural*)
  a piece of jewelry = una alhaja, una joya

Jewish *adjective*
  = judío/judía

jigsaw *noun*
  a jigsaw = un rompecabezas, un puzzle

job *noun*
  • (*a post*)
  a job = un empleo, un trabajo
  • (*a task*)
  a job = una tarea

jogging *noun*
  jogging = jogging (*masculine*), footing
  (*masculine*)
  to go jogging = salir a hacer jogging, salir a
  hacer footing

join *verb*
  • (*to connect*) = unir
  • (*to meet up with*)
  I'll join you in half an hour = los encuentro
  dentro de media hora
  may I join you? = ¿lo puedo acompañar?
  • (*become a member of*)
  to join a club/an organization = hacerse
  socio de un club/una organización
  to join the army = alistarse en el ejército

join in
  to join in a game = participar en un juego

joke
  1 *noun*
  a joke = (*verbal*) un chiste
  (*practical*) = una broma
  2 *verb* = bromear

journalist *noun*
  a journalist = un/una periodista

journey *noun*
  a journey = un viaje

joy *noun*
  joy = alegría (*feminine*)

judge
  1 *noun*
  • (*in a court*)
  a judge = un juez/una jueza
  • (*at a sporting event*)
  a judge = un juez/una jueza
  • (*in a competition*)
  the judges = los miembros del jurado
  2 *verb* = juzgar

jug *noun*
  a jug = una jarra

juice *noun*
  juice = jugo (*masculine*), zumo (*masculine*)
  (*Spa*)
  fruit juice = jugo de frutas, zumo de frutas
  (*Spa*)

July *noun* ▶ p. 192
  July = julio (*masculine*)

jump
  1 *verb* = saltar
  he jumped across the stream = cruzó el
  arroyo de un salto
  to jump rope (*US English*) = saltar a la
  cuerda, saltar a la comba (*Spa*)
  2 *noun*
  a jump = un salto

jump out
  he jumped out of the window = saltó por la
  ventana

jumper *noun* (*British English*)
  a jumper = un suéter, un pulóver, un jersey
  (*Spa*)

June *noun* ▶ p. 192
  June = junio (*masculine*)

junior *adjective*
  • (*of lower rank*)
  (*if it's a person*) = subalterno/subalterna
  (*if it's a position*) = de subalterno
  • (*younger*) = más joven

jury *noun*
  the jury = el jurado

just[1] *adverb*
  • (*very recently*)
  I have just arrived = acabo de llegar, recién
  llego (*Lat Am*)
  I saw him just now = lo vi hace un
  momento, recién lo vi (*Lat Am*)
  • (*immediately*)
  just before the weekend = justo antes del
  fin de semana
  • (*exactly*)
  it's just what I wanted = es justo lo que
  quería

J

- (*barely*) = justo
  I got there just in time = llegué justo a
  tiempo
- (*at this or that very moment*)
  I was just about to phone = estaba a punto
  de llamar
- (*equally*)
  he's just as clever as she is = es tan listo
  como ella

just² *adjective*
= justo/justa

justice *noun*
justice = justicia (*feminine*)

Kk

kangaroo *noun*
a kangaroo = un canguro

karate *noun*
karate = kárate (*masculine*), karate
(*masculine*) (*Lat Am*)

keen *adjective*
(*eager, enthusiastic*)
he is a keen footballer = es un futbolista
entusiasta
a keen student = un alumno aplicado/una
alumna aplicada
he is keen on football = le encanta el fútbol

keep *verb*
- (*not to throw away, to reserve for use*) =
  guardar
- (*to cause to remain*)
  to keep the house clean = mantener la
  casa limpia
  to keep someone waiting = hacer esperar a
  alguien
- (*to detain*)
  what kept you? = ¿por qué tardaste?
  they kept him in hospital = lo dejaron
  ingresado, lo dejaron internado (*SC*)
- (*to store*) = guardar
  where do you keep the cups? = ¿dónde
  guardas las tazas?
- (*not break*)
  to keep a promise = cumplir una promesa
  to keep a secret = guardar un secreto
- (*to maintain*)
  to keep the accounts = llevar la
  contabilidad
- (*to continue*)
  to keep walking = seguir caminando
  to keep going = seguir
- (*to remain*)
  to keep calm = mantener la calma

- (*of food: to stay in good condition*) =
  conservarse
keep back = retener
  he kept the children back after school =
  retuvo a los chicos después de las clases
keep down
  to keep down prices = mantener bajos los
  precios
  keep your voice down = no levantes la voz
keep off
  'keep off the grass' = 'prohibido pisar el
  césped'
keep on
  to keep on [walking | talking | singing ...] =
  seguir [caminando | hablando | cantando ...]
keep out
  keep out of the kitchen! = ¡no entres en la
  cocina!
keep up
  **he finds it hard to keep up with the other
  pupils** = le resulta difícil mantenerse al
  nivel de los demás alumnos

kennel, kennels (*British English*) *noun*
(*where dogs are kept while their owners are
away*)
  a kennel, kennels = una residencia canina,
  un hotel de perros

kerb *noun* (*British English*)
  the kerb = el bordillo (de la acera), el borde
  de la banqueta (*Mex*), el cordón de la
  vereda (*R Pl*)

kettle *noun*
  a kettle = una pava, una tetera (para
  calentar agua)

key *noun*
- **a key** = una llave
- (*on a computer or piano*)
  a key = una tecla
key in = teclear

keyhole *noun*
  a keyhole = un ojo de la cerradura

kick
1 *verb*
  to kick someone = darle una patada a
  alguien
  he kicked the ball = pateó la pelota
2 *noun*
  a kick = una patada
kick off
  (*in a football match*)
  to kick off = empezar un partido
kick out
  to kick someone out = echar a alguien

kid *noun*
- (*a young goat*)
  a kid = un cabrito/una cabrita, un
  choto/una chota (*Spa*)

- (*a child*)
  a kid = un niño/una niña, un chaval�/una chavala� (*Esp*), un chavalo�/una chavala� (*C Am*), un escuincle�/una escuincla� (*Mex*), un pibe�/una piba� (*R Pl*)

kidnap *verb*
= secuestrar

kill *verb*
= matar
to kill oneself = suicidarse

killer *noun*
a killer = un asesino/una asesina

kilometer *noun* (*US English*),
kilometre (*British English*)
a kilometer = un kilómetro

kind
1 *adjective*
(*if it's a person or gesture*) = amable
to be kind to someone = ser amable con alguien
2 *noun*
a kind [of fish | novel | hotel ...] = un tipo [de pescado | de novela | de hotel ...]
all kinds of animals = todo tipo de animal

king *noun*
a king = un rey

kingdom *noun*
a kingdom = un reino

kiss
1 *verb* = besar
2 *noun*
a kiss = un beso

kitchen *noun*
a kitchen = una cocina

kite *noun*
a kite = una cometa, un papalote (*Mex*), un barrilete (*R Pl*)

kitten *noun*
a kitten = un gatito/una gatita

knee *noun* ▶ p. 235
the knee = la rodilla

kneel *verb*
to kneel (down) (*to get down on one's knees*) = arrodillarse
(*to be on one's knees*) = estar arrodillado/arrodillada

knife *noun*
a knife = un cuchillo

knit *verb*
= tejer, hacer punto (*Spa*)
she knitted a scarf = hizo una bufanda, tejió una bufanda (*Lat Am*)

knock
1 *verb*
to knock at the door = llamar a la puerta, golpear a la puerta (*Lat Am*), tocar a la puerta (*Lat Am*)
he knocked his head against the door = se dio un golpe en la cabeza contra la puerta
he knocked the vase off the table = tiró el florero de la mesa
2 *noun*
a knock = un golpe
a knock on the head = un golpe en la cabeza
there was a knock at the door = llamaron a la puerta

knock down
he was knocked down by a car = lo atropelló un coche
to knock down a door = derribar una puerta

knock out
(*to make unconscious*) = dejar sin sentido

knock over = tirar
he knocked over the vase = tiró el florero

knot *noun*
a knot = un nudo

know *verb*
- (*to be acquainted with*) = conocer
  I don't know him = no lo conozco
- (*to understand, to possess knowledge of*) = saber
  how do you know that? = ¿cómo lo sabes?
  I don't know how to drive = no sé manejar
  let me know if you have any more news = avísame si recibes más noticias

knowledge *noun*
- (*learning*)
  knowledge (*in general*) = saber (*masculine*)
  (*facts known by a particular person*) = conocimientos (*masculine plural*)
- (*awareness*)
  knowledge = conocimiento (*masculine*)
  not to my knowledge = no que yo sepa

K
L

Ll

laboratory *noun*
a laboratory = un laboratorio

lace *noun*
- (*the material*)
  lace = encaje (*masculine*)
- (*on a shoe*)
  a lace = un cordón, una agujeta (*Mex*)

lack
1 *noun*
a lack of food = una falta de comida
2 *verb*
he lacks confidence = le falta confianza en sí mismo

ladder *noun*
a ladder = una escalera de mano

lady *noun*
a lady = una dama

lake *noun*
a lake = un lago

lamb *noun*
a lamb = un cordero

lamp *noun*
a lamp = una lámpara

lampshade *noun*
a lampshade = una pantalla (de lámpara)

land
1 *noun*
• (*as opposed to sea*)
land = tierra (*feminine*)
• (*farmland*)
land = tierra (*feminine*)
• (*property*)
a piece of land = un terreno
2 *verb*
• (*of an aircraft*) = aterrizar
• (*from a ship*) = desembarcar
• (*to fall*) = ir a parar
the ball landed on the roof = la pelota fue a parar en el tejado

landlady *noun*
a landlady = una dueña
my landlady = la dueña de la casa que alquilo

landlord *noun*
a landlord = un dueño
my landlord = el dueño de la casa que alquilo

landscape *noun*
a landscape = un paisaje

language *noun*
• (*of a particular nation*)
a language = un idioma, una lengua
• (*as a general concept or system*)
language = lenguaje (*masculine*)
• (*way of speaking or expressing oneself*)
language = lenguaje (*masculine*)
bad language = malas palabras (*feminine plural*) (*Lat Am*), palabrotas (*feminine plural*)

lap *noun*
to sit on someone's lap = sentarse en las rodillas de alguien

large *adjective*
= grande

! *Note that* **grande** *becomes* **gran** *when it is used before a singular noun*
a large garden = un jardín grande, un gran jardín
a large sum of money = una gran cantidad de dinero

last
1 *pronoun*
the last = el último/la última
the week before last = la semana antepasada
2 *adjective*
• (*final*) = último/última (! *before noun*)
the last episode in the series = el último capítulo de la serie
• (*previous*)
last Tuesday = el martes pasado
in my last letter = en mi última carta
3 *adverb*
• (*in final position*)
he came last in the race = quedó en último lugar en la carrera, terminó último en la carrera (*SC*)
• (*most recently*)
I was last here in 1978 = la última vez que estuve aquí fue en 1978
4 *verb* = durar

late
1 *adjective*
• (*not on time*)
sorry I'm late = perdón por llegar tarde
the train was two hours late = el tren llegó con dos horas de retraso, el tren llegó dos horas atrasado (*Lat Am*)
• (*far into the day or night*)
to have a late lunch = comer tarde, almorzar tarde (*Lat Am*)
• (*toward the end of*)
in late September = a fines de septiembre
in the late 1930s = hacia el final de la década de los treinta
2 *adverb*
• (*not on time*) = tarde
they arrived late = llegaron tarde
they arrived half an hour late = llegaron con media hora de retraso, llegaron media hora atrasados (*Lat Am*)
• (*far into the day or night*)
it's getting late = se hace tarde

later *adverb*
= más tarde
later on = más tarde
see you later! = ¡hasta luego!

latest *adjective*
(*most recent*) = último/última
the latest fashion = la última moda

Latin *noun* ▶ p. 245
Latin = latín (*masculine*)

Latin America *noun* ▶ p. 187
Latin America = América Latina (*feminine*), Latinoamérica (*feminine*)

Languages

Note that the names of languages in Spanish are always written with a small letter, not a capital as in English; also, Spanish often uses the definite article with languages while English does not.

In the following examples, the name of any language may be substituted for **Spanish** and **español**:

Spanish is a Romance language   = el español es una lengua románica
to translate something into Spanish = traducir algo al español

There are exceptions:

Spanish is spoken in Chile   = en Chile se habla español
I speak Spanish   = hablo español

The article is never used after **en**:

*he said it **in** Spanish*   = lo dijo **en** español

When **Spanish** means *in Spanish* or *of the Spanish*, it is translated by **español/española**:

a Spanish movie   = una película española
a Spanish word   = una palabra española

If you wish to make it clear that you mean *in Spanish* and not *from Spain,* use **en español**:

a Spanish book   = un libro en español
a Spanish program   = un programa en español

When *Spanish* means *relating to Spanish* or *about Spanish*, it is translated by **de español**:

a Spanish class   = una clase de español
a Spanish dictionary   = un diccionario de español

but

a Spanish-English dictionary   = un diccionario español-inglés

L

Latin American *adjective* ▶ **p. 187**
= latinoamericano/latinoamericana

laugh
1 *verb* = reírse
  they laughed at him = se rieron de él
2 *noun*
  a laugh = una risa

laughter *noun*
  laughter = risas (*feminine plural*)

laundry *noun*
• (*a shop or a firm*)
  a laundry = una lavandería, un lavadero
  (*R Pl*)
• (*washing*)
  the laundry (*clean*) = la ropa limpia
  (*dirty*) = la ropa sucia
  to do the laundry = lavar la ropa, hacer la
  colada (*Spa*)

law *noun*
• (*a regulation*)
  a law = una ley
• (*a set of rules in a country*)
  the law = la ley
  it's against the law = está prohibido por la
  ley
• (*as a university subject*)
  law = derecho (*masculine*)

lawn *noun*
  a lawn = un césped, un pasto (*Lat Am*), una
  grama (*C Am*)

lawnmower *noun*
  a lawnmower = una cortadora de céseped,
  una cortadora de pasto (*Lat Am*), un
  cortagrama (*C Am*)

lawyer *noun*
  a lawyer = un abogado/una abogada

lay *verb*
• (*to put*) = poner
  she laid her hand on his shoulder = le puso
  la mano en el hombro
• (*to set*)
  to lay the table = poner la mesa
• (*of a chicken*)
  to lay an egg = poner un huevo

lazy *adjective*
= perezoso/perezosa

lead¹
1 *verb*
• (*to guide or escort*) = llevar
  he led me into the garden = me llevó al
  jardín
• (*to cause*)
  this led him to believe that she was right =
  esto le hizo llegar a creer que tenía razón

R Pl River Plate area   SC Southern Cone   Spa Spain

- (*to result in*)
  this led to an accident = esto resultó en un accidente
- (*to have or conduct*) = llevar
  to lead an active life = llevar una vida activa
- (*to be ahead or in front*)
  they were leading by two goals = iban ganando por dos goles

2 *noun*
  (*in a match or contest*)
  to be in the lead = llevar la delantera
- (*initiative*)
  to take the lead = tomar la iniciativa
- (*British English—for a dog*)
  a lead = una correa
- (*a wire*)
  a lead = un cable

lead² *noun*
- (*the metal*)
  lead = plomo (*masculine*)
- (*in a pencil*)
  the lead = la mina

leader *noun*
- (*of a group or political party*)
  a leader = un/una líder
- (*of a gang*)
  a leader = un/una cabecilla

leaf *noun*
  a leaf = una hoja

leak
1 *verb*
  (*if it's a container*) = gotear, perder (*R Pl*)
  the roof is leaking = hay una gotera en el techo
2 *noun*
  a leak (*in a roof*) = una gotera
  (*in a container*) = un agujero

lean
1 *verb*
  to lean against/on something = apoyarse contra/en algo
  she leaned out of the window = se asomó por la ventana
2 *adjective*
  (*if it's meat*) = magro/magra
lean back = echarse hacia atrás

leap
1 *verb* = saltar, brincar
2 *noun*
  a leap = un salto, un brinco

learn *verb*
  = aprender

leash *noun*
  a leash = una correa

least
1 *adjective*
  they have the least money = son los que tienen menos dinero

2 *pronoun*
- **it was the least I could do** = fue lo menos que pude hacer
- **at least**
  (*at the minimum*) = por lo menos
  he's at least thirty = tiene por lo menos treinta años
3 *adverb*
  (*when used with adjectives or nouns*)
  the least expensive shop = la tienda menos cara
  the least difficult question = la pregunta menos difícil
- (*when used with verbs*)
  I like that color the least = ese color es el que menos me gusta

leather
1 *noun*
  leather = cuero (*masculine*), piel (*feminine*) (*Spa*)
2 *adjective* = de cuero, de piel (*Spa*)

leave
1 *verb*
- (*to depart from*)
  the train left London at 11 o'clock = el tren salió de Londres a las once
  she left the room = se fue del cuarto
  he left home when he was 18 = se fue de la casa a los 18 años
  to leave school = dejar los estudios
  she left her husband = dejó a su marido
- (*to depart*) = irse, marcharse (*Spa*)
  he left the next day = se fue al día siguiente, se marchó al día siguiente (*Spa*)
- (*to put or deposit*) = dejar
  I left my keys on the table = dejé mis llaves sobre la mesa
  he didn't leave a message = no dejó recado
- (*to postpone*) = dejar
  leave it until tomorrow = déjalo para mañana
- (*to allow to remain*) = dejar
  she left the window open = dejó la ventana abierta
- (*to remain*)
  to be left = quedar
  we have ten minutes left = nos quedan diez minutos
2 *noun*
  (*authorized absence*) = permiso (*masculine*), licencia (*feminine*) (*Lat Am*)
  to be on leave = estar de permiso, estar de licencia (*Lat Am*)
leave behind
  (*not take with one*) = dejar
leave out
- (*not to show or mention*) = omitir
- (*to exclude*) = excluir
leave over
  to be left over = quedar

lecture noun
- (British English—in a university)
  a lecture = una clase
- (a public talk)
  a lecture = una conferencia

left
1 noun
  left = izquierda (feminine)
  the first street on your left = la primera
    calle a tu izquierda
2 adjective = izquierdo/izquierda
3 adverb = a la izquierda, hacia la izquierda

left-handed adjective
= zurdo/zurda

leg noun
- (of a person) ▶ p. 235
  a leg = una pierna
- (of an animal, a bird)
  a leg = una pata
- (of a chair or table)
  a leg = una pata
- (of a pair of trousers)
  a leg = una pierna
- (of meat)
  a leg of lamb = una pierna de cordero

legal adjective
= legal

leisure noun
  leisure = ocio (masculine)

lemon noun
  a lemon = un limón

lemonade noun
- (made with fresh lemons)
  lemonade = limonada (feminine)
- (British English—fizzy drink)
  lemonade = gaseosa (feminine)

lend verb
= prestar

length noun
- (in measurement)
  length = largo (masculine), longitud
    (feminine)
  to be 30 cm in length = medir 30
    centímetros de largo, tener 30
    centímetros de largo
- (duration)
  length = duración (feminine)

lens noun
- (for spectacles)
  a lens = una lente
- (on a camera)
  a lens = un objetivo

Leo noun
- (the sign)
  Leo = Leo
  I'm Leo = soy Leo, soy de Leo
- (a person)
  a Leo = un/una leo

leopard noun
  a leopard = un leopardo

less
1 adjective = menos
  less money = menos dinero
  I have less work than he does = tengo
    menos trabajo que él
2 pronoun = menos
  to cost less = costar menos
  they have less than you = tienen menos
    que ustedes
  in less than half an hour = en menos de
    media hora
3 adverb = menos
  we travel less in the winter = viajamos
    menos en el invierno
  less and less = cada vez menos
4 preposition = menos
  less 10% discount = menos 10% de
    descuento

lesson noun
  a lesson = una clase

let¹ verb
- (used in suggestions)
  let's eat = comamos
  let's go home = vamos a casa
  let's go! = ¡vámonos!
- (to allow) = dejar
  to let someone in = dejarle entrar a alguien
  let me help him = deja que yo lo ayude
let down
  (to disappoint) = fallar
let go
  (to stop holding, to release) = soltar
  let go of me! = ¡suéltame!
  he let the prisoners go = soltó a los
    prisioneros
let in
  (to allow to penetrate)
  to let in the rain = dejar entrar la lluvia
let off
  (not to punish) = perdonar
let out
- (to allow to go out)
  let me out! = ¡déjame salir!
  he let the cat out = dejó salir al gato
- (to utter)
  to let out a scream = soltar un grito
- (to release)
  to let a prisoner out = soltar a un
    prisionero

let² verb (British English)
= alquilar
  'to let' = 'se alquila'

letter noun
  a letter = una carta

letter box noun
  a letter box = un buzón

lettuce noun
  a lettuce = una lechuga

L

level
1 *noun*
  a level = un nivel
  at sea level = a nivel del mar
2 *adjective*
• *(flat or even)* = plano/plana, parejo/pareja
  (Lat Am)
  a level teaspoonful of sugar = una
  cucharada rasa de azúcar
• *(at same height)*
  level with the ground = al nivel del suelo

liar *noun*
  a liar = un mentiroso/una mentirosa

Libra *noun*
• *(the sign)*
  Libra = Libra
  I'm Libra = soy Libra, soy de Libra
• *(a person)*
  a Libra = un/una libra

library *noun*
  a library = una biblioteca

license *(US)*, **licence** *(GB)* noun
  (for driving or fishing)
  a license = un permiso, una licencia

license number *noun (US English)*
  a license number = un número de
  matrícula, un número de patente *(SC)*

license plate *noun (US English)*
  a license plate = una matrícula, una plata
  (Lat Am), una patente *(SC)*

lick *verb*
  = lamer

lid *noun*
  a lid = una tapa

lie
1 *verb*
• *(on the ground or on a bed etc)* = tenderse
  he was lying on the sofa = estaba tendido
  en el sofá
• *(to be situated)* = encontrarse
  the village lies in a valley = el pueblo se
  encuentra en un valle
• *(not tell the truth)* = mentir
2 *noun*
  a lie = una mentira
  to tell a lie = mentir
lie down = tenderse, recostarse

life *noun*
  life = vida *(feminine)*

lift
1 *verb* = levantar
  he lifted his arm = levantó el brazo
2 *noun*
• *(British English—an elevator)*
  a lift = un ascensor

• *(in a car)*
  he gave me a lift to the station = me llevó
  hasta la estación en coche, me dio un
  aventón hasta la estación *(Mex)*
lift up = levantar

light
1 *noun*
• *(brightness)*
  light = luz *(feminine)*
• *(in a room , on a machine)*
  a light = una luz
• *(in a street)*
  a light = un farol, una farola *(Spa)*
• *(for traffic)*
  traffic lights = semáforo *(masculine)*
  the lights are green = el semáforo está (en)
  verde
• *(for a cigarette)*
  have you got a light? = ¿tienes fuego?
• *(on a vehicle)*
  the lights = las luces
2 *adjective*
• *(not nighttime)*
  it's already light = ya es de día
• *(if it's a color or piece of clothing)* =
  claro/clara
  light blue = azul claro
• *(not heavy)* = ligero/ligera, liviano/liviana
  (Lat Am)
3 *verb*
• *(with a match)* = encender, prender *(Lat
  Am)*
• *(illuminate)* = iluminar

light bulb *noun*
  a light bulb = una bombilla, una bombita
  (R Pl), una bujía *(C Am)*, un foco *(Mex)*

lighthouse *noun*
  a lighthouse = un faro

lightning *noun*
  a flash of lightning = un relámpago

like[1] *preposition* = como
  people like you and me = la gente como tú
  y yo
  what's it like? = ¿cómo es?

  ! Note that como *becomes* cómo *in*
  questions

like[2] *verb*
• *(to be keen on)*
  I like [swimming | reading | dancing …] = me
  gusta [nadar | leer | bailar …]
  I like Paul but I don't like Peter = me gusta
  Paul pero no Peter
• *(to wish)* = querer
  I would like a coffee please = quiero un
  café por favor
  would you like some cake? = ¿quieres un
  poco de pastel?
  if you like = si quieres

likely *adjective*
= probable
it is likely that he will come = es probable
que venga

> ! *Note the use of the subjunctive after* **es probable que**

limit
1 *noun*
a limit = un límite
2 *verb* = limitar

limited *adjective*
= limitado/limitada

limp *verb*
= cojear, renguear (*Lat Am*)

line
1 *noun*
a line = una línea
a straight line = una línea recta
• (*in poetry*)
a line = un verso
• (*US English—a queue*)
a line = una cola
to stand in line = hacer cola
• (*a row*)
a line = una fila, una hilera
• (*for fishing*)
a line = un sedal
• (*of a telephone*)
a line = una línea
• **a railroad line, a railway line** (*a route*) = una
línea de ferrocarril
(*a track*) = una vía de ferrocarril
2 *verb*
• (*to border*)
an avenue lined with trees = una avenida
bordeada de árboles
• (*with material*) = forrar

linen *noun*
• (*the fabric*)
linen = lino (*masculine*)
• (*for household use*)
linen (*for a bed*) = ropa blanca (*feminine*),
ropa de cama (*feminine*)
(*for a table*) = mantelería (*feminine*)

link
1 *noun*
• (*a connection*)
a link = una conexión
• (*in a chain*)
a link = un eslabón
2 *verb*
• (*to connect physically*) = conectar
to link A to B = conectar A a B
• (*to establish a relation between*) =
relacionar

lion *noun*
a lion = un león

lip *noun*
a lip = un labio

lipstick *noun*
lipstick = lápiz de labios (*masculine*), lápiz
labial (*masculine*) (*Lat Am*)

liquid *noun*
a liquid = un líquido

Lisbon *noun* ▶ p. 187
Lisbon = Lisboa (*feminine*)

list *noun*
a list = una lista

listen *verb*
= escuchar

liter *noun* (*US English*)
a liter = un litro

literature *noun*
literature = literatura (*feminine*)

litre *noun* (*British English*) ▶ liter

litter *noun*
• (*garbage*)
litter = basura (*feminine*)
• (*of puppies, kittens etc*)
a litter = una camada

little[1]
1 *adjective* = poco/poca
little [time | wine | money ...] = poco [tiempo |
vino | dinero ...]
a little [wine | money | Spanish ...] = un poco
de [vino | dinero | español ...]
2 *pronoun*
a little = un poco
I only ate a little = sólo comí un poco
3 *adverb* = poco
a little (bit) = un poco
a little (bit) **slow** = un poco lento
little by little = poco a poco

little[2] *adjective*
= pequeño/pequeña
a little house = una casa pequeña
a little dog = un perrito

live[1] *verb*
= vivir
he lives in London = vive en Londres
live on
that's not enough to live on = eso no es
suficiente para vivir

live[2]
1 *adjective*
• (*alive*) = vivo/viva
• (*of a broadcast or performance*)
this program is live = este programa es en
directo, este programa es en vivo
2 *adverb*
to be transmitted live = transmitirse en
directo, transmitirse en vivo

lively *adjective*
• (*if it's a person, imagination*) = vivo/viva
• (*if it's a party, discussion*) = animado/
animada

living *noun*
  to make a living = ganarse la vida

living room *noun*
  a living room = una sala (de estar), un living (*Lat Am*), un salón (*Spa*)

load
1 *noun*
• (*on a truck etc*)
  a load = una carga
• (*a lot of*)
  loads of [food | money | work ...] = cantidad de [comida | dinero | trabajo ...], montones de [comida | dinero | trabajo ...]
2 *verb*
  to load a truck = cargar un camión
  to load a camera = poner un rollo en una cámara

loaf *noun*
  a loaf (of bread) = un pan

loan *noun*
  a loan = un préstamo

lobster *noun*
  a lobster = una langosta, un bogavante (*Spa*)

local *adjective*
  the local newspapers = los periódicos locales
  the local shops = las tiendas del barrio
  the local people = los lugareños

location *noun*
  a location = una situación

lock
1 *verb* = cerrar (con llave)
2 *noun*
  a lock = una cerradura, un cerrojo
lock in = encerrar
  I got locked in = me quedé encerrado
lock up
  to lock up a house = cerrar una casa con llave

locker *noun*
• (*in a locker room*)
  a locker = un armario, un locker (*Lat Am*)
• (*at a bus or railroad station*)
  a locker = una (casilla de la) consigna automática

locker room *noun* (*American English*)
  a locker room = un vestuario, un vestidor (*Mex*)

log *noun*
  a log = un tronco
  (*as fuel*) = un leño

logical *adjective*
  = lógico/lógica

London *noun* ▶ **p. 187**
  London = Londres

lonely *adjective*
  a lonely person = una persona sola
  a lonely life = una vida solitaria
  to feel lonely = sentirse solo/sola

long
1 *adjective* = largo/larga
  to have long hair = tener el pelo largo
  how long is this room? = ¿cuánto mide de largo este cuarto?
  the room is 20 meters long = el cuarto tiene 20 metros de largo
  how long is the movie? = ¿cuánto dura la película?
  the movie is two hours long = la película dura dos horas
  he has been ill for a long time = hace mucho que está enfermo
2 *adverb*
• long ago = hace mucho
  I won't be long = no tardo, no demoro (*Lat Am*)
  it doesn't take long = no lleva mucho tiempo, no se demora nada (*Lat Am*)
• as long as (*provided that*) = con tal de que
  as long as the weather is nice all will be well = con tal de que haga buen tiempo todo estará bien

> **!** Note the use of the subjunctive after con tal de que

look
1 *verb* = mirar
  to look at a picture = mirar un cuadro
  he looked out of the window = miró por la ventana
• (*to appear*)
  he looks tired = parece cansado
  he looks well = tiene buena cara
  she looks like her mother = se parece a la madre
2 *noun*
• (*appearance*)
  the look = el aspecto
  I don't like the look of the house = no me gusta el aspecto que tiene la casa
• (*an expression*)
  a look = una cara
  a look of sadness = una cara triste
look after = cuidar
look around
• he looked around = miró a su alrededor
• (*to inspect*)
  they're coming to look around the house = vienen a ver la casa
look back = mirar hacia atrás
look for = buscar
look forward to
  I am looking forward to meeting him = tengo muchas ganas de conocerlo
look out
  look out! = ¡cuidado!
  look out for snakes = cuidado con las serpientes

look up
(*to search for*) = buscar

loose *adjective*
• (*if it's a knot or a screw*) = flojo/floja,
   suelto/suelta
• (*if it's a tooth*)
   this tooth is loose = tengo este diente flojo
• (*if it's clothes*) = suelto/suelta,
   holgado/holgada

lorry *noun* (*British English*)
   a lorry = un camión

lose *verb*
   = perder

loss *noun*
   a loss = una pérdida

lost *adjective*
   = perdido/perdida
   to get lost = perderse

lot *pronoun*
   he drinks a lot = bebe mucho
   a lot of money = mucho dinero
   a lot of patience = mucha paciencia
   **I don't need a lot—three or four will be
      enough** = no necesito muchos—con tres o
      cuatro basta
   there's not a lot left = no queda mucho

loud *adjective*
   (*if it's a sound*) = fuerte
   to have a loud voice = tener una voz fuerte
   to say something in a loud voice = decir
      algo en voz alta
   the music was too loud = la música estaba
      demasiado fuerte

loudspeaker *noun*
   a loudspeaker = un altavoz, un
      (alto)parlante (*Lat Am*)

lounge *noun*
• (*in a hotel*)
   a lounge = un salón
• (*in an airport*)
   the departure lounge = la sala de embarque
• (*US English—a bar*)
   a lounge = un bar
• (*British English—in a house*)
   a lounge = una sala (de estar), un living
      (*Lat Am*), un salón (*Spa*)

love
1 *verb*
• (*if it's a person*) = querer, amar
   they love each other = se quieren, se aman
• (*if it's a thing or activity*)
   I love chocolate = el chocolate me encanta
   I love reading = me encanta leer

2 *noun*
   love = amor (*masculine*)
   to be in love = estar enamorado/enamorada

lovely *adjective*
   (*beautiful*) = precioso/preciosa, lindo/linda
      (*Lat Am*)

low
1 *adjective* = bajo/baja
2 *adverb* = bajo

lower
1 *adjective*
   at a lower price = a un precio más bajo
2 *verb* = bajar

loyal *adjective*
   (*if it's a friend or customer*) = fiel

luck *noun*
   luck = suerte (*feminine*)
   good luck! = i(buena) suerte!

lucky *adjective*
   to be lucky = tener suerte
   a lucky number = un número de la suerte

luggage *noun*
   luggage = equipaje (*masculine*)

lump *noun*
• (*on the body*)
   a lump = un bulto
• (*as the result of a blow to the head*)
   a bump = un chichón
• (*in a sauce or liquid*)
   a lump = un grumo
• (*of coal, cheese etc*)
   a lump = un trozo
• (*of sugar*)
   a lump = un terrón

lunch *noun*
   lunch = almuerzo (*masculine*), comida
      (*feminine*) (*Mex, Spa*)
   to have lunch = almorzar, comer (*Mex,
      Spa*)

lung *noun* ▶ **p. 235**
   a lung = un pulmón

Luxembourg *noun* ▶ **p. 187**
   Luxembourg = Luxemburgo (*masculine*)

luxury
1 *noun*
   luxury = lujo (*masculine*)
2 *adjective* = de lujo

L

Mm

machine *noun*
a machine = una máquina

machinery *noun*
machinery = maquinaria (*feminine*)

mad *adjective*
* (*crazy*) = loco/loca
* (*very angry*) = furioso/furiosa
* (*enthusiastic, keen*)
  to be mad about someone = estar loco/loca
  por alguien
  he's mad about sports = es un fanático de
  los deportes

magazine *noun*
a magazine = una revista

magic
1 *noun*
  magic = magia (*feminine*)
2 *adjective* = mágico/mágica

magnet *noun*
a magnet = un imán

magnificent *adjective* =
magnífico/magnífica

magnifying glass *noun*
a magnifying glass = una lupa

maiden name *noun*
a maiden name = un apellido de soltera

mail
1 *noun*
* (*the system*)
  the mail = el correo
* (*letters, packages*)
  the mail = la correspondencia, el correo
2 *verb* (*US English*)
  to mail a letter to someone = mandarle una
  carta a alguien

mailbox *noun* (*US English*)
a mailbox = un buzón

mailman *noun* (*US English*)
a mailman = un cartero

main *adjective*
= principal

main course *noun*
the main course = el plato principal, el
plato fuerte

main road *noun* (*British English*)
a main road = una carretera principal

maintain *verb*
* (*to preserve*) = mantener
* (*to take care of*)
  to maintain a house = ocuparse del
  mantenimiento de una casa

maize *noun*
maize = maíz (*masculine*)

major
1 *adjective*
  a major event = un acontecimiento muy
  importante
  a major crisis = una crisis seria
2 *noun*
  a major = un/una mayor (*Lat Am*), un/una
  comandante (*Spa*)
3 *verb* (*US English*)
  to major in Spanish = especializarse en
  español

majority *noun*
a majority = una mayoría

make

> **!** *The word* make *can often be translated
> by* hacer. *This entry covers the most
> frequent uses of* make, *but to find
> translations for other expressions like* to
> make a fuss, to make a mistake, to make
> sure *etc, look up the entries at* fuss,
> mistake, sure *etc*

1 *verb*
  to make = hacer
  to make [a cake | the bed | noise …] = hacer
  [un pastel | la cama | ruido …]
  to make a phone call = hacer una llamada
  telefónica
  to make friends = hacer amigos
  to make oneself understood = hacerse
  entender
  to make breakfast = preparar el desayuno
  to be made of [wood | plastic | gold …] = ser
  de [madera | plástico | oro …]
  'made in Argentina' = 'industria argentina'
  'made in Mexico/Spain' = 'hecho en
  México/España'
* (*to cause a particular reaction*)
  to make someone happy = hacer feliz a
  alguien
  to make someone [sad | tired | annoyed …] =
  [entristecer | cansar | enojar …] a alguien
  it makes you thirsty = da sed
* (*to have someone do something*)
  to make someone wait = obligar a alguien
  a esperar
* (*to earn*)
  to make a lot of money = ganar mucho
  dinero
  to make a living = ganarse la vida
2 *noun*
  a make = una marca

make do
  to make do with something = arreglárselas
  con algo

make out
* (*to understand*) = entender
* (*to write out*) = hacer

make up
* (*to be friends again*) = reconciliarse, hacer
  las paces
* (*to invent*) = inventar

makeup noun
  makeup = maquillaje (*masculine*)
  to put on makeup = maquillarse

male
1 adjective
- (*when talking about animals*) = macho/macha
- (*when talking about humans*) = masculino/masculina

2 noun
- (*a man*)
  a male = un hombre
- (*an animal*)
  a male = un macho

man noun
- a man = un hombre
- (*all human beings*)
  man = el hombre

manage verb
- (*to run*) = dirigir
  to manage a shop = dirigir una tienda
- (*to be able*)
  to manage to find work = lograr encontrar trabajo
- (*to cope*) = arreglárselas

manager noun
  a manager (*of a company, a department*) = un director/una directora
  (*of a shop*) = un/una gerente
  (*of a soccer team*) = un entrenador/una entrenadora, un director técnico/una directora técnica (*Lat Am*)

manner noun
- (*a way*)
  a manner = una manera
- (*an attitude*)
  a manner = una actitud

manners noun
  manners = modales (*masculine plural*)
  it's bad manners not to say hello = es de mala educación no saludar

manual noun
  a manual = un manual

manufacture verb
  = fabricar

many
1 adjective
- (*a lot of*) = muchos/muchas
- (*when used with* how, too, so, as)
  how many plates? = ¿cuántos platos?
  how many cups? = ¿cuántas tazas?
  there are too many cars = hay demasiados coches
  there are so many things to do here = hay tantas cosas que hacer aquí
  I got as many presents as you did = recibí tantos regalos como tú

2 pronoun
  are there many left? = ¿quedan muchos/muchas?
  I've got too many = tengo demasiados/demasiadas
  how many? = ¿cuántos/cuántas?
  as many as you like = todo lo que quieras
  there were too many of them = había demasiados/demasiadas

map noun
  a map (*of a country, or region*) = un mapa
  (*of a transport system*) = un plano
  a street map of New York = un plano de Nueva York

marble noun
- (*the rock*)
  marble = mármol (*masculine*)
- (*used in a game*)
  a marble = una canica, una bolita (*S Am*)

march
1 verb
- (*in the army*) = marchar
- (*in a demonstration*) = manifestarse
2 noun
  a march = una marcha

March noun ▶ **p. 192**
  March = marzo (*masculine*)

M

margarine noun
  margarine = margarina (*feminine*)

margin noun
  a margin = un margen

mark
1 noun
- a mark (*on a surface*) = una mancha
  (*on a person's body*) = una marca
- (*a grade*)
  a mark = una nota
- (*in races*)
  on your marks! = ¡a sus marcas!
2 verb
- (*to stain*) = manchar
- (*to correct*)
  to mark the homework = corregir los deberes
- (*to indicate*) = señalar, marcar

market
1 noun
- (*the place*)
  a market = un mercado
- (*the system of trade, the people or things concerned*)
  the market = el mercado
  the Spanish market = el mercado español
2 verb
  (*to sell*) = comercializar

marmalade noun
  marmalade = mermelada (*feminine*)

---

marriage noun
- (the institution)
  marriage = matrimonio (masculine)
- (a ceremony)
  a marriage = un casamiento

married adjective
  to be married to someone = estar casado/casada con alguien
  to get married = casarse

marry verb
  to marry someone, to get married to someone = casarse con alguien

marvelous (US English), **marvellous** (British English) adjective
  = maravilloso/maravillosa

masculine
1 noun (in grammar)
  the masculine = el masculino
2 adjective = masculino/masculina

mash verb
  = hacer puré de, moler (Mex), chafar (Spa), pisar (R Pl)

mashed potatoes noun
  mashed potatoes = puré de papas (Lat Am), puré de patatas (Spa)

mask noun
- (in a ceremony, for disguise)
  a mask = una máscara
- (in sports)
  a mask = una careta

mass noun
- (a large number)
  a mass of people = una gran cantidad de gente
- (in a church)
  a mass = una misa

massive adjective
  = enorme

mast noun
  (on a ship, for flags)
  a mast = un mástil

master
1 noun
- (an owner of a dog)
  a master = un amo
- (British English—a teacher)
  a master (in primary school) = un maestro
  (in secondary school) = un profesor
2 verb
  to master a language = dominar un idioma

masterpiece noun
  a masterpiece = una obra maestra

mat noun
  a mat (at a door) = un felpudo

  (in a bathroom) = una alfombrita, una alfombrilla (Spa), un tapete del baño (Méx)

match
1 noun
- (a game)
  a match = un partido
- (a matchstick)
  a match = un fósforo, una cerilla (Spa)
2 verb
  the shoes match the skirt = los zapatos hacen juego con la falda

matchbox noun
  a matchbox = una caja de fósforos, una caja de cerillas (Spa)

mate
1 noun (British English)
  (a friend)
  a mate = un amigo/una amiga
2 verb = aparearse

material noun
- (a substance)
  a material = un material
- (cloth)
  a material = una tela
- (written information)
  material = material (masculine)

math noun (US English)
  math = matemáticas (feminine plural)

mathematics noun
  mathematics = matemáticas (feminine plural)

maths noun (British English) ▶ math

matter
1 noun
- (a situation, an event)
  a matter = un asunto
- (a question)
  it's only a matter of time = sólo es cuestión de tiempo
- (the problem)
  what's the matter? = ¿qué pasa?
  what's the matter with her? = ¿qué le pasa?
2 verb = importar
  it doesn't matter = no importa

mattress noun
  a mattress = un colchón

mature adjective
  = maduro/madura

maximum
1 adjective = máximo/máxima
2 noun
  the maximum = el máximo

may verb
- (when talking about a possibility)
  they may be able to come = es posible que vengan
  she may not have seen him = es posible que no lo haya visto

---

C Am Central America   Lat Am Latin America   Mex Mexico

! *Note the use of the subjunctive after* es
posible que
- (*when asking for or giving permission*)
  may I come in? = ¿puedo entrar?
  you may sit down = pueden sentarse

May *noun* ▶ p. 192
  May = mayo (*masculine*)

maybe *adverb*
  = quizás, tal vez, a lo mejor
  maybe he'll arrive later = quizás llegue más
  tarde, tal vez llegue más tarde, a lo mejor
  llega más tarde

! *Note the use of the subjunctive after*
quizás *and* tal vez

mayor *noun*
  a mayor = un alcalde/una alcaldesa

maze *noun*
  a maze = un laberinto

me *pronoun*
- (*when used as a direct object*) = me
  they know/don't know me = me
  conocen/no me conocen

! *Note that* me *comes before the verb in
Spanish*

- (*when used as an indirect object*) = me
  he never talks to me = no me habla nunca
  he wrote me a letter = me escribió una
  carta

! *Note that* me *comes before the verb in
Spanish*

  don't send them to me! = ¡no me los
  mandes!

- (*when used as an indirect object pronoun
  together with a direct object pronoun*) =
  me
  you have to give them to me = tienes que
  dármelos, me los tienes que dar
  he said it to me = me lo dijo

! *Note that* me *comes before the direct
object pronoun*

- (*when telling someone to do something*) =
  me
  help me! = ¡ayúdame!
  give the money to me = dame el dinero
  give them to me! = ¡dámelos!

! *Note that* me *comes after the verb in
Spanish*

- (*when telling someone not to do
  something*) = me
  don't leave me! = ¡no me dejes!
  don't send them to me! = ¡no me los
  mandes!

! *Note that* me *comes before the verb in
Spanish*

- (*when used after prepositions*) = mí
  did you buy it for me? = ¿lo compraste
  para mí?
  come with me = ven conmigo
- (*when used with* to be)
  it's me = soy yo

meadow *noun*
  a meadow = un prado, una pradera

meal *noun*
  a meal = una comida
  to go out for a meal = salir a comer (fuera)

mean
  1 *verb*
- (*when talking about the sense of
  something*) = querer decir
  what does that mean? = ¿qué quiere decir
  eso?
- (*to have as a result*)
  it means giving up my job = significa que
  tengo que dejar el trabajo
- (*to intend*)
  I meant to tell you the news but I forgot =
  tenía la intención de contarte la noticia
  pero se me olvidó
  she didn't mean to upset you = no quiso
  ofenderte
- (*to intend to say*) = querer decir
  what do you mean by that? = ¿qué quieres
  decir con eso?
  I know what you mean = entiendo
- (*to be of importance or value*)
  her work means a lot to her = su trabajo es
  muy importante para ella
  to be meant to
  I'm meant to collect the books = se supone
  que tengo que recoger los libros
  it's meant to be a dictionary for beginners
  = se supone que es un diccionario para
  principiantes
  2 *adjective*
- (*not generous*) = tacaño/tacaña
- (*nasty, unkind*) = malo/mala

meaning *noun*
  a meaning = un significado

means *noun*
- (*a way*)
  a means = un medio
  a means of transport = un medio de
  transporte
- (*when talking about money*)
  means = medios (económicos) (*masculine
  plural*), recursos (*masculine*)
  he lives beyond his means = lleva un tren
  de vida que no se puede costear

meanwhile *adverb*
  (*during this time*) = mientras tanto

measles *noun*
  measles = sarampión (*masculine*)

measure
  1 *verb* = medir
  the window measures 40 cm by 60 cm = la
  ventana mide 40 centímetros por 60
  centímetros

M

2 noun
(a step)
a measure = una medida
to take measures to do something = tomar medidas para hacer algo

measurement noun
(of a person)
measurements = medidas (feminine plural)
to take someone's measurements = tomarle las medidas a alguien

meat noun
meat = carne (feminine)

mechanical adjective
= mecánico/mecánica

medal noun
a medal = una medalla

media noun
the media = los medios de comunicación

medical adjective
= médico/médica

medicine noun
• (the subject, the profession)
medicine = medicina (feminine)
• (a drug)
a medicine = un medicamento, una medicina

Mediterranean noun
the Mediterranean = el Mediterráneo

medium adjective
= mediano/mediana

meet verb
• (by accident or appointment) = encontrar
she met him in the bar = lo encontró en el bar
to meet during the vacation = encontrarse durante las vacaciones
• (to make the acquaintance of) = conocer
have you met Liz? = ¿conoces a Liz?
Nicky, meet Carol = Nicky, te presento a Carol
pleased to meet you! = ¡encantado/encantada!
• (to wait for) = esperar
is there someone meeting you at the station? = ¿alguien te espera en la estación?
• (to fetch)
(when going to a place) = ir a buscar,
(when coming to a place) = venir a buscar
• (to have a formal meeting) = reunirse
meet up
• (after being apart) = encontrarse
• (regularly) = verse

meeting noun
a meeting = una reunión

melon noun
a melon = un melón

melt verb
• (to become liquid)
(of ice, butter, snow, metal) = fundirse
(of wax) = derretirse
• (to make liquid)
(if it's butter, ice, metal) = fundir
(if it's wax) = derretirse

member noun
a member (of a committee or international organization) = un/una miembro
(of a club) = un socio/una socia
a member of staff (in a school) = un/una miembro del personal docente
(in a bank, firm) = un empleado/una empleada

memory noun
• (the ability to remember)
memory = memoria (feminine)
to have a good/bad memory = tener buena/mala memoria
• (of a person, place or time)
a memory = un recuerdo

mend verb
• (to fix) = arreglar
to have the roof mended = hacer arreglar el tejado
• (by sewing) = coser, arreglar

mental adjective
= mental

mention verb = mencionar
she mentioned that she is looking for another job = dijo que está buscando otro trabajo
thank you very much—don't mention it! = muchas gracias—¡no hay de qué!

menu noun
a menu = un menú

mercy noun
mercy = clemencia (feminine)

merry-go-round noun
a merry-go-round = unos caballitos, un carrusel (Lat Am), una calesita (R Pl), un tiovivo (Spa)

mess noun
a mess = un desorden
your room is in a mess = tu cuarto está todo desordenado
to make a mess in the kitchen = dejar la cocina hecha un desastre
mess around, mess about (British English) = tontear

message noun
a message = un mensaje
(when phoning) = un recado

messenger
a messenger = un mensajero/una mensajera

metal
1 *noun*
  a metal = un metal
2 *adjective* = metálico/metálica

meter *noun*
• (*for gas, electricity, water*)
  a meter = un contador, un medidor (*Lat Am*)
• (*US English—a measure*)
  a meter = un metro

method *noun*
  a method = un método
  a method of payment = una forma de pago

metre *noun* (*British English*)
  a metre = un metro

Mexico *noun* ▶ p. 187
  Mexico = México (*masculine*)

microphone *noun*
  a microphone = un micrófono

microscope *noun*
  a microscope = un microscopio

microwave (**oven**) *noun*
  a microwave (**oven**) = un microondas

midday *noun* ▶ p. 319
  midday = mediodía (*masculine*)
  at midday = al mediodía

middle *noun*
  the middle = el medio
  in the middle of the road = en medio de la calle
  in the middle of August = a mediados de agosto
  I'm in the middle of cooking something = estoy preparando algo

middle-aged *adjective*
  = de mediana edad (**!** *never changes*)

Middle Ages *noun*
  the Middle Ages = la Edad Media

midnight *noun*
  midnight = medianoche (*feminine*)
  at midnight = a medianoche

midwife *noun*
  a midwife = una partera

might *verb*
• (*when talking about a possibility*)
  she might be right = puede que tenga razón
  will you come?—I might = ¿vas a venir?—quizás
  we might miss the plane = a lo mejor perdemos el avión

> **!** *Note the use of the subjunctive after* puede que

• (*when implying that something did not happen*)
  she might have warned us = podría habernos avisado

mild *adjective*
• (*not harsh*)
  a mild winter = un invierno no muy frío
• (*gentle on the hair, skin*) = suave
• (*not strong in taste*)
  a mild cheese = un queso suave
  a mild curry = un curry no muy picante
• (*not serious*)
  a mild infection = una infección leve

mile *noun*
  a mile = una milla

military *adjective*
  = militar

milk
1 *noun*
  milk = leche
2 *verb* = ordeñar

million *number*
  one million, a million = un millón
  a million inhabitants = un millón de habitantes
  three million dollars = tres millones de dólares

millionaire *noun*
  a millionaire = un millonario/una millonaria

mince
1 *noun* (*British English*)
  mince = carne molida, carne picada (*R Pl, Spa*)
2 *verb* = moler, picar (*R Pl, Spa*)

mind
1 *noun*
• (*when talking about a person's thoughts*)
  the mind = la mente
  what's on your mind? = ¿qué es lo que te preocupa?
  I can't get it out of my mind = no puedo quitármelo de la cabeza
• (*when talking about a person's opinions or attitudes*)
  to make up one's mind to live alone = decidirse vivir solo
  to change one's mind = cambiar de opinión
2 *verb*
• (*when expressing an opinion*)
  there's a lot of noise but I don't mind = hay mucho ruido pero no me importa
  she doesn't mind the heat = el calor no le molesta
  I wouldn't mind a drink = no me vendría mal un trago

M

- (*in polite questions or requests*)
  do you mind if I smoke? = ¿te importa si fumo?
  would you mind closing the window? = ¿le importaría cerrar la ventana?
- (*when telling someone to be careful*)
  mind the steps! = ¡cuidado con las escaleras!
- (*to take care of*) = cuidar
  to mind the children = cuidar a los niños
  to mind the shop = atender la tienda
- (*to worry*)
  never mind, I'll get the next train = no te preocupes, tomaré el próximo tren

mine[1] *pronoun*
  (*singular*) = mío/mía
  (*plural*) = míos/mías
  mine is here = el mío/la mía está aquí
  a friend of mine = un amigo mío

mine[2] *noun*
- (*for coal, metals*)
  a mine = una mina
- (*type of bomb*)
  a mine = una mina

miner *noun*
  a miner = un minero/una minera

mineral *noun*
  a mineral = un mineral

mineral water *noun*
  a mineral water = un agua mineral (*feminine*)

minimum
1 *adjective* = mínimo/mínima
2 *noun*
  the minimum = el mínimo

miniskirt *noun*
  a miniskirt = una minifalda

minister *noun*
- (*in government*)
  a minister = un ministro/una ministra, un secretario/una secretaria (*Mex*)
- (*in religion*)
  a minister = un pastor/una pastora

ministry *noun*
  a ministry = un ministerio, una secretaría (*Mex*)

minor
1 *adjective*
  some minor changes = unos pequeños cambios
  a minor injury = una herida leve
2 *noun*
  a minor = un/una menor (de edad)

minority *noun*
  a minority = una minoría

mint *noun*
- (*the herb*)
  mint = menta

- (*a sweet*)
  a mint = una pastilla de menta

minus *preposition*
  = menos
  six minus three is three (6 − 3 = 3) = seis menos tres es igual a tres (6 − 3 = 3)

minute *noun* ▶ **p. 319**
  a minute = un minuto

minutes *noun*
  the minutes = el acta
  to take the minutes = levantar el acta

miracle *noun*
  a miracle = un milagro

mirror *noun*
  a mirror (*on a wall*) = un espejo
  (*on a vehicle*) = un (espejo) retrovisor

mischievous *adjective*
  = travieso/traviesa

miserable *adjective*
- (*unhappy*) = triste
- (*depressing*)
  the weather's miserable = el tiempo está pésimo

miss *verb*
- (*to fail to hit*)
  to miss the target = no dar en el blanco
  the stone just missed her head = la piedra por poco le da en la cabeza
  you missed! = ¡fallaste!
- (*to fail to see*)
  you can't miss it = lo va a ver enseguida
- (*to fail to take*)
  to miss an opportunity = perder una oportunidad
  he missed the chance to work abroad = perdió la oportunidad de trabajar al extranjero
- (*to fail to understand*)
  you've missed the point = no lo has entendido
- (*to feel sad not to see*) = echar de menos, extrañar (*Lat Am*)
  I miss you = te echo de menos, te extraño
- (*to fail to catch*) = perder
  to miss a train = perder un tren
  to miss a party = perder una fiesta

Miss *noun*
  = señorita

missile *noun*
  a missile = un misil

missing *adjective*
  to be missing = faltar
  the missing jewels = las joyas desaparecidas
  to go missing (*British English*) = desaparecer

mist noun
  mist = neblina (feminine)

mistake noun
  a mistake = un error
  to make a mistake = cometer un error
  a spelling mistake = una falta de ortografía
  by mistake = por error

misunderstand verb
  = entender mal

misunderstanding noun
  a misunderstanding = un malentendido

mix verb
• (to put together) = mezclar
• (to go together) = mezclarse
  oil doesn't mix with water = el aceite no se
    mezcla con el agua

mix up
  (to get confused)
  to mix up the two languages, to get the
    two languages mixed up = confundir los
    dos idiomas

mixture noun
  a mixture = una mezcla

moan verb
• (to groan) = gemir
• (to complain) = quejarse

model noun
• (of a train, a car, a building)
  a model = un modelo, una maqueta
• (of fashions)
  a model = un/una modelo

modern adjective
  = moderno/moderna

mole noun
• (the animal)
  a mole = un topo
• (a spot on the skin)
  a mole = un lunar

mom noun (US English)
  Mom = mamá✻ (feminine)

moment noun
  a moment = un momento
  it will be ready in a moment = estará listo
    enseguida
  at the moment = en este momento

mommy noun (US English)
  my mommy = mi mamá✻

Monday noun ▶ p. 192
  Monday = lunes (masculine)

money noun
  money = dinero (masculine), plata
    (feminine) (S Am)

monkey noun
  a monkey = un mono/una mona

monster noun
  a monster = un monstruo

month noun ▶ p. 192
  a month = un mes

monument noun
  a monument = un monumento

mood noun
• (a humor)
  to be in a good/bad mood = estar de
    buen/mal humor
• (a bad humor)
  he's in a mood = está de mal humor

moody adjective
  to be moody (unpredictable) = ser
    temperamental
  (in a bad mood) = estar de mal humor

moon noun
  the moon = la luna

moonlight noun
  the moonlight = la luz de la luna

moor
1 noun
  a moor = un páramo
2 verb
  to moor a boat = amarrar un barco

moral adjective
  = moral

more
1 adjective = más
  more [friends | books | time ...] = más [amigos |
    libros | tiempo ...]
  I have more work than him = tengo más
    trabajo que él
  there's no more bread = no hay más pan
  he bought two more tickets = compró dos
    boletos más
2 pronoun = más
  to cost more = costar más
  I did more than you = hice más que tú
  more than = más de
  there were more than 20 people = había
    más de 20 personas
  I can't tell you any more = no te puedo
    decir más
  we need more (of them/of it) = necesitamos
    más
3 adverb
• (when comparing) = más
  it's more complicated than that = es más
    complicado que eso
• (when talking about time)
  he doesn't live here any more = ya no vive
    aquí
• more and more = cada vez más
• more or less = más o menos

M

morning noun ▶ p. 319
  a morning = una mañana
  Friday morning = el viernes en la mañana,
    el viernes por la mañana (Spa)
  in the morning = en la mañana, por la
    mañana (Spa)
  tomorrow morning = mañana por la
    mañana
  at six o'clock in the morning = a las seis de
    la mañana
  good morning = buenos días

mosquito noun
  a mosquito = un mosquito, un zancudo
    (Lat Am)

most
1 adjective
• (the majority of) = la mayoría de, la mayor
    parte de
• (in superlatives)
  who has the most money? = ¿quién es el
    que tiene más dinero?
2 pronoun
• = la mayoría, la mayor parte
• at (the) most = como mucho
3 adverb
• (in superlatives) = más
  the most expensive shop in London = la
    tienda más cara de Londres
  the most difficult problems = los problemas
    más difíciles
• most of all
  I like this one most of all = éste es el que
    más me gusta
  most of all I want to visit Buenos Aires = lo
    que más quisiera es visitar Buenos Aires

mostly adverb
  (for the most part)
  the students are mostly Japanese = la
    mayoría de los estudiantes son japoneses

moth noun
  a moth = una mariposa de la luz, una
    palomilla
  (in clothes) = una polilla

mother noun
  a mother = una madre

mother-in-law noun
  a mother-in-law = una suegra

motive noun
  a motive = un motivo

motor noun
  a motor = un motor

motorbike noun
  a motorbike = una motocicleta, una moto

motorist noun
  a motorist = un/una automovilista

motor racing noun
  motor racing = carreras automovilísticas
    (feminine plural)

motorway noun (British English)
  a motorway = una autopista

mountain noun
  a mountain = una montaña

mouse noun
  a mouse = un ratón, una laucha (SC)

moustache (British English)
  a moustache = un bigote

mouth noun
• (of a person, an animal) ▶ p. 235
  the mouth = la boca
• (of a cave, tunnel)
  the mouth = la entrada
• (of a river)
  the mouth = la desembocadura

move
1 verb
• (to make a movement) = moverse
  I can't move = no puedo moverme
  when the train is moving = cuando el tren
    está en marcha
• (to put elsewhere)
  to move the television = cambiar de lugar
    la televisión
  could you move the chair (out of the way)?
    = ¿podrías quitar la silla de en medio?
• (to make a movement with) = mover
  to move one's head = mover la cabeza
  don't move the camera = no muevas la
    cámara
• (to act) = actuar
  to move fast = actuar rápido
• to move (house) (British English) =
    mudarse de casa
• (to touch, to move emotionally) = conmover
  to be moved = estar conmovido/conmovida
2 noun
• (a movement)
  a move = un movimiento
• (a step, a decision)
  a good move = una buena decisión
  to make the first move = dar el primer paso
• (a change of location)
  a move = una mudanza
• (in a game)
  it's your move = te toca mover
move around
• (to travel around) = moverse
• (to put elsewhere) = cambiar de lugar
  to move the furniture around = cambiar los
    muebles de lugar
move away
• (to live elsewhere) = mudarse
• (to make a movement away) = alejarse
move back = retroceder
move forward = avanzar
move in = mudarse
move out = irse
move over = correrse

movement noun
- **a movement** = un movimiento
- (a group)
  a movement = un movimiento
  the women's movement = el movimiento
  feminista

movie noun (US English)
  a movie = una película

mow verb
  = cortar

MP noun (British English)
  an MP = un diputado/una diputada

Mr noun
  = Señor, Sr.

Mrs noun
  = Señora, Sra.

Ms noun
  = Señora, Sra.

much
1 adverb
- (a lot) = mucho
  her house is much smaller than ours = su
  casa es mucho más pequeña que la
  nuestra
- (often) = mucho
  they don't go out much = no salen mucho
- (when used with very, too or so)
  I don't like driving very much = no me
  gusta mucho manejar
  you talk too much = hablas demasiado
  she loves her so much = la quiere tanto
2 pronoun = mucho
  how much does it cost? = ¿cuánto cuesta?
3 adjective = mucho/mucha
  there isn't much water = no hay mucha
  agua
- (when used with very, too, so or how)
  she doesn't eat very much meat = no come
  mucha carne
  I spent too much money = gasté demasiado
  dinero
  don't use so much salt = no pongas tanta
  sal
  how much coffee? = ¿cuánto café?
  how much milk? = ¿cuánta leche?

mud noun
  mud = barro (masculine), fango
  (masculine)

mug
1 noun
  a mug = una taza (alta y sin platillo), un
  tarro (Mex)
2 verb = atracar

mule noun
  a mule = una mula

multiply verb
  (in arithmetic) = multiplicar
  to multiply 10 by 10 = multiplicar 10 por 10

mumble verb
  = farfullar

mum noun (British English)
  Mum = mamá✱ (feminine)

mummy noun (British English)
  (mother)
  my mummy = mi mamá✱

murder
1 noun
  a murder = un asesinato
2 verb = asesinar

murderer noun
  a murderer = un asesino/una asesina

muscle noun
  a muscle = un músculo

museum noun
  a museum = un museo

mushroom noun
  (edible)
  a mushroom = un champiñón

music noun
  music = música

musical
1 adjective
  to be musical (to have talent) = ser
  músico/música
2 noun
  a musical = un musical

musician noun
  a musician = un músico/una música

Muslim
1 noun
  a Muslim = un musulmán/una musulmana
2 adjective = musulmán/musulmana

mussel noun
  a mussel = una mejillón

must verb

> **!** The verbs deber and tener que are
> used to translate must

- (when stressing the importance of
  something)
  you must go to the doctor = tienes que ir al
  médico, debes ir al médico
  she must do the exam in June = tiene que
  dar el examen en junio
- (when assuming that something is true)
  it must be nice to live there = debe (de) ser
  lindo vivir allí
- (when talking about what you intend to do)
  I must phone her this evening = tengo que
  llamarla esta tarde

mustache noun (US English)
  a mustache = un bigote

mutton noun
  mutton = carne de ovino (feminine)

M

my *adjective*
= mi (+ *singular*), mis (+ *plural*)

> **!** *For* my *used with parts of the body,*
> ▶ **p. 235**

myself *pronoun*
* (*when translated by a reflexive verb in Spanish*)
  I didn't hurt myself = no me hice daño, no me lastimé (*Lat Am*)
  I bought myself a hat = me compré un sombrero
* (*when used for emphasis*)
  I told them myself = se lo dije yo mismo/yo misma
  I did it all by myself = lo hice yo solo

mysterious *adjective*
= misterioso/misteriosa

mystery *noun*
* a mystery = un misterio
* (*a story*)
  a mystery = una novela de misterio

Nn

nail
1 *noun*
* (*for use in hanging, attaching, repairing*)
  a nail = un clavo
* (*on the fingers or toes*)
  a nail = una uña
2 *verb* = clavar

nail polish, nail varnish (*British English*) *noun*
nail polish = esmalte de uñas (*masculine*)

naïve *adjective*
= ingenuo/ingenua

naked *adjective*
= desnudo/desnuda

name
1 *noun*
* (*of a person*)
  a name = un nombre
  what's your name? = ¿cómo te llamas?, ¿cómo se llama?
  my name is Joan = me llamo Joan
* (*of a book, play or film*)
  a name = un título
2 *verb* = ponerle nombre a
  a man named Bob Jones = un hombre llamado Bob Jones

napkin *noun*
a napkin = un servilleta

nappy *noun* (*British English*)
a nappy = un pañal

narrow *adjective*
= estrecho/estrecha, angosto/angosta (*Lat Am*)

nasty *adjective*
* (*unkind*) = malo/mala
  to be nasty to someone = ser malo/mala con alguien
* (*unpleasant*) = desagradable

nation *noun*
a nation = una nación

national *adjective*
= nacional

national anthem *noun*
a national anthem = un himno nacional

native
1 *adjective*
  his native language = su lengua materna
  a native Spanish speaker = un hablante nativo de español
2 *noun*
  a native = un nativo/una nativa

natural *adjective*
* (*not artificial*) = natural
* (*normal*) = normal, natural

naturally *adverb*
= naturalmente

nature *noun*
* (*the natural world*)
  nature = naturaleza (*feminine*)
* (*part of a person's personality*)
  nature = carácter (*masculine*)

naughty *noun*
= travieso/traviesa

navel *noun*
the navel = el ombligo

navy *noun*
the navy = la armada

navy blue *adjective* ▶ **p. 183**
= azul marino (**!** *never changes*)

near
1 *preposition* = cerca de
  it's near the station = está cerca de la estación
2 *adverb*
  they live quite near = viven muy cerca
  to move nearer = acercarse
3 *adjective*
  the school is quite near = la escuela está bastante cerca
  the nearest shops = las tiendas más cercanas
  in the near future = en un futuro próximo

C Am Central America   Lat Am Latin America   Mex Mexico

nearby *adverb*
= cerca

nearly *adverb*
= casi
I'm nearly ready = estoy casi listo
we're nearly there = ya casi llegamos, ya
casi hemos llegado
I nearly forgot = por poco me olvido

nearsighted *adjective*
= miope, corto/corta de vista

neat *adjective*
• (*if it's a person*) = pulcro/pulcra,
prolijo/prolija (*R Pl*)
• (*tidy*)
your room is always very neat = tu cuarto
siempre está muy ordenado

necessary *adjective*
= necesario/necesaria

neck *noun*
• (*of a person*) ▶ **p. 235**
the neck = el cuello
the back of the neck = la nuca
• (*of a garment*)
the neck = el cuello, el escote

necklace *noun*
a necklace = un collar

need
1 *verb*
• (*to have to*)
you didn't need to ask for permission = no
tenías que pedir permiso
you needn't pay now = no hace falta que
pagues ahora
they'll need to come early = tendrán que
venir temprano
you needn't have come = no hacía falta
que vinieras

! *Note the use of the subjunctive after* no
hace falta que

• (*to want*) = necesitar
to need money = necesitar dinero
we need to talk to her = tenemos que
hablar con ella
2 *noun*
there's no need (for you) to worry = no
tienes por qué preocuparte
I'll do it—there's no need, it's done = yo lo
hago—no hace falta, ya está hecho

needle *noun*
a needle = una aguja

negative
1 *adjective* = negativo/negativa
2 *noun*
(*of a photo*)
a negative = una negativa

neglect *verb*
to neglect a child = desatender a un niño
to neglect a house = descuidar

negotiations *noun*
negotiations = negociaciones (*feminine
plural*)

neighbor (*US English*), **neighbour**
(*British English*) *noun*
a neighbor = un vecino/una vecina

neither
1 *conjunction*
• (*in* neither . . . nor *sentences*)
she speaks neither Spanish nor English =
no habla (ni) español ni inglés
they drink neither coffee nor tea = no
beben (ni) café ni té
• (*nor*)
I can't sleep—neither can I = no puedo
dormir—yo tampoco
2 *adjective*
neither book is useful = ninguno de los
libros es útil
neither girl answered = ninguna de las
chicas contestó
3 *pronoun* = ninguno/ninguna
neither of them is coming = ninguno (de
ellos) viene, no viene ninguno (de ellos)

nephew *noun*
a nephew = un sobrino

nerve *noun*
• a nerve = un nervio
• (*courage*)
nerve = valor (*masculine*)
to have the nerve to refuse = tener el valor
de rehusar
(*when criticizing*) = tener la frescura de
rehusar

nerves *noun*
nerves = nervios (*masculine plural*)
to get on someone's nerves = ponerle los
nervios de punta a alguien

nervous *adjective*
= nervioso/nerviosa

nest *noun*
a nest = un nido

net
1 *noun*
a net = una red
2 *adjective* = neto/neta

Netherlands *noun* ▶ **p. 187**
the Netherlands = los Países Bajos

nettle *noun*
a nettle = una ortiga

network *noun*
a network = una red

neutral
1 *adjective*
• (*impartial*) = neutral
• (*not bright*) = neutro/neutra
a neutral color = un color neutro

N

2 *noun*
(*when driving*)
to be in neutral = estar en punto muerto

never *adverb*
• (*not ever*)
they never come to see us = nunca vienen
a vernos, no vienen nunca a vernos
never again! = ¡jamás!
I'll never go back there again = no volveré
allí nunca, nunca volveré allí
• (*when used for emphasis*)
I never knew that = no lo sabía
she never even apologized = nunca se
disculpó siquiera

nevertheless *adverb*
= sin embargo

new *adjective*
= nuevo/nueva

newborn *adjective*
a newborn baby = un bebé recién nacido

news *noun*
• a piece of news = una noticia
have you heard the news? = ¿te enteraste
de lo que pasó?
have you any news of John? = ¿sabes algo
de John?
• (*on radio, TV*)
the news = las noticias

newsagent *noun* (*British English*)
▶ newsdealer

newscaster *noun*
a newscaster = un locutor/una locutora

newsdealer *noun* (*US English*)
a newsdealer = un vendedor/una
vendedora de periódicos

newspaper *noun*
a newspaper = un periódico, un diario

newsreader *noun* (*British English*)
a newsreader = un locutor/una locutora

New Year *noun*
the New Year = el Año Nuevo
Happy New Year! = ¡Feliz Año Nuevo!

New Year's (*US English*), **New
Year's Day** (*British English*) *noun*
New Year's (Day) = el día de Año Nuevo

New Zealand *noun* ▶ p. 187
New Zealand = Nueva Zelanda (*feminine*),
Nueva Zelandia (*feminine*) (*Lat Am*)

next
1 *adjective*
• (*when talking about what is still to come*) =
próximo/próxima
the next train = el próximo tren
she's leaving next Friday = se va el viernes
que viene

• (*when talking about what followed*) =
siguiente
I took the next train = tomé el tren
siguiente
the next day = el día siguiente
• (*in a line*)
who's next? = ¿quién sigue?
I'm next = (yo) soy el siguiente
2 *adverb*
• (*in the past*) = luego, después
what happened next? = ¿y luego qué
pasó?, ¿y después qué pasó?
• (*now*) = ahora
what'll we do next? = ¿qué vamos a hacer
ahora?
• (*in the future*)
when you next go to Leeds, give Gary a
call = la próxima vez que vas a Leeds,
lláma a Gary
• next to
we live next to the school = vivimos al lado
de la escuela
3 *pronoun*
they're coming the week after next =
vienen la semana que viene no, la
siguiente

next door *adverb*
= al lado
they live next door = viven al lado

nice *adjective*
• (*enjoyable*) = agradable, lindo/linda
(*Lat Am*)
it's nice to be able to relax = es agradable
poder descansar
I had a nice time = lo pasé bien
• (*pleasant, kind*) = simpático/simpática
to be nice to someone = ser amable con
alguien
• (*attractive*) = bonito/bonita, lindo/linda (*Lat
Am*)
you look very nice in that suit = ese traje te
queda muy bien
• (*tasty*) = bueno/buena
the meal was nice = la comida estuvo
buena

nickname *noun*
a nickname = un apodo

niece *noun*
a niece = una sobrina

night *noun* ▶ p. 319
a night = una noche
to work at night = trabajar de noche
I didn't sleep last night = no dormí anoche

nightclub *noun*
a nightclub = un club (nocturno)

nightdress, nightie *noun*
a nightdress = un camisón

nightmare *noun*
a nightmare = una pesadilla

nil *noun* (*British English*)
(*in sport*)
nil = cero (*masculine*)

nine *number* ▶ **p. 154, p. 319**
nine = nueve (*masculine*) (**!** *never changes*) *see also* **five**

nineteen *number* ▶ **p. 154, p. 319**
nineteen = diecinueve (*masculine*) (**!** *never changes*) *see also* **five**

ninety *number* ▶ **p. 154**
ninety = noventa (*masculine*) (**!** *never changes*) *see also* **five**

ninth
1 *adjective* = noveno/novena
2 *noun* ▶ **p. 192**
(*a part*)
a ninth = una novena parte

no
1 *exclamation*
no = no
no thanks = no gracias
2 *adjective*
• (*not any*)
we have no money = no tenemos dinero
where is he?—I've no idea = ¿dónde está? —no tengo idea
• (*when refusing permission*)
no smoking = prohibido fumar
no talking! = ¡silencio!
• (*when used for emphasis*)
there is no time to argue = no hay tiempo para discutir
it's no problem = no hay problema
3 *adverb*
he no longer works here = ya no trabaja aquí

nobody ▶ **no one**

nod *verb*
to nod (one's head) (*to say 'yes'*) = asentir con la cabeza
(*to make a sign*) = indicar con la cabeza

noise *noun*
noise = ruido (*masculine*)

noisy *adjective*
= ruidoso/ruidosa
it's too noisy here = hay demasiado ruido aquí

none *pronoun*
= ninguno/ninguna
none of the girls went to the class = ninguna de las chicas fue a la clase
none of what he says is true = nada de lo que dice es cierto
there's none left = no queda ninguno
I have none, I've got none = no tengo

nonsense *noun*
nonsense = tonterías (*feminine plural*)

noodles *noun*
noodles = fideos (*masculine plural*)

noon *noun*
noon = mediodía (*masculine*)
at noon = al mediodía

no one *pronoun* (*also* **nobody**)
no one = nadie
no one saw him = nadie lo vio
there's no one in the office = no hay nadie en la oficina

nor *conjunction*

> **!** *For translations of* nor *when used in combination with* neither, *look at the entry for* neither *in this dictionary*

I don't like him—nor do I = no me gusta—a mí tampoco
she didn't understand anything and nor did we = ella no entendió nada y nosotros tampoco

normal
1 *adjective* = normal
2 *noun*
to get back to normal = volver a la normalidad

normally *adverb*
= normalmente

north
1 *noun*
the north = el norte
in the north of France = en el norte de Francia
2 *adverb*
we went north = fuimos hacia el norte
it is north of Madrid = está al norte de Madrid
3 *adjective*
= norte (**!** *never changes*)
the north coast = la costa norte
the north wind = el viento norte

North America *noun* ▶ **p. 187**
North America = Norteamérica (*feminine*), América del Norte (*feminine*)

northeast *noun*
the northeast = el noreste

Northern Ireland *noun* ▶ **p. 187**
Northern Ireland = Irlanda del Norte (*feminine*)

northwest *noun*
the northwest = el noroeste

Norway *noun* ▶ **p. 187**
Norway = Noruega (*feminine*)

Norwegian ▶ **p. 187, p. 245**
1 *adjective* = noruego/noruega
2 *noun*
• (*a person*)
a Norwegian = un noruego/una noruega

N

* (*the language*)
Norwegian = noruego (*masculine*)

nose *noun* ▶ p. 235
the nose = la nariz

nostril *noun*
a nostril = una ventana de la nariz

not
1 *adverb* = no
she's not at home = no está en casa
has he not phoned you?, hasn't he phoned you? = ¿no te ha llamado?
I hope not = espero que no
2 not at all
* (*in no way*)
he's not at all worried = no está nada preocupado
* (*don't mention it*)
thanks a lot—not at all = muchas gracias—de nada

note
1 *noun*
* (*to remind oneself*)
a note = una nota
to make a note of an address = anotar una dirección
to take note of a name = tomar nota de un nombre
* (*a short letter*)
a note = una nota
* (*British English—paper money*)
a note = un billete
* (*in music*)
a note = una nota
2 *verb*
to note that something has happened = notar que algo ha pasado
note down = apuntar

notebook *noun*
* (*an exercise book*)
a notebook = un cuaderno
* (*for shorthand*)
a notebook = una libreta

nothing *pronoun*
nothing = nada
nothing has changed = nada ha cambiado
nothing happens in this town = no pasa nada en esta ciudad
there's nothing else to say = no hay nada más que decir
they do nothing but complain = no hace más que quejarse

notice
1 *verb* = notar
2 *noun*
* (*a written sign*)
a notice = un letrero

* (*advance warning*)
notice = aviso (*masculine*)
without any notice = sin previo aviso
to give two month's notice = avisar con dos meses de antelación
to cancel something at short notice = cancelar algo con muy poca antelación
to hand in one's notice = presentar su renuncia
he was given his notice = lo despidieron
* (*attention*)
to take notice of someone = hacerle caso a alguien

novel *noun*
a novel = una novela

November *noun* ▶ p. 192
November = noviembre (*masculine*)

now *adverb*
= ahora
we have to do it now = tenemos que hacerlo ahora
do it right now = hazlo ahora
it's three weeks now since she wrote us = ya hace tres semanas que nos escribió
I should have told you before now = tendría que habértelo dicho antes
from now on = a partir de ahora
now and again, now and then = de vez en cuando

nowhere *adverb*
where are you going this summer? —nowhere = ¿adónde vas este verano?—a ningún lado
there's nowhere to sit = no hay dónde sentarse

nuclear *adjective*
= nuclear

nude *adjective*
= desnudo/desnuda
in the nude = desnudo/desnuda

nuisance *noun*
* (*an annoying person*)
a nuisance = un pesado/una pesada
* (*an annoying thing, situation*)
it's a nuisance having to pay in cash = es una molestia tener que pagar en efectivo, es un fastidio tener que pagar en efectivo
what a nuisance! = ¡qué molestia!, ¡que fastidio!

numb *adjective*
(*due to the cold*) = entumecido/entumecida
to go numb = entumecerse
my hands are numb = tengo las manos entumecidas

number *noun*
* a number = un número
I gave him my number = le di mi número

- *(when talking about quantities)*
  a number of people = varias personas
  they don't want to leave for a number of reasons = no quieren irse por una serie de razones

numberplate *noun (British English)*
  a numberplate = una matrícula, una placa *(Lat Am)*, una patente *(SC)*

nun *noun*
  a nun = una monja

nurse *noun*
  a nurse = un enfermero/una enfermera

nursery *noun*
- *(for children)*
  a nursery = una guardería
- *(for plants)*
  a nursery = un vivero

nursery school *noun*
  a nursery school = un parvulario, un kindergarten *(AmL)*

nut *noun*
- *(a nut)* = un fruto seco
- *(for use with a bolt)*
  a nut = una tuerca

nylon *noun*
  nylon = nylon *(masculine)*

Oo

oak *noun*
  (the tree)
  an oak = un roble

oar *noun*
  an oar = un remo

obedient *adjective*
  = obediente

obey *verb*
  = obedecer

object
1 *noun*
- *(a thing)*
  an object = un objeto
- *(an aim)*
  an object = un objetivo
2 *verb*
  to object to something = oponerse a algo

(handwritten: → pronoun *me lo nos / te los / la / las)*

objection *noun*
  an objection = una objeción

oblige *verb*
- *(to require)*
  to oblige someone to do something = obligar a alguien a hacer algo
  to be obliged to give up work = verse obligado/obligada a dejar el trabajo
- *(to be grateful)*
  I'd be much obliged if you could help me = le quedaría muy agradecido si pudiera ayudarme

obscene *adjective*
  = obsceno/obscena

obsessed *adjective*
  = obsesionado/obsesionada

obsession *noun*
  an obsession = una obsesión

obstacle *noun*
  an obstacle = un obstáculo

obstinate *adjective*
  = obstinado/obstinada

obstruct *verb*
- *(to slow down)*
  to obstruct the traffic = bloquear el tráfico
- *(to block)*
  to obstruct the road = obstruir la carretera

obtain *verb*
  = obtener, conseguir

obvious *adjective*
  = obvio/obvia

obviously *adverb*
  = obviamente

occasion *noun*
  an occasion = una ocasión

occasionally *adverb*
  = de vez en cuando

occupy *verb*
- *(to live in)* = ocupar
- *(to take)* = ocupar
  the seats are occupied = los asientos están ocupados
- *(to keep busy)*
  to keep oneself occupied = entretenerse
  it keeps me occupied = me entretiene

occur *verb*
- *(to take place)* = ocurrir
- *(to cross someone's mind)*
  it never occurred to me = nunca se me ocurrió

ocean *noun*
  the ocean = el océano

o'clock *adverb* ▶ p. 319
  it's 5 o'clock = son las cinco

October *noun* ▶ p. 192
  October = octubre *(masculine)*

(handwritten: comes before verb)

octopus *noun*
an octopus = un pulpo

odd *adjective*
* (*strange*) = raro/rara, extraño/extraña
* (*not matching*) = desparejado/desparejada
odd socks = calcetines desparejados
the odd one out = la excepción
* (*when talking about numbers*) = impar
an odd number = un número impar

odor (*US English*), **odour** (*British English*)
noun
an odor = un olor

of *preposition*
* of = de
it's in the center of London = estó en el
centro de Londres
have you heard of her? = ¿has oído hablar
de ella?
of the = del (*masculine*), de la (*feminine*),
de los/las (*plural*)
the names of the pupils = los nombres de
los estudiantes
* (*when talking about quantities*)
a kilo of apples = un kilo de manzanas
a glass of wine = una copa de vino
the flowers were lovely so we bought
some of them = las flores eran bonitas así
que compramos algunas
there are a lot of them = son
muchos/muchas
* (*US English—when talking about time*)
▶ **p. 319**
it's ten (minutes) of five = son diez para
las cinco (*Lat Am*), son las cinco menos diez
(*R Pl, Spa*)

off

! Off *is often used in combinations with
verbs, for example,* fall off, get off, go off,
take off. *To find the correct translations
for this type of verb, look up the separate
dictionary entries at* fall, get, go, take *etc*

---

1 *adverb*
* (*leaving*)
I'm off = me voy
* (*away*)
the coast is a long way off = la costa está
muy lejos de aquí
the town is about 30 km off = la ciudad está
a unos 30 kilómetros de aquí
* to take a day off = tomar un día libre
* (*not working, switched off*)
the lights are all off = todas las luces están
apagadas
why is the television off? = ¿por qué está
apagada la televisión?
the water's off = el agua está cortada
* (*canceled*)
the match is off because of the bad
weather = el partido está cancelado
debido al mal tiempo

2 *adjective*
the milk is off = la leche está cortada
I think the meat is off = creo que la carne
está mala
3 *preposition*
* (*away from*)
just off the coast of Florida = a poca
distancia de la costa de Florida
three feet off the ground = a tres pies del
suelo
* (*near*)
the bathroom's off the bedroom = el baño
da al dormitorio
it's just off Oxford Street = está en una
bocacalle de Oxford Street

offence *noun* (*British English*) ▶ offense

offend *verb*
= ofender

offense (*US English*) *noun*
* (*a crime*)
an offense = un delito
* to take offense = ofenderse

offer
1 *verb* = ofrecer
I offered her a sweet = le ofrecí un
caramelo
to offer to water the plants = ofrecerse a
regar las plantas
2 *noun*
an offer = una oferta

office *noun*
* an office = una oficina
* a doctor's office (*US English*) = un
consultorio, una consulta

office hours *noun*
office hours = horas de oficina (*feminine
plural*)

officer *noun*
an officer (*in the army or navy*) = un/una
oficial
(*in the police force*) = un/una policía

official
1 *adjective* = oficial
2 *noun*
an official (*in the public service*) = un
funcionario/una funcionaria
(*in a party, a union*) = un/una dirigente

often *adverb*
= a menudo

oil
1 *noun*
* (*for fuel*)
oil = petróleo (*masculine*)
* (*for a vehicle*)
oil = aceite (*masculine*)
* (*for cooking, in medicine, for the skin*)
oil = aceite (*masculine*)
2 *verb* = lubricar

ointment *noun*
  an ointment = un ungüento

okay, OK
1 *adjective*
* (*when asking or giving opinions*)
  is it okay if I smoke? = ¿está bien si fumo?
  it's okay to invite them = está bien si los invitas
* (*when talking about health*) = bien
  are you okay? = ¿estás bien?
2 *exclamation* = ¡bueno!, ¡okey! (*Lat Am*), ¡vale! (*Spa*)

old *adjective*
* (*not new, not young*) = viejo/vieja
  an old man/woman = un viejo/una vieja
* (*when talking about a person's age*)
    ▶ **p. 154**
  how old are you? = ¿cuántos años tienes?, ¿qué edad tienes?
  a three-year old girl = una niña de tres años
  her older sister = su hermana mayor
  to be the oldest = ser el/la mayor
* (*previous*)
  that's my old address = esa es mi antigua dirección
* (*long-standing*)
  an old friend = un viejo amigo

old-fashioned *adjective*
* (*outdated*)
  = anticuado/anticuada
* (*traditional*)
  = tradicional

olive *noun*
* (*the fruit*)
  an olive = una aceituna
* (*the tree*)
  an olive (**tree**) = un olivo

olive oil *noun*
  olive oil = aceite de oliva (*masculine*)

Olympics *noun*
  the Olympics = los juegos Olímpicos

omelet (*US English*), **omelette** (*British English*) *noun*
  an omelet = una omelette, una tortilla francesa (*Spa*)

on

> **!** On *is often used in combinations with verbs, for example,* count on, get on, keep on. *To find the correct translations for this type of verb, look up the separate dictionary entries for* count, get, keep *etc*

1 *preposition*
* **on** = en, sobre
  it's on the table = está en la mesa, está sobre la mesa
  there's a spot on the carpet = la alfombra tiene una mancha
  to fall on the floor = caerse al suelo
  I like the picture on the wall = me gusta el cuadro en la pared
  to live on Park Avenue = vivir en Park Avenue

* (*when talking about transport*) = en
  to travel on the train = viajar en tren
* (*about*) = sobre
  a book on Africa = un libro sobre (el) África
* (*when talking about time*)
  she was born on the 6th of December = nació el 6 de diciembre
  I'll be there on Saturday = estaré allí el sábado
  they go to the gym on Mondays = van al gimnasio los lunes
* (*when talking about the media*)
  on television = en la televisión
  I heard it on the radio = lo oí por la radio
* (*using*)
  to be on antibiotics = estar tomando antibióticos
  to be on drugs = drogarse
  the clock runs on batteries = el reloj funciona con pilas
2 *adverb*
* (*when talking about what one wears*)
  to have a hat on = llevar un sombrero
* (*working, switched on*) = encendido/encendida, prendido/prendida (*Lat Am*)
* (*taking place, due to take place*)
  there's a lecture on in there = hay una conferencia allí
  I don't have anything on that day = no tengo ningún compromiso ese día
* (*showing*)
  what's on at the Renoir? = ¿que dan en el Renoir?, ¿que ponen en el Renoir? (*Spa*)
* (*when talking about time*)
  from Tuesday on = a partir del martes

once
1 *adverb*
* (*one time*) = una vez
  once a day = una vez al día
  once in a while = de vez en cuando
* (*in the old days*)
  once upon a time there was a princess = érase una vez una princesa
* **at once**
  (*immediately*) = inmediatamente
  (*at the same time*) = al mismo tiempo, a la vez
2 *conjunction* = una vez que
  I feel better once I'm sitting down = me siento mejor una vez que estoy sentado

one
1 *number* ▶ **p. 154, p. 319**
  one = uno/una

> **!** *Note that* uno *becomes* un *before a masculine singular noun*

  one child = un niño/una niña
  one of my colleagues = uno/una de mis colegas

2 *adjective*
(*the only*)
she's the one person who can persuade him = es la única persona que lo puede persuadir
it's the one thing that annoys me = es la única cosa que me fastidia
3 *pronoun*
I need a cigarette—have you got one? = necesito un cigarrillo—¿tienes?
the cakes are delicious—I'll have another one = los pasteles están deliciosos—voy a comer otro
• (*when referring to a specific person or thing*)
I've decided to wear the black one = he decidido llevar el negro
he's the one who told me to be quiet = es él quien me dijo que me callara
which one? = ¿cuál?
this one = éste/ésta
• (*when used as a personal pronoun*) = uno/una
one never knows = uno nunca sabe
• one by one = uno a uno, uno por uno

one another *pronoun*
to love one another = quererse el uno al otro
to help one another = ayudarse el uno al otro

oneself *pronoun*
• (*when translated by a reflexive verb in Spanish*) = se
to enjoy oneself = divertirse
to hurt oneself = hacerse daño
• (*when used for emphasis*) = uno mismo/una misma

one-way street *noun*
a one-way street = una calle de sentido único, una calle de un solo sentido

one-way ticket *noun* (*US English*)
a one-way ticket (*on a ship or plane*) = un pasaje de ida (*Lat Am*), un billete de ida (*Spa*)
(*on a bus or train*) = un boleto de ida (*Lat Am*), un billete de ida (*Spa*)

onion *noun*
an onion = una cebolla

only
1 *adverb*
• only = sólo, solamente
it's only a game = es sólo un juego
he only reads novels = solamente lee novelas
the lift is for staff only = el ascensor es sólo para el personal
only I saw them = soy el único que los vio
• I've only just arrived = acabo de llegar, recién acabo de llegar (*Lat Am*)
she had only just bought a car = acababa de comprar un coche, recién acababa de comprar un coche (*Lat Am*)

2 *adjective* = único/única
they are our only neighbors = son nuestros únicos vecinos
she was the only one who didn't speak English = era la única que no hablaba inglés
an only child = un hijo único/una hija única

onto *preposition*
the vase fell onto the sofa = el florero cayó sobre el sofá
my room looks onto the garden = mi cuarto da al jardín

open
1 *verb*
• to open = abrir
• (*to start*) = the movie opens next week = la película se estrena la semana que viene
2 *adjective*
• (*not closed*) = abierto/abierta
• (*frank*) = abierto/abierta, franco/franca

opener *noun*
an opener (*for bottles*) = un abrebotellas, un destapador (*Lat Am*)
(*for cans*) = un abrelatas

opening hours *noun*
opening hours = horario comercial (*masculine*)

opera *noun*
an opera = una ópera

operate *verb*
• (*to make something work*) = manejar, operar
to operate a machine = manejar una máquina, operar una máquina
• (*to carry out an operation*) = operar
to operate on someone = operar a alguien

operation *noun*
an operation = una operación
he had an operation = lo operaron

operator *noun*
an operator = un/una telefonista, un operador/una operadora

opinion *noun*
an opinion = una opinión
in my opinion = en mi opinión

opponent *noun*
• (*in a contest*)
an opponent = un/una contrincante
• (*of a government, a regime*)
an opponent = un opositor/una opositora

opportunity *noun*
an opportunity = una oportunidad, una ocasión
to have an opportunity to go abroad = tener la oportunidad de ir al extranjero
to take the opportunity to go to Boston = aprovechar la ocasión para ir a Boston

oppose *verb*
= oponerse a
to be opposed to something = oponerse a
algo

opposite
1 *preposition*
= enfrente de, frente a
it's opposite the park = está enfrente del
parque, está frente al parque
2 *adjective*
he was walking in the opposite direction =
caminaba en dirección opuesta
I sat on the opposite side of the room = me
senté al otro lado de la habitación
3 *adverb* = enfrente
who lives opposite? = ¿quién vive
enfrente?
4 *noun*
the opposite = lo contrario

opposition *noun*
opposition = oposición (*feminine*)

optician *noun*
• (*selling glasses*)
an optician = un óptico/una óptica
• (*British English—an eye specialist*)
an optician = un/una oculista

optimistic *adjective*
= optimista

or *conjunction*
• **or** = o

> **!** *Note that the usual translation* o
> *becomes* u *when it precedes a word*
> *beginning with* o *or* ho-

with or without milk? = ¿con o sin leche?
one or the other = uno u otro
we'll stay here or at Philip's = nos vamos a
quedar aquí o en casa de Philip
• (*in negative sentences*)
I can't come today or tomorrow = no puedo
ir ni hoy ni mañana
he doesn't speak Spanish or English = no
habla ni español ni inglés

orange ▶ p. 183
1 *noun*
• (*the fruit*)
an orange = una naranja
• (*the color*)
orange = naranja (*masculine*)
2 *adjective*
= naranja (**!** *never changes*)

orchard *noun*
an orchard = un huerto

orchestra *noun*
an orchestra = una orquesta

order
1 *verb*
• (*to tell*)
to order someone to leave = ordenarle a
alguien que se vaya

> **!** *Note the use of the subjunctive after*
> ordenarle a alguien que

• (*to ask for*) = pedir
**you have to order the flowers the day
before** = hay que pedir las flores el día
anterior
to order white wine = pedir vino blanco
are you ready to order? = ¿ya han decidido
lo que van a pedir?
• (*to reserve*)
to order a book = encargar un libro
to order a taxi = llamar un taxi
2 *noun*
• (*an instruction*)
an order = una orden
• (*a request*)
an order = un pedido
to place an order for something = hacer un
pedido de algo, encargar algo
• (*the way something is arranged*)
order = orden (*masculine*)
in alphabetical order = en orden alfabético
• (*control*)
order = orden (*masculine*)
• **in order to** = para

ordinary *adjective*
(*not unusual*) = normal
an ordinary family = una familia normal
I was wearing my ordinary clothes =
llevaba la ropa de todos los días

organ *noun*
• (*the musical instrument*)
an organ = un órgano
• (*part of the body*)
an organ = un órgano

organization *noun*
an organization = una organización

organize *verb*
• (*to arrange*) = organizar
to get organized = organizarse
• (*to tidy*) = ordenar

original *adjective*
= original

ornament *noun*
an ornament = un adorno

orphan *noun*
an orphan = un huérfano/una huérfana

other
1 *adjective* = otro/otra (+ *singular*), =
otros/otras (+ *plural*)
they sold the other shop = vendieron la
otra tienda
she met them the other day = los conoció
el otro día
2 *pronoun*
the others = los otros/las otras
3 *adverb*
other than = aparte de
no one other than you knows = nadie sabe
aparte de ti

O

---

otherwise *conjunction*
= si no
it's not dangerous, otherwise I wouldn't go
= no es peligroso, si no no me iría

ought *verb*
• (*when talking about what should be done*)
we ought to fix the radiator = deberíamos
arreglar el radiador
you ought not to say things like that = no
deberías decir semejantes cosas
• (*when saying that something is likely to
happen*)
they ought to arrive tomorrow = deberían
llegar mañana
• (*when implying that something did not
happen*)
someone ought to have gone with them =
alguien debería haberlos acompañado

our *adjective*
= nuestro/nuestra (+ *singular*),
nuestros/nuestra (+ *plural*)

> ! For our *used with parts of the body,*
> ▶ **p. 235**

ours *pronoun*
(*singular*) = nuestro/nuestra
(*plural*) = nuestros/nuestras
ours is blue = el nuestro/la nuestra es azul
a friend of ours = un amigo nuestro

ourselves *pronoun*
• (*when translated by a reflexive verb in
Spanish*)
we didn't hurt ourselves = no nos hicimos
daño, no nos lastimamos (*Lat Am*)
we bought ourselves a new car = nos
compramos un coche nuevo
• (*when used for emphasis*)
we organized everything ourselves = lo
organizamos todo nosotros
mismos/nosotras mismas
we like to be by ourselves = nos gusta
estar solos/solas

out *adverb*

> ! Out *is often used in combinations with
> verbs, for example,* blow out, come out,
> find out, give out. *To find the correct
> translations for this type of verb, look up
> the separate dictionary entries for* blow,
> come, find, give *etc*

• (*outside*) = fuera, afuera (*Lat Am*)

> ! Note that it is not always necessary to
> translate out in this sense

they're out there = están fuera, están
afuera
she's out in the garden = está en el jardín
to go out = salir
I'm looking for the way out = estoy
buscando la salida

• (*absent*)
he's out, so you'll come back later = no está, así que tendrás que volver más
tarde
someone called while you were out =
alguien llamó cuando no estabas
• (*available to the public*)
the book will be out in November = el libro
saldrá en noviembre
• (*not lighted, not on*) = apagado/apagada
out of
• (*from*)
to walk out of the building = salir del
edificio
to take a pencil out of the drawer = sacar
un lápiz del cajón
• (*away from*)
it's good to get out of the city = es bueno
salir de la ciudad

outdoor *adjective*
• (*if it's a pool*) = descubierto/descubierta, al
aire libre
• (*taking place outside*)
outdoor games = juegos al aire libre

outdoors *adverb*
= al aire libre

outfit *noun*
an outfit = un conjunto

outlaw *noun*
an outlaw = un forajido/una forajida

outlook *noun*
• (*an attitude*)
an outlook = una actitud
• (*for the future*)
the outlook = las perspectivas (*feminine
plural*)
the outlook for the future is excellent = las
perspectivas para el futuro son excelentes

outside
1 *noun*
the outside = el exterior
2 *preposition*
• (*in front of*)
I'll see you outside the theater = te veo
fuera del teatro, te veo afuera del teatro
(*Lat Am*)
• (*beyond*)
outside the city = fuera de la ciudad
3 *adverb* = fuera, afuera (*Lat Am*)
4 *adjective* = exterior

oval *adjective*
= ovalado/ovalada, oval

oven *noun*
an oven = un horno

over

> ! Over *is often used in combinations with
> verbs, for example,* get over, hand over,
> move over, roll over. *To find the correct
> translations for this type of verb, look up
> the separate dictionary entries for* get,
> hand, move, roll *etc*

1 *preposition*
  to wear a sweater over a shirt = usar un
    suéter encima de una camisa
• (*across*)
  the bridge over the river = el puente sobre
    el río
  it's over there = está allí
  come over here = ven aquí
• (*above*) = encima de
  the office is over a bookshop = la oficina
    está encima de una librería
  young people over 18 = los jóvenes
    mayores de 18 años
• (*during*)
  we saw them over the weekend = lo vimos
    durante el fin de semana
  we'll be in Italy over the summer =
    pasaremos el verano en Italia
• (*using*)
  over the phone = por teléfono
• (*everywhere*)
  I've looked all over the house for my keys
    = he buscado mis llaves por toda la casa
2 *adverb*
• (*finished*)
  the term is over = el trimestre ha
    terminado
  is the movie over? = ¿terminó la película?
• (*to one's home*)
  to ask someone over = invitar a alguien (a
    casa)
• (*when something is repeated*)
  to start all over again = volver a empezar
  I've told him over and over again = se lo he
    dicho una y otra vez

overcast *adjective*
  an overcast sky = un cielo cubierto

overcoat *noun*
  an overcoat = un abrigo, un sobretodo
    (*R Pl*)

overdose *noun*
  an overdose = una sobredosis

overdraft *noun*
  an overdraft = un sobregiro, un descubierto

overlook *verb*
  my room overlooks the sea = mi cuarto da
    al mar

overtake *verb* (*British English*)
  (*of a car*)
  = adelantar, rebasar (*Mex*)

overthrow *verb*
  = derrocar

overweight *adjective*
• (*if it's a person*) = demasiado gordo/gorda
• (*if it's baggage*)
  your case is overweight = su maleta pesa
    más de la cuenta, su maleta tiene
    sobrepeso (*Lat Am*)

owe *verb*
  = deber
  to owe money to someone = deberle
    dinero a alguien

owl *noun*
  an owl = un búho, un tecolote (*Mex*)

own
1 *adjective* = propio/propia
  she has her own house = tiene su propia
    casa
2 *pronoun*

! Note that, when describing objects,
people etc, the translations given for the
pronouns mine, yours, his, hers or theirs
work for my own, your own, his own etc.
To work out which translation to use, find
out whether the object, person etc which
is being described is masculine,
feminine or plural

• **I didn't use his pencil, I have my own** = no
    usé su lápiz, tengo el mío
  **they lent us their chairs because our own
    are broken** = nos prestaron sus sillas
    porque las nuestras están rotas
  they have a house of their own = tienen su
    propia casa
• **on one's own** = solo/sola
  she lives on her own now = ahora vive sola
3 *verb* = tener
  she owns two houses = tiene dos casa
  he owns a shop = es dueño de una tienda
  who owns that dog? = ¿de quién es ese
    perro?

own up = confesarse culpable

owner *noun*
  an owner = un dueño/una dueña

oxygen *noun*
  oxygen = oxígeno (*masculine*)

oyster *noun*
  an oyster = una ostra, un ostión (*Mex*)

ozone layer *noun*
  the ozone layer = la capa de ozono

Pp

Pacific *noun*
  the Pacific = el Pacífico

pack
1 *verb* = hacer la(s) maleta(s), empacar (*Lat
    Am*)

2 *noun*
  a pack = un paquete
  a pack of cigarettes = un paquete de
    cigarrillos, una cajetilla de cigarrillos
  a pack of cards (*British English*) = una
    baraja, un mazo de cartas (*SC*)
pack up
  to pack up one's belongings = recoger sus
    bártulos

package *noun*
  a package = un paquete

packed *adjective*
  = lleno/llena

packet *noun*
  a packet = un paquete

page *noun*
  a page = una página

pain *noun*
  pain = dolor (*masculine*)
  I have a pain in my back = me duele la
    espalda
  to be in pain = tener dolores

painful *adjective*
  = doloroso/dolorosa

paint
1 *noun*
  paint = pintura (*feminine*)
2 *verb* = pintar

paintbrush *noun*
  a paintbrush (*for art*) = un pincel
    (*for decorating*) = una brocha

painter *noun*
  a painter = un pintor/una pintora

painting *noun*
• (*a picture*)
  a painting = un cuadro
• (*the activity*)
  painting = pintura (*feminine*)

pair *noun*
• (*of objects*)
  a pair = un par
• (*of people, animals*)
  a pair = una pareja

pajamas *noun* (*US English*)
  pajamas = un pijama, un/una piyama (*Lat Am*)

Pakistan *noun* ▶ **p. 187**
  Pakistan = Paquistán (*masculine*)

palace *noun*
  a palace = un palacio

pale *adjective*
  = pálido/pálida
  to go pale, to turn pale = palidecer

pancake *noun*
  a pancake = un crep, un panqueque (*Lat Am*), una crepa (*Mex*)

panic *verb*
  = dejarse llevar por el pánico

panties *noun* (*US English*)
  panties = calzones (*masculine plural*)
    (*S Am*), pantaletas (*feminine plural*)
    (*Mex*), bragas (*feminine plural*) (*Spa*)

pantihose *noun* (*US English*)
  ▶ pantyhose

pants *noun*
• (*US English—trousers*)
  pants = pantalones (*masculine plural*)
• (*British English—underwear*)
  pants (*men's*) = calzoncillos (*masculine plural*)
  (*women's*) ▶ panties

pantyhose *noun*
  pantyhose = panty (*masculine*), medias
    (*feminine plural*) (*Spa*), pantimedias
    (*feminine plural*) (*Mex*), medias
    bombacha (*feminine plural*) (*R Pl*)

paper *noun*
• (*for writing or drawing on*)
  paper = papel (*masculine*)
  a piece of paper = un papel
• (*a newspaper*)
  a paper = un periódico, un diario

parade
1 *noun*
  a parade = un desfile
2 *verb*
  to parade through the streets = desfilar
    por las calles

parcel *noun* (*British English*)
  a parcel = un paquete

parents *noun*
  parents = padres (*masculine plural*)

park
1 *noun*
• (*in a town*)
  a park = un parque
• (*US English—a stadium*)
  a park = un estadio
2 *verb* = estacionar, aparcar (*Spa*)
  to park a car = estacionar un coche,
    aparcar un coche (*Spa*)

parking lot *noun* (*US English*)
  a parking lot = un estacionamiento, un
    aparcamiento (*Spa*)

parking meter *noun*
  a parking meter = un parquímetro

parliament *noun*
  a parliament = un parlamento

parrot *noun*
  a parrot = un loro, un papagayo

part *noun*
• a part = una parte
  a part [of the book | the movie | the time …] =
    una parte [del libro | de la película | del
    tiempo …]
• (*a piece for a machine, a car*)
  a part = una pieza
• (*a section*)
  a part (*in a program*) = una parte
  (*in a series*) = un capítulo
• (*a role*)
  a part = un papel
  to play the part of **Tommy** = hacer el papel
    de Tommy
• to take part in a demonstration = participar
    en una manifestación

participate *verb*
  = participar, tomar parte
  to participate in something = participar en
    algo, tomar parte en algo

particular
1 *adjective*
  (*specific*)
  we don't sell that particular model = no
    vendemos ese modelo en particular
  in this particular case = en este caso
    particular
2 *noun*
  in particular = en particular

partner *noun*
• (*in a relationship*)
  a partner = un compañero/una compañera
• (*in dancing, sport*)
  a partner = una pareja

part-time *adverb*
  = a tiempo parcial

party *noun*
• (*a social event*)
  a party = una fiesta
• (*a political organization*)
  a party = un partido

pass *verb*
• (*to go past*) = pasar
  a lot of cars passed = pasaron muchos
    coches
  to pass the school = pasar (por) delante de
    la escuela
  to pass a car = adelantar un coche, rebasar
    un carro (*Mex*)
  to pass someone in the street = cruzarse
    con alguien en la calle
• (*to give*) = pasar
  pass me the salt, please = pásame la sal,
    por favor
• (*in football, rugby etc*) = pasar

• (*to spend*) = pasar
  to pass the time [reading | painting | listening
    to the radio …] = pasar el tiempo [leyendo |
    pintando | escuchando el radio …]
• (*to succeed in an exam*) = aprobar
  to pass an exam = aprobar un examen
pass on = pasar
  to pass on a message to someone =
    pasarle un mensaje a alguien

passage *noun*
  a passage (*indoors*) = un pasillo
  (*outdoors*) = un pasaje

passenger *noun*
  a passenger = un pasajero/una pasajera

passport *noun*
  a passport = pasaporte

past
1 *noun*
  the past = el pasado
2 *adjective*
  (*last*) = último/última (**!** *before the noun*)
  the past few days have been very difficult
    = los últimos días han sido muy difíciles
3 *preposition* ▶ **p. 319**
• (*British English—when talking about time*)
  it's twenty past four = son las cuatro y
    veinte
  it's past eleven = son las once pasadas
• (*by*)
  I went past your house = pasé por delante
    de tu casa
  she walked straight past me = pasó de
    largo por mi lado
• (*beyond*)
  it's just past the traffic lights = queda un
    poco más allá del semáforo
4 *adverb*
  to go past, to walk past = pasar

pastry *noun*
  pastry = masa (*feminine*)

patch *noun*
• (*on a garment*)
  a patch = un parche
• (*on a tire*)
  a patch = un parche
• (*an area*)
  a patch of ground = un área (*feminine*) de
    terreno

path *noun*
  a path = un camino, un sendero

patient
1 *noun*
  a patient = un/una paciente
2 *adjective* = paciente

pattern *noun*
• (*a design*)
  a pattern = un diseño
• (*when making garments*)
  a pattern = un patrón, un molde (*SC*)

P

pavement noun (British English)
a pavement = una acera, una banqueta (Mex), una vereda (SC)

paw noun
a paw = una pata

pay
1 verb
• to pay = pagar
to pay for the shopping = pagar las compras
he paid for my meal = me pagó la comida
• (when talking about wages)
I'm paid $5 an hour = me pagan 5 dólares la hora
• (to give)
to pay someone a visit = hacerle una visita a alguien
to pay someone a compliment = hacerle un cumplido a alguien
2 noun
pay = sueldo (masculine)
pay back
to pay someone back = devolverle el dinero a alguien

PE noun
PE = educación física (feminine)

pea noun
a pea = una arveja, un guisante (Spa), un chícharo (Mex)

peace noun
peace = paz (feminine)

peach noun
a peach = un durazno, un melocotón (Spa)

peacock noun
a peacock = un pavo real

peanut noun
a peanut = un maní, un cacahuate (Mex), un cacahuete (Spa)

pear noun
a pear = una pera

pearl noun
a pearl = una perla

pebble noun
a pebble = un guijarro, una piedrecita, una piedrita (Lat Am)

pedestrian noun
a pedestrian = un peatón/una peatona

pedestrian crossing noun
a pedestrian crossing = un paso de peatones

peel verb
= pelar

pen noun
a pen = una pluma

penalty noun
a penalty (in US football) = un castigo
(in soccer) = un penalty, un penal (Lat Am)
(in rugby) = un penalty

pencil noun
a pencil = un lápiz

pencil case noun
a pencil case = un estuche para lápices, una cartuchera (R Pl), un plumier (Spa)

pencil sharpener noun
a pencil sharpener = un sacapuntas

pen pal noun
a pen pal = un amigo/una amiga por correspondencia

penknife noun
a penknife = una navaja, un cortaplumas

pensioner noun
a pensioner = un jubilado/una jubilada

people noun
people (in general) = gente (feminine)
(if counting) = personas (feminine plural)
we met very nice people = conocimos a gente muy simpática
there were three people waiting = había tres personas esperando

pepper noun
• (the spice)
pepper = pimienta (feminine)
• (the vegetable)
a pepper = un pimiento, un pimentón (S Am), un ají (R Pl)

per preposition
per person = por persona

per cent, percent
1 noun
per cent = porcentaje (masculine)
2 adverb = por ciento

percentage noun
a percentage = un porcentaje

perfect adjective
= perfecto/perfecta
it's the perfect place for a picnic = es el lugar ideal para un picnic

perform verb
• (to do)
to perform a task = ejecutar una tarea
• (to act) = actuar
• (to play) = tocar

perfume noun
perfume = perfume (masculine)

perhaps adverb
= quizás, tal vez, a lo mejor
perhaps he'll arrive later = quizás llegue más tarde, tal vez llegue más tarde, a lo mejor llega más tarde

! Note the use of the subjunctive after
quizás and tal vez

period noun
• (in time)
  a period = un período
• (in history)
  a period = una época
• (in a woman's cycle)
  a period = una regla, un período
  to have one's period = estar con la regla,
  estar con el período
• (a school lesson)
  a period = una clase
• (in punctuation—US English)
  a period = un punto

permanent adjective
= permanente

permission noun
  permission = permiso (masculine)

person noun
  a person = una persona

personal adjective
= personal

personality noun
  a personality = una personalidad

persuade verb
= persuadir
  to persuade someone to give up smoking
  = persuadir a alguien para que deje de
  fumar

! Note the use of the subjunctive after
persuadir a alguien para que

pessimistic adjective
= pesimista

pet noun
  a pet = un animal doméstico

petrol noun (British English)
  petrol = gasolina (feminine), nafta
  (feminine) (R Pl)

petrol station noun (British English)
  a petrol station = una gasolinera, una
  estación de nafta (R Pl)

pharmacist noun
  a pharmacist = un farmacéutico/una
  farmacéutica

pharmacy noun
  a pharmacy = una farmacia

phone
1 noun
  a phone = un teléfono
  he's on the phone = está hablando por
  teléfono
2 verb = llamar (por teléfono)
  to phone for a taxi = llamar para pedir un
  taxi

phone book noun
  a phone book = una guía telefónica, un
  directorio (Lat Am)

phone booth, phone box (British
English) noun
  a phone booth = una cabina telefónica

phone call noun
  a phone call = una llamada (telefónica)

phonecard noun
  a phonecard = una tarjeta telefónica

phone number noun
  a phone number = un número de teléfono

photo noun
  a photo = una foto
  to take a photo = sacar una foto

photocopier noun
  a photocopier = una fotocopiadora

photocopy
1 noun
  a photocopy = una fotocopia
2 verb = fotocopiar

photograph noun
  a photograph = una fotografía

photographer noun
  a photographer = un fotógrafo/una
  fotógrafa

physical adjective
= físico/física

physics noun
  physics = física (feminine)

piano noun
  a piano = un piano

pick verb
• (to choose) = elegir, escoger
• (to collect)
  to pick strawberries = recoger fresas
  to pick flowers = recoger flores, cortar
  flores (SC)
pick up
• (to lift)
  to pick up the clothes from the floor =
  recoger la ropa del suelo, alzar la ropa del
  suelo (Lat Am)
  to pick up a baby = levantar a un bebé,
  alzar a un bebé (Lat Am)
  to pick up the phone = agarrar el teléfono,
  coger el teléfono (Spa)
• (to collect) = recoger

picnic noun
  a picnic = un picnic

picture noun
• **a picture** (painted) = un cuadro
  (drawn) = un dibujo
• (a photograph)
  a picture = una foto

* (a movie)
  a picture = una película

piece noun
* (a bit)
  a piece = un pedazo, un trozo
  a piece of cheese = un pedazo de queso, un trozo de queso
  a piece of string = un cordel
* (a part of a machine)
  a piece = una pieza
  to take a machine to pieces = desarmar una máquina
* (a broken part)
  a piece = un pedazo, un trozo
  to fall to pieces = hacerse pedazos
* (a coin) = una moneda
  a 50-pence piece = una moneda de 50 peniques
* (other uses)
  a piece of furniture = un mueble
  a piece of advice = un consejo

pierce verb
  she's had her ears pierced = se ha hecho agujeros en las orejas

pig noun
  a pig = un cerdo, un chancho (Lat Am)

pigeon noun
  a pigeon = una paloma

pile
  a pile = un montón, una pila

pill noun
* (a tablet)
  a pill = una pastilla, una píldora
* (a method of contraception)
  the pill = la píldora

pillow noun
  a pillow = una almohada

pilot noun
  a pilot = un/una piloto

pimple noun
  a pimple = un grano, una espinilla (Lat Am)

pin noun
  a pin = un alfiler

pinch verb
  = pellizcar
  he pinched my arm = me pellizcó el brazo
  my shoes are pinching = mis zapatos me aprietan

pineapple noun
  a pineapple = una piña, un ananá (R Pl)

pine tree noun
  a pine tree = un pino

pink adjective ▶ p. 183
  = rosa (**!** never changes), rosado/rosada

pint noun
  (the quantity)
  a pint = una pinta

  ! Note that a pint = 0.57 l in Britain and 0.47 l in the US

  a pint of milk = una pinta de leche

pipe noun
* (for gas, water)
  a pipe = una cañería, un caño
* (for smoking)
  a pipe = una pipa

pirate noun
  a pirate = un pirata

Pisces noun
* (the sign)
  Pisces = Piscis
  I'm Pisces = soy Piscis, soy de Piscis
* (a person)
  a Pisces = un/una piscis

pitch noun (British English)
  a pitch = un campo, una cancha (Lat Am)
  a football pitch = un campo de fútbol, una cancha de fútbol

pity
1 noun
* (when showing regret)
  it's a pity you can't come = es una lástima que no puedas venir

  ! Note the use of the subjunctive after es una lástima que

  what a pity! = ¡qué lástima!
2 verb
  to pity someone = tenerle lástima a alguien

place
1 noun
* **a place** = un lugar, un sitio
  it's the best place to buy fruit = es el mejor lugar para comprar frutas
  they come from all over the place = vienen de todas partes
* (a home)
  at Alison's place = en casa de Alison, donde Alison (Lat Am), en lo de Alison (R Pl)
  I'd like a place of my own = quisiera tener mi propia casa
* (in a line or queue, in a car park)
  a place = un lugar
* (on a team, in a firm)
  a place = un puesto
* (in a contest)
  a place = un puesto, un lugar
  to take first place = obtener el primer puesto, obtener el primer lugar
2 verb
* (to position carefully) = colocar

- (*in a race*)
  this victory places her among the top three
  = este triunfo la sitúa entre las tres
  primeras

plain *adjective*
- (*simple*) = sencillo/sencilla
- (*not good-looking*) = feucho/feucha✱

plait *noun*
  a plait = una trenza

plan
1 *noun*
- (*an arrangement*)
  a plan = un plan
- (*a map*)
  a plan = un plano
2 *verb*
- (*to prepare, to organize*)
  to plan [a trip | a timetable | a meeting ...] =
  planear [un viaje | un horario | una reunión ...]
- (*to intend*)
  I'm planning to go to Scotland = pienso ir a
  Escocia

plane *noun*
  a plane = un avión

planet *noun*
  a planet = un planeta

plant
1 *noun*
  a plant = una planta
2 *verb* = plantar

plaster *noun*
- (*a powder, a mixture*)
  plaster = yeso (*masculine*)
  his leg is in plaster = tiene la pierna
  enyesada, tiene la pierna escayolada
  (*Spa*)
- (*on walls*)
  plaster = revoque (*masculine*)
- (*British English—for a cut, a wound*)
  a plaster = una curita®, una tirita® (*Spa*)

plastic
1 *noun*
  plastic = plástico (*masculine*)
2 *adjective* = de plástico

plate *noun*
  a plate = un plato

platform *noun*
  a platform = un andén

play
1 *verb*
- (*to have fun*) = jugar
  to play with friends = jugar con amigos
  to play cards = jugar a las cartas
- (*when talking about sports*) = jugar
  to play [football | cricket | tennis ...] = jugar
  [fútbol | cricket | tenis ...], jugar [al fútbol | al
  cricket | al tenis ...] (*R Pl, Spa*)
  France is playing (against) Ireland =
  Francia juega contra Irlanda

- (*if it's music*) = tocar
  to play [the flute | the piano | the drums ...] =
  tocar [la flauta | el piano | la batería ...]
- (*to put on*) = poner
  to play [a video | a CD | a record ...] = poner
  [un video | un CD | un disco ...]
- (*when talking about theater, cinema*)
  to play Hamlet = hacer el papel de Hamlet
2 *noun*
  a play = una obra de teatro

player *noun*
  a player = un jugador/una jugadora
  a tennis player = un jugador/una jugadora
  de tenis

playground *noun*
(*British English—of a school*)
  a playground = un patio de recreo

please *adverb*
  = por favor

pleased *adjective*
- (*satisfied*) = satisfecho/satisfecha
  I'm very pleased with myself = estoy muy
  satisfecha conmigo misma
- (*happy*) = contento/contenta
  he's very pleased with the results = está
  muy contento con los resultados
  pleased to meet you = mucho gusto en
  conocerlo/conocerla

plenty *pronoun*
  to have [plenty of time | plenty of money | plenty
  of friends ...] = tener [mucho tiempo | mucho
  dinero | muchos amigos ...]

plot *noun*
- (*a plan*)
  a plot = un complot
- (*the story in a movie, novel, play*)
  a plot = un argumento

plug *noun*
- (*on an appliance*)
  a plug = un enchufe
- (*in a sink or bath*)
  a plug = un tapón
  plug in = enchufar
  to plug in the radio = enchufar la radio

plum *noun*
  a plum = una ciruela

plumber *noun*
  a plumber = un plomero/una plomera (*Lat
  Am*), un fontanero/una fontanera (*Spa*)

plus *preposition*
  = más
  three plus three is six (3 + 3 = 6) = tres
  más tres son seis (3 + 3 = 6)

pocket *noun*
  a pocket = un bolsillo, una bolsa (*Mex*)

pocket money *noun* (*British English*)
  pocket money = dinero de bolsillo
  (*masculine*), mesada (*feminine*) (*Lat Am*)

P

poem *noun*
a poem = un poema

poet *noun*
a poet = un/una poeta

point
1 *noun*
* (*a statement in a discussion*)
a point = una observación
* (*the most important idea*)
to get to the point = ir al grano
the point is that ... = la cuestión es que ...
that's not the point = no se trata de eso
* (*the use*)
there's no point in [arguing | shouting |
rushing ...] = no sirve de nada [discutir |
gritar | darse prisa ...]
* (*talking about time*)
to be on the point of [moving | leaving | selling
the house ...] = estar a punto de [mudarse |
irse | vender la casa ...]
* (*the sharp end*)
the point = la punta
* (*in a contest, a game*)
a point = un punto
2 *verb*
(*to indicate*)
to point one's finger at someone = apuntar
a alguien con el dedo
to point at [a house | a street | a store ...] =
señalar [una casa | una calle | una tienda ...]
point out = señalar

poison
1 *noun*
poison = veneno (*masculine*)
2 *verb* = envenenar

Poland *noun* ▶ p. 187
Poland = Polonia (*feminine*)

pole *noun*
a pole = un poste

police *noun*
the police = la policía

policeman *noun*
a policeman = un policía

police station *noun*
a police station = una comisaría

policewoman *noun*
a policewoman = una policía

polish *verb*
to polish one's shoes = limpiarse los
zapatos, lustrarse los zapatos (*Lat Am*),
embolarse los zapatos (*Mex*)
to polish the car = darle brillo al coche,
sacarle brillo al coche

polite *adjective*
= bien educado/educada, cortés

political *adjective*
= político/política

politician *noun*
a politician = un político/una política

politics *noun*
politics = política (*feminine*)

pollution *noun*
pollution = contaminación (*feminine*)

pond *noun*
a pond (*man-made*) = un estanque
(*natural*) = una laguna

pony *noun*
a pony = un poni

ponytail *noun*
a ponytail = una cola de caballo

pool *noun*
* (*a swimming pool*)
a pool = una piscina, una alberca (*Mex*),
una pileta (*R Pl*)
* (*on the ground, the floor*)
a pool of water = un charco de agua
* (*the game*)
pool = billar americano (*masculine*), pool
(*masculine*)

poor *adjective*
* (*having little money*) = pobre
* (*not satisfactory*)
a poor result = un resultado pobre
* (*expressing sympathy*) = pobre (**!** before
the noun)
the poor boy is exhausted = el pobre chico
está agotado

popular *adjective*
a popular hobby = un pasatiempo popular
she's very popular = tiene muchos amigos

population *noun*
the population = la población

pork *noun*
pork = carne de cerdo (*feminine*), carne de
puerco (*feminine*) (*Mex*)

port *noun*
a port = un puerto

porter *noun*
a porter (*at a station, airport*) = un
maletero, un mozo
(*at a hotel, apartment block*) = un portero

Portugal *noun* ▶ p. 187
Portugal = Portugal (*masculine*)

Portuguese ▶ p. 187, p. 245
1 *adjective* = portugués/portuguesa
2 *noun*
* (*the people*)
the Portuguese = los portugueses
* (*the language*)
Portuguese = portugués (*masculine*)

positive *adjective*
= positivo/positiva

---

possibility *noun*
  a possibility = una posibilidad

possible *adjective*
  = posible
  I did as much as possible = hice todo lo
    posible
  they came as quickly as possible =
    vinieron lo más rápido posible

post¹ (*British English*)
1 *noun*
• (*the system*)
  the post = el correo
• (*letters, packages*)
  the post = la correspondencia, el correo
2 *verb* = echar al correo
  I posted the letter yesterday = eché la carta
    al correo ayer

post² *noun*
  (*a pole*)
  a post = un poste

postbox *noun* (*British English*)
  a postbox = un buzón

postcard *noun*
  a postcard = una tarjeta postal, una postal

postcode *noun* (*British English*)
  a postcode = un código postal

poster *noun*
  a poster = un cartel, un póster

postman *noun* (*British English*)
  a postman = un cartero

post office *noun*
  a post office = un correo, una oficina de
    correos

postpone *verb*
  = aplazar, posponer, postergar (*Lat Am*)

pot *noun*
• (*for jam, honey*)
  a pot = un tarro
• (*for cooking*)
  a pot = una olla
• (*for a plant*)
  a pot = una maceta, un tiesto

potato *noun*
  a potato = una papa (*Lat Am*), una patata
    (*Spa*)

pottery *noun*
  pottery = cerámica (*feminine*)

pound *noun*
• (*the currency*)
  a pound = una libra
• (*the measurement*)
  a pound = una libra

  ! *Note that a pound = 453.6 g*

pour *verb*
• (*from a container*) = echar
• (*to serve*) = servir
  she poured me a vodka = me sirvió un
    vodka
• (*to rain*)
  it's pouring (**with rain**) = está lloviendo a
    cántaros

powder *noun*
  powder = polvo (*masculine*)

power *noun*
• (*control, influence*)
  power = poder (*masculine*)
  to be in power = estar en el poder
• (*electricity*)
  power = electricidad (*feminine*)

power cut *noun*
  a power cut = un apagón

practical *adjective*
  = práctico/práctica

practice (*US English*), **practise** (*British
English*) *verb*
  = practicar

practice *noun*
  practice (*training, rehearsal*) = práctica
    (*feminine*)

praise *verb*
  = elogiar

pram *noun* (*British English*)
  a pram = un cochecito

prawn *noun*
  a prawn = un camarón (*Lat Am*), una
    gamba (*Spa*)

prayer *noun*
  a prayer = una oración

precious *adjective*
  = precioso/preciosa

precise *adjective*
• (*accurate*) = exacto/exacta
• (*specific*) = preciso/precisa
  at that precise moment = en ese preciso
    momento

prefer *verb*
  = preferir
  to prefer chocolate to vanilla = preferir el
    chocolate a la vainilla
  I'd prefer to phone = preferiría llamar por
    teléfono

pregnant *adjective*
  = embarazada

prejudice *noun*
  a prejudice = un prejuicio

P

prepare verb
- (to get something or someone ready) = preparar
- (to get ready) = prepararse

prepared adjective
- (willing)
  to be prepared to wait = estar dispuesto/dispuesta a esperar
- (ready) = listo/lista

prescription noun
  a prescription = una receta

present
1 noun
- (a gift)
  a present = un regalo
  to give someone a present = hacerle un regalo a alguien
- (now)
  the present = el presente
  at present = en este momento
2 verb
- (to give)
  to present a prize to someone = entregarle un premio a alguien
- (on radio or TV)
  to present a program = presentar un programa

president noun
  a president = un presidente/una presidenta

press
1 verb = apretar
2 noun
  the press = la prensa

pressure noun
  pressure = presión (feminine)
  to put pressure on someone = presionar a alguien

pretend verb
  = fingir

pretty
1 adjective = bonito/bonita, lindo/linda (Lat Am)
2 adverb = bastante

prevent verb
  to prevent a war = evitar una guerra
  to prevent someone from working = impedir que alguien trabaje

  ! Note the use of the subjunctive after impedir que

previous adjective
  = anterior
  the previous day = el día anterior

price noun
  a price = un precio

pride noun
  pride = orgullo (masculine)

priest noun
  a priest = un cura

primary school noun
  a primary school = una escuela primaria

prime minister noun
  the prime minister = el primer mininstro/la primera ministra

prince noun
  a prince = un príncipe

princess noun
  a princess = una princesa

principal noun
  a principal (in a school) = un director/una directora
  (at a university) = un rector/una rectora

print
1 verb = imprimir
2 noun
- (of a photo)
  a print = una copia
- (in a book)
  the print = la letra

prison noun
  a prison = una cárcel

prisoner noun
- (a captive)
  a prisoner = un prisionero/una prisionera
- (in jail)
  a prisoner = un preso/una presa

private
1 adjective = privado/privada
2 noun
  in private
  he told me in private = me lo dijo en confianza
  the meeting was held in private = la reunión se celebró en privado

prize noun
  a prize = un premio

probably adverb
  = probablemente

problem noun
  a problem = un problema

process noun
  a process = un proceso
  to be in the process of writing a letter = estar escribiendo una carta

produce
1 verb
- (to make) = producir
  the company produces soft drinks = la compañía produce refrescos
- (to create)
  to produce a movie = producir una película
  to produce a play = poner en escena una obra de teatro

C Am Central America   Lat Am Latin America   Mex Mexico

2 *noun*
produce = productos (*masculine plural*)

product *noun*
a product = un producto

production *noun*
production = producción (*feminine*)

profession *noun*
a profession = una profesión

professional *adjective*
= profesional

professor *noun*
a professor = un catedrático/una
catedrática

profit *noun*
profit = ganancias (*feminine plural*),
beneficios (*masculine plural*)
to make a profit = obtener ganancias,
obtener beneficios

program[1] *noun*
(*for a computer*)
a program = un programa

program[2] (*US English*), **programme**
(*British English*)
1 *noun*
• (*on radio, TV*)
a program = un programa
• (*for a play, a concert*)
a program = un programa
2 *verb* = programar

progress *noun*
progress = progreso (*masculine*)
to make progress (*of a student*) = hacer
progresos
(*of a patient*) = mejorar

project *noun*
a project = un proyecto
(*at school*) = un trabajo

promise
1 *verb* = prometer
to promise to do something = prometer
hacer algo
2 *noun*
a promise = una promesa

pronounce *verb*
= pronunciar

proof *noun*
proof = prueba (*feminine*), pruebas
(*feminine plural*)
I have proof that they lied = tengo pruebas
de que mintieron

properly *adverb*
= bien

property *noun*
property = propiedad (*feminine*)

protect *verb*
= proteger

protest *verb*
= protestar

proud *adjective*
= orgulloso/orgullosa
she's proud of her work = está orgullosa de
su trabajo

prove *verb*
= probar

provide *verb*
to provide a meal = proporcionar una
comida
to provide work for people = dar trabajo a
la gente

provided *conjunction*
I'll lend you my jacket provided you wash
the dishes = te presto mi chaqueta con
tal de que friegues los platos

> **!** *Note the use of the subjunctive after*
> con tal de que

psychiatrist *noun*
a psychiatrist = un/una psiquiatra

pub *noun* (*British English*)
a pub = un bar

public
1 *noun*
• the public = el público
• in public = en público
2 *adjective*
= público/pública

public holiday *noun*
a public holiday = un día festivo, un día
feriado (*Lat Am*)

public transportation (*US English*),
public transport (*British English*) *noun*
public transportation = transporte público
(*masculine*)

pudding *noun* (*British English*)
a pudding = un postre

puddle *noun*
a puddle = un charco

pull *verb*
• to pull = tirar de, jalar (*Lat Am*)
to pull (on) a rope = tirar de una cuerda,
jalar una cuerda
he pulled my hair = me tiró del pelo, me
jaló el pelo
• (*to take out*)
to pull a handkerchief out of one's pocket
= sacar un pañuelo del bolsillo
to pull someone out of the river = sacar a
alguien del río
pull down
• (*to knock down*) = echar abajo, tumbar
(*Mex*)

P

- (*to lower*) = bajar
pull out
  to pull a tooth out = sacar una muela
pull up
- (*to stop*) = parar
- (*to remove*)
  to pull up a plant = arrancar una planta

pullover *noun*
  a pullover = un suéter, un pulóver, un
    jersey (*Spa*)

pump *noun*
  a pump = una bomba
  a gasoline pump (*US English*), a petrol
    pump (*British English*) = un surtidor

pumpkin *noun*
  a pumpkin = una calabaza, un zapallo (*SC*)

punch *verb*
  = darle un puñetazo a
  she punched him in the face = le dio un
    puñetazo en la cara

punctual *adjective*
  = puntual

puncture *noun*
  a puncture = un pinchazo, una
    ponchadura (*Mex*)

punish *verb*
  = castigar

pupil *noun*
  a pupil = un alumno/una alumna

puppet *noun*
  a puppet = una marioneta, un títere

puppy *noun*
  a puppy = un cachorro/una cachorra

pure *adjective*
  = puro/pura

purple *adjective* ▶ p. 183
  = morado/morada

purpose *noun*
  a purpose = un propósito
  on purpose = a propósito

purse *noun*
- (*for money*)
  a purse = un monedero
- (*US English—a handbag*)
  a purse = una cartera, un bolso (*Spa*), una
    bolsa (*Mex*)

push *verb*
  = empujar
  to push someone out of the way = apartar
    a alguien de un empujón

pushchair *noun* (*British English*)
  a pushchair = una sillita de paseo, una
    carreola (*Mex*), un changuito® (*R Pl*)

put *verb*
  = poner
  to put the cards on the table = poner las
    cartas sobre la mesa
  don't put sugar in my coffee = no me
    pongas azúcar en el café
  to put someone in prison = meter a alguien
    en la cárcel
put away = guardar
put back
- (*to return to its place*) = volver a poner
  to put a book back on the shelf = volver a
    poner un libro en el estante
- (*to change the time*)
  to put the clocks back = atrasar los relojes
put down
- (*on a surface*) = dejar
  put your cases down here = deja tus
    maletas aquí
- to put the phone down = colgar el teléfono
put forward
  to put forward the clocks = adelantar los
    relojes
put off
- (*to delay*) = aplazar, posponer, postergar
    (*Lat Am*)
- (*British English—to switch off*) = apagar
put on
- (*when dressing*) = ponerse
- (*to switch on*)
  to put the lights on = encender las luces,
    prender las luces (*Lat Am*)
  to put a CD on = poner un CD
put out
  (*to extinguish*) = apagar
put up
- to put one's hand up (*in class*) = levantar
    la mano
- to put a sign up = poner un letrero
- to put up a tent = armar una carpa
- (*to increase*) = aumentar
  to put the rent up = aumentar el alquiler
- (*to give someone a place to stay*) = alojar
put up with = aguantar, soportar

puzzle *noun*
  a puzzle = un rompecabezas (! *never
    changes*)

pyjamas *noun* (*British English*)
  pyjamas = un pijama, un/una piyama (*Lat
    Am*)

qualified *adjective*
(*having certificates*) = titulado/titulada

quality *noun*
quality = calidad (*feminine*)

quantity *noun*
a quantity = una cantidad

quarrel
1 *noun*
a quarrel = una pelea
2 *verb* = pelearse

quarter
1 *noun*
a quarter = un cuarto
a quarter of an hour = un cuarto de hora
2 *pronoun*
• (*when talking about quantities, numbers*)
a quarter of the population = la cuarta
parte de la población
• (*when talking about time*) ▶ **p. 319**
an hour and a quarter = una hora y cuarto
it's a quarter after five, it's (a) quarter past
five (*British English*) = son las cinco y
cuarto

quay *noun*
a quay = un muelle

queen *noun*
a queen = una reina

question
1 *noun*
• (*a request for information*)
a question = una pregunta
• (*a problem, matter*)
a question = una cuestión, un asunto
2 *verb*
• (*to interrogate*) = interrogar
• (*to doubt*) = cuestionar

queue (*British English*)
1 *noun*
a queue = una cola
2 *verb* = hacer cola

quick *adjective*
= rápido/rápida

quickly *adverb*
• (*speedily*) = rápido, rápidamente
• (*promptly*) = pronto

quiet
1 *adjective*
• (*silent*)
a quiet street = una calle silenciosa
be quiet! = ¡cállense!
quiet please! = ¡silencio, por favor!

• (*not talkative*) = callado/callada
• (*calm*) = tranquilo/tranquila
2 *noun*
quiet = silencio (*masculine*)

quietly *adverb*
to speak quietly = hablar en voz baja
to play quietly = jugar sin hacer ruido

quit *verb*
• (*to resign*) = dejar el trabajo
• (*US English—to give up*)
to quit smoking = dejar de fumar

quite *adverb*
• (*fairly*) = bastante
• (*completely*)
you're quite right = tienes toda la razón
are you quite sure? = ¿estás
completamente seguro?
• (*exactly*)
is it true?—not quite = ¿es cierto?—no
exactamente

quiz *noun*
a quiz = un concurso

rabbit *noun*
a rabbit = un conejo

race
1 *noun*
• (*a contest*)
a race = una carrera
• (*in horse-racing*)
the races = las carreras de caballos
• (*an ethnic group*)
a race = una raza
2 *verb*
• to race (**against**) **someone** = echarle una
carrera a alguien, jugarle una carrera a
alguien (*R Pl*)
• (*to take part in a contest*) = correr

racecourse *noun*
a racecourse = un hipódromo

racetrack *noun*
a racetrack (*for runners*) = una pista de
atletismo
(*for cars*) = un circuito

racket, racquet *noun*
a racket = una raqueta

Q
R

radiator noun
  a radiator = un radiador

radio noun
  a radio = un radio (Lat Am), una radio (SC, Spa)
  I heard it on the radio = lo oí por el radio, lo oí por la radio

radish noun
  a radish = un rábano

rage noun
  rage = furia (feminine)

raid
1 verb
  to raid a bank = asaltar un banco
  the police raided the building = la policía hizo una redada en el edificio
2 noun
  a raid (by thieves) = un atraco
  (by the police) = una redada

rail noun
• (for holding on to)
  a rail = un pasamanos
• (for trains)
  the rails = los rieles, los railes (Spa)

railroad (US English), **railway** (British English) noun
• (a track)
  a railroad, a railway = una vía férrea
• (the rail system)
  the railroad, the railway = el ferrocarril

railroad station (US English),
railway station (British English) noun
  a railroad station, a railway station = una estación de ferrocarril

rain
1 noun
  rain = lluvia (feminine)
2 verb = llover

rainbow noun
  a rainbow = un arco íris

raincoat noun
  a raincoat = un impermeable

raise verb
• (to lift) = levantar
  to raise one's hand = levantar la mano
• (to increase) = aumentar
  to raise prices = aumentar los precios
• to raise one's voice = levantar la voz
• to raise a subject = sacar un tema
• to raise a child = criar a un niño

raisin noun
  a raisin = una pasa

range noun
• (a selection)
  a range (of goods) = una línea
  (of prices) = una gama

• (of mountains)
  a range = una cadena

rare adjective
  (not common) = poco común

raspberry noun
  a raspberry = una frambuesa

rat noun
  a rat = una rata

rather adverb
• (when saying what one would prefer)
  I'd rather leave = preferiría irme
  I'd rather you came with me = preferiría que vinieras conmigo

  ! Note that the subjunctive is used after preferiría que

• (quite) = bastante

raw adjective
  = crudo/cruda

razor noun
  a razor (cutthroat) = una navaja de afeitar, una navaja de rasurar (Mex)
  (with safety blade) = una cuchilla de afeitar, un rastrillo (Mex)
  (electric) = una máquina de afeitar, una máquina de rasurar (Mex), una maquinilla de afeitar (Spa)

razor blade noun
  a razor blade = una cuchilla

reach verb
• (to arrive at) = llegar a
  to reach a decision = llegar a una decisión
• (to be delivered to)
  the letter never reached her = la carta nunca le llegó
• (by stretching)
  I can't reach the shelf = no alcanzo al estante
• (to contact by phone) = contactar
  you can reach me at this number = me puedes contactar llamando a este número

react verb
  = reaccionar

read verb
  = leer
  read out = leer en voz alta
  read through
  (once) = leer
  (a second time) = releer

ready adjective
  (prepared) = listo/lista
  are you ready to leave? = ¿estás listo para irte?
  to get ready = prepararse, aprontarse (SC)

real adjective
• (not imagined) = real, verdadero/verdadera
  in real life = en la vida real

- (*actual*) = verdadero/verdadera
  is that his real name? = ¿es ése su nombre verdadero?
- (*not artificial*) = auténtico/auténtica
  are they real diamonds? = ¿son diamantes auténticos?
- (*when used for emphasis*) = verdadero/verdadera
  it was a real disaster = fue un verdadero desastre

realize *verb*
= darse cuenta
I didn't realize (that) he was your boss = no me di cuenta de que era tu jefe

really *adverb*
it's really easy = es facilísimo
I don't really know them = en realidad no los conozco
really? = ¿de verdad?

rear
1 *noun*
the rear (*of a building*) = la parte trasera
(*of a train*) = los últimos vagones
2 *adjective*
the rear door = la puerta trasera
the rear wheel = la rueda de atrás
3 *verb*
(*if it's a child*) = criar

reason *noun*
a reason = una razón
there's no reason to get annoyed = no hay por qué enojarse

reassure *verb*
= tranquilizar

receipt *noun*
a receipt = un recibo

receive *verb*
= recibir

recent *adjective*
= reciente

recently *adverb*
= recientemente

reception *noun*
- (*in a hotel, hospital, company*)
  a reception = una recepción
- (*a formal event*)
  a reception = una recepción

receptionist *noun*
a receptionist = un/una recepcionista

recipe *noun*
a recipe = una receta

recognize *verb*
= reconocer

recommend *verb*
= recomendar

record
1 *noun*
- (*of events*)
  a record = un registro
  to keep a record of something = llevar un registro de algo
- (*information*)
  the records (*historical, public*) = los archivos
  (*personal, medical*) = el historial
- (*for playing music*)
  a record = un disco
- (*in sport*)
  a record = un récord
2 *verb*
(*on a tape*) grabar

recorder *noun*
a recorder = una flauta dulce

record player *noun*
a record player = un tocadiscos

recover *verb*
(*recuperate*) = recuperarse

rectangle *noun*
a rectangle = un rectángulo

recycle *verb*
= reciclar

red *adjective* ▶ p. 183
= rojo/roja, colorado/colorada (*SC*)
to go red = ponerse rojo/roja, ponerse colorado/colorada
to have red hair = ser pelirrojo/pelirroja
red wine = vino tinto

reduce *verb*
to reduce prices = rebajar los precios
to reduce the number of employees = reducir el número de empleados
to reduce speed = disminuir la velocidad

reduction *noun*
- (*in numbers, size, spending*)
  a reduction = una reducción
- (*in prices*)
  a reduction = una rebaja

redundant *adjective* (*British English*)
he was made redundant = lo despidieron por reducción del personal, quedó cesante

refer *verb*
- (*to mention*)
  to refer to a subject = hacer referencia a un tema
- (*to allude*)
  to refer to someone = referirse a alguien

referee *noun*
(*in a match, a dispute*)
a referee = un árbitro/una árbitra

R

reflect *verb*
= reflejar
the lights were reflected in the water = las luces se reflejaban en el agua

reflection *noun*
a reflection = un reflejo

refreshing *adjective*
= refrescante

refrigerator *noun*
a refrigerator = un refrigerador (*Lat Am*), un frigorífico (*Spa*), una heladera (*R Pl*)

refugee *noun*
a refugee = un refugiado/una refugiada

refuse¹ *verb*
= rechazar
he refused my offer = rechazó mi oferta
to refuse to listen = negarse a escuchar

refuse² *noun*
refuse = residuos (*masculine plural*), desperdicios (*masculine plural*)

regards *noun*
give her my regards = dale saludos de mi parte, dale recuerdos de mi parte

region *noun*
a region = una región

registration number *noun* (*British English*)
a registration number = un número de matrícula, una matrícula

regret
1 *verb* = arrepentirse de
he regrets that he can't come = lamenta no poder venir
2 *noun*
to have regrets = arrepentirse

regular *adjective*
to take regular exercise = hacer ejercicio con regularidad
a regular customer = un cliente habitual

regularly *adverb*
= con regularidad

rehearsal *noun*
a rehearsal = un ensayo

rehearse *verb*
= ensayar

reject *verb*
= rechazar

relationship *noun*
a relationship = una relación
to have a good relationship with one's parents = llevarse bien con sus padres

relative *noun*
a relative = un/una pariente, un familiar

relax *verb*
= relajarse

relaxed *adjective*
= relajado/relajada

release *verb*
(*to free*) = liberar

reliable *adjective*
a reliable person = una persona de confianza
a reliable car = un coche fiable

relieved *adjective*
= aliviado/aliviada

religion *noun*
religion = religión (*feminine*)

religious *adjective*
= religioso/religiosa

rely *verb*
to rely on
• (*to depend on*) = depender de
• (*to count on*) = contar con
can we rely on you? = ¿podemos contar contigo?

remain *verb*
• (*to continue to be*) = seguir
we have remained friends = seguimos siendo amigos
• (*to continue to stay*) = quedarse
they will remain here until December = se quedarán aquí hasta diciembre
• (*to be left*) = quedar
is this all that remains? = ¿es esto todo lo que queda?

remark *noun*
a remark = un comentario

remarkable *adjective*
= extraordinario/extrordinaria

remember *verb*
= acordarse de, recordar
I remember writing down the address = recuerdo haber anotado la dirección
to remember to water the plants = acordarse de regar las plantas

remind *verb*
to remind someone to buy milk = recordarle a alguien que compre leche

! *Note the use of the subjunctive after* recordarle a alguien que

she reminds me of my sister = me recuerda a mi hermana

remove *verb*
= quitar

rent
1 *verb* = alquilar, rentar (*Mex*)
2 *noun*
the rent = el alquiler, la renta (*Méx*)

rent out = alquilar, rentar (*Mex*)

rental *noun*
  car rental (*US English*) = alquiler de coches (*masculine*)

repair *verb*
  = arreglar
  to have a bicycle repaired = hacer arreglar una bicicleta

repeat *verb*
  = repetir

replace *verb*
  to replace a teacher = sustituir a un profesor
  they replaced the fence with a wall = cambiaron la cerca por una pared

reply
1 *verb* = responder, contestar
2 *noun*
  a reply = una respuesta, una contestación

report
1 *verb*
• (*to tell about*)
  to report an accident = informar de un accidente
• (*in the news*)
  to report on an event = informar sobre un acontecimiento
• (*to complain about*)
  to report someone (to someone) = denunciar a alguien (a alguien)
2 *noun*
• (*in the news*)
  a report = una noticia
• (*in a newspaper*)
  a report = un reportaje
• (*an official document*)
  a report = un informe, un reporte (*Mex*)
• (*British English—at school*)
  a (**school**) report = un boletín de notas, un reporte (*Mex*)

report card *noun* (*US English*)
  a report card = un boletín de notas, un reporte (*Mex*)

reporter *noun*
  a reporter = un/una periodista, un reportero/una reportera

represent *verb*
  = representar

republic *noun*
  a republic = una república

request *noun*
  a request = una petición

rescue *verb*
  (*from danger*) = rescatar, salvar

resemble *verb*
  = parecerse a
  they resemble each other = se parecen

resent *verb*
  to resent someone = guardarle rencor a alguien
  he resented her success = le molestaba que ella tuviera éxito

  ! *Note that the subjunctive is used after* le molestaba que

reservation *noun*
  a reservation = una reserva, una reservación (*Lat Am*)

reserve *verb*
  = reservar

resign *verb*
  = renunciar, dimitir

resist *verb*
  = resistir

respect
1 *verb* = respetar
2 *noun*
  respect = respeto (*masculine*)

responsibility *noun*
  responsibility = responsabilidad (*feminine*)

responsible *adjective*
  = responsable
  to be responsible for the damage = ser responsable del daño
  to be responsible for organizing a trip = ser responsable de organizar un viaje

rest
1 *noun*
• (*what is left*)
  the rest of them have gone = los demás se han ido
  the rest of the class = el resto de la clase
  we spent the rest of the day in the garden = pasamos el resto del día en el jardín
• (*a break*)
  a rest = un descanso
  to have a rest = descansar
2 *verb* = descansar

restaurant *noun*
  a restaurant = un restaurante, un restaurant

result *noun*
  a result = un resultado
  as a result of the accident = como consecuencia del accidente

resumé *noun* (*American English*)
  a resumé = un currículum, un historial personal

retire *verb*
  = jubilarse

return *verb*
• (*to go back, to come back*) = volver, regresar
• (*to give back*) = devolver, regresar (*Mex*)

R

return ticket *noun* (*British English*)
   a return ticket (*on a ship or plane*) = un
      pasaje de ida y vuelta (*Lat Am*), un billete
      de ida y vuelta (*Spa*), un boleto (de viaje)
      redondo (*Mex*)
   (*on a bus or train*) = un boleto de ida y
      vuelta (*Lat Am*), un billete de ida y vuelta
      (*Spa*), un boleto (de viaje) redondo (*Mex*)

reveal *verb*
   to reveal a secret = revelar un secreto

revenge *noun*
   revenge = venganza (*feminine*)

revolution *noun*
   a revolution = una revolución

reward
   1 *noun*
   a reward = una recompensa
   2 *verb* = recompensar

rhythm *noun*
   rhythm = ritmo (*masculine*)

rib *noun*
   a rib = una costilla

ribbon *noun*
   a ribbon = una cinta

rice *noun*
   rice = arroz (*masculine*)

rich *adjective*
   = rico/rica

rid: to get rid of *verb*
   to get rid of something = deshacerse de
      algo
   to get rid of someone = quitarse a alguien
      de encima

ride
   1 *verb*
   to go riding = ir a montar a caballo, ir a
      andar a caballo (*Lat Am*)
   to ride a horse = montar a un caballo
   to ride a bike = montar en bici, andar en
      bici (*Lat Am*)
   2 *noun*
   to go for a ride = ir a dar una vuelta, ir a
      dar un paseo

ridiculous *adjective*
   = ridículo/ridícula

right
   1 *adjective*
   • (*not left*) = derecho/derecha
   • (*honest, good*)
   it's not right to steal = no está bien robar
   • (*correct*) = correcto/correcta
   the right answer = la respuesta correcta
   you're right = tienes razón
   that's right = eso es
   2 *noun*

• (*the direction*)
   right = derecha (*feminine*)
   the first street on the right = la primera
      calle a la derecha
• (*what one is entitled to do*)
   a right = un derecho
   human rights = derechos humanos
      (*masculine plural*)
   3 *adverb*
   = a la derecha, hacia la derecha

right-handed *adjective*
   = diestro/diestra

ring
   1 *verb*
   • (*British English—to phone*) = llamar
   to ring for a taxi = llamar un taxi
   • (*to make a sound*) = sonar
   the bell rang = sonó el timbre
   the phone's ringing = está sonando el
      teléfono
   to ring the bell = tocar el timbre
   2 *noun*
   • (*a piece of jewelry*)
   a ring = un anillo
   a wedding ring = una alianza, un anillo de
      boda
   • (*a circle*)
   a ring = un círculo
   ring back (*British English*) = volver a llamar
   ring up (*British English*) = llamar

rinse *verb*
   = enjuagar

ripe *adjective*
   = maduro/madura

rise *verb*
   • (*of smoke, water, a plane*) = subir
   • (*of prices*) = aumentar
   • (*of the sun or the moon*) = salir

risk
   1 *noun*
   a risk = un riesgo
   2 *verb*
   to risk one's life = arriesgar la vida
   to risk losing one's job = correr el riesgo de
      perder el trabajo

rival *noun*
   a rival = un/una rival

river *noun*
   a river = un río

road *noun*
   a road (*in town*) = una calle
   (*out of town*) = una carretera
   the road to London = la carretera que va a
      Londres

road sign *noun*
   a road sign = una señal vial, una señal de
      tránsito (*Lat Am*)

roar *verb*
- (*of a lion, an engine*) = rugir
- (*of a person*)
  to roar with laughter = reírse a carcajadas

roast
1 *verb* = asar
2 *adjective* = asado/asada

roast beef *noun*
  roast beef = rosbif (*masculine*)

rob *verb*
  to rob someone = robarle a alguien
  they robbed her of her savings = le robaron los ahorros
  to rob a bank = asaltar un banco

robbery *noun*
  a robbery = un robo

robot *noun*
  a robot = un robot

rock *noun*
- (*the material*)
  rock = roca (*feminine*)
- (*a large stone*)
  a rock = una roca
- (*music*)
  rock = rock (*masculine*)

rocket *noun*
  a rocket = un cohete

role *noun*
  a role = un papel

roll
1 *verb* = rodar
  the ball rolled under the car = la pelota rodó debajo del coche
2 *noun*
- (*of paper, cloth, plastic*)
  a roll = un rollo
  a roll of film = un rollo, un carrete, una película
- (*bread*)
  a roll = un pancito, un panecillo (*Spa*), un bolillo (*Mex*)
  roll about, roll around = rodar
  roll out = estirar
  roll over = darse la vuelta, voltearse (*Lat Am*), darse vuelta (*SC*)
  roll up
  to roll up one's sleeves = arremangarse

roller skate *noun*
  a roller skate = un patín

roller skating *noun*
  roller skating = patinaje (*masculine*)
  to go roller skating = ir a patinar

Romania *noun* ▶ **p. 187**
  Romania = Rumania (*feminine*)

romantic *adjective*
  = romántico/romántica

roof *noun*
  a roof = un tejado, un techo (*Lat Am*)

room *noun*
- **a room** = una habitación, una pieza (*Lat Am*)
  (*for sleeping*) = un dormitorio, un cuarto, una pieza (*Lat Am*), una recámara (*Lat Am*)
  (*for teaching, holding meetings*) = una sala
- (*space*)
  room = espacio (*masculine*), lugar (*masculine*)

root *noun*
  a root = una raíz

rope *noun*
  a rope = una cuerda

rose *noun*
  a rose = una rosa

rot *verb*
  = pudrir

rotten *adjective*
  = podrido/podrida

rough *adjective*
- (*not smooth*) = áspero/áspera
  to have rough skin = tener la piel áspera
- (*not gentle*) = brusco/brusca
  don't be so rough! = ¡no seas tan brusco!
- (*not exact, precise*)
  a rough figure = una cifra aproximada
- **a rough sea** = un mar agitado

round

> **!** Often **round** occurs in combinations with verbs. For more information, see the note at **around**

1 *preposition* (*British English*) = alrededor de
  to be sitting round a table = estar sentados/sentadas alrededor de una mesa
2 *adverb* (*British English*)
  to go round and round = dar vueltas y vueltas
  to invite someone round = invitar a alguien a casa
3 *noun*
  a round (*in a quiz*) = una vuelta
  (*in boxing*) = un round, un asalto
4 *adjective* = redondo/redonda

roundabout *noun* (*British English*)
- (*for traffic*)
  a roundabout = una rotonda, una glorieta (*Mex, Spa*)
- (*in an amusement park*)
  a roundabout = unos caballitos, un carrusel (*Lat Am*), una calesita (*R Pl*), un tiovivo (*Spa*)

round-trip ticket *noun* (*US English*)
  a round-trip ticket (*on a ship or plane*) = un pasaje de ida y vuelta (*Lat Am*), un billete de ida y vuelta (*Spa*), un boleto (de viaje) redondo (*Mex*)

R

(*on a bus or train*) = un boleto de ida y
vuelta (*Lat Am*), un billete de ida y vuelta
(*Spa*), un boleto (de viaje) redondo (*Mex*)

route *noun*
  a route = un camino, una ruta
  (*of a bus*) = un recorrido

routine *noun*
  a routine = una rutina

row¹
1 *noun*
* a row (*of trees, houses*) = una hilera
  (*of people, seats*) = una fila
* to be absent five days in a row = faltar tres
  días seguidos
2 *verb* = remar

row² *noun*
  (*quarrel*)
  a row = una pelea
  to have a row with someone = tener una
  pelea con alguien

royal *adjective*
  = real

rub *verb*
  to rub one's eyes = restregarse los ojos
rub out = borrar

rubber *noun*
* (*the material*)
  rubber = goma (*feminine*), caucho
  (*masculine*), hule (*masculine*) (*Mex*)
* (*British English—an eraser*)
  a rubber = una goma de borrar

rubber band *noun*
  a rubber band = una goma (elástica), una
  liga (*Mex*), una gomita (*R Pl*)

rubbish *noun* (*British English*)
* (*garbage*)
  rubbish = basura (*feminine*)
* (*poor quality goods*)
  rubbish = porquerías (*feminine plural*)
* (*nonsense*)
  rubbish = tonterías (*feminine plural*)

rubbish bin *noun* (*British English*)
  a rubbish bin = un cubo de la basura, un
  tacho de la basura (*SC*), un bote de la
  basura (*Mex*)

rucksack *noun*
  a rucksack = una mochila

rude *adjective*
* (*not polite*) = maleducado/maleducada,
  grosero/grosera
  to be rude to someone = ser
  grosero/grosera con alguien
* (*vulgar*) = grosero/grosera
  a rude word = una grosería, una palabrota

rug *noun*
  a rug = una alfombra, un tapete (*Mex*)

rugby *noun* ▶ p. 306
  rugby = rugby (*masculine*)

ruin
1 *verb*
* (*to destroy*) = destruir
* (*to spoil*) = arruinar, estropear
  to ruin a meal = arruinar una comida,
  estropear una comida
* (*to damage*) = estropear
  you'll ruin your shoes = vas a estropear tus
  zapatos
2 *noun*
  a ruin = una ruina

rule
1 *noun*
  a rule = una regla, una norma
  it's against the rules to smoke in the
  building = está prohibido fumar en el
  edificio
2 *verb* = gobernar

ruler *noun*
* (*for measuring*)
  a ruler = una regla
* (*a leader*)
  a ruler = un/una gobernante

rumor (*US English*), **rumour** (*British
English*) *noun*
  a rumor = un rumor

run
1 *verb*
* to run = correr
  to run after someone = correr tras alguien
  to run a race = correr una carrera
* (*to manage*) = dirigir
  to run a company = dirigir una compañía
* (*to work, to operate*)
  it runs on batteries = funciona con pilas
  the system runs well = el sistema funciona
  bien
* (*to organize*) = organizar
  to run a competition = organizar un
  concurso
* (*when talking about transport*)
  the trains don't run after 12 o'clock = no
  hay trenes después de las doce
* (*to flow*) = correr
  to leave the water running = dejar el agua
  corriendo
* (*to fill with water*)
  to run a bath = preparar un baño
* (*of colors*) = desteñirse
  (*of makeup*) = correrse
2 *noun*
  to go for a run = salir a correr
run around, **run about** (*British English*)
  = corretear
run away = huir
run off = salir corriendo

C Am Central America   Lat Am Latin America   Mex Mexico

run out
  we ran out of milk = quedamos sin leche
run over = atropellar

rush
1 *verb*
  (*to hurry*)
  to rush out of the house = salir de la casa
    corriendo
  she was rushed to hospital = fue
    trasladada rápidamente al hospital
2 *noun*
  to be in a rush = tener mucha prisa, estar
    muy apurado/apurada (*Lat Am*)

rush hour *noun*
  the rush hour = la hora pico (*Lat Am*), la
    hora punta (*Spa*)

Russia *noun* ▶ p. 187
  Russia = Rusia (*feminine*)

Russian ▶ p. 187, p. 245
1 *adjective* = ruso/rusa
2 *noun*
• (*a person*)
  a Russian = un ruso/una rusa
• (*the language*)
  Russian = ruso (*masculine*)

rusty *adjective*
  = oxidado/oxidada

Ss

sad *adjective*
  = triste

saddle *noun*
  a saddle (*on a horse*) = una silla de montar,
    una montura
  (*on a bicycle*)= un asiento, un sillín

safe
1 *adjective*
• (*without risk, free from danger*) =
    seguro/segura
  a safe place = un lugar seguro
  it's not safe for children = es peligroso para
    los niños
  to feel safe = sentirse seguro/segura
• (*unharmed*)
  safe and sound = sano y salvo/sana y salva
2 *noun*
  a safe = una caja fuerte

safety *noun*
  safety = seguridad (*feminine*)

Sagittarius *noun*
• (*the sign*)
  Sagittarius = Sagitario
  I'm Sagittarius = soy Sagitario, soy de
    Sagitario
• (*a person*)
  a Sagittarius = un/una sagitario

sail
1 *noun*
  a sail = una vela
  to set sail = zarpar, hacerse a la mar
2 *verb* = ir en barco, navegar
  to go sailing = salir a navegar

sailboat *noun* (*US English*)
  a sailboat = un velero, un barco de vela

sailing boat *noun* (*British English*)
▶ sailboat

sailor *noun*
  a sailor = un marinero

saint *noun*
  a saint = un santo/una santa

salad *noun*
  a salad = una ensalada

salary *noun*
  a salary = un sueldo

sale *noun*
• to put a house up for sale = poner una casa
    en venta, poner una casa a la venta
  to be on sale (*US English*) = estar en
    liquidación
  (*British English*) = estar a la venta
  'for sale' = 'se vende'
• (*with reduced prices*)
  a sale = una liquidación, unas rebajas

salesclerk *noun* (*US English*)
  a salesclerk = un empleado/una empleada
    (*Lat Am*), un dependiente/una
    dependienta (*Spa*), un vendedor/una
    vendedora (*SC*)

salmon *noun*
  salmon = salmón (*masculine*)

salt *noun*
  salt = sal (*feminine*)

same
1 *adjective* = mismo/misma
  she's got the same coat as me = tiene el
    mismo abrigo que yo
  they go to the same school = van a la
    misma escuela
  it's all the same to me = me da igual
  the houses all look the same = las casa son
    todas parecidas
2 *pronoun*
  the same = lo mismo

sand *noun*
  sand = arena (*feminine*)

S

sandal noun
a sandal = una sandalia

sandwich noun
a sandwich = un sándwich

Santa (Claus) noun
Santa (Claus) = Papá Noel (masculine)

satellite TV noun
satellite TV = televisión vía satélite

satisfactory adjective
= satisfactorio/satisfactoria

satisfied adjective
= satisfecho/satisfecha

Saturday noun ▶ p. 192
Saturday = sábado (masculine)

sauce noun
a sauce = una salsa

saucepan noun
a saucepan = una cacerola, un cazo (Spa)

saucer noun
a saucer = un platillo

sausage noun
a sausage = una salchicha

save verb
• (to rescue) = salvar
  they saved his life = le salvaron la vida
• (to avoid spending)
  to save (up) = ahorrar
• (to avoid wasting) = ahorrar
  to save [time | money | energy ...] = ahorrar
  [tiempo | dinero | energía ...]
• (to keep) = guardar
  he saved me a piece of cake = me guardó
  un pedazo de pastel
• (to spare)
  it saved me a lot of work = me ahorró
  mucho trabajo
• (in computing) = guardar

savings noun
savings = ahorros (masculine plural)

saw noun
a saw = una sierra

saxophone noun
a saxophone = un saxofón, un saxófono

say verb
= decir
he said to wait here = dijo que
  esperáramos aquí

! Note the use of the subjunctive after
decir que

scandal noun
a scandal = un escándalo

scare verb
= asustar

scared adjective
to be scared = tener miedo
to be scared of someone/something =
  tenerle miedo a alguien/algo

scarf noun
a scarf (long) = una bufanda
  (square) = un pañuelo

scenery noun
scenery = paisaje (masculine)

school noun
• (in primary, secondary education)
  a school = una escuela, un colegio
• (for learning languages, learning to drive)
  a school = una academia
• (US English—a university)
  a school = una universidad

schoolboy noun
a schoolboy = un colegial, un escolar

schoolchild noun
a schoolchild = un colegial/una colegiala,
  un/una escolar

schoolgirl noun
a schoolgirl = una colegiala, una escolar

science noun
science = ciencia (feminine)
to study science = estudiar ciencias

scientist noun
a scientist = un científico/una científica

scissors noun
scissors = tijeras (feminine plural)
a pair of scissors = unas tijeras

score verb
= marcar
to score a goal = marcar un gol

Scorpio noun
• (the sign)
  Scorpio = Escorpio
  I'm Scorpio = soy Escorpio, soy de Escorpio
• (a person)
  a Scorpio = un/una escorpio

Scotch tape® noun (US English)
Scotch tape = cinta Scotch® (feminine),
  cinta Durex® (feminine) (Lat Am), cello
  (masculine) (Spa)

Scotland noun ▶ p. 187
Scotland = Escocia (feminine)

Scottish adjective ▶ p. 187
= escocés/escocesa

scratch verb
• (when itchy) = rascarse
  to scratch one's arm = rascarse el brazo
• (to hurt) = arañar, rasguñar
• (to mark, to damage) = rayar

scream verb
= gritar

---

screen *noun*
a screen = una pantalla

screw *noun*
a screw = un tornillo

sea *noun*
the sea = el mar

seafood *noun*
seafood = mariscos (*masculine plural*),
marisco (*masculine*) (*Spa*)

seagull *noun*
a seagull = una gaviota

seal *noun*
a seal = una foca

search *verb*
• to search = buscar
  to search for someone = buscar a alguien
• (*to examine a place, a person*) = registrar,
  catear (*Mex*)

seasick *adjective*
to be seasick = estar mareado/mareada

seaside *noun*
the seaside = la costa, la playa

season *noun*
• (*autumn, winter, summer or spring*)
  a season = una estación
• (*for a specific activity*)
  a season = una temporada
  strawberries are in season = es temporada
  de fresas

seat *noun*
• (*a chair, a bench, on transport*)
  a seat = un asiento
• (*in a theater, a cinema*)
  a seat = una localidad

seatbelt *noun*
a seatbelt = un cinturón de seguridad

second
1 *adjective* = segundo/segunda
2 *noun* ▶ p. 192, p. 319
• (*in order*)
  the second = el segundo/la segunda
• (*when talking about time*)
  a second = un segundo
3 *adverb* = en segundo lugar
  to come second = quedar en segundo
  lugar

secondary school *noun*
a secondary school = un colegio de
enseñanza secundaria

second-hand *adjective*
= de segunda mano (**!** *never changes*)

secret
1 *adjective* = secreto/secreta
2 *noun*
• a secret = un secreto
• in secret = en secreto

secretary *noun*
a secretary = un secretario/una secretaria

see *verb*
• to see = ver
  I can't see them = no los veo
  see you tomorrow! = ¡hasta mañana!
  what time?—let's see = ¿a qué hora?—a ver
• (*to make sure*)
  to see that the work is finished quickly =
  asegurarse de que el trabajo se termine
  rápido

  ! *Note the use of the subjunctive after*
  asegurarse de que

• (*to accompany*)
  I'll see you home = te voy a acompañar a
  casa
see out
to see someone out = acompañar a
alguien a la puerta
see to = ocuparse de

seem *verb*
• (*to appear*)
  she seems happy = parece contenta, se ve
  contenta (*Lat Am*)
  they seem to be looking for someone =
  parece que están buscando a alguien
• (*when talking about one's impressions*)
  it seems (that) there are a lot of problems
  = parece que hay muchos problemas

seldom *adverb*
= rara vez

self-confident *adjective* = seguro/segura
de sí mismo/misma

selfish *adjective*
= egoísta

sell *verb*
= vender
stamps sold here = los sellos se venden
aquí

sellotape® *noun* (*British English*)
Sellotape = cinta Scotch® (*feminine*), cinta
Durex® (*feminine*) (*Lat Am*), cello
(*masculine*) (*Spa*)

semidetached *adjective*
a semidetached house = una casa pareada,
una casa adosada

send *verb*
= mandar
to send a package to someone = mandarle
un paquete a alguien, enviarle un
paquete a alguien
he sent me a letter = me mandó un carta
to send someone to buy the paper =
mandar a alguien a comprar el diario
send away
they sent him away = le dijeron que se
fuera
send back = devolver

S

send for = mandar a buscar, mandar llamar (*Lat Am*)
  they sent for the doctor = mandaron a buscar al médico, mandaron llamar al médico

senior *adjective*
* (*higher in rank*)
  those in senior positions = quienes ocupan puestos de responsabilidad
  I need to ask advice from a senior colleague = tengo que consultar a un superior
* (*older*)
  the senior members of a club = los socios más antiguos de un club

senior high school (*US English*) *noun*
  a senior high school = un colegio secundario

sense *noun*
* (**common**) **sense** = sentido común (*masculine*)
* (*allowing one to see, hear, smell etc*)
  a sense = un sentido
* (*a meaning*)
  a sense = un sentido
  it doesn't make sense = no tiene sentido

sensible *adjective*
* (*if it's a person*) = sensato/sensata
* (*if it's a decision*) = prudente
* (*if it's clothes*) = cómodo y práctico/cómoda y práctica

sensitive *adjective*
* (*if it's a person*) = sensible
* (*if it's a situation*) = delicado/delicada

sentence
1 *noun*
* (*in grammar*)
  a sentence = una frase
* (*for a crime*)
  the maximum sentence = la pena máxima
  a life sentence = una condena a cadena perpetua
2 *verb* = sentenciar

separate
1 *adjective* = separado/separada
2 *verb*
* **to separate** = separar
* (*if it's a couple*) = separarse

separately *adjective*
= por separado

September *noun* ▶ **p. 192**
  September = septiembre (*masculine*), setiembre (*masculine*)

serial *noun*
  (*on radio, television*)
  a serial = una serie

series *noun*
  a series = una serie

serious
* (*causing worry*) = grave
  a serious accident = un accidente grave
* (*if it's someone's personality*) = serio/seria

serve *verb*
* (*British English—in a shop*) = atender
  are you being served? = ¿lo/la atienden?
* (*at table*) = servir
* (*in sport*) = servir, sacar

service *noun*
* (*which people need or find useful*)
  a service = un servicio
* (*in a shop*)
  the service = el servicio
* (*a religious ceremony*)
  a service = un oficio religioso

service station *noun*
  a service station = una estación de servicio

serviette *noun* (*British English*)
  a serviette = una servilleta

set
1 *noun*
* (*a collection*)
  a set of keys = un juego de llaves
  a set of stamps = una serie de sellos
* (*in tennis*)
  a set = un set
2 *verb*
* (*to decide on*) = fijar
  to set [a date | a time | a price ...] = fijar [una fecha | una hora | un precio ...]
* (*to adjust*) = poner
  to set an alarm clock = poner un despertador
  to set a video = poner un video
* (*in school*)
  to set homework = mandar los deberes, dejar tareas (*Mex*)
  to set an exam = poner un examen
* (*to be responsible for*)
  to set a record = establecer un récord
  to set a good example = dar buen ejemplo
* (*if it's a story, movie*)
  the novel is set in Paris = la novela está ambientada en París
* (*of the sun*) = ponerse
set off
* (*to leave*) = salir
* **to set off a bomb** = hacer explotar una bomba
set up
  to set up in business = poner un negocio

settle *verb*
* (*to end*)
  to settle an argument = resolver una discusión
* **to settle a bill** = pagar una cuenta
* (*to make one's home*) = establecerse

seven number ▶ p. 154, p. 319
  seven = siete (*masculine*) (! *never changes*) *see also* five

seventeen number ▶ p. 154, p. 319
  seventeen = diecisiete (*masculine*) (! *never changes*) *see also* five

seventh
1 *adjective* = séptimo/séptima
2 *noun* ▶ p. 192
• (*a part*)
  a seventh = una séptima parte

seventy noun ▶ p. 154
  seventy = setenta (*masculine*) (! *never changes*) *see also* five

several adjective
  = varios/varias

severe adjective
• (*if it's an illness or injury*) = grave
  (*if it's pain*) = fuerte
• (*harsh*) = severo/severa

sew verb
  = coser

sewing machine noun
  a sewing machine = una máquina de coser

sex noun
  sex = sexo (*masculine*)
  to have sex = tener relaciones sexuales

shade noun
• (*out of the sun*)
  shade = sombra (*feminine*)
  to sit in the shade = sentarse a la sombra
• (*a color*)
  a shade = un tono
• (*for a lamp*)
  a shade = una pantalla

shadow noun
  a shadow = una sombra

shake verb
• **to shake** = sacudir
  to shake a bottle = agitar una botella
  to shake hands with someone = darle la mano a alguien
• **to shake one's head** = negar con la cabeza
• (*with cold, fear, shock*) = temblar
  he was shaking with fear = temblaba de miedo
• (*during an explosion, earthquake*) = temblar

shall verb

> ! When referring to the future, Spanish uses the future tense of the verb to translate **shall** + verb: **I shall leave** = me iré

• (*when talking about the future*)
  I shall see you next Tuesday = te veré el martes que viene

• (*when making suggestions*)
  shall we go to the cinema? = ¿vamos al cine?

shame noun
• **shame** = vergüenza (*feminine*)
• (*when expressing regret*)
  what a shame = ¡qué lástima!

shampoo noun
  shampoo = champú (*masculine*)

shape noun
• (*a form*)
  a shape = una forma
  in the shape of a cross = en forma de cruz
• (*when talking about health*)
  to be in good shape = estar en forma
  to get into shape = ponerse en forma

share
1 *verb* = compartir
2 *noun*
  a share = una parte
  to pay one's share = pagar su parte
  share out = repartir, distribuir

shark noun
  a shark = un tiburón

sharp adjective
• (*able to cut*) = afilado/afilada, filoso/filosa (*Lat Am*)
• (*sudden*) = cerrado/cerrada
  a sharp bend = una curva cerrada
• (*clever*) = despierto/despierta
• (*harsh, aggressive*)
  a sharp comment = un comentario cáustico
  a sharp reply = una respuesta cortante
• (*violent*)
  a sharp pain = un dolor agudo
• (*in taste*) = ácido/ácida

shave verb
  = afeitarse, rasurarse (*Mex*)

she pronoun
  she = ella
  she went to the theater = fue al teatro
  she **did it** = ella lo hizo
  he works in London but she doesn't = él trabaja en Londres pero ella no

> ! Although ella is given as the translation of **she**, it is in practice used only for emphasis, or to avoid ambiguity

sheep noun
  a sheep = una oveja

sheet noun
• (*for a bed*)
  a sheet = una sábana
• (*of paper*)
  a sheet = una hoja

shelf noun
  a shelf (*for books, ornaments*) = un estante

S

(*in an oven*) = una parrilla
a set of shelves = unos estantes, una
  estantería

shell *noun*
  a shell (*of an egg, a nut*) = una cáscara
  (*of a crab, a snail, a tortoise*) = un
    caparazón
  (*of a sea mollusk*) = una concha

shelter
1 *noun*
• (*from rain, danger*)
  to take shelter = refugiarse
• (*for homeless people*)
  a shelter = un refugio
2 *verb*
• (*to take shelter*) = refugiarse
• (*to help*) = proteger

shine *verb*
• (*to give out light*) = brillar
• **to shine a light on someone** = alumbrar a
    alguien con una luz

ship *noun*
  a ship = un barco

shirt *noun*
  a shirt = una camisa

shiver *verb*
  = temblar, tiritar

shock
1 *noun*
• (*an upsetting experience*)
  a shock = un shock
  to get a shock = llevarse un shock
• (*a scare*)
  what a shock you gave me! = ¡qué susto
    me diste!
• (*the medical state*)
  to be in shock = estar en estado de shock
• (*from electricity*)
  a shock = una descarga
2 *verb*
• (*to upset*) = conmocionar
• (*to cause a scandal*) = escandalizar

shoe *noun*
  a shoe = un zapato

shoelace *noun*
  a shoelace = un cordón, una agujeta (*Mex*)

shoot *verb*
• (*using a weapon*)
  to shoot someone = pegarle un tiro a
    alguien
  they shot him in the leg = le pegaron un
    tiro en la pierna
• (*to move very fast*)
  to shoot past = pasar como un bólido

shop
1 *noun*
  a shop = una tienda, un negocio (*SC*)

2 *verb*
  to go shopping = ir de compras

shop assistant *noun* (*British English*)
  a shop assistant = un empleado/una
    empleada (*Lat Am*), un dependiente/una
    dependienta (*Spa*), un vendedor/una
    vendedora (*SC*)

shopkeeper *noun* (*British English*)
  a shopkeeper = un/una comerciante

shopping *noun*
  shopping = compras (*feminine plural*)
  to do the shopping = hacer la compra,
    hacer los mandados (*Mex*), hacer las
    compras (*SC*)

shopping cart *noun* (*US English*)
  a shopping cart = un carrito

shopping mall (*US English*),
shopping centre (*British English*) *noun*
  a shopping mall, a shopping centre = un
    centro comercial

shopping trolley *noun* (*British English*)
  a shopping trolley = un carrito

shop window *noun*
  a shop window = un escaparate, una
    vidriera (*Lat Am*), un aparador (*Mex*)

shore *noun*
• (*the coast*)
  the shore = la costa, la ribera
• (*the edge of the sea*)
  the shore = la orilla
• (*dry land*)
  to go on shore = bajar a tierra (firme)

short *adjective*
• (*not lasting long*) = corto/corta
  a short visit = una visita corta
  a short speech = un breve discurso
• (*not long*) = corto/corta
  to have short hair = tener el pelo corto
• (*not tall*) = bajo/baja
• (*lacking*)
  to be short of money/time = andar
    corto/corta de dinero/tiempo
• **in short** = en resumen

short cut *noun*
  a short cut = un atajo

shortly *adverb*
• (*soon*) = dentro de poco
• (*not long*)
  shortly before we left = poco antes de que
    nos fuéramos

shorts *noun*
• (*short trousers*)
  shorts = shorts (*masculine plural*)
  a pair of shorts = unos shorts
• (*US English—men's underwear*)
  shorts = calzoncillos (*masculine plural*)

shortsighted *adjective* (*British English*)
= miope, corto/corta de vista

shot *noun*
- (*from a gun*)
  a shot = un disparo, un tiro
- (*in sports*)
  a shot (*in football*) = un tiro, un disparo
  (*in tennis, golf, cricket*) = un tiro

should *verb*
- (*when talking about what ought to be done*)
  she should learn to drive = debería
    aprender a manejar
  you shouldn't have said that = no deberías
    haber dicho eso
- (*when saying something is likely to
    happen*)
  it shouldn't be too difficult = no debería ser
    demasiado difícil
- (*when implying that something, though
    likely, didn't happen*)
  the letter should have arrived yesterday =
    la carta debería haber llegado ayer

shoulder *noun* ▶ p. 235
  the shoulder = el hombro

shout
1 *verb* = gritar
2 *noun*
  a shout = un grito

shovel *noun*
  a shovel = una pala

show
1 *verb*
- (*to let someone see*) = mostrar, enseñar
  I'll show you how it works = te muestro
    cómo funciona
- (*to go with*)
  I'll show you to your room = le acompaño a
    su cuarto
- (*to be on TV, at the cinema*)
  the movie is showing at the Phoenix =
    están dando la película en el Phoenix,
    ponen la película en el Phoenix (*Spa*)
2 *noun*
- **a show** (*on a stage*) = un espectáculo
  (*on TV, radio*) = un programa
- (*an exhibition*)
  a show = una exposición
  to be on show = estar expuesto/expuesta
show off = lucirse

shower *noun*
- (*for washing*)
  a shower = una ducha, una regadera (*Mex*)
  to take a shower (*US English*), **to have a
    shower** (*British English*) = ducharse
- (*rain*)
  a shower = un chaparrón, un chubasco

shrimp *noun*
  a shrimp = un camarón

shrink *verb*
= encogerse

shut
1 *adjective* = cerrado/cerrada
2 *verb* = cerrar
shut down = cerrar
shut up
  (*to be quiet*) = callarse
  shut up! = ¡cállate!

shy *adjective*
= tímido/tímida

sick *adjective*
- (*ill*) = enfermo/enferma
  to be sick = estar enfermo/enferma
  (*if one vomits*) = vomitar
  to feel sick = tener ganas de vomitar
  to get sick (*US English*) = caer
    enfermo/enferma, enfermarse (*Lat Am*)
- (*fed up*)
  he's sick of work = está harto del trabajo

sickness *noun*
  a sickness = una enfermedad

side *noun*
- **a side** = un lado
  on my right side = a mi derecha
  by the side of the river = a la orilla del río
- (*of a person's body*)
  the side = el costado, el lado
- (*in a conflict, a contest*)
  to take sides = tomar partido
- (*a team*)
  a side = un equipo

sidewalk *noun* (*US English*)
  a sidewalk = una acera, una banqueta
  (*Mex*), una vereda (*SC*)

sigh *verb*
= suspirar

sight *noun*
- **sight** = vista (*feminine*)
  to lose sight of someone = perder a
    alguien de vista
- **to see the sights** = visitar los lugares de
    interés

sightseeing *noun*
  to go sightseeing = visitar los lugares de
    interés

sign
1 *noun*
- (*a mark*)
  a sign = un signo
- (*for traffic*)
  a sign = una señal
- (*a notice*)
  a sign = un letrero
2 *verb* = firmar

signal
1 *noun*
  a signal = una señal

S

2 *verb*
- (*to make signs*) = hacer señas
- (*when driving*) = poner el intermitente

signature *noun*
  a signature = una firma

signpost *noun*
  a signpost = una señal

silence *noun*
  silence = silencio (*masculine*)

silent *adjective*
  a silent night = una noche silenciosa
  he remained silent = se quedó callado

silk *noun*
  silk = seda (*feminine*)

silly *adjective*
  = tonto/tonta

silver
1 *noun*
  silver = plata (*feminine*)
2 *adjective* = de plata

similar *adjective*
  = parecido/parecida

simple *adjective*
  = sencillo/sencilla

since
1 *preposition* = desde
  I haven't seen him since yesterday = no lo
    he visto desde ayer
  she has been living here since 1988 = vive
    aquí desde 1988
  I haven't been feeling well since Monday =
    desde el lunes que no me siento bien
2 *conjunction*
- (*from the time when*) = desde que
  since she left = desde que se fue
  it's ten years since she died = hace diez
    años que se murió
- (*because*)
  since she was ill, she couldn't go = como
    estaba enferma, no pudo ir
3 *adverb* = desde entonces
  I haven't seen them since = no los he visto
    desde entonces

sincere *adjective*
  = sincero/sincera

sing *verb*
  = cantar

singer *noun*
  a singer = un/una cantante

single
1 *adjective*
- (*one*) = solo/sola (**!** *before noun*)
  we visited three towns in a single day =
    visitamos tres ciudades en un solo día
  not a single word = ni una palabra

- (*when used for emphasis*)
  every single day = todos los días sin
    excepción
  there wasn't a single person = no había ni
    una sola persona
- (*without a partner*) = soltero/soltera
2 *noun*
  (*in tennis*)
  singles = individuales (*masculine plural*),
    singles (*masculine plural*) (*Lat Am*)

single bed *noun*
  a single bed = una cama individual, una
    cama de una plaza (*Lat Am*)

single room *noun*
  a single room = una habitación individual

single ticket *noun* (*British English*)
  a single ticket (*on a ship or plane*) = un
    pasaje de ida (*Lat Am*), un billete de ida
    (*Spa*)
  (*on a bus or train*) = un boleto de ida
    (*Lat Am*), un billete de ida (*Spa*)

sink
1 *noun*
  a sink (*in a kitchen*) = un fregadero, un
    lavaplatos (*Mex*), una pileta (*R Pl*)
  (*in a bathroom*) = un lavabo, un lavamanos,
    un lavatorio (*SC*)
2 *verb* = hundirse

sister *noun*
  a sister = una hermana

sister-in-law *noun*
  a sister-in-law = una cuñada

sit *verb*
- (*to take a seat*) = sentarse
  he sat down on the floor = se sentó en el
    suelo
  to be sitting on the floor = estar
    sentado/sentada en el suelo
  sit down = sentarse
  to be sitting down = estar sentado/sentada
  sit up = ponerse derecho/derecha

situated *adjective*
  = situado/situada
  it is situated near the town center = está
    situado cerca del centro de la ciudad, está
    ubicado cerca del centro de la ciudad
    (*Lat Am*)

situation *noun*
  a situation = una situación

six *number* ▶ **p. 154, p. 319**
  six = seis (*masculine*) (**!** *never changes*)
  see also five

sixteen *number* ▶ **p. 154, p. 319**
  sixteen = dieciseis (*masculine*) (**!** *never
    changes*) *see also* five

sixth
1 *adjective* = sexto/sexta

2 *noun* ▶ **p. 192**
  (*a part*)
  a sixth = una sexta parte

sixty *noun* ▶ **p. 154**
  sixty = sesenta (*masculine*) (**!** *never
    changes*) *see also* **five**

size *noun*
• (*when talking about clothes*)
  a size (*of garment*) = una talla, un talle
    (*R Pl*)
  (*of shoe*) = un número
  what size do you take? (*in clothes*) = ¿qué
    talla tiene?, ¿qué talle tiene?
  (*in shoes*) = ¿qué número calza?
• (*when talking about how big something is*)
  the size (*of a building, a wardrobe*) = el
    tamaño
  (*of a problem, an operation*) = la magnitud

skating *noun*
  skating = patinaje (*masculine*)

skating rink *noun*
  a skating rink = una pista de patinaje

skeleton *noun*
  a skeleton = un esqueleto

sketch *noun*
• (*a drawing*)
  a sketch = un bosquejo
  (*rougher*) = un esbozo
• (*a funny scene*)
  a sketch = un sketch

ski
1 *noun*
  a ski = un esquí
2 *verb*
  to go skiing = ir a esquiar

skiing *noun*
  skiing = esquí (*masculine*)

skillful (*US English*), **skilful** (*British
English*) *adjective*
  = habilidoso/habilidosa
  to be skillful at sewing = ser
    habilidoso/habilidosa para la costura

skill *noun*
• (*the quality*)
  skill = habilidad (*feminine*)
• (*a particular ability*)
  typing is a very useful skill = saber escribir
    a máquina es muy útil

skin *noun*
  skin = piel (*feminine*)
  to have dry skin = tener la piel seca

skip *verb*
• (*to give little jumps*) = brincar
• (*with a rope*)
  to skip rope (*US English*), **to skip** (*British
    English*) = saltar a la cuerda, saltar a la
    comba (*Spa*)

• (*to miss*) = saltarse
  to skip a page = saltarse una página

skirt *noun*
  a skirt = una falda, una pollera (*SC*)

sky *noun*
  the sky = el cielo

skyscraper *noun*
  a skyscraper = un rascacielos

slap *verb*
  to slap someone (*on the arm, the leg*) =
    darle una palmada a alguien
  (*in the face*) = darle una bofetada a alguien,
    darle una cachetada a alguien (*Lat Am*)

sled (*US English*), **sledge** (*British
English*)
  a sled = un trineo

sleep
1 *noun*
  sleep = sueño
  to go to sleep = dormirse
2 *verb*
• (*to be asleep*) = dormir
• (*to have sex*)
  to sleep with someone = acostarse con
    alguien

sleeping bag *noun*
  a sleeping bag = un saco de dormir, una
    bolsa de dormir (*R Pl*)

sleepy *adjective*
  to be sleepy, to feel sleepy = tener sueño

sleet *noun*
  sleet = aguanieve (*feminine*)

sleeve *noun*
  a sleeve = una manga

slice
1 *noun*
  a slice (*of bread*) = una rebanada
  (*of meat*) = una tajada
  (*of cheese*) = un trozo, un pedazo
  (*of lemon, cucumber*) = una rodaja
2 *verb*
  to slice bread = cortar pan en rebanadas

slide
1 *verb*
• (*intentionally*) = deslizarse
• (*accidentally*) = resbalarse
  the plates slid off the table = los platos se
    resbalaron y cayeron al suelo
2 *noun*
• (*an image*)
  a slide = una diapositiva
• (*in a playground*)
  a slide = un tobogán, una rebaladilla (*Mex*)

slightly *adverb*
  = ligeramente

S

slim adjective
= delgado/delgada

slip verb
* (to slide, to fall) = resbalarse
 it just slipped out of my hands = se me resbaló de las manos
* (to go quietly)
 he slipped out of the room = salió de la habitación sin que lo vieran

slipper noun
 a slipper = una zapatilla, una pantufla (Lat Am)

slippery adjective
= resbaladizo/resbaladiza

slow adjective
* (not fast) = lento/lenta
* (if it's a clock or watch) = atrasado/atrasada
 the clock is 20 minutes slow = el reloj está 20 minutos atrasado

slowly adverb
= lentamente, despacio

sly adjective
= astuto/astuta

small adjective
= pequeño/pequeña, chico/chica (Lat Am)

smart adjective
* (clever) = listo/lista
* (British English—elegant) = elegante

smash verb
 (to break) = romper
smash up = destrozar

smell
1 noun
* (an odor)
 a smell = un olor
* **the sense of smell** = el olfato
2 verb = oler
 to smell of soap = oler a jabón

smelly adjective
 to be smelly = oler mal

smile
1 verb = sonreír
 to smile at someone = sonreírle a alguien
2 noun
 a smile = una sonrisa

smoke
1 noun
 smoke = humo (masculine)
2 verb = fumar

smooth adjective
 (if it's cloth, stone) = liso/lisa
 (if it's skin) = suave

snack noun
 a snack = un tentempié

snail noun
 a snail = un caracol

snake noun
 a snake = una serpiente

sneaker noun (US English)
 a sneaker = una zapatilla de deporte, un tenis

sneeze verb
= estornudar

snore verb
= roncar

snow
1 noun
 snow = nieve (feminine)
2 verb = nevar

snowball noun
 a snowball = una bola de nieve

snowflake noun
 a snowflake = un copo de nieve

snowman noun
 a snowman = un muñeco de nieve

so
1 adverb
 he's so happy = está tan contento
 they speak so fast = hablan tan rápido
 he worries so much = se preocupa tanto
 she has so many clothes = tiene tanta ropa
 I've so much work to do = tengo tanto trabajo que hacer
* (also)
 I'm fifteen and so is he = tengo quince años y él también
 if you go, so will I = si vas tú, voy yo también
* (other uses)
 I think so = creo que sí
 I'm afraid so = me temo que sí
 I told you so = te lo dije
 so what? = ¿y qué?
 and so on = etcétera
2 conjunction
* **so that** = para que
 be quiet so that I can work = cállate para que yo pueda trabajar

 ! Note the use of the subjunctive after para que

* **so as** = para
 we left early so as not to miss the train = salimos temprano para no perder el tren
* (therefore) = así que, de manera que
 he wasn't at home so I called again = no estaba en casa, así que volví a llamar más tarde, no estaba en casa, de manera que volví a llamar más tarde

soap noun
 soap = jabón (masculine)

soccer noun ▶ p. 306
  soccer = fútbol (*masculine*), futbol
  (*masculine*) (*Mex*)

social adjective
  = social

sock noun
  a sock = un calcetín

sofa noun
  a sofa = un sofá

soft adjective
• (*not hard or tough*) = blando/blanda
• (*not harsh or severe*) = suave
  a soft light = una luz suave
• (*not strict*) = blando/blanda, indulgente

soft drink noun
  a soft drink = un refresco

software noun
  software = software (*masculine*)

soil noun
  soil = tierra (*feminine*)

soldier noun
  a soldier = un/una soldado

sole noun
• (*of the foot*)
  the sole = la planta
• (*of a shoe*)
  a sole = una suela

solicitor noun (*British English*)
  a solicitor = un abogado/una abogada

solution noun
  a solution = una solución

solve verb
  to solve a problem = solucionar un
    problema
  to solve a mystery = resolver un misterio

some
1 adjective
• (*an amount or a number of*)
  I have to buy some bread = tengo que
    comprar pan
  have some water = toma un poco de agua
  we bought some beer = compramos
    cerveza
  she ate some strawberries = comió unas
    fresas
• (*certain*) = algunos/algunas
  some people don't like traveling by plane
    = a algunas personas no les gusta viajar
    en avión
2 pronoun
• (*an amount or number*)
  I need some nails—I know where you can
    find some = necesito unos clavos—yo sé
    dónde puedes encontrar algunos
  have some more = toma más

• (*certain people or things*) =
    algunos/algunas
  some are very expensive = algunos son
    muy caros
  some (of them) are Italian = algunos son
    italianos

somebody, **someone** pronoun
  = alguien

something pronoun
  = algo

sometimes adverb
  = a veces

somewhere adverb
  to go somewhere else = ir a otro lado
  I saw your pen somewhere = vi tu pluma
    en algún lado

son noun
  a son = un hijo

song noun
  a song = una canción

son-in-law noun
  a son-in-law = un yerno

soon adverb
  = pronto
  see you soon! = ¡hasta pronto!
  the sooner the better = cuanto antes mejor
  as soon as possible = lo más pronto
    posible, lo antes posible

sore adjective
  = dolorido/dolorida
  my legs are sore = tengo las piernas
    doloridas
  she has a sore throat = le duele la garganta

sorry
1 exclamation
• (*when apologizing*)
  sorry! = ¡lo siento!, ¡perdón!
• (*when asking someone to repeat*)
  sorry? = ¿cómo?
2 adjective
• (*when apologizing*)
  I'm sorry I'm late = siento llegar tarde
  to say sorry = pedir perdón
• (*when expressing regret*)
  I'm sorry you can't come = siento que no
    puedas venir

  ❗ *Note the use of the subjunctive after*
  sentir que

• (*to feel pity for*)
  I feel sorry for them = los compadezco

sort
1 noun
  a sort = un tipo
  it's a sort of bird = es un tipo de pájaro

S

2 *verb*
to sort the papers = ordenar los documentos
to sort the books into piles = separar los libros en montones
sort out
* (*to solve*) = solucionar
* (*to organize*) = ordenar
* (*to pick out*)
to sort out the old clothes from the new = separar la ropa vieja de la nueva

sound
1 *noun*
* (*a noise*)
a sound = un ruido
* (*of an instrument, a bell*)
a sound = un sonido
I heard the sound of voices = oí unas voces
* (*of a radio, a television*)
the sound = el sonido
2 *verb*
it sounds interesting = suena interesante
it sounds like a piano = suena como un piano

soup *noun*
a soup = una sopa

sour *adjective*
= agrio/agria

south
1 *noun*
the south = el sur
in the south of France = en el sur de Francia
2 *adverb*
we went south = fuimos hacia el sur
it is south of Newark = está al sur de Newark
3 *adjective*
= sur (**!** *never changes*)
the south coast = la costa sur
the south wind = el viento del sur

South Africa *noun* ▶ **p. 187**
South Africa = Sudáfrica (*feminine*)

southeast *noun*
the southeast = el sureste

southwest *noun*
the southwest = el suroeste

souvenir *noun*
a souvenir = un recuerdo

space *noun*
* (*room*)
space = espacio (*masculine*), lugar (*masculine*), sitio (*masculine*)
* (*outer space*)
space = espacio (*masculine*)
* (*a gap*)
a space = un espacio

spade *noun*
a spade = una pala

Spain *noun* ▶ **p. 187**
Spain = España (*feminine*)

Spaniard *noun* ▶ **p. 187**
a Spaniard = un español/una española

Spanish ▶ **p. 187, p. 245**
1 *adjective* = español/española
2 *noun*
* (*the language*)
Spanish = español (*masculine*), castellano (*masculine*)
* (*the people*)
the Spanish = los españoles

spare
1 *adjective*
* (*extra*) = de más
to have a spare key = tener una llave de más
I've got a spare ticket = tengo un boleto de más
spare time = tiempo libre
2 *verb*
* to have money to spare = tener dinero de sobra
* (*from a bad experience*)
you can spare me the details = te puedes ahorrar los detalles

spare room *noun*
a spare room = un cuarto de huéspedes

speak *verb*
= hablar
who's speaking, please? (*on the phone*) = ¿quién habla?
speak up = hablar más fuerte

special *adjective*
= especial

specialty (*US English*), **speciality** (*British English*) *noun*
a specialty = una especialidad

spectator *noun*
a spectator = un espectador/una espectadora

speech *noun*
a speech = un discurso

speed
1 *noun*
speed = velocidad (*feminine*)
2 *verb*
* (*to travel fast*)
to speed away = alejarse a toda velocidad
* (*to drive too fast*) = ir a exceso de velocidad
speed up = acelerar

speed limit *noun*
a speed limit = una velocidad máxima, un límite de velocidad

spell *verb*
* (*when speaking*) = deletrear
* (*when writing*) = escribir
  how do you spell it? = ¿cómo se escribe?

spelling *noun*
  spelling = ortografía (*feminine*)

spend *verb*
* (*to pay money*) = gastar
* (*to pass*)
  to spend time reading = pasar el tiempo
  leyendo

spider *noun*
  a spider = una araña

spill *verb*
  = derramar
  the milk spilled everywhere = la leche se
  derramó por todas partes

spinach *noun*
  spinach = espinacas (*feminine plural*)

spine *noun* ▶ **p. 235**
  the spine = la columna vertebral

spit *verb*
  = escupir

spite: in spite of *preposition*
  = a pesar de
  we went out in spite of the weather =
  salimos a pesar del tiempo

spiteful *adjective*
* (*mean*)
  a spiteful person = una persona mala
  a spiteful comment = un comentario
  malicioso
* (*resentful*) = rencoroso/rencorosa

spoil *verb*
* (*to ruin*) = arruinar, estropear
* (*as a parent*) = mimar, malcriar

sponge *noun*
  a sponge = una esponja

sponge cake *noun*
  a sponge cake = un bizcocho, un
  bizcochuelo (*SC*)

spoon *noun*
  a spoon = una cuchara

sport *noun* ▶ **p. 306**
  a sport = un deporte

sports center (*US English*), **sports centre** (*British English*) *noun*
  a sports center = un centro deportivo

spot
1 *noun*
* (*on an animal*)
  a spot = una mancha
* (*British English—pimple*)
  a spot = un grano, una espinilla (*Lat Am*)
* (*a place*)
  a spot = un lugar, un sitio
  I had to decide on the spot = tuve que
  decidir en ese mismo momento
2 *verb* = ver, divisar
  he spotted her in the crowd = la vio entre
  el gentío, la divisó entre el gentío
  to spot a mistake = descubrir un error

sprain *verb*
  to sprain one's ankle = hacerse un
  esguince en el tobillo

spring *noun*
  spring = primavera (*feminine*)
  in spring = en primavera

spy
1 *noun*
  a spy = un/una espía
2 *verb*
  to spy on someone = espiar a alguien

square
1 *noun*
* (*the shape*)
  a square = un cuadrado
* (*in a town*)
  a square = una plaza
2 *adjective* = cuadrado/cuadrada

squash
1 *noun*
* (*the sport*) ▶ **p. 306**
  squash = squash (*masculine*)
* (*British English—a drink*)
  orange squash = naranjada (*feminine*)
2 *verb* = aplastar

squeak *verb*
  (*of an animal*) = chillar
  (*of a door*) = chirriar
  (*of a shoe*) = crujir

squeeze *verb*
  to squeeze a lemon = exprimir un limón
  he squeezed her hand = le apretó la mano

squirrel *noun*
  a squirrel = una ardilla

stable *noun*
  a stable = una caballeriza

stadium *noun*
  a stadium = un estadio

staff *noun*
  the staff (*of a company*) = el personal
  (*of a school, college*) = el personal docente

stage *noun*
* (*a phase*)
  a stage = una etapa
* (*in a theater*)
  a stage = un escenario

S

Sports and games

Spanish normally uses the definite article with names of sports and games:

football	= **el** fútbol
bridge	= **el** bridge
chess	= **el** ajedrez

Names of games and sports follow the same pattern as **chess** in the following phrases:

to play chess	= jugar ajedrez, jugar al ajedrez (*RPI, Spa*)
he beat me at chess	= me ganó al ajedrez
to win at chess	= ganar al ajedrez
she's good at chess	= juega bien ajedrez, juega bien al ajedrez (*RPI, Spa*)

Players and events

| a chess player | = un jugador ajedrez |

but

| I'm not a chess player | = no juego ajedrez, no juego al ajedrez (*RPI, Spa*) |

| a chess champion | = un campeón de ajedrez |
| a chess championship | = un campeonato de ajedrez |

| a game of chess | = una partida de ajedrez, un partido de ajedrez (*Lat Am*) |

but

| a game of football | = un partido de fútbol |

---

stain
1 *noun*
 a stain = una mancha
2 *verb* = manchar

stairs *noun*
 the stairs = la escalera

stamp *noun*
• (*for an envelope*)
 a stamp = un sello, una estampilla (*Lat Am*), un timbre (*Mex*)
• (*on a document, a passport*)
 a stamp = un sello

stand *verb*
• **to be standing** = estar de pie, estar parado/parada (*Lat Am*)
• (*to step*)
 to stand on a nail = pisar un clavo
• (*to bear*)
 I can't stand German = no soporto el alemán
 I can't stand him = no lo aguanto, no lo soporto
stand back = apartarse
stand for = significar
 what does SA stand for? = ¿qué significa SA?
stand out = destacarse
stand up
 to stand up = ponerse de pie, levantarse, pararse (*Lat Am*)
stand up for = defender
 to stand up for oneself = defenderse

star *noun*
• (*in space*)
 a star = una estrella
• (*a famous person*)
 a star = una estrella

stare *verb*
 to stare at someone = mirar fijamente a alguien

start
1 *verb*
• (*to begin*) = empezar, comenzar
 to start work, to start working = empezar a trabajar, comenzar a trabajar
• (*to set up*)
 to start a business = abrir un negocio
• (*to begin working*)
 the car won't start = el coche no arranca
• (*to put into action*)
 to start a car = arrancar un coche
 to start a machine = hacer funcionar una máquina
2 *noun*
 a start = un comienzo
 at the start of the week = al principio de la semana
start off = empezar
 to start off by painting the walls = empezar por pintar las paredes
start over (*US English*) = volver a empezar

state *noun*
• (*a territory*)
 a state = un estado
• (*a government*)
 the State = el Estado
• (*the condition something or someone is in*)
 a state = un estado
 to be in a bad state (of repair) = estar en mal estado

---

statement *noun*
  a statement = una declaración

station *noun*
• (*for trains*)
  a station = una estación
• (*a channel*)
  a station (*on radio*) = una emisora, una
    estación (*Lat Am*)
  (*on TV*) = un canal

stationery *noun*
  stationery = artículos de papelería
    (*masculine plural*)

statue *noun*
  a statue = una estatua

stay
1 *verb* = quedarse
  we stayed there for a week = nos
    quedamos allí una semana
  to stay with friends = quedarse con amigos
2 *noun*
  a stay = una estadía (*Lat Am*), una estancia
    (*Mex, Spa*)
stay in = quedarse en casa
stay out
  to stay out late = volver tarde
stay up = quedarse levantado/levantada

steady *adjective*
• (*continuous*) = constante
• (*not likely to move*) = firme

steak *noun*
  a steak = un bistec, un filete, un churrasco
    (*S Am*), un bife (*R Pl*)

steal *verb*
  = robar
  to steal money from someone = robarle
    dinero a alguien

steam *noun*
  steam = vapor (*masculine*)
steam up = empañarse

steel *noun*
  steel = acero (*masculine*)

steep *adjective*
  = empinado/empinada

steering wheel *noun*
  a steering wheel = un volante

step
1 *noun*
• (*when walking*)
  a step = un paso
  to take a step = dar un paso
• (*in stairs, at a door*)
  a step = un escalón
• (*in a series of actions*)
  to take steps = tomar medidas
2 *verb*
  to step in a puddle = pisar un charco
step aside = hacerse a un lado

stepbrother *noun*
  a stepbrother = un hermanastro

stepfather *noun*
  a stepfather = un padrastro

stepmother *noun*
  a stepmother = una madrastra

stepsister *noun*
  a stepsister = una hermanastra

stereo *noun*
  a stereo = un estéreo

stewardess *noun*
  a stewardess = una azafata, una aeromoza
    (*Lat Am*)

stick
1 *verb*
• (*using glue or tape*) = pegar
• (*to become attached*) = pegar
• (*to get blocked*)
  the door is stuck = la puerta está atascada
2 *noun*
• (*a piece of wood*)
  a stick = un palo
• (*for walking*)
  a stick = un bastón
stick out = sobresalir
  his ears stick out = tiene las orejas salidas

stiff *adjective*
• (*not soft, not supple*)
  a stiff material = una tela tiesa
  to have stiff legs (*after sport, walking*) =
    tener las piernas entumecidas
• (*not easy to use*)
  to be stiff (*if it's a door, a drawer*) = ser
    difícil de abrir

still[1] *adverb*
  = todavía, aún

still[2]
1 *adverb*
  to sit/stand still = quedarse
    tranquilo/tranquila
2 *adjective*
  the lake was still = el lago estaba en calma

sting *verb*
  = picar

stir *verb*
  = revolver, remover (*Spa*)

stomach *noun* ▶ **p. 235**
  the stomach = el estómago

stomachache *noun*
  stomachache = dolor de estómago
    (*masculine*)

stone *noun*
  a stone = una piedra

stop
1 *verb*

S

- (*to put an end to*)
  to stop smoking = dejar de fumar
  stop it! = ¡basta ya!
- (*to prevent*)
  to stop someone from leaving = impedir
  que alguien se vaya

  ! *Note the use of the subjunctive after*
  impedir que

- (*to cease moving*) = parar
  the bus didn't stop = el autobús no paró
- (*to cease, to stop operating*)
  it's stopped raining = ha dejado de llover
  the clock stopped = el reloj se paró
2 *noun*
  a (bus) stop = una parada, un paradero
  (*Lat Am*)

store *noun*
  a store = una tienda

storekeeper *noun* (*US English*)
  a storekeeper = un/una comerciante

storey *noun* (*British English*)
  a storey = un piso, una planta

storm *noun*
  a storm = una tormenta

story[1] *noun*
- **a story** = una historia
- (*in a newspaper*)
  a story = un artículo
- (*a rumor*)
  a story = un rumor

story[2] *noun* (*US English*)
  a story = un piso, una planta

straight
1 *adjective*
- (*not curved*) = recto/recta
  a straight line = una línea recta
- (*not curly*) = liso/lisa
- (*in the right position*)
  the picture isn't straight = el cuadro no está
  derecho, el cuadro está chueco (*Lat Am*)
- (*honest*)
  a straight question = una pregunta directa
2 *adverb*
- (*erect*) = derecho
  sit up straight = ponte derecho
- (*without delay*) = directamente

strange *adjective*
- (*odd*) = raro/rara, extraño/extraña
  **it's strange that she doesn't come here
  any more** = es raro que no venga más por
  aquí

  ! *Note the use of the subjunctive after* es
  raro que

- (*which or whom one doesn't know*) =
  desconocido/desconocida

stranger *noun*
  a stranger (*a person one hasn't met before*)
  = un desconocido/una desconocida

(*from another place*) = un forastero/una
  forastera

straw *noun*
- (*for feeding animals*)
  straw = paja (*feminine*)
- (*for drinking through*)
  a straw = una pajita, una paja, un popote
  (*Mex*), una caña (*Spa*)

strawberry *noun*
  a strawberry = una fresa, una frutilla (*SC*)

stream *noun*
  a stream = un riachuelo, un arroyo

street *noun*
  a street = una calle

streetlamp *noun*
  a streetlamp = un farol, una farola (*Spa*)

strength *noun*
  strength = fuerza (*feminine*)

stress *noun*
  stress = estrés (*masculine*), tensión
  (*feminine*)

stretch *verb*
  = estirar
  to stretch one's legs (*by walking*) = estirar
  las piernas

strict *adjective*
  = estricto/estricta

strike *noun*
  a strike = una huelga, un paro (*Lat Am*)
  to go on strike = ir a la huelga, ir al paro
  (*Lat Am*)

string *noun*
  string = cordel (*masculine*), bramante
  (*masculine*) (*Spa*), mecate (*masculine*)
  (*Mex*), piolín (*masculine*) (*R Pl*)

striped *adjective*
  = rayado/rayada

stroke *verb*
  = acariciar

stroller *noun* (*US English*)
  a stroller = una sillita de paseo, una
  carreola (*Mex*), un changuito® (*R Pl*)

strong *adjective*
- (*having physical, mental strength*) = fuerte
- (*not easily damaged*) = fuerte, resistente
- (*having force, power*) = fuerte
  a strong wind = un viento fuerte
  strong coffee = café fuerte, café cargado
- (*obvious, noticeable*)
  a strong Spanish accent = un acento
  español muy marcado
  a strong smell of garlic = un fuerte olor a
  ajo

stubborn *adjective*
  = terco/terca

student *noun*
a student (*at university*) = un/una
  estudiante
(*at school*) = un alumno/una alumna

study
1 *verb* = estudiar
to study to be a teacher = estudiar
  docencia
2 *noun*
a study = un estudio

stuff
1 *noun*
• stuff (*things, belongings*) = cosas (*feminine plural*)
2 *verb*
(*to put*) = poner
she stuffed her clothes in the drawer =
  puso la ropa en el cajón

stuffing *noun*
stuffing = relleno (*masculine*)

stupid *adjective*
= tonto/tonta

style *noun*
• (*a way of dressing, behaving*)
  a style = un estilo
  to have style = tener estilo
• (*a design, a type*)
  a style = un diseño
• (*a fashion*)
  a style = una moda

stylish *adjective*
= elegante

subject *noun*
• (*of a conversation*)
  a subject = un tema
  to change the subject = cambiar de tema
• (*being studied*)
  a subject (*at school, college*) = una
   asignatura, una materia (*Lat Am*)
  (*for an essay, a report*) = un tema

suburb *noun*
a suburb = un barrio residencial de las
  afueras, una colonia (*Mex*)

subway *noun*
• (*US English—the rail system*)
  the subway = el metro, el subterráneo
  (*R Pl*)
• (*British English—an underground passage*)
  a subway = un paso subterráneo

succeed *verb*
to succeed in doing something = lograr
  hacer algo

success *noun*
success = éxito (*masculine*)

successful *adjective*
to be successful = tener éxito

such
1 *adjective*
there's no such thing as ghosts = no
  existen los fantasmas
I said no such thing! = ¡yo no dije tal cosa!
2 *adverb*
they have such a lot of money = tienen
  tanto dinero
I've never seen such a mess = nunca vi
  semejante desorden

suddenly *adverb*
= de repente, de golpe

suffer *verb*
= sufrir
to suffer from headaches = sufrir de
  dolores de cabeza

sugar *noun*
sugar = azúcar (*masculine or feminine*)

suggest *verb*
= sugerir

suggestion *noun*
a suggestion = una sugerencia

suit
1 *noun*
a suit = un traje
2 *verb*
• (*to be convenient*) = convenirle a
  does Friday suit you? = ¿le conviene el
   viernes?
• (*to look well on*)
  the hat suits you = el sombrero te queda
   bien

suitable *adjective*
= apropiado/apropiada

suitcase *noun*
a suitcase = una maleta, una petaca (*Mex*),
  una valija (*R Pl*)

sum *noun*
• (*an amount*)
  a sum of money = una cantidad de dinero
• (*in arithmetic*)
  a sum = una suma
sum up = resumir

summer *noun*
summer = verano (*masculine*)
in summer = en (el) verano

sun *noun*
the sun = el sol

sunbathe *verb*
= tomar el sol, asolearse (*Lat Am*)

sunburned, sunburnt *adjective*
to get sunburned = quemarse

Sunday *noun* ▶ p. 192
Sunday = domingo (*masculine*)

S

sunglasses *noun*
  sunglasses = gafas de sol (*feminine plural*),
  lentes de sol (*masculine plural*) (*Lat Am*),
  anteojos de sol (*masculine plural*)
  (*Lat Am*)

sunny *adjective*
  a sunny day = un día de sol
  it's going to be sunny = va a hacer sol

sunrise *noun*
  sunrise = salida del sol (*feminine*)

sunset *noun*
  sunset = puesta de(l) sol (*feminine*)

sunshine *noun*
  sunshine = sol (*masculine*)

suntan *noun*
  a suntan = un bronceado
  to get a suntan = broncearse

supermarket *noun*
  a supermarket = un supermercado

superstitious *adjective*
  = supersticioso/supersticiosa

supper *noun*
  a supper = una cena, una comida (*Lat Am*)

support *verb*
• (*to back*) = apoyar
• (*to hold, to help physically*)
  the roof is supported by these columns =
  el tejado se apoya en estas columnas

supporter *noun*
  a supporter (*of a team*) = un/una hincha
  (*of a party*) = un partidario/una partidaria

suppose *verb*
• (*to imagine*) = suponer, imaginarse
  I suppose so = supongo que sí, me
  imagino que sí
• (*to be meant to*)
  we're supposed to start at 8 o'clock = se
  supone que tenemos que empezar a las
  ocho

sure *adjective*
• (*certain*) = seguro/segura
  I'm sure he said 9 o'clock = estoy segura de
  que dijo las nueve
  are you sure? = ¿estás seguro?
  to make sure that the door is closed =
  asegurarse de que la puerta esté cerrada
• (*bound*)
  he's sure to win = seguro que va a ganar
• **to be sure of oneself** = estar seguro/ segura
  de sí mismo/misma

surf *verb*
  = hacer surf

surface *noun*
  a surface = una superficie

surgeon *noun*
  a surgeon = un cirujano/una cirujana

surgery *noun*
• (*an operation*)
  to have surgery = operarse, someterse a
  una intervención quirúrgica
• (*British English—the place*)
  a surgery = un consultorio, una consulta

surname *noun*
  a surname = un apellido

surprise
1 *noun*
  surprise = sorpresa (*feminine*)
  to take someone by surprise = sorprender
  a alguien
2 *verb* = sorprender

surprised *adjective*
  = sorprendido/sorprendida
  I'm not surprised = no me sorprende

surround *verb*
  = rodear

survey *noun*
  a survey = una encuesta, un sondeo

survive *verb*
  = sobrevivir
  to survive an accident = salir con vida de
  un accidente

suspect *verb*
  = sospechar
  they suspect him of lying = sospechan que
  miente

suspicious *adjective*
• (*mistrustful*) = desconfiado/desconfiada
  to be suspicious of someone = desconfiar
  de alguien
• (*arousing suspicion*) =
  sospechoso/sospechosa

swan *noun*
  a swan = un cisne

swap *verb*
  to swap something for something =
  cambiar algo por algo

sweat
1 *noun*
  sweat = transpiracion (*feminine*), sudor
  (*masculine*)
2 *verb* = transpirar, sudar

sweater *noun*
  a sweater = un suéter, un pulóver, un
  jersey (*Spa*)

Swede *noun* ▶ **p. 187**
  a Swede = un sueco/una sueca

Sweden *noun* ▶ **p. 187**
  Sweden = Suecia (*feminine*)

Swedish ▶ **p. 187, p. 245**
1 *adjective*
  = sueco/sueca

---

2 *noun*
　Swedish = sueco (*masculine*)

sweep *verb*
　= barrer

sweet
1 *adjective*
* (*tasting of sugar*) = dulce,
　azucarado/azucarada
　(*not bitter or dry*) = dulce
　to have a sweet tooth = ser goloso/golosa
* (*if it's a smell*) = agradable
* (*kind, gentle*) = dulce
* (*cute*) = rico/rica
2 *noun* (*British English*)
* (*confectionery*)
　a sweet = un caramelo, un dulce (*Mex*)
* (*a dessert*)
　a sweet = un postre

swim
1 *verb* = nadar
2 *noun*
　to go for a swim = ir a nadar

swimming *noun*
　swimming = natación (*feminine*)

swimming pool *noun*
　a swimming pool = una piscina, una
　alberca (*Mex*), una pileta (*R Pl*)

swimsuit *noun*
　a swimsuit = un traje de baño, un bañador
　(*Spa*), una malla (*R Pl*)

swimming trunks *noun*
　swimming trunks = traje de baño
　(*masculine*), bañador (*masculine*) (*Spa*)

swing
1 *verb*
* (*to move back and forth*) = balancearse
　to swing by one's hands from a tree =
　balancearse colgando de un árbol
* (*to move something back and forth*) =
　balancear
　to swing one's legs = balancear las piernas
2 *noun*
　a swing = un columpio, una hamaca (*R Pl*)

Swiss ▶ p. 187
1 *adjective*
　= suizo/suiza
2 *noun*
　the Swiss = los suizos

switch
1 *noun*
　a switch = un interruptor
2 *verb* = cambiar
　to switch seats = cambiar de asiento
　to switch from English to Spanish = pasar
　del inglés al español
switch off = apagar
switch on = encender, prender (*Lat Am*)

Switzerland *noun* ▶ p. 187
　Switzerland = Suiza (*feminine*)

sympathetic *adjective*
　= comprensivo/comprensiva

symptom *noun*
　a symptom = un síntoma

syringe *noun*
　a syringe = una jeringa, una jeringuilla

system *noun*
　a system = un sistema

Tt

table *noun*
　a table = una mesa

tablet *noun*
　a tablet = una pastilla, un comprimido

table tennis *noun* ▶ p. 306
　table tennis = ping-pong (*masculine*), tenis
　de mesa (*masculine*)

tackle *verb*
* (*in soccer*) = entrarle a
* (*in American football, rugby*) = placar

tactful *adjective*
　= diplomático/diplomática

tail *noun*
　a tail (*of a horse, a fish, a bird*) = una cola
　(*of a dog, a pig*) = un rabo

take *verb*
* (*to take hold of*) = tomar, agarrar (*Lat Am*)
　to take someone by the hand = tomar a
　alguien de la mano, agarrar a alguien de
　la mano
* (*to carry with one*) = llevar
　I'll take the letters to Jack = yo le llevo las
　cartas a Jack
* (*to accompany, to bring*) = llevar
　to take someone home = llevar a alguien a
　casa
* (*to remove*)
　to take a book off the shelf = tomar un
　libro del estante
* (*to cope with, to bear*) = aguantar
　I can't take any more = no aguanto más
* (*when talking about what is necessary*)
　it takes [time | courage | patience ...] = hace
　falta [tiempo | valentía | paciencia ...]
　it takes two hours to get to London = se
　tarda dos horas en llegar a Londres
* (*to accept*) = aceptar
　we don't take checks = no aceptamos
　cheques

- (*to react to*)
  she took it the wrong way = se lo tomó a mal
- **take the first turn on the right** = tome la primera a la derecha
- **to take an exam** = hacer un examen, examinarse (*Spa*), dar un examen (*SC*)
- (*to wear*)
  to take a size 10 (*in clothes*) = usar la talla 14, usar el talle 14 (*R Pl*)
  to take a size 5 (*in shoes*) = calzar un número 5
- (*if it's a medicine or drugs*) = tomar
  I don't take sugar in my coffee = no le pongo azúcar al café

take apart = desmontar, desarmar
take away
  (*to carry or lead away*) = llevarse
take back = devolver, regresar (*Mex*)
take down
  (*to remove*)
  to take down a poster = quitar un cartel
take off
- (*from an airport*) = despegar
- (*to remove*)
  to take off one's clothes = quitarse la ropa
  I took off my shoes = me quité los zapatos
take out
- (*from a box, a pocket, a bag*) = sacar
- (*from a bank account*) = sacar, retirar
take part = participar
  to take part in something = participar en algo, tomar parte en algo
take place = tener lugar
take up
  to take up time = llevar tiempo
  to take up space = ocupar espacio

talented *adjective*
= talentoso/talentosa

talk
1 *verb*
- (*to speak*) = hablar
  to talk to someone = hablar con alguien
  they were talking about you = estaban hablando de ti
  to talk to oneself = hablar solo/sola
- (*to chat*) = hablar, platicar (*Mex*)
2 *noun*
- (*a conversation*)
  a talk = una conversación, una plática (*Mex*)
- (*about a special subject*)
  a talk = una charla, una plática

talkative *adjective*
= hablador/habladora

tall *adjective*
= alto/alta
  how tall is he? = ¿cuánto mide?
  he's 2 meters tall = mide dos metros

tame *adjective*
- (*by nature*) = manso/mansa
- (*domesticated*) = domado/domada

tan *noun*
  a tan = un bronceado
  to get a tan = broncearse

tank *noun*
- (*in a car, for water*)
  a tank = un tanque
- (*vehicle*)
  a tank = un tanque

tanned *adjective*
= bronceado/bronceada

tap
1 *noun* (*British English*)
  a tap = una llave, una canilla (*R Pl*), un grifo (*Spa*)
2 *verb*
  to tap on the door = dar un golpecito en la puerta

tape
1 *noun*
- (*for a tape recorder, a video*)
  a tape = una cinta
- (*for repairs, sticking*)
  tape = cinta adhesiva (*feminine*)
2 *verb* = grabar

tape measure *noun*
  a tape measure = una cinta métrica

tape recorder *noun*
  a tape recorder = un grabador, una grabadora

target *noun*
  a target = un blanco, un objetivo

task *noun*
  a task = una tarea

taste
1 *noun*
- (*when eating, drinking*)
  a taste = un sabor, un gusto
- (*when talking about preferences*)
  taste = gusto (*masculine*)
2 *verb*
- (*when describing a flavor*)
  it tastes bitter = tiene un sabor amargo
  it tastes like cabbage = sabe a repollo
- (*to try*) = probar

Taurus *noun*
- (*the sign*)
  Taurus = Tauro
  I'm Taurus = soy Tauro, soy de Tauro
- (*a person*)
  a Taurus = un/una tauro

tax *noun*
  a tax = un impuesto

taxi *noun*
  a taxi = un taxi

tea *noun*
- *(the product)*
  tea = té
- *(a cup of tea)*
  a tea = un té
- *(British English—a meal)*
  tea *(in the afternoon)* = té *(masculine)*
  (in the evening) = cena *(feminine)*, comida
  (feminine) *(Lat Am)*

teach *verb*
- *(to help someone to learn skills)*
  to teach someone (how) to read =
  enseñarle a leer a alguien
- *(to work as a teacher)* = enseñar

teacher *noun*
  a teacher *(in a primary school)* = un
  maestro/una maestra
  (in a secondary school) = un profesor/una
  profesora

team *noun*
  a team = un equipo

teapot *noun*
  a teapot = una tetera

tear[1] *verb*
- *(to cause damage to)*
  to tear a piece of paper = romper un papel
  to tear a page out of a book = arrancar una
  página de un libro
- *(to become damaged)* = romperse
  tear off = arrancar
  tear up = romper

tear[2] *noun*
(when crying)
  a tear = una lágrima

tease *verb*
  to tease someone = tomarle el pelo a
  alguien

teaspoon *noun*
  a teaspoon = una cucharita

technical *adjective*
  = técnico/técnica

teenager *noun*
  a teenager = un/una adolescente

telegram *noun*
  a telegram = un telegrama

telephone *noun*
  a telephone = un teléfono

telephone call *noun*
  a telephone call = una llamada (telefónica)

telephone directory *noun*
  a telephone directory = una guía
  telefónica, un directorio *(Lat Am)*

telescope *noun*
  a telescope = un telescopio

television *noun*
  a television = un televisor
  I saw it on television = lo vi en la televisión

tell *verb*
- *(to say to)* = decir
  tell me the truth = dime la verdad
- *(to recount, to relate)* = contar
  to tell a joke = contar un chiste
- *(when giving instructions)*
  to tell someone to do something = decirle
  a alguien que haga algo

  > **!** Note the use of the subjunctive after
  > decirle a alguien que

- *(to work out, to know)*
  I can tell (that) she's annoyed = sé que está
  enojada
- *(when making distinctions)*
  to tell the difference = notar la diferencia
  to tell which is which = distinguir cuál es
  cuál
- *(to reveal)*
  don't tell anyone = no le cuentes a nadie
  tell off = regañar, reñir *(Spa)*, retar *(SC)*

temper *noun*
  to be in a temper = estar furioso/furiosa
  to lose one's temper = perder los estribos

temperature *noun*
  a temperature = una temperatura
  to have a temperature = tener fiebre, tener
  calentura, tener temperatura *(SC)*
  to take someone's temperature = tomarle
  la temperatura a alguien

temporary *adjective*
- *(if it's a job)* = eventual, temporal
- *(if it's accommodation)* = temporal,
  temporario/temporaria *(Lat Am)*

ten *number* ▶ **p. 154, p. 319**
  ten = diez *(masculine)* *(**!** never changes)*
  see also **five**

tennis *noun* ▶ **p. 306**
  tennis = tenis

tense *adjective*
  = tenso/tensa

tent *noun*
  a tent = una tienda, una carpa *(Lat Am)*

tenth
1 *adjective*
  = décimo/décima
2 *noun* ▶ **p. 192**
  (a part)
  a tenth = una décima parte

term *noun*
  (at school, university)
  a term = un trimestre

T

terrible adjective
(very bad)
the film is terrible = la película es espantosa
I've got a terrible headache = tengo un
terrible dolor de cabeza

terrified adjective
= aterrorizado/aterrorizada

terror noun
terror = terror (masculine)

test
1 verb
• (to try out) = probar
• (in school, college)
to test the students = hacerles una prueba
a los estudiantes
2 noun
• (of a person or a person's ability)
a test = un test
(in school, college) = una prueba
a driving test = un examen de conducir, un
examen de manejar (Lat Am)
• (for medical reasons)
a blood test = un análisis de sangre
an eye test = un examen de la vista

textbook noun
a textbook = un libro de texto

than
1 preposition
• (in comparisons) = que
he is stronger than me = es más fuerte que
yo
I've got more money than you = tengo más
dinero que tú
• (when talking about quantities) = de
more than half the pupils = más de la
mitad de los alumnos
less than $100 = menos de cien dólares
2 conjunction
he's older than I am = es mayor que yo

thank verb
to thank someone = darle las gracias a
alguien
thank you = gracias

thanks
1 exclamation
thanks! = ¡gracias!
2 noun
thanks to = gracias a

that

> ! See the usage note on **that** for more
> detailed information

1 pronoun
what's that? = ¿qué es eso?
who's that? = ¿quién es él/ella?
is that Joe? = ¿ése es Joe?
that's how they make butter = así es como
se hace la mantequilla
that's not true = eso no es cierto
that's the kitchen = allí está la cocina

2 adjective
= ese/esa
• (if it's more distant or in the remote past) =
aquél/aquella
I know that girl = conozco a esa chica
he didn't go to work that day = no fue a
trabajar aquél día

the definite article

> ! See the usage note on **the** for
> translations

theater (US English), **theatre** (British
English) noun
a theater = un teatro

their adjective
= su (+ singular), sus (+ plural)

> ! For **their** used with parts of the body,
> ▶ p. 235

theirs pronoun
(singular) = suyo/suya
(plural) = suyos/suyas
theirs is blue = el suyo/la suya es azul, el/la
de ellos es azul
a friend of theirs = un amigo suyo, un
amigo de ellos

them pronoun
• (when used as a direct object) = los/las
I know them = los/las conozco
I don't know them = no los/las conozco

> ! Note that **los** and **las** come before the
> verb in Spanish; when talking about
> mixed groups, the masculine form **los** is
> used

• (when used as an indirect object) = les
I never talk to them = nunca les hablo
I wrote them a letter = les escribí una carta

> ! Note that **les** comes before the verb in
> Spanish

• (when used as an indirect object pronoun
together with a direct object pronoun) =
se
I gave it to them = se lo di
I'm not going to say it to them = no se lo
voy a decir

> ! Note that **se** comes before the direct
> object pronoun

• (when telling someone to do something)
catch them! = ¡atrápenlos!/¡atrápenlas!
give them the money = dales el dinero
give it to them = dáselo

> ! Note that **los, las, les,** and **se** come after
> the verb in Spanish

• (when telling someone not to do
something)
don't look at them! = ¡no los/las mires!
don't give them my phone number! = ¡no
les des mi número de teléfono!
don't show it to them! = ¡no se lo muestres!

That

As an adjective **that** is translated by:

    ese + masculine singular noun   **ese** libro
    esa + feminine singular noun   **esa** mesa

Note that the gender and number agree with the noun that follows.

To refer to something more distant or something that occurred in the remote past, the following forms are used:

    aquel + masculine singular noun   **aquel** libro
    aquella + feminine singular noun   **aquella** época

As a pronoun

In Spanish, pronouns reflect the gender and number of the noun that they represent. So **that** meaning *that one* is translated by **ése** or **aquél** for a masculine singular noun, **ésa** or **aquélla** for a feminine singular noun, and **those** is translated by **ésos** or **aquéllos** for a masculine plural noun and by **ésas** or **aquéllas** for a feminine plural noun:

    that is my favorite   **aquélla** es la que más me gusta

When used to mean **who** or **which**, **that** is translated by **que** when it is the subject or direct object:

    *the woman **that** bought them*   la mujer **que** los compró
    *the books **that** I bought*   los libros **que** compré

When followed by a preposition, **that** is translated by **el que** when representing a masculine singular noun, by **la que** when representing a feminine singular noun, by **los que** when representing a masculine plural noun, and by **las que** when representing a feminine plural noun:

    *the chair **that** he was sitting on*   la silla en **la que** estaba sentado
    *the children **that** I bought the books for* los niños para **los que** compré los libros

Where **that** as a pronoun is used to refer to something which is not specified for gender, it is translated by the neuter **eso** or **aquello**, according to context:

    *what's **that**?*   = ¿qué es **eso**?
    *what's **that** over there?*   = ¿qué es **aquello** que se ve allá?

As a conjunction

When used as a conjunction, **that** can always be translated by **que**:

    *he said **that** he would go*   dijo **que** iría

! Note that los, las, les, *and* se *come after the verb in Spanish*

- (*when used after prepositions and with* to be) = ellos/ellas
  we bought it for them = lo compramos para ellos/ellas
  I have nothing against them = no tengo nada en contra de ellos/ellas, no tengo nada en contra suya
  they had their dog with them = tenían el perro consigo
  it's them = son ellos

themselves *pronoun*
- (*when translated by a reflexive verb in Spanish*)
  they didn't hurt themselves = no se hicieron daño, no se lastimaron (*Lat Am*)
  they bought themselves a new car = se compraron un coche nuevo

- (*when used for emphasis*)
  they said it themselves = ellos mismos/ellas mismas lo dijeron
  they did it all by themselves = lo hicieron ellos solos/ellas solas

then *adverb*
- (*at that point in time*)= entonces
  I was living in Germany then = entonces yo vivía en Alemania
- (*after, next*) = después, luego

there
1 *pronoun*
  there is = hay
  there are = hay
  there is a problem = hay un problema
  there are no shops = no hay tiendas
  there was no room = no había lugar
  there will be a lot of people = habrá mucha gente

T

R Pl River Plate area   SC Southern Cone   Spa Spain

The

In Spanish the definite article agrees in gender and number with the noun that follows, so **the** is translated as follows:

el + masculine singular noun	**el** perro
la + feminine singular noun	**la** silla
los + masculine plural noun	**los** papeles
las + feminine plural noun	**las** mujeres

When **el** follows the preposition **de** the two words combine to form one word **del**:

los hijos **del** profesor (*not* los hijos **de el** profesor)

Similarly, when **el** follows the preposition **a** the two words combine to form **al**:

fuimos **al** colegio (*not* fuimos **a el** colegio)

In general, when the definite article is used in English, it is also used in Spanish. There are however important exceptions:

Before the ordinal number in titles of kings, popes, etc

*Elizabeth **the** Second*	= Isabel Segunda
*Henry **the** Eighth*	= Enrique Octavo

There are some occasions where there is no definite article in English but it is needed in Spanish.

There are two main cases of this:

a) with generic and abstract nouns when they are the subject of a sentence:

modesty is a good virtue	= **la** modestia es una buena virtud
silk is very delicate	= **la** seda es muy delicada
international Communism	= **el** comunismo internacional
blue is my favourite color	= **el** azul es mi color favorito

b) with nouns that refer to the members of a group:

children are often very selfish	= **los** niños son a menudo muy egoístas
Brazilians speak Portuguese	= **los** brasileños hablan portugués

---

2 *adverb*
- (*when talking about location*) (*close by*) = ahí
  (*further away*) = allí, ahí (*Lat Am*)
  (*less precise, further*) = allá
  put the books there = pon los libros ahí
  go over there = vete allí
  when do we get there? = ¿cuándo llegamos allá?
- (*when drawing attention*)
  there they are = allí están
  there you are, there you go = toma

therefore *adverb*
= por lo tanto

thermometer *noun*
a thermometer = un termómetro

these
1 *adjective*
= estos/estas
these books aren't mine = estos libros no son míos
2 *pronoun*
= éstos/éstas
what are these? = ¿qué son éstos/éstas?
these are your things = éstas son tus cosas

they *pronoun*
- **they** = ellos/ellas

  ! *When talking about mixed groups the masculine form* **ellos** *is used*

  they went to the theater = fueron al teatro
  they **did it** = ellos/ellas lo hicieron

  ! *Although* **ellos** *and* **ellas** *are given as translations of* **they***, they are in practice used for emphasis, or to avoid ambiguity*

- (*when talking in an impersonal or vague way about people*)
  that's how they make butter = así es como se hace la mantequilla
  they've dug up the road = han levantado la calle

thick *adjective*
- (*if it's a fabric, a book*) = grueso/gruesa
  (*if it's a soup, a sauce*) = espeso/espesa
- (*stupid*) = burro✱/burra✱

thief *noun*
a thief = un ladrón/una ladrona

thigh *noun* ▶ p. 235
the thigh = el muslo

---

thin adjective
• (not thick)
a thin slice of ham = una tajada fina de jamón
a thin sauce = una salsa clara
• (not fat) = delgado/delgada
to get thin = adelgazar

thing noun
• a thing = un cosa
I've got things to do = tengo cosas que hacer
the best thing would be to call = lo mejor sería llamarlo
I can't hear a thing = no oigo nada
• (belongings)
things = cosas (feminine plural)
• (when talking about a situation)
how are things? = ¿qué tal?

think verb
• (when talking about opinions) = pensar, creer
what do you think? = ¿tú qué piensas?
I think it's unfair = pienso que es injusto
will they come?—I don't think so = ¿van a venir?—pienso que no
• (to concentrate on an idea) = pensar
think hard before answering = piénsalo bien antes de contestar
• (to remember)
I can't think of his name = no recuerdo su nombre
• (to take into account, to have in mind)
to think of someone = pensar en alguien
I hadn't thought of that = eso no se me había ocurrido
• (to have vague plans to)
I'm thinking of leaving school = estoy pensando dejar los estudios
• (to have an idea about)
to think of a solution = encontrar una solución

third
1 adjective = tercero/tercera

> ! Note that tercero becomes tercer when it appears before a masculine singular noun

2 noun ▶ p. 192
• (in a series)
the third = el tercero/la tercera
• (a part)
a third = una tercera parte, un tercio
3 adverb = en tercer lugar
to come third = terminar en tercer lugar

thirsty adjective
to be thirsty = tener sed

thirteen number ▶ p. 154, p. 319
thirteen = trece (masculine) (! never changes) see also five

thirty noun ▶ p. 154, p. 319
thirty = treinta (masculine) (! never changes) see also five

this
1 adjective = este/esta
I like this garden = me gusta este jardín
who is this woman? = ¿quién es esta mujer?
2 pronoun = éste/ésta (masculine/feminine), esto (neuter)
this (one) is mine = éste es el mío/ésta es la mía
what's this? = ¿qué es esto?

thorn noun
a thorn = una espina

those
1 adjective = esos/esas
(if it's more distant or in the remote past) = aquellos/aquellas
those keys are Pete's = esas llaves son de Pete
in those times = en aquellos tiempos
2 pronoun = ésos/ésas
(if it's more distant or in the remote past) = aquéllos/aquéllas
those (ones) cost five dollars and those (ones) over there ten dollars = ésos cuestan cinco dólares y aquéllos (de allá) diez dólares
those who have been less fortunate = los que no han tenido tanta suerte

though conjunction
= aunque

thought noun
a thought = un pensamiento

thousand number
one thousand, a thousand = mil
four thousand pounds = cuatro mil libras

thread noun
thread = hilo (masculine)

threat noun
a threat = una amenaza

threaten verb
= amenazar

three number ▶ p. 154, p. 319
three = tres (masculine) (! never changes) see also five

throat noun ▶ p. 235
the throat = la garganta

through preposition

> ! Through is often used in combinations with verbs, for example, get through, go through. To find the correct translations for this type of verb, look up the separate dictionary entries at get, go etc

• (from one side to the other)
to drive through the desert = cruzar el desierto en coche

* (*via, by way of*) = por
  to go through the town center = pasar por
  el centro de la ciudad
  to look through a window = mirar por una
  ventana
* (*past*)
  to go through customs = pasar por la
  aduana
* (*when talking about time*)
  right through the day = todo el día
  from Friday through to Sunday = de
  viernes a domingo
  open April through September (*US
  English*) = abierto/abierta desde abril
  hasta septiembre

throw *verb*
* (*to hurl*)
  to throw a ball = tirar una pelota, aventar
  una pelota (*Mex*)
  she threw stones at him = le tiró piedras, le
  aventó piedras (*Mex*)
  she threw the book on the floor = tiró el
  libro al suelo
* **to throw a party** = dar una fiesta
  throw away, throw out = tirar

thumb *noun* ▶ **p. 235**
  the thumb = el pulgar

thunder *noun*
  thunder = truenos (*masculine plural*)

thunderstorm *noun*
  a thunderstorm = una tormenta eléctrica

Thursday *noun* ▶ **p. 192**
  Thursday = jueves (*masculine*)

ticket *noun*
  a ticket (*for a bus, a train*) = un boleto (*Lat
  Am*), un billete (*Spa*)
  (*for a plane*) = un pasaje
  (*for a theater, a museum*) = una entrada

tickle *verb*
  to tickle someone = hacerle cosquillas a
  alguien

tide *noun*
  the tide = la marea
  the tide is in/out = la marea está alta/baja
  a high/low tide = una marea alta/baja

tidy *adjective*
  = ordenado/ordenada, prolijo/prolija (*R Pl*)
  tidy up = ordenar

tie
1 *verb* = atar, amarrar (*Lat Am*)
  he tied the dog to a tree = ató el perro a un
  árbol, amarró el perro a un árbol
  (*Lat Am*)
  to tie a package (up) with string = atar un
  paquete con cuerda, amarrar un paquete
  con cuerda (*Lat Am*)
2 *noun*
* (*worn with a shirt*)
  a tie = una corbata

* (*in sport*)
  a tie = un empate
  tie up = atar, amarrar (*Lat Am*)

tiger *noun*
  a tiger = un tigre

tight *adjective*
  a tight dress (*fitting closely*) = un vestido
  ajustado
  (*uncomfortable*) = un vestido apretado
  these shoes are too tight = estos zapatos
  me aprietan

tights *noun* (*British English*)
  tights = panty (*masculine*), medias
  (*feminine plural*) (*Spa*), pantimedias
  (*feminine plural*) (*Mex*), medias
  bombacha (*feminine plural*) (*R Pl*)

tile *noun*
  a tile (*on a wall*) = un azulejo
  (*on a floor*) = una baldosa

till[1] ▶ until

till[2] *noun*
  a till = una caja

timber *noun*
  timber = madera (*feminine*)

time *noun* ▶ **p. 319**
* **time** = tiempo (*masculine*)
  we haven't seen them for a long time =
  hace mucho tiempo que no los vemos
* (*when talking about a specific hour or
  period of time*)
  the time = la hora
  to arrive on time = llegar a tiempo
  it's time we left = es hora de irnos
* (*a moment*)
  at times = a veces
  we arrived at the right time = llegamos en
  un buen momento
  for the time being = por el momento, de
  momento
* (*a period in the past*)
  a time = una época
* (*an experience*)
  we had a good time = lo pasamos bien
* (*an occasion*)
  a time = una vez
  several times a day = varias veces al día
  the first time we met = la primera vez que
  nos encontramos
  from time to time = de vez en cuando
* (*when comparing*)
  three times more expensive = tres veces
  más caro

times *preposition*
  three times four is twelve (3 × 4 = 12) =
  tres (multiplicado) por cuatro (son) doce
  (3 × 4 = 12)

timetable *noun*
  a timetable = un horario

C Am Central America   **Lat Am** Latin America   **Mex** Mexico

Time of day

What time is it?

what time is it?	= ¿qué hora es?
can you tell me the time?	= ¿me dice(s) la hora?, ¿me da(s) la hora?
do you have the time?	= ¿tiene(s) hora?

It is ...

it is one o'clock	= es la una
it is three o'clock	= son las tres
it is exactly one o'clock	= es la una en punto
it is exactly three o'clock	= son las tres en punto

Note that **y** is used for times **after** the hour

it is 1:15	= es la una **y** cuarto
it is 6:20	= son las seis **y** veinte
it is 2:30	= son las dos **y** media

For times **before** the hour **para** is used in Latin America (with the exception of the River Plate area) and **menos** is used in Spain and the River Plate. Note the different constructions:

it's 7:45	= son un cuarto **para** las ocho (*Lat Am excluding R Pl*)
	= son las ocho **menos** cuarto (*Spa, R Pl*)
it's 4:50	= son diez **para** las cinco (*Lat Am excluding R Pl*)
	= son las cinco **menos** diez (*Spa, R Pl*)

a.m./p.m.

To specify a.m. or p.m. Spanish adds one of the following:

in the morning	= de la mañana
in the afternoon/evening	= de la tarde
in the evening/at night	= de la noche
in the morning (early hours)	= de la madrugada

De la tarde is used from midday until about 8 p.m. and **de la madrugada** is used for the early hours of the morning, between 2a.m. and 5 a.m.

Midday

twelve o'clock midday	= las doce del mediodía

Note that **el mediodía** refers in Spanish to the hours between 12 and 3 o'clock in the afternoon:

It's one o'clock (p.m.)	= es la una del mediodía

When?

Spanish always uses the word **a**, whether or not English includes the word **at**. The only exception is when there is another preposition present, as in **alrededor de las tres** (about three o'clock), **antes de las tres** (before three o'clock):

what *time did you arrive?*	= ¿**a** qué hora llegaste?	
at *two o'clock*	= **a** las dos	
at about *one o'clock*	= **alrededor de** la una	= **sobre** la una (*Spa*)
Just after *three*	= **a** las tres **y pico**	
it must be ready **by** *five*	= tiene que estar listo **para** las cinco	
it is open **from** *nine* **to** *five*	= está abierto **de** nueve **a** cinco	

The 24-hour clock

This is used a lot more in Spanish than it is in English (in timetables etc):

21:30 (9:30 p.m.)	= las veintiuna treinta
13:15 (1:15 p.m.)	= las trece quince

When the time is on the hour, you add the word **horas**:

17:00 (5 p.m.)	= las diecisiete horas

T

tin *noun*
- (*the metal*)
  tin = estaño (*masculine*)
- (*British English—a can*)
  a tin = una lata, un bote (*Spa*)

tin opener *noun* (*British English*)
  a tin opener = un abrelatas

tiny *adjective*
  = minúsculo/minúscula

tip *noun*
- (*the point, the end*)
  the tip = la punta
- (*given in a hotel, restaurant*)
  a tip = una propina
- (*a piece of advice*)
  a tip = un consejo

tire *noun* (*US English*)
  a tire = un neumático, una llanta (*Lat Am*),
  una goma (*R Pl*)

tired *adjective*
- (*needing rest*) = cansado/cansada
  to get tired = cansarse
- (*needing a change*) = harto/harta
  I'm tired of being a waitress = estoy harta
  de ser camarera

tissue *noun*
  a tissue = un pañuelo de papel

to
1 *preposition*
- (*talking about destination*) = a
  we went to London = fuimos a Londres
  they went to the airport = fueron al
  aeropuerto
  move a little to the right = córrete un poco
  hacia la derecha
- (*talking about position*)
  to the left/right of something = a la
  izquierda/derecha de algo
  to the north of Madrid = al norte de Madrid
- (*as far as, until*) = hasta
  she can count to ten = sabe contar hasta
  diez
  I can't stay to the end = no puedo
  quedarme hasta el final ▶ from
- (*when used with the indirect object*)
  give the book to me = dame el libro
  I gave it to Rachel = se lo di a Rachel
  what did you say to him/them? = ¿qué
  le/les dijiste?
- (*talking about proportion, relation*)
  Barcelona won by two goals to one =
  Barcelona ganó por dos (goles) a uno
  there's a ten to one chance of . . . = hay
  una probabilidad de uno en diez de . . .
- (*indicating a reaction, showing an attitude*)
  to my horror . . . = para mi horror . . .
  to the best of my knowledge = que yo sepa
- (*indicating belonging to*) = de
  the key to the front door = la llave de la
  puerta de la calle

- (*British English—when talking about time*)
  ▶ **p. 319**
  it's ten (minutes) to five = son diez para las
  cinco (*Lat Am*), son las cinco menos diez
  (*R Pl, Spa*)
2 *used in infinitives*
- **to sing/sew/go** = cantar/coser/ir
  it's easy to do = es fácil de hacer
  she had to do it = tuvo que hacerlo
  I tried to phone you = traté de llamarte
  she was the first to arrive = fue la primera
  en llegar
  he has a lot to do = tiene mucho que hacer
- (*in order to*) = para
  I do it to save money = lo hago para
  ahorrar dinero

toast *noun*
  toast = tostadas (*feminine plural*), pan
  tostado (*masculine*)

toaster *noun*
  a toaster = una tostadora

today *adverb*
  = hoy

toe *noun* ▶ **p. 235**
  a toe = un dedo (del pie)

together *adverb*
  = juntos/juntas

toilet *noun*
  a toilet = un baño (*Lat Am*), un servicio
  (*Spa*)

toilet paper *noun*
  toilet paper = papel higiénico

tomato *noun*
  a tomato = un tomate, un jitomate (*Mex*)

tomorrow *noun*
  tomorrow = mañana

tongue *noun* ▶ **p. 235**
  the tongue = la lengua

tonight *adverb*
  = esta noche

too *adverb*
- (*also*) = también
  I'm going too = yo voy también
- (*more than is necessary or desirable*)
  it's too big = es demasiado grande
  there were too many people = había
  demasiada gente
  I ate too much = comí demasiado
- (*very*) = muy
  I'm not too sure = no estoy muy segura

tool *noun*
  a tool = una herramienta

tooth *noun* ▶ **p. 235**
  a tooth = un diente

toothache *noun*
  to have toothache = tener dolor de muela

toothbrush *noun*
  a toothbrush = un cepillo de dientes

toothpaste *noun*
  toothpaste = pasta de dientes (*feminine*)

top
1 *noun*
• (*the highest part*)
  the top of the hill = la cumbre de la colina
  at the top of the stairs = en lo alto de la
    escalera
  at the top of the page = en la parte superior
    de la página
  the socks are on top of the radiator = los
    calcetines están encima del radiador, los
    calcetines están sobre el radiador
• (*a cover, a lid*)
  a top (*on a bottle, a pan*) = una tapa
    (*on a pen*) = el capuchón
• (*the highest level*)
  to be at the top of the class = ser el
    primero/la primera de la clase
2 *adjective* = superior, de arriba
  the top shelf = el estante superior, el
    estante de arriba

torch *noun* (*British English*)
  a torch = una linterna

tortoise *noun*
  a tortoise = una tortuga

total
1 *noun*
  a total = un total
2 *adjective* = total

touch
1 *verb* = tocar
2 *noun*
  [to be | get | stay ...] **in touch with someone** =
    [estar | ponerse | mantenerse ...] en contacto
    con alguien

tough *adjective*
• (*not soft, not sensitive*) = duro/dura
  to be tough with someone = ser duro/dura
    con alguien
• (*difficult*) = difícil
• (*severe*) = severo/severa
  a tough law = una ley severa

tour *noun*
• (*by a team, band, theater group*)
  a tour = una gira
  to be on tour = estar de gira
• (*by tourists, pupils, visitors*)
  a tour = una visita

tourism *noun*
  tourism = turismo (*masculine*)

tourist *noun*
  a tourist = un/una turista

toward(s) *preposition*
• (*when talking about place, time*) = hacia

• (*when talking about attitudes*)
  his attitude toward her = su actitud para
    con ella

towel *noun*
  a towel = una toalla

tower *noun*
  a tower = una torre

town *noun*
  a town = una ciudad
  to go into town = ir a la ciudad

town hall *noun*
  the town hall = el ayuntamiento, la
    intendencia (*Mex*)

toy *noun*
  a toy = un juguete

track *noun*
• (*a path*)
  a track = un sendero
• (*for sports*)
  a track = una pista
• (*the rails*)
  the track(s) = la vía férrea
• (*left by a person, animal, vehicle*)
  a track = una pista, unas huellas

tracksuit *noun*
  a tracksuit = un equipo de deportes, unos
    pants (*Mex*), un chándal (*Spa*), un
    jogging (*R Pl*)

trade *noun*
• (*business*)
  trade = comercio (*masculine*)
• (*a profession*)
  a trade = un oficio

traffic *noun*
  traffic = tráfico (*masculine*), tránsito
    (*masculine*) (*Lat Am*)

traffic circle *noun* (*US English*)
  a traffic circle = una rotonda, una glorieta
    (*Mex, Spa*)

traffic jam *noun*
  a traffic jam = un embotellamiento, un
    atasco

traffic lights *noun*
  the traffic lights = el semáforo

trailer *noun* (*US English*)
  a trailer = una caravana, un rulot (*Esp*),
    una casa rodante (*SC*)

train
1 *noun*
  a train = un tren
2 *verb*
• (*to teach, to prepare*)
  to train an employee = capacitar a un
    empleado/una empleada

T

R Pl River Plate area   **SC** Southern Cone   **Spa** Spain

* (*to learn a job*)
  to train as a doctor/teacher = estudiar medicina/docencia
* (*for a sporting event*) = entrenarse

trainer *noun*
* (*sports coach*)
  a trainer = un entrenador/una entrenadora
* (*British English—sports shoe*)
  a trainer = una zapatilla de deporte, un tenis

tramp *noun*
  a tramp = un vagabundo/una vagabunda

translate *verb*
  = traducir

translator *noun*
  a translator = un traductor/una traductora

transport, transportation (*US English*) *noun*
  transport = transporte (*masculine*)
  a means of transport = un medio de transporte

trap *noun*
  a trap = una trampa

trash *noun* (*US English*)
  trash = basura (*feminine*)

trash can *noun* (*US English*)
  a trash can = un cubo de la basura, un tacho de la basura (*SC*), un bote de la basura (*Mex*)

travel *verb*
  = viajar

travel agency *noun*
  a travel agency = una agencia de viajes

traveler (*US English*), **traveller** (*British English*)
  a traveler = un viajero/una viajera

traveler's check (*US English*), **traveller's cheque** (*British English*) *noun*
  a traveler's check = un cheque de viaje

tray *noun*
  a tray = una bandeja

treat *verb*
* (*to deal with, to behave with*) = tratar
  he treated me badly = me trató mal
* (*to provide medical care for*) = tratar
* (*to pay for*)
  he treated me to lunch = me invitó a almorzar

treatment *noun*
  treatment = tratamiento (*masculine*)

tree *noun*
  a tree = un árbol

tremble *verb*
  = temblar

trial *noun*
  a trial = un proceso

triangle *noun*
  a triangle = un triángulo

trick
1 *noun*
* (*a joke*)
  a trick = una broma
  to play a trick on someone = hacerle una broma a alguien
* (*a means of deceiving*)
  a trick = una trampa
* (*to entertain*)
  a trick = un truco
2 *verb* = engañar

trip
1 *noun*
  a trip (*abroad*) = un viaje
  (*a day out*) = una excursión
2 *verb*
  to trip (**up**) = tropezar
  to trip someone (**up**) = hacerle una zancadilla a alguien

trouble *noun*
* (*difficulties*)
  trouble = problemas (*masculine plural*)
  to be in trouble = estar en apuros
  to get someone into trouble = meter a alguien en problemas
* (*an effort*)
  to take the trouble to do something = molestarse en hacer algo

trousers *noun*
  trousers = pantalones (*masculine plural*)

trout *noun*
  a trout = una trucha

truck *noun* (*US English*)
  a truck = un camión

true *adjective*
  is it true that he's leaving? = ¿es cierto que se va?
  it's a true story = es una historia verídica
  to come true = hacerse realidad

trumpet *noun*
  a trumpet = una trompeta

trunk *noun*
* (*of a tree*)
  a trunk = un tronco
* (*a large case*)
  a trunk = un baúl
* (*of an elephant*)
  a trunk = una trompa
* (*US English—of a car*)
  the trunk = el maletero, la cajuela (*Mex*), el baúl (*R Pl*)

---

trust *verb*
= confiar en
to trust a friend = confiar en un amigo
I don't trust them = no me fío de ellos

truth *noun*
the truth = la verdad

try *verb*
• (*to attempt*) = intentar
to try to understand = intentar entender
• (*to test*) = probar
to try (out) a recipe = probar una receta
to try (on) a pair of trousers = probarse
unos pantalones
• (*to taste*) = probar
• (*in court*) = juzgar

T-shirt *noun*
a T-shirt = una camiseta

tube *noun*
a tube = un tubo

Tuesday *noun* ▶ p. 192
Tuesday = martes (*masculine*)

tuna *noun*
tuna = atún (*masculine*)

tunnel *noun*
a tunnel = un túnel

turkey *noun*
a turkey = un pavo, un guajolote (*Mex*)

Turkey *noun* ▶ p. 187
Turkey = Turquía (*feminine*)

turn
1 *verb*
• (*to move one's body*) = volverse, voltearse
(*Lat Am*), darse vuelta (*SC*)
• (*to change direction*) = doblar
to turn right = doblar a la derecha
to turn the corner = doblar la esquina
• (*to twist*) = girar
to turn the handle = girar la manilla
• (*to become*)
to turn into a butterfly = transformarse en
una mariposa
to turn red = ponerse rojo/roja
2 *noun*
• (*a bend*)
a turn = una curva
• (*a change of direction*)
a turn = una vuelta, un giro
• (*in games*)
whose turn is it? = ¿a quién le toca?
it's my turn = me toca a mí
turn around, turn round (*British English*)
• (*to face the other way*) = darse la vuelta,
volverse, voltearse (*Lat Am*), darse vuelta
(*SC*)
• (*to change the position of*)
to turn the table around = dar la vuelta a la
mesa, voltear la mesa (*Lat Am*), dar
vuelta la mesa (*SC*)

turn back = volver, regresar
turn down
• (*to lower*) = bajar
to turn down the volume = bajar el
volumen
• (*to reject*) = rechazar
turn off = apagar
to turn [the light | the oven | the radio ...] off =
apagar [la luz | el horno | la radio ...]
to turn the faucet/tap off = cerrar la llave
turn on = encender, prender (*Lat Am*)
to turn on the TV = encender el televisor,
prender el televisor
to turn the faucet/tap on = abrir la llave
turn over
• (*to roll over*) = darse la vuelta, voltearse
(*Lat Am*), darse vuelta (*SC*)
• to turn over the page = dar la vuelta a la
página, dar vuelta la página
(*SC*)
turn up
• (*shorten*)
(*if it's trousers*) = acortar
(*if it's a hem*) = subir
• (*to increase*) = subir
to turn up the heating = subir la calefacción
• (*British English—arrive*) = aparecer

turtle *noun*
• a (**sea**) **turtle** = una tortuga marina
• (*US English—a tortoise*)
a turtle = una tortuga

TV *noun*
a TV = un televisor
I saw it on TV = lo vi en la televisión

twelve *number* ▶ p. 154, p. 319
twelve = doce (*masculine*) (**!** *never
changes*) *see also* five

twenty *number* ▶ p. 154, p. 319
twenty = veinte (*masculine*) (**!** *never
changes*) *see also* five

twice *adverb*
= dos veces
twice a week = dos veces por semana
twice as many people = el doble de
gente

twin
1 *noun*
a twin = un mellizo/una melliza, un
gemelo/una gemela (*Spa*)
2 *adjective*
my twin brother = mi hermano mellizo, mi
hermano gemelo (*Spa*)

twist *verb*
• (*to bend out of shape*) = retorcer
• (*to injure*)
to twist one's ankle = torcerse el tobillo
• (*of a road, a river*)
to twist and turn = serpentear

T

two *number* ▶ **p. 154, p. 319**
  two = dos (*masculine*) (**!** *never changes*)
  see also five

type
1 *noun*
  a type = un tipo
  he's not my type = no es mi tipo
2 *verb* = escribir a máquina

typewriter *noun*
  a typewriter = una máquina de escribir

typical *adjective*
  = típico/típica

typist *noun*
  a typist = un mecanógrafo/una
  mecanógrafa

tyre *noun* (*British English*)
  a tyre = un neumático, una llanta (*Lat Am*),
  una goma (*R Pl*)

Uu

ugly *adjective*
  = feo/fea

umbrella *noun*
  an umbrella = un paraguas

unbearable *adjective*
  = insoportable

unbelievable *adjective*
  = increíble

uncle *noun*
  an uncle = un tío

uncomfortable *adjective*
  = incómodo/incómoda

unconscious *adjective*
  = inconsciente

under *preposition*
• under = debajo de, abajo de (*Lat Am*)
  to hide under the bed = eesconderse debajo
  de la cama, esconderse abajo de la cama
• (*below*)
  to go under the bridge = pasar por debajo
  del puente, pasar por abajo del puente
• (*less than*)
  to earn under $3 an hour = ganar menos de
  3 dólares la hora
  children under 5 = los niños menores de
  cinco años

underground
1 *adjective* = suterráneo/suterránea

2 *noun* (*British English*)
  the underground = el metro, el subterráneo
  (*R Pl*)

underline *verb*
  = subrayar

underneath
1 *adverb* = debajo, abajo
2 *preposition* = debajo de, abajo de (*Lat Am*)

underpass *noun*
  an underpass (*for traffic*) = un paso
  inferior
  (*for pedestrians*) = un paso subterráneo

undershirt *noun* (*US English*)
  an undershirt = una camiseta

understand *verb*
  = entender
  to make oneself understood = hacerse
  entender

understanding *adjective*
  = comprensivo/comprensiva

underwater *adjective*
  = submarino/submarina

underwear *noun*
  underwear = ropa interior (*feminine*)

undo *verb*
  (*if it's a button*) = desabrochar
  (*if it's a zipper*) = abrir
  (*if it's a knot or shoelace*) = desatar,
  desamarrar (*R Pl*)

undress *verb*
  = desvestirse

unemployed *adjective*
  = desempleado/desempleada,
  desocupado/desocupada, parado/parada
  (*Spa*)

unemployment *noun*
  unemployment = desempleo (*masculine*),
  desocupación (*feminine*), paro
  (*masculine*) (*Spa*)

unfair *adjective*
  = injusto/injusta

unfortunate *adjective*
  = desafortunado/desafortunada

unfortunately *adverb*
  = desafortunadamente

unfriendly *adjective*
• (*if it's a person*) = antipático/antipática
• (*if it's a place*) = hostil

ungrateful *adjective*
  = desagradecido/desagradecida

unhappy *adjective*
• (*sad*) = triste
• (*not satisfied*) = descontento/descontenta

C Am Central America   Lat Am Latin America   Mex Mexico

unhealthy *adjective*
- (*if it's food*) = malo/mala para la salud
- (*if it's a person*) = de mala salud
- (*if it's conditions*) = poco saludable

uniform *noun*
  a uniform = un uniforme

union *noun*
  a union = un sindicato

unique *adjective*
  = único/única

United Kingdom *noun* ▶ **p. 187**
  the United Kingdom = el Reino Unido

United States (**of America**) *noun*
▶ **p. 187**
  the United States (**of America**) = los
    Estados Unidos

universe *noun*
  the universe = el universo

university *noun*
  a university = una universidad

unkind *adjective*
  (*if it's a person, an action*)
  to be unkind = ser cruel
  an unkind remark = un comentario
    hiriente

unknown *adjective*
  = desconocido/desconocida

unless *conjunction*
  = a no ser que
  he won't come unless you're there = no
    vendrá a no ser que estés tú

  ! *Note that the subjunctive is used after* a
  no ser que

unlock *verb*
  = abrir

unlucky *adjective*
- (*having bad luck*) =
  desafortunado/desafortunada
  you were unlucky = tuviste mala suerte
- (*bringing bad luck*)
  it's unlucky to walk under a ladder = pasar
    debajo de una escalera trae mala suerte

unpack *verb*
  = deshacer las maletas, desempacar (*Lat
    Am*)

unsuccessful *adjective*
  to be unsuccessful in doing something =
    no lograr hacer algo
  the movie was unsuccessful = la película
    fracasó

unsuitable *adjective*
  unsuitable clothing = ropa inapropiada
  he is unsuitable for the job = no es la
    persona indicada para el trabajo

untidy *adjective*
  (*in habits*) = desordenado/desordenada,
    desprolijo/desprolija (*R Pl*)
  (*in appearance*) = descuidado/descuidada,
    desprolijo/desprolija (*R Pl*)
  your room is untidy = tu cuarto está
    desordenado

until
  1 *preposition* = hasta
  2 *conjunction* = hasta que
  we'll stay until they come = nos
    quedaremos hasta que vengan

  ! *Note the use of the subjunctive after*
  hasta que

unusual *adjective*
- (*rare*) = poco común, fuera de lo corriente
  it's unusual to see so few people = es raro
    ver a tan poca gente
- (*different, out of the ordinary*) =
    distintivo/distintiva

up

  ! Up *is often used in combinations with
  verbs, for example,* blow up, give up, sit
  up. *To find the correct translations for this
  type of verb, look up the separate
  dictionary entries at* blow, give, sit *etc*

  1 *preposition*
  to go up the street = subir por la calle
  she ran up the stairs = subió las escaleras
    corriendo
  2 *adverb*
  up in the sky = en el cielo
  to go up = subir
  to go up to Scotland = ir a Escocia
  up there = allí arriba
  put the picture a bit further up = pon el
    cuadro un poco más arriba
  3 *adjective*
- (*out of bed*)
  he's not up yet = no se ha levantado
    todavía
  to be up all night = pasar la noche en vela
- (*wrong*)
  what's up? = ¿qué pasa?
  up to
- (*well enough*)
  to be up to going out = sentirse con fuerzas
    para salir
- (*when talking about who is responsible*)
  it's up to me to decide = me corresponde a
    mí decidir
- (*until*) = hasta

upset
  1 *adjective*
  to be upset (*annoyed*) = estar
    disgustado/disgustada, estar
    molesto/molesta
  (*distressed*) = estar alterado/alterada
  to get upset (*annoyed*) = disgustarse
  (*distressed*) = alterarse

U

2 *verb*
* (*to make someone unhappy*) = molestar
* (*to annoy*) = disgustar

upside down *adverb*
= al revés

upstairs *adverb*
= arriba
he's upstairs = está arriba
to go upstairs = subir

urgent *adjective*
= urgente

us *pronoun*
* (*when used as a direct object*) = nos
they know/don't know us = nos conocen/no
nos conocen

> ! *Note that* nos *comes before the verb in
> Spanish*

* (*when used as an indirect object*) = nos
he never talks to us = no nos habla nunca
they wrote us a letter = nos escribió una
carta

> ! *Note that* nos *comes before the verb in
> Spanish*

* (*when used as an indirect object pronoun
together with a direct object pronoun*) =
nos
you have to give them to us = nos los
tienes que dar, tienes que dárnoslos
he said it to us = nos lo dijo

> ! *Note that* nos *comes before the direct
> object pronoun*

* (*when telling someone to do something*)
help us! = ¡ayúdanos!
give the money to us = danos el dinero
give them to us! = ¡dánoslos!

> ! *Note that* nos *comes after the verb in
> Spanish*

* (*when telling someone not to do
something*)
don't leave us! = ¡no nos dejes!
don't send them to us! = ¡no nos los
mandes!

> ! *Note that* nos *comes after the verb in
> Spanish*

* (*when used after prepositions and with to
be*) = nosotros/nosotras
did you buy it for us? = ¿lo compraste para
nosotros?
come with us = ven con nosotros
it's us = somos nosotros

> ! *Note that, when talking about mixed
> groups, the masculine form* nosotros *is
> used*

USA *noun* ▶ p. 187
the USA = los EEUU, los EE UU
(*in spoken language*) = los Estados Unidos,
USA✶ (*masculine*)

use
1 *verb*
* (*to make use of*) = usar
he uses this room as an office = usa este
cuarto como oficina
* (*to use up*)
to use gas = consumir gasolina
2 *noun*
* to make use of a room = hacer uso de un
cuarto
to have the use of the car = poder usar el
coche
* (*when talking about what is useful*)
to be of use to someone = serle útil a
alguien
to be of no use = no servir
what's the use of complaining? = ¿de qué
sirve quejarse?

use up
to use up all the money = gastar todo el
dinero
to use up the milk = acabar la leche

used
1 *verb*

> ! *Note that the imperfect tense in
> Spanish is generally used to translate*
> used to + *verb:* she used to live in
> London = vivía en Londres

I used to read a lot = leía mucho
there used to be a castle here = antes
había un castillo aquí
2 *adjective*
to be used to animals = estar
acostumbrado/acostumbrada a los
animales
to get used to a new job = acostumbrarse a
un trabajo nuevo

useful *adjective*
= útil

useless *adjective*
= inútil

usual *adjective*
* (*if it's a method*) =
acostumbrado/acostumbrada
* (*if it's a place, route*) = de siempre
* (*if it's clothes*) = de costumbre

usually *adverb*
= normalmente

vacant *adjective*
a vacant room = un cuarto libre
the post is vacant = el puesto está vacante

vacation *noun* (*US English*)
a vacation = unas vacaciones
to go on vacation = ir de vacaciones

vacuum *verb* = pasar la aspiradora,
aspirar (*Lat Am*)
to vacuum a room = pasar la aspiradora
por un cuarto, aspirar un cuarto

vacuum cleaner *noun*
a vacuum cleaner = una aspiradora, un
aspirador

vain *adjective*
= vanidoso/vanidosa

valley *noun*
a valley = un valle

valuable *adjective*
= valioso/valiosa

van *noun*
a van = una furgoneta, una camioneta, una
vagoneta (*Mex*)

variety *noun*
variety = variedad (*feminine*)
there are a variety of flavors = hay varios
sabores

various *adjective*
= varios/varias

vary *verb*
= variar

vase *noun*
a vase (*for flowers*) = un florero
(*ornamental*) = un jarrón

veal *noun*
veal = ternera (*feminine*)

vegetable *noun*
a vegetable = una verdura

vegetarian *noun*
a vegetarian = un vegetariano/una
vegetariana

vein *noun*
a vein = una vena

velvet *noun*
velvet = terciopelo (*masculine*)

very
1 *adverb* = muy
to eat very little = comer muy poco
we like them very much = nos gustan
mucho
for the very first time = por primera vez

2 *adjective*
to stay to the very end = quedarse hasta el
fin
you are the very person I wanted to see =
eres justo la persona que quería ver

vest *noun*
• (*US English—a waistcoat*)
a vest = un chaleco
• (*British English—a piece of underwear*)
a vest = una camiseta

vet *noun*
a vet = un veterinario/una veterinaria

vicious *adjective*
• (*if it's an attack*) = feroz, salvaje
• (*if it's a dog*) = fiero/fiera

victory *noun*
a victory = una victoria

video
1 *noun*
• (*a recorded film, program, event*)
a video = un video, un vídeo (*Spa*)
• ▶ video cassette, video recorder
2 *verb* = grabar

video camera *noun*
a video camera = una videocámara

videocassette *noun*
a videocassette = un videocasete

video recorder *noun*
a video recorder = un aparato de video, un
aparato de vídeo (*Spa*)

view *noun*
• a view = una vista
you're blocking my view = me estás
tapando
• (*an opinion, an attitude*)
a view = una opinión
a point of view = un punto de vista

village *noun*
a village = un pueblo

vinegar *noun*
vinegar = vinagre (*masculine*)

vineyard *noun*
a vineyard = una viña

violent *adjective*
= violento/violenta

violin *noun*
a violin = un violín

Virgo *noun*
• (*the sign*)
Virgo = virgo
I'm Virgo = soy Virgo, soy de Virgo
• (*a person*)
a Virgo = un/una virgo

visit
1 *verb* = visitar
  to visit Bilbao = visitar Bilbao
  we visited Helen yesterday = fuimos a ver
    a Helen ayer
  to visit with someone (*US English*) = ir a
    ver a alguien
2 *noun*
  a visit = una visita
  to pay someone a visit = hacerle una visita
    a alguien

visitor *noun*
* (*a guest*)
  a visitor = una visita
  to have visitors = tener visitas
* (*a tourist*)
  a visitor = un/una visitante

vocabulary *noun*
  vocabulary = vocabulario (*masculine*)

voice *noun*
  a voice = una voz
  to speak in a low voice = hablar en voz
    baja

volleyball *noun* ▶ p. 306
  volleyball = vóleibol (*masculine*)

vomit *verb*
  = vomitar

vote
1 *noun*
  (*a ballot*)
  a vote = un voto
2 *verb* = votar
  I did not vote for her = no voté por ella

wage *noun*
  a wage = un sueldo

waist *noun*
  the waist = la cintura

waistcoat *noun* (*British English*)
  a waistcoat = un chaleco

wait *verb*
* **to wait** = esperar
  to wait for something/someone = esperar
    algo/a alguien
  to wait for someone to leave = esperar a
    que alguien se vaya

  ! *Note the use of the subjunctive after*
  esperar a que

  I can't wait to see them = me muero de
    ganas de verlos
* (*in a restaurant*)
  to wait on table (*US English*), **to wait at**
    table (*British English*) = atender una mesa
wait up
  to wait up for someone = esperar a alguien
    levantado/levantada

waiter *noun*
  a waiter = un camarero, un mesero (*Lat*
    Am), un mozo (*SC*)

waiting room *noun*
  a waiting room = una sala de espera

waitress *noun*
  a waitress = una camarera, una mesera
    (*Lat Am*)

wake *verb*
  = despertar
wake up = despertarse
  he woke me up = me despertó

Wales *noun* ▶ p. 187
  Wales = (el País de) Gales

walk
1 *verb*
* (*rather than run*) = caminar, andar
* (*rather than drive or ride*) = ir a pie
* (*for pleasure*) = pasear
  to walk the dog = sacar al perro a pasear
2 *noun*
  a walk = un paseo
  to go for a walk = ir a pasear
  it's five minutes walk from here = está a
    cinco minutos de aquí a pie
walk around = pasear
  to walk around the town = pasear por la
    ciudad
walk back = volver a pie, regresar a pie

wall *noun*
  a wall (*freestanding*) = un muro
  (*of a city*) = una muralla
  (*of a room, a building*) = una pared, una
    muralla (*Chi*)

wallet *noun*
  a wallet = una billetera, un billetero

wallpaper *noun*
  wallpaper = papel de empapelar
    (*masculine*)

wander *verb*
  to wander around town = pasear por la
    ciudad
wander away, wander off = alejarse

want *verb*
* **to want** = querer
  he wants to go out = quiere salir
  I want you to come with me = quiero que
    me acompañes

  ! *Note the use of the subjunctive after*
  querer que
* (*to need*) = necesitar

C Am Central America   Lat Am Latin America   Mex Mexico

war *noun*
a war = una guerra

wardrobe *noun*
a wardrobe = un armario, un ropero

warm *adjective*
• (*not cold*)
the water is warm = el agua está tibia
the climate is warm = el clima está cálido
to feel warm, to be warm = tener calor
it's warm in here = hace calor aquí dentro
to get warm = calentarse
• (*enthusiastic*)
a warm reception = una acogida cálida
warm up
• (*to get warm*) = calentarse
• (*for a sporting event*) = hacer ejercicios de calentamiento
• (*to make warm*) = calentar

warn
= advertir
I warned him not to take the car = le advertí que no llevara el coche

! Note the use of the subjunctive after advertir que

warning *noun*
• (*a piece of advice*)
a warning = una advertencia
• (*prior notice*)
they arrived without warning = llegaron sin avisar

wash *verb*
• (*to clean*) = lavar
to wash one's clothes = lavar la ropa
to wash one's face = lavarse la cara
to wash the dishes = fregar los platos, lavar los trastes (*C Am, Mex*)
• (*to clean oneself*) = lavarse
wash up
• (*US English—to clean oneself*) = lavarse
• (*British English—to do the dishes*) = fregar los platos, lavar los trastes (*C Am, Mex*)

washbowl (*US English*), **washbasin** (*British English*) *noun*
a washbowl = un lavamanos, un lavabo, un lavatorio (*SC*)

washing *noun*
the washing (*dirty*) = la ropa para lavar
(*clean*) = la ropa lavada
to do the washing = lavar la ropa, hacer la colada (*Spa*)

washing machine *noun*
a washing machine = una máquina de lavar, una lavadora, un lavarropas (*R Pl*)

washing-up *noun* (*British English*)
to do the washing-up = fregar los platos, lavar los trastes (*C Am, Mex*)

wasp *noun*
a wasp = una avispa

waste
1 *verb*
to waste electricity = despilfarrar la electricidad
we're wasting time = estamos perdiendo el tiempo
2 *noun*
it's a waste of money = es tirar el dinero
a waste of time = una pérdida de tiempo

watch
1 *verb*
• (*to look at*) = mirar
to watch television = ver la televisión, mirar televisión
• (*to keep under observation*) = vigilar
• (*to pay attention to*)
watch what you're doing = mira lo que haces
2 *noun*
a watch = un reloj
watch out = tener cuidado
watch out! = ¡cuidado!

water
1 *noun*
water = agua (*feminine*)
the water's cold = el agua está fría
2 *verb* = regar

waterfall *noun*
a waterfall (*small*) = una cascada
(*large*) = una catarata

wave
1 *verb*
• (*to signal with one's hand*)
to wave to someone = saludar a alguien con la mano
to wave goodbye = hacer adiós con la mano
• (*to direct*)
the policeman waved them on = el policía les hizo señas de que siguieran
2 *noun*
(*on the sea*)
a wave = una ola

way *noun*
• (*a manner, a method*)
a way = una forma, una manera, un modo
he does it the wrong way = no lo hace bien
that's not the way to do it = no se hace así
I like the way she dresses = me gusta como se viste
I prefer to do it my way = prefiero hacerlo a mi manera
• (*a route, a road*)
a way = un camino
on the way to Leeds = de camino a Leeds
where's the way out? = ¿dónde está la salida?
to lose one's way = perderse
• (*a direction*)
they went that way = fueron por ahí
this way! = ¡por aquí!

- (*someone's route*)
  to be in the way = estorbar
  to get out of the way = apartarse
- (*when talking about distances*)
  it's a long way from here = está muy lejos
  de aquí
- (*what one wants*)
  she likes to get her own way = le gusta
  salirse con la suya
- by the way = a propósito

we *pronoun*
  we = nosotros/nosotras

> ! *When talking tabout mixed groups the
> masculine form* **nosotros** *is used*
> we went to the theater = fuimos al teatro
> *we* did it = nosotros/nosotras lo hicimos

> ! *Although* **nosotros** *and nosotras are
> given as translations of* **we***, they are in
> practice used only for emphasis*

weak *adjective*
- (*not healthy*) = débil
- (*not good or able*) = flojo/floja
- (*having very little power*) = débil
- (*with very little taste*)
  weak coffee = café poco cargado

wealthy *adjective*
  = rico/rica

wear *verb*
- (*to be dressed in*)
  to be wearing trousers = llevar pantalones
  to wear black = vestirse de negro
- (*to put on*) = ponerse
wear out
  to wear one's shoes out = gastar los
  zapatos
  to wear someone out = agotar a alguien

weather *noun*
  the weather = el tiempo
  what's the weather like? = ¿qué tiempo
  hace?, ¿cómo está el tiempo?
  the weather is [bad | nice | hot …] = hace [mal
  tiempo | buen tiempo | calor …]

weather forecast *noun*
  the weather forecast = el pronóstico del
  tiempo

wedding *noun*
  a wedding = una boda

Wednesday *noun* ▶ p. 192
  Wednesday = miércoles (*masculine*)

week *noun*
  a week = una semana

weekend *noun*
  a weekend = un fin de semana

weigh *verb*
  = pesar
  what do you weigh? = ¿cuánto pesas?

weight *noun*
  weight = peso
  to put on weight = engordar
  to lose weight = adelgazar

weird *adjective*
  = raro/rara, extraño/extraña

welcome
1 *verb*
  to welcome someone = darle la bienvenida
  a alguien
2 *adjective*
- (*when receiving people*)
  to be welcome = ser bienvenido/bienvenida
  welcome to the United States =
  bienvenidos a los Estados Unidos
- (*when acknowledging thanks*)
  thanks—you're welcome = gracias—de
  nada

well
1 *adverb*
- well = bien
  he is well paid = le pagan bien
- as well = también
  as well as = además de
  we may as well go home = más vale que
  vayamos a casa

> ! *Note the use of the subjunctive after*
> más vale que

2 *adjective*
  to feel well = sentirse bien
  I'm very well = estoy muy bien

well-known *adjective*
  = conocido/conocida

Welsh ▶ p. 187, p. 245
1 *adjective* = galés/galesa
2 *noun*
- (*the people*)
  the Welsh = los galeses
- (*the language*)
  Welsh = galés (*masculine*)

west
1 *noun*
  the west = el oeste
  in the west of England = en el oeste de
  Inglaterra
2 *adverb*
  we went west = fuimos hacia el oeste
  it is west of London = está al oeste de
  Londres
3 *adjective*
  = oeste (! *never changes*)
  the west coast = la costa oeste
  a west wind = un viento del oeste

West Indies *noun* ▶ p. 187
  the West Indies = las Antillas

wet *adjective*
* (*moist*) = mojado/mojada
  to get wet = mojarse
  she got her feet wet = se mojó los pies
* (*if it's the weather*) = lluvioso/lluviosa

what
1 *pronoun*
* **do what you want** = haz lo que quieras
  what we need is a timetable = lo que
  necesitamos es un horario
* (*used in questions*)
  what do you want? = ¿qué quieres?
  what's her phone number? = ¿cuál es su
  número de teléfono?
  what's this button for? = ¿para qué sirve
  este botón?
  what's the Spanish for 'boring'? = ¿cómo
  se dice 'boring' en español?
  what's she like? = ¿cómo es?
  what if I don't get there on time? = ¿y si no
  llego a tiempo?
2 *adjective*
  do you know what train to take? = ¿sabes
  qué tren hay que tomar?
  what a great idea! = ¡qué buena idea!

whatever *pronoun*
* (*when anything is possible*)
  take whatever you want = toma lo que
  quieras
* (*when it doesn't matter*)
  **whatever they do, it won't change
  anything** = hagan lo que hagan, no va a
  cambiar nada

wheat *noun*
  wheat = trigo (*masculine*)

wheel *noun*
  a wheel = una rueda

wheelchair *noun*
  a wheelchair = una silla de ruedas

when
1 *adverb* = cuándo
  when did she leave? = ¿cuándo se fue?
  I don't know when the film starts = no sé
  cuándo empieza la película
2 *conjunction* = cuando
  I was asleep when the phone rang = estaba
  dormida cuando sonó el teléfono
3 *pronoun*
  (*used in questions*) = cuándo
  until when? = ¿hasta cuándo?

where
1 *adverb* = dónde
  where are you going? = ¿dónde vas?
  do you know where he is? = ¿sabes dónde
  está?
2 *conjunction* = donde
  that's where she fell = allí es donde se cayó
  I'll leave the key where you can see it =
  voy a dejar la llave donde la puedes ver

whether *conjunction*
  = si

which
1 *pronoun*
* **the house which I told you about** = la casa
  de la que te hablé
* (*used in questions*)
  which of the girls is his sister? = ¿cuál de
  las chicas es su hermana?
  do you know which she chose? = ¿sabes
  cuál eligió?
2 *adjective*
  in which European city is it? = ¿en qué
  ciudad europea está?, ¿en cuál ciudad
  europea está?
  ask her which chapters we have to read =
  pregúntale qué capítulos hay que leer,
  pregúntale cuáles capítulos hay que leer

while
1 *conjunction* = mientras
2 *noun*
  a while ago = hace un rato
  after a while = después de un rato

whisper *verb*
  = susurrar

whistle
1 *verb* = silbar
2 *noun*
* (*an instrument*)
  a whistle = un silbato
* (*a sound*)
  a whistle = un silbido

white *adjective* ▶ p. 183
  = blanco/blanca

who *pronoun*
* **my friend who lives in Miami** = mi amigo
  que vive en Miami
  those who can't come by car = los que no
  pueden venir en coche
* (*used in questions*) = quién
  who did he buy the book for? = ¿para
  quién compró el libro?

whole
1 *noun*
  the whole of the country = todo el país
  we're staying the whole of August = nos
  quedamos todo agosto
2 *adjective* = entero/entera
  three whole weeks = tres semanas enteras

whom *pronoun*
* **the person to whom I spoke on the phone**
  = la persona con la que hablé por
  teléfono
* (*used in questions*)
  whom did you meet? = ¿a quién conociste?

whose
1 *pronoun*

- **the boy whose bike was stolen** = el chico al que le robaron la bicicleta
  the woman whose house I'm buying = la mujer cuya casa voy a comprar
- (*used in questions*)
  whose is the dog? = ¿de quién es el perro?

2 *adjective*
  whose car is that? = ¿de quién es ese coche?
  do you know whose jacket this is? = ¿sabes de quién es esta chaqueta?

why

1 *adverb*
- (*used in questions*) = por qué
  why did you do that? = ¿por qué hiciste eso?
  why not? = ¿por qué no?
- (*when making suggestions*)
  why don't we go away this weekend? = ¿por qué no vamos a algún lado este fin de semana?

2 *conjunction*
  that's why I can't stand him = por eso es que no lo aguanto

wide

1 *adjective*
- (*in size*) = ancho/ancha
  how wide is it? = ¿cuánto tiene de ancho?, ¿cuánto mide de ancho?
  the room is 10 meters wide = el cuarto tiene 10 metros de ancho
- (*in range*) = amplio/amplia (**!** before the noun)
  a wide range of games = una amplia gama de juegos

2 *adverb*
  to open the window wide = abrir la ventana de par en par

wife *noun*
  a wife = una esposa, una mujer

wild *adjective*
- (*if it's an animal*) = salvaje
- (*if it's a plant*) = silvestre
- (*noisy, out of control*)
  to go wild = volverse loco/loca

will *verb*
- (*when talking about the future*)

  > **!** When referring to the future, the future tense is not always the first option for translating **will** + verb into Spanish. The present tense of **ir** + **a** + verb is common in Latin American countries

  she won't agree = no aceptará, no va a aceptar
  it will be sunny tomorrow = mañana hará sol, mañana va a hacer sol
  what will we do? = ¿qué vamos a hacer?
- (*in invitations and requests*)
  will you have some coffee? = ¿quiere un café?
  won't you stay for dinner? = ¿se queda a cenar?

- (*when making assumptions*)
  they won't know what's happened = no sabrán lo que ha pasado
- (*in short questions and answers*)
  that will be cheaper, won't it? = ¿eso será más barato, no?
  will it be ready?—yes it will = ¿estará listo? —sí

win *verb*
  = ganar

wind *noun*
  the wind = el viento

window *noun*
  a window (*in a house*) = una ventana
  (*in a shop*) = un escaparate, una vidriera (*Lat Am*), un aparador (*Mex*)
  (*in a vehicle*) = una ventanilla

windy *adjective*
  a windy day = un día de viento
  it's windy = hace viento

wine *noun*
  wine = vino (*masculine*)

wing *noun*
  a wing = un ala (*feminine*)

winter *noun*
  winter = invierno (*masculine*)
  in winter = en invierno

wipe *verb*
  = limpiar
  to wipe one's nose = limpiarse la nariz
wipe up = limpiar

wise *adjective*
- (*if it's a person*) = sabio/sabia
- (*if it's a decision, a choice*) = acertado/acertada

wish

1 *noun*
- **a wish** = un deseo
  to make a wish = pedir un deseo
- (*in greetings*)
  best wishes, Helen = saludos de Helen, un abrazo de Helen

2 *verb*
- (*expressing what one would like*)
  I wish they would come = ojalá (que) vinieran

  > **!** Note the use of the subjunctive after ojalá (que)

  she wished she hadn't told him = lamentó habérselo dicho
- (*in greetings*) = desear

with *preposition*

  > **!** Note that **with** is used after many adjectives, eg to be angry with someone, to be pleased with something. To find the translation, look up the separate dictionary entries at **angry**, **pleased** etc

• **with** = con
  to go out with friends = salir con amigos
  I'm living with my parents = vivo con mis
    padres
• (*when describing*)
  a girl with black hair = una chica de pelo
    negro
  his clothes were covered with mud = su
    ropa estaba cubierta de barro
• (*as a result of*)
  trembling with fear = temblando de miedo

without *preposition*
  = sin
  we got in without paying = entramos sin
    pagar

wolf *noun*
  a wolf = un lobo

woman *noun*
  a woman = una mujer

wonder
1 *verb*
• (*to ask oneself*) = preguntarse
  I wonder why? = ¿me pregunto por qué?
• (*in polite requests*)
  I wonder if you could help me? = ¿me
    podría ayudar?
2 *noun*
  it's a wonder that no one was injured = es
    asombroso que nadie resultara herido
  it's no wonder he's always late = no es de
    extrañar que siempre llegue tarde

  ! *Note the use of the subjunctive after* es
  asombroso que *and* no es de extrañar
  que

wonderful *adjective*
  = maravilloso/maravillosa

wood *noun*
• (*timber*)
  wood = madera (*feminine*)
• (*a small forest*)
  a wood = un bosque

wool *noun*
  wool = lana (*feminine*)

word *noun*
  a word = una palabra
  I didn't say a word = yo no dije nada
  in other words you don't want to go = es
    decir que no quieres ir

word processor *noun*
  a word processor = un procesador de
    textos

work
1 *verb*
• (*to have or do a job*) = trabajar
• (*to operate properly*) = funcionar
  the TV isn't working = la televisión no
    funciona

• (*to be successful*) (*of an idea, a trick*) =
    resultar
  (*of a medicine, a treatment, a plan*) = surtir
    efecto
• (*to use, to operate*)
  do you know how to work the computer? =
    ¿sabes manejar la computadora?
2 *noun*
• **work** = trabajo (*masculine*)
  to be out of work = estar sin trabajo
  it's hard work learning German = es difícil
    aprender alemán
• (*by an artist, a musician*)
  a work = una obra
work out
• (*to solve*)
  to work out a problem = resolver un
    problema
• (*to understand*) = entender
• (*to calculate*) = calcular
• (*to go well*) = salir bien
work up
  to get worked up = exaltarse

worker *noun*
  a worker (*in a factory*) = un obrero/una
    obrera
  (*in an office, a bank*) = un empleado/una
    empleada

world *noun*
  the world = el mundo

World Cup *noun*
  the World Cup = la Copa Mundial

worm *noun*
  a worm = un gusano

worried *adjective*
  = preocupado/preocupada
  to be worried about someone =
    preocuparse por alguien

worry *verb*
• (*to be worried*) = preocuparse
• (*to make someone worried*) = preocupar
  it's worrying me = me preocupa

worse *adjective*
  = peor
  this book is worse than the others = este
    libro es peor que los demás
  to get worse = empeorar

worst
1 *noun*
  the worst = el/la peor
2 *adjective* = peor
  the worst hotel in town = el peor hotel de la
    ciudad

worth *adjective*
  to be worth $100 = valer 100 dólares
  how much is it worth? = ¿cuánto vale?
  it's not worth the trouble = no vale la pena

W

would *verb*

> **!** *Spanish usually uses verbs in the conditional to translate* would *or* 'd + *verb:* I would buy, I'd buy = compraría

- (*when talking about hypothetical rather than real situations*)
  If I had more money, I would buy a car = si tuviera más dinero, me compraría un coche
- (*in reported speech*)
  I thought you'd forget to come = pensé que te olvidarías de venir
- (*to be prepared to*)
  he wouldn't listen to me = no me quería escuchar
- (*when talking about wishes*)
  I'd like a beer = me gustaría una cerveza, quisiera una cerveza
- (*when asking, offering, or advising*)
  would you switch the television off? = ¿podrías apagar la televisión?
  would you like something to eat? = ¿quieres comer algo?

wrap *verb*
= envolver

wreck *verb*
= destrozar

wrestling *noun*
wrestling = lucha (*feminine*)

wrist *noun* ▶ p. 235
the wrist = la muñeca

write *verb*
= escribir
to write a letter = escribir una carta
to write someone a check = hacerle un cheque a alguien
write back = contestar
write down = apuntar
write out = escribir

writing *noun*
(*written material*)
to put something in writing = poner algo por escrito

writing pad *noun*
a writing pad = un bloc

wrong
1 *adjective*
- (*not as it should be*)
  there's something wrong = pasa algo
  what's wrong? = ¿qué pasa?
  what's wrong with you? = ¿qué te pasa?, ¿qué tienes?
- (*not proper or suitable*)
  I took the wrong key = llevé la llave equivocada
  to go the wrong way = equivocarse de camino

- (*not correct*)
  a wrong answer = una respuesta equivocada
  you're wrong = estás equivocado/equivocada
- (*not good, not honest*)
  it's wrong to steal = robar está mal
  she hasn't done anything wrong = no ha hecho nada malo

2 *adverb*
to get the time wrong = equivocarse de hora
everything went wrong = todo salió mal

Xx

X-ray
1 *noun*
an X-ray = una radiografía
I had an X-ray = me hicieron una radiografía
2 *verb* = hacer una radiografía de

Yy

yacht *noun*
a yacht = un yate

yard *noun*
- (*when measuring*)
  a yard = una yarda

  > **!** *Note that a yard = 0.9144 m*

- (*US English—a garden*)
  a yard = un jardín
- (*of a school*)
  a yard = un patio
- (*British English—of a house*)
  a yard = un patio

yawn *verb*
= bostezar

year *noun* ▶ p. 154, p. 192
- **a year** = un año
  he's lived there for years = hace años que vive allí
- (*when talking about age*)
  to be 15 years old, to be 15 years of age = tener 15 años
  a four-year old = un niño/una niña de cuatro años

C Am Central America   **Lat Am** Latin America   **Mex** Mexico

You

In English **you** is used to address everybody, whereas Spanish has four forms: **tú**, **vosotros** (feminine form **vosotras**), **usted**, and **ustedes**.

Generally speaking, the pronoun **tú** and the **tú** form of the verb are used between friends and family, between people on first-name terms, among young people even if they do not know each other, and when addressing children and animals.

The pronouns **usted** and the **usted** form of the verb are used when addressing an older person, someone in authority, or, in general, as a show of respect.

Ustedes and vosotros

In Latin America, the Canary Islands and parts of Andalusia, **ustedes** is the plural of both **usted** and **tú**. In the rest of Spain, the informal plural, that is, the plural form of **tú**, is **vosotros**, which takes the second person plural form of the verb.

Vos

In some Latin American countries, the form **vos** is used instead of **tú**. This usage is known as **voseo** and is common in the River Plate and parts of Central America.

• (*in a school system*)
  the first year, year 1 = el primer curso, el
      primer año

yell
1 *verb* = gritar
2 *noun*
  a yell = un grito

yellow *adjective* ▶ p. 183
  = amarillo/amarilla

yes *adverb*
  yes = sí
  are you coming with us?—yes I am =
      ¿vienes con nosotros?—sí

yesterday *adverb*
  = ayer

yet
1 *adverb* = todavía
  not yet = todavía no
  have they arrived yet? = ¿han llegado ya?
2 *conjunction* = pero

yield *verb*
  to yield one's right of way (*US
      English—when driving*) = ceder el paso

yoghurt *noun*
  yoghurt = yogur (*masculine*)

you *pronoun*
• (*when used as the subject*)
  (*informal—singular*) = tú, vos (*R Pl*)
  (*informal—plural*) = ustedes,
      vosotros/vosotras (*Spa*)

  ! *When talking about mixed groups the*
  masculine form **vosotros** *is used*

  (*formal—singular*) = usted

  (*formal—plural*) = ustedes
  you are my best friends = ustedes son mis
      mejores amigos, (vosotros) sois mis
      mejores amigos (*Spa*)
  you **did it** = tú lo hiciste
  I was singing and you were playing the
      piano = yo cantaba y usted tocaba el
      piano
  be quiet, you two = ustedes dos: ¡cállense!,
      vosotros dos: ¡callaos! (*Spa*)
  poor you! = ¡pobrecito!/¡pobrecita!

  ! *Note that the main translations given*
  above are in practice used only for
  emphasis, or to avoid ambiguity

• (*when used as a direct object*)
  (*informal—singular*) = te
  (*informal—plural*) = los/las, os (*Spa*)
  (*formal—singular*) = lo/la, le/la (*Spa*)
  (*formal—plural*) = los/las, les/las (*Spa*)
  I know/don't know you = te conozco/no te
      conozco
  did he see you? = ¿los/las vio?, ¿les/las vio?
      (*Spa*)

  ! *Note that the direct object pronoun*
  comes before the verb in Spanish

• (*when used as an indirect object*)
  (*informal—singular*) = te
  (*informal—plural*) = les, os (*Spa*)
  (*formal—singular*) = le
  (*formal—plural*) = les
  he gave you the book = les dio el libro, os
      dio el libro (*Spa*)
  I wrote you a letter = le escribí una carta

  ! *Note that the indirect object pronoun*
  comes before the verb in Spanish

• (*when used as an indirect object pronoun*
  together with a direct object pronoun)
  (*informal—singular*) = te

X
Y

R Pl River Plate area   **SC** Southern Cone   **Spa** Spain

(informal—plural) = se, os *(Spa)*
(formal—singular) = se
(formal—plural) = se
I gave it to you = se lo di
I'm not going to say it to you = no te lo voy
a decir

> **!** *Note that the indirect object pronoun*
> *comes before the direct object pronoun*
> *in Spanish*

• *(when used after prepositions)*
(informal—singular) = ti, vos *(R Pl)*
(informal—plural) = ustedes,
vosotros/vosotras *(Spa)*
(formal—singular) = usted
(formal—plural) = ustedes
we bought it for you = lo compramos para
ustedes
a letter for you = una carta para usted
he arrived after you = llegó después de ti
I'll go with you = iré contigo
• *(when talking in an impersonal or vague*
way about people)
(when used as the subject)
you can't do that here = no se puede hacer
eso aquí, uno no puede hacer eso aquí, no
puedes hacer eso aquí *(Spa)*
(when used as a direct object)
**people stop you in the street and ask for
money** = la gente lo para a uno en la calle
y le pide dinero, la gente te para en la
calle y te pide dinero *(Spa)*
(when used as an indirect object)
they can cause you a lot of trouble = le
pueden a uno crear muchos problemas,
te pueden crear muchos problemas *(Spa)*

young *adjective*
= joven
a young lady = una joven
young people = los jóvenes
she is a year younger than me = tiene un
año menos que yo, es un año menor que
yo
a younger brother/sister = un
hermano/una hermana menor

your *adjective*
• *(belonging to one person)*
(informal) = tu (+ *singular*), tus (+ *plural*)
(formal) = su (+ *singular*), sus (+ *plural*)
• *(belonging to more than one person)*
(informal) = su (+ *singular*), sus (+ *plural*),
vuestro/vuestra (+ *singular*) *(Spa)*,
vuestros/vuestras (+ *plural*) *(Spa)*
(formal) = su (+ *singular*), sus (+ *plural*)
• *(one's)*
if your name begins with A ... = si el
nombre de uno empieza con A ..., si tu
nombre empieza con A ... *(Spa)*
**you have to take your shoes off in a
mosque** = hay que quitarse los zapatos
en una mezquita

> **!** *For* your *used with parts of the body,*
> ▶ **p. 235**

yours *pronoun*
• *(belonging to one person)*
(informal—singular) = tuyo/tuya
(informal—plural) = tuyos/tuyas
(formal—singular) = suyo/suya
(formal—plural) = suyos/suyas
yours is blue = el tuyo/la tuya es azul
a friend of yours = un amigo suyo
• *(belonging to more than one person)*
(informal—singular) = suyo/suya,
vuestro/vuestra *(Spa)*
(informal—plural) = suyos/suyas,
vuestros/vuestras *(Spa)*
(formal—singular) = suyo/suya
(formal—plural) = suyos/suyas
yours are blue = los suyos/las suyas son
azules
a friend of yours = un amigo suyo, un
amigo vuestro *(Spa)*

yourself *pronoun*
• *(when translated by a reflexive verb in*
Spanish)
(informal)
did you hurt yourself? = ¿te hiciste daño?,
¿te lastimaste? *(Lat Am)*
describe yourself = descríbete
(formal)
did you hurt yourself? = ¿se hizo daño?,
¿se lastimó? *(Lat Am)*
describe yourself = descríbase
• *(when used for emphasis)*
(informal) = tú mismo/tú misma
(formal) = usted mismo/usted misma
by yourself = solo/sola
• *(oneself)* = uno mismo/una misma

yourselves *pronoun*
• *(when translated by a reflexive verb in*
Spanish)
(informal)
did you hurt yourselves? = ¿se hicieron
daño *or* se lastimaron? *(Lat Am)*, ¿os
hicisteis daño? *(Spa)*
(formal)
did you hurt yourselves? = ¿se hicieron
daño?, ¿se lastimaron? *(Lat Am)*
• *(when used for emphasis)*
(informal) = ustedes mismos/mismas,
vosotros mismos/vosotras mismas *(Spa)*
(formal) = ustedes mismos/mismas
by yourselves = solos/solas

youth *noun*
(a young man)
a youth = un joven

youth club *noun*
a youth club = un club de jóvenes

youth hostel *noun*
a youth hostel = un albergue juvenil

Zz

zebra *noun*
  a **zebra** = una cebra

zebra crossing *noun* (*British English*)
  a **zebra crossing** = un paso de cebra

zero *noun*
  a **zero** = un cero

zip (*British English*) *noun* ▶ zipper

zip code *noun* (*US English*)
  a **zip code** = un código postal

zipper *noun* (*US English*)
  a **zipper** = una cremallera, un cierre (*Lat Am*), un zíper (*Mex*)

zodiac *noun*
  the **zodiac** = el zodíaco, el zodiaco

zone *noun*
  a **zone** = una zona

zoo *noun*
  a **zoo** = un zoológico, un zoo (*Spa*)

Z

Spanish verb tables

Present indicative
canto = *I sing, I'm singing*

Imperfect indicative
cantaba = *I was singing, I used to sing*

Past simple indicative
canté = *I sang*

Future indicative
cantaré = *I will sing*

Conditional (present)
si hubiera un coro, cantaría =
if there was a choir, I would sing

Present subjunctive
es posible que cante = *he might sing*

Imperfect subjunctive
aunque yo cantara = *even if I sang*

Imperative
canta/cantad = *sing!*

Verbs ending in -ar

1 hablar

Present indicative	Conditional (present)
hablo	hablaría
hablas	hablarías
habla	hablaría
hablamos	hablaríamos
habláis	hablaríais
hablan	hablarían

Imperfect indicative	Present subjunctive
hablaba	hable
hablabas	hables
hablaba	hable
hablábamos	hablemos
hablabais	habléis
hablaban	hablen

Past simple indicative	Imperfect subjunctive*
hablé	hablara
hablaste	hablaras
habló	hablara
hablamos	habláramos
hablasteis	hablarais
hablaron	hablaran

Future indicative	Imperative
hablaré	habla (tú)
hablarás	hable (usted)
hablará	hablemos (nosotros)
hablaremos	hablad (vosotros)
hablaréis	hablen (ustedes)
hablarán	

Gerund
hablando

Past participle
hablado

* all **-ar** verbs have an alternative form of the Imperfect subjunctive in which the **-ara** ending is replaced by **-ase**, eg: hablase, hablases, hablase, hablásemos, hablaseis, hablasen

2 sacar   formed as **1 hablar** except:

Past simple indicative	Present subjunctive
saqué	saque
sacaste	saques
sacó	saque
sacamos	saquemos
sacasteis	saquéis
sacaron	saquen

	Imperative
	saca (tú)
	saque (usted)
	saquemos (nosotros)
	sacad (vosotros)
	saquen (ustedes)

3 pagar   formed as **1 hablar** except:

Past simple indicative	Present subjunctive
pagué	pague
pagaste	pagues
pagó	pague
pagamos	paguemos
pagasteis	paguéis
pagaron	paguen

	Imperative
	paga (tú)
	pague (usted)
	paguemos (nosotros)
	pagad (vosotros)
	paguen (ustedes)

4 cazar formed as 1 hablar except:

Past simple indicative	Present subjunctive
cacé	cace
cazaste	caces
cazó	cace
cazamos	cacemos
cazasteis	cacéis
cazaron	cacen

	Imperative
	caza (tú)
	cace (usted)
	cacemos (nosotros)
	cazad (vosotros)
	cacen (ustedes)

5 empezar formed as 1 hablar except:

Present indicative	Present subjunctive
empiezo	empiece
empiezas	empieces
empieza	empiece
empezamos	empecemos
empezáis	empecéis
empiezan	empiecen

Past simple indicative	Imperative
empecé	empieza (tú)
empezaste	empiece (usted)
empezó	empecemos (nosotros)
empezamos	empezad (vosotros)
empezasteis	empiecen (ustedes)
empezaron	

6 contar formed as 1 hablar except:

Present indicative	Present subjunctive
cuento	cuente
cuentas	cuentes
cuenta	cuente
contamos	contemos
contáis	contéis
cuentan	cuenten

	Imperative
	cuenta (tú)
	cuente (usted)
	contemos (nosotros)
	contad (vosotros)
	cuenten (ustedes)

7 pensar formed as 1 hablar except:

Present indicative	Present subjunctive
pienso	piense
piensas	pienses
piensa	piense
pensamos	pensemos
pensáis	penséis
piensan	piensen

	Imperative
	piensa (tú)
	piense (usted)
	pensemos (nosotros)
	pensad (vosotros)
	piensen (ustedes)

8 regar formed as 1 hablar except:

Present indicative	Present subjunctive
riego	riegue
riegas	riegues
riega	riegue
regamos	reguemos
regáis	reguéis
riegan	rieguen

Past simple indicative	Imperative
regué	riega (tú)
regaste	riegue (usted)
regó	reguemos (nosotros)
regamos	regad (vosotros)
regasteis	rieguen (ustedes)
regaron	

9 colgar formed as 1 hablar except:

Present indicative	Present subjunctive
cuelgo	cuelgue
cuelgas	cuelgues
cuelga	cuelgue
colgamos	colguemos
colgáis	colguéis
cuelgan	cuelguen

Past simple indicative	Imperative
colgué	cuelga (tú)
colgaste	cuelgue (usted)
colgó	colguemos (nosotros)
colgamos	colgad (vosotros)
colgasteis	cuelguen (ustedes)
colgaron	

10 forzar formed as 1 hablar except:

Present indicative	Present subjunctive
fuerzo	fuerce
fuerzas	fuerces
fuerza	fuerce
forzamos	forcemos
forzáis	forcéis
fuerzan	fuercen

Past simple indicative	Imperative
forcé	fuerza (tú)
forzaste	fuerce (usted)
forzó	forcemos (nosotros)
forzamos	forzad (vosotros)
forzasteis	fuercen (ustedes)
forzaron	

11 actuar formed as 1 hablar except:

Present indicative	Present subjunctive
actúo	actúe
actúas	actúes
actúa	actúe
actuamos	actuemos
actuáis	actuéis
actúan	actúen

	Imperative
	actúa (tú)
	actúe (usted)
	actuemos (nosotros)
	actuad (vosotros)
	actúen (ustedes)

12 jugar formed as 1 hablar except:

Present indicative	Present subjunctive
juego	juegue
juegas	juegues
juega	juegue
jugamos	juguemos
jugáis	juguéis
juegan	jueguen

Past simple indicative	Imperative
jugué	juega (tú)
jugaste	juegue (usted)
jugó	juguemos (nosotros)
jugamos	jugad (vosotros)
jugasteis	jueguen (ustedes)
jugaron	

13 vaciar formed as 1 hablar except:

Present indicative	Present subjunctive
vacío	vacíe
vacías	vacíes
vacía	vacíe
vaciamos	vaciemos
vaciáis	vaciéis
vacían	vacíen

Imperative
vacía (tú)
vacíe (usted)
vaciemos (nosotros)
vaciad (vosotros)
vacíen (ustedes)

14 andar formed as 1 hablar except:

Past simple indicative	Imperfect subjunctive
anduve	anduviera
anduviste	anduvieras
anduvo	anduviera
anduvimos	anduviéramos
anduvisteis	anduvierais
anduvieron	anduvieran

15 dar formed as 1 hablar except:

Present indicative	Present subjunctive
doy	dé
das	des
da	dé
damos	demos
dais	deis
dan	den

Past simple indicative	Imperfect subjunctive
di	diera
diste	dieras
dio	diera
dimos	diéramos
disteis	dierais
dieron	dieran

16 estar formed as 1 hablar except:

Present indicative	Present subjunctive
estoy	esté
estás	estés
está	esté
estamos	estemos
estáis	estéis
están	estén

Past simple indicative	Imperfect subjunctive
estuve	estuviera
estuviste	estuvieras
estuvo	estuviera
estuvimos	estuviéramos
estuvisteis	estuvierais
estuvieron	estuvieran

Imperative
está (tú)
esté (usted)
estemos (nosotros)
estad (vosotros)
estén (ustedes)

Verbs ending in -er

17 meter

Present indicative	Conditional (present)
meto	metería
metes	meterías
mete	metería
metemos	meteríamos
metéis	meteríais
meten	meterían

Imperfect indicative	Present subjunctive
metía	meta
metías	metas
metía	meta
metíamos	metamos
metíais	metáis
metían	metan

Past simple indicative	Imperfect subjunctive*
metí	metiera
metiste	metieras
metió	metiera
metimos	metiéramos
metisteis	metierais
metieron	metieran

Future indicative	Imperative
meteré	mete (tú)
meterás	meta (usted)
meterá	metamos (nosotros)
meteremos	meted (vosotros)
meteréis	metan (ustedes)
meterán	

Gerund
metiendo

Past Participle
metido

* all -er verbs have an alternative form of the Imperfect subjunctive in which the -era ending is replaced by -ese, eg: metiese, metieses, metiese, metiésemos, metieseis, metiesen

18 vencer formed as 17 meter except:

Present indicative	Present subjunctive
venzo	venza
vences	venzas
vence	venza
vencemos	venzamos
vencéis	venzáis
vencen	venzan

Imperative
vence (tú)
venza (usted)
venzamos (nosotros)
venced (vosotros)
venzan (ustedes)

19 conocer formed as 17 meter except:

present indicative	Present subjunctive
conozco	conozca
conoces	conozcas
conoce	conozca
conocemos	conozcamos
conocéis	conozcáis
conocen	conozcan

Imperative
conoce (tú)
conozca (usted)
conozcamos (nosotros)
conoced (vosotros)
conozcan (ustedes)

20 coger formed as 17 meter except:

Present indicative	Present subjunctive
cojo	coja
coges	cojas
coge	coja
cogemos	cojamos
cogéis	cojáis
cogen	cojan

Imperative
coge (tú)
coja (usted)
cojamos (nosotros)
coged (vosotros)
cojan (ustedes)

21 entender formed as 17 meter except:

Present indicative	Present subjunctive
entiendo	entienda
entiendes	entiendas
entiende	entienda
entendemos	entendamos
entendéis	entendáis
entienden	entiendan

Imperative
entiende (tú)
entienda (usted)
entendamos (nosotros)
entended (vosotros)
entiendan (ustedes)

22 mover formed as 17 meter except:

Present indicative	Present subjunctive
muevo	mueva
mueves	muevas
mueve	mueva
movemos	movamos
movéis	mováis
mueven	muevan

Imperative
mueve (tú)
mueva (usted)
movamos (nosotros)
moved (vosotros)
muevan (ustedes)

23 torcer formed as 17 meter except:

Present indicative	Present subjunctive
tuerzo	tuerza
tuerces	tuerzas
tuerce	tuerza
torcemos	torzamos
torcéis	torzáis
tuercen	tuerzan

Imperative
tuerce (tú)
tuerza (usted)
torzamos (nosotros)
torced (vosotros)
tuerzan (ustedes)

24 volver formed as 17 meter except:

Past participle
vuelto

Present indicative
vuelvo
vuelves
vuelve
volvemos
volvéis
vuelven

Present subjunctive
vuelva
vuelvas
vuelva
volvamos
volváis
vuelvan

Imperative
vuelve (tú)
vuelva (usted)
volvamos (nosotros)
volved (vosotros)
vuelvan (ustedes)

25 oler formed as 17 meter except:

Present indicative	Present subjunctive
huelo	huela
hueles	huelas
huele	huela
olemos	olamos
oléis	oláis
huelen	huelan

Imperative
huele (tú)
huela (usted)
olamos (nosotros)
oled (vosotros)
huelan (ustedes)

26 leer formed as 17 meter except:

Gerund
leyendo

Past participle
leído

Past simple indicative
leí
leíste
leyó
leímos
leísteis
leyeron

Imperfect subjunctive
leyera
leyeras
leyera
leyéramos
leyerais
leyeran

27 caber formed as 17 meter except:

Present indicative
quepo
cabes
cabe
cabemos
cabéis
caben

Past simple indicative
cupe
cupiste
cupo
cupimos
cupisteis
cupieron

Future indicative
cabré
cabrás
cabrá
cabremos
cabréis
cabrán

Conditional (present)
cabría
cabrías
cabría
cabríamos
cabríais
cabrían

Present subjunctive
quepa
quepas
quepa
quepamos
quepáis
quepan

Imperfect subjunctive
cupiera
cupieras
cupiera
cupiéramos
cupierais
cupieran

28 caer formed as 17 meter except:

Gerund
cayendo

Past participle
caído

Present indicative
caigo
caes
cae
caemos
caéis
caen

Past simple indicative
caí
caíste
cayó
caímos
caísteis
cayeron

Present subjunctive
caiga
caigas
caiga
caigamos
caigáis
caigan

Imperfect subjunctive
cayera
cayeras
cayera
cayéramos
cayerais
cayeran

Imperative
cae (tú)
caiga (usted)
caigamos (nosotros)
caed (vosotros)
caigan (ustedes)

29 haber formed as 17 meter except:

Present indicative
he
has
ha
habemos
habéis
han

Past simple indicative
hube
hubiste
hubo
hubimos
hubisteis
hubieron

Future indicative
habré
habrás
habrá
habremos
habréis
habrán

Conditional (present)
habría
habrías
habría
habríamos
habríais
habrían

Present subjunctive
haya
hayas
haya
hayamos
hayáis
hayan

Imperfect subjunctive
hubiera
hubieras
hubiera
hubiéramos
hubierais
hubieran

30 hacer formed as 17 meter except:

Past participle
hecho

Present indicative
hago
haces
hace
hacemos
hacéis
hacen

Past simple indicative
hice
hiciste
hizo
hicimos
hicisteis
hicieron

Future indicative
haré
harás
hará
haremos
haréis
harán

Conditional (present)
haría
harías
haría
haríamos
haríais
harían

Present subjunctive
haga
hagas
haga
hagamos
hagáis
hagan

Imperfect subjunctive
hiciera
hicieras
hiciera
hiciéramos
hicierais
hicieran

Imperative
haz (tú)
haga (usted)
hagamos (nosotros)
haced (vosotros)
hagan (ustedes)

31 poder formed as 17 meter except:

Present indicative
puedo
puedes
puede
podemos
podéis
pueden

Past simple indicative
pude
pudiste
pudo
pudimos
pudisteis
pudieron

Future indicative
podré
podrás
podrá
podremos
podréis
podrán

Conditional (present)
podría
podrías
podría
podríamos
podríais
podrían

Present subjunctive
pueda
puedas
pueda
podamos
podáis
puedan

Imperfect subjunctive
pudiera
pudieras
pudiera
pudiéramos
pudierais
pudieran

Imperative
puede (tú)
pueda (usted)
podamos (nosotros)
poded (vosotros)
puedan (ustedes)

32 poner formed as **17 meter** except:

Past participle
puesto

Present indicative
pongo
pones
pone
ponemos
ponéis
ponen

Past simple indicative
puse
pusiste
puso
pusimos
pusisteis
pusieron

Future indicative
pondré
pondrás
pondrá
pondremos
pondréis
pondrán

Conditional (present)
pondría
pondrías
pondría
pondríamos
pondríais
pondrían

Present subjunctive
ponga
pongas
ponga
pongamos
pongáis
pongan

Imperfect subjunctive
pusiera
pusieras
pusiera
pusiéramos
pusierais
pusieran

Imperative
pon (tú)
ponga (usted)
pongamos (nosotros)
poned (vosotros)
pongan (ustedes)

34 querer formed as **17 meter** except:

Present indicative
quiero
quieres
quiere
queremos
queréis
quieren

Past simple indicative
quise
quisiste
quiso
quisimos
quisisteis
quisieron

Future indicative
querré
querrás
querrá
querremos
querréis
querrán

Conditional (present)
querría
querrías
querría
querríamos
querríais
querrían

Present subjunctive
quiera
quieras
quiera
queramos
queráis
quieran

Imperfect subjunctive
quisiera
quisieras
quisiera
quisiéramos
quisierais
quisieran

Imperative
quiere (tú)
quiera (usted)
queramos (nosotros)
quered (vosotros)
quieran (ustedes)

33 traer formed as **17 meter** except:

Gerund
trayendo

Past participle
traído

Present indicative
traigo
traes
trae
traemos
traéis
traen

Past simple indicative
traje
trajiste
trajo
trajimos
trajisteis
trajeron

Present subjunctive
traiga
traigas
traiga
traigamos
traigáis
traigan

Imperfect subjunctive
trajera
trajeras
trajera
trajéramos
trajerais
trajeran

Imperative
trae (tú)
traiga (usted)
traigamos (nosotros)
traed (vosotros)
traigan (ustedes)

35 saber formed as **17 meter** except:

Present indicative
sé
sabes
sabe
sabemos
sabéis
saben

Past simple indicative
supe
supiste
supo
supimos
supisteis
supieron

Future indicative
sabré
sabrás
sabrá
sabremos
sabréis
sabrán

Conditional (present)
sabría
sabrías
sabría
sabríamos
sabríais
sabrían

Present subjunctive
sepa
sepas
sepa
sepamos
sepáis
sepan

Imperfect subjunctive
supiera
supieras
supiera
supiéramos
supierais
supieran

Imperative
sabe (tú)
sepa (usted)
sepamos (nosotros)
sabed (vosotros)
sepan (ustedes)

36 ser   formed as **17 meter** except:

Gerund	Present subjunctive
siendo	sea
	seas
Past participle	sea
sido	seamos
	seáis
Present indicative	sean
soy	
eres	**Imperfect subjunctive**
es	fuera
somos	fueras
sois	fuera
son	fuéramos
	fuerais
Imperfect indicative	fueran
era	
eras	**Imperative**
era	sé (tú)
éramos	sea (usted)
erais	seamos (nosotros)
eran	sed (vosotros)
	sean (ustedes)
Past simple indicative	
fui	
fuiste	
fue	
fuimos	
fuisteis	
fueron	

37 tener   formed as **17 meter** except:

Present indicative	Present subjunctive
tengo	tenga
tienes	tengas
tiene	tenga
tenemos	tengamos
tenéis	tengáis
tienen	tengan
Past simple indicative	**Imperfect subjunctive**
tuve	tuviera
tuviste	tuvieras
tuvo	tuviera
tuvimos	tuviéramos
tuvisteis	tuvierais
tuvieron	tuvieran
Future indicative	**Imperative**
tendré	ten (tú)
tendrás	tenga (usted)
tendrá	tengamos (nosotros)
tendremos	tened (vosotros)
tendréis	tengan (ustedes)
tendrán	
Conditional (present)	
tendría	
tendrías	
tendría	
tendríamos	
tendríais	
tendrían	

38 valer   formed as **17 meter** except:

Present indicative	Present subjunctive
valgo	valga
vales	valgas
vale	valga
valemos	valgamos
valéis	valgáis
valen	valgan
Future indicative	**Imperfect subjunctive**
valdré	valiera
valdrás	valieras
valdrá	valiera
valdremos	valiéramos
valdréis	valierais
valdrán	valieran
Conditional (present)	**Imperative**
valdría	vale (tú)
valdrías	valga (usted)
valdría	valgamos (nosotros)
valdríamos	valed (vosotros)
valdríais	valgan (ustedes)
valdrían	

39 ver   formed as **17 meter** except:

Gerund	Present subjunctive
viendo	vea
	veas
Past participle	vea
visto	veamos
	veáis
Present indicative	vean
veo	
ves	**Imperative**
ve	ve (tú)
vemos	vea (usted)
veis	veamos (nosotros)
ven	ved (vosotros)
	vean (ustedes)
Imperfect indicative	
veía	
veías	
veía	
veíamos	
veíais	
veían	
Past simple indicative	
vi	
viste	
vio	
vimos	
visteis	
vieron	

40 romper   formed as **17 meter** except:

Past participle
roto

Verbs ending in -ir

41 partir

Gerund
partiendo

Past participle
partido

Present indicative
parto
partes
parte
partimos
partís
parten

Imperfect indicative
partía
partías
partía
partíamos
partíais
partían

Past simple indicative
partí
partiste
partió
partimos
partisteis
partieron

Future indicative
partiré
partirás
partirá
partiremos
partiréis
partirán

Conditional (present)
partiría
partirías
partiría
partiríamos
partiríais
partirían

Present subjunctive
parta
partas
parta
partamos
partáis
partan

Imperfect subjunctive*
partiera
partieras
partiera
partiéramos
partierais
partieran

Imperative
parte (tú)
parta (usted)
partamos (nosotros)
partid (vosotros)
partan (ustedes)

* all **-ir** verbs have an alternative form of the Imperfect subjunctive in which the **-era** ending is replaced by **-ese**, eg: partiese, partieses, partiese, partiésemos, partieseis, partiesen

42 distinguir formed as 41 partir except:

Present indicative
distingo
distingues
distingue
distinguimos
distinguís
distinguen

Present subjunctive
distinga
distingas
distinga
distingamos
distingáis
distingan

Imperative
distingue (tú)
distinga (usted)
distingamos (nosotros)
distinguid (vosotros)
distingan (ustedes)

43 reducir formed as 41 partir except:

Present indicative
reduzco
reduces
reduce
reducimos
reducís
reducen

Past simple indicative
reduje
redujiste
redujo
redujimos
redujisteis
redujeron

Present subjunctive
reduzca
reduzcas
reduzca
reduzcamos
reduzcáis
reduzcan

Imperfect subjunctive
redujera
redujeras
redujera
redujéramos
redujerais
redujeran

Imperative
reduce (tú)
reduzca (usted)
reduzcamos (nosotros)
reducid (vosotros)
reduzcan (ustedes)

44 dirigir formed as 41 partir except:

Present indicative
dirijo
diriges
dirige
dirigimos
dirigís
dirigen

Present subjunctive
dirija
dirijas
dirija
dirijamos
dirijáis
dirijan

Imperative
dirige (tú)
dirija (usted)
dirijamos (nosotros)
dirigid (vosotros)
dirijan (ustedes)

45 corregir formed as 41 partir except:

Present indicative
corrijo
corriges
corrige
corregimos
corregís
corrigen

Past simple indicative
corregí
corregiste
corrigió
corrigieron
corregisteis
corrigieron

Present subjunctive
corrija
corrijas
corrija
corrijamos
corrijáis
corrijan

Imperative
corrige (tú)
corrija (usted)
corrijamos (nosotros)
corregid (vosotros)
corrijan (ustedes)

46 sentir formed as 41 partir except:

Gerund	Present subjunctive
sintiendo	sienta
	sientas
Present indicative	sienta
siento	sintamos
sientes	sintáis
siente	sientan
sentimos	
sentís	**Imperfect subjunctive**
sienten	sintiera
	sintieras
Past simple indicative	sintiera
sentí	sintiéramos
sentiste	sintierais
sintió	sintieran
sentimos	
sentisteis	**Imperative**
sintieron	siente (tú)
	sienta (usted)
	sintamos (nosotros)
	sentid (vosotros)
	sientan (ustedes)

47 adquirir formed as 41 partir except:

Present indicative	Present subjunctive
adquiero	adquiera
adquieres	adquieras
adquiere	adquiera
adquirimos	adquiramos
adquirís	adquiráis
adquieren	adquieran
	Imperative
	adquiere (tú)
	adquiera (usted)
	adquiramos (nosotros)
	adquirid (vosotros)
	adquieran (ustedes)

48 pedir formed as 41 partir except:

Gerund	Present subjunctive
pidiendo	pida
	pidas
Present indicative	pida
pido	pidamos
pides	pidáis
pide	pidan
pedimos	
pedís	**Imperfect subjunctive**
piden	pidiera
	pidieras
Past simple indicative	pidiera
pedí	pidiéramos
pediste	pidierais
pidió	pidieran
pedimos	
pedisteis	**Imperative**
pidieron	pide (tú)
	pida (usted)
	pidamos (nosotros)
	pedid (vosotros)
	pidan (ustedes)

49 dormir formed as 41 partir except:

Gerund	Present subjunctive
durmiendo	duerma
	duermas
Past participle	duerma
dormido	durmamos
	durmáis
Present indicative	duerman
duermo	
duermes	**Imperfect subjunctive**
duerme	durmiera
dormimos	durmieras
dormís	durmiera
duermen	durmiéramos
	durmierais
	durmieran
Past simple indicative	
dormí	**Imperative**
dormiste	duerme (tú)
durmió	duerma (usted)
dormimos	durmamos (nosotros)
dormisteis	dormid (vosotros)
durmieron	duerman (ustedes)

50 reír formed as 41 partir except:

Gerund	Conditional (present)
riendo	reiría
	reirías
Past participle	reiría
reído	reiríamos
	reiríais
Present indicative	reirían
río	
ríes	**Present subjunctive**
ríe	ría
reímos	rías
reís	ría
ríen	riamos
	riáis
Imperfect indicative	rían
reía	
reías	**Imperfect subjunctive**
reía	riera
reíamos	rieras
reíais	riera
reían	riéramos
	rierais
Past simple indicative	rieran
reí	
reíste	**Imperative**
rió	ríe (tú)
reímos	ría (usted)
reísteis	riamos (nosotros)
rieron	reíd (vosotros)
	rían (ustedes)
Future indicative	
reiré	
reirás	
reirá	
reiremos	
reiréis	
reirán	

51 huir formed as 41 partir except:

Gerund
huyendo

....

Past participle
huido

....

Present indicative
huyo
huyes
huye
huimos
huís
huyen

Past simple indicative
huí
huiste
huyó
huimos
huisteis
huyeron

Present subjunctive
huya
huyas
huya
huyamos
huyáis
huyan

Imperfect subjunctive
huyera
huyeras
huyera
huyéramos
huyerais
huyeran

....

Imperative
huye (tú)
huya (usted)
huyamos (nosotros)
huid (vosotros)
huyan (ustedes)

52 prohibir formed as 41 partir except:

Present indicative
prohíbo
prohíbes
prohíbe
prohibimos
prohibís
prohíben

Present subjunctive
prohíba
prohíbas
prohíba
prohibamos
prohibáis
prohíban

....

Imperative
prohíbe (tú)
prohíba (usted)
prohibamos (nosotros)
prohibid (vosotros)
prohíban (ustedes)

53 decir formed as 41 partir except:

Gerund
diciendo

....

Past participle
dicho

....

Present indicative
digo
dices
dice
decimos
decís
dicen

Past simple indicative
dije
dijiste
dijo
dijimos
dijisteis
dijeron

....

Future indicative
diré
dirás
dirá
diremos
diréis
dirán

Conditional (present)
diría
dirías
diría
diríamos
diríais
dirían

....

Present subjunctive
diga
digas
diga
digamos
digáis
digan

....

Imperfect subjunctive
dijera
dijeras
dijera
dijéramos
dijerais
dijeran

....

Imperative
di (tú)
diga (usted)
digamos (nosotros)
decid (vosotros)
digan (ustedes)

54 **ir** formed as **41 partir** except:

Gerund
yendo

Past participle
ido

Present indicative
voy
vas
va
vamos
vais
van

Imperfect indicative
iba
ibas
iba
íbamos
ibais
iban

Past simple indicative
fui
fuiste
fue
fuimos
fuisteis
fueron

Present subjunctive
vaya
vayas
vaya
vayamos
vayáis
vayan

Imperfect subjunctive
fuera
fueras
fuera
fuéramos
fuerais
fueran

Imperative
ve (tú)
vaya (usted)
vayamos (nosotros)
id (vosotros)
vayan (ustedes)

55 **oír** formed as **41 partir** except:

Gerund
oyendo

Past participle
oído

Present indicative
oigo
oyes
oye
oímos
oís
oyen

Imperfect indicative
oía
oías
oía
oíamos
oíais
oían

Past simple indicative
oí
oíste
oyó
oímos
oísteis
oyeron

Future indicative
oiré
oirás
oirá
oiremos
oiréis
oirán

Conditional (present)
oiría
oirías
oiría
oiríamos
oiríais
oirían

Present subjunctive
oiga
oigas
oiga
oigamos
oigáis
oigan

Imperfect subjunctive
oyera
oyeras
oyera
oyéramos
oyerais
oyeran

Imperative
oye (tú)
oiga (usted)
oigamos (nosotros)
oíd (vosotros)
oigan (ustedes)

56 **salir** formed as **41 partir** except:

Present indicative
salgo
sales
sale
salimos
salís
salen

Past simple indicative
salí
saliste
salió
salimos
salisteis
salieron

Future indicative
saldré
saldrás
saldrá
saldremos
saldréis
saldrán

Conditional (present)
saldría
saldrías
saldría
saldríamos
saldríais
saldrían

Present subjunctive
salga
salgas
salga
salgamos
salgáis
salgan

Imperfect subjunctive
saliera
salieras
saliera
saliéramos
salierais
salieran

Imperative
sal (tú)
salga (usted)
salgamos (nosotros)
salid (vosotros)
salgan (ustedes)

57 seguir formed as **41 partir** except:

Gerund
siguiendo

Present indicative
sigo
sigues
sigue
seguimos
seguís
siguen

Past simple indicative
seguí
seguiste
siguió
seguimos
seguisteis
siguieron

Present subjunctive
siga
sigas
siga
sigamos
sigáis
sigan

Imperfect subjunctive
siguiera
siguieras
siguiera
siguiéramos
siguierais
siguieran

Imperative
sigue (tú)
siga (usted)
sigamos (nosotros)
seguid (vosotros)
sigan (ustedes

58 venir formed as **41 partir** except:

Gerund
viniendo

Present indicative
vengo
vienes
viene
venimos
venís
vienen

Past simple indicative
vine
viniste
vino
vinimos
vinisteis
vinieron

Future indicative
vendré
vendrás
vendrá
vendremos
vendréis
vendrán

Conditional (present)
vendría
vendrías
vendría
vendríamos
vendríais
vendrían

Present subjunctive
venga
vengas
venga
vengamos
vengáis
vengan

Imperfect subjunctive
viniera
vinieras
viniera
viniéramos
vinierais
vinieran

Imperative
ven (tú)
venga (usted)
vengamos (nosotros)
venid (vosotros)
vengan (ustedes)

59 abrir formed as **41 partir** except:

Past participle
abierto

60 escribir formed as **41 partir** except:

Past participle
escrito

61 freír formed as **41 partir** except:

Gerund
friendo

Past participle
frito

Present indicative
frío
fríes
fríe
freímos
freís
fríen

Imperfect indicative
freía
freías
freía
freíamos
freíais
freían

Past simple indicative
freí
freíste
frió
freímos
freísteis
frieron

Future indicative
freiré
freirás
freirá
freiremos
freiréis
freirán

Conditional (present)
freiría
freirías
freiría
freiríamos
freiríais
freirían

Present subjunctive
fría
frías
fría
friamos
friáis
frían

Imperfect subjunctive
friera
frieras
friera
friéramos
frierais
frieran

Imperative
fríe (tú)
fría (usted)
friamos (nosotros)
freíd (vosotros)
frían (ustedes)

62 morir formed as **41 partir** except:

Gerund
muriendo

Past participle
muerto

Present indicative
muero
mueres
muere
morimos
morís
mueren

Past simple indicative
morí
moriste
murió
morimos
moristeis
murieron

Present subjunctive
muera
mueras
muera
muramos
muráis
mueran

Imperfect subjunctive
muriera
murieras
muriera
muriéramos
murierais
murieran

63 pudrir formed as **41 partir** except:

past participle
podrido

64 reunir formed as **41 partir** except:

Present indicative
reúno
reúnes
reúne
reunimos
reunís
reúnen

Present subjunctive
reúna
reúnas
reúna
reunamos
reunáis
reúnan

....

Imperative
reúne (tú)
reúna (usted)
reunamos (nosotros)
reunid (vosotros)
reúnan (ustedes)

65 ceñir formed as **41 partir** except:

Gerund
ciñendo

....

Present indicative
ciño
ciñes
ciñe
ceñimos
ceñís
ciñen

....

Past simple indicative
ceñí
ceñiste
ciñó
ceñimos
ceñisteis
ciñeron

Present subjunctive
ciña
ciñas
ciña
ciñamos
ciñáis
ciñan

....

Imperfect subjunctive
ciñera
ciñeras
ciñera
ciñéramos
ciñerais
ciñeran

....

Imperative
ciñe (tú)
ciña (usted)
ciñamos (nosotros)
ceñid (vosotros)
ciñan (ustedes)